Networks, Crowds, and Markets

Over the past decade there has been a growing public fascination with the complex connectedness of modern society. This connectedness is found in many incarnations: in the rapid growth of the Internet, in the ease with which global communication takes place, and in the ability of news and information as well as epidemics and financial crises to spread with surprising speed and intensity. These are phenomena that involve networks, incentives, and the aggregate behavior of groups of people; they are based on the links that connect us and the ways in which our decisions can have subtle consequences for others.

This introductory undergraduate textbook takes an interdisciplinary look at economics, sociology, computing and information science, and applied mathematics to understand networks and behavior. It describes the emerging field of study that is growing at the interface of these areas, addressing fundamental questions about how the social, economic, and technological worlds are connected.

David Easley is the Henry Scarborough Professor of Social Science and the Donald C. Opatrny '74 Chair of the Department of Economics at Cornell University. He was previously an Overseas Fellow of Churchill College, Cambridge. His research is in the fields of economics, finance, and decision theory. In economics, he focuses on learning, wealth dynamics, and natural selection in markets. In finance, his work focuses on market microstructure and asset pricing. In decision theory, he works on modeling decision making in complex environments. He is a Fellow of the Econometric Society and is Chair of the NASDAQ-OMX Economic Advisory Board.

Jon Kleinberg is the Tisch University Professor in the Computer Science Department at Cornell University. He is a member of the National Academy of Engineering and the American Academy of Arts and Sciences. His research focuses on issues at the interface of networks and information, with an emphasis on the social and information networks that underpin the Web and other online media. He is the recipient of MacArthur, Packard, and Sloan Foundation Fellowships; the Nevanlinna Prize; the ACM-Infosys Foundation Award; and the National Academy of Sciences Award for Initiatives in Research.

Networks, Crowds, and Markets

Reasoning about a Highly Connected World

David Easley

Cornell University

Jon Kleinberg

Cornell University

CAMBRIDGE
UNIVERSITY PRESS

CAMBRIDGE UNIVERSITY PRESS
Cambridge, New York, Melbourne, Madrid, Cape Town, Singapore,
São Paulo, Delhi, Dubai, Tokyo, Mexico City

Cambridge University Press
32 Avenue of the Americas, New York, NY 10013-2473, USA

www.cambridge.org
Information on this title: www.cambridge.org/9780521195331

First published 2010

Printed in the United States of America

A catalog record for this publication is available from the British Library.

Library of Congress Cataloging in Publication data

Easley, David.
Networks, crowds, and markets : reasoning about a highly connected world / David
Easley, Jon Kleinberg.
     p.   cm.
Includes bibliographical references and index.
ISBN 978-0-521-19533-1 (hardback)
1. Telecommunication – Social aspects.   2. Information society.   I. Kleinberg, Jon.
II.   Title.
HM851.E24   2010
303.48′33–dc22   2009050314

ISBN 978-0-521-19533-1 Hardback

Contents

Part II   Game Theory

Part III   Markets and Strategic Interaction in Networks

Part IV   Information Networks and the World Wide Web

Part V   Network Dynamics: Population Models

Part VI Network Dynamics: Structural Models

Part VII Institutions and Aggregate Behavior

Preface

Over the past decade, there has been a growing public fascination with the complex "connectedness" of modern society. This connectedness is found in many incarnations: in the rapid growth of the Internet and the Web, in the ease with which global communication now takes place, and in the ability of news and information as well as epidemics and financial crises to spread around the world with surprising speed and intensity. These are phenomena that involve networks, incentives, and the aggregate behavior of groups of people; they are based on the links that connect us and the ways in which each of our decisions can have subtle consequences for the outcomes of everyone else.

Motivated by these developments in the world, there has been a coming-together of multiple scientific disciplines in an effort to understand how highly connected systems operate. Each discipline has contributed techniques and perspectives that are characteristically its own, and the resulting research effort exhibits an intriguing blend of these different flavors. From computer science and applied mathematics has come a framework for reasoning about how complexity arises, often unexpectedly, in systems that we design; from economics has come a perspective on how people's behavior is affected by incentives and by their expectations about the behavior of others; and from sociology and the social sciences have come insights into the characteristic structures and interactions that arise within groups and populations. The resulting synthesis of ideas suggests the beginnings of a new area of study, focusing on the phenomena that take place within complex social, economic, and technological systems.

This book grew out of a course that we developed at Cornell, designed to introduce this topic and its underlying ideas to a broad student audience at an introductory level. The central concepts are fundamental and accessible ones, but they are dispersed across the research literatures of the many different fields contributing to the topic. The principal goal of this book is therefore to bring the essential ideas together in a single unified treatment and to present them in a way that requires as little background knowledge as possible.

Overview. The book is intended to be used at the introductory undergraduate level, and as such it has no formal prerequisites beyond a level of comfort with basic mathematical definitions at a precalculus level. In keeping with the introductory style, many of the ideas are developed in special cases and through illustrative examples; our goal is to take concepts and theories that are complex in their full generality and to provide simpler formulations where the essential ideas still come through.

In our use of the book, we find that many students are also interested in pursuing some of these topics more deeply, and so it is useful to provide pathways that lead from the introductory formulations into the more advanced literature on these topics. With this in mind, we provide optional sections labeled *Advanced Material* at the ends of most chapters. These advanced sections are qualitatively different from the other sections in the book; some draw on more advanced mathematics, and their presentation is at a more challenging level of conceptual complexity. Aside from the additional mathematical background required, however, even these advanced sections are self-contained; they are also strictly optional, in the sense that nothing elsewhere in the book depends on them.

Synopsis. The first chapter of the book provides a detailed description of the topics and issues that we cover. Here we give a briefer summary of the main focus areas.

The book is organized into seven parts of three to four chapters each. Parts I and II discuss the two main theories that underpin our investigations of networks and behavior: *graph theory*, which studies network structure, and *game theory*, which formulates models of behavior in environments where people's decisions affect each other's outcomes. Part III integrates these lines of thought into an analysis of the network structure of markets and the notion of power in such networks. Part IV pursues a different integration, discussing the World Wide Web as an information network, the problem of Web search, and the development of the markets that currently lie at the heart of the search industry. Parts V and VI study the dynamics of some of the fundamental processes that take place within networks and groups, including the ways in which people are influenced by the decisions of others. Part V pursues this topic at an aggregate scale, where we model interactions between an individual and the population as a whole. Part VI continues the analysis at the more fine-grained level of network structure, beginning with the question of influence and moving on to the dynamics of search processes and epidemics. Finally, Part VII considers how we can interpret fundamental social institutions – including markets, voting systems, and property rights – as mechanisms for productively shaping some of the phenomena we've been studying.

Use of the Book. The book is designed for teaching as well as for any reader who finds these topics interesting and wants to pursue them independently at a deeper level.

Several different types of courses can be taught from this book. When we teach from it at Cornell, the students in our class come from many different majors and have a wide variety of technical backgrounds; this diversity in the audience has served as our primary calibration in setting the introductory level of the book. Our course includes a portion of the material from each chapter; for the sake of concreteness, we provide the approximate weekly schedule we follow below. (There are three 50-minute lectures each week, except that weeks 6 and 7 of our course contain only two lectures each. In each lecture, we don't necessarily include all the details from each indicated section.)

Week 1: Chapters 1; 2.1–2.3; 3.1–3.3, 3.5; 4.1
Week 2: Chapters 5.1–5.3; 6.1–6.4; 6.5–6.9
Week 3: Chapters 8.1–8.2; 9.1–9.6; 10.1–10.2
Week 4: Chapters 10.3; 10.4–10.5; 11.1–11.2
Week 5: Chapters 11.3–11.4; 12.1–12.3; 12.5–12.6
Week 6: Chapters 12.7–12.8; 13
Week 7: Chapter 14.1–14.2; 14.3–14.4
Week 8: Chapter 15.1–15.2; 15.3–15.4; 15.5–15.6, 15.8
Week 9: Chapter 16.1–16.2; 16.3–16.4; 16.5–16.7
Week 10: Chapters 17.1–17.2; 17.3–17.5; 18
Week 11: Chapters 19.1–19.2; 19.3; 19.4, 19.6
Week 12: Chapter 22.1–22.4; 22.5–22.9; 7.1–7.4
Week 13: Chapters 20.1–20.2; 20.3–20.6; 21.1–21.5
Week 14: Chapters 23.1–23.5; 23.6–23.9; 24

There are many other paths that a course could follow through the book. First, a number of new courses are being developed at the interface of computer science and economics, focusing particularly on the role of economic reasoning in the design and behavior of modern computing systems. The book can be used for such courses in several ways, building on four chapters as a foundation: Chapter 2 on graphs, Chapter 6 on games, Chapter 9 on auctions, and Chapter 10 on matching markets. From here, a more expansive version of such a course could cover the remainder of Parts II and III, all of Parts IV and V, Chapter 19, and portions of Part VII. A more focused and potentially shorter version of such a course concerned principally with auctions, markets, and the online applications of these ideas could be constructed from Chapters 2, 6, 9, 10, 13, 15, 17, 18, and 22, and drawing on parts of Chapters 11, 12, 14, 16, and 19. When these courses are taught at a more advanced level, the advanced sections at the ends of most of these chapters would be appropriate material; depending on the exact level of the course, the text of many of these chapters could be used to lead into the more advanced analysis in their respective final sections.

In a different but related direction, new courses are also being developed on the topic of social computing and information networks. The book can be used for courses of this type by emphasizing Chapters 2–6, 13, 14, 17–20, and 22; many such courses also include sponsored search markets as part of their coverage of the Web, which can be done by including Chapters 9, 10, and 15 as well. The advanced sections in the book can play a role here too, depending on the level of the course.

Finally, portions of the book can serve as self-contained modules in courses on broader topics. To pick just a few examples, one can assemble such modules on network algorithms (Sections 2.3, 3.6, 5.5, 8.3, 10.6, 14.2, 14.3, 14.6, 15.9, 20.3, 20.4, and 20.7); applications of game theory (Chapters 6–9 and 11; Sections 12.9, 15.3–15.6, 19.2, 19.3, 19.5–19.7, and 23.7–23.9); social network analysis (Chapters 2–5; Sections 12.1–12.3 and 12.5–12.8; and Chapters 18–20); the role of information in economic settings (Chapters 16 and 22, and Sections 23.6–23.10); and the analysis of large-scale network data sets (Sections 2.3, 3.2, 3.3, 3.6, 4.4, 5.3, 13.3, 13.4, 14.2–14.5, 18.2, 18.5, and 20.5). Most of these modules use graphs and/or games as fundamental building blocks; for students not already familiar with these topics, Chapters 2 and 6, respectively, provide self-contained introductions.

Acknowledgments. Our work on this book took place in an environment at Cornell that was particularly conducive to interaction between computing and the social sciences. Our collaboration began as part of a project with Larry Blume, Eric Friedman, Joe Halpern, Dan Huttenlocher, and Éva Tardos funded by the National Science Foundation, followed by a campus-wide "theme project" on networks sponsored by Cornell's Institute for the Social Sciences, with a group that included Larry and Dan together with John Abowd, Geri Gay, Michael Macy, Kathleen O'Connor, Jeff Prince, and David Strang. Our approach to the material in the book draws on perspectives – ways of thinking about these topics and ways of talking about them – that we've learned and acquired from this interdisciplinary set of colleagues, a group that includes some of our closest professional collaborators.

The course on which the book is based grew out of discussions that were part of the Cornell theme project; the two of us had taught distinct portions of this material separately in graduate courses that we had developed, and Michael Kearns's *Networked Life* course at University of Pennsylvania demonstrated the vibrancy and relevance this material could have for an introductory undergraduate audience as well. We were intrigued by the prospect of combining different perspectives that hadn't previously appeared together – a process that would be educational not only to the students in the course but to us as well. Creating and teaching this new interdisciplinary course was made possible by the support of our departments, Computer Science and Economics, and by support from the Solomon Fund at Cornell University.

Once the book had begun to take shape, we benefited enormously from the feedback, suggestions, and experiences of colleagues who taught from early drafts of it. In particular, we thank Daron Acemoglu (MIT), Lada Adamic (Michigan), Allan Borodin (Toronto), Noshir Contractor (Northwestern), Jason Hartline (Northwestern), Nicole Immorlica (Northwestern), Ramesh Johari (Stanford), Samir Khuller (Maryland), Jure Leskovec (Stanford), David Liben-Nowell (Carleton), Peter Monge (USC), Asu Ozdaglar (MIT), Vijay Ramachandran (Colgate), R. Ravi (CMU), Chuck Severance (Michigan), Aravind Srinivasan (Maryland), and Luis von Ahn (CMU). The graduate and undergraduate teaching assistants in our own teaching of this subject have been very helpful as well; we thank Alex Ainslie, Lars Backstrom, Jacob Bank, Vlad Barash, Burak Bekdemir, Anand Bhaskar, Ben Cole, Bistra Dilkina, Eduard Dogaru, Ram Dubey, Ethan Feldman, Ken Ferguson, Narie Foster, Eric Frackleton, Christie Gibson, Vaibhav Goel, Scott Grabnic, Jon Guarino, Fahad Karim, Koralai Kirabaeva, Tian Liang, Austin Lin, Fang Liu, Max Mihm, Sameer Nurmohamed, Ben Pu, Tal Rusak, Mark Sandler, Stuart Tettemer, Ozgur Yonter, Chong-Suk Yoon, and Yisong Yue.

In addition to the instructors who used early drafts, a number of other people provided extensive comments on portions of the book, leading to many improvements in the text: Lada Adamic, Robert Kerr, Evie Kleinberg, Gueorgi Kossinets, Stephen Morris, David Parkes, Rahul Sami, Andrew Tomkins, and Johan Ugander. We also thank a further set of colleagues, in addition to those already listed, who have provided very useful advice and suggestions on this project as it has proceeded: Bobby Kleinberg, Gene Kleinberg, Lillian Lee, Maureen O'Hara, Prabhakar Raghavan, and Steve Strogatz.

It has been a pleasure to be able to work with the editorial team at Cambridge University Press. Lauren Cowles, our main point of contact at Cambridge, has been an amazing source of advice and help, and we likewise very much appreciate the contributions of Scott Parris and David Tranah to this project, and Peggy Rote and her colleagues at Aptara for their work on the production of the book.

Finally, a profound thanks goes to our families, in continuing appreciation of their support and many other contributions.

David Easley
Jon Kleinberg
Ithaca, 2010

CHAPTER 1

Overview

The past decade has seen a growing public fascination with the complex "connected-ness" of modern society. At the heart of this fascination is the idea of a *network* – a pattern of interconnections among a set of things – and one finds networks appearing in discussion and commentary on an enormous range of topics. The diversity of con-texts in which networks are invoked is in fact so vast that it's worth deferring precise definitions for a moment while we first recount a few of the more salient examples.

To begin with, the social networks we inhabit – the collections of social ties among friends – have grown steadily in complexity over the course of human history, due to technological advances facilitating distant travel, global communication, and digital interaction. The past half-century has seen these social networks depart even more radically from their geographic underpinnings – an effect that has weakened the tradi-tionally local nature of such structures but enriched them in other dimensions.

no more geo-ties

The information we consume has a similarly networked structure: these structures too have grown in complexity, as a landscape with a few purveyors of high-quality information (publishers, news organizations, the academy) has become crowded with an array of information sources of wildly varying perspectives, reliabilities, and motivating intentions. Understanding any one piece of information in this environment depends on understanding the way it is endorsed by and refers to other pieces of information within a large network of links.

Our technological and economic systems have also become dependent on networks of enormous complexity. This has made the behavior of these systems increasingly difficult to reason about and increasingly risky to tinker with. It has made them suscep-tible to disruptions that spread through the underlying network structures, sometimes turning localized breakdowns into cascading failures or financial crises.

The imagery of networks has made its way into many other lines of discussion as well: Global manufacturing operations now have networks of suppliers, Web sites have networks of users, and media companies have networks of advertisers. In such formulations, the emphasis is often less on the structure of the network itself than on its complexity as a large, diffuse population that reacts in unexpected ways to the actions of central authorities. The terminology of international conflict has come to reflect this

1

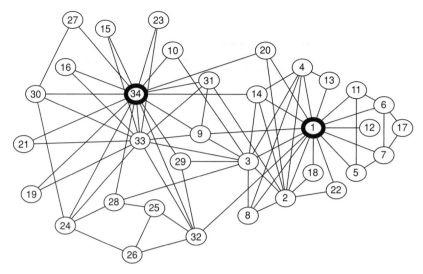

Figure 1.1. The social network of friendships within a 34-person karate club [421]. (Drawing from the *Journal of Anthropological Research*.)

as well: for example, the picture of two opposing, state-supported armies gradually morphs, in U.S. presidential speeches, into images of a nation facing "a broad and adaptive terrorist network" [296] or "at war against a far-reaching network of violence and hatred" [328].

1.1 Aspects of Networks

How should we think about networks, at a more precise level, to bring all these issues together? In the most basic sense, a network is any collection of objects in which some pairs of these objects are connected by *links*. This definition is very flexible: depending on the setting, many different forms of relationships or connections can be used to define links.

Because of this flexibility, it is easy to find networks in many domains, including the ones we've just been discussing. As a first example of what a network looks like, Figure 1.1 depicts the social network among thirty-four people in a university karate club studied by the anthropologist Wayne Zachary in the 1970s. The people are represented by small circles, and lines join the pairs of people who are friends outside the context of the club. This is the typical way in which networks will be drawn in this book, with lines joining the pairs of objects that are connected by links.

Later in this chapter we'll discuss some of the things one can learn from a network such as the one in Figure 1.1, as well as from larger examples such as the ones shown in Figures 1.2–1.4. These larger examples depict e-mail exchanges among employees of a company (Figure 1.2); loans among financial institutions (Figure 1.3); and links among blogs on the Web (Figure 1.4). In each case, links indicate the pairs that are connected (specifically, people connected by e-mail exchange, financial institutions by a borrower–lender relationship, and blogs via a link on the Web from one to the other, respectively).

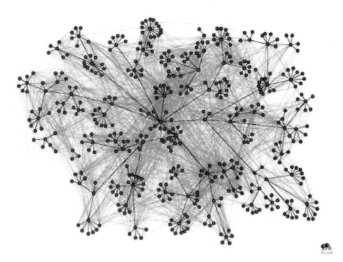

Figure 1.2. Social networks based on communication and interaction can be constructed from the traces left by online data. In this case, the pattern of e-mail communication among 436 employees of the Hewlett Packard Research Lab is superimposed on the official organizational hierarchy [6]. (Image from http://www-personal.umich.edu/ladamic/img/hplabsemailhierarchy.jpg, courtesy of Elsevier Science and Technology Journals.)

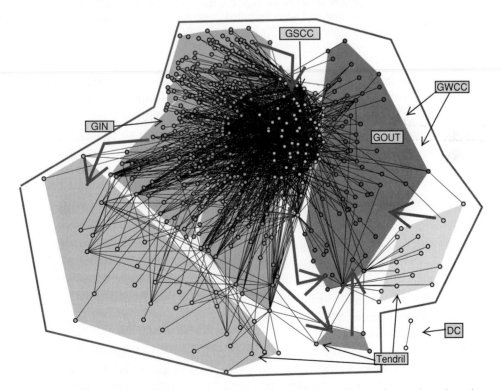

Figure 1.3. The network of loans among financial institutions can be used to analyze the roles that different participants play in the financial system and how the interactions among these roles affect the health of individual participants and the system as a whole. The network is annotated in a way that reveals its dense core, according to a scheme that we describe in Chapter 13. (Image from Bech and Atalay, [50].)

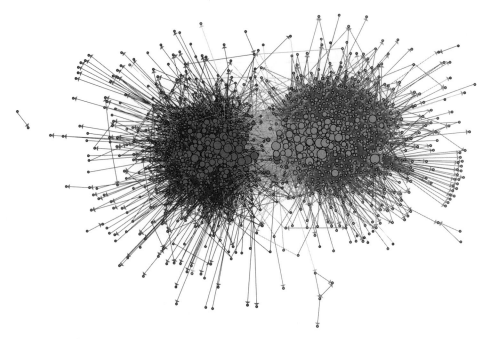

Figure 1.4. The links among Web pages can reveal densely knit communities and prominent sites. In this case, the network structure of political blogs prior to the 2004 U.S. presidential election reveals two natural and well-separated clusters [5]. (Image from Association for Computing Machinery, Inc.; http://www-personal.umich.edu/ ladamic/img/politicalblogs.jpg.)

Simply from their visual appearance, we can already see some of the complexity inherent in network structures. It is generally difficult to summarize succinctly the whole network; some parts are more or less densely interconnected, sometimes with central "cores" containing most of the links and sometimes with natural splits into multiple tightly-linked regions. Participants in the network can be more central or more peripheral; they can straddle the boundaries of different tightly-linked regions or sit squarely in the middle of one. Developing a language for talking about the typical structural features of networks is an important first step in understanding them.

Behavior and Dynamics. But the structure of the network is only a starting point. When people talk about the "connectedness" of a complex system, in general they are really talking about two related issues. One is connectedness at the level of structure – who is linked to whom – and the other is connectedness at the level of *behavior* – the fact that each individual's actions have implicit consequences for the outcomes of everyone in the system.

This means that, in addition to a language for discussing the structure of networks, we also need a framework for reasoning about behavior and interaction in network contexts. And just as the underlying structure of a network can be complex, so too can the coupled behavior of its inhabitants. If individuals have strong incentives to achieve good outcomes, then they not only will appreciate that their outcomes depend on how others behave, but they also take this into account in planning their own actions.

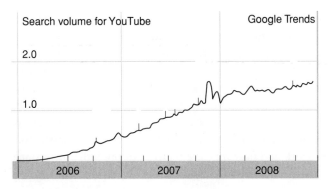

Figure 1.5. The rapidly growing popularity of YouTube is characteristic of the way in which new products, technologies, or innovations rise to prominence through feedback effects in the behavior of many individuals across a population. The plot depicts the number of Google queries for YouTube over time. The image comes from the site Google Trends (http://www.google.com/trends?q=youtube); by design, the units on the *y*-axis are suppressed in the output from this site.

As a result, models of networked behavior must take strategic behavior and strategic reasoning into account.

A fundamental point here is that, in a network setting, you should evaluate your actions not in isolation but with the expectation that the world will react to what you do. This means that cause-and-effect relationships can become quite subtle. Changes in a product, a Web site, or a government program can seem like good ideas when evaluated using the assumption that everything else will remain static, but in reality such changes can easily create incentives that shift behavior across the network in ways that were initially unintended.

Moreover, such effects are at work whether we are able to see the network or not. When a large group of people is tightly interconnected, these people often respond in complex ways that are only apparent at the population level, even though these effects may come from implicit networks that we do not directly observe. Consider, for example, the way in which new products, Web sites, or celebrities rise to prominence (as illustrated, for example, by Figures 1.5 and 1.6, which show the growth in popularity

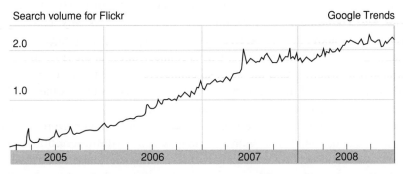

Figure 1.6. This companion to Figure 1.5 shows the rise of the social media site Flickr; the growth in popularity has a very similar pattern to that of other sites, including YouTube. (Image from Google Trends, http://www.google.com/trends?q=flickr.)

of the social media sites YouTube and Flickr, respectively, over the past several years). What we see in these figures is a growing awareness and adoption of a new innovation that is visible in aggregate, across a whole population. What are the underlying mechanisms that lead to such success? Standard refrains are often invoked in these situations: the rich get richer, winners take all, small advantages are magnified to a critical mass, and new ideas get attention that becomes "viral." But the rich don't always get richer and small advantages don't always lead to success. Some social networking sites flourish, like Facebook, while others, like SixDegrees.com, vanish. To understand how these processes work and how they are realized through the interconnected actions of many people, we need to study the dynamics of aggregate behavior.

A Confluence of Ideas. Understanding highly connected systems, then, requires a set of ideas for reasoning about network structure, strategic behavior, and the feedback effects they produce across large populations. These are ideas that have traditionally been dispersed across many different disciplines. However, in parallel with the increasing public interest in networks, there has been a coming-together of scientific fields around the topic of network research. Each of these fields brings important ideas to the discussion, and a full understanding seems to require a synthesis of perspectives from all of them.

One of the central goals in this book is to help bring about such a synthesis, by combining approaches that have traditionally been pursued separately. From computer science, applied mathematics, and operations research we draw on a language for talking about the complexity of network structure, information, and systems with interacting agents. From economics we draw on models for the strategic behavior of individuals who interact with each other and operate as members of larger aggregates. From sociology – particularly the more mathematical aspects concerned with social networks – we draw on a broad set of theoretical frameworks for talking about the structure and dynamics of social groups.

And the overall picture can help fill in pieces that are arguably missing from the intellectual landscape of each of these disciplines. Economics has developed rich theories for the strategic interaction among small numbers of parties, as well as for the cumulative behavior of large, homogeneous populations. The challenge is that much of economic life takes place in the complex spectrum between these extremes, with macroscopic effects that arise from an intricate pattern of localized interactions. Sociology has developed some of the fundamental insights into the structure of social networks, but its network methodology has been refined in the domains and scales where data collection has traditionally been possible – primarily, well-defined groups with tens to hundreds of people. The explosion of new contexts in which we find network data and network applications – including enormous, digitally mediated ones – leads to new opportunities for how we can pose questions, formulate theories, and evaluate predictions about social networks. Computer science, with the rise of the Web and social media, has had to deal with a world in which the design constraints on large computing systems are not just technological but also human – imposed by the complex feedback effects that human audiences create when they collectively use the Web for communication, self-expression, and the creation of knowledge. A fully satisfactory theory of network structure and behavior has the potential to address the simultaneous challenges encountered by all these fields.

A recurring theme underlying these challenges is the way in which networks span many different levels of scale and resolution. There are interesting questions that reach from the scale of small groups, such as the thirty-four–person social network in Figure 1.1, all the way up to the level of whole societies or economies, or to the body of global knowledge represented by the Web. In this book we examine networks both at the level of explicit structures, like those in Figures 1.1–1.4, and at the level of aggregate effects, like the popularity curves in Figures 1.5 and 1.6. As we look at networks of increasing scales, it becomes correspondingly more appropriate to take aggregate models into account. But the ability to work with massive network data sets has also enriched the picture, making it possible to study networks with billions of interacting items at a level of resolution where each connection is recorded. When an Internet search engine identifies the most useful pages from an index of the entire Web, for example, it is doing precisely this in the context of a specific task. Ultimately, it is an ongoing and challenging scientific problem to bridge these vastly different levels of scale so that predictions and principles from one level can be reconciled with those of others.

1.2 Central Themes and Topics

With this set of ideas in mind, we now introduce some of the main topics considered in this book and the ways in which these topics reinforce the underlying principles of networks. We begin with the two main bodies of theory that we will be building on: graph theory and game theory. These are theories of structure and behavior, respectively. Graph theory is the study of network structure, while game theory provides models of individual behavior in settings where outcomes depend on the behavior of others.

Graph Theory. In our discussion of graph theory, we focus particularly on some of the fundamental ideas from social network analysis, framing a number of graph-theoretic concepts in these terms. The networks in Figures 1.1 and 1.2 hint at some of these ideas. In the corporate e-mail communication network from Figure 1.2, for example, the communication is balanced between staying within small organizational units and cutting across organizational boundaries. This is an example of a much more general principle in social networks – that *strong ties*, representing close and frequent social contacts, tend to be embedded in tightly-linked regions of the network, whereas *weak ties*, representing more casual and distinct social contacts, tend to cross between these regions. Such a dichotomy suggests a way of thinking about social networks in terms of their dense pockets of strong ties and the ways in which they interact with each other through weaker ties. In a professional setting, it suggests a strategy for navigating one's way through the social landscape of a large organization by finding the *structural holes* between parts of the network that interact very little with each other. At a global scale, it suggests some of the ways in which weak ties can act as "shortcuts" that link together distant parts of the world, resulting in the phenomenon colloquially known as *six degrees of separation*.

Social networks can also capture the sources of conflict within a group. For example, latent conflicts are at work in the karate club social network from Figure 1.1. The people labeled 1 and 34 (the darker circles) are particularly central in the network of

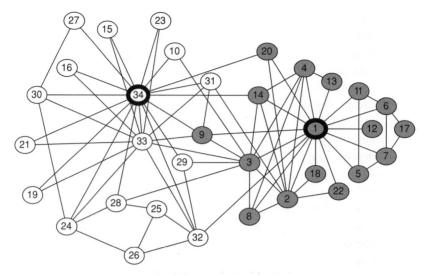

Figure 1.7. From the social network of friendships in the karate club from Figure 1.1, we can find clues to the latent schism that eventually split the group into two separate clubs (indicated by the two different shadings of individuals in the drawing).

friendships, with many connections to other people. On the other hand, they are not friends with each other, and in fact most people are only friends with one or the other of them. These two central people were, respectively, the instructor and the student founder of the club, and this pattern of noninteracting clusters was the most visible symptom of a conflict between them and their factions that ultimately splintered the group into two rival karate clubs, as shown in Figure 1.7. Later we will see how the theory of *structural balance* can be used to reason about how fissures in a network may arise from the dynamics of conflict and antagonism at a purely local level.

Game Theory. Our discussion of game theory starts from the observation that there are numerous settings in which a group of people must simultaneously choose how to act, knowing that the outcome will depend on the decisions made by all of them. One natural example is the problem of choosing a driving route through a network of highways at a time when traffic is heavy. For a driver in such a situation, the delays experienced depend on the pattern of traffic congestion arising not just from the driver's choice of route, but also from the choices made by all other drivers. In this example, the network plays the role of a shared resource, and the combined actions of its users can either congest this resource or use it more efficiently. In fact, the interactions among people's behavior can lead to counterintuitive effects; for example, adding resources to a transportation network can in fact create incentives that seriously undermine its efficiency, in a phenomenon known as *Braess's Paradox* [76].

Another example that will recur in several settings throughout the book is the problem of bidding in an auction. If a seller is trying to sell a single item using an auction, then the success of any one bidder in the auction (whether she gets the item, and how much she pays) depends not just on how she bids but also on how everyone else bids; an optimal bidding strategy should take this into account. Here too, counterintuitive effects are at work: for example, if the seller introduces more aggressive pricing rules into the auction, he can make the strategic behavior of the bidders much more complex, and in particular induce optimal bidding that offsets whatever gains he might have expected to make from the new rules. Auctions represent a basic kind of economic interaction that we will generalize to more complex patterns of interactions in networks.

Auctions

As a general part of our investigation of game theory, we abstract such situations with interdependent behavior into a common framework, wherein a collection of individuals must each commit to a *strategy*, thereby receiving a *payoff* that depends on the strategies chosen by everyone. Interpreting our preceding examples in this light, we see that the strategies available to a driver on a set of highways consist of the different options for routes he can take, and the payoff to this driver is based on his resulting travel time. In an auction, the strategies are the different choices for how to bid, and the payoff to a bidder is the difference between the value of the goods she receives and the price she pays. This general framework allows us to make predictions about how people will behave in a range of such situations. A fundamental part of this framework is the notion of *equilibrium* – a state that is "self-reinforcing" in that it provides no individual with an incentive to unilaterally change his or her strategy, even if that individual knows how others will behave.

Markets and Strategic Interaction in Networks. Once we have developed graph theory and game theory, we can combine them to produce richer models of behavior in networks. One natural setting for this exploration is in models of trade and other forms of economic activity. The interactions among buyers and sellers, or pairs of counterparties to a trade or loan, naturally forms a network. In Figure 1.3 we saw an example of such a network, with links between banks engaging in a loan. Figure 1.8 shows another example: a network representation of international trade among twenty-eight countries [262], in which the size of each country depicts its total amount of trade, and the thickness of each link connecting two countries indicates the amount of trade between them.

Where do these networks come from? In some cases, they are the traces of what happens when each participant seeks out the best trading partner it can find guided by how highly it values different trading opportunities. In other cases, they also reflect fundamental underlying constraints in the market that limit the access of certain participants to each other. In modern markets, these constraints could be institutional restrictions based on regulations; in other settings, they could be based on physical constraints like geography. For example, Figure 1.9 shows a map of trade routes in medieval Europe: when the physical movement of goods is costly and difficult, the economic outcome for different cities can depend significantly on where they are located in the underlying transportation network.

In all these settings, the network structure encodes a lot about the pattern of trade, and the success levels of different participants are affected by their positions in the network. Having a powerful position, however, depends not just on having many connections providing different options, but also on more subtle features – such as the power of the other individuals to which one is connected. Later we will see that this idea of network positions conferring power has been extended much more broadly and reaches beyond

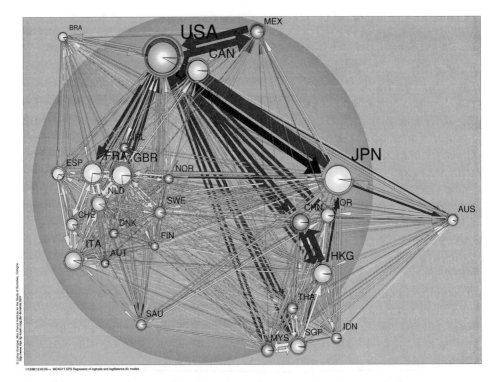

Figure 1.8. In a network representing international trade, one can look for countries that occupy powerful positions and derive economic benefits from these positions [262]. (Image from Carnegie Mellon University; http://www.cmu.edu/joss/content/articles/volume4/KrempelPlumper.html.)

just economic exchange to suggest how power imbalances in many forms of social relationships may have their roots in the network patterns formed by the relationships.

Information Networks. The information we deal with online has a fundamental network structure. Links among Web pages, for example, can help us understand how these pages are related, how they are grouped into different communities, and which pages are the most prominent or important. Figure 1.4 illustrates some of these issues: it shows a network of links among political blogs constructed by Lada Adamic and Natalie Glance in the period leading up to the 2004 U.S. presidential election [5]. Although the network in the figure is too large to be able to see clearly the detailed structure around individual blogs, the image and its layout do convey the clear separation of the blogging network into two large clusters, which turn out to closely correspond to the sets of liberal and conservative blogs, respectively. From more detailed analysis of the raw linkage data underlying the image, it is possible to pick out the prominent blogs within each of these clusters.

Current Web search engines such as Google make extensive use of network structure in evaluating the quality and relevance of Web pages. To produce search results, these sites evaluate the prominence of a Web page based not just on the number of links it receives but on more subtle aspects of its position in the network. For example, a page

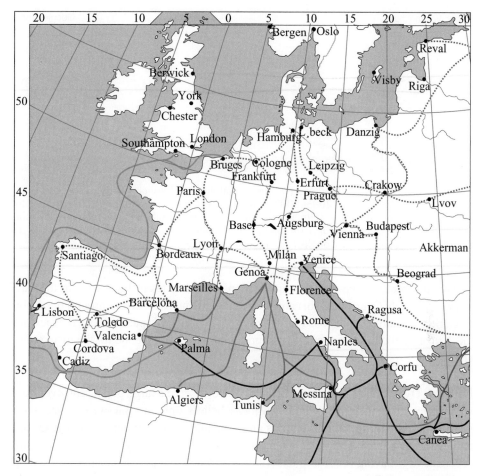

Figure 1.9. In some settings, such as this map of medieval trade routes, physical networks constrain the patterns of interaction, giving certain participants an intrinsic economic advantage based on their individual network positions. (Image from http://upload.wikimedia.org/wikipedia/commons/e/e1/Late_Medieval_Trade_Routes.jpg.)

can be viewed as more prominent if it receives links from pages that are themselves prominent; this is a circular notion in which prominence is defined in terms of itself, but we will see later that this circularity can be resolved through careful definitions that are based on a kind of equilibrium in the link structure.

The interaction between search engines and the authors of Web pages is also a compelling example of a system where connectedness at the level of behavior produces interesting effects. Whenever a search engine introduces a new method for evaluating Web pages and deciding which pages to rank highly in its results, the creators of Web content react: they optimize what they put on the Web to try to achieve a high rank under the new method. As a result, changes to a search engine can never be designed under the assumption that the Web will remain static; rather, the Web inevitably adapts to the ways in which search engines evaluate content, and search methods must be developed with these feedback effects in mind.

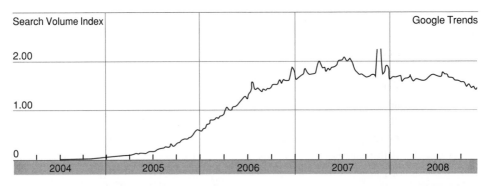

Figure 1.10. Cascading adoption of a new technology or service (in this case, the social networking site MySpace in 2005–2008) can be the result of individual incentives to use the most widespread technology – either based on the informational effects of seeing many other people adopt the technology or based on the direct benefits of adopting what many others are already using. (Image from Google Trends, http://www.google.com/trends?q=myspace.)

This inherently game-theoretic interaction existed in latent form even in the early days of the Web. Over time it became more explicit and formalized through the design of markets for advertising based on search, with advertising space allocated by auction mechanisms. Today such markets are a principal source of revenue for the main search engines.

Network Dynamics: Population Effects. If we observe a large population over time, we see a recurring pattern by which new ideas, beliefs, opinions, innovations, technologies, products, and social conventions are constantly emerging and evolving. Collectively, we can refer to these as social *practices* [382] (e.g., holding opinions, purchasing products, or behaving according to certain principles) that people can choose to adopt or not. As we watch a group or society over time, we see that new practices can be introduced that either become popular or remain obscure; meanwhile, established practices can persist or potentially fade over time. Thinking back to Figures 1.5 and 1.6, recall that they show the adoption of particular practices over time – the use of two very popular social media sites (taking the total number of Google queries for these sites over time as proxies for their popularity). Figure 1.10 depicts an analogous curve for the social networking site MySpace, where we see a life cycle of rapid adoption followed by a slower period of decline, as MySpace's dominance was challenged by newer competitors, including Facebook.

The way in which new practices spread through a population depends in large part on the fact that people *influence* each other's behavior. In short, as you see more and more people doing something, you generally become more likely to do it, too. Understanding this process, and what its consequences are, is a central issue for our understanding of networks and aggregate behavior.

At a surface level, one could hypothesize that people imitate the decisions of others simply because of an underlying human tendency to *conform*: we have a fundamental inclination to behave as we see others behaving. This observation is clearly important, but as an explanation it leaves some crucial questions unresolved. In particular, by taking imitation as a given, we miss the opportunity to ask *why* people are influenced by the behavior of others. This is a broad and difficult question, but in fact it is possible to identify multiple reasons why even purely rational agents – individuals with no a priori desire to conform to what others are doing – nonetheless copy the behavior of others.

One class of reasons is based on the fact that the behavior of others conveys *information*. You may have some private information on which to base a decision between alternatives, but if you see many people making a particular choice, it is natural to assume that they too have their own information, and to try to infer how other people are evaluating different choices from how they are behaving. In the case of a Web site like YouTube or Flickr, the observation that a lot of people use it can suggest that these people know something about its quality. Similarly, seeing that a certain restaurant is extremely crowded every weekend can suggest that many people think highly of it. But this sort of reasoning raises surprisingly subtle issues: as many people make decisions sequentially over time, the later decisions can be based in complex ways on a mixture of private information and inferences from what has already happened, so that the actions of a large set of people can in fact be based on surprisingly little genuine information. In an extreme form of this phenomenon we may get *information cascades*, where even rational individuals can choose to abandon their private information and follow a crowd.

There is a completely different but equally important class of reasons why people may imitate the behavior of others – when a direct benefit can be gained from aligning one's behavior with that of others, regardless of whether they are making the best decision. Let's go back to our examples of social networking and media-sharing sites. If the value of such sites is in the potential to interact with others, to have access to a wide range of content, and to have a large audience for the content you post, then these types of sites become more and more valuable as people join them. In other words, regardless of whether YouTube had better features than its competitors, once it became the most popular video-sharing site, there was *by definition* an added value in using it. Such *network effects* amplify the success of products and technologies that are already doing well; in a market where network effects are at work, the leader can be difficult to displace. Still, this type of dominance is not necessarily permanent; as we will see later, it is possible for a new technology to displace an old one if it offers something markedly different or when it starts in a part of the network where there is room for the new technology to take hold. *holes in the network?*

These considerations show how popularity as a general phenomenon is governed by a "rich get richer" feedback process in which popularity tends to build on itself. It is possible to build mathematical models for this process that include predictions for the distribution of popularity that are borne out by empirical data – a picture in which society's attention is divided between a small number of prominent items and a "long tail" of more obscure ones.

Network Dynamics: Structural Effects. As we've just seen, the question of how people influence each other's behavior is already quite subtle even when the actual structure of the underlying network is left implicit. But taking network structure into account provides important further insights into how such kinds of influence take place. The underlying mechanisms, based on information and direct benefits, are present both

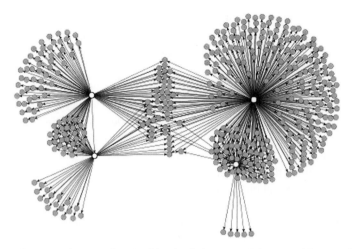

Figure 1.11. When people are influenced by the behaviors of their neighbors in the network, the adoption of a new product or innovation can cascade through the network structure. Here, e-mail recommendations for a Japanese graphic novel spread in a kind of informational or social contagion. (Image from Leskovec et al., [271]).

at the level of whole populations and at a local level in the network, between an individual and his or her set of friends or colleagues. In many cases you may care more about aligning your own behavior with the behavior of your immediate neighbors in the social network, rather than with the population as a whole.

When individuals have incentives to adopt the behavior of their neighbors in the network, there can be *cascading* effects, in which a new behavior starts with a small set of initial adopters and then spreads radially outward through the network. Figure 1.11 shows a small example, in which e-mail recommendations for a particular Japanese graphic novel spread outward from four initial purchasers. By reasoning about the underlying network structure, we will see how it becomes possible for a superior technology to displace a universally used but inferior one, if the superior technology starts in a portion of the network where it can make progress incrementally, a few people at a time. We will also find that the diffusion of technologies can be blocked by the boundary of a densely connected cluster in the network – a "closed community" of individuals who have a high amount of linkage among themselves, and hence are resistant to outside influences.

Cascading behavior in a network is sometimes referred to as "social contagion" because it spreads from one person to another in the style of a biological epidemic. Figure 1.12 reinforces this analogy; it shows the beginning of a tuberculosis outbreak [16] and forms a visual counterpart to the social cascade in Figure 1.11. There are fundamental differences in the underlying mechanisms between social and biological contagion; social contagion tends to involve decision making on the part of the affected individuals, whereas biological contagion is based on the chance of catching a disease-causing pathogen through contact with another individual. But the network-level dynamics are similar, and insights from the study of biological epidemics are also useful in thinking about the processes by which things spread in networks.

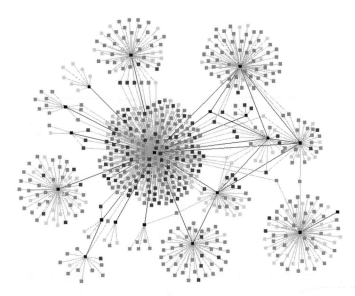

Figure 1.12. The spread of an epidemic disease (such as the tuberculosis outbreak shown here) is another form of cascading behavior in a network. The similarities and contrasts between biological and social contagion lead to interesting research questions. (Image from the American Public Health Association; [16].)

The act of spreading, which transmits both ideas and diseases, is just one kind of dynamic process that takes place in networks. A different process that we also consider is *search* – the way people can explore chains of social contacts for information or referrals to others. The surprising effectiveness with which people are able to accomplish such tasks, confirmed by both experiments and everyday experience, suggests characteristic patterns of structure at the network level that help facilitate these types of activities.

Institutions and Aggregate Behavior. Once we have developed some of the basic forces underlying networks and strategic behavior, we can ask how the *institutions* designed by a society can, in effect, channel these forces to produce certain kinds of overall outcomes. Our notion of an institution here is very broad. It can be any set of rules, conventions, or mechanisms that serves to synthesize individual actions into a pattern of aggregate behavior. We've already discussed particular examples of this process: for example, the way in which a particular auction mechanism leads to bidding behavior and hence prices; or the way in which the Internet search industry has become a significant influence on how Web content is created.

Applications of this kind of analysis to fundamental social institutions can be very informative in a number of settings. As a first setting, we consider markets and their role in aggregating and conveying information. In a financial market, for example, the market price serves to aggregate individuals' beliefs about the value of the assets being traded. In this sense, the overall behavior of the market serves to synthesize the information that is held by many participants; consequently, when people speak of what the market "expects," they are really referring to the expectations that can be read out of this composite of information.

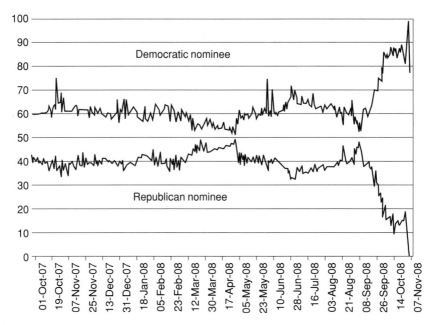

Figure 1.13. Prediction markets, as well as markets for financial assets such as stocks, can synthesize individual beliefs about future events into a price that captures the aggregate of these beliefs. The plot here depicts the varying price over time for two assets that paid $1 in the respective events that the Democratic or Republican nominee won the 2008 U.S. presidential election. (Image from Iowa Electronic Markets, http://iemweb.biz.uiowa.edu/graphs/graph_PRES08_WTA.cfm.)

How this synthesis works depends on how the market is designed and on the kind of individual and aggregate behavior that results. Nor are such issues restricted to markets for financial assets such as stocks. Recent work, for example, has explored the design of *prediction markets* that use a market mechanism to provide predictions of future events such as the outcomes of elections. Here, market participants purchase assets that pay a fixed amount if a certain event takes place. In this way, the price of the asset reflects an aggregate estimate of the probability of the event, and such estimates have been found to be highly accurate in a number of cases – the market's aggregate predictions have often outperformed the opinions of expert analysts. Figure 1.13 shows an example from the 2008 U.S. presidential election: the upper curve depicts the price over time for an asset that paid $1 in the event that the Democratic party nominee won the election, and the lower curve depicts the corresponding price for the Republican party nominee. Note that the market was already functioning before the identities of these nominees were known, and it shows a clear aggregate reaction to certain events such as the contentious end of the Democratic primary process between Obama and Clinton (in early May) and the Republican National Convention (in early September), both of which brought the prices for the opposing predictions close to equality before they diverged once and for all as the actual election neared.

Voting is another social institution that aggregates behavior across a population. Although markets and voting systems both seek a synthesis of individual beliefs or preferences, there are some fundamental contrasts in the settings where they are generally applied. We have just outlined a view of markets as aggregators of beliefs about the probabilities of future events. In this view, each individual belief that forms an ingredient of the market's consensus is ultimately confirmed as correct or incorrect, based on whether or not certain relevant future events actually happen. Voting systems, on the other hand, are typically applied to cases where each individual has a preference or prioritization over a set of arbitrary and subjective choices for which there may be no eventual way to say that any one is "right" or "wrong." The problem is then to synthesize a cumulative social preference that reconciles, as well as possible, the conflicting priorities of the individuals in the population. In our analysis of voting, we will explore a long history of work showing that the task of producing such a social preference is fraught with unavoidable difficulties. Results that formalize such difficulties began with work of eighteenth-century French philosophers, and came fully into focus with Arrow's Impossibility Theorem in the 1950s.

This perspective on institutions is a natural one for social systems that are highly interconnected. Whenever the outcomes across a population depend on an aggregate of everyone's behavior, the design of the underlying institutions can have a significant effect on how this behavior is shaped and on the resulting consequences for society.

Looking Ahead. Examples, phenomena, and principles such as those discussed in this chapter will motivate the ways in which we analyze networks, behavior, and population-level dynamics throughout the book. Understanding whether a principle holds across many settings will involve formulating and reasoning about mathematical models and also reasoning qualitatively about these models and searching for their broader implications. In this way, we hope to develop a network perspective as a powerful way of looking at complex systems in general – a way of thinking about social dynamics, economic interaction, online information, designed technology, and natural processes, and approaching such systems with an eye toward their patterns of internal structure and the rich feedback effects that result.

PART ONE
Graph Theory and Social Networks

CHAPTER 2

Graphs

In this first part of the book we develop some of the basic ideas behind graph theory – the study of network structure. This approach allows us to formulate basic network properties in a unifying language. The central definitions discussed here are simple enough that we can describe them relatively quickly at the outset; after this, we consider some fundamental applications of the definitions.

2.1 Basic Definitions

Graphs: Nodes and Edges. A *graph* is a way of specifying relationships among a collection of items. A graph consists of a set of objects, called *nodes*, with certain pairs of these objects connected by links called *edges*. For example, the graph in Figure 2.1(a) consists of four nodes labeled A, B, C, and D; node B is connected to each of the other three nodes by edges, and nodes C and D are also connected by an edge. We say that two nodes are *neighbors* if they are connected by an edge. Figure 2.1 shows the typical way to draw a graph: a small circle represents each node, and a line connects each pair of nodes that are linked by an edge.

When looking at Figure 2.1(a), think of the relationship between the two ends of an edge as being symmetric; the edge simply connects them to each other. In many settings, however, we want to express asymmetric relationships – for example, that *A points to B* but not vice versa. For this purpose, we define a *directed graph* to consist of a set of nodes, as before, together with a set of *directed edges*; each directed edge is a link from one node to another, and the direction is important. Directed graphs are generally drawn as in Figure 2.1(b), with edges represented by arrows. When we want to emphasize that a graph is not directed, we can refer to it as an *undirected graph*, but in general the graphs we discuss will be undirected unless noted otherwise.

Graphs as Models of Networks. Graphs are useful because they serve as mathematical models of network structures. With this in mind, it is useful before going further to replace the toy examples in Figure 2.1 with a real example. Figure 2.2 depicts the

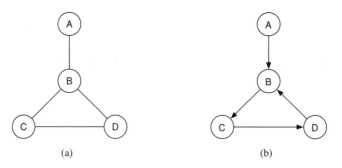

Figure 2.1. Two graphs: (a) an undirected graph on four nodes and (b) a directed graph on four nodes.

network structure of the Internet – originally called the Advanced Research Projects Agency Network (ARPANET) – from December 1970 [214], when it had only thirteen sites. Nodes represent computing hosts, and an edge joins two nodes in this drawing if there is a direct communication link between them. Ignoring the superimposed map of the United States (and the circles indicating blown-up regions in Massachusetts and Southern California), we can see that the rest of the image is simply a depiction of this thirteen-node graph using the same dots-and-lines style from Figure 2.1. Note that to show the pattern of connections, the actual placement or layout of the nodes is immaterial; all that matters is which nodes are linked to which other nodes. Thus, Figure 2.3 shows a different drawing of the same thirteen-node ARPANET graph.

Graphs play a role whenever it is useful to represent how things are either physically or logically linked to one another in a network structure. The thirteen-node

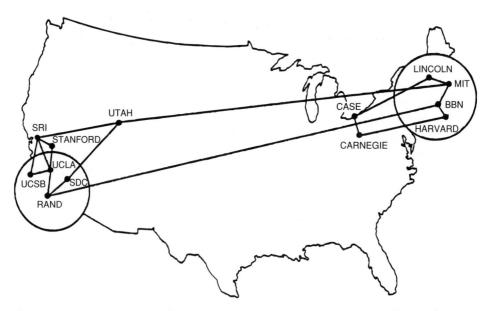

Figure 2.2. A network depicting the sites on the Internet, then known as the ARPANET, in December 1970. (Image from F. Heart, A. McKenzie, J. McQuillian, and D. Walden, [214]; available online at http://som.csudh.edu/cis/lpress/history/arpamaps/.)

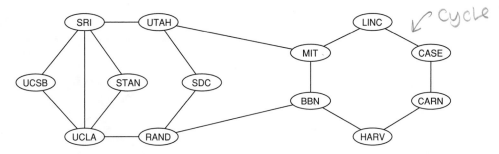

Figure 2.3. An alternate drawing of the thirteen-node Internet graph from December 1970.

ARPANET in Figures 2.2 and 2.3 is an example of a *communication network,* in which nodes are computers or other devices that can relay messages and the edges represent direct links along which messages can be transmitted. In Chapter 1, we saw examples from two other broad classes of graph structures: *social networks,* in which nodes are people or groups of people, and edges represent some kind of social interaction; and *information networks,* in which the nodes are information resources such as Web pages or documents, and edges represent logical connections such as hyperlinks, citations, or cross references. The list of areas in which graphs play a role is of course much broader than what can be enumerated here; Figure 2.4 gives a few more examples, and also shows that many images we encounter on a regular basis have graphs embedded in them.

2.2 Paths and Connectivity

We now turn to some of the fundamental concepts and definitions surrounding graphs. An enormous range of graph-theoretic notions have been studied, perhaps because graphs are so simple to define and work with. Indeed, the social scientist John Barnes once described graph theory as a "terminological jungle, in which any newcomer may plant a tree" [45]. Fortunately, for our purposes, we can get under way with just a brief discussion of some of the most central concepts.

Paths. Although we've been discussing examples of graphs in many different areas, there are clearly some common themes in the use of graphs across these areas. Perhaps foremost among these is the idea that things often travel across the edges of a graph, moving from node to node in sequence: for example, a passenger taking a sequence of airline flights, a piece of information being passed from person to person in a social network, or a computer user or a piece of software visiting a sequence of Web pages by following links.

This idea motivates the definition of a *path* in a graph: a path is simply a sequence of nodes with the property that each consecutive pair in the sequence is connected by an edge. Sometimes it is also useful to think of the path as containing not just the nodes but also the sequence of edges linking these nodes. For example, the sequence of nodes MIT, BBN, RAND, UCLA is a path in the Internet graph from Figures 2.2 and 2.3, as is the sequence CASE, LINCOLN, MIT, UTAH, SRI, UCSB. As we have defined it here, a path

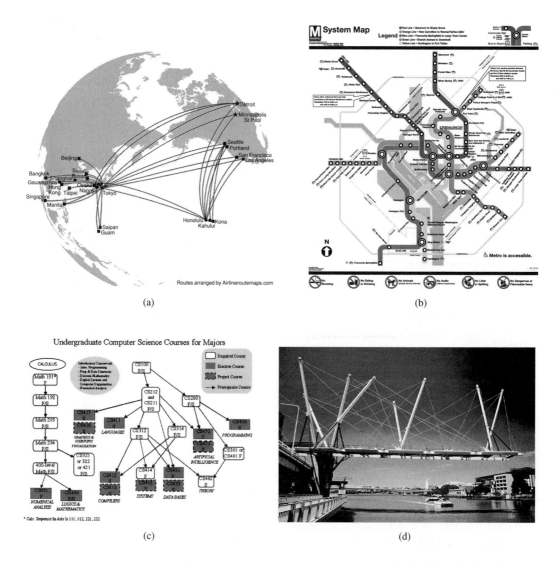

Figure 2.4. Images of graphs arising in different domains. The depictions of (a) airline and (b) subway systems are examples of *transportation networks*, in which nodes are destinations and edges represent direct connections. Much of the terminology surrounding graphs derives from metaphors based on transportation through a network of roads, rail lines, or airline flights. The prerequisites among college courses in part (c) is an example of a *dependency network*, in which nodes are tasks and directed edges indicate that one task must be performed before another. The design of complex software systems and industrial processes often requires the analysis of enormous dependency networks, with important consequences for efficient scheduling in those settings. The bridge in part (d) is an example of a *structural network*, which has joints as nodes and physical linkages as edges. The internal frameworks of mechanical structures such as buildings, vehicles, or human bodies are based on such networks, and the area of *rigidity theory*, which is at the intersection of geometry and mechanical engineering, studies the stability of such structures from a graph-based perspective [388]. (Image sources: (a) www.airlineroutemaps.com/USA/Northwest_Airlines_asia_pacific.shtml, (b) www.wmata.com/metrorail/systemmap.cfm, (c) www.cs.cornell.edu/ugrad/flowchart.htm, (d) The State of Queensland – Department of Public Works 2009.)

can repeat nodes: for example, SRI, STAN, UCLA, SRI, UTAH, MIT is a path. But most paths we consider will not do this; if we want to emphasize that the path we are discussing does not repeat nodes, we can refer to it as a *simple path.* ← no repetitions

Cycles. A particularly important kind of nonsimple path is a *cycle*, which informally is a "ring" structure such as the sequence of nodes LINC, CASE, CARN, HARV, BBN, MIT, LINC on the right-hand side of Figure 2.3. More precisely, a cycle is a path with at least three edges, in which the first and last nodes are the same, but otherwise all nodes are distinct. There are many cycles in Figure 2.3: SRI, STAN, UCLA, SRI is as short an example as possible according to our definition (because it has exactly three edges), while SRI, STAN, UCLA, RAND, BBN, MIT, UTAH, SRI is a significantly longer example.

In fact, every edge in the 1970 ARPANET belongs to a cycle, and this was by design: if any edge were to fail (e.g., if a construction crew accidentally cut through the cable), there would still be a way to get from any node to any other node. More generally, cycles in communication and transportation networks are often present to allow for redundancy; they provide for alternative routes that go the "other way" around the cycle. In a social network of friendships, we also often notice cycles in everyday life, even if we don't refer to them as such. When you discover, for example, that your wife's cousin's close friend from high school is in fact someone who works with your brother, this is a cycle – consisting of you, your wife, her cousin, his high school friend, his coworker (i.e., your brother), and finally back to you.

Connectivity. Given a graph, it is natural to ask whether every node can reach every other node by a path. With this in mind, we say that a graph is *connected* if, for every pair of nodes, there is a path between them. For example, the thirteen-node ARPANET graph is connected; and more generally, one expects most communication and transportation networks to be connected – or at least to aspire to be connected – since the goal is to move traffic from one node to another.

However, there is no a priori reason to expect graphs in other settings to be connected. For example, in a social network, one could easily imagine that there might exist two people for which it is not possible to construct a path from one to the other. Figures 2.5 and 2.6 show examples of disconnected graphs. The first is a simple made-up example, while the second is built from the collaboration graph at a biological research center [134]: nodes represent researchers, and there is an edge between two nodes if the researchers appear jointly on a coauthored publication. (Thus, the edges in Figure 2.6 represent a particular formal definition of collaboration – joint authorship of a published paper – and do not attempt to capture the network of more informal interactions that presumably take place at the research center.)

Components. Figures 2.5 and 2.6 make visually apparent a basic fact about disconnected graphs: if a graph is not connected, then it breaks apart naturally into a set of connected "pieces" – groups of nodes with the property that each group is connected when considered as a graph in isolation, and no two groups overlap. The graph in Figure 2.5 consists of three such pieces: one consisting of nodes A and B, one consisting of nodes C, D, and E, and one consisting of the rest of the nodes. The network in

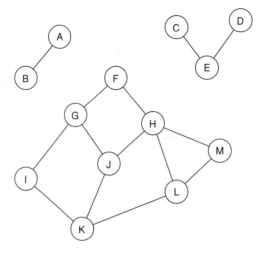

Figure 2.5. A graph with three connected components.

Figure 2.6 also consists of three pieces: one piece of three nodes, one of four nodes, and one that is much larger.

To make this notion precise, we say that a *connected component* of a graph (often shortened to the term *component*) is a subset of the nodes such that (i) every node in the subset has a path to every other and (ii) the subset is not part of some larger set with the property that every node can reach every other. Notice how both conditions (i) and (ii) are necessary to formalize the intuitive meaning we intend: condition (i) says that the component is indeed internally connected, and condition (ii) says that it is really a free-standing "piece" of the graph, not a connected part of a larger piece. (For example, we would not think of the set of nodes F, G, H, and J in Figure 2.5 as forming a component, because this set violates part (ii) of the definition. Although there are

[handwritten margin notes: 1. every node has a path to the other; 2. not part of larger subset where each node can reach each other]

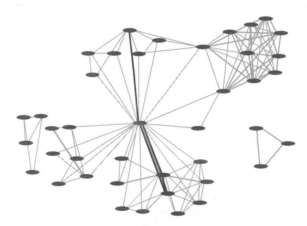

Figure 2.6. The collaboration graph of the biological research center Structural Genomics of Pathogenic Protozoa (SGPP; [134]), which consists of three distinct connected components. This graph was part of a comparative study of the collaboration-pattern graphs of nine research centers supported by the National Institutes of Health's Protein Structure Initiative; SGPP was an intermediate case between centers whose collaboration graph was connected and centers for which the graph was fragmented into many small components. (Image from BioMed Central.)

paths among all pairs of nodes in the set, this set belongs to the larger set consisting of F–M, in which all pairs are also linked by paths.)

Dividing a graph into its components is of course only a first, global way of describing its structure. Within a given component, there may be a richer internal structure that is important to an interpretation of the network. For example, thinking about the largest component from Figure 2.6, in light of the collaborations that it represents, one notices certain suggestive features of the structure: a prominent node at the center and tightly-knit groups linked to this node but not to each other. One way to formalize the role of the prominent central node is to observe that the largest connected component would break apart into three distinct components if this node were removed. Analyzing a graph in this way – in terms of its densely connected regions and the boundaries between them – is a powerful way of thinking about network structure, and it will be a central topic in Chapter 3.

Giant Components. There is a useful qualitative way of thinking about the connected components of typical large networks, for which it helps to begin with the following thought experiment. Consider the social network of the entire world, with a link between two people if they are friends. Now, of course, this is a graph that we don't actually have explicitly recorded anywhere, but it is one where we can use our general intuitions to answer some basic questions.

First, is this global friendship network connected? Presumably not. After all, connectivity is a fairly brittle property in that the behavior of a single node (or a small set of nodes) can negate it. For example, a single person with no living friends would constitute a one-node component in the global friendship network, and hence the graph would not be connected. Or the canonical "remote tropical island," consisting of people who have had no contact with the outside world, would also be a small component in the network, again showing that it is not connected.

But there is something more going on here. If you're a typical reader of this book, then you have friends who grew up in other countries. You're in the same component as all of these friends, since you have a path (containing a single edge) to each of them. Now, if you consider, say, the parents of these friends, your friends' parents' friends, their friends and descendants, then all of these people are in the same component as well – and by now, we're talking about people who have never heard of you, may well not share a language with you, may have never traveled anywhere near where you live, and may have had enormously different life experiences. So even though the global friendship network may not be connected, the component you inhabit seems very large indeed – it reaches into most parts of the world, includes people from many different backgrounds, and seems in fact likely to contain a significant fraction of the world's population.

This is in fact true when one looks across a range of network data sets. Large, complex networks often have what is called a *giant component*, which is a deliberately informal term for a connected component that contains a significant fraction of all nodes. Moreover, when a network contains a giant component, it almost always contains only one. To see why, let's go back to the example of the global friendship network and try to imagine that there were two giant components, each with hundreds of millions of people. All it would take is a single edge from someone in the first of these components

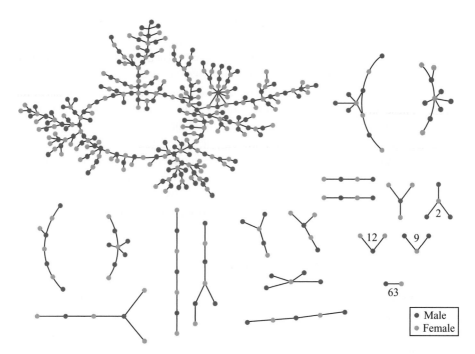

Figure 2.7. A network in which the nodes are students in a large American high school, and an edge joins any two who had a romantic relationship at some point during the 18-month period in which the study was conducted [49]. (Image from The University of Chicago Press.)

to someone in the second, and the two giant components would merge into a single component. In most cases, it's essentially inconceivable that some such edge wouldn't form, and hence two coexisting giant components are something one almost never sees in real networks. When a giant component exists, it is thus generally unique and distinguishable as a component that dwarfs all others.

In fact, in some of the rare cases when two giant components have coexisted for a long time in a real network, their merging has been sudden, dramatic, and ultimately catastrophic. For example, Jared Diamond's book *Guns, Germs, and Steel* [130] devotes much of its attention to the cataclysm that befell the civilizations of the Western Hemisphere when European explorers began arriving in it roughly half a millennium ago. One can view this development from a network perspective as follows: 5,000 years ago, the global social network likely contained two giant components – one in the Americas and one in the Europe–Asia land mass. Because of this division, technology evolved independently in the two components and, perhaps even worse, human diseases also evolved independently; when the two components finally came in contact, the technology and diseases of one quickly and disastrously overwhelmed the other.

The notion of giant components is also useful for reasoning about networks on much smaller scales. The collaboration network in Figure 2.6 is one simple example; another interesting example is depicted in Figure 2.7, which shows the romantic relationships in an American high school over an 18-month period [49]. (These edges were not all present at once; rather, there is an edge between two people if they were romantically involved at any point during the time period.) The fact that this graph contains such a large component is significant when one thinks about the spread of sexually transmitted diseases, which was a focus of the researchers performing the study. A high school student may have had a single partner over this time period and nevertheless – without realizing it – may have been part of this large component and hence part of many paths of potential transmission. As Bearman, Moody, and Stovel note in their analysis of this network, "These structures reflect relationships that may be long over, and they link individuals together in chains far too long to be the subject of even the most intense gossip and scrutiny. Nevertheless, they are real: like social facts, they are invisible yet consequential macrostructures that arise as the product of individual agency."

2.3 Distance and Breadth-First Search

In addition to simply asking whether two nodes are connected by a path, it is also interesting in most settings to ask how *long* such a path is; in transportation, Internet communication, or the spread of news and diseases, it is often important whether something flowing through a network has to travel just a few hops or many.

To be able to talk about this notion precisely, we define the *length* of a path to be the number of steps it contains from beginning to end – in other words, the number of edges in the sequence that comprises it. Thus, for example, the path MIT, BBN, RAND, UCLA in Figure 2.3 has length 3, while the path MIT, UTAH has length 1. Using the notion of a path's length, we can talk about whether two nodes are close together or far apart in a graph. In particular, the *distance* between two nodes in a graph is defined as the length of the shortest path between them. For example, the distance between the nodes LINC and SRI is 3, although to believe this you have to first convince yourself that there is no length 1 or length 2 path between them.

Breadth-First Search. For a graph like the one in Figure 2.3, we can generally figure out the distance between two nodes just by looking at the picture, but for graphs that are even somewhat more complicated, we need some systematic method to determine distances.

The most natural way to do this – and also the most efficient way to calculate distances for a large network data set using a computer – is the way you would probably do it if you really needed to trace out distances in the global friendship network (and had the unlimited patience and cooperation of everyone in the world). This procedure is pictured in Figure 2.8.

1. First declare all of your actual friends to be at a distance of 1.
2. Then find all of *their friends* (not counting people who are already friends of yours), and declare these to be at a distance of 2.
3. Then find all of *their* friends (again, not counting people whom you've already found at distances of 1 and 2) and declare these to be at a distance of 3.
(. . .) Continuing in this way, search in successive layers, each of which represents the next distance out. Each new layer is built from all those nodes that (i) have not already been discovered in earlier layers and (ii) have an edge to some node in the previous layer.

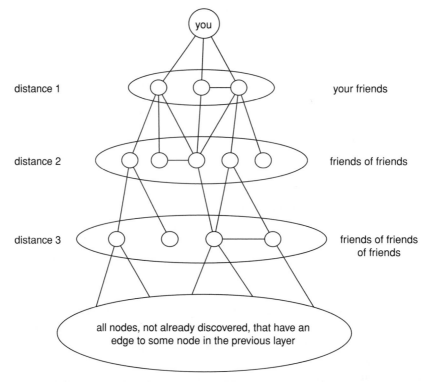

distance 1 — your friends

distance 2 — friends of friends

distance 3 — friends of friends of friends

all nodes, not already discovered, that have an edge to some node in the previous layer

you

Figure 2.8. Breadth-first search discovers the distances to nodes one "layer" at a time; each layer is built of nodes that have an edge to at least one node in the previous layer.

This technique is called *breadth-first search*, since it searches the graph outward from a starting node, reaching the closest nodes first. In addition to providing a method of determining distances, it can also serve as a useful conceptual framework to organize the structure of a graph, arranging the nodes based on their distances from a fixed starting point.

Of course, despite the social-network metaphor we used to describe breadth-first search, the process can be applied to any graph: one just keeps discovering nodes in a layer-by-layer fashion, building each new layer from the nodes that are connected to at least one node in the previous layer. For example, Figure 2.9 shows how to discover all distances from the node MIT in the thirteen-node ARPANET graph from Figure 2.3.

The Small-World Phenomenon. As with our discussion of the connected components in a graph, there is something qualitative we can say, beyond the formal definitions, about distances in typical large networks. If we go back to our thought experiments on the global friendship network, we see that the argument explaining why you belong to a giant component in fact asserts something stronger: not only are there paths of friends connecting you to a large fraction of the world's population, but these paths are surprisingly *short*. Take the example of a friend who grew up in another country: following a path through this friend, to his or her parents, and to their friends, you have followed only three steps and ended up in a different part of the world, in a different generation, with people who have very little in common with you.

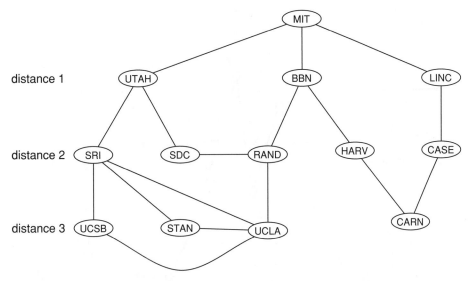

distance 1

distance 2

distance 3

Figure 2.9. The layers arising from a breadth-first of the December 1970 ARPANET, starting at the node MIT.

This idea has been termed the *small-world phenomenon* – the idea that the world looks "small" when you think of how short a path of friends it takes to get from you to almost anyone else. It is also known, perhaps more memorably, as the *six degrees of separation*; this phrase comes from the play of this title by John Guare [200], and in particular from the line uttered by one of the play's characters: "I read somewhere that everybody on this planet is separated by only six other people. Six degrees of separation. Between us and everyone else on this planet."

The first experimental study of this notion – and the origin of the number "six" in the pop-cultural mantra – was performed by Stanley Milgram and his colleagues in the 1960s [297, 391]. Lacking any of the massive social-network data sets available today, and with a budget of only $680, Milgram set out to test the speculative idea that people are really connected in the global friendship network by short chains of friends. To this end, he asked a collection of 296 randomly chosen "starters" to try forwarding a letter to a "target" person – a stockbroker who lived in a suburb of Boston. The starters were each given some personal information about the target (including his address and occupation) and were asked to forward the letter to someone they knew on a first-name basis, with the same instructions, to eventually reach the target as quickly as possible. Each letter thus passed through the hands of a sequence of friends in succession, and each thereby formed a chain of people that closed in on the stockbroker outside Boston.

Figure 2.10 shows the distribution of path lengths among the sixty-four chains that succeeded in reaching the target; the median length was six – the number that made its way two decades later into the title of Guare's play. That so many letters reached their destination, and by such short paths, was a striking fact when it was first discovered, and it remains so today. Of course, it is worth noting a few caveats about the experiment. First, the experiment clearly does not establish a statement quite as bold as "six degrees of separation between us and everyone else on this planet": the paths were just to a

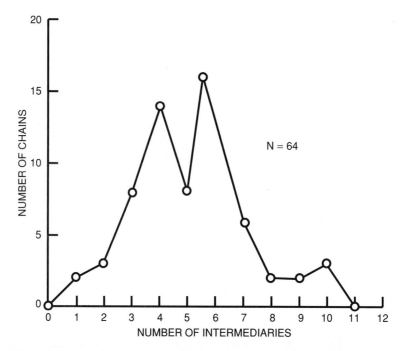

Figure 2.10. A histogram from Travers and Milgram's paper on their small-world experiment [391]. For each possible length (labeled "number of intermediaries" on the x-axis), the plot shows the number of successfully completed chains of that length. In total, sixty-four chains reached the target person, with a median chain length of six. (Image from the American Sociological Association.)

single, fairly affluent target; many letters never arrived; and attempts to re-create the experiment have been problematic due to lack of participation [255]. Second, one can ask how useful these short paths really are to people in society: even if you can reach someone through a short chain of friends, is this fact useful to you? Does it mean you're truly socially "close" to them? Milgram himself mused about this in his original paper [297]; his observation, paraphrased slightly, was that if we think of each person as the center of their own social "world," then "six short steps" becomes "six worlds apart" – a change in perspective that makes six sound like a much larger number.

Despite these caveats, the experiment and the phenomenon that it hints at have formed a crucial aspect in our understanding of social networks. In the years since the initial experiment, the overall conclusion has been accepted in a broad sense: social networks tend to have very short paths between essentially arbitrary pairs of people. And even if your six-step connections to chief executive officers and political leaders don't yield immediate payoffs on an everyday basis, the existence of all of these short paths has substantial consequences for the potential speed with which information, diseases, and other kinds of contagion can spread through society, as well as for the potential access that the social network provides to opportunities and to people with very different characteristics. All these issues, and their implications for the processes that take place in social networks, are rich enough that we will devote Chapter 20 to a more detailed study of the small-world phenomenon and its consequences.

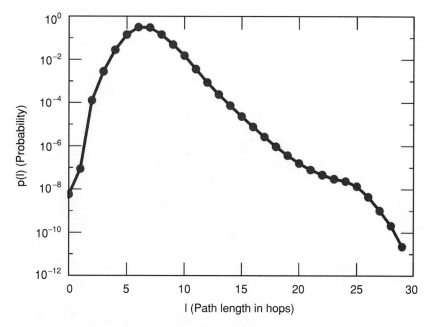

Figure 2.11. The distribution of distances in the graph of all active Microsoft Instant Messenger user accounts, in which an edge joins two users if they communicated at least once during a month-long observation period [273].

Instant Messaging, Paul Erdös, and Kevin Bacon. One reason for the current empirical consensus that social networks generally are "small worlds" is that this notion has been increasingly confirmed in settings where we do have full data available on the network structure. Milgram was forced to resort to an experiment in which letters served as "tracers" through a global friendship network that he had no hope of fully mapping on his own; but for other kinds of social network data in which the full graph structure is known, one can just load it into a computer and perform a breadth-first search procedure to determine what typical distances look like.

One of the largest such computational studies was performed by Jure Leskovec and Eric Horvitz [273]. They analyzed the 240 million active user accounts on Microsoft Instant Messenger (IM) and built a graph in which each node corresponds to a user. There is an edge between two users if they engaged in a two-way conversation at any point during a month-long observation period. As employees of Microsoft at the time, Leskovec and Horvitz had access to a complete snapshot of the system for the month under study, so there were no concerns about missing data. This graph turned out to have a giant component containing almost all of the nodes, and the distances within this giant component were very small. Indeed, the distances in the IM network closely corresponded to the numbers from Milgram's experiment, with an estimated average distance of 6.6 and an estimated median of 7. Figure 2.11 shows the distribution of distances averaged over a random sample of 1,000 users: breadth-first search was performed separately from each of these 1,000 users, and the results from these 1,000 nodes were combined to produce the plot in the figure. The reason for this estimation by sampling users is computational: the graph was so large that performing

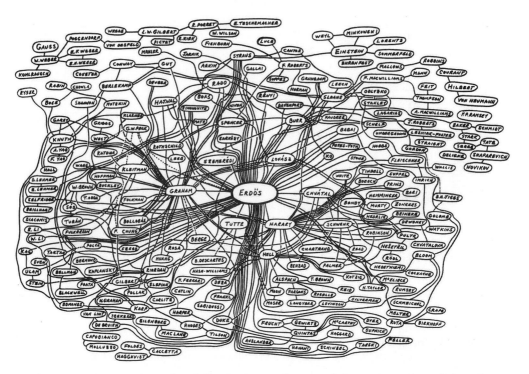

Figure 2.12. Ron Graham's hand-drawn picture of a part of the mathematics collaboration graph, centered on Paul Erdös [189]. (Image courtesy of Ron Graham.)

breadth-first search from every single node would have taken an astronomical amount of time. Producing plots like this efficiently for massive graphs is an interesting research topic in itself [338].

In a sense, the plot in Figure 2.11 starts to approximate, in a striking way, what Milgram and his colleagues were trying to understand – the distribution of how far apart we all are in the full global friendship network. At the same time, reconciling the structure of such massive data sets with the underlying networks they are trying to measure is an issue that comes up here, as it will many times throughout the book. In this case, enormous as the Microsoft IM study was, it remains some distance away from Milgram's goal: it only tracks people who are technologically endowed enough to have access to instant messaging and, rather than basing the graph on who is truly friends with whom, it can only observe who talks to whom during an observation period.

Turning to a smaller scale – at the level of hundreds of thousands of people rather than hundreds of millions – researchers have also discovered very short paths in collaboration networks within professional communities. In the domain of mathematics, for example, people often speak of the itinerant mathematician Paul Erdös, who published roughly 1,500 papers during his career, as a central figure in the collaborative structure of the field. To make this precise, we can define a collaboration graph as we did for Figure 2.6, in this case with nodes corresponding to mathematicians, and edges connecting pairs of mathematicians who have jointly authored a paper. (While Figure 2.6 concerned a single research lab, we are now talking about collaboration within the entire field of mathematics.) Figure 2.12 shows a small hand-drawn piece of the collaboration graph, with paths leading to Paul Erdös [189]. Now, a mathematician's *Erdös number* is the distance from him or her to Erdös in this graph [198]. The point is that most mathematicians have Erdös numbers of at most 4 or 5, and – extending the collaboration graph to include coauthorship across all the sciences – most scientists in other fields have Erdös numbers that are comparable or only slightly larger: Albert Einstein's is 2; Enrico Fermi's is 3; Noam Chomsky's and Linus Pauling's are each 4; and Francis Crick's and James Watson's are 5 and 6, respectively. The world of science is truly a small one in this sense.

Inspired by some mixture of the Milgram experiment, John Guare's play, and a compelling belief that Kevin Bacon was the center of the Hollywood universe, three students at Albright College in Pennsylvania sometime around 1994 adapted the idea of Erdös numbers to the collaboration graph of movie actors and actresses: nodes are performers, an edge connects two performers if they've appeared together in a movie, and a performer's *Bacon number* is his or her distance in this graph to Kevin Bacon [372]. Using cast lists from the Internet Movie Database (IMDb), it is possible to compute Bacon numbers for all performers via breadth-first search; and as with mathematics, it's a small world indeed. The average Bacon number, for all performers in the IMDb, is approximately 2.9, and it is a challenge to find one that's larger than 5. Indeed, it's fitting to conclude with a movie enthusiast's description of his late-night attempts to find the largest Bacon number in the IMDb by hand: "With my life-long passion for movies, I couldn't resist spending many hours probing the dark recesses of film history until, at about 10 AM on Sunday, I found an incredibly obscure 1928 Soviet pirate film, *Plenniki Morya*, starring P. Savin with a Bacon number of 7, and whose supporting cast of 8 appeared nowhere else" [197]. One is left with the image of a long exploration that arrives finally at the outer edge of the movie world – in the early history of film, in the Soviet Union – and yet in another sense, only eight steps from where it started.

2.4 Network Data Sets: An Overview

The explosion of research on large-scale networks in recent years has been fueled to a significant extent by the increasing availability of large, detailed network data sets. We've seen examples of such data sets throughout these first two chapters, and it is useful at this point to step back and think more systematically about where people have been getting the data that they employ in large-scale studies of networks.

To put this in perspective, we note first of all that there are several distinct reasons why you might study a particular network data set. One reason is that you may care about the actual domain that the data set comes from, so that fine-grained details of the data are potentially as interesting as the broad picture. Another reason is that you may be using the data set as a proxy for a related network that is impossible to measure – for example, in the way the Microsoft IM graph from Figure 2.11 gave us information about distances in a social network of a scale and character that begins to approximate the global friendship network. A third possibility is that you may be looking for network properties that appear to be common across many different domains, and so finding a similar effect in unrelated settings can suggest that it has a certain universal nature, with possible explanations that are not tied to the specifics of any one of the domains.

Of course, all three of these motivations are often at work simultaneously, to varying degrees, in the same piece of research. For example, the analysis of the Microsoft IM graph gave us insight into the global friendship network. However, at a more specific level, the researchers performing the study were also interested in the dynamics of instant messaging in particular, and at a more general level, the results of the IM graph analysis fit into the broader framework of small-world phenomena that span many domains.

As a final point, here we are concerned with sources of data on networks that are *large*. If one wants to study a social network on 20 people – say, within a small company, or a fraternity or sorority, or a karate club as in Figure 1.1 – then one strategy is to interview all the people involved and to ask them who their friends are. But if we want to study the interactions among 20,000 people, or 20,000 individual nodes of some other kind, then we need to be more opportunistic in where we look for data: except in unusual cases, we can't simply go out and collect everything by hand, and so we need to think about settings in which the relevant information has in some essential way already been collected for us.

With this in mind, let's consider some of the main sources of large-scale network data that people have used for research. The resulting list is far from exhaustive, and the categories are not truly distinct – a single data set can easily exhibit characteristics from several.

Collaboration Graphs. Collaboration graphs record who works with whom in a specific setting; coauthorships among scientists and coappearance in movies by actors and actresses are two examples of collaboration graphs that we discussed in Section 2.3. Another example that has been extensively studied by sociologists is the graph of highly placed people in the corporate world, with an edge joining two if they have served together on the board of directors of the same Fortune 500 company [301]. The online world provides new instances: the Wikipedia collaboration graph (connecting two Wikipedia editors if they've ever edited the same article) [122, 246] and the World of Warcraft (WoW) collaboration graph (connecting two WoW users if they've ever taken part together in the same raid or other activity) [419] are just two examples.

Sometimes a collaboration graph is studied to learn about the specific domain it comes from; for example, sociologists who study the business world have a substantive interest in the relationships among companies at the director level, as expressed via comembership on boards. On the other hand, while there is a research community that studies the sociological context of scientific research, a broader community of people is interested in scientific coauthorship networks precisely because they form detailed, predigested snapshots of a rich form of social interaction that unfolds over a long period of time [318]. By using online bibliographic records, one can often track the patterns of collaboration within a field across a century or more, and thereby attempt to extrapolate how the social structure of collaboration may work across a range of harder-to-measure settings as well.

Who-Talks-to-Whom Graphs. The Microsoft IM graph is a snapshot of a large community engaged in several billion conversations over the course of a month. In this way, it captures the "who-talks-to-whom" structure of the community. Similar data sets have been constructed from the e-mail logs within a company [6] or a university [259], and also from records of phone calls: researchers have studied the structure of *call graphs* in which each node is a phone number, and there is an edge between two phone numbers if they were engaged in a phone call over a given observation period [1, 334]. One can also use the fact that mobile phones with short-range wireless technology can detect other similar devices nearby. By equipping a group of experimental subjects with such devices and studying the traces they record, researchers can thereby build "face-to-face" graphs that represent physical proximity: a node in such a graph is a person carrying one of the mobile devices, and an edge joins two people if they were detected to be in close physical proximity over a given observation period [141, 142].

In almost all of these kinds of data sets, the nodes represent customers, employees, or students of the organization that maintains the data. These individuals generally have strong expectations of privacy, not necessarily even appreciating how easily one can reconstruct details of their behavior from the digital traces they leave behind when communicating by e-mail, instant messaging, or phone. As a result, the style of research performed on this kind of data is generally restricted in specific ways that protect the privacy of the individuals involved. Such privacy considerations have also become a topic of significant discussion in settings in which companies try to use this type of data for marketing, or when governments try to use it for intelligence-gathering purposes [315].

Related to this kind of who-talks-to-whom data, economic network measurements recording the "who-transacts-with-whom" structure of a market or financial community have been used to study the ways in which different levels of access to market participants can lead to different levels of market power and different prices for goods. This empirical work has in turn motivated more mathematical investigations of how a network structure limiting access between buyers and sellers can affect outcomes [63, 176, 232, 261], which will be a focus of our discussion in Chapters 10–12.

Information Linkage Graphs. Snapshots of the Web are central examples of network data sets; nodes are Web pages and directed edges represent links from one page to another. Web data stands out both in its scale and in the diversity of what the nodes represent: billions of little pieces of information with links wiring them together. And clearly it is not just the information that is of interest, but the social and economic structures that stand behind the information: hundreds of millions of personal pages on social-networking and blogging sites, and hundreds of millions more representing companies and governmental organizations trying to engineer their external images in a crowded network.

A network on the scale of the full Web can be daunting to work with; simply manipulating the data effectively can become a research challenge in itself. As a result, much network research has been done on interesting, well-defined subsets of the Web, including the linkages among bloggers [264], among pages on Wikipedia [404], among pages on social-networking sites such as Facebook or MySpace [185], and among discussions and product reviews on shopping sites [201].

The study of information linkage graphs significantly predates the Web: the field of *citation analysis* has, since the early part of the twentieth century, studied the network structure of citations among scientific papers or patents, as a way of tracking the evolution of science [145]. Citation networks are still popular research data sets today for the same reason that scientific coauthorship graphs are: even if you don't have a substantive interest in the social processes by which science gets done, citation networks are very clean data sets that can easily span many decades.

Technological Networks. Although the Web is built on a lot of sophisticated technology, it would be a mistake to think of it primarily as a technological network: it is really a projection onto a technological backdrop of ideas, information, and social and economic structure created by humans. But as we noted in the opening chapter, there has been a convergence of social and technological networks in recent years, and many interesting network data sets come from the more overtly technological end of the spectrum, in which nodes represent physical devices and edges represent physical connections between them. Examples include the interconnections among computers on the Internet [155] or among generating stations in a power grid [411].

Even physical networks like these are ultimately economic networks as well, representing the interactions among the competing organizations, companies, regulatory bodies, and other economic entities that shape them. On the Internet, this relationship is made particularly explicit by a two-level view of the network. At the lowest level, nodes are individual routers and computers, and an edge indicates that two devices actually have a physical connection to each other. But, at a higher level, these nodes are grouped into what are essentially little "nation-states" termed *autonomous systems*, each one controlled by a different Internet service provider. There is then a who-transacts-with-whom graph on the autonomous systems, known as the *AS graph*, that represents the data-transfer agreements these Internet service providers make with each other.

Networks in the Natural World. Graph structures also abound in biology and the other natural sciences, and network research has devoted particular attention to several different types of biological networks. The following are three examples at three different scales, from the population level down to the molecular level.

1. As a first example, *food webs* represent the who-eats-whom relationships among species in an ecosystem [137]: there is a node for each species, and a directed edge from node A to node B indicates that members of A consume members of B. Understanding the structure of a food web as a graph can help in reasoning about issues such as *cascading extinctions*: if certain species become extinct, then species that rely on them for food also risk becoming extinct if they do not have alternative food sources; these extinctions can propagate through the food web as a chain reaction.

2. Another heavily studied network in biology is the structure of neural connections within an organism's brain: the nodes are neurons, and an edge represents a

connection between two neurons [380]. The global brain architecture for simple organisms like *C. elegans*, with 302 nodes and roughly 7,000 edges, has essentially been completely mapped [3], but obtaining a detailed network picture for brains of higher organisms is far beyond the current state of the art. However, significant insight has been gained by studying the structure of specific modules within a complex brain and understanding how they relate to one another.

3. A final example is the set of networks that make up a cell's metabolism. There are many ways to define these networks, but roughly, the nodes are compounds that play a role in a metabolic process, and the edges represent chemical interactions among them [43]. Researchers hope that analysis of these networks can shed light on the complex reaction pathways and regulatory feedback loops that take place inside a cell, and perhaps suggest "network-centric" attacks on pathogens that disrupt their metabolism in targeted ways.

2.5 Exercises

1. One reason for graph theory's power as a modeling tool is the fluidity with which one can use it to formalize the properties of large systems using the language of graphs, and then to systematically explore their consequences. In this first set of questions, we work through an example of this process using the concept of a *pivotal* node.

   Recall from earlier in the chapter that a *shortest path* between two nodes is a path of the minimum possible length. We say that a node X is *pivotal* for a pair of distinct nodes Y and Z if X lies on every shortest path between Y and Z (and X is not equal to either Y or Z).

   For example, in the graph in Figure 2.13, node B is pivotal for two pairs: the pair consisting of A and C, and the pair consisting of A and D. [Notice that B is not pivotal for the pair consisting of D and E because two different shortest paths connect D and E, one of which (using C and F) does not pass through B. Therefore, B is not on *every* shortest path between D and E.] As another example, note that node D is not pivotal for any pairs.

   (a) Give an example of a graph in which *every* node is pivotal for at least one pair of nodes. Explain your answer.

   (b) Give an example of a graph in which *every* node is pivotal for at least two different pairs of nodes. Explain your answer.

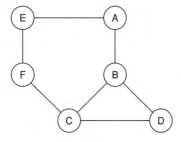

Figure 2.13. In this example, node B is pivotal for two pairs: the pair consisting of A and C, and the pair consisting of A and D; node D is not pivotal for any pairs.

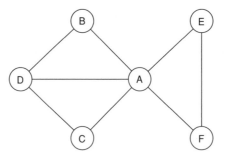

Figure 2.14. Node A is a gatekeeper; node D is a local gatekeeper but not a gatekeeper.

(c) Give an example of a graph having at least four nodes in which there exists a single node X that is pivotal for *every* pair of nodes (not counting pairs that include X). Explain your answer.

2. In the next set of questions, we consider a related cluster of definitions that seek to formalize the idea that certain nodes can play a "gatekeeping" role in a network. The first definition is the following. We say that a node X is a *gatekeeper* if, for some other two nodes Y and Z, every path from Y to Z passes through X. For example, in the graph in Figure 2.14, node A is a gatekeeper, because it lies on every path from B to E. (It also lies on every path between other pairs of nodes – for example, the pair D and E, as well as other pairs.)

   This definition has a certain "global" flavor, because it requires that we think about paths in the full graph to decide whether a particular node is a gatekeeper. A more "local" version of this definition could involve only looking at the neighbors of a node. The following is a way to make this definition precise: we say that a node X is a *local gatekeeper* if there are two neighbors of X, say Y and Z, that are not connected by an edge. (That is, for X to be a local gatekeeper, there should be two nodes Y and Z such that Y and Z each have edges to X, but not to each other.) For example, in Figure 2.14, on the one hand, node A is a local gatekeeper in addition to being a gatekeeper; node D, on the other hand, is a local gatekeeper but not a gatekeeper. (Node D has neighbors B and C, which are not connected by an edge; however, every pair of nodes – including B and C – can be connected by a path that does not go through D.)

   So we have two new definitions: *gatekeeper* and *local gatekeeper*. When faced with new mathematical definitions, a strategy that is often useful is to explore them first through examples and then to assess them at a more general level and try to relate them to other ideas and definitions. Let's try this in the next two questions.

   (a) Give an example (together with an explanation) of a graph in which more than half of all nodes are gatekeepers.

   (b) Give an example (together with an explanation) of a graph in which there are no gatekeepers but in which every node is a local gatekeeper.

3. When we think about a single aggregate measure to summarize the distances between the nodes in a given graph, two natural quantities come to mind. One is the *diameter*, which we define to be the maximum distance between any pair of nodes in the graph. Another is the *average distance*, which, as the term suggests, is the average distance over all pairs of nodes in the graph.

In many graphs, these two quantities are close to each other in value. But there are graphs where they can be very different.

(a) Describe an example of a graph where the diameter is more than three times as large as the average distance.

(b) Describe how you could extend your construction to produce graphs in which the diameter exceeds the average distance by as large a factor as you would like. (That is, for every number c, can you produce a graph in which the diameter is more than c times as large as the average distance?)

CHAPTER 3

Strong and Weak Ties

One of the powerful roles that networks play is to bridge the local and the global – to offer explanations for how simple processes at the level of individual nodes and links can have complex effects that ripple through a population as a whole. In this chapter, we consider some fundamental social network issues that illustrate this theme: how information flows through a social network, how different nodes can play structurally distinct roles in this process, and how these structural considerations shape the evolution of the network itself over time. These themes all play central roles throughout the book, adapting themselves to different contexts as they arise. Our context in this chapter begins with the famous "strength of weak ties" hypothesis from sociology [190] and explores outward from this point to more general settings.

Let's begin with some backgound and a motivating question. As part of his Ph.D. thesis research in the late 1960s, Mark Granovetter interviewed people who had recently changed employers to learn how these people had discovered their new jobs [191]. In keeping with earlier research, Granovetter found that many people learned information leading to their current jobs through personal contacts. But perhaps more strikingly, these personal contacts were often described by interview subjects as acquaintances rather than close friends. This fact is a bit surprising: your close friends presumably have the most motivation to help you when you're between jobs, so why is it so often your more distant acquaintances who are actually to thank for crucial information leading to your new job?

The answer that Granovetter proposed to this question is striking in the way it links two different perspectives on distant friendships – one structural, focusing on the way these friendships span different portions of the full network, and the other interpersonal, considering the purely local consequences that follow from a friendship between two people being either strong or weak. In this way, the answer transcends the specific setting of job-seeking and offers a way of thinking about the architecture of social networks more generally. To get at this broader view, we first develop some general principles about social networks and their evolution, and then we return to Granovetter's question.

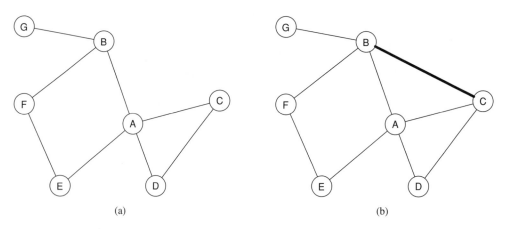

Figure 3.1. The formation of the edge between B and C illustrates the effects of triadic closure, since they have a common neighbor, A. Parts (a) and (b) illustrate the network before and after the B-C edge forms, respectively.

3.1 Triadic Closure

In Chapter 2, our discussions treated networks largely as static structures: we take a snapshot of the nodes and edges at a particular moment in time, and then we ask about paths, components, distances, and so forth. While this style of analysis forms the basic foundation for thinking about networks – and indeed, many data sets are inherently static, offering us only a single snapshot of a network – it is also useful to think about how a network evolves over time. In particular, what are the mechanisms by which nodes arrive and depart, and by which edges form and vanish?

The precise answer, of course, varies depending on the type of network being considered, but one of the most basic principles is the following:

> If two people in a social network have a friend in common, then there is an increased likelihood that they will become friends themselves at some point in the future [347].

We refer to this principle as *triadic closure*, and it is illustrated in Figure 3.1. If nodes B and C have a friend A in common, then the formation of an edge between B and C produces a situation in which all three nodes A, B, and C have edges connecting each other – a structure we refer to as a *triangle* in the network. The term "triadic closure" comes from the fact that the B-C edge has the effect of "closing" the third side of this triangle. If we observe snapshots of a social network at two distinct points in time, then in the later snapshot we generally find a significant number of new edges that have formed through this triangle-closing operation, between two people who had a common neighbor in the earlier snapshot. Figure 3.2, for example, shows the new edges we might see from watching the network in Figure 3.1 over a longer time span.

The Clustering Coefficient. The basic role of triadic closure in social networks has motivated the formulation of simple social network measures to capture its prevalence. One of these measures is the *clustering coefficient* [320, 411]. The clustering coefficient

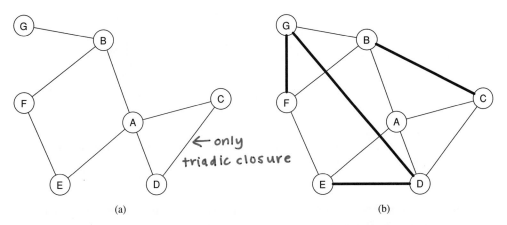

Figure 3.2. If we watch a network for a longer span of time, we can see multiple edges forming; some form through triadic closure while others (such as the D-G edge) form even though the two endpoints have no neighbors in common. The network is illustrated (a) before and (b) after new edges form.

of a node A is defined as the probability that two randomly selected friends of A are friends with each other. In other words, it is the fraction of pairs of A's friends that are connected to each other by edges. For example, the clustering coefficient of node A in Figure 3.2(a) is 1/6 (because there is only the single C-D edge among the six pairs of friends B-C, B-D, B-E, C-D, C-E, and D-E), and it increases to 1/2 in the second snapshot of the network in Figure 3.2(b) (because there are now the three edges B-C, C-D, and D-E among the same six pairs). In general, the clustering coefficient of a node ranges from 0 (when none of the node's friends are friends with each other) to 1 (when all of the node's friends are friends with each other). The more strongly the process of triadic closure operates in the neighborhood of the node, the higher the clustering coefficient will tend to be.

Reasons for Triadic Closure. Triadic closure is intuitively very natural, and essentially everyone can find examples from their own experience. Moreover, experience suggests some of the basic reasons why triadic closure operates. One reason why B and C are more likely to become friends, when they have a common friend A, is simply based on the *opportunity* for B and C to meet: if A spends time with both B and C, then there is an increased chance that they will end up knowing each other and potentially becoming friends. A second, related reason is that, in the process of forming a friendship, the fact that each of B and C is friends with A (provided they are mutually aware of this) gives them a basis for *trusting* each other that may be lacking in an arbitrary pair of unconnected people.

A third reason is based on the *incentive* that A may have to bring B and C together: if A is friends with B and C, then it becomes a source of latent stress in these relationships if B and C are not friends with each other. This premise is based in theories dating back to early work in social psychology [217]; it also has empirical reflections that show up in natural but troubling ways in public-health data. For example, Bearman and Moody [48] have found that teenage girls who have a low clustering coefficient in

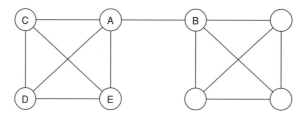

Figure 3.3. The A-B edge is a *bridge,* meaning that its removal would place A and B in distinct components. Bridges provide nodes with access to parts of the network that are unreachable by other means.

their network of friends are significantly more likely to contemplate suicide than those whose clustering coefficient is high.

3.2 The Strength of Weak Ties

So how does all this relate to Mark Granovetter's interview subjects telling him with such regularity that their best job leads came from acquaintances rather than close friends? In fact, triadic closure turns out to be one of the crucial ideas needed to unravel what's going on.

Bridges and Local Bridges. Let's start by positing that information about good jobs is something that is relatively scarce; hearing about a promising job opportunity from someone suggests that they have access to a source of useful information that you don't. Now consider this observation in the context of the simple social network drawn in Figure 3.3. The person labeled A has four friends in this picture, but one of her friendships is qualitatively different from the others: A's links to C, D, and E connect her to a tightly-knit group of friends who all know each other, while the link to B seems to reach into a different part of the network. We could speculate, then, that the structural peculiarity of the link to B translates into differences in the role it plays in A's everyday life: while the tightly-knit group of nodes A, C, D, and E all tend to be exposed to similar opinions and similar sources of information, A's link to B offers her access to things she otherwise wouldn't necessarily hear about.

To make precise the sense in which the A-B link is unusual, we introduce the following definition. An edge that joins two nodes A and B in a graph is called a *bridge* if deleting the edge would cause A and B to lie in two different components. In other words, this edge is literally the only route between its endpoints, the nodes A and B.

Now, if our discussion in Chapter 2 about giant components and small-world properties taught us anything, it's that bridges are presumably extremely rare in real social networks. You may have a friend from a very different background, and it may seem that your friendship is the only thing that bridges your world and his, but one expects in reality that there will be other, hard-to-discover, multistep paths that also span these worlds. In other words, if we were to look at Figure 3.3 as it is embedded in a larger, ambient social network, we would likely see a picture that looks like Figure 3.4.

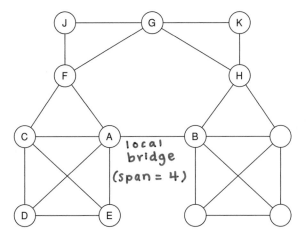

Figure 3.4. The A-B edge is a local bridge of span 4, since the removal of this edge would increase the distance between A and B to 4.

In Figure 3.4, the A-B edge is not the only path that connects its two endpoints; though they may not realize it, A and B are also connected by a longer path through F, G, and H. This kind of structure is arguably much more common than a bridge in real social networks, and we use the following definition to capture it. We say that an edge joining two nodes A and B in a graph is a *local bridge* if its endpoints A and B have no friends in common – in other words, deleting the edge would increase the distance between A and B to a value strictly more than 2. We say that the *span* of a local bridge is the distance its endpoints would be from each other if the edge were deleted [190, 407]. Thus, in Figure 3.4, the A-B edge is a local bridge with span 4; we can also check that no other edge in this graph is a local bridge, because for every other edge in the graph, the endpoints would still be at a distance of 2 if the edge were deleted. Notice that the definition of a local bridge already makes an implicit connection with triadic closure, in that the two notions form conceptual opposites: an edge is a local bridge precisely when it does not form the side of any triangle in the graph.

Local bridges, especially those with reasonably large spans, still play roughly the same role as bridges, though in a less extreme way; they provide their endpoints with access to parts of the network – and hence sources of information – that they would otherwise be far away from. And so this is the first network context in which to interpret Granovetter's observation about job-seeking: we might expect that, if a node like A is going to get truly new information – the kind that leads to a new job – it might come unusually often (though certainly not always) from a friend connected by a local bridge. The closely-knit groups to which you belong, although they are filled with people eager to help, are also filled with people who know roughly the same things that you do.

The Strong Triadic Closure Property. Of course, Granovetter's interview subjects didn't say, "I learned about the job from a friend connected by a local bridge." If we believe that local bridges are overrepresented in the set of people providing job leads, how

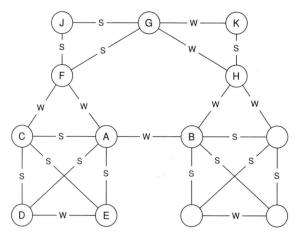

Figure 3.5. Each edge of the social network from Figure 3.4 is labeled as either a *strong tie* (S) or a *weak tie* (W) to indicate the strength of the relationship. The labeling in the figure satisfies the Strong Triadic Closure property at each node: if the node has strong ties to two neighbors, then these neighbors must have at least a weak tie between them.

does this fact relate to the observation that distant acquaintances are overrepresented as well?

To talk about this in any detail, <u>we must be able to distinguish between different levels of *strength* in the links of a social network</u>. We will deliberately refrain from trying to define "strength" precisely, but we mean it to align with the idea that stronger links represent closer friendships and greater frequency of interaction. In general, links can have a wide range of possible strengths, but for conceptual simplicity – and to match the friend–acquaintance dichotomy that we're trying to explain – we will categorize all links in the social network as belonging to one of two types: *strong ties* (the stronger links, corresponding to friends) and *weak ties* (the weaker links, corresponding to acquaintances).[1]

Once we have decided on a classification of links into strong and weak ties, we can take a social network and label each edge as either strong or weak. For example, assuming we asked the nodes in the social network of Figure 3.4 to report which of their network neighbors were close friends and which were acquaintances, we could get an annotated network as shown in Figure 3.5.

---

[1] In addition to the difficulty in reducing a range of possible link strengths to a two-category strong/weak distinction, there are many other subtleties in this type of classification. For example, in the discussion here, we will consider this division of links into strong and weak ties to be fixed in a single snapshot of the network. In reality, of course, the strength of a particular link can vary across different times and different situations. For example, an employee of a company who is temporarily assigned to work with a new division of the company for a few months may find that her full set of available social-network links remains roughly the same, but that her links to people within the new division have been temporarily strengthened (because of the sudden close proximity and increased contact), while the links to her old division have been temporarily weakened. Similarly, a high school student may find that links to fellow members of a particular sports team constitute strong ties while that sport is in season, but that some of these links – to the teammates he knows less well outside of the team – become weak ties in other parts of the year. Again, for our purposes, we consider a single distinction between strong and weak ties that holds throughout the analysis.

It is useful to go back and think about triadic closure in terms of this division of edges into strong and weak ties. If we recall the arguments supporting triadic closure, based on opportunity, trust, and incentive, they all act more powerfully when the edges involved are strong ties than when they are weak ties. This suggests the following qualitative assumption:

> If a node A has edges to nodes B and C, then the B-C edge is especially likely to form if A's edges to B and C are both strong ties.

To enable more concrete analysis, Granovetter suggested a more formal (and somewhat more extreme) version of this assumption, as follows.

> We say that a node A violates the Strong Triadic Closure property if it has strong ties to two other nodes B and C, and there is no edge at all (either a strong or weak tie) between B and C. We say that a node A satisfies the Strong Triadic Closure property if it does not violate it.

violating vs. satisfying

We can check that no node in Figure 3.5 violates the Strong Triadic Closure property; hence, all nodes satisfy the property. However, if the A-F edge were to be a strong tie rather than a weak tie, then nodes A and F would both violate the Strong Triadic Closure property: node A would now have strong ties to nodes E and F without there being an E-F edge, and node F would have strong ties to both A and G without the presence of an A-G edge. As a further check on the definition, notice that with the edges labeled as in Figure 3.5, node H satisfies the Strong Triadic Closure property: node H couldn't possibly violate the property because it only has a strong tie to one other node.

Clearly the Strong Triadic Closure property is too extreme for us to expect it hold across all nodes of a large social network. But it is a useful step as an abstraction to reality, making it possible to reason further about the structural consequences of strong and weak ties. In the same way that an introductory physics course might assume away the effects of air resistance in analyzing the flight of a ball, proposing a slightly too-powerful assumption in a network context can also lead to cleaner and conceptually more informative analysis. For now, then, we continue figuring out where the assumption leads in this case; later, we'll return to the question of its role as a modeling assumption.

Local Bridges and Weak Ties. We now have a purely local, interpersonal distinction between kinds of links – whether they are weak ties or strong ties – as well as a global, structural notion – whether they are local bridges or not. On the surface, there is no direct connection between the two notions, but in fact by using triadic closure we can establish a connection via the following claim:

> *Claim:* If a node A in a network satisfies the Strong Triadic Closure property and is involved in at least two strong ties, then any local bridge it is involved in must be a weak tie.

In other words, under the assumption of the Strong Triadic Closure property and a sufficient number of strong ties, the local bridges in a network are necessarily weak ties.

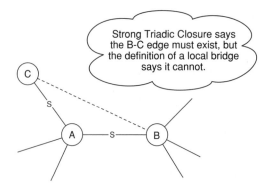

Figure 3.6. If a node satisfies Strong Triadic Closure and is involved in at least two strong ties, then any local bridge it is involved in must be a weak tie. The figure illustrates the reason why: if the A-B edge is a strong tie, then there must also be an edge between B and C, meaning that the A-B edge cannot be a local bridge.

We're going to justify this claim as a mathematical statement – that is, it will follow logically from the definitions thus far, without our having to invoke any as-yet-unformalized intuitions about what social networks ought to look like. In this way, it's a different kind of claim from our argument in Chapter 2 that the global friendship network likely contains a giant component. That was a thought experiment (albeit a very convincing one) that required us to believe various empirical statements about the network of human friendships – empirical statements that could later be confirmed or refuted by collecting data on large social networks. Here, on the other hand, we have constructed a small number of specific mathematical definitions – particularly local bridges and the Strong Triadic Closure property – and we can now justify the claim directly from these definitions.

The argument is actually very short, and it proceeds by contradiction. Take some network, and consider a node A that satisfies the Strong Triadic Closure property and is involved in at least two strong ties. Now suppose A is involved in a local bridge – say, to a node B – that is a strong tie. We want to argue that this is impossible, and the crux of the argument is depicted in Figure 3.6. First, since A is involved in at least two strong ties, and the edge to B is only one of these ties, A must have a strong tie to some other node, which we'll call C. Now we ask: Is there an edge connecting B and C? Since the edge from A to B is a local bridge, A and B must have no friends in common, and so the B-C edge must not exist. But this contradicts Strong Triadic Closure, which says that since the A-B and A-C edges are both strong ties, the B-C edge must exist. This contradiction shows that our initial premise – the existence of a local bridge that is a strong tie – cannot hold, finishing the argument.

This argument completes the connection we've been looking for between the local property of tie strength and the global property of serving as a local bridge. As such, it provides a way to think about how interpersonal properties of social-network links are related to broader considerations about the network's structure. But because the argument is based on some strong assumptions (mainly Strong Triadic Closure, since the other assumption is very mild), it is also worth reflecting on the role played by simplifying assumptions in this type of result.

First, simplifying assumptions are useful when they lead to statements that are robust in practice, making sense as qualitative conclusions that hold in approximate forms even when the assumptions are relaxed. This is the case here: the mathematical argument can be summarized more informally and approximately as saying that, in real life, a local bridge between nodes A and B tends to be a weak tie because, if it weren't, triadic closure would tend to produce short-cuts to A and B that would eliminate its role as a local bridge. Again, one is tempted to invoke the analogy to freshman physics: even if the assumptions used to derive the perfectly parabolic flight of a ball don't hold exactly in the real world, the conclusions about flight trajectories are a very useful, conceptually tractable approximation to reality.

Second, when the underlying assumptions are stated precisely, as they are here, it becomes possible to test them on real-world data. In the past few years researchers have studied the relationship of tie strength and network structure quantitatively across large populations, and they have shown that the conclusions described here in fact hold in an approximate form. We describe some of this empirical research in the next section.

Finally, this analysis provides a concrete framework for thinking about the initially surprising fact that life transitions such as a new jobs are often rooted in contact with distant acquaintances. The argument is that these links are the social ties that connect us to new sources of information and new opportunities, and their conceptual "span" in the social network (the local bridge property) is directly related to their weakness as social ties. This dual role – as weak connections but also valuable conduits to hard-to-reach parts of the network – is the surprising strength of weak ties.

3.3 Tie Strength and Network Structure in Large-Scale Data

The arguments connecting tie strength with the structural properties of the underlying social network make intriguing theoretical predictions about the organization of social networks in real life. For many years after Granovetter's initial work, however, these predictions remained relatively untested on large social networks because of the difficulty in finding data that reliably captured the strengths of edges in large-scale, realistic settings.

This state of affairs began to change rapidly once detailed traces of digital communication became available. Such "who-talks-to-whom" data exhibits the two ingredients we need for an empirical evaluation of hypotheses about weak ties: the network structure of communication among pairs of people, and the total time that two people spend talking to each other, which can be used as a proxy for the strength of the tie – the more time spent communicating during the course of an observation period, the stronger we can declare the tie to be.

In one of the more comprehensive studies of this type, Onnela et al. studied the who-talks-to-whom network maintained by a cell phone provider that covered roughly 20% of a national population [334]. The nodes correspond to cell phone users, and an edge joins two nodes if they made phone calls to each other in both directions over an 18-week observation period. Because the cell phones in this population are generally used for personal communication rather than business purposes, and because the lack of a central directory means that cell phone numbers are generally exchanged among people who already know each other, the underlying network can be viewed as a reasonable sampling of the conversations occurring within a social network representing a significant fraction of one country's population. Moreover, the data set exhibits many of the broad structural features of large social networks discussed in Chapter 2, including a *giant component* – a single connected component containing most (in this case 84%) of the individuals in the network.

Generalizing the Notions of Weak Ties and Local Bridges. The theoretical formulation in the preceding section is based on two definitions that impose sharp dichotomies on the network: an edge is either a strong tie or a weak tie, and it is either a local bridge or it isn't. For both of these definitions, it is useful to have versions that exhibit smoother gradations when we go to examine real data on a large scale.

We have just indicated a way to do this for tie strength: we can make the strength of an edge a numerical quantity by defining it to be the total number of minutes spent on phone calls between the two ends of the edge. It is also useful to sort all the edges by tie strength, so that for a given edge we can ask what percentile it occupies in this ordering of edges sorted by strength.

Because a very small fraction of the edges in the cell phone data constitute local bridges, it makes sense to soften this definition as well, so that we can view certain edges as being "almost" local bridges. To do this, we define the *neighborhood overlap* of an edge connecting A and B to be the ratio

$$\frac{\text{number of nodes who are neighbors of } both \text{ A and B}}{\text{number of nodes who are neighbors of } at \ least \ one \ of \text{ A or B}}, \qquad (3.1)$$

where in the denominator we do not count A or B themselves (even though A is a neighbor of B and B is a neighbor of A). As an example of how this definition works, consider the edge A-F in Figure 3.4. The denominator of the neighborhood overlap for A-F is determined by the nodes B, C, D, E, G, and J, because each of these nodes is a neighbor of at least one of A or F. Of these, only C is a neighbor of both A and F, so the neighborhood overlap is $1/6$.

The key feature of this definition is that this ratio in question is zero precisely when the numerator is zero and, hence, when the edge is a local bridge. So the notion of a local bridge is contained within this definition – local bridges are the edges of neighborhood overlap zero; hence, edges with very small neighborhood overlap can be thought of as being "almost" local bridges. (Intuitively, edges with very small neighborhood overlap consist of nodes that travel in "social circles" that have almost no one in common.) For example, this definition views the A-F edge as much closer to being a local bridge than the A-E edge, which accords with intuition.

Empirical Results on Tie Strength and Neighborhood Overlap. Using these definitions, we can formulate some fundamental quantitative questions based on Granovetter's theoretical predictions. First, we can ask how the neighborhood overlap of an edge depends on its strength; the strength of weak ties predicts that neighborhood overlap should grow as tie strength grows.

In fact, this dependence is borne out extremely cleanly by the data. Figure 3.7 shows the neighborhood overlap of edges as a function of their percentile in the sorted order of all edges by tie strength. Thus, as we go to the right on the x-axis, we get edges of greater

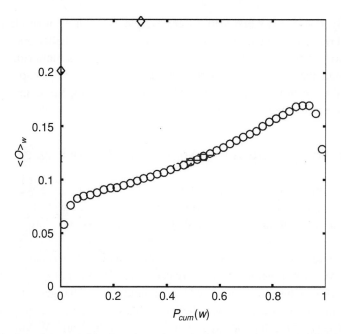

Figure 3.7. A plot of the neighborhood overlap of edges as a function of their percentile in the sorted order of all edges by tie strength. The fact that overlap increases with increasing tie strength is consistent with the theoretical predictions from Section 3.2 [334]. (Image from the National Academy of Sciences, USA.)

and greater strength, and because the curve rises in a strikingly linear fashion, we also get edges of greater and greater neighborhood overlap. The relationship between these quantities thus aligns well with the theoretical prediction.[2]

The measurements underlying Figure 3.7 describe a connection between tie strength and network structure at a local level – in the neighborhoods of individual nodes. It is also interesting to consider how this type of data can be used to evaluate the more global picture suggested by the theoretical framework – that weak ties serve to link together different tightly knit communities that each contain a large number of stronger ties. Here, Onnela et al. provided an indirect analysis to address this question, as follows. They first deleted edges from the network one at a time, starting with the strongest ties and working downward in order of tie strength. The giant component shrank steadily as they did this, reducing in size gradually due to the elimination of connections among the nodes. Onnela et al. then tried the same thing but starting from the weakest ties and working upward in order of tie strength. In this case, they found that the giant component shrank more rapidly; moreover, its remnants broke apart abruptly once a critical number of weak ties had been removed. This outcome is consistent with a picture in which the weak ties provide the more crucial connective structure for holding together disparate communities and for keeping the global structure of the giant component intact.

---

[2] It is of course interesting to note the deviation from this trend at the very right-hand edge of the plot in Figure 3.7, corresponding to the edges of greatest possible tie strength. It is not clear what causes this deviation, but it is certainly plausible that these extremely strong edges are associated with people who are using their cell phones in some unusual fashion.

Ultimately, this is just a first step toward evaluating theories of tie strength on network data of this scale, and it illustrates some of the inherent challenges: given the size and complexity of the network, we cannot simply look at the structure and "see what's there." Indirect measures must generally be used and, because one knows relatively little about the meaning or significance of any particular node or edge, it remains an ongoing research challenge to draw richer and more detailed conclusions as well.

3.4 Tie Strength, Social Media, and Passive Engagement

As an increasing amount of social interaction moves online, the way in which we maintain and access our social networks begins to change as well. For example, as is well known to users of social-networking tools, people maintain large explicit lists of friends in their profiles on these Web sites; this contrasts with the ways in which such friendship circles were once much more implicit, and in fact relatively difficult for individuals even to enumerate or mentally access [244]. What effect does this have on social network structure more broadly? Understanding the changes arising from these forms of technological mediation is a challenge that was articulated early in the general public's adoption of the Internet by researchers including Barry Wellman [413, 414], and these issues have continued to broaden in scope between then and now.

Tie strength can provide an important perspective on such questions by providing a language for asking how online social activity is distributed across different kinds of links and, in particular, how it is distributed across links of different strengths. When we see people maintaining hundreds of friendship links on a social-networking site, we can ask how many of these links correspond to strong ties that involve frequent contact and how many correspond to weak ties that are activated relatively rarely.

Tie Strength on Facebook. Researchers have begun to address such questions of tie strength using data from some of the most active social media sites. At Facebook, Cameron Marlow and his colleagues analyzed the friendship links reported in each user's profile and asked to what extent each link was actually *used* for social interaction, beyond simply being reported in the profile [286]. In other words, where are the strong ties among a user's friends? To make this question precise using the data they had available, they defined three categories of links based on usage over a one-month observation period:

1. A link represents *reciprocal (mutual) communication* if the user both sent messages to the friend at the other end of the link and also received messages from the friend during the observation period.
2. A link represents *one-way communication* if the user sent one or more messages to the friend at the other end of the link (whether or not these messages were reciprocated).
3. A link represents a *maintained relationship* if the user followed information about the friend at the other end of the link, whether or not actual communication took place; "following information" in this case means either clicking on content via Facebook's News Feed service (which provides information about the friend) or visiting the friend's profile more than once.

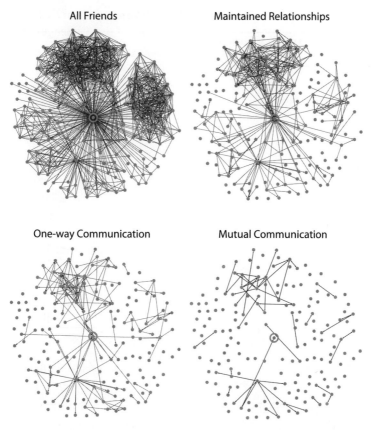

Figure 3.8. Four different views of a Facebook user's network neighborhood, showing the structure of links corresponding respectively to all declared friendships, maintained relationships, one-way communication, and reciprocal (i.e., mutual) communication, all over a one-month observation period. (Image from [286].)

Notice that these three categories are not mutually exclusive. Indeed, the links classified as reciprocal communication always belong to the set of links classified as one-way communication.

This stratification of links by their use lets us understand how a large set of declared friendships on a site like Facebook translates into an actual pattern of more active social interaction, corresponding approximately to the use of stronger ties. To get a sense of the relative volumes of these different kinds of interaction through an example, Figure 3.8 shows the network neighborhood of a sample Facebook user, consisting of all his friends, and all links among his friends. The upper-left diagram shows the set of all declared friendships in this user's profile; the other three diagrams show how the set of links becomes sparser once we consider only maintained relationships, one-way communication, or reciprocal communication. Moreover, as we restrict to stronger ties, certain parts of the network neighborhood thin out much faster than others. For example, in the neighborhood of the sample user in Figure 3.8, we see two distinct regions with a particularly large amount of triadic closure: one in the upper part of the drawing, and one on the right-hand side of the drawing. However, when we restrict to

Active Network Sizes

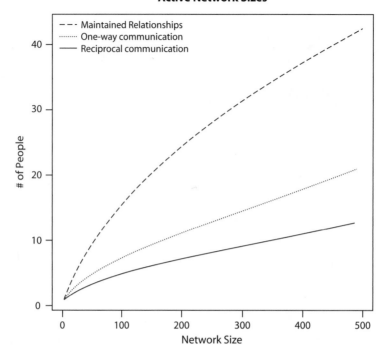

Figure 3.9. The number of links corresponding to maintained relationships, one-way communication, and reciprocal communication as a function of the total neighborhood size for users on Facebook. (Image from [286].)

links representing communication or a maintained relationship, many more of the links survive in the upper region than in the right-hand region. One could conjecture that the right-hand region represents a set of friends from some earlier phase of the user's life (perhaps from high school) who declare each other as friends but do not actively remain in contact; the upper region, on the other hand, consists of more recent friends (perhaps coworkers) for whom there is more frequent contact.

We can make the relative abundance of these different types of links quantitative through the plot in Figure 3.9. On the x-axis is the total number of friends declared by a user, and the curves then show the (smaller) numbers of other link types as a function of this total. Several interesting conclusions can be drawn from this figure. First, the figure confirms that, even for users who report very large numbers of friends on their profile pages (on the order of 500), the number with whom they actually communicate is generally between 10 and 20, and the number they follow even passively (e.g., by reading about them) is less than 50. But beyond this observation, Marlow and his colleagues draw a further conclusion about the power of media like Facebook to enable this kind of *passive engagement*, in which one keeps up with friends by reading news about them even in the absence of communication. They argue that this passive network occupies an interesting middle ground between the strongest ties maintained by regular communication and the weakest ties from one's distant past, preserved only in lists on social-networking profile pages. They write, "The stark contrast between reciprocal

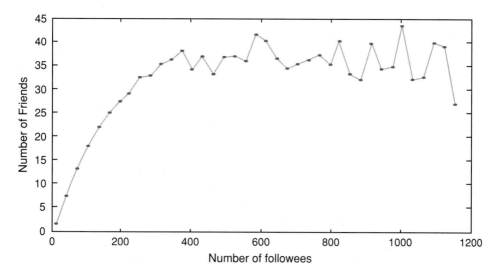

Figure 3.10. The total number of a user's strong ties (defined by multiple directed messages) as a function of the number of followees he or she has on Twitter. (Image from First Monday and [222].)

and passive networks shows the effect of technologies such as News Feed. If these people were required to talk on the phone to each other, we might see something like the reciprocal network, where everyone is connected to a small number of individuals. Moving to an environment where everyone is passively engaged with each other, some event, such as a new baby or engagement can propagate very quickly through this highly connected network."

Tie Strength on Twitter. Similar lines of investigation have been carried out recently on the social media site Twitter, where individual users engage in a form of *microblogging* by posting very short, 140-character public messages known as "tweets." Twitter also includes social-network features, and these enable one to distinguish between stronger and weaker ties: each user can specify a set of other users whose messages he or she will follow, and each user can also direct messages specifically to another user. (In the latter case, the message remains public for everyone to read, but it is marked with a notation indicating that it is intended for a particular user.) Thus, the former kind of interaction defines a social network based on more passive, weak ties: it is very easy for a user to follow many people's messages without ever directly communicating with any of them. The latter kind of interaction – especially when we look at users directing multiple messages to others – corresponds to a stronger kind of direct relationship.

In a style analogous to the work of Marlow et al., Huberman, Romero, and Wu analyzed the relative abundance of these two kinds of links on Twitter [222]. Specifically, for each user they considered the number of users whose messages she followed (her "followees"), and then they defined her strong ties to consist of the users to whom she had directed at least two messages over the course of an observation period. Figure 3.10 shows how the number of strong ties varies as a function of the number of followees. As we saw for Facebook, even for users who maintain very large numbers of weak ties online, the number of strong ties remains relatively modest, in this case stabilizing at a value below 50 even for users with more than 1,000 followees.

There is another useful way to think about the contrast between the ease of forming links and the relative scarcity of strong ties in environments like Facebook and Twitter. By definition, each strong tie requires a continuous investment of time and effort to maintain, and so even people who devote a lot of their energy to building strong ties will eventually reach a limit – imposed simply by the hours available in a day – on the number of ties that they can maintain in this way. The formation of weak ties is governed by much milder constraints – they must be established at their outset but not necessarily maintained continuously – and so it is easier for someone to accumulate them in large numbers. We will encounter this distinction again in Chapter 13 when we consider how social networks differ at a structural level from information networks such as the World Wide Web.

Understanding the effect that online media have on the maintenance and use of social networks is a complex problem for which the underlying research is only in its early stages. But some of these preliminary studies already highlight the ways in which networks of strong ties can still be relatively sparse even in online settings where weak ties abound, and how the nature of the underlying online medium can affect how different links are used for conveying information.

3.5 Closure, Structural Holes, and Social Capital

The discussion thus far suggests a general view of social networks in terms of tightly-knit groups and the weak ties that link them. The analysis has focused primarily on the roles that different kinds of edges of a network play in this structure: a few edges span different groups while most are surrounded by dense patterns of connections.

A lot of further insight can be gained by asking about the roles that different *nodes* play in this structure as well. In social networks, access to edges that span different groups is not equally distributed across all nodes: some nodes are positioned at the interfaces between multiple groups, with access to boundary-spanning edges, while others are positioned in the middle of a single group. What is the effect of this heterogeneity? Following the expositional lead of social-network researchers including Ron Burt [87], we can formulate an answer to this question as a story about the different experiences that nodes have in a network like the one in Figure 3.11 – particularly in the contrast between the experience of a node such as A, who sits at the center of a single tightly-knit group, and node B, who sits at the interface between several groups.

Embeddedness. Let's start with node A. Node A's set of network neighbors has been subject to considerable triadic closure; A has a high clustering coefficient. (Recall that the clustering coefficient is the fraction of pairs of neighbors who are themselves neighbors.)

To talk about the structure around A, it is useful to introduce an additional definition. We define the *embeddedness* of an edge in a network to be the number of common neighbors shared by the two endpoints. Thus, for example, the A-B edge has an

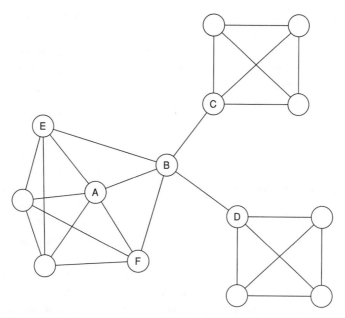

Figure 3.11. The contrast between densely-knit groups and boundary-spanning links is reflected in the different positions of nodes A and B in the underyling social network.

embeddedness of 2, because A and B have the two common neighbors E and F. This definition relates to two notions from earlier in the chapter. First, the embeddedness of an edge is equal to the numerator in the ratio that defines the *neighborhood overlap* in Equation (3.1) from Section 3.3. Second, we observe that local bridges are precisely the edges that have an embeddedness of zero, since they were defined as those edges whose endpoints have no neighbors in common.

In the example shown in Figure 3.11, what stands out about A is the way in which all of his edges have significant embeddedness. A long line of research in sociology has argued that, if two individuals are connected by an embedded edge, it is easier for them to trust one another and to have confidence in the integrity of the transactions (social, economic, or otherwise) that take place between them [117, 118, 193, 194, 395]. Indeed, the presence of mutual friends puts the interactions between two people "on display" in a social sense, even when they are carried out in private; in the event of misbehavior by one of the two parties to the interaction, there is the potential for social sanctions and reputational consequences from their mutual friends. As Granovetter writes, "My mortification at cheating a friend of long standing may be substantial even when undiscovered. It may increase when a friend becomes aware of it. But it may become even more unbearable when our mutual friends uncover the deceit and tell one another" [194].

No similar kind of deterring threat exists for edges with zero embeddedness, since there is no one who knows both people involved in the interaction. In this respect, the interactions that B has with C and D are much riskier than the embedded interactions experienced by A. Moreover, the constraints on B's behavior are made complicated by the fact that she is subject to potentially contradictory norms and expectations from the different groups with which she associates [116].

Structural Holes. Thus far we have been discussing the advantages that accrue for node A in Figure 3.11 from the closure in his network neighborhood, and the embedded edges that result. But a related line of research in sociology, catalyzed by the influential work of Burt [86], has argued that network positions such as that of node B, at the end of multiple local bridges, confer a distinct set of equally fundamental advantages.

The canonical setting for this argument is the social network within an organization or company, consisting of people who are in some ways collaborating on common objectives and in other ways implicitly competing for career advancement. Note that, although we may be thinking about settings involving a formal organizational hierarchy – encoding who reports to whom – we are interested in the more informal network of who knows whom, and who talks to whom on a regular basis. Empirical studies of managers in large corporations have correlated an individual's success within a company with his or her access to local bridges [86, 87]. At a more abstract level, the central arguments behind these studies are also supported by the network principles we have been discussing, as we now explore further.

Going back to the network in Figure 3.11, imagine that the network represents the interaction and collaboration among managers in a large company. In Burt's language, node B, with her multiple local bridges, spans a *structural hole* in the organization – the "empty space" in the network between two sets of nodes that do not otherwise interact closely. (Unlike the term "local bridge," which has a precise mathematical definition in terms of the underlying graph, we will keep the term "structural hole" somewhat informal in this discussion.) The argument is that B's position offers advantages in several dimensions relative to A's position. The first kind of advantage, following the observations in the previous section, is an informational one: B has early access to information that originates in multiple, noninteracting parts of the network. Any one person has a limited amount of energy they can invest in maintaining contacts across the organization, and B is investing her energy efficiently by reaching out to different groups rather than basing all her contacts in the same group.

A second, related kind of advantage is based on the way in which standing at one end of a local bridge can be an amplifier for creativity [88]. Experience from many domains suggests that innovations often arise from the unexpected synthesis of multiple ideas, with each of the ideas perhaps well known by itself, but well known in distinct and unrelated bodies of expertise. Thus, B's position at the interface between several noninteracting groups gives her not only access to the combined information from these groups but also the opportunity for novel ideas by combining these disparate sources of information in new ways.

Finally, B's position in the network provides an opportunity for a kind of social "gatekeeping": She regulates the access of both C and D to the tightly-knit group to which she belongs, and she controls the ways in which her own group learns about information coming from C and D's groups. This position provides B with a source of power in the organization, and one could imagine that certain people in this situation might try to prevent triangles from forming around the local bridges they are a part of. For example, another edge from C or D into B's group would reduce B's gatekeeping role.

This last point highlights a sense in which the interests of node B and of the organization as a whole may not be aligned. For the functioning of the organization, accelerating the flow of information between groups could be beneficial, but this building of bridges would come at the expense of B's latent power at the boundaries of these groups. It also emphasizes that our analysis of structural holes is primarily a static one: we look at the network at a single point in time and consider the effects of the local bridges. How long these local bridges last before triadic closure produces short-cuts around them, and the extent to which people in an organization are consciously, strategically seeking out local bridges and trying to maintain them, is less well understood; it is a topic of ongoing research [90, 188, 252, 259].

Ultimately, then, there are trade-offs in the relative positions of A and B. The position of B at the interface between groups means that her interactions are less embedded within a single group and less protected by the presence of mutual network neighbors. On the other hand, this riskier position provides her with access to information that resides in multiple groups and with the opportunity both to regulate the flow of this information and to synthesize it in new ways.

Closure and Bridging as Forms of Social Capital.   All of these arguments are framed in terms of individuals and groups deriving benefits from an underlying social structure or social network; as such, they are naturally related to the notion of *social capital* [117, 118, 279, 342, 344]. Social capital is a term that has been in increasingly widespread use, but it is a famously difficult one to define [138]. In Alejandro Portes's review of the topic, he writes, "Consensus is growing in the literature that social capital stands for the ability of actors to secure benefits by virtue of membership in social networks or other social structures" [342].

The formulation of the term "social capital" is designed to suggest its role as part of an array of different forms of capital, all of which serve as tangible or intangible resources that can be mobilized to accomplish tasks. James Coleman and others speak of social capital alongside *physical capital* (the implements and technologies that help perform work) and *human capital* (the skills and talents that individual people bring to a job or goal) [118]. Pierre Bourdieu offers a related but distinct taxonomy, which considers social capital in relation to *economic capital* (consisting of monetary and physical resources) and *cultural capital* (the accumulated resources of a culture that exist at a level beyond any one individual's social circle, conveyed through education and other broad social institutions) [17, 75].

Borgatti, Jones, and Everett [74], summarizing discussions within the sociology community, have observed two important sources of variation in the use of the term "social capital." First, social capital is sometimes viewed as a property of a group; some groups function more effectively than others because of favorable properties of their social structures or networks. Alternately, it has also been considered a property of an individual. Used in this latter sense, a person can have more or less social capital depending on his or her position in the underlying social structure or network. A second, related source of terminological variation is based on whether social capital is a property that is purely intrinsic to a group – based only on the social interactions among the group's members – or if it is also based on the interactions of the group with the outside world.

A view at this level of generality does not yet specify what kinds of network structures are the most effective for creating social capital, and the discussion earlier in this section highlights several different perspectives on the question. The writings of Coleman and others on social capital emphasize the benefits of triadic closure and embedded edges for the reasons discussed earlier: they enable the enforcement of norms and reputational effects, and hence can help protect the integrity of social and economic transactions. Burt, on the other hand, discusses social capital as a tension between *closure* and *brokerage*: the former refers to Coleman's conception and the latter refers to benefits arising from the ability to "broker" interactions at the interface between different groups, across structural holes.

In addition to the structural distinctions between these perspectives, their contrasts also illustrate different focuses on groups versus individuals and on the activity within a group versus its contacts with a larger population. The contrasts are also related to Robert Putnam's dichotomy between *bonding capital* and *bridging capital* [344]; these terms, although intended informally, correspond roughly to the kinds of social capital arising respectively from connections within a tightly-knit group and from connections between such groups.

The notion of social capital thus provides a framework for thinking about social structures as facilitators of effective action by individuals and groups, and a way of focusing discussions of the different kinds of benefits conferred by different structures. Networks are at the heart of such discussions, both in the way they produce closed groups where transactions can be trusted and in the way they link different groups and thereby enable the fusion of different sources of information residing in these groups.

3.6 Advanced Material: Betweenness Measures and Graph Partitioning

This is the first in a series of sections throughout the book labeled "Advanced Material." Each of these sections comes at the end of a chapter and explores mathematically more sophisticated aspects of some of the models developed earlier in the chapter. They are strictly optional, in that nothing later in the book builds on them. Also, although these sections are technically more involved, they are written to be completely self-contained, except where specific pieces of mathematical background are needed; this necessary background is noted at the beginnings of the sections where it is required.

In this section, we formulate more concrete mathematical definitions for some of the basic concepts from earlier in the chapter. The discussion in this chapter has articulated a way of thinking about networks in terms of tightly-knit regions and the weaker ties that link them together. We have formulated precise definitions for some of the underlying concepts, such as the clustering coefficient and the definition of a local bridge. In the process, however, we have refrained from trying to delineate precisely what we mean by a "tightly-knit region," and how to formally characterize such regions.

For our purposes so far, it has been useful to be able to speak in this more general, informal way about tightly-knit regions; it helps to be flexible since the exact characterization of the notion may differ depending on the different domains in which we encounter it. But there are also settings in which it is valuable to have a more precise,

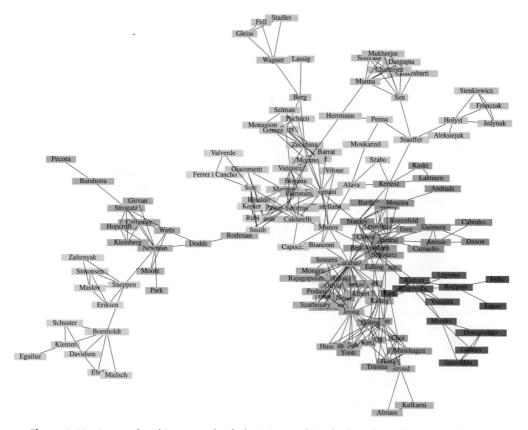

Figure 3.12. A coauthorship network of physicists and applied mathematicians working on networks [322]. Within this professional community, more tightly-knit subgroups are evident from the network structure. (Image from the American Physical Society.)

formal definition. In particular, a formal definition can be crucial if we are faced with a network data set and actually want to identify densely connected groups of nodes within it.

Therefore, the focus here is to describe a method that can take a network and break it down into a set of tightly-knit regions, with sparser interconnections between the regions. We will refer to this problem as *graph partitioning*, and the constituent parts into which the network is divided are the *regions* arising from the partitioning method. Formulating a method for graph partitioning will implicitly require working out a set of definitions for all these notions that are both mathematically tractable and also useful on real data sets.

To give a sense for what we might hope to achieve from such a method, let's consider two examples. The first, shown in Figure 3.12, depicts the coauthorships among a set of physicists and applied mathematicians working on networks [322]. Recall that we discussed coauthorship networks in Chapter 2 as a way of encoding the collaborations within a professional community. It is clear from the picture that there are tightly-knit groups within this community, and some people sit on the boundaries of their respective groups. Indeed it resembles, at a somewhat larger scale, some of the pictures of tightly

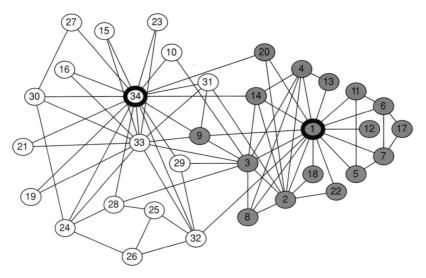

Figure 3.13. A karate club studied by Wayne Zachary [421]. A dispute during the course of the study caused it to split into two clubs, indicated by the shading of the nodes. Could the boundaries of the two clubs have been predicted from the network structure? (Image from the *Journal of Anthropological Research.*)

knit groups and weak ties that we drew in schematic form earlier in examples such as Figure 3.11. Is there a general way to pull these groups out of the data, beyond using just our visual intuition?

A second example, in Figure 3.13, is a picture of the social network of a karate club studied by Wayne Zachary [421] and discussed in Chapter 1: a dispute between the president (node 34) and the instructor (node 1) led the club to split into two rival clubs. Figure 3.13 shows the network structure, with the membership in the two clubs after the division indicated by the shaded and unshaded nodes. Now, a natural question is whether the structure itself contains enough information to predict the fault line. In other words, did the split occur along a weak interface between two densely connected regions? Unlike the network in Figure 3.12, or in some of the earlier examples in the chapter, the two conflicting groups here are still heavily interconnected. So to identify the division in this case, we need to look for more subtle signals in the way that edges between the groups effectively occur at lower "density" than edges within the groups. We will see that in fact this is possible, both for the definitions considered here and for other definitions.

A. A Method for Graph Partitioning

Many different approaches have been developed for the problem of graph partitioning, and for networks with clear divisions into tightly-knit regions, there are often many methods that will prove to be effective. While these methods can differ considerably in their specifics, it is useful to identify the different general styles that motivate their designs.

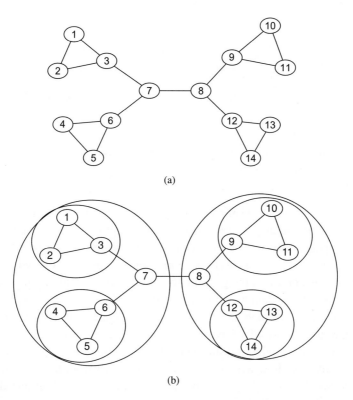

(a)

(b)

Figure 3.14. (a) A sample network and (b) tightly-knit regions and their nested structure. In many networks, there are tightly-knit regions that are intuitively apparent, and they can even display a *nested* structure, with smaller regions nesting inside larger ones.

General Approaches to Graph Partitioning. One class of methods focuses on identifying and removing the "spanning links" between densely connected regions. Once these links are removed, the network begins to fall apart into large pieces; within these pieces, further spanning links can be identified, and the process continues. We will refer to these as *divisive* methods of graph partitioning, because they divide up the network as they go.

An alternate class of methods starts from the opposite end of the problem, focusing on the most tightly-knit parts of the network, rather than on the connections at their boundaries. Such methods find nodes that are likely to belong to the same region and merge them together. Once this is done, the network consists of a large number of merged chunks, each containing the seeds of a densely connected region; the process then looks for chunks that should be further merged together, and in this way the regions are assembled "bottom-up." We refer to these as *agglomerative* methods of graph partitioning, because they glue nodes together into regions as they go.

To illustrate the conceptual differences between these two approaches, consider the simple graph in Figure 3.14(a). Intuitively, as indicated in Figure 3.14(b), there is a broad separation between one region, consisting of nodes 1–7, and another region, consisting of nodes 8–14. Within each of these regions, there is a further split: on the left into nodes 1–3 and nodes 4–6, and on the right into nodes 9–11 and nodes 12–14.

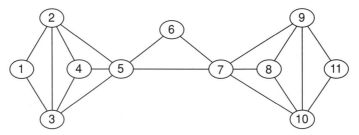

Figure 3.15. A network can display tightly-knit regions even when there are no bridges or local bridges along which to separate it.

Note how this simple example already illustrates that the process of graph partitioning can usefully be viewed as producing regions in the network that are naturally *nested*: larger regions potentially contain several smaller, even more densely connected regions "nested" within them. This is of course a familiar picture from everyday life, where, for example, a separation of the global population into national groups can be further subdivided into subpopulations within particular local areas within countries.

In fact, a number of graph partitioning methods will find the nested set of regions indicated in Figure 3.14(b). Divisive methods will generally proceed by breaking apart the graph first at the 7-8 edge and subsequently at the remaining edges into nodes 7 and 8. Agglomerative methods will arrive at the same result from the opposite direction, first by merging the four triangles into clumps and then by finding that the triangles themselves can be naturally paired off.

This is a good point at which to make the discussion more concrete, and to do so we focus on a particular divisive method proposed by Girvan and Newman [184, 322]. The Girvan–Newman method has been applied very widely in recent years, and to social network data in particular. Again, however, we emphasize that graph partitioning is an area in which an especially wide range of different approaches is in use. The approach we discuss is an elegant and particular widely used one; however, understanding the types of methods that work best in different situations remains a subject of active research.

The Notion of Betweenness. To motivate the design of a divisive method for graph partitioning, let's think about some general principles that might lead us to remove the 7-8 edge first in Figure 3.14(a).

A first idea, motivated by the discussion earlier in this chapter, is that because bridges and local bridges often connect weakly interacting parts of the network, we should try removing these bridges and local bridges first. This idea is in fact along the right lines; the problem is simply that it's not strong enough, for two reasons. First, when there are several bridges, we need to decide which to remove first. As we see in Figure 3.14(a), where there are five bridges, certain bridges can produce more reasonable splits than others. Second, there can be graphs where no edge is even a local bridge, because every edge belongs to a triangle – yet there is still a natural division into regions. Figure 3.15 shows a simple example, where we may want to identify nodes 1–5 and nodes 7–11 as tightly-knit regions despite the fact that there are no local bridges to remove.

However, if we think more generally about what bridges and local bridges are doing, then we can arrive at a notion that forms the central ingredient of the Girvan–Newman method. Local bridges are important because they form part of the shortest path between pairs of nodes in different parts of the network; without a particular local bridge, paths between many pairs of nodes may have to be "re-routed" a longer distance. We therefore define an abstract notion of "traffic" on the network and look for the edges that carry the most of this traffic. Like crucial bridges and highway arteries, we might expect these edges to link different densely connected regions, and hence to be good candidates for removal in a divisive method.

We define our notion of traffic as follows. For every pair of nodes A and B in the graph that are connected by a path, we imagine having one unit of fluid "flow" along the edges from A to B. (If A and B belong to different connected components, then no fluid flows between them.) The flow between A and B divides itself evenly along all the possible *shortest* paths from A to B: so if there are k shortest paths between A and B, then $1/k$ units of flow pass along each path.

We define the *betweenness* of an edge to be the total amount of flow it carries, taking into account the flow between all pairs of nodes using this edge. For example, we can determine the betweenness of each edge in Figure 3.14(a) as follows:

- First consider the 7-8 edge. For each node A in the left half of the graph, and for each node B in the right half of the graph, their full unit of flow passes through the 7-8 edge. On the other hand, no flow passing between pairs of nodes that both lie in the same half uses this edge. As a result, the betweenness of the 7-8 edge is $7 \times 7 = 49$.
- The 3-7 edge carries the full unit of flow from each node among 1, 2, and 3 to each node among 4–14. Thus, the betweenness of this edge is $3 \times 11 = 33$. The same goes for the edges 6-7, 8-9, and 8-12.
- The 1-3 edge carries all the flow from node 1 to every other except node 2. As a result, its betweennness is 12. By strictly symmetric reasoning, the other edges linked from nodes 3, 6, 9, and 12 into their respective triangles have a betweenness of 12 as well.
- Finally, the 1-2 edge only carries flow between its endpoints, so its betweenness is 1. This also holds for edges 4-5, 10-11, and 13-14.

Thus, betweenness has picked out the 7-8 edge as the one that carries the most traffic.

In fact, the idea of using betweenness to identify important edges draws on a long history in sociology, where most people attribute its first explicit articulation to Linton Freeman [73, 168, 169]. Its use by sociologists has traditionally focused more on nodes than on edges, where the definition is the same: the betweenness of a node is the total amount of flow that it carries, when a unit of flow between each pair of nodes is divided up evenly over shortest paths. Like edges of high betweenness, nodes of high betweenness occupy critical roles in the network structure. Indeed, because carrying a large amount of flow suggests a position at the interface between tightly-knit groups, there are clear relationships of betweenness with our earlier discussions of nodes that span structural holes in a social network [86].

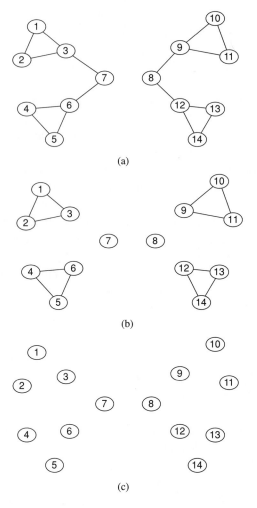

Figure 3.16. The three steps (a)–(c) of the Girvan–Newman method applied to the network from Figure 3.14(a).

The Girvan–Newman Method: Successively Deleting Edges of High Betweenness.
Edges of high betweenness are the edges that, over all pairs of nodes, carry the highest volume of traffic along shortest paths. Based on the premise that these edges are the most "vital" for connecting different regions of the network, it is natural to try to remove these first. This approach is the crux of the Girvan–Newman method, which can now be summarized as follows:

1. Find the edge of highest betweenness – or multiple edges of highest betweenness, if there is a tie – and remove these edges from the graph. This may cause the graph to separate into multiple components. If so, this is the first level of regions in the partitioning of the graph.
2. Now recalculate all betweennesses, and again remove the edge or edges of highest betweenness. This procedure may break some of the existing components into smaller components; if so, these are regions nested within the larger regions.

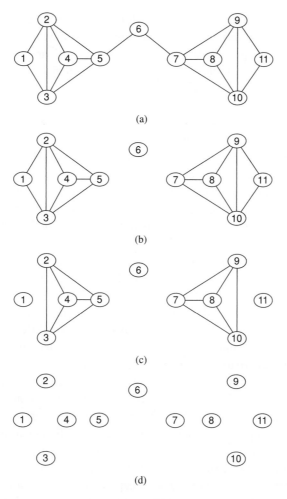

Figure 3.17. The four steps (a)–(d) of the Girvan–Newman method applied to the network from Figure 3.15.

... Proceed in this way as long as edges remain in the graph, in each step recalculating all betweennesses and removing the edge or edges of highest betweenness.

Thus, as the graph falls apart first into large pieces and then into smaller ones, the method naturally exposes a nested structure in the tightly-knit regions. In Figures 3.16 and 3.17 we show how the method operates on the graphs from Figures 3.14(a) and 3.15, respectively. Note how smaller regions emerge from larger ones as edges are successively removed.

The sequence of steps in Figure 3.17 in fact exposes some interesting points about how the method works:

- When we calculate the betweenness in the first step, the 5-7 edge carries all the flow from nodes 1–5 to nodes 7–11, for a betweenness of 25. The 5-6 edge, on the other hand, only carries flow from node 6 to each of nodes 1–5, for a betweenness of 5 (and similarly for the 6-7 edge).

- Once the 5-7 edge is deleted, however, all the betweennesses for the second step are recalculated. At this point, all 25 units of flow that used to be on this deleted edge have shifted onto the path through nodes 5, 6, and 7, and so the betweenness of the 5-6 edge (and also the 6-7 edge) has increased to $5 + 25 = 30$. This is why these two edges are deleted next.

In their original presentation of the method, Girvan and Newman showed its effectiveness at partitioning a number of real network data sets into intuitively reasonable sets of regions. For example, on Zachary's karate club network in Figure 3.13, when the method is used to remove edges until the graph first separates into two pieces, the resulting partition agrees with the actual split that occurred in the club except for a single person – node 9 in the figure. In real life, node 9 went with the instructor's club, even though the graph partitioning analysis here would predict that he would join the president's club.

Zachary's original analysis of the karate club employed a different approach, which also used the network structure. He first supplemented the network with numerical estimates of tie strength for the edges, based on his empirical study of the relationships within the karate club. He then identified a set of edges of minimum total strength whose removal would place node 1 and node 34 (the rival leaders) in different connected components, and he predicted this as the split. The approach Zachary used – deleting edges of minimum total strength to separate two specified nodes – is known as the problem of finding a *minimum cut* in a graph, and it has the been the subject of extensive research and applications [8, 164, 253]. In the karate club network, this minimum-cut approach produced the same split as the Girvan–Newman method: it agreed with the split that actually occurred except for the outcome of node 9, an alignment of predictions that emphasizes how different approaches to graph partitioning can produce corresponding results. It is also interesting to note that Zachary traced the anomalous nature of node 9 to a fact that the network structure could not capture: at the time of the actual split, the person corresponding to node 9 was three weeks away from completing a four-year quest to obtain a black belt, which he could only do with the instructor (node 1).

Among the other examples discussed by Girvan and Newman, they provide a partition of the coauthorship network from Figure 3.12, with the top level of regions suggested by the different shadings of the nodes in that figure.

Ultimately, it is a challenge to rigorously evaluate graph partitioning methods and to formulate ways of asserting that one is better than another, both because the goal is hard to formalize and because different methods may be more or less effective on different kinds of networks. Moreover, a line of recent work by Leskovec et al. has argued that, in real social-network data, it is much easier to separate a tightly-knit region from the rest of the network when it is relatively small – on the order of at most a few hundred nodes [275]. Studies on a range of different social and information networks suggest that, beyond this size, sets of nodes become much more "inextricable" from the rest of the network, raising the prospect that graph partitioning approaches on this type of data may produce qualitatively different results for small networks and small regions than for large ones. This is an area of ongoing investigation.

In the remainder of this section, we address a final important issue: how to actually compute the betweenness quantities that are needed to make the Girvan–Newman method work.

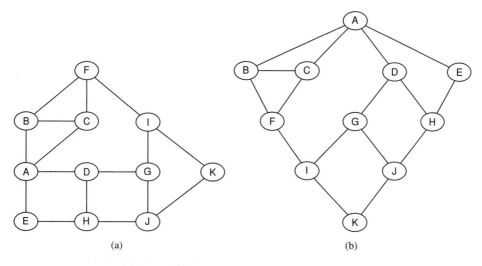

Figure 3.18. The first step in the efficient method for computing betweenness values is to perform a breadth-first search of the network. (a) A sample network and (b) the results of breadth-first search from node A are shown; over the course of the method, breadth-first search is performed from each node in turn.

B. Computing Betweenness Values

To perform the Girvan–Newman method, we need a way to find the edges of highest betweenness in each step. This is done by computing all the betweennesses of all edges and then looking for the ones with the highest values. The tricky part is that the definition of betweenness involves reasoning about the set of *all* the shortest paths between pairs of nodes. Since there could be a very large number of such shortest paths, how can we efficiently compute betweenness without the overhead of actually listing out all such paths? Finding a reasonable answer to this question is crucial for implementing the method on a computer to work with data sets of any reasonable size.

In fact, there is a clever way to compute betweennesses efficiently [77, 317], and it is based on the notion of breadth-first search from Section 2.3. We consider the graph from the perspective of one node at a time; for each given node, we compute how the total flow from that node to all others is distributed over the edges. If we do this computation for every node, then we can simply add up the flows from all of them to get the betweennesses on every edge.

So let's consider how we would determine the flow from one node to all other nodes in the graph. As an example, we'll look at the graph in Figure 3.18(a), focusing on how the flow from node A reaches all other nodes. We do this in the following three high-level steps, which we describe in more detail next:

1. Perform a breadth-first search of the graph, starting at A.
2. Determine the number of shortest paths from A to each other node.
3. Based on these numbers, determine the amount of flow from A to all other nodes that use each edge.

For the first step, recall that breadth-first search divides a graph into *layers* starting at a given node (A in our case), in which all the nodes in layer d have distance d

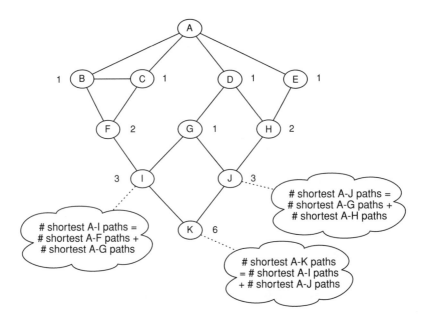

Figure 3.19. The second step in computing betweenness values is to count the number of shortest paths from a starting node A to all other nodes in the network. This can be done by adding up counts of shortest paths, moving downward through the breadth-first search structure.

from A. Moreover, the shortest paths from A to a node X in layer d are precisely the paths that move downward from A to X one layer at a time, thereby taking exactly d steps. Figure 3.18(b) shows the result of a breadth-first search from A in our graph, with the layers placed horizontally going downward from A. Thus, for example, some inspection of the figure shows that there are two shortest paths (each of length 2) from A to F: one using nodes A, B, and F, and the other using nodes A, C, and F.

Counting Shortest Paths. Now, let's consider the second step: determining the number of shortest paths from A to each other node. There is a remarkably clean way to do this, by working down through the layers of the breadth-first search.

To motivate this, consider a node like I in Figure 3.18(b). All shortest paths from A to I must take their last step through either F or G, because these are the two nodes above I in the breadth-first search. (For terminological convenience, we will say that a node X is *above* a node Y in the breadth-first search if X is in the layer immediately preceding Y, and X has an edge to Y.) Moreover, to be a shortest path to I, a path must first be a shortest path to one of F or G, and then take this last step to I. It follows that the number of shortest paths from A to I is precisely the number of shortest paths from A to F, plus the number of shortest paths from A to G.

We can use this as a general method to count the number of shortest paths from A to all other nodes, as depicted in Figure 3.19. Each node in the first layer is a neighbor of A, and so it has only one shortest path from A: the edge leading straight from A to it. So we give each of these nodes a count of 1. Now, as we move down through the breadth-first search layers, we apply the reasoning discussed above to conclude that the number of shortest paths to each node should be the *sum* of the number of shortest paths to all nodes directly above it in the breadth-first search. Working downward

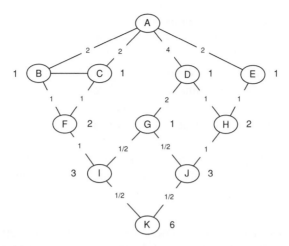

Figure 3.20. The final step in computing betweenness values is to determine the flow values from a starting node A to all other nodes in the network. This is done by working up from the lowest layers of the breadth-first search and dividing up the flow above a node in proportion to the number of shortest paths coming into it on each edge.

through the layers, we thus get the number of shortest paths to each node, as shown in Figure 3.19. Note that, by the time we get to deeper layers, it may not be so easy to determine these numbers by visual inspection – for example, to immediately list the six different shortest paths from A to K – but it is quite easy when they are built up layer-by-layer in this way.

Determining Flow Values. Finally, we come to the third step: computing how the flow from A to all other nodes spreads out across the edges. Here too we use the breadth-first search structure, but this time working up from the lowest layers. We first show the idea in Figure 3.20 for our running example, and then describe the general procedure.

- Let's start at the bottom with node K. A single unit of flow arrives at K, and an equal number of the shortest paths from A to K come through nodes I and J, so this unit of flow is equally divided over the two incoming edges. Therefore we put a half-unit of flow on each of these edges.
- Now, working upward, the total amount of flow arriving at I is equal to the one unit actually destined for I plus the half-unit passing through to K, for a total of 3/2. How does this 3/2 amount of flow get divided over the edges leading upward from I, to F and G, respectively? We see from the second step that there are twice as many shortest paths from A through F as through G, so twice as much of the flow should come from F. Therefore we put one unit of the flow on F, and a half-unit of the flow on G, as indicated in the figure.
- We continue in this way for each other node, working upward through the layers of the breadth-first search.

From this, it is not hard to describe the principle in general. When we get to a node X in the breadth-first search structure, working up from the bottom, we add up all the flow traveling on edges directly below X, plus 1 for the flow destined for X itself. (Because we are proceeding from the bottom up, we will know how much flow is traveling on each edge below X by the time we get to X.) We then divide this total flow up over the edges leading upward from X, in proportion to the number of shortest paths coming through each. You can check that applying this principle leads to the numbers shown in Figure 3.20.

We are now essentially done. We build one of these breadth-first structures from *each* node in the network, determine flow values from the node using this procedure, and then we sum up the flow values to get the betweenness value for each edge. Notice that we are counting the flow between each pair of nodes X and Y twice: once when we do the breadth-first search from X and once when we do it from Y. Therefore, at the end we divide everything by 2 to cancel out this double counting. Finally, using these betweenness values, we can identify the edges of highest betweenness for purposes of removing them in the Girvan–Newman method.

Final Observations. The method just described can be used to compute the betweennesses of nodes as well as edges. In fact, this is already happening in the third step: notice that we implicitly keep track of the amounts of flow through the nodes as well as through the edges, and this is what is needed to determine the betweennesses of the nodes.

The original Girvan–Newman method described here, based on repeated removal of high-betweenness edges, is a good conceptual way to think about graph partitioning, and it works well for networks of moderate size (up to a few thousand nodes). However, for larger networks, the need to recompute betweenness values at every step becomes computationally very expensive. In view of this, a number of different alternatives have been proposed to more efficiently identify similar sets of tightly-knit regions. These include methods of approximating the betweenness [34] and related but more efficient graph partitioning approaches using divisive and agglomerative methods [35, 321]. Finding fast partitioning methods that can scale to very large network data sets remains a topic of considerable interest.

3.7 Exercises

1. In two to three sentences, explain what triadic closure is and how it plays a role in the formation of social networks. You can draw a schematic picture if you find it useful.

2. Consider the graph in Figure 3.21, in which each edge – except the edge connecting nodes B and C – is labeled as a strong tie (S) or a weak tie (W).

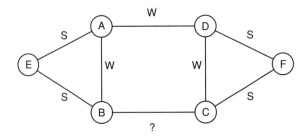

Figure 3.21. A graph with a labeling of the edges as strong or weak ties, for Exercise 2.

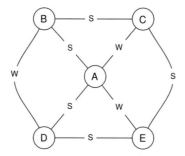

Figure 3.22. A graph with a labeling of the edges as strong or weak ties, for Exercise 3.

According to the theory of strong and weak ties, using the Strong Triadic Closure assumption, how would you expect the edge connecting B and C to be labeled? Give a brief (one- to three-sentence) explanation for your answer.

3. In the social network depicted in Figure 3.22, in which each edge is labeled as either a strong or weak tie, which nodes satisfy the Strong Triadic Closure property from this chapter, and which do not? Provide an explanation for your answer.

4. In the social network depicted in Figure 3.23, in which each edge is labeled as either a strong or weak tie, which two nodes violate the Strong Triadic Closure property? Provide an explanation for your answer.

5. In the social network depicted in Figure 3.24, in which each edge is labeled as either a strong or weak tie, which nodes satisfy the Strong Triadic Closure property from this chapter, and which do not? Provide an explanation for your answer.

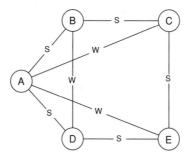

Figure 3.23. A graph with a labeling of the edges as strong or weak ties, for Exercise 4.

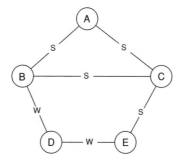

Figure 3.24. A graph with a labeling of the edges as strong or weak ties, for Exercise 5.

CHAPTER 4

Networks in Their Surrounding Contexts

In Chapter 3 we considered some of the typical structures that characterize social networks, and some of the typical processes that affect the formation of links in the network. Our discussion in Chapter 3 focused primarily on the network as an object of study in itself, relatively independent of the broader world in which it exists.

However, the contexts in which a social network is embedded will generally have significant effects on its structure. Each individual in a social network has a distinctive set of personal characteristics, and similarities and compatibilities between two people's characteristics can strongly influence whether a link forms between them. Each individual also engages in a set of behaviors and activities that can shape the formation of links within the network. These considerations suggest what we mean by a network's *surrounding contexts*: factors that exist outside the nodes and edges of a networks, but which nonetheless affect how the network's structure evolves.

In this chapter we consider how such effects operate and what they imply about the structure of social networks. Among other observations, we will find that the surrounding contexts affecting a network's formation can, to some extent, be viewed in network terms. By expanding the network to represent the contexts together with the individuals, we will see in fact that several different processes of network formation can be described in a common framework.

4.1 Homophily

One of the most basic notions governing the structure of social networks is *homophily* – the principle that we tend to be similar to our friends. Typically, your friends don't look like a random sample of the underlying population. Viewed collectively, your friends are generally similar to you along racial and ethnic dimensions; they are similar in age; and they are also similar in characteristics that are more or less mutable, including the places they live, their occupations, their levels of affluence, and their interests, beliefs, and opinions. Clearly most of us have specific friendships that cross all these

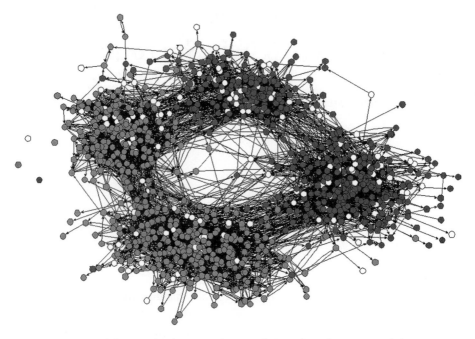

Figure 4.1. Homophily can divide a social network into densely connected, homogeneous parts that are weakly connected to each other. In this social network from a town's middle school and high school, two such divisions in the network are apparent: one based on race (with students of different races drawn as differently colored circles) and the other based on friendships in the middle and high schools, respectively [304]. (Image from the University of Chicago Press.)

boundaries; but in aggregate, the pervasive fact is that links in a social network tend to connect people who are similar to one another.

This observation has a long history; as McPherson, Smith-Lovin, and Cook note in their extensive review of research on homophily [294], the underlying idea can be found in the writings of Plato ("similarity begets friendship") and Aristotle (people "love those who are like themselves"), as well as in proverbs such as "birds of a feather flock together." The role of homophily in modern sociological research was catalyzed in large part by the influential work of Lazarsfeld and Merton in the 1950s [269].

Homophily provides us with a first, fundamental illustration of how a network's surrounding contexts can drive the formation of its links. Consider the basic contrast between a friendship that forms because two people are introduced through a common friend and a friendship that forms because two people attend the same school or work for the same company. In the first case, a new link is added for reasons that are *intrinsic* to the network itself; we need not look beyond the network to understand where the link came from. In the second case, the new link arises for an equally natural reason, but one that makes sense only when we look at the contextual factors beyond the network itself – at some of the social environments (in this case schools and companies) to which the nodes belong.

Often, when we look at a network, such contexts capture some of the dominant features of its overall structure. Figure 4.1, for example, depicts the social network within a particular town's middle school and high school (encompassing grades 7–12) [304]; in this image (produced by the study's author, James Moody), students of different races are drawn as differently colored circles. Two dominant divisions within the network are apparent. One division is based on race (from left to right in the figure); the other, based on age and school attendance, separates students in the middle school from those in the high school (from top to bottom in the figure). There are many other structural details in this network, but the effects of these two contexts stand out when the network is viewed at a global level.

Of course, there are strong interactions between intrinsic and contextual effects on the formation of any single link; they both operate concurrently in the same network. For example, the principle of triadic closure – that triangles in the network tend to "close" as links form between friends of friends – is supported by a number of mechanisms that range from the intrinsic to the contextual. In Chapter 3 we motivated triadic closure by hypothesizing intrinsic mechanisms: when individuals B and C have a common friend A, then there are increased opportunities and sources of trust on which to base their interactions, and A will also have incentives to facilitate their friendship. However, social contexts also provide natural bases for triadic closure: since A-B and A-C friendships already exist, the principle of homophily suggests that B and C are each likely to be similar to A in a number of dimensions, and hence quite possibly similar to each other as well. As a result, based purely on this similarity, there is an elevated chance that a B-C friendship will form; this is true even if neither of them is aware that the other one knows A.

The point isn't that any one basis for triadic closure is the "correct" one. Rather, as more and more of the factors that drive the formation of links in a social network are taken into account, it inevitably becomes difficult to attribute any individual link to a single factor. And ultimately, one expects most links to in fact arise from a combination of several factors – partly due to the effect of other nodes in the network, and partly due to the surrounding contexts.

Measuring Homophily. When we see striking divisions within a network like the one in Figure 4.1, it is important to ask whether they are "genuinely" present in the network itself, and not simply an artifact of how it is drawn. To make this question concrete, we need to formulate it more precisely: given a particular characteristic of interest (like race, or age), is there a simple test that can be applied to a network to estimate whether it exhibits homophily according to this characteristic?

Since the example in Figure 4.1 is too large to inspect by hand, we consider this question using a smaller example on which we can develop some intuition. Suppose in particular that we have the friendship network of an elementary-school classroom, and we suspect that it exhibits homophily by gender: boys tend to be friends with boys, and girls tend to be friends with girls. For example, the graph in Figure 4.2 shows the friendship network of a (small) hypothetical classroom in which the three shaded nodes are girls and the six unshaded nodes are boys. If there were no cross-gender edges at all, then the question of homophily would be easy to resolve: it would be present in an extreme sense. But we expect that homophily should be a more subtle effect that is visible mainly in aggregate – as it is, for example, in the real data from Figure 4.1. Is the network in Figure 4.2 consistent with homophily?

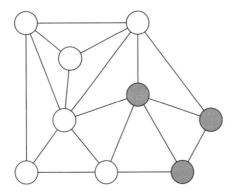

Figure 4.2. Using a numerical measure, one can determine whether small networks such as this one (with nodes divided into two types) exhibit homophily.

There is a natural numerical measure of homophily that we can use to address questions like this [202, 319]. To motivate the measure (using the example of gender from Figure 4.2), we first ask the following question: What would it mean for a network *not* to exhibit homophily by gender? It would mean that the proportion of male and female friends that a person has looks like the background male/female distribution in the full population. Here is a closely related formulation of this "no-homophily" definition that is a bit easier to analyze: If we were to randomly assign each node a gender according to the gender balance in the real network, then the number of cross-gender edges should not change significantly relative to what is seen in the real network. That is, in a network with no homophily, friendships are being formed as though random mixing were occurring across the given characteristic.

Thus, suppose we have a network in which a fraction p of all individuals are male, and a fraction q of all individuals are female. Consider a given edge in this network. If we independently assign each node the gender *male* with probability p and the gender *female* with probability q, then both ends of the edge will be male with probability p^2, and both ends will be female with probability q^2. On the other hand, if the first end of the edge is male and the second end is female, or vice versa, then we have a cross-gender edge, so this happens with probability $2pq$.

Therefore, the test for homophily according to gender can be summarized as follows:

> *Homophily Test:* If the fraction of cross-gender edges is significantly less than $2pq$, then there is evidence for homophily.

In Figure 4.2, for example, 5 of the 18 edges in the graph are cross-gender edges. Since $p = 2/3$ and $q = 1/3$ in this example, we should be comparing the fraction of cross-gender edges to the quantity $2pq = 4/9 = 8/18$. In other words, with no homophily, one should expect to see 8 cross-gender edges rather than 5, and so this example shows some evidence of homophily.

A few points should be noted here. First, the number of cross-gender edges in a random assignment of genders will deviate somewhat from its expected value of $2pq$; therefore, to perform the test in practice one needs a working definition of "significantly less than." Standard measures of statistical significance (quantifying the significance of a deviation below a mean) can be used for this purpose. Second, it is also easily possible for a network to have a fraction of cross-gender edges that is significantly *more than* $2pq$. In such a case, we say that the network exhibits *inverse homophily*. The network of romantic relationships in Figure 2.7 from Chapter 2 provides a clear example of inverse homophily; almost all the relationships reported by the high school students in the study involved opposite-sex partners rather than same-sex partners, so almost all the edges are cross-gender.

Finally, it's easy to extend the homophily test to any underlying characteristic (race, ethnicity, age, native language, political orientation, and so forth). When the characteristic can only take two possible values (say, one's voting preference in a two-candidate election), then we can draw a direct analogy to the case of two genders and use the same formula, $2pq$. When the characteristic can take on more than two possible values, we still perform a general version of the same calculation. For this case, we say that an edge is *heterogeneous* if it connects two nodes that are different according to the characteristic in question. We then ask how the number of heterogeneous edges compares to what we'd see if we were to randomly assign values for the characteristic to all nodes in the network – using the proportions from the real data as probabilities. In this way, even a network in which the nodes are classified into many groups can be tested for homophily using the same underlying comparison to a baseline of random mixing.

4.2 Mechanisms Underlying Homophily: Selection and Social Influence

The fact that people tend to have links to others who are similar to them is a statement about the structure of social networks; on its own, it does not propose an underlying mechanism by which ties among similar people are preferentially formed.

In the case of immutable characteristics such as race or ethnicity, the tendency of people to form friendships with others who are like them is often termed *selection*, in that people are selecting friends with similar characteristics. Selection may operate at several different scales and with different levels of intentionality. In a small group, when people choose friends who are most similar from among a clearly delineated pool of potential contacts, active choice is clearly taking place. In other cases, and at more global levels, selection can be more implicit. For example, when people live in neighborhoods, attend schools, or work for companies that are relatively homogeneous compared to the population at large, the social environment already favors opportunities to form friendships with others like oneself. For this discussion, we refer to all these effects cumulatively as selection.

When we consider how immutable characteristics interact with network formation, the order of events is clear: a person's attributes are determined at birth, and they play a role in how this person's connections are formed over the course of his or her life. With characteristics that are more mutable, on the other hand – behaviors, activities, interests, beliefs, and opinions – the feedback effects between people's individual characteristics and their links in the social network become significantly more complex. The process of selection still operates, and individual characteristics still affect the connections that are formed. But now another process comes into play as well: people may modify their behaviors to bring them more closely into alignment with the behaviors of their friends. This process has been variously described as *socialization* [233] and *social influence* [170], since the existing social connections in a network influence the individual characteristics of the nodes. Social influence can be viewed as the reverse of selection: with selection, the individual characteristics drive the formation of links, while with social influence, the existing links in the network serve to shape people's (mutable) characteristics.[1]

The Interplay of Selection and Social Influence. When we look at a single snapshot of a network and see that people tend to share mutable characteristics with their friends, it can be very hard to sort out the distinct effects and relative contributions of selection and social influence. Have the people in the network adapted their behaviors to become more like their friends, or have they sought out people who were already like them? Such questions can be addressed by using *longitudinal* studies of a social network, in which both the social connections and the behaviors within a group are tracked over a period of time. Fundamentally, this approach makes it possible to see the behavioral changes that occur after changes in an individual's network connections, as opposed to the changes to the network that occur after an individual changes his or her behavior.

This type of methodology has been used, for example, to study the processes that lead pairs of adolescent friends to have similar outcomes in terms of scholastic achievement and delinquent behavior such as drug use [92]. Empirical evidence confirms the intuitive fact that teenage friends are similar to each other in their behaviors, and both selection and social influence have a natural resonance in this setting: teenagers seek out social circles composed of people like them, and peer pressure causes them to conform to behavioral patterns within their social circles. What is much harder to resolve is how these two effects interact, and whether one is more strongly at work than the other. As longitudinal behavior relevant to this question became available, researchers began to quantify the relative impact of these different factors. A line of work beginning with Cohen and Kandel has suggested that, while both effects are present in the data, the outsized role that earlier informal arguments had accorded to peer pressure (i.e., social influence) is actually more moderate; the effect of selection here is in fact comparable to (and sometimes greater than) the effect of social influence [114, 233].

Understanding the tension between these different forces can be important, not just for identifying underlying causes but also for reasoning about the effect of possible interventions one might attempt in the system [21, 396]. For example, once we find that illicit drug use displays homophily across a social network – where students show a greater likelihood of using drugs when their friends do – we can ask about the effects of a program that targets certain high school students and influences them to stop using drugs. To the extent that the observed homophily is based on some amount of social influence, such a program could have a broad impact across the social network by causing the friends of these targeted students to stop using drugs as well. But one must

---

[1] Other cognitive effects are at work as well; for example, people may systematically misperceive the characteristics of their friends as being more in alignment with their own than they really are [224]. We will not focus explicitly on such effects in our discussion here.

be careful; if the observed homophily is arising instead almost entirely from selection effects, then the program may not reduce drug use beyond the students it directly targets: as these students stop using drugs, they change their social circles and form new friendships with students who don't use drugs, but the drug-using behavior of other students is not strongly affected.

Another example of research that addresses this subtle interplay of factors is the work of Christakis and Fowler on the effect of social networks on health-related outcomes. In one recent study using longitudinal data involving roughly 12,000 people, Christakis and Fowler tracked obesity status and social network structure over a 32-year period [108]. They found that obese and nonobese people clustered in the network in a fashion consistent with homophily, according to the numerical measure described in Section 4.1: people tend to be more similar in obesity status to their network neighbors than in a version of the same network where obesity status is assigned randomly. The problem is then to distinguish among several hypotheses for why this clustering is present:

(i) Is it because of selection effects, in which people are choosing to form friendships with others of similar obesity status?

(ii) Is it because of the confounding effects of homophily according to other characteristics, in which the network structure indicates existing patterns of similarity in other dimensions that correlate with obesity status?

(iii) Or is it because changes in the obesity status of a person's friends was exerting a (presumably behavioral) influence that affected his or her future obesity status?

Statistical analysis in Christakis and Fowler's paper is used to argue that, even accounting for the effects of types (i) and (ii), there is significant evidence for an effect of type (iii) as well: that obesity is a health condition displaying a form of social influence, with changes in your friends' obesity status in turn having a subsequent effect on you. This evidence suggests the intriguing prospect that obesity (and perhaps other health conditions with a strong behavioral aspect) may exhibit some amount of "contagion" in a social sense: you don't necessarily catch it from your friends the way you catch the flu, but it nonetheless can spread through the underlying social network via the mechanism of social influence.

These examples, and this general style of investigation, show how careful analysis is needed to distinguish among different factors contributing to an aggregate conclusion: even when people tend to be similar to their neighbors in a social network, it may not be clear why. The point is that an observation of homophily is often not an endpoint in itself but rather the starting point for deeper questions – questions that address why the homophily is present, how its underlying mechanisms will affect the further evolution of the network, and how these mechanisms interact with possible outside attempts to influence the behavior of people in the network.

4.3 Affiliation

Thus far, we have been discussing contextual factors that affect the formation of links in a network, based on similarities in characteristics of the nodes and on behaviors

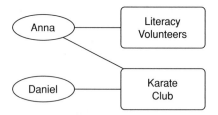

Figure 4.3. An affiliation network is a bipartite graph that shows which individuals are affiliated with which groups or activities. Here, Anna participates in both of the social foci on the right, while Daniel participates in only one.

and activities that the nodes engage in. These surrounding contexts have been viewed, appropriately, as existing "outside" the network. But in fact, it is possible to put these contexts into the network itself, by working with a larger network that contains both people and contexts as nodes. Through such a network formulation, we obtain additional insight into some broad aspects of homophily and see how the simultaneous evolution of contexts and friendships can be put on a common network footing with the notion of triadic closure from Chapter 3.

In principle we could represent any context in this way, but for the sake of concreteness we focus on how to represent the set of activities in which a person takes part, and how these activities affect the formation of links. We take a very general view of the notion of an "activity" here. Being part of a particular company, organization, or neighborhood; frequenting a particular place; or pursuing a particular hobby or interest – these are all activities that, when shared between two people, tend to increase the likelihood that they will interact and hence form a link in the social network [78, 161]. Adopting terminology introduced by Scott Feld, we'll refer to such activities as *foci* – "focal points" of social interaction – constituting "social, psychological, legal, or physical entit[ies] around which joint activities are organized (e.g., workplaces, voluntary organizations, hangouts, etc.)" [161].

Affiliation Networks. As a first step, we can represent the participation of a set of people in a set of foci using a graph as follows. There is a node representing each person and each focus, and person A is connected to focus X by an edge if A participates in X. A very simple example of such a graph is depicted in Figure 4.3, showing two people (Anna and Daniel) and two foci (working for a literacy tutoring organization, and belonging to a karate club). The graph indicates that Anna participates in both of the foci, while Daniel participates in only one.

Such a graph is referred to as an *affiliation network*, since it represents the affiliation of people (drawn on the left) with foci (drawn on the right) [78, 323]. More generally, affiliation networks are examples of a class of graphs called *bipartite graphs*. We say that a graph is bipartite if its nodes can be divided into two sets in such a way that every edge connects a node in one set to a node in the other set. (In other words, no edges join nodes that belong to the same set; all edges go between the two sets.) Bipartite graphs are very useful for representing data in which the items under study are divided into two categories, and we want to understand how the items in one category are associated with the items in the other. In the case of affiliation networks, the two

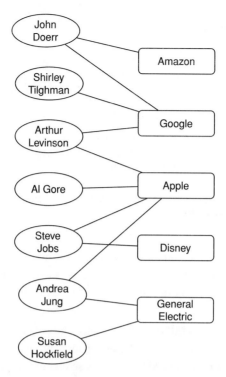

Figure 4.4. One type of affiliation network that has been widely studied involves the member-ships of people on corporate boards of directors [301]. A very small portion of this network (as of mid-2009) is shown here. The structural pattern of memberships can reveal subtleties in the interactions among both the board members and the companies.

categories are the people and the foci, with each edge connecting a person to a focus in which he or she participates. Bipartite graphs are often drawn, as in Figure 4.3, with the two different sets of nodes as two parallel vertical columns, and the edges crossing between the two columns.

Affiliation networks are studied in a range of settings where researchers want to understand the patterns of participation in structured activities. As one example, these networks have received considerable attention in studying the composition of boards of directors of major corporations [301]. Boards of directors are relatively small advisory groups populated by high-status individuals, and since many board members serve on multiple boards, the overlaps in their participation have a complex structure. These overlaps can be naturally represented by an affiliation network; as the example in Figure 4.4 shows, there is a node for each person and a node for each board, and each edge connects a person to a board.

Affiliation networks defined by boards of directors have the potential to reveal interesting relationships on both sides of the graph. Two companies are implicitly linked by having the same person sit on both their boards; we can thus learn about possible conduits for the flow of information and influence between different companies. Two people, on the other hand, are implicitly linked by serving together on a board, and so we learn about particular patterns of social interaction among some of the most powerful members of society. Of course, even the complete affiliation network of people and

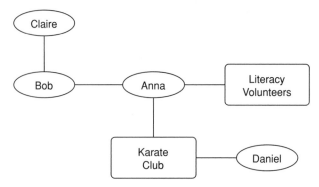

Figure 4.5. A social-affiliation network shows both the friendships between people and their affiliation with different social foci.

boards (of which Figure 4.4 is only a small piece) still misses other important contexts that these people inhabit; for example, the seven people in Figure 4.4 include the presidents of two major universities and a former vice president of the United States.[2]

Coevolution of Social and Affiliation Networks. It is clear that both social networks and affiliation networks change over time: new friendship links are formed, and people become associated with new foci. Moreover, these changes represent a kind of *coevolution* that reflects the interplay between selection and social influence: if two people participate in a shared focus, they are provided with an opportunity to become friends; and if two people are friends, they can influence each other's choice of foci.

There is a natural network perspective on these ideas, which begins from a network representation that slightly extends the notion of an affiliation network. As before, we have nodes for people and nodes for foci, but we now introcuce two distinct kinds of edges as well. The first kind of edge functions as an edge in a social network: it connects two people and indicates friendship (or alternatively some other social relation, like professional collaboration). The second kind of edge functions as an edge in an affiliation network: it connects a person to a focus and indicates the participation of the person in the focus. We will call such a network a *social-affiliation network*, reflecting the fact that it simultaneously contains a social network on the people and an affiliation network on the people and foci. Figure 4.5 depicts a simple social-affiliation network.

Once we have social-affiliation networks as our representation, we can appreciate that a range of different mechanisms for link formation can all be viewed as types

---

[2] The structure of this network changes over time as well, and sometimes in ways that reinforce the points in our present discussion. For example, the board memberships shown in Figure 4.4 are taken from the middle of 2009; by the end of 2009, Arthur Levinson had resigned from the board of directors of Google (thus removing one edge from the graph). As part of the news coverage of this resignation, the chair of the U.S. Federal Trade Commission, Jon Leibowitz, explicitly invoked the notion of overlaps in board membership, saying, "Google, Apple and Mr. Levinson should be commended for recognizing that overlapping board members between competing companies raise serious antitrust issues, and for their willingness to resolve our concerns without the need for litigation. Beyond this matter, we will continue to monitor companies that share board members and take enforcement actions where appropriate" [219].

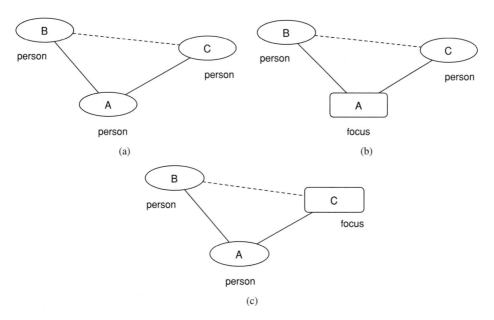

Figure 4.6. Each of (a) triadic closure, (b) focal closure, and (c) membership closure corresponds to the closing of a triangle in a social-affiliation network.

of *closure processes* in that they involve "closing" the third edge of a triangle in the network. In particular, suppose we have two nodes, B and C, with a common neighbor in the network, A, and suppose that an edge forms between B and C. As Figure 4.6 illustrates, there are several possible interpretations of this situation, depending on whether A, B, and C are people or foci:

(i) If A, B, and C each represent a person, then the formation of the link between B and C is triadic closure, just as in Chapter 3 [see Figure 4.6(a)].

(ii) If B and C represent people, but A represents a focus, then the formation of the B-C edge corresponds to something different: the tendency of two people to form a link when they have a focus in common [see Figure 4.6(b)]. This is an aspect of the more general principle of selection, when a person forms links to others who share characteristics with him or her. To emphasize the analogy with triadic closure, this process has been called *focal closure* [259].

(iii) If A and B are people, and C is a focus, then we have the formation of a new affiliation: B takes part in a focus in which her friend A is already involved [see Figure 4.6(c)]. This is a kind of social influence, in which B's behavior comes into closer alignment with that of her friend A. Continuing the analogy with triadic closure, we will refer to this kind of link formation as *membership closure*.

Thus, three very different underlying mechanisms – reflecting triadic closure and aspects of selection and social influence – can be unified in this type of network as kinds of closure: the formation of a link in cases where the two endpoints already have a neighbor in common. Figure 4.7 shows all three kinds of closure processes at work: triadic closure leads to a new link between Anna and Claire; focal closure leads to a

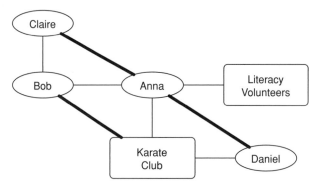

Figure 4.7. In a social-affiliation network containing both people and foci, edges can form under the effect of several different kinds of closure processes: two people with a friend in common, two people with a focus in common, or a person joining a focus that a friend is already involved in.

new link between Anna and Daniel; and membership closure leads to Bob's affiliation with the karate club. Oversimplifying the mechanisms at work, we can summarize them in the following succinct way:

> (i) *Bob introduces Anna to Claire.*
> (ii) *Karate introduces Anna to Daniel.*
> (iii) *Anna introduces Bob to Karate.*

4.4 Tracking Link Formation in Online Data

In this chapter and the previous one, we have identified a set of different mechanisms that lead to the formation of links in social networks. These mechanisms are good examples of social phenomena that are clearly at work in small-group settings but have traditionally been very hard to measure quantitatively. A natural research strategy is to try tracking these mechanisms as they operate in large populations, where an accumulation of many small effects can produce something observable in the aggregate. However, given that most of the forces responsible for link formation go largely unrecorded in everyday life, it is a challenge to select a large, clearly delineated group of people (and social foci) and to accurately quantify the relative contributions that these different mechanisms make to the formation of real network links.

The availability of data from large online settings with clear social structure has made it possible to attempt some preliminary research along these lines. As we emphasized in Chapter 2, any analysis of social processes based on such online data sets must come with a number of caveats. In particular, it is never clear a priori how much one can extrapolate from digital interactions to interactions that are not computer mediated, or even from one computer-mediated setting to another. Of course, this problem of extrapolation is present whenever one studies phenomena in a model system, online or not, and the kinds of measurements enabled by these large data sets represent interesting first steps toward a deeper quantitative understanding of how mechanisms

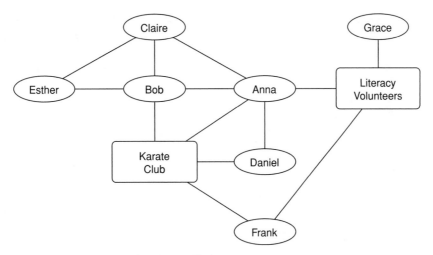

Figure 4.8. A larger network that contains the example from Figure 4.7. Pairs of people can have more than one friend (or more than one focus) in common. How does this increase the likelihood that an edge forms between them?

of link formation operate in real life. Exploring these questions in a broader range of large data sets is an important problem, and one that will become easier as such data sets become increasingly abundant.

Triadic Closure. With this background in mind, let's start with some questions about triadic closure. Here's a first, basic numerical question: how much more likely is a link to form between two people in a social network if they already have a friend in common? (In other words, how much more likely is a link to form if it has the effect of closing a triangle?)

Second, along the same lines as the first question, how much more likely is an edge to form between two people if they have *multiple* friends in common? For example, in Figure 4.8, Anna and Esther have two friends in common, while Claire and Daniel only have one friend in common. How much more likely is the formation of a link in the first of these two cases? If we go back to the arguments for why triadic closure operates in social networks, we see that all of these arguments are qualitatively strengthened as two people have more friends in common: there are more sources of opportunity and trust for the interaction, there are more people with an incentive to bring them together, and the evidence for homophily is arguably stronger.

We can address these questions empirically by using network data as follows:

(i) Take two snapshots of the network at different times.
(ii) For each k, identify all pairs of nodes who have exactly k friends in common in the first snapshot, but who are not directly connected by an edge.
(iii) Define $T(k)$ to be the fraction of these pairs that have formed an edge by the time of the second snapshot. This is an empirical estimate for the probability that a link will form between two people with k friends in common.
(iv) Plot $T(k)$ as a function of k to illustrate the effect of common friends on the formation of links.

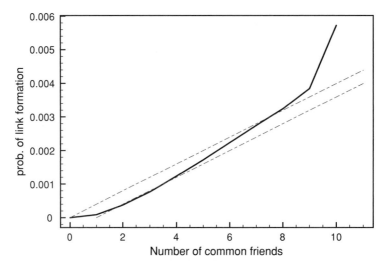

Figure 4.9. Quantifying the effects of triadic closure in an e-mail data set [259]. The curve determined from the data is shown in the solid black line; the dotted curves show a comparison to probabilities computed according to two simple baseline models in which common friends provide independent probabilities of link formation. (Image from the American Association for the Advancement of Science.)

Note that $T(0)$ is the rate at which link formation happens when it does not close a triangle, while the values of $T(k)$ for larger k determine the rate at which link formation happens when it does close a triangle. Thus, the comparison between $T(0)$ and these other values addresses the most basic question about the power of triadic closure.

Kossinets and Watts computed the function $T(k)$ using a data set encoding the full history of e-mail communication among roughly 22,000 undergraduate and graduate students over a one-year period at a large U.S. university [259]. This is a "who-talks-to-whom" type of data set, as discussed in Chapter 2; from the communication traces, Kossinets and Watts constructed a network that evolved over time, joining two people by a link at a given instant if they had exchanged e-mail in each direction at some point in the past 60 days. They then determined an "average" version of $T(k)$ by taking multiple pairs of snapshots: they built a curve for $T(k)$ on each pair of snapshots using the aforementioned procedure, and then they averaged all the curves they obtained. In particular, the observations in each snapshot were one day apart, so their computation gives the average probability that two people form a link per day as a function of the number of common friends they have.

Figure 4.9 shows a plot of this curve (in the solid black line). The first thing one notices is the clear evidence for triadic closure: $T(0)$ is very close to 0, after which the probability of link formation increases steadily as the number of common friends increases. Moreover, for much of the plot, this probability increases in a roughly linear fashion as a function of the number of common friends, with an upward bend away from a straight-line shape. The curve turns upward in a particularly pronounced way from 0 to 1 to 2 friends; having two friends in common produces significantly more than twice the effect on link formation compared to having a single common friend. (The upward effect from 8 to 9 to 10 friends is also significant, but it occurs on a much smaller subpopulation, since many fewer people in the data have this many friends in common without having already formed a link.)

To interpret this plot more deeply, it helps to compare it to an intentionally simplified baseline model, which describes what one might have expected the data to look like in the presence of triadic closure. Suppose that, for some small probability p, each common friend that two people have gives them an independent probability p of forming a link each day. So if two people have k friends in common, the probability that they fail to form a link on any given day is $(1 - p)^k$; this is because each common friend fails to cause the link to form with probability $1 - p$, and these k trials are independent. Since $(1 - p)^k$ is the probability that the link fails to form on a given day, the probability that it does form, according to our simple baseline model, is

$$T_{\text{baseline}}(k) = 1 - (1 - p)^k.$$

This baseline curve is plotted in Figure 4.9 as the upper dotted line, for a value of p chosen so that it approximately aligns with the real curve. Given the small absolute effect of the first common friend in the data, we also show a comparison to the curve $1 - (1 - p)^{k-1}$, which just shifts the simple baseline curve one unit to the right. Again, the point is not to propose this baseline as an explanatory mechanism for triadic closure, but rather to look at how the real curve compares to it. Both the real curve and the baseline curve are close to linear, and hence qualitatively similar; but the fact that the real curve turns upward while the baseline curve turns slightly downward indicates that the assumption of independent effects from common friends is too simple to be fully supported by the data.

A still larger and more detailed study of these effects was conducted by Leskovec et al. [272], who analyzed properties of triadic closure in the online social networks of LinkedIn, Flickr, Del.icio.us, and Yahoo! Answers. It remains an interesting question to try understanding the similarities and variations in triadic closure effects across social interaction in a range of different settings.

Focal and Membership Closure. Using the same approach, we can compute probabilities for the other kinds of closure discussed earlier – specifically,

- for *focal closure*, what is the probability that two people form a link as a function of the number of foci they are jointly affiliated with?
- for *membership closure*, what is the probability that a person becomes involved with a particular focus as a function of the number of friends who are already involved in it?

As an example of the first of these kinds of closure, using Figure 4.8, Anna and Grace have one activity in common while Anna and Frank have two in common. As an example of the second, Esther has one friend who belongs to the karate club while Claire has two. How do these distinctions affect the formation of new links?

For focal closure, Kossinets and Watts supplemented their university e-mail data set with information about the class schedules for each student. In this way, each class became a focus, and two students shared a focus if they had taken a class together. They could then compute the probability of focal closure by direct analogy with their computation for triadic closure, determining the probability of link formation per day

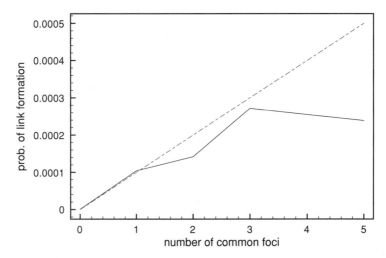

Figure 4.10. Quantifying the effects of focal closure in an e-mail data set [259]. Again, the curve determined from the data is shown as the solid black line, while the dotted curve provides a comparison to a simple baseline. (Image from the American Association for the Advancement of Science.)

as a function of the number of shared foci. Figure 4.10 shows a plot of this function. A single shared class turns out to have roughly the same absolute effect on link formation as a single shared friend, but after this point the curve for focal closure behaves quite differently from the curve for triadic closure: it turns downward and appears to approximately level off rather than turning slightly upward. Thus, subsequent shared classes after the first produce a "diminishing returns" effect. Comparing to the same kind of baseline, in which the probability of link formation with k shared classes is $1 - (1 - p)^k$ (shown as the dotted curve in Figure 4.10), we see that the real curve turns downward more significantly than this independent model. Again, it is an interesting open question to understand how this effect generalizes to other types of shared foci and to other domains.

For membership closure, the analogous quantities have been measured in other online domains that possess both person-to-person interactions and person-to-focus affiliations. Figure 4.11 is based on the blogging site LiveJournal, where friendships are designated by users in their profiles and where foci correspond to membership in user-defined communities [32]; thus, the plot shows the probability of joining a community as a function of the number of friends who have already done so. Figure 4.12 shows a similar analysis for Wikipedia [122]. Here, the social-affiliation network contains a node for each Wikipedia editor who maintains a user account and *user talk page* on the system. An edge joins two such editors if they have communicated, meaning that one editor has written on the user talk page of the other. Each Wikipedia article defines a focus – an editor is associated with a focus corresponding to a particular article if he or she has edited the article. Thus, the plot in Figure 4.12 shows the probability that a person edits a Wikipedia article as a function of the number of prior editors of that article with whom he or she has communicated.

As with triadic and focal closure, the probabilities in both Figures 4.11 and 4.12 increase with the number k of common neighbors, representing friends associated with

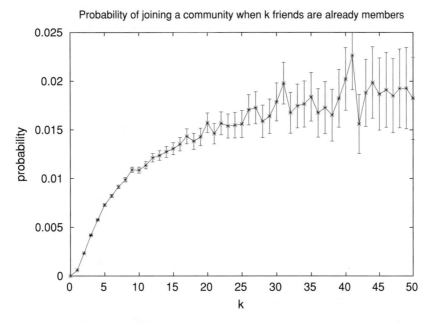

Figure 4.11. Quantifying the effects of membership closure in a large online data set: The plot shows the probability of joining a LiveJournal community as a function of the number of friends who are already members [32].

the foci. The marginal effect diminishes as the number of friends increases, but the effect of subsequent friends remains significant. Moreover, in both sources of data, there is an initial *increasing* effect similar to what we saw with triadic closure: the probability of joining a LiveJournal community or editing a Wikipedia article is more than twice as great when you have two connections into the focus rather than one. In other words,

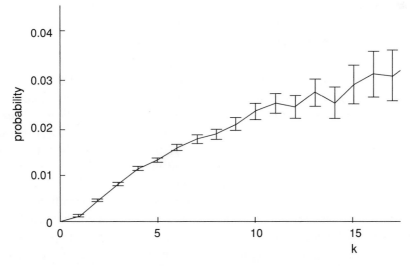

Figure 4.12. Quantifying the effects of membership closure in a large online data set: The plot shows the probability of editing a Wikipedia articles as a function of the number of friends who have already done so [122].

the connection to a second person in the focus has a particularly pronounced effect, and after this point the diminishing marginal effect of connections to further people takes over.

Of course, multiple effects can operate simultaneously on the formation of a single link. For example, in the network from Figure 4.8, triadic closure makes a link between Bob and Daniel more likely because of their shared friendship with Anna; focal closure also makes this link more likely because of the shared membership of Bob and Daniel in the karate club. If a link does form between them, it will not necessarily be clear a priori how to attribute it to these two distinct effects. This is also a reflection of an issue we discussed in Section 4.1 when describing some of the mechanisms behind triadic closure. Because the principle of homophily suggests that friends tend to have many characteristics in common, the existence of a friend shared between two people is often indicative of other, possibly unobserved, sources of similarity (such as shared foci in this case) that by themselves may also make link formation more likely.

Quantifying the Interplay Between Selection and Social Influence. As a final illustration of how we can use large-scale online data sets to track processes of link formation, let's return to the question of how selection and social influence work together to produce homophily, which we considered in Section 4.2. Using the Wikipedia data discussed earlier in this section, we ask: How do similarities in behavior between two Wikipedia editors relate to their pattern of social interaction over time [122]?

To make this question precise, we need to define both the social network and an underlying measure of behavioral similarity. As before, the social network consists of all Wikipedia editors who maintain talk pages, and there is an edge connecting two editors if they have communicated, with one writing on the talk page of the other. An editor's behavior corresponds to the set of articles she has edited. There are a number of natural ways to define numerical measures of similarity between two editors based on their actions; a simple one is to declare their similarity to be the value of the following ratio:

$$\frac{\text{number of articles edited by } \textit{both } \text{A and B}}{\text{number of articles edited by } \textit{at least one of } \text{A or B}}. \tag{4.1}$$

For example, if editor A has edited the Wikipedia articles on "Ithaca, NY" and "Cornell University," and editor B has edited the articles on "Cornell University" and "Stanford University," then their similarity under this measure is $1/3$, since they have jointly edited one article (Cornell) out of three that they have edited in total (Cornell, Ithaca, and Stanford). Note the close similarity to the definition of *neighborhood overlap* used in Section 3.3; indeed, the measure in Equation (4.1) is precisely the neighborhood overlap of two editors in the bipartite affiliation network of editors and articles, consisting only of edges from editors to the articles they have edited.[3]

Pairs of Wikipedia editors who have communicated are significantly more similar in their behavior than pairs of Wikipedia editors who have not communicated, so we have a case where homophily is clearly present. Therefore, we are set up to address the question of selection and social influence: Does the homophily arise because editors

---

[3] For technical reasons, a minor variation on this simple similarity measure is used for the results that follow. However, since this variation is more complicated to describe, and the differences are not significant for our purposes, we can think of similarity as consisting of the numerical measure just defined.

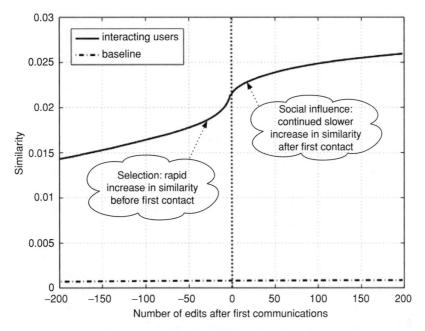

Figure 4.13. The average similarity of two editors on Wikipedia, relative to the time (0) at which they first communicated [122]. Time, on the x-axis, is measured in discrete units, where each unit corresponds to a single Wikipedia action taken by either of the two editors. The curve increases both before and after the first contact at time 0, indicating that both selection and social influence play a role; the increase in similarity is steepest just before time 0.

are forming connections with those who have edited the same articles (selection), or is it because editors are led to the articles of those they talk to (social influence)?

Because every action on Wikipedia is recorded and time-stamped, it is not hard to get an initial picture of this interplay, using the following method. For each pair of editors A and B who have ever communicated, record their similarity over time, where "time" in this case moves in discrete units, advancing by one "tick" whenever either A or B performs an action on Wikipedia (editing an article or communicating with another editor). Next, declare *time 0* for the pair A-B to be the point at which they first communicated. This results in many curves showing similarity as a function of time – one for each pair of editors who ever communicated – and each is shifted so that time is measured for each one relative to the moment of first communication. Averaging all these curves yields the single plot in Figure 4.13, which shows the average level of similarity relative to the time of first interaction, over all pairs of editors who have ever interacted on Wikipedia [122].

There are a number of things to notice about this plot. First, similarity is clearly increasing both before and after the moment of first interaction, indicating that both selection and social influence are at work. However, the the curve is not symmetric around time 0; the period of fastest increase in similarity clearly occurs before 0, indicating a particular role for selection: there is an especially rapid rise in similarity, on average, just before two editors meet.[4] Also note that the levels of similarity

---

[4] To make sure that these editors have significant histories on Wikipedia, this plot is constructed using only pairs of editors who each had at least 100 actions both before and after their first interaction with each other.

depicted in the plot are much higher than for pairs of editors who have not interacted: the dashed line at the bottom of the plot shows similarity over time for a random sample of noninteracting pairs; it is both far lower and also essentially constant as time moves forward.

At a higher level, the plot in Figure 4.13 once again illustrates the trade-offs involved in working with large-scale online data. On the one hand, the curve is remarkably smooth because so many pairs are being averaged, and so differences between selection and social influence show up that are genuine, but too subtle to be noticeable at smaller scales. On the other hand, the effect being observed is an aggregate one: it is the average of the interaction histories of many different pairs of individuals, and it does not provide more detailed insight into the experience of any one particular pair.[5] A goal for further research is clearly to find ways of formulating more complex, nuanced questions that can still be meaningfully addressed for large data sets.

Overall, then, these analyses represent early attempts to quantify some of the basic mechanisms of link formation at a very large scale, using online data. Although these analyses are promising in revealing that the basic patterns indeed show up strongly in the data, they raise many further questions. In particular, it is natural to ask whether the general shapes of the curves in Figures 4.9–4.13 are similar across different domains – including domains that are less technologically mediated – and whether these curve shapes can be explained at a simpler level by more basic underlying social mechanisms.

4.5 A Spatial Model of Segregation

One of the most readily perceived effects of homophily is in the formation of ethnically and racially homogeneous neighborhoods in cities. Traveling through a metropolitan area, one finds that homophily produces a natural spatial signature; people live near others like them, and as a consequence they open shops, restaurants, and other businesses oriented toward the populations of their respective neighborhoods. The effect is also striking when superimposed on a map, as Figure 4.14 by Möbius and Rosenblat [302] illustrates. Their images depict the percentage of African Americans per city block in Chicago for the years 1940 and 1960; in their notation, blocks drawn lighter in the map have the lowest percentages, while blocks drawn darker in the map have the highest percentages.

This pair of figures also shows how concentrations of different groups can intensify over time, emphasizing that this is a process with a dynamic aspect. Using the principles considered thus far, we now discuss how simple mechanisms based on similarity and selection can provide insight into the observed patterns and their dynamics.

The Schelling Model. A famous model introduced by Thomas Schelling [365, 366] shows how global patterns of spatial segregation can arise from the effect of homophily

---

[5] Because the individual histories being averaged took place at many distinct points in Wikipedia's history, it is also natural to ask whether the aggregate effects operated differently in different phases of this history. This is a natural question for further investigation, but initial tests – based on studying these types of properties on Wikipedia data sets built from different periods – show that the main effects have remained relatively stable over time.

(a)   (b)

Figure 4.14. The tendency of people to live in racially homogeneous neighborhoods produces spatial patterns of segregation that are apparent both in everyday life and when superimposed on a map – as here, in these maps of Chicago from (a) 1940 and (b) 1960 [302]. In the notation of the paper that presented this data, blocks drawn lighter in the map have populations with the lowest percentages of African-Americans, while blocks drawn darker in the map have populations with the highest percentages of African-Americans.

operating at a local level. Many factors contribute to segregation in real life, but Schelling's model focuses on an intentionally simplified mechanism to illustrate how the forces leading to segregation are remarkably robust – they can operate even when no one individual explicitly wants a segregated outcome.

The general formulation of the model is as follows. We assume a population of individuals, whom we'll call *agents*, in which each agent is of type X or O. We think of the two types as representing some (immutable) characteristic that can serve as the basis for homophily – race, ethnicity, country of origin, or native language, for example. The agents reside in the cells of a grid, intended as a stylized model of the two-dimensional geography of a city. As illustrated in Figure 4.15(a), we will assume that some cells of the grid contain agents while others are unpopulated. A cell's *neighbors* are the cells that touch it, including diagonal contact; thus, a cell that is not on the boundary of the grid has eight neighbors. We can equivalently think of the neighbor relationships as defining a graph: the cells are the nodes, and we place an edge between two cells that are neighbors on the grid. In this view, the agents thus occupy the nodes of a graph that are arranged in this gridlike pattern, as shown in Figure 4.15(b). For ease of visualization, however, we will continue to draw things using a geometric grid rather than a graph.

The fundamental constraint driving the model is that each agent wants to have at least some other agents of its own type as neighbors. We assume that there is a threshold t common to all agents: if an agent discovers that fewer than t of its neighbors are of

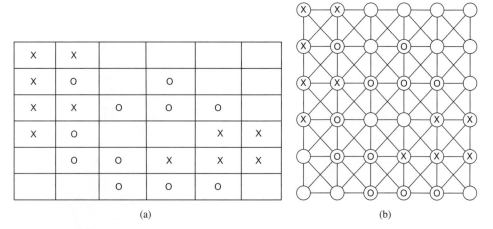

Figure 4.15. In Schelling's segregation model, agents of two different types (X and O) occupy cells on a grid (a). The neighbor relationships among the cells can be represented very simply as a graph (b). Agents care about whether they have at least some neighbors of the same type.

the same type as itself, then it has an interest in moving to a new cell. We will call such an agent *unsatisfied* with its current location. For example, in Figure 4.16(a), we indicate with an asterisk all the agents that are unsatisfied in the arrangement from Figure 4.15(a), when the threshold t is equal to 3. [In Figure 4.16(a) we have also added a number after each agent, which is simply to provide each with a unique name; the key distinction is still whether each agent is of type X or type O.]

The Dynamics of Movement. Thus far, we have simply specified a set of agents that want to move, given an underlying threshold; we now discuss how this gives the model its dynamic aspect. Agents move in a sequence of *rounds*: in each round, we consider the unsatisfied agents in some order; for each one in turn, we move it to an unoccupied cell where it will be satisfied. After this, the round of movement has come to an end, representing a fixed time period during which unsatisfied agents have changed where they live. These new locations may cause different agents to be unsatisfied, which leads to a new round of movement.

The literature on this model gives numerous variations in the specific details of how the movement of agents within a round is handled. For example, the agents can be scheduled to move in a random order, or in an order that sweeps downward along rows of the grid; they can move to the nearest location that satisfies them or to a random one. There also needs to be a way of handling situations in which an agent is scheduled to move but there is *no* cell to make it satisfied. In such a case, the agent can be left where it is or moved to a completely random cell. Research has found that the qualitative results of the model tend to be quite similar however these issues are resolved, and different investigations of the model have tended to resolve them differently.

For example, Figure 4.16(b) shows the results of one round of movement, starting from the arrangement in Figure 4.16(a), when the threshold t is 3. Unsatisfied agents are scheduled to move by considering them one row at a time and working downward through the grid, and each agent moves to the nearest cell that will make

X1*	X2*				
X3	O1*		O2		
X4	X5	O3	O4	O5*	
X6*	O6			X7	X8
	O7	O8	X9*	X10	X11
		O9	O10	O11*	

(a)

X3	X6	O1	O2		
X4	X5	O3	O4		
	O6	X2	X1	X7	X8
O11	O7	O8	X9	X10	X11
	O5	O9	O10*		

(b)

Figure 4.16. After arranging agents in cells of the grid (a), we first determine which agents are *unsatisfied*, with fewer than t other agents of the same type as neighbors. In one round, each of these agents moves to a cell where they will be satisfied (b); this may cause other agents to become unsatisfied, in which case a new round of movement begins.

it satisfied. [The unique name of each agent in the figure allows us to see where it has moved in Figure 4.16(b) relative to the initial state in Figure 4.16(a).] Notice that in some concrete respects, the pattern of agents has become more "segregated" after this round of movement. For example, in Figure 4.16(a), there is only a single agent with no neighbors of the opposite type. After this first round of movement, however, there are six agents in Figure 4.16(b) with no neighbors of the opposite type. As we will see, this increasing level of segregation is the key behavior to emerge from the model.

Larger Examples. Small examples of the type in Figures 4.15 and 4.16 are helpful in working through the details of the model by hand, but at such small scales it is difficult to see the kinds of typical patterns that arise. Computer simulation is very useful to identify such patterns at larger scales.

Many online computer programs make it possible to simulate the Schelling model; as with the published literature on the model, they all tend to differ slightly from each

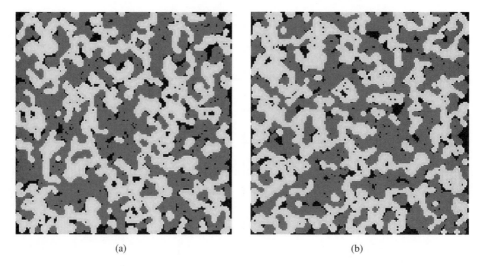

(a)   (b)

Figure 4.17. Two runs of a simulation of the Schelling model with a threshold t of 3, on a 150×150 grid with $10,000$ agents of each type. In each image, there is a dot for each cell of the grid; black dots indicate cells that are empty, and the two intermediate shades of grey indicate cells occupied by the two different type of agents.

other in their specifics. Here we discuss some examples from a simulation written by Luke [282], which is like the version of the model discussed thus far except that unsatisfied agents move to a random location.

In Figure 4.17, we show the results of simulating the model on a grid with 150 rows and 150 columns, 10,000 agents of each type, and 2,500 empty cells. The threshold t is equal to 3, as in our earlier examples. The two images depict the results of two different runs of the simulation, each with different random starting patterns of agents. In each case, the simulation reached a point (shown in the figures) at which all agents were satisfied, after roughly fifty rounds of movement.

Because of the different random starts, the final arrangement of agents is different in the two cases, but the qualitative similarities reflect the fundamental consequences of the model. By seeking out locations near other agents of the same type, the model produces large homogeneous regions, interlocking with each other as they stretch across the grid. In the midst of these regions are large numbers of agents who are surrounded on all sides by other agents of the same type – and in fact at some distance from the nearest agent of the opposite type. The geometric pattern has become segregated, much as in the maps of Chicago from Figure 4.14.

Interpretations of the Model. We've now seen how the model works, what it looks like at relatively large scales, and how it produces spatially segregated outcomes. But what broader insights into homophily and segregation does it suggest?

The first and most basic insight is that spatial segregation is taking place even though no individual agent is actively seeking it. Sticking to our focus on a threshold of $t = 3$, we see that, although agents want to be near others like them, their requirements are not particularly draconian. For example, an agent would be perfectly happy to be in the minority among its neighbors, with five neighbors of the opposite type and three of its

X	X	O	O	X	X
X	X	O	O	X	X
O	O	X	X	O	O
O	O	X	X	O	O
X	X	O	O	X	X
X	X	O	O	X	X

Figure 4.18. With a threshold of 3, it is possible to arrange agents in an integrated pattern: all agents are satisfied, and everyone who is not on the boundary of the grid has an equal number of neighbors of each type.

own type. Nor are the requirements globally incompatible with complete integration of the population. By arranging agents in a checkerboard pattern as shown in Figure 4.18, we can make each agent satisfied, and all agents not on the boundary of the grid have exactly four neighbors of each type. This is a pattern that can be continued on as large a grid as we want.

Thus, segregation does not happen because it has been subtly built into the model; agents are willing to be in the minority, and they could all be satisfied if only we were able to carefully arrange them in an integrated pattern. The problem is that, from a random start, it is very hard for the collection of agents to find such integrated patterns. Much more typically, agents attach themselves to clusters of others like themselves, and these clusters grow as other agents follow suit. Moreover, a compounding effect occurs as the rounds of movement unfold, in which agents who fall below their threshold depart for more homogeneous parts of the grid, causing previously satisfied agents to fall below their thresholds and move as well – an effect that Schelling describes as the progressive "unraveling" of more integrated regions [366]. In the long run, this process tends to cause segregated regions to grow at the expense of more integrated ones. The overall effect is one in which the local preferences of individual agents have produced a global pattern that none of them necessarily intended.

This point is ultimately at the heart of the model: although segregation in real life is amplified by a genuine desire within some fraction of the population to belong to large clusters of similar people – either to avoid people who belong to other groups, or to acquire a critical mass of members from one's own group – such factors are not necessary for segregation to occur. The underpinnings of segregation are already present in a system where individuals simply want to avoid being in too extreme a minority in their own local area.

The process operates even more powerfully when we raise the threshold t in our examples from 3 to 4. Even with a threshold of 4, nodes are willing to have an equal number of neighbors of each type, and a slightly more elaborate checkerboard example in the spirit of Figure 4.18 shows that, with careful placement, the agents can be arranged so that all are satisfied and most still have a significant number

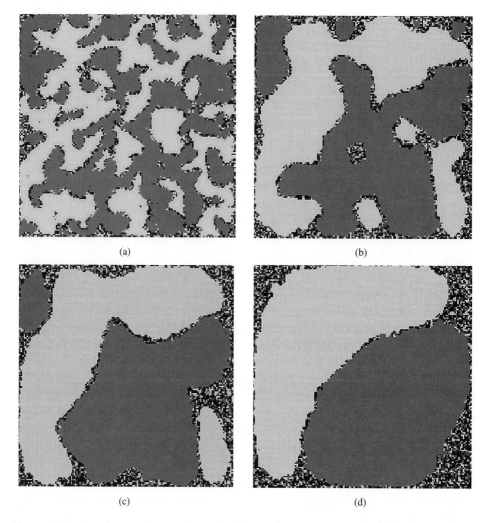

Figure 4.19. Four intermediate points, after (a) 20, (b) 150, (c) 350, and (d) 800 steps, in a simulation of the Schelling model with a threshold $t = 4$, on a 150×150 grid with $10,000$ agents of each type. As the rounds of movement progress, large homogeneous regions on the grid grow at the expense of smaller, narrower regions. In each image, there is a dot for each cell of the grid; black dots indicate cells that are empty, and the two intermediate shades of grey indicate cells occupies by the two different types of agents.

of neighbors of the opposite type. Now, not only is an integrated pattern very hard to reach from a random starting arrangement, but any vestige of integration among the two types tends to collapse completely over time. As one example, Figure 4.19 shows four intermediate points in one run of a simulation with threshold 4 and other properties the same as before (a 150×150 grid with 10,000 agents of each type and random movement by unsatisfied agents). Figure 4.19(a) shows that, after 20 rounds of movement, we have an arrangement of agents that roughly resembles what we saw with a lower threshold of 3. However, this arrangement does not last long: crucially, the long tendrils where one type interlocks with the other quickly wither and retract, leaving the more homogeneous regions shown after 150 rounds in Figure 4.19(b). This pulling back continues, passing through a phase with a large and a small region of each type after 350 rounds [Figure 4.19(c)] eventually to a point where there is only a single significant region of each type, after roughly 800 rounds [Figure 4.19(d)]. Note that this is not the end of the process, since agents remain around the edges still looking for places to move, but by this point the overall two-region layout has become very stable. Finally, we stress that this figure corresponds to just a single run of the simulation – but computational experiments show that the sequence of events it depicts, leading to almost complete separation of the two types, is very robust when the threshold is this high.

Viewed at a still more general level, the Schelling model is an example of how characteristics that are fixed and unchanging (such as race or ethnicity) can become highly correlated with other characteristics that are mutable. In this case, the mutable characteristic is the decision about where to live, which over time conforms to similarities in the agents' (immutable) types, producing segregation. But there are other, nonspatial manifestations of the same effect, in which beliefs and opinions become correlated across racial or ethnic lines, and for similar underlying reasons: as homophily draws people together along immutable characteristics, there is a natural tendency for mutable characteristics to change in accordance with the network structure.

As a final point, although the model is mathematically precise and self-contained, the discussion has been carried out in terms of simulations and qualitative observations. This is because rigorous mathematical analysis of the Schelling model appears to be quite difficult, and it is largely an open research question. For partial progress on analyzing properties of the Schelling model, see the work of Young [420], who compares properties of different arrangements in which all agents are satisfied; Möbius and Rosenblat [302], who perform a probabilistic analysis; and Vinković and Kirman [401], who develop analogies to models for the mixing of two liquids and other physical phenomena.

4.6 Exercises

1. Consider the social network represented in Figure 4.20. Suppose that this social network was obtained by observing a group of people at a particular point in time and recording all their friendship relations. Now suppose that we come back at some point in the future and observe it again. According to the theories based on empirical studies of triadic closure in networks, which new edge is most likely to be present? (That is, which pair of nodes, among those that do not currently have an edge connecting them, are most likely to be linked by an edge when we return to take the second observation?) Provide a brief explanation for your answer.

2. Given a bipartite affiliation graph that shows the membership of people in different social foci, researchers sometimes create a *projected graph* on just the people, in which we join two people when they have a focus in common.

   (a) Draw the projected graph for the example of memberships on corporate boards of directors from Figure 4.4. Here the nodes should be the seven people in the figure, and an edge should join any two who serve on a board of directors together.

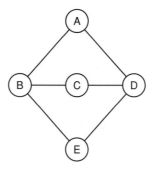

Figure 4.20. A social network with nodes representing people and edges representing friend-ships at a moment in time, for Exercise 1.

> (b) Give an example of two different affiliation networks – on the same set of people, but with different foci – so that the projected graphs from these two different affiliation networks are the same. This shows how information can be "lost" when moving from the full affiliation network to just the projected graph on the set of people.

3. Consider the affiliation network in Figure 4.21, with six people labeled A–F, and three foci labeled X, Y, and Z.

> (a) Draw the projected graph of just the six people as in Exercise 2, joining two people when they share a focus.
> (b) In the resulting network of people, can you identify a sense in which the triangle on nodes A, C, and E has a qualitatively different meaning than the other triangles that appear in the network? Explain.

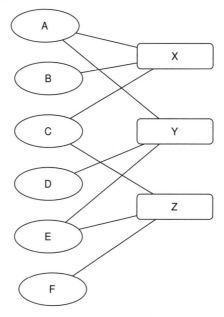

Figure 4.21. An affiliation network on six people, labeled A–F, and three foci, labeled X, Y, and Z, for Exercise 3.

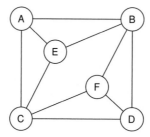

Figure 4.22. A graph of people arising from an (unobserved) affiliation network, for Exercise 4.

4. Given a network showing pairs of people who share activities, we can try to reconstruct an affiliation network consistent with this information.

    For example, suppose that you are trying to infer the structure of a bipartite affiliation network, and by indirect observation you've obtained the projected network on just the set of people, constructed as in Exercise 2: an edge joins each pair of people who share a focus. This projected network is shown in Figure 4.22.

    (a) Draw an affiliation network involving these six people, together with four foci that you should define, whose projected graph is the graph shown in Figure 4.22.

    (b) Explain why any affiliation network capable of producing the projected graph in Figure 4.22 must have at least four foci.

CHAPTER 5

Positive and Negative Relationships

In our discussion of networks thus far, we have generally viewed the relationships contained in these networks as having positive connotations – links have typically indicated such things as friendship, collaboration, sharing of information, or membership in a group. The terminology of online social networks reflects a largely similar view, through its emphasis on the connections one forms with friends, fans, followers, and so forth. But in most network settings, there are also negative effects at work. Some relations are friendly, but others are antagonistic or hostile; interactions between people or groups are regularly beset by controversy, disagreement, and sometimes outright conflict. How should we reason about the mix of positive and negative relationships that take place within a network?

Here we describe a rich part of social network theory that involves taking a network and annotating its links (i.e., its edges) with positive and negative signs. Positive links represent friendship while negative links represent antagonism, and an important problem in the study of social networks is to understand the tension between these two forces. The notion of *structural balance* that we discuss in this chapter is one of the basic frameworks for doing this.

In addition to introducing some of the basics of structural balance, our discussion in this chapter serves a second, methodological purpose: it illustrates a nice connection between local and global network properties. A recurring issue in the analysis of networked systems is the way in which *local* effects – phenomena involving only a few nodes at a time – can have global consequences that are observable at the level of the network as a whole. Structural balance offers a way to capture one such relationship in a very clean way, and by purely mathematical analysis: we will consider a simple definition abstractly and find that it inevitably leads to certain macroscopic properties of the network.

5.1 Structural Balance

We focus here on perhaps the most basic model of positive and negative relationships, since it captures the essential idea. Suppose we have a social network on a set of

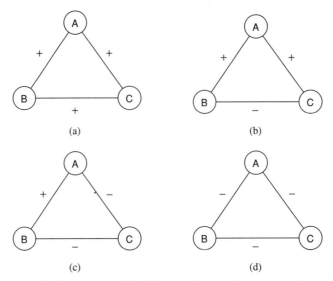

Figure 5.1. Structural balance: each labeled triangle must have one or three positive edges. (a) A, B, and C are mutual friends: balanced. (b) A is friends with B and C, but they don't get along with each other: not balanced. (c) A and B are friends and C is a mutual enemy: balanced. (d) A, B, and C are mutual enemies: not balanced.

people, in which everyone knows everyone else – so we have an edge joining each pair of nodes. Such a network is called a *clique*, or a *complete graph*. We then *label* each edge with either + or −; a + label indicates that its two endpoints are friends, while a − label indicates that its two endpoints are enemies.

Because there's an edge connecting each pair of nodes, we are assuming that each pair of people are either friends or enemies – no two people are indifferent to one another or unaware of each other. Thus, the model under consideration makes the most sense for a group of people small enough to have this level of mutual awareness (e.g., a classroom, a small company, a sports team, or a fraternity or sorority) or for a setting such as international relations, in which the nodes are countries and each country has an official diplomatic position toward every other country.[1]

The principles underlying structural balance are based on theories in social psychology dating back to the work of Heider in the 1940s [216] and generalized and extended to the language of graphs beginning with the work of Cartwright and Harary in the 1950s [97, 126, 204]. The crucial idea is the following. If we look at any two people in the group in isolation, the edge between them can be labeled + or −; that is, they are either friends or enemies. But when we look at sets of *three* people at a time, certain configurations of +'s and −'s are socially and psychologically more plausible than others. In particular, there are four distinct ways (up to symmetry) to label the three edges among three people with +'s and −'s (see Figure 5.1). We can distinguish among these four possibilities as follows.

1. Given a set of people A, B, and C, having three pluses among them [as in Figure 5.1(a)] is a very natural situation: it corresponds to three people who are mutual friends.

[1] Later, in Section 5.5, we will consider the more general setting in which not every pair of nodes is necessarily connected by an edge.

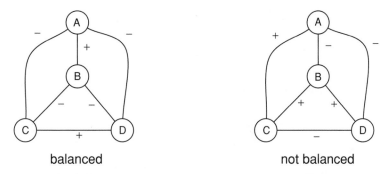

balanced   not balanced

Figure 5.2. The labeled four-node complete graph on the left is balanced; the graph on the right is not.

2. Having a single plus and two minuses in the relations among the three people is also very natural: it means that two of the three are friends, and they have a mutual enemy in the third [see Figure 5.1(c)].

3. The other two possible labelings of the triangle of A, B, and C introduce some amount of psychological "stress" or "instability" into the relationships. A triangle with two pluses and one minus corresponds [as in Figure 5.1(b)] to a person A who is friends with each of B and C, but B and C don't get along with each other. In this type of situation, there would be implicit forces pushing A to try to get B and C to become friends (thus turning the B-C edge label to +); or else for A to side with one of B or C against the other (turning one of the edge labels out of A to a −).

4. Similarly, there are sources of instability in a configuration where each of A, B, and C are mutual enemies [as in Figure 5.1(d)]. In this case, there would be forces motivating two of the three people to "team up" against the third (turning one of the three edge labels to a +).

Based on this reasoning, we refer to triangles with one or three +'s as *balanced*, since they are free of these sources of instability, and we refer to triangles with zero or two +'s as *unbalanced*. The argument by structural balance theorists is that, because unbalanced triangles are sources of stress or psychological dissonance, people strive to minimize them in their personal relationships, and hence they will be less abundant in real social settings than balanced triangles.

Defining Structural Balance for Networks. So far we have been talking about struc- tural balance for groups of three nodes. But it is easy to create a definition that naturally generalizes this to complete graphs on an arbitrary number of nodes, with edges labeled by pluses and minuses.

Specifically, we say that a labeled complete graph is balanced if every one of its triangles is balanced – that is, if it obeys the following:

> Structural Balance Property: For *every* set of three nodes, if we consider the three edges connecting them, either all three of these edges are labeled +, or exactly one of them is labeled +.

For example, consider the two labeled four-node networks in Figure 5.2. The one on the left is balanced, because we can check that each set of three nodes satisfies the

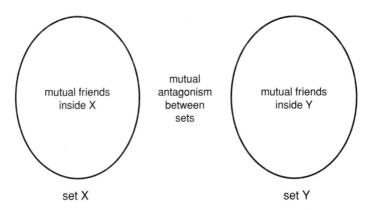

Figure 5.3. If a complete graph can be divided into two sets of mutual friends, with complete mutual antagonism between the two sets, then it is balanced. Furthermore, this is the only way for a complete graph to be balanced (other than graphs with all edges positive).

Structural Balance property. On the other hand, the one on the right is not balanced, since among the three nodes, A, B, and C, there are exactly two edges labeled +, in violation of structural balance. (The triangle on B, C, D also violates the condition.)

The definition of balanced networks here represents the limit of a social system that has eliminated all unbalanced triangles. As such, it is a fairly extreme definition – for example, one could instead propose a definition only requiring that at least some large percentage of all triangles were balanced, allowing a few triangles to be unbalanced.[2] But the version with all triangles balanced is a fundamental first step in thinking about this concept; and as we will see next, it turns out to have very interesting mathematical structure that in fact helps to inform the conclusions of more complicated models as well.

5.2 Characterizing the Structure of Balanced Networks

At a general level, what does a balanced network (i.e., a balanced labeled complete graph) look like? Given any specific example, we can check all triangles to make sure that they each obey the balance conditions, but it would be much better to have a simple conceptual description of what a balanced network looks like in general.

One way for a network to be balanced is if everyone likes each other; in this case, all triangles have three + labels. On the other hand, the left-hand side of Figure 5.2 suggests a slightly more complicated way for a network to be balanced: it consists of two groups of friends (A, B and C, D), with negative relations between people in different groups. This is actually true in general: suppose we have a labeled complete graph in which the nodes can be divided into two groups, X and Y, such that each pair of people in X likes each other, each pair of people in Y likes each other, and everyone in X is the enemy of everyone in Y. (See the schematic illustration in Figure 5.3.) You can check that such a network is balanced: a triangle contained entirely in one group or the

---

[2] We consider this type of weaker definition in Section 5.5.

other has three + labels, and a triangle with two people in one group and one in the other has exactly one + label.

So this describes two basic ways to achieve structural balance: either everyone likes each other, or the world consists of two groups of mutual friends with complete antagonism between the groups. The surprising fact is the following: these are the *only* ways to have a balanced network. We formulate this fact precisely as the following *Balance Theorem*, proved by Frank Harary in 1953 [97, 204]:

> The Balance Theorem: If a labeled complete graph is balanced, then either all pairs of nodes are friends, or else the nodes can be divided into two groups, X and Y, such that each pair of people in X likes each other, each pair of people in Y likes each other, and everyone in X is the enemy of everyone in Y.

The Balance Theorem is not at all an obvious fact, nor should it be initially clear why it is true. Essentially, we're taking a purely *local* property – namely the Structural Balance property, which applies to only three nodes at a time – and showing that it implies a strong *global* property: either everyone gets along, or the world is divided into two battling factions.

We're now going to show why this claim is in fact true.

Proving the Balance Theorem. Establishing the claim requires a proof: We're going to suppose we have an arbitrary labeled complete graph, assume only that it is balanced, and conclude either that everyone is friends, or that there are sets X and Y as described in the claim. Recall that we've worked through a proof in earlier in the book, in Chapter 3, where we used simple assumptions about triadic closure in a social network to conclude that all local bridges in the network must be weak ties. Our proof here will be somewhat longer, but still very natural and straightforward – we use the definition of balance to directly derive the conclusion of the claim.

To start, suppose we have a labeled complete graph, and all we know is that it's balanced. We have to show that it has the structure in the claim. If it has no negative edges at all, then everyone is friends, and we're all set. Otherwise, at least one negative edge is present, and we must somehow come up with a division of the nodes into sets of mutual friends X and Y, with complete antagonism between them. The difficulty is that, knowing so little about the graph itself other than that it is balanced, it's not clear how we're supposed to identify X and Y.

Let's pick any node in the network – we'll call it A – and consider things from A's perspective. Every other node is either a friend of A or an enemy of A. Thus, natural candidates to try for the sets X and Y would be to define X to be A and all its friends, and to define Y to be all the enemies of A. This is indeed a division of all the nodes, since every node is either a friend or an enemy of A.

Recall what we must show in order for these two sets, X and Y, to satisfy the conditions of the claim:

  (i) Every two nodes in X are friends.
 (ii) Every two nodes in Y are friends.
(iii) Every node in X is an enemy of every node in Y.

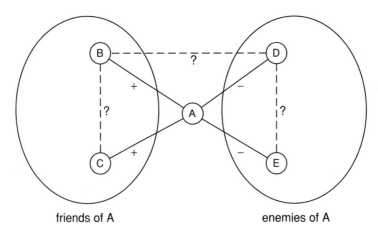

Figure 5.4. A schematic illustration of our analysis of balanced networks. (There may be other nodes not illustrated here.)

We now argue that each of these conditions is in fact true for our choice of X and Y. This will mean that X and Y do satisfy the conditions of the claim, and it will complete the proof. The rest of the argument, establishing conditions (i), (ii), and (iii), is illustrated schematically in Figure 5.4.

For condition (i), we know that A is friends with every other node in X. How about two other nodes in X (let's call them B and C) – must they be friends? We know that A is friends with both B and C, so if B and C were enemies of each other, then A, B, and C would form a triangle with two + labels: a violation of the balance condition. Since we know the network is balanced, this can't happen, so it must be that B and C are in fact friends. Since B and C were the names of any two nodes in X, we have concluded that every two nodes in X are friends.

Let's try the same kind of argument for condition (ii). Consider any two nodes in Y (let's call them D and E) – must they be friends? We know that A is enemies with both D and E, so if D and E were enemies of each other, then A, D, and E would form a triangle with no + labels: a violation of the balance condition. Since we know the network is balanced, this can't happen, so it must be that D and E are in fact friends. Since D and E were the names of any two nodes in Y, we have concluded that every two nodes in Y are friends.

Finally, let's check condition (iii). Following the style of our arguments for conditions (i) and (ii), consider a node in X (call it B) and a node in Y (call it D) – must they be enemies? We know A is friends with B and enemies with D, so if B and D were friends, then A, B, and D would form a triangle with two + labels: a violation of the balance condition. Since we know the network is balanced, this can't happen, so it must be that B and D are in fact enemies. Since B and D were the names of any node in X and any node in Y, we have concluded that every such pair constitutes a pair of enemies.

So in conclusion, by assuming only that the network is balanced, we have described a division of the nodes into two sets, X and Y, and we have checked conditions (i), (ii), and (iii) required by the claim. This completes the proof of the Balance Theorem.

5.3 Applications of Structural Balance

Structural balance has grown into a large area of study, and we've only described a simple but central example of the theory. In Section 5.5, we discuss two extensions to the basic theory: one to handle graphs that are not necessarily complete, and one to describe the structure of complete graphs that are "approximately balanced" in the sense that most but not all of their triangles are balanced.

Recent research has also looked at dynamic aspects of structural balance theory, modeling how the set of friendships and antagonisms in a complete graph – in other words, the labeling of the edges – might evolve over time as the social network implicitly seeks out structural balance. Antal, Krapivsky, and Redner [20] study a model in which we start with a random labeling (choosing + or − randomly for each edge); we then repeatedly look for a triangle that is not balanced and flip one of its labels to make it balanced. This dynamic process, where the pattern of signs in the network evolves over time, captures a situation in which people continually reassess their likes and dislikes of others as they strive for structural balance. The mathematics here becomes quite complicated and turns out to resemble the mathematical models one uses for certain physical systems as they reconfigure to minimize their energy [20, 287].

In the remainder of this section, we consider two further areas in which the ideas of structural balance are relevant: international relations, where the nodes are different countries, and online social media sites, where users can express positive or negative opinions about each other.

International Relations. International politics represents a setting in which it is natural to assume that a collection of nodes all have opinions (positive or negative) about one another – here the nodes are nations, and + and − labels indicate alliance or animosity, respectively. Research in political science has shown that structural balance can sometimes provide an effective explanation for the behavior of nations during various international crises. For example, Moore [306], describing the conflict over Bangladesh's separation from Pakistan in 1972, explicitly invokes structural balance theory when he writes, "The United States's somewhat surprising support of Pakistan . . . becomes less surprising when one considers that the USSR was China's enemy, China was India's foe, and India had traditionally bad relations with Pakistan. Since the U.S. was at that time improving its relations with China, it supported the enemies of China's enemies. Further reverberations of this strange political constellation became inevitable: North Vietnam made friendly gestures toward India, Pakistan severed diplomatic relations with those countries of the Eastern Bloc which recognized Bangladesh, and China vetoed the acceptance of Bangladesh into the U.N."

Antal, Krapivsky, and Redner use the shifting alliances preceding World War I as another example of structural balance in international relations (see Figure 5.5). This example also reinforces the fact that structural balance is not necessarily a good thing: because its global outcome often involves two implacably opposed alliances, the search for balance in a system can sometimes be seen as a slide into a hard-to-resolve opposition between two sides.

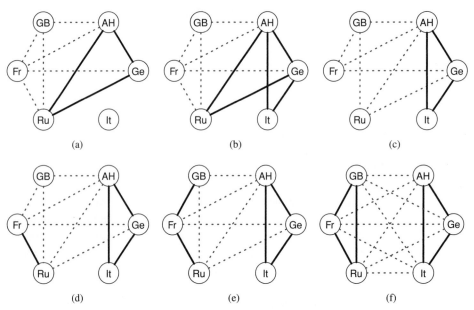

Figure 5.5. The evolution of alliances in Europe, 1872–1907 (the abbreviations GB, Fr, Ru, It, Ge, and AH stand for Great Britain, France, Russia, Italy, Germany, and Austria-Hungary, respectively): (a) Three Emperors' League, 1872–1881; (b) Triple Alliance, 1882; (c) German–Russian Lapse, 1890; (d) French–Russian Alliance, 1891–1994; (e) Entente Cordiale, 1904; (f) British Russian Alliance, 1907. Solid dark edges indicate friendship while dotted edges indicate enmity. Note how the network slides into a balanced labeling – and into World War I. (This figure and example are from Antal et al. [20] and Elsevier Science and Technology Journals.)

Trust, Distrust, and Online Ratings. A growing source for network data with both positive and negative edges comes from user communities on the Web, where people can express positive or negative sentiments about each other. Examples include the technology news site Slashdot, where users can designate each other as a "friend" or a "foe" [266], and online product-rating sites such as Epinions, where a user can evaluate different products and also express *trust* or *distrust* of other users.

Guha et al. [201] performed an analysis of the network of user evaluations on Epinions; their work identified an interesting set of issues that show how the trust–distrust dichotomy in online ratings has both similarities and differences with the friend–enemy dichotomy in structural balance theory. One difference is based on a simple structural distinction: we have been considering structural balance in the context of undirected graphs, whereas user evaluations on a site like Epinions form a directed graph. That is, when user A expresses trust or distrust of user B, we don't necessarily know what B thinks of A, or whether B is even aware of A.

A more subtle difference between trust–distrust and friend–enemy relations becomes apparent when thinking about how we should expect triangles on three Epinions users to behave. Certain patterns are easy to reason about: for example, if user A trusts user B, and user B trusts user C, then it is natural to expect that A trusts C. Such triangles with three forward-pointing positive edges make sense here, by analogy with the all-positive (undirected) triangles of structural balance theory. But what if A distrusts B and B distrusts C? Should we expect A to trust or to distrust C? There are intuitively appealing arguments in both directions. If we think of distrust fundamentally as a kind of enemy relationship, then the arguments from structural balance theory would suggest that A should trust C; otherwise we would have a triangle with three negative edges. On the other hand, if A's distrust of B expresses A's belief that she is more knowledgeable and competent than B – and if B's distrust of C reflects a corresponding belief by B – then we might well expect that A distrusts C, perhaps even more strongly than she distrusts B.

It is reasonable to expect that these two different interpretations of distrust may each apply, simply in different settings. And both might apply in the context of a single product-rating site like Epinions. For example, among users who are primarily rating best-selling books by political commentators, trust–distrust evaluations between users may become strongly aligned with agreement or disagreement in these users' own political orientations. In such a case, if A distrusts B and B distrusts C, this may suggest that A and C are close to each other on the underlying political spectrum, and so the prediction of structural balance theory that A should trust C may apply. On the other hand, among users who are primarily rating consumer electronics products, trust–distrust evaluations may largely reflect the relative expertise of users about the products (their respective features, reliability, and so forth). In such a case, if A distrusts B and B distrusts C, we may conclude that A is far more expert than C, and so A should distrust C as well.

Ultimately, understanding how these positive and negative relationships work is important for understanding the role they play on social Web sites where users register subjective evaluations of each other. Research is only beginning to explore these fundamantal questions, including the ways in which theories of balance – as well as related theories – can be used to shed light on these issues in large-scale data sets [274].

5.4 A Weaker Form of Structural Balance

In studying models of positive and negative relationships in networks, researchers have also formulated alternate notions of structural balance, by revisiting the original assumptions we used to motivate the framework.

In particular, our analysis began from the claim that among three people, there are two kinds of structures that are inherently unbalanced: a triangle with two positive edges and one negative edge [as in Figure 5.1(b)] and a triangle with three negative edges [as in Figure 5.1(d)]. In each of these cases, we argued that the relationships within the triangle contained a latent source of stress that the network might try to resolve. The underlying arguments in the two cases, however, were fundamentally different. In a triangle with two positive edges, we have the problem of a person whose two friends don't get along; in a triangle with three negative edges, there is possibility that two of the nodes will ally themselves against the third.

James Davis and others have argued that, in many settings, the first of these factors may be significantly stronger than the second [127]: we may see friends of friends trying to reconcile their differences [resolving the lack of balance in Figure 5.1(b)], but

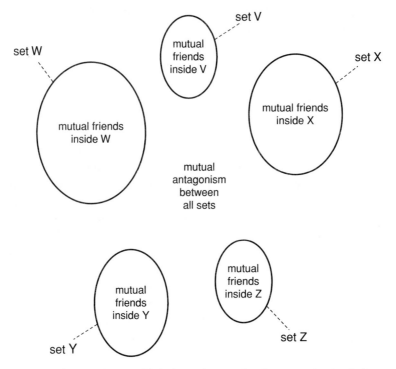

Figure 5.6. A complete graph is weakly balanced precisely when it can be divided into multiple sets of mutual friends, with complete mutual antagonism occurring between each pair of sets.

at the same time there could be less of a force leading any two of three mutual enemies [(as in Figure 5.1(d)] to become friendly. Therefore, it becomes natural to ask what structural properties arise when we rule out only triangles with exactly two positive edges, while allowing triangles with three negative edges to be present in the network.

Characterizing Weakly Balanced Networks. More precisely, we will say that a complete graph, with each edge labeled by $+$ or $-$, is *weakly balanced* if the following property holds:

> Weak Structural Balance Property: There is no set of three nodes such that the edges among them consist of exactly two positive edges and one negative edge.

Since weak balance imposes less of a restriction on what the network can look like, we should expect to see a broader range of possible structures for weakly balanced networks – beyond what the Balance Theorem required for networks that were balanced under our original definition. And indeed, Figure 5.6 indicates a new kind of structure that can arise. Suppose the nodes can be divided into an arbitrary number of groups (possibly more than two), in such a way that two nodes are friends when they belong to the same group and enemies when they belong to different groups. Then we can check that such a network is weakly balanced: in any triangle that contains at least two positive edges, all three nodes must belong to the same group. Therefore, the third edge of this triangle must be positive as well – in other words, the network contains no triangles with exactly two + edges.

Just as the Balance Theorem established that all balanced networks must have a simple structure, an analogous result holds for weakly balanced networks: they must have the structure depicted in Figure 5.6, with any number of groups:

> Characterization of Weakly Balanced Networks: If a labeled complete graph is weakly balanced, then its nodes can be divided into groups in such a way that every two nodes belonging to the same group are friends, and every two nodes belonging to different groups are enemies.

The fact that this characterization is true provided another early motivation for studying weak structural balance. The original Cartwright–Harary notion of balance predicted only dichotomies (or mutual consensus) as its basic social structure, and thus did not provide a model for reasoning about situations in which a network is divided into more than two factions. Weak structural balance makes this possible, since weakly balanced complete graphs can contain any number of opposed groups of mutual friends [127].

Proving the Characterization. It is not hard to give a proof of this characterization, following the structure of our proof for the Balance Theorem and making appropriate changes where necessary. Starting with a weakly balanced complete graph, the characterization requires that its nodes be divided into groups of mutual friends, such that all relations between nodes in different groups are negative. We construct this division as follows.

First, we pick any node A and consider the set consisting of A and all its friends. Let's call this set of nodes X. We'd like to make X our first group, and for this to work, we need to establish two conditions:

(i) All of A's friends are friends with each other. (This way, we have indeed produced a group of mutual friends.)
(ii) A and all his friends are enemies with everyone else in the graph. (This way, the people in this group will be enemies with everyone in other groups, regardless of how we divide up the rest of the graph.)

Fortunately, ideas that we already used inside the proof of the Balance Theorem can be adapted to our new setting here to establish conditions (i) and (ii). The idea is shown in Figure 5.7. First, for condition (i), let's consider two nodes, B and C, who are both friends with A. If B and C were enemies of each other, then the triangle on nodes A, B, and C would have exactly two + labels, which would violate weak structural balance. Therefore, B and C must indeed be friends with each other.

For condition (ii), we know that A is enemies with all nodes in the graph outside X, since the group X is defined to include all of A's friends. How about an edge between a node B in X and a node D outside X? If B and D were friends, then the triangle on nodes A, B, and D would have exactly two + labels; again, a violation of weak structural balance would occur. Therefore, B and D must be enemies.

Since properties (i) and (ii) hold, we can remove the set X – consisting of A and all his friends – from the graph and declare it to be the first group. We now have a smaller

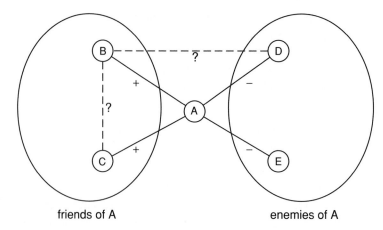

Figure 5.7. A schematic illustration of our analysis of weakly balanced networks. (There may be other nodes not illustrated here.)

complete graph that is still weakly balanced. We find a second group in this graph and proceed to remove groups in this way until all the nodes have been assigned to a group. Since each group consists of mutual friends by property (i), and each group has only negative relations with everyone outside the group by property (ii), this proves the characterization.

It is interesting to reflect on this proof in relation to the proof of the Balance Theorem – particularly the contrast reflected by the small differences between Figures 5.4 and 5.7. In proving the Balance Theorem, we had to reason about the sign of the edge between D and E to show that the enemies of the set X themselves formed a set Y of mutual friends. In characterizing weakly balanced complete graphs, on the other hand, we made no attempt to reason about the D-E edge, because weak balance imposes no condition on it: two enemies of A can be either friends or enemies. As a result, the set of enemies in Figure 5.7 might not be a set of mutual friends when only weak balance holds; it may consist of multiple groups of mutual friends, and as we extract these groups one by one over the course of the proof, we recover a structure with potentially many factions, as illustrated schematically in Figure 5.6.

5.5 Advanced Material: Generalizing the Definition of Structural Balance

In this section, we consider more general ways of formulating the idea of structural balance in a network. In particular, our definition of structural balance thus far has been fairly demanding in two respects:

1. It applies only to complete graphs. We require that each person knows and has an opinion (positive or negative) on everyone else. What if only some pairs of people know each other?
2. The Balance Theorem, which shows that structural balance implies a global division of the world into two factions [97, 204], only applies to the case in which *every*

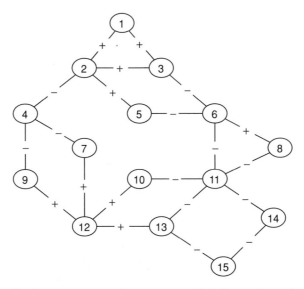

Figure 5.8. In graphs that are not complete, we can still define notions of structural balance when the edges that are present have positive or negative signs, indicating friend or enemy relations, respectively.

triangle is balanced. Can we relax this requirement to say that, if *most* triangles are balanced, then the world can be *approximately* divided into two factions?

In the two parts of this section, we discuss a pair of results that address these questions. The first is based on a graph-theoretic analysis involving the notion of breadth-first search from Chapter 2, while the second is typical of a style of proof known as a "counting argument." Throughout this section, we focus on the original definition of structural balance from Sections 5.1 and 5.2 rather than the weaker version from Section 5.4.

A. Structural Balance in Arbitrary (Noncomplete) Networks

First, let's consider the case of a social network that is not necessarily complete; that is, there are only edges between certain pairs of nodes, but each of these edges is still labeled with + or −. So now there are three possible relations between each pair of nodes: a positive edge, indicating friendship; a negative edge, indicating enmity; or the absence of an edge, indicating that the two endpoints do not know each other. Figure 5.8 depicts an example of such a signed network.

Defining Balance for General Networks. Drawing on what we've learned from the special case of complete graphs, what would be a good definition of balance for this more general kind of structure? The Balance Theorem suggests that structural balance can be viewed in either of two equivalent ways: a *local* view, as a condition on each triangle of the network, or a *global* view, as a requirement that the world be divided into two mutually opposed sets of friends. Each of these views suggests a way of defining structural balance for general signed graphs.

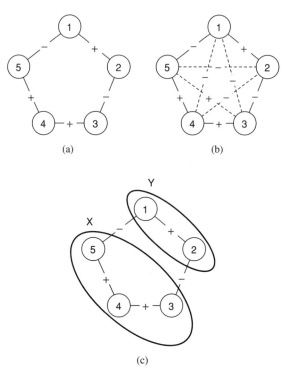

Figure 5.9. Two equivalent ways are used to define structural balance for an arbitary graph that, as in (a), may not be complete. One definition asks whether it is possible to (b) fill in the remaining edges to produce a signed complete graph that is balanced. The other definition asks whether it is possible to (c) divide the nodes into two sets, X and Y, so that all edges inside X and inside Y are positive, and all edges between X and Y are negative.

1. One option would be to treat balance for noncomplete networks as a problem of filling in "missing values." Imagine, as a thought experiment, that all people in the group in fact do know and have an opinion on each other; the graph under consideration is not complete only because we have failed to observe the relations between some of the pairs. We could then say that the graph is balanced if it is possible to fill in all the missing labeled edges in such a way that the resulting signed complete graph is balanced. In other words, a (noncomplete) graph is balanced if it can be "completed" by adding edges to form a signed complete graph that is balanced.

   For example, Figure 5.9(a) shows a graph with signed edges, and Figure 5.9(b) shows how the remaining edges can be "filled in" to produce a balanced complete graph: we declare the missing edge between nodes 3 and 5 to be positive and the remaining missing edges to be negative, and this causes all triangles to be balanced.

2. Alternately, we could take the more global view of structural balance as implying a division of the network into two mutually opposed sets of friends. With this in mind, we could define a signed graph to be balanced if it is possible to divide the nodes into two sets, X and Y, such that any edge with both ends inside X or both ends inside Y is positive, and any edge with one end in X and the other in Y is

negative. That is, people in X are all mutual friends to the extent that they know each other, and the same is true for people in Y; people in X are all enemies of people in Y to the extent that they know each other.

Continuing the example from Figure 5.9(a), Figure 5.9(c) shows how to divide this graph into two sets with the desired properties.

This example hints at a principle that is true in general: these two ways of defining balance are equivalent. An arbitrary signed graph is balanced under the first definition if and only if it is balanced under the second definition.

This is actually not hard to see. If a signed graph is balanced under the first definition, then after filling in all the missing edges appropriately, we have a signed complete graph to which we can apply the Balance Theorem. This approach divides the network into two sets, X and Y, that satisfy the properties of the second definition. Reasoning in the other direction, if a signed graph is balanced under the second definition, then, after finding a division of the nodes into sets X and Y, we can fill in positive edges inside X and inside Y, and fill in negative edges between X and Y, and then we can check that all triangles will be balanced. So this approach gives a "filling in" that satisfies the first definition.

The fact that the two definitions are equivalent suggests a certain "naturalness" to the definition, since there are fundamentally different ways to arrive at it. This equivalence also means that we are free to use either definition, depending on which is more convenient in a given situation. As the example in Figure 5.9 suggests, the second definition is generally more useful to work with, because it tends to be much easier to think about dividing the nodes into two sets than to reason about filling in edges and checking triangles.

Characterizing Balance for General Networks. Conceptually, however, something is not fully satisfying about either definition: the definitions themselves do not provide much insight into how to easily check whether a graph is balanced or not balanced. After all, there are lots of ways to choose signs for the missing edges, or to choose ways of splitting the nodes into sets X and Y. And if a graph is not balanced, so that there is no way to do these things successfully, what could you show someone to convince them of this fact? To take just a small example to suggest some of the difficulties, it may not be obvious from a quick inspection of Figure 5.8 that this is not a balanced graph – or that if we change the edge connecting nodes 2 and 4 to be positive instead of negative, it becomes a balanced graph.

In fact, however, all these problems can be remedied if we explore the consequences of the definitions a little further. What we show now is a simple characterization of balance in general signed graphs, also due to Harary [97, 204]; the proof also provides an easy method for checking whether a graph is balanced.

The characterization is based on considering the following question: what prevents a graph from being balanced? Figure 5.10 shows a graph that is not balanced, obtained from Figure 5.9(a) by changing the sign of the edge from node 4 to node 5. The figure also illustrates a reason why the graph is not balanced: If we start at node 1 and try to divide the nodes into sets X and Y, then our choices are forced at every step. Suppose we initially decide that node 1 should belong to X. (For the first node, it doesn't matter,

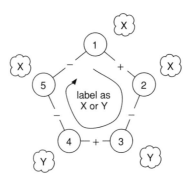

Figure 5.10. If a signed graph contains a cycle with an odd number of negative edges, then it is not balanced. Indeed, if we pick one of the nodes and try to place it in X, then following the set of friend/enemy relations around the cycle produces a conflict by the time we get to the starting node.

by symmetry.) Then, because node 2 is friends with node 1, it too must belong to X. Node 3, an enemy of 2, must therefore belong to Y; hence, node 4, a friend of 3, must belong to Y as well. And node 5, an enemy of 4, must belong to X. The problem is that, if we continue this reasoning one step further, node 1, an enemy of 5, should belong to Y – but we had already decided at the outset to put it into X. We had no freedom of choice during this process – so this shows that there is no way to divide the nodes into sets X and Y to satisfy the mutual-friend/mutual-enemy conditions of structural balance. Hence, the signed graph in Figure 5.10 is not balanced.

The reasoning in the previous paragraph sounds elaborate, but in fact it follows a simple principle: we were walking around a cycle, and every time we crossed a negative edge we had to change the set into which we were putting nodes. The difficulty was that getting back around to node 1 required crossing an *odd number* of negative edges, and so our original decision to put node 1 into X clashed with the eventual conclusion that node 1 ought to be in Y.

This principle applies in general: if the graph contains a cycle with an odd number of negative edges, then this implies that the graph is not balanced. Indeed, if we start at any node A in the cycle and place it in one of the two sets, and then we walk around the cycle and place the other nodes where they must go, the identity of the set where we're placing nodes switches an odd number of times as we go around the cycle. Thus, we end up with the "wrong set" by the time we make it back to A.

A cycle with an odd number of negative edges is thus a very simple-to-understand reason why a graph is not balanced: You can show someone such a cycle and immediately convince him or her that the graph is not balanced. For example, the cycle in Figure 5.8 consisting of nodes 2, 3, 6, 11, 13, 12, 9, and 4 contains five negative edges, thus supplying a succinct reason why this graph is not balanced. But are there other, more complex reasons why a graph is not balanced?

In fact, though it may seem initially surprising, cycles with an odd number of negative edges are the only obstacles to balance. This is the crux of the following claim [97, 204]:

> *Claim:* A signed graph is balanced if and only if it contains no cycle with an odd number of negative edges.

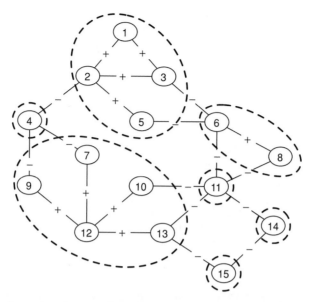

Figure 5.11. To determine if a signed graph is balanced, the first step is to consider only the positive edges, to find the connected components using just these edges, and to declare each of these components to be a *supernode*. In any balanced division of the graph into X and Y, all nodes in the same supernode must be placed in the same set.

We now show how to prove this claim. The proof proceeds by designing a method that analyzes the graph and either finds a division into the desired sets X and Y or else finds a cycle with an odd number of negative edges.

Proving the Characterization: Identifying Supernodes. Let's recall what we're trying to do: Find a division of the nodes into sets X and Y so that all edges inside X and Y are positive, and all edges crossing between X and Y are negative. When we produce a partition into sets X and Y with these properties it is called a *balanced division*. We now describe a procedure that searches for a balanced division of the nodes into sets X and Y; either it succeeds, or it stops with a cycle containing an odd number of negative edges. Because these are the only two possible outcomes for the procedure, this will provide a proof of the claim.

The procedure works in two main steps: the first step is to convert the graph to a reduced form that only contains negative edges, and the second step is to solve the problem on this reduced graph. The first step works as follows. Notice that whenever two nodes are connected by a positive edge, they must belong to the same set, either X or Y, in a balanced division. So we begin by considering what the connected components of the graph would be if we were to consider only positive edges. These components can be viewed as a set of contiguous "blobs" in the overall graph, as shown in Figure 5.11. We will refer to each of these blobs as a *supernode*: each supernode is connected internally via positive edges, and the only edges going between two different supernodes are negative. (If there were a positive edge linking two different supermodes, then we should have combined them together into a single supernode.)

Now, if any supernode contains a negative edge between some pair of nodes A and B, then we already have a cycle with an odd number of negative edges, as illustrated

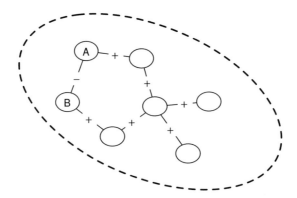

Figure 5.12. Suppose a negative edge connects two nodes, A and B, that belong to the same supernode. Because there is also a path consisting entirely of positive edges that connect A and B through the inside of the supernode, putting this negative edge together with the all-positive path produces a cycle with an odd number of negative edges.

in the example of Figure 5.12. Consider a path of positive edges that connects A and B inside the supernode, and then close off a cycle by including the negative edge that joins A and B. This cycle has only a single negative edge, linking A and B, and so it shows that the graph is not balanced.

If there are no negative edges inside any of the supernodes, then there is no "internal" problem with declaring each supernode to belong entirely to one of X or Y. Therefore, the problem is now to assign a single label "X" or "Y" to each supernode in such a way that these choices are all consistent with each other. Because these decisions are now taking place at the level of supernodes, we create a new version of the problem in which each supernode is "collapsed" down to a single node that represents it, and there is an edge joining two of these representative nodes whenever there is an edge in the original graph between members of their corresponding supernodes. Figure 5.13 shows how this works for the example of Figure 5.11: We essentially forget about the individual nodes inside the supernodes, and a new graph is built at the level of the large "blobs." Of course, having done so, we can draw the graph in a less blob-like way, as in Figure 5.14.

We now enter the second step of the procedure, using this *reduced graph*, whose nodes are the supernodes of the original graph.

Proving the Characterization: Breadth-First Search of the Reduced Graph. Recall that only negative edges occur between supernodes (since a positive edge between two supernodes would have merged them together into a single supernode). As a result, our reduced graph has only negative edges. The remainder of the procedure will produce one of two possible outcomes:

1. The first possible outcome involves labeling each node in the reduced graph as either X or Y in such a way that every edge has endpoints with opposite labels. From this labeling we can create a balanced division of the original graph, by labeling each node the way its supernode is labeled in the reduced graph.

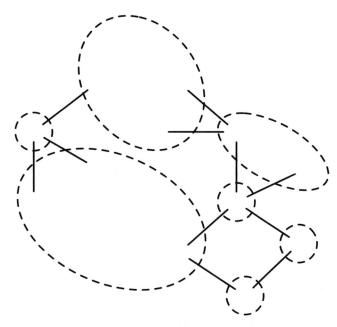

Figure 5.13. The second step in determining if a signed graph is balanced is to look for a labeling of the supernodes so that adjacent supernodes (which necessarily contain mutual enemies) receive opposite labels. For this purpose, we can ignore the original nodes of the graph and consider a *reduced graph*, whose nodes are the supernodes of the original graph.

2. The second possible outcome is to find a cycle in the reduced graph that has an odd number of edges. We can then convert this cycle to a (potentially longer) cycle in the original graph with an odd number of negative edges: The cycle in the reduced graph connects supernodes, and it corresponds to a set of negative edges in the original graph. We can simply "stitch together" these negative edges using paths that consist entirely of positive edges that pass through the insides of the supernodes. This path will contain an odd number of negative edges in the original graph.

   For example, the odd-length cycle in Figure 5.14 consisting of nodes A through E can be realized in the original graph as the darkened negative edges shown in

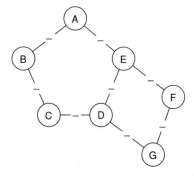

Figure 5.14. A more standard drawing of the reduced graph from the previous figure. A negative cycle is visually apparent in this drawing.

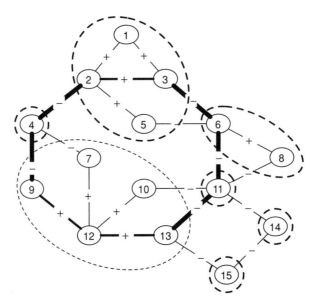

Figure 5.15. Having found a negative cycle through the supernodes, we can then turn it into a cycle in the original graph by filling in paths of positive edges through the inside of the supernodes. The resulting cycle has an odd number of negative edges.

Figure 5.15. These darkened negative edges can then be grown into a cycle in the original graph by including paths through the supernodes – in this example using the additional nodes 3 and 12.

In fact, this version of the problem, in which the underlying graph has only negative edges, is known in graph theory as the problem of determining whether a graph is *bipartite*: whether its nodes can be divided into two groups (in this case X and Y) so that each edge goes from one group to the other. We saw bipartite graphs when we considered affiliation networks in Chapter 4, but in the discussion in that chapter, the fact that the graphs were bipartite was apparent from the ready-made division of the nodes into people and social foci. Here, on the other hand, we are handed a graph "in the wild" with no prespecified division into two sets, and we want to know if it is possible to identify such a division. We now show a way to do this using the idea of breadth-first search from Chapter 2, resulting either in the division we seek or in a cycle of odd length.

We simply perform breadth-first search starting from any "root" node in the graph, producing a set of layers at increasing distances from this root. Figure 5.16 shows this process for the reduced graph in Figure 5.14, with node G as the starting root node. Now, because edges cannot jump over successive layers in breadth-first search, each edge either connects two nodes in adjacent layers or connects two nodes in the same layer. If all edges are of the first type – connecting nodes in adjacent layers – then we can find the desired division of nodes into sets X and Y: we simply declare all nodes in even-numbered layers to belong to X and all nodes in odd-numbered layers to belong

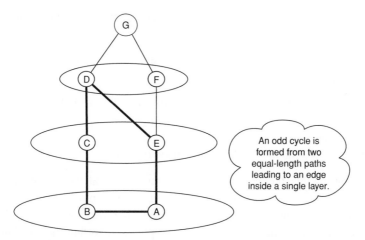

An odd cycle is formed from two equal-length paths leading to an edge inside a single layer.

Figure 5.16. When we perform a breadth-first search of the reduced graph, either there is an edge that connects two nodes in the same layer or there isn't. If there isn't, then we can produce the desired division into X and Y by putting alternate layers in different sets. If such an edge does exist (such as the edge joining A and B in the figure), then we can take two paths of the same length leading to the two ends of the edge, which together with the edge itself forms an odd cycle.

to Y. Because edges only go between adjacent layers, all edges have one end in X and the other end in Y, as desired.

Otherwise, there is an edge connecting two nodes that belong to the same layer. Let's call these two nodes A and B (as they are in Figure 5.16). For each of these two nodes, a path descends layer by layer from the root to the node. Consider the last node that is common to these two paths – let's call this node D (as it is in Figure 5.16). The D-A path and the D-B path have the same length k, so a cycle created from these two paths plus the A-B edge must have length $2k + 1$: an odd number. This is the odd cycle we seek.

And this completes the proof. To recap: If all edges in the reduced graph connect nodes in adjacent layers of the breadth-first search, then we have a way to label the nodes in the reduced graph, as X and Y, which in turn provides a balanced division of the nodes in the original graph into X and Y. In this case, we have established that the graph is balanced. Otherwise, there is an edge connecting two nodes in the same layer of the breadth-first search, in which case we produce an odd cycle in the reduced graph as in Figure 5.16. In this case, we can convert this to a cycle in the original graph containing an odd number of negative edges, as in Figure 5.15. Because these are the only two possibilities, the claim has been proved.

B. Approximately Balanced Networks

We now return to the case in which the graph is complete, so that every node has a positive or negative relation with every other node, and we think about a different way of generalizing the characterization of structural balance.

First let's write down the original Balance Theorem again, with some additional formatting to make its logical structure clear.

Claim: If all triangles in a labeled complete graph are balanced, then either

(a) all pairs of nodes are friends, or else
(b) the nodes can be divided into two groups, X and Y, such that

    (i) every pair of nodes in X like each other,
    (ii) every pair of nodes in Y like each other, and
    (iii) every node in X is the enemy of every node in Y.

The conditions of this theorem are fairly extreme, in that we require every single triangle to be balanced. What if we only know that most triangles are balanced? It turns out that the conditions of the theorem can be relaxed in a very natural way, allowing us to prove statements like the following one. We phrase it so that the wording remains completely parallel to that of the Balance Theorem.

Claim: If at least 99.9% of all triangles in a labeled complete graph are balanced, then either

(a) there is a set consisting of at least 90% of the nodes in which at least 90% of all pairs are friends, or else
(b) the nodes can be divided into two groups, X and Y, such that

    (i) at least 90% of the pairs in X like each other,
    (ii) at least 90% of the pairs in Y like each other, and
    (iii) at least 90% of the pairs with one end in X and the other end in Y are enemies.

This statement is true, although the choice of numbers is very specific. The following is a more general statement that includes both the original Balance Theorem and the preceding claim as special cases.

Claim: Let ε be any number such that $0 \leq \varepsilon < \frac{1}{8}$, and define $\delta = \sqrt[3]{\varepsilon}$. If at least $1 - \varepsilon$ of all triangles in a labeled complete graph are balanced, then either

(a) there is a set consisting of at least $1 - \delta$ of the nodes in which at least $1 - \delta$ of all pairs are friends, or else
(b) the nodes can be divided into two groups, X and Y, such that

    (i) at least $1 - \delta$ of the pairs in X like each other,
    (ii) at least $1 - \delta$ of the pairs in Y like each other, and
    (iii) at least $1 - \delta$ of the pairs with one end in X and the other end in Y are enemies.

Notice that the Balance Theorem is the case in which $\varepsilon = 0$, and the other claim above is the case in which $\varepsilon = 0.001$ (since, in this latter case, $\delta = \sqrt[3]{\varepsilon} = 0.1$).

We now prove this last claim. The proof is self-contained, but it is most easily read with some prior experience in what is sometimes called the analysis of "permutations and combinations" – counting the number of ways to choose particular subsets of larger sets.

The proof loosely follows the style of the proof we used for the Balance Theorem: We will define the two sets X and Y to be the friends and enemies, respectively, of a designated node A. Things are trickier here, however, because not all choices of A give us the structure we need – in particular, if a node is personally involved in too many unbalanced triangles, then splitting the graph into its friends and enemies may give a very disordered structure. Consequently, the proof consists of two steps. We first find a "good" node that is not involved in too many unbalanced triangles. We then show that if we divide the graph into the friends and enemies of this good node, we have the desired properties.

Warmup: Counting Edges and Triangles. Before launching into the proof itself, let's consider some basic counting questions that will show up as ingredients in the proof. Recall that we have a complete graph, with an (undirected) edge joining each pair of nodes. If N is the number of nodes in the graph, how many edges are there? We can count this quantity as follows. There are N possible ways to choose one of the two endpoints, and then $N - 1$ possible ways to choose a different node as the other endpoint, for a total of $N(N - 1)$ possible ways to choose the two endpoints in succession. If we write down a list of all these possible pairs of endpoints, then an edge with endpoints A and B appears twice on the list: once as AB and once as BA. In general, each edge appears twice on the list, and so the total number of edges is $N(N - 1)/2$.

A very similar argument lets us count the total number of triangles in the graph. Specifically, there are N ways to pick the first corner, then $N - 1$ ways to pick a different node as the second corner, and then $N - 2$ ways to pick a third corner different from the first two. This yields a total of $N(N - 1)(N - 2)$ sequences of three corners. If we write down this list of $N(N - 1)(N - 2)$ sequences, then a triangle with corners A, B, and C appears six times: as ABC, ACB, BAC, BCA, CAB, and CBA. In general, each triangle appears six times in this list, and so the total number of triangles is

$$\frac{N(N - 1)(N - 2)}{6}.$$

The First Step: Finding a "Good" Node. Now let's move on to the first step of the proof, which is to find a node that isn't involved in too many unbalanced triangles.

Since we are assuming that at most an ε fraction of all triangles are unbalanced, and the total number of triangles in the graph is $N(N - 1)(N - 2)/6$, it follows that the total number of unbalanced triangles is at most $\varepsilon N(N - 1)(N - 2)/6$. Suppose we define the *weight* of a node to be the number of unbalanced triangles it belongs to; thus, a node of low weight – a node that is in relatively few unbalanced triangles – is precisely what we seek.

One way to count the total weight of all nodes would be to list, for each node, the unbalanced triangles to which it belongs and then to look at the length of all these lists combined. In these combined lists, each unbalanced triangle will appear three times – once in the list for each of its corners – and so the total weight of all nodes is exactly three times the number of unbalanced triangles. As a result, the total weight of all nodes is at most $3\varepsilon N(N - 1)(N - 2)/6 = \varepsilon N(N - 1)(N - 2)/2$.

There are N nodes, so the *average* weight of a node is at most $\varepsilon(N - 1)(N - 2)/2$. It's not possible for all nodes to have weights that are strictly above the average, so there is at least one node whose weight is equal to or below the average. Let's pick

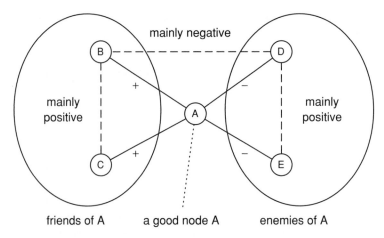

Figure 5.17. The characterization of approximately balanced complete graphs follows from an analysis similar to the proof of the original Balance Theorem. However, we have to be more careful in dividing the graph by first finding a "good" node that is not involved in too many unbalanced triangles.

one such node and call it A. Node A will be our "good" node: a node whose weight is at most $\varepsilon(N-1)(N-2)/2$.[3] Since $(N-1)(N-2) < N^2$, this good node is in at most $\varepsilon N^2/2$ triangles, and, because the algebra is a bit simpler with this slightly larger quantity, we will use it in the rest of the analysis.

The Second Step: Splitting the Graph According to the Good Node. By analogy with the proof of the Balance Theorem, we divide the graph into two sets: a set X consisting of A and all its friends, and a set Y consisting of all the enemies of A, as illustrated in Figure 5.17. Now, using the definition of unbalanced triangles and the fact that node A is not involved in too many of them, we can argue that there are relatively few negative edges inside each of X and Y, and relatively few positive edges between them. Specifically, this works as follows:

- Each negative edge connecting two nodes in X creates a distinct unbalanced triangle involving node A. Since at most $\varepsilon N^2/2$ unbalanced triangles involve A, there are at most $\varepsilon N^2/2$ negative edges inside Y.
- A closely analogous argument applies to Y: Each negative edge connecting two nodes in Y creates a distinct unbalanced triangle involving node A, and so there are at most $\varepsilon N^2/2$ negative edges inside Y.
- And, finally, an analogous argument applies to edges with one end in X and the other end in Y. Each such edge that is positive creates a distinct unbalanced triangle involving A, and so there are at most $\varepsilon N^2/2$ positive edges with one end in X and the other end in Y.

---

[3] This is a very common trick in counting arguments, and it is referred to as the *pigeonhole principle*: we compute the average value of a set of objects and then argue that there must be at least one node that is equal to the average or below. (Also, of course, there must be at least at least one object that is equal to the average or above, although this observation isn't useful for our purposes here.)

We now consider several possible cases, depending on the sizes of the sets X and Y. Essentially, if either X or Y consists of almost the entire graph, then we show that alternative (a) in the claim holds. Otherwise, if each of X and Y contain a nonnegligible number of nodes, then we show that alternative (b) in the claim holds. We're also going to assume, to make the calculations simpler, that N is even and that the quantity δN is a whole number, although this is not in fact necessary for the proof.

To start, let x be the number of nodes in X and let y be the number of nodes in Y. Suppose first that $x \geq (1 - \delta)N$. Since $\varepsilon < \frac{1}{8}$ and $\delta = \sqrt[3]{\varepsilon}$, it follows that $\delta < \frac{1}{2}$, and so $x > \frac{1}{2}N$. Now, recall our earlier counting argument that gave a formula for the number of edges in a complete graph in terms of its number of nodes. In this case, X has x nodes, so it has $x(x - 1)/2$ edges. Since $x > \frac{1}{2}N$, this number of edges is at least $(\frac{1}{2}N + 1)(\frac{1}{2}N)/2 \geq (\frac{1}{2}N)^2/2 = N^2/8$. There are at most $\varepsilon N^2/2$ negative edges inside X, and so the fraction of negative edges inside X is at most

$$\frac{\varepsilon N^2/2}{N^2/8} = 4\varepsilon = 4\delta^3 < \delta,$$

where we use the facts that $\varepsilon = \delta^3$ and $\delta < \frac{1}{2}$. Thus, we conclude that if X contains at least $(1 - \delta)N$ nodes, then it is a set containing at least a $1 - \delta$ fraction of the nodes in which at least $1 - \delta$ of all pairs are friends, satisfying part (a) in the conclusion of the claim.

The same argument can be applied if Y contains at least $(1 - \delta)N$ nodes. Thus, we are left with the case in which both X and Y contain strictly fewer than $(1 - \delta)N$ nodes, and in this case we will show that part (b) in the conclusion of the claim holds. First, of all the edges with one end in X and the other in Y, what fraction are positive? The total number of edges with one end in X and the other end in Y can be counted as follows: There are x ways to choose the end in X, and then y ways to choose the end in Y, for a total of xy such edges. Now, because each of x and y are less than $(1 - \delta)N$, and they add up to N, the product xy is at least $(\delta N)(1 - \delta)N = \delta(1 - \delta)N^2 \geq \delta N^2/2$, where the last inequality follows from the fact that $\delta < \frac{1}{2}$. There are at most $\varepsilon N^2/2$ positive edges with one end in X and the other in Y, which, as a fraction of the total, is at most

$$\frac{\varepsilon N^2/2}{\delta N^2/2} = \frac{\varepsilon}{\delta} = \delta^2 < \delta.$$

Finally, what fraction of edges inside each of X and Y are negative? Let's calculate this fraction for X; the argument for Y is exactly the same. There are $x(x - 1)/2$ edges inside X in total, and because we are considering the case where $x > \delta N$, this total number of edges is at least $(\delta N + 1)(\delta N)/2 \geq (\delta N)^2/2 = \delta^2 N^2/2$. There are at most $\varepsilon N^2/2$ negative edges inside X; as a fraction of the total, this value is at most

$$\frac{\varepsilon N^2/2}{\delta^2 N^2/2} = \frac{\varepsilon}{\delta^2} = \delta.$$

Thus, the division of nodes into sets X and Y satisfies all the requirements in conclusion (b) of the claim, and so the proof is complete.

As a final comment on the claim and its proof, one might feel that the difference between $1 - \varepsilon$ in the assumption of the claim and $1 - \sqrt[3]{\varepsilon}$ is a bit excessive: As we saw earlier, when $\varepsilon = 0.001$, we need to assume that 99.9% of all triangles are balanced in order to get sets with a 90% density of edges having the correct sign. But in fact, it is possible to construct examples showing that this relationship between ε and δ is essentially the best one can do. In short, the claim provides the kind of approximate version of the Balance Theorem that we wanted at a qualitative level, but we must assume a fairly small fraction of unbalanced triangles to be able to start drawing strong conclusions.

5.6 Exercises

1. Suppose that a team of anthropologists is studying a set of three small villages that neighbor one another. Each village has thirty people, consisting of two to three extended families. Everyone in each village knows all the people in their own village as well as the people in the other villages.

   When the anthropologists build the social network of the people in all three villages taken together, they find that each person is friends with all the other people in their own village, and enemies with everyone in the two other villages. This gives them a network of ninety people (i.e., thirty in each village), with positive and negative signs on its edges.

   According to the definitions in this chapter, is this network of ninety people balanced? Give a brief explanation for your answer.

2. Consider the network shown in Figure 5.18: An edge exists between each pair of nodes, with five of the edges corresponding to positive relationships and the other five of the edges corresponding to negative relationships.

   Each edge in this network participates in three triangles – one formed by each of the additional nodes that is not already an endpoint of the edge. (For example, the A-B edge participates in a triangle on A, B, and C; a triangle on A, B, and D; and a triangle on A, B, and E. We can list triangles for the other edges in a similar way.)

   For each edge, how many of the triangles in which it participates are balanced and how many are unbalanced? (Notice that, because of the symmetry of the network, the answer is the same for each positive edge, and also for each negative edge; so it is enough to consider this question for one of the positive edges and one of the negative edges.)

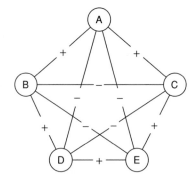

Figure 5.18. A network with five positive edges and five negative edges.

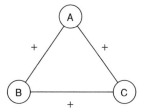

Figure 5.19. A three-node social network in which all pairs of nodes know each other, and all pairs of nodes are friendly toward each other.

3. When we think about structural balance, we can ask what happens when a new node tries to join a network with existing friendship and hostility. In Figures 5.19–5.22, each pair of nodes is either friendly or hostile, as indicated by the + or − label on each edge.

   First, consider the three-node social network in Figure 5.19, in which all pairs of nodes know each other and all pairs of nodes are friendly toward each other. Now, a fourth node, D, wants to join this network and establish either positive or negative relations with each existing node A, B, and C. It wants to do this in such a way that it doesn't become involved in any unbalanced triangles (i.e., after adding D and the labeled edges from D, there are no unbalanced triangles that contain D.) Is this possible?

   In fact, in this example, there are two ways for D to accomplish this outcome, as indicated in Figure 5.20. First, D can become friends with all existing nodes; in this way, all the triangles containing it have three positive edges, and so they are balanced. Alternatively, it can become enemies with all existing nodes; in this way, each triangle containing it has exactly one positive edge, and again these triangles would be balanced.

   So for this network, it was possible for D to join without becoming involved in any unbalanced triangles. However, the same is not necessarily possible for other networks.

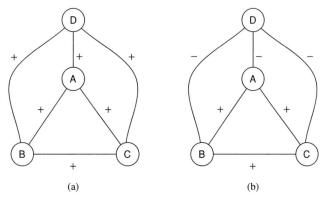

(a)   (b)

Figure 5.20. There are two distinct ways in which node D can join the social network from Figure 5.19 without becoming involved in any unbalanced triangles: (a) by becoming friends with all nodes or (b) by becoming enemies with all nodes.

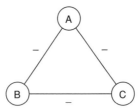

Figure 5.21. All three nodes are mutual enemies.

We now consider this kind of question for some other networks.

(a) Consider the three-node social network in Figure 5.21, in which all pairs of nodes know each other and each pair is either friendly or hostile as indicated by the + or − label on each edge. A fourth node, D, wants to join this network and establish either positive or negative relations with each existing node A, B, and C. Can node D do this in such a way that it doesn't become involved in any unbalanced triangles?

- If there is a way for D to do this, tell how many different such ways there are and give an explanation. (That is, how many different possible labelings of the edges out of D have the property that all triangles containing D are balanced?)
- If there is no such way for D to do this, give an explanation of why not.

(In this and subsequent questions, it is possible to work out an answer by reasoning about the new node's options without having to check all possibilities.)

(b) For a different network, consider the three-node social network in Figure 5.22, in which all pairs of nodes know each other and each pair is either friendly or hostile as indicated by the + or − label on each edge. A fourth node, D, wants to join this network and establish either positive or negative relations with each existing node A, B, and C. Can node D do this in such a way that it doesn't become involved in any unbalanced triangles?

- If there is a way for D to do this, tell how many different such ways there are, and give an explanation. (That is, how many different possible labelings of the edges out of D have the property that all triangles containing D are balanced?)
- If there is no such way for D to do this, give an explanation of why not.

(c) Using what you've worked out in Questions 2 and 3, consider the following question. Take *any* labeled complete graph – on any number of nodes –

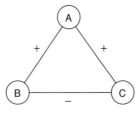

Figure 5.22. Node A is friends with nodes B and C, who are enemies with each other.

that is not balanced (i.e., it contains at least one unbalanced triangle). (Recall that a labeled complete graph is a graph in which an edge exists between each pair of nodes, and each edge is labeled with either $+$ or $-$.) A new node, X, wants to join this network by attaching to each node using a positive or negative edge. When, if ever, is it possible for X to do this in such a way that it does not become involved in any unbalanced triangles? Give an explanation for your answer. (*Hint: Think about any unbalanced triangle in the network, and how X must attach to the nodes in it.*)

4. Together with some anthropologists, you're studying a sparsely populated region of a rain forest, where 50 farmers live along a 50-mile-long stretch of river. Each farmer lives on a tract of land that occupies a 1-mile stretch of the river bank, so their tracts exactly divide up the 50 miles of river bank that they collectively cover. (The numbers are chosen to be simple and to make the story easy to describe.)

   The farmers all know each other, and after interviewing them, you've discovered that each farmer is friends with all the other farmers that live at most 20 miles from him or her, and is enemies with all the farmers that live more than 20 miles from him or her.

   You build the signed complete graph corresponding to this social network, and you wonder whether it satisfies the Structural Balance property. This is the question: is the network structurally balanced or not? Provide an explanation for your answer.

PART TWO
Game Theory

CHAPTER 6

Games

In the opening chapter of the book, we emphasized that the "connectedness" of a complex social, natural, or technological system really means two things: first, an underlying structure of interconnecting links, and second, an interdependence in the behaviors of the individuals who inhabit the system, so that the outcome for any one depends at least implicitly on the combined behaviors of all. The first issue – network structure – was addressed in the first part of the book using graph theory. In this second part of the book, we study interconnectedness at the level of behavior, developing basic models for this in the language of *game theory*.

Game theory is designed to address situations in which the outcomes of a person's decisions depend not just on how they choose among several options, but also on the choices made by the people with whom they interact. Game-theoretic ideas arise in many contexts. Some contexts are literally games; for example, choosing how to target a soccer penalty kick and choosing how to defend against it can be modeled using game theory. Other settings are not usually called games, but they can be analyzed with the same tools. Examples include the pricing of a new product when other firms have similar new products, deciding how to bid in an auction, choosing a route on the Internet or through a transportation network, deciding whether to adopt an aggressive or a passive stance in international relations, or choosing whether to use performance-enhancing drugs in a professional sport. In these examples, each decision-maker's outcome depends on the decisions made by others. This introduces a strategic element that game theory is designed to analyze.

As we will see later in Chapter 7, game-theoretic ideas are also relevant to settings where no one is overtly making decisions. Evolutionary biology provides perhaps the most striking example. A basic principle is that mutations are more likely to succeed in a population when they improve the fitness of the organisms that carry the mutation. But often, this fitness cannot be assessed in isolation; rather, it depends on what all the other (nonmutant) organisms are doing and how the mutant's behavior interacts with the nonmutants' behaviors. In such situations, reasoning about the success or failure of the mutation involves game-theoretic definitions, and in fact very closely resembles the process of reasoning about decisions made by intelligent actors. Similar kinds of reasoning have been applied to the success or failure of new cultural practices and conventions – it depends on the existing patterns of behavior into which they are introduced. These examples show that the ideas of game theory are broader than just a model of how people reason about their interactions with others; game theory more generally addresses the question of which behaviors tend to sustain themselves when carried out in a larger population.

Game-theoretic ideas appear in many places throughout the book. Chapters 8 and 9 describe two initial and fundamental applications: to network traffic, where travel time depends on the routing decisions of others; and to auctions, where the success of a bidder depends on how the other bidders behave. We will see many further examples later in the book, including the ways in which prices are set in markets and the ways in which people choose to adopt new ideas in situations where the payoffs to adoption decisions are affected by what others are doing.

As a first step, then, we begin with a discussion of the basic ideas behind game theory. For now, this discussion will involve descriptions of situations in which people interact with one another, initially without an accompanying graph structure. Once these ideas are in place, we will bring graphs back into the picture in subsequent chapters and begin to consider how structure and behavior can be studied simultaneously.

6.1 What Is a Game?

Game theory is concerned with situations in which decision-makers interact with one another, and in which each participant's satisfaction with the outcome depends not just on his or her own decisions but on the decisions made by everyone. To help make the definitions concrete, it's useful to start with an example.

A First Example. Suppose that you're a college student, and you have two large pieces of work due the next day: an exam and a presentation. You need to decide whether to study for the exam or to prepare for the presentation. For simplicity, and to make the example as clean as possible, we'll impose a few assumptions. First, we assume you can either study for the exam or prepare for the presentation, but not both. Second, we assume you have an accurate estimate of the expected grade you'll get under the outcomes of different decisions.

The outcome of the exam is easy to predict: if you study, then your expected grade is a 92, while if you don't study, then your expected grade is an 80.

The presentation is a bit more complicated to think about. For the presentation, you're doing it jointly with a partner. If both you and your partner prepare for the presentation, then the presentation will go extremely well, and your expected joint grade is a 100. If just one of you prepares (and the other doesn't), you'll get an expected joint grade of 92. If neither of you prepares, your expected joint grade is 84.

The challenge in reasoning about this decision is that your partner also has the same exam the next day, and we'll assume that he has the same expected outcome for it: 92 if he studies, and 80 if he doesn't. He also has to choose between studying for the exam and preparing for the presentation. We'll assume that neither of you is able to contact

Your Partner

		Presentation	Exam
You	Presentation	90, 90	86, 92
	Exam	92, 86	88, 88

Figure 6.1. Exam or presentation?

the other, so you can't jointly discuss what to do; each of you needs to make a decision independently, knowing that the other will also be making a decision.

Both of you are interested in maximizing the average grade you get, and we can use the preceding discussion to work out how this average grade is determined by the way the two of you invest your efforts:

- If both of you prepare for the presentation, you'll both get 100 on the presentation and 80 on the exam, for an average of 90.
- If both of you study for the exam, you'll both get 92 on the exam and 84 on the presentation, for an average of 88.
- If one of you studies for the exam while the other prepares for the presentation, the result is as follows.
  - The one who prepares for the presentation gets a 92 on the presentation but only an 80 on the exam, for an average of 86.
  - On the other hand, the one who studies for the exam still gets a 92 on the presentation; since it's a joint grade, this person benefits from the fact that one of the two of you prepared for it. This person also gets a 92 on the exam, through studying, and so gets an average of 92.

A simple table can be used to summarize all these outcomes, as follows. We represent your two choices – to prepare for the presentation or to study for the exam – as the rows of a 2 × 2 table. We represent your partner's two choices as the columns. So each box in this table represents a decision by each of you. In each box, we record the average grade you each receive: first yours, then your partner's. Writing all this down, we have the table shown in Figure 6.1.

This describes the set-up of the situation; now you need to figure out what to do: prepare for the presentation or study for the exam? Clearly, your average grade depends not just on which of these two options you choose, but also on what your partner decides. Therefore, as part of your decision, you have to reason about what your partner is likely to do. Thinking about the strategic consequences of your own actions, where you need to consider the effect of decisions by others, is precisely the kind of reasoning that game theory is designed to facilitate. So before moving on to the actual outcome of this exam-or-presentation scenario, it is useful to introduce some of the basic definitions of game theory and then continue the discussion in this language.

Basic Ingredients of a Game. The situation we've just described is an example of a *game*. For our purposes, a game is any situation with the following three aspects:

1. There is a set of participants, whom we call the *players*. In our example, you and your partner are the two players.

2. Each player has a set of options for how to behave; we will refer to these options as the player's possible *strategies*. In the example, you and your partner each have two possible strategies: to prepare for the presentation or to study for the exam.

3. For each choice of strategies, each player receives a *payoff* that can depend on the strategies selected by everyone. The payoffs are generally numbers, and each player prefers larger payoffs to smaller payoffs. In our current example, the payoff to each player is the average grade he or she gets on the exam and the presentation. We will generally write the payoffs in a *payoff matrix* as in Figure 6.1.

Our interest is in reasoning about how players will behave in a given game. For now we focus on games with only two players, but the ideas apply equally well to games with any number of players. Our discussion will focus primarily on simple, one-shot games – games in which the players simultaneously and independently choose their actions, and they do so only once. In Section 6.10 at the end of this chapter, we discuss how to reinterpret the theory to deal with dynamic games, in which actions can be played sequentially over time.

6.2 Reasoning about Behavior in a Game

Once we write down the description of a game, consisting of the players, the strategies, and the payoffs, we can ask how the players are likely to behave – that is, how they go about selecting strategies.

Underlying Assumptions. In order to make this question tractable, we begin with a few assumptions. First, we assume everything that a player cares about is summarized in the player's payoffs. For the exam-or-presentation game described in Section 6.1, the two players are solely concerned with maximizing their own average grade. However, nothing in the framework of game theory requires that players care only about personal rewards. For example, a player who is altruistic may care about both his or her own benefit and also the other player's benefit. If so, then the payoffs should reflect this; once the payoffs have been defined, they should constitute a complete description of each player's evaluation of each of the possible outcomes of the game.

We also assume that each player knows everything about the structure of the game. To begin with, this assumption means that each player knows his or her own list of possible strategies. It seems reasonable in many settings to assume that each player also knows who the other player is (in a two-player game), the strategies available to this other player, and what his or her payoff will be for any choice of strategies. In the exam-or-presentation game in particular, this assumption means that you realize you and your partner are each faced with the choice of studying for the exam or preparing for the presentation, and you have an accurate estimate of the expected outcome under different courses of action. There has been considerable research on how to analyze games in which the players have much less knowledge about the underlying structure, and in fact John Harsanyi shared the 1994 Nobel Prize in Economics for his work on games with incomplete information [208].

Finally, we suppose that each individual chooses a strategy to maximize her own payoff, given her beliefs about the strategy used by the other player. This model of individual behavior, which is usually called *rationality*, actually combines two ideas. The first idea is that each player wants to maximize her own payoff. Since each individual's payoff is defined to be whatever the individual cares about, this hypothesis seems reasonable. The second idea is that each player actually succeeds in selecting the optimal strategy. In simple settings, and for games played by experienced players, this too seems reasonable. In complex games, or for games played by inexperienced players, it is surely less reasonable. It is interesting to consider players who make mistakes and learn from the play of the game. There is an extensive literature that analyzes problems of this sort [175], but we do not consider these issues here.

Reasoning about Behavior in the Exam-or-Presentation Game. Let's go back to the exam-or-presentation game and ask how we should expect you and your partner – the two players in the game – to behave.

We first focus on this question from your point of view. (The reasoning for your partner is symmetric, because the game looks the same from his point of view.) It would be easier to decide what to do if you could predict what your partner would do, but to begin with, let's consider what you should do for each possible choice of strategy by your partner.

- First, if you knew your partner was going to study for the exam, then you would get a payoff of 88 by also studying, and a payoff of only 86 by preparing for the presentation. So in this case, you should study for the exam.
- On the other hand, if you knew that your partner was going to prepare for the presentation, then you'd get a payoff of 90 by also preparing for the presentation, but a payoff of 92 by studying for the exam. So in this case too, you should study for the exam.

This approach of considering each of your partner's options separately turns out to be a very useful way of analyzing the present situation: it reveals that, no matter what your partner does, you should study for the exam.

When a player has a strategy that is strictly better than all other options, regardless of what the other player does, we will refer to it as a *strictly dominant strategy*. When a player has a strictly dominant strategy, we should expect that he or she will definitely play it. In the exam-or-presentation game, studying for the exam is also a strictly dominant strategy for your partner (by the same reasoning), and so we should expect that the outcome will be for both of you to study, each getting an average grade of 88.

So this game has a very clean analysis, and it's easy to see how to end up with a prediction for the outcome. Despite this fact, there's something striking about the conclusion. If you and your partner could somehow agree that you would both prepare for the presentation, you would each get an average grade of 90; in other words, you would each be better off. But, despite the fact that you both understand this potential improvement, the payoff of 90 cannot be achieved by rational play. The preceding reasoning makes it clear why not: even if you were to personally commit to preparing

Suspect 2

		NC	C
Suspect 1	NC	−1, −1	−10, 0
	C	0, −10	−4, −4

Figure 6.2. Prisoner's Dilemma.

for the presentation – hoping to achieve the outcome where you both get 90 – and even if your partner knew you were doing this, your partner would still have an incentive to study for the exam so as to achieve a still-higher payoff of 92 for himself.

This result depends on our assumption that the payoffs truly reflect everything each player values in the outcome – in this case, that you and your partner each only care about maximizing your own respective average grades. If, for example, you also cared about the grade that your partner received, then the payoffs in this game would look different, and the outcome could be different. Similarly, if you cared about the fact that your partner would be angry at you for not preparing for the joint presentation, then this too should be incorporated into the payoffs, again potentially affecting the results. But with the payoffs as they are, we are left with the interesting situation in which there is an outcome that is better for both of you – an average grade of 90 each – and yet it cannot be achieved by rational play of the game.

A Related Story: The Prisoner's Dilemma. The outcome of the exam-or-presentation game is closely related to one of the most famous examples in the development of game theory, the *Prisoner's Dilemma*. Here is how this example works.

Suppose that two suspects have been apprehended by the police and are being interrogated in separate rooms. The police strongly suspect that these two individuals are responsible for a robbery, but there is not enough evidence to convict either of them of the robbery. However, they both resisted arrest and can be charged with that lesser crime, which would carry a 1-year sentence. Each of the suspects is told the following story. "If you confess, and your partner doesn't confess, then you will be released and your partner will be charged with the crime. Your confession will be sufficient to convict him of the robbery and he will be sent to prison for 10 years. If you both confess, then we don't need either of you to testify against the other, and you will both be convicted of the robbery. (Although in this case your sentence will be less – only 4 years – because of your guilty plea.) Finally, if neither of you confesses, then we can't convict either of you of the robbery, so we will charge each of you with resisting arrest. Your partner is being offered the same deal. Do you want to confess?"

To formalize this story as a game we need to identify the players, the possible strategies, and the payoffs. The two suspects are the players, and each has to choose between two possible strategies – *Confess* (C) or *Not-Confess* (NC). Finally, the payoffs can be summarized from the preceding story as in Figure 6.2. (Note that the payoffs are all zero or less, since there are no good outcomes for the suspects, only different gradations of bad outcomes.)

Athlete 2

		Don't Use Drugs	Use Drugs
Athlete 1	Don't Use Drugs	3, 3	1, 4
	Use Drugs	4, 1	2, 2

Figure 6.3. Performance-enhancing drugs.

As in the exam-or-presentation game, we can consider how one of the suspects – say Suspect 1 – should reason about his options.

- If Suspect 2 were going to confess, then Suspect 1 would receive a payoff of −4 by confessing and a payoff of −10 by not confessing. So in this case, Suspect 1 should confess.
- If Suspect 2 were not going to confess, then Suspect 1 would receive a payoff of 0 by confessing and a payoff of −1 by not confessing. So in this case too, Suspect 1 should confess.

So confessing is a strictly dominant strategy – it is the best choice regardless of what the other player chooses. As a result, we should expect both suspects to confess, each getting a payoff of −4.

We therefore have the same striking phenomenon as in the exam-or-presentation game: there is an outcome that the suspects know to be better for both of them – in which they both choose not to confess – but under rational play of the game there is no way for them to achieve this outcome. Instead, they end up with an outcome that is worse for both of them. And here too, it is important that the payoffs reflect everything about the outcome of the game; if, for example, the suspects could credibly threaten each other with retribution for confessing, thereby making confessing a less desirable option, then this could affect the payoffs and potentially the outcome.

Interpretations of the Prisoner's Dilemma. The Prisoner's Dilemma has been the subject of a huge amount of literature since its introduction in the early 1950s [343, 346], since it serves as a highly streamlined depiction of the difficulty in establishing cooperation in the face of individual self-interest. While no model this simple can precisely capture complex scenarios in the real world, the Prisoner's Dilemma has been used as an interpretive framework for many different real-world situations.

For example, the use of performance-enhancing drugs in professional sports has been modeled as a case of the Prisoner's Dilemma game [210, 367]. Here the athletes are the players, and the two possible strategies are to use performance-enhancing drugs or not. If you use drugs while your opponent doesn't, you'll get an advantage in the competition, but you'll suffer long-term harm (and may get caught). If we consider a sport where it is difficult to detect the use of such drugs, and we assume athletes in such a sport view the downside as a smaller factor than the benefits in competition, we can capture the situation with numerical payoffs that might look as follows, in Figure 6.3. (The numbers are arbitrary here; we are only interested in their relative sizes.)

Your Partner

		Presentation	Exam
You	*Presentation*	98, 98	94, 96
	Exam	96, 94	92, 92

Figure 6.4. Exam-or-presentation game with an easier exam.

Here, the best outcome (with a payoff of 4) is to use drugs when your opponent doesn't, since this maximizes your chances of winning. However, the payoff to both using drugs (2) is worse than the payoff to both not using drugs (3), since in both cases you're evenly matched, but in the former case you're also causing harm to yourself. We can now see that using drugs is a strictly dominant strategy, and so we have a situation where the players use drugs even though they understand that there's a better outcome for both of them.

More generally, situations of this type are often referred to as *arms races*, in which two competitors use an increasingly dangerous arsenal of weapons simply to remain evenly matched. In the preceding example, the performance-enhancing drugs play the role of the weapons, but the Prisoner's Dilemma has also been used to interpret literal arms races between opposing nations, where the weapons correspond to the nations' military arsenals.

To wrap up our discussion of the Prisoner's Dilemma, we should note that it only arises when the payoffs are aligned in a certain way; as we will see in the remainder of the chapter, there are many situations in which the structure of the game and the resulting behavior look very different. Indeed, even simple changes to a game can change it from an instance of the Prisoner's Dilemma to something more benign. For example, returning to the exam-or-presentation game, suppose that we keep everything the same as before, except that we make the exam much easier, so that you'll get a 100 on it if you study or a 96 if you don't. Then we can check that the payoff matrix now becomes the table of values shown in Figure 6.4.

Furthermore, we can check that with these new payoffs, preparing for the presentation now becomes a strictly dominant strategy; we can expect that both players will play this strategy and both will benefit from this decision. The downsides of the previous scenario no longer appear: like other dangerous phenomena, the Prisoner's Dilemma only manifests itself when the conditions are right.

6.3 Best Responses and Dominant Strategies

In reasoning about the games in the previous section, we used two fundamental concepts that will be central to our discussion of game theory. As such, it is useful to define them carefully here, and then delve further into some of their implications.

The first concept is the idea of a *best response*: it is the best choice of one player, given a belief about what the other player will do. For instance, in the exam-or-presentation game, we determined the best choice of one player in response to each possible choice of his or her partner.

We can make this concept precise with a bit of notation, as follows. If S is a strategy chosen by Player 1, and T is a strategy chosen by Player 2, then there is an entry in the payoff matrix corresponding to the pair of chosen strategies (S, T). We will write $P_1(S, T)$ to denote the payoff to Player 1 as a result of this pair of strategies, and $P_2(S, T)$ to denote the payoff to Player 2 as a result of this pair of strategies. Now, we say that a strategy S for Player 1 is a *best response* to a strategy T for Player 2 if S produces at least as good a payoff as any other strategy paired with T:

$$P_1(S, T) \geq P_1(S', T)$$

for all other strategies S' of Player 1. Naturally, there is a completely symmetric definition for Player 2, which we won't write here. (In what follows, we present the definitions from Player 1's point of view, but there are direct analogues for Player 2 in each case.)

Notice that this definition allows for multiple different strategies of Player 1 to be tied as the best response to strategy T, which can make it difficult to predict which of these multiple different strategies Player 1 will use. We can emphasize that one choice is uniquely the best against T as follows; we say that a strategy S of Player 1 is a *strict best response* to a strategy T for Player 2 if S produces a strictly higher payoff than any other strategy paired with T:

$$P_1(S, T) > P_1(S', T)$$

for all other strategies S' of Player 1. When a player has a strict best response to T, this strategy is clearly the one we should expect her to play when faced with T.

The second concept, which was central to our analysis in the previous section, is that of a strictly dominant strategy. We can formulate its definition in terms of best responses as follows:

- We say that a *dominant strategy* for Player 1 is a strategy that is a best response to every strategy of Player 2.
- We say that a *strictly dominant strategy* for Player 1 is a strategy that is a strict best response to every strategy of Player 2.

In the previous section, we made the observation that if a player has a strictly dominant strategy, then we can expect him or her to use it. The notion of a dominant strategy is slightly weaker, since it can be tied as the best option against some opposing strategies. As a result, a player could potentially have multiple dominant strategies, in which case it may not be obvious which one should be played.

The analysis of the Prisoner's Dilemma was facilitated by the fact that both players had strictly dominant strategies, and so it was easy to reason about what was likely to happen. But most settings won't be this clear-cut; we now begin to look at games that lack strictly dominant strategies.

A Game in Which Only One Player Has a Strictly Dominant Strategy. As a first step, let's consider a setting in which one player has a strictly dominant strategy and the other one doesn't. As a concrete example, we consider the following story.

Suppose two firms are each planning to produce and market a new product; these two products will directly compete with each other. Let's imagine that the population

Firm 2

		Low-Priced	Upscale
Firm 1	Low-Priced	.48, .12	.60, .40
	Upscale	.40, .60	.32, .08

Figure 6.5. Marketing strategy.

of consumers can be cleanly divided into two market segments: people who would only buy a low-priced version of the product and people who would only buy an upscale version. Let's also assume that the profit any firm makes on a sale of either a low-priced or an upscale product is the same. So, to keep track of profits, it's good enough to keep track of sales. Each firm wants to maximize its profit, or equivalently its sales, and to do this it has to decide whether its new product will be low-priced or upscale.

This game has two players – Firm 1 and Firm 2 – and each has two possible strategies: to produce a low-priced product or an upscale one. To determine the payoffs, here is how the firms expect the sales to work out:

- People who prefer a low-priced version account for 60% of the population, and people who prefer an upscale version account for 40% of the population.
- Firm 1 is the much more popular brand, and so when the two firms directly compete in a market segment, Firm 1 gets 80% of the sales and Firm 2 gets 20% of the sales. (If a firm is the only one to produce a product for a given market segment, it gets all the sales.)

Based on this description of the market, we can determine payoffs for different choices of strategies as follows:

- If the two firms target different market segments, they each get all the sales in that segment. The one that targets the low-priced segment gets a payoff of .60 and the one that targets the upscale segment gets .40.
- If both firms target the low-priced segment, then Firm 1 gets 80% of it, for a payoff of .48, and Firm 2 gets 20% of it, for a payoff of .12.
- Analogously, if both firms target the upscale segment, then Firm 1 gets a payoff of $(.8)(.4) = .32$ and Firm 2 gets a payoff of $(.2)(.4) = .08$.

This description of the game is summarized in the payoff matrix in Figure 6.5.

Notice that in this game, Firm 1 has a strictly dominant strategy: for Firm 1, *Low-Priced* is a strict best response to each strategy of Firm 2. On the other hand, Firm 2 does not have a dominant strategy: *Low-Priced* is its best response when Firm 1 plays *Upscale*, and *Upscale* is its best response when Firm 1 plays *Low-Priced*.

Still, it is not hard to make a prediction about the outcome of this game. Since Firm 1 has a strictly dominant strategy in *Low-Priced*, we can expect Firm 1 to play it. Now, what should Firm 2 do? If Firm 2 knows Firm 1's payoffs, and knows that Firm 1 wants to maximize profits, then Firm 2 can confidently predict that Firm 1 will play *Low-Priced*. Then, since *Upscale* is the strict best response by Firm 2 to *Low-Priced*, we can predict that Firm 2 will play *Upscale*. So our overall prediction of play in this marketing game is *Low-Priced* by Firm 1 and *Upscale* by Firm 2, resulting in payoffs of .60 and .40, respectively.

Note that, although we've described the reasoning in two steps – first the strictly dominant strategy of Firm 1, and then the best response of Firm 2 – the context is still a game in which the players move simultaneously: both firms are developing their marketing strategies concurrently and in secret. It is simply that the reasoning about strategies naturally follows this two-step logic, resulting in a prediction about how the simultaneous play will occur. It's also interesting to note the intuitive message of this prediction. Firm 1 is so strong that it can proceed without regard to Firm 2's decision; given this, Firm 2's best strategy is to stay safely out of the way of Firm 1.

Finally, we should also note how this marketing strategy game makes use of the knowledge we assume players have about the game being played and about each other. In particular, we assume that each player knows the entire payoff matrix. And in reasoning about this specific game, it is important that Firm 2 knows that Firm 1 wants to maximize profits, and that Firm 2 knows that Firm 1 knows its own profits. In general, we will assume that the players have *common knowledge* of the game: they know the structure of the game, they know that each of them knows the structure of the game, they know that each of them knows that each of them knows, and so on. While we will not need the full technical content of common knowledge in anything we do here, it is an underlying assumption and a topic of research in the game theory literature [28]. As mentioned earlier, it is still possible to analyze games in situations where common knowledge does not hold, but the analysis becomes more complex [208]. It's also worth noting that the assumption of common knowledge is a bit stronger than we need for reasoning about simple games such as the Prisoner's Dilemma, in which strictly dominant strategies for each player imply a particular course of action regardless of what the other player is doing.

6.4 Nash Equilibrium

When neither player in a two-player game has a strictly dominant strategy, we need some other way to predict what is likely to happen. In this section, we develop methods for doing this; the result will be a useful framework for analyzing games in general.

An Example: A Three-Client Game. To frame the question, it helps to think about a simple example of a game that lacks strictly dominant strategies. Like our previous example, it is a marketing game played between two firms; however, it has a slightly more intricate setup. Suppose two firms each hope to do business with one of three large clients, A, B, and C. Each firm has three possible strategies: whether to approach A, B, or C. The results of their two decisions will work out as follows:

- If the two firms approach the same client, then the client will give half its business to each.
- Firm 1 is too small to attract business on its own, so if it approaches one client while Firm 2 approaches a different one, then Firm 1 gets a payoff of 0.

Firm 2

		A	B	C
	A	4, 4	0, 2	0, 2
Firm 1	B	0, 0	1, 1	0, 2
	C	0, 0	0, 2	1, 1

Figure 6.6. Three-client game.

- If Firm 2 approaches client B or C on its own, it will get their full business. However, A is a larger client, and will only do business with the firms if both approach A.
- Because A is a larger client, doing business with it is worth 8 (and, hence, 4 to each firm if it's split), whereas doing business with B or C is worth 2 (and hence 1 to each firm if it's split).

From this description, we can work out the payoff matrix in Figure 6.6.

If we study how the payoffs in this game work, we see that neither firm has a dominant strategy. Indeed, each strategy by each firm is a strict best response to some strategy by the other firm. For Firm 1, A is a strict best response to strategy A by Firm 2, B is a strict best response to B, and C is a strict best response to C. For Firm 2, A is a strict best response to strategy A by Firm 1, C is a strict best response to B, and B is a strict best response to C. So how should we reason about the outcome of play in this game?

Defining Nash Equilibrium. In 1950, John Nash proposed a simple but powerful principle for reasoning about behavior in general games [313, 314], and its underlying premise is the following: even when there are no dominant strategies, we should expect players to use strategies that are best responses to each other. More precisely, suppose that Player 1 chooses a strategy S and Player 2 chooses a strategy T. We say that this pair of strategies (S, T) is a *Nash equilibrium* if S is a best response to T, and T is a best response to S. This concept is not one that can be derived purely from rationality on the part of the players; instead, it is an *equilibrium* concept. The idea is that if the players choose strategies that are best responses to each other, then no player has an incentive to deviate to an alternative strategy – the system is in a kind of equilibrium state, with no force pushing it toward a different outcome. Nash shared the 1994 Nobel Prize in Economics for his development and analysis of this idea.

To understand the idea of Nash equilibrium, we should first ask why a pair of strategies that are not best responses to each other would not constitute an equilibrium. The answer is that the players cannot both believe that these strategies would actually be used in the game, since they know that at least one player would have an incentive to deviate to another strategy. So a Nash equilibrium can be thought of as an equilibrium in beliefs. If each player believes that the other player will actually play a strategy that is part of a Nash equilibrium, then she has an incentive to play her part of the Nash equilibrium.

		Your Partner	
		PowerPoint	Keynote
You	PowerPoint	1, 1	0, 0
	Keynote	0, 0	1, 1

Figure 6.7. Coordination game.

Let's consider the three-client game from the perspective of Nash equilibrium. If Firm 1 chooses A and Firm 2 chooses A, then we can check that Firm 1 is playing a best response to Firm 2's strategy, and Firm 2 is playing a best response to Firm 1's strategy. Hence, the pair of strategies (A, A) forms a Nash equilibrium. Moreover, we can check that this is the only Nash equilibrium. No other pair of strategies are best responses to each other.[1]

This discussion also suggests two ways to find Nash equilibria. The first is simply to check all pairs of strategies and ask, for each pair, whether the individual strategies are best responses to each other. The second is to compute each player's best response(s) to each strategy of the other player and then find strategies that are mutual best responses.

6.5 Multiple Equilibria: Coordination Games

For a game with a single Nash equilibrium, such as the three-client game in the previous section, it seems reasonable to predict that the players will play the strategies in this equilibrium: under any other play of the game, at least one player will not be using a best response to what the other is doing. Some natural games, however, can have more than one Nash equilibrium, and in this case it becomes difficult to predict how rational players will actually behave in the game. We consider some fundamental examples of this problem here.

A Coordination Game. A simple but central example is the following *coordination game*, which we can motivate through the following story. Suppose you and a partner are each preparing slides for a joint project presentation; you can't reach your partner by phone, and you need to start working on the slides now. You have to decide whether to prepare your half of the slides in PowerPoint or in Apple's Keynote software. Either would be fine, but it will be much easier to merge your slides with your partner's if you use the same software.

So we have a game in which you and your partner are the two players; choosing PowerPoint or choosing Keynote form the two strategies, and the payoffs are shown in Figure 6.7.

This is called a *coordination game* because the two players' shared goal is really to coordinate on the same strategy. Coordination games arise in many settings. For

[1] In this discussion, each player only has three available strategies: A, B, or C. Later in this chapter, we will introduce the possibility of more complex strategies in which players can randomize over their available options. Using this more complex formulation of possible strategies, we will find additional equilibria for the three-client game.

Your Partner

		PowerPoint	Keynote
You	PowerPoint	1, 1	0, 0
	Keynote	0, 0	2, 2

Figure 6.8. Unbalanced coordination game.

example, two manufacturing companies that work together extensively must decide whether to configure their machinery in metric or English units of measurement; two platoons in the same army must decide whether to attack an enemy's left or right flank; two people trying to find each other in a crowded mall must decide whether to wait at the north end or the south end of the mall. In each case, either choice can be fine, provided that both participants make the same choice.

The underlying difficulty is that the game has two Nash equilibria – (PowerPoint, PowerPoint) and (Keynote, Keynote) in our example from Figure 6.7. If the players fail to coordinate on one of the Nash equilibria, perhaps because one player expects PowerPoint to be played and the other expects Keynote, then they receive low payoffs. So what do the players do?

This remains a subject of considerable discussion and research, but some proposals have received attention in the literature. Thomas Schelling [364] introduced the idea of a *focal point* as a way to resolve this difficulty. He noted that in some games there are natural reasons (possibly outside the payoff structure of the game) that cause the players to focus on one of the Nash equilibria. For example, suppose two drivers are approaching each other at night on an undivided country road. Each driver has to decide whether to move over to the left or to the right. If the drivers coordinate – making the same choice of side – then they pass each other, but if they fail to coordinate, then they get a severely low payoff due to the resulting collision. Fortunately, social convention can help the drivers decide what to do in this case: if this game is being played in the United States, convention strongly suggests that they should move to the right, whereas if the game is being played in England, convention strongly suggests that they should move to the left. In other words, social conventions, while often arbitrary, can sometimes be useful in helping people coordinate among multiple equilibria.

Variants on the Basic Coordination Game. One can enrich the structure of our basic coordination game to capture a number of related issues surrounding the problem of multiple equilibria. To take a simple extension of our previous example, suppose that both you and your project partner each prefer Keynote to PowerPoint. You still want to coordinate, but you now view the two alternatives as unequal. This situation gives us the payoff matrix for an *unbalanced coordination game*, shown in Figure 6.8.

Notice that (PowerPoint, PowerPoint) and (Keynote, Keynote) are still both Nash equilibria for this game, despite the fact that one of them gives higher payoffs to both players. (The point is that if you believe your partner will choose PowerPoint, you still should choose PowerPoint as well.) Here, Schelling's theory of focal points suggests that we can use a feature *intrinsic* to the game – rather than an arbitrary social convention – to make a prediction about which equilibrium will be chosen by the

	Your Partner	
	PowerPoint	Keynote
You PowerPoint	1, 2	0, 0
Keynote	0, 0	2, 1

Figure 6.9. Battle of the sexes.

players. That is, we can predict that when the players have to choose, they will select strategies so as to reach the equilibrium that gives higher payoffs to both of them. (To take another example, consider the two people trying to meet at a crowded mall. If the north end of the mall has a bookstore they both like, while the south end consists of a loading dock, the natural focal point would be the equilibrium in which they both choose the north end.)

Things get more complicated if you and your partner don't agree on which software you prefer, as shown in the payoff matrix of Figure 6.9.

In this case, the two equilibria still correspond to the two different ways of coordinating, but your payoff is higher in the (Keynote, Keynote) equilibrium, while your partner's payoff is higher in the (PowerPoint, PowerPoint) equilibrium. This game is traditionally called the *Battle of the Sexes*, because of the following motivating story. A husband and wife want to see a movie together, and they need to choose between a romantic comedy and an action movie. They want to coordinate on their choice, but the (Romance, Romance) equilibrium gives a higher payoff to one of them while the (Action, Action) equilibrium gives a higher payoff to the other.

In Battle of the Sexes, it can be hard to predict the equilibrium that will be played using either the payoff structure or some purely external social convention. Rather, it helps to know something about conventions that exist between the two players themselves, suggesting how they resolve disagreements when they prefer different ways of coordinating.

It's worth mentioning one final variation on the basic coordination game, which has attracted attention in recent years. This is the Stag Hunt game [374]; the name is motivated by the following story from the writings of Rousseau. Suppose that two people are out hunting; if they work together, they can catch a stag (which would be the highest-payoff outcome), but on their own each can catch a hare. The tricky part is that if one hunter tries to catch a stag on his own, he will get nothing, while the other one can still catch a hare. Thus, the hunters are the two players, their strategies are Hunt Stag and Hunt Hare, and the payoffs are shown in Figure 6.10.

This situation is quite similar to the unbalanced coordination game, except that if the two players miscoordinate, the one who was trying for the higher-payoff outcome gets

	Hunter 2	
	Hunt Stag	Hunt Hare
Hunter 1 Hunt Stag	4, 4	0, 3
Hunt Hare	3, 0	3, 3

Figure 6.10. Stag Hunt game.

		Your Partner	
		Presentation	Exam
You	Presentation	90, 90	82, 88
	Exam	88, 82	88, 88

Figure 6.11. Exam-or-presentation game (Stag Hunt version).

penalized more than the one who was trying for the lower-payoff outcome. (In fact, the one trying for the lower-payoff outcome doesn't get penalized at all.) As a result, the challenge in reasoning about which equilibrium will be chosen is based on the trade-off between the high payoff of one and the mild consequences of miscoordination from the other.

It has been argued that the Stag Hunt game captures some of the intuitive challenges that are also raised by the Prisoner's Dilemma. The structures are clearly different, since the Prisoner's Dilemma has strictly dominant strategies; both, however, have the property that players can benefit if they cooperate with each other, but risk suffering if they try cooperating while their partner doesn't. Another way to see some of the similarities between the two games is to notice that if we go back to the original exam-or-presentation game from Section 6.1 and make one small change, then we end up changing it from an instance of the Prisoner's Dilemma to something closely resembling the Stag Hunt game. Specifically, suppose that we keep the grade outcomes the same as in Section 6.1, except that we require both you and your partner to prepare for the presentation in order to have any chance of a better grade. That is, if you both prepare, you both get a 100 on the presentation, but if at most one of you prepares, you both get the base grade of 84. With this change, the payoffs for the exam-or-presentation game become what is shown in Figure 6.11.

We now have a structure that closely resembles the Stag Hunt game: coordinating on (Presentation, Presentation) or (Exam, Exam) are both equilibria, but if you attempt to go for the higher-payoff equilibrium, you risk getting a low grade if your partner opts to study for the exam.

6.6 Multiple Equilibria: The Hawk–Dove Game

Multiple Nash equilibria also arise in a different but equally fundamental kind of game, in which the players engage in a kind of "anticoordination" activity. Probably the most basic form of such a game is the *Hawk-Dove game*, which is motivated by the following story.

Suppose two animals are engaged in a contest to decide how a piece of food will be divided between them. Each animal can choose to behave aggressively (the *Hawk* strategy) or passively (the *Dove* strategy). If the two animals both behave passively, they divide the food evenly, and each gets a payoff of 3. If one behaves aggressively while the other behaves passively, then the aggressor gets most of the food, obtaining a payoff of 5, while the passive one only gets a payoff of 1. But if both animals behave

Animal 2

		D	H
Animal 1	D	3, 3	1, 5
	H	5, 1	0, 0

Figure 6.12. Hawk–Dove game.

aggressively, then they destroy the food (and possibly injure each other), each getting a payoff of 0. Thus, we have the payoff matrix in Figure 6.12.

This game has two Nash equilibria: (D, H) and (H, D). Without knowing more about the animals we cannot predict which of these equilibria will be played. So, as in the coordination games we looked at earlier, the concept of Nash equilibrium helps to narrow down the set of reasonable predictions, but it does not provide a unique prediction.

The Hawk–Dove game has been studied in many contexts. For example, suppose we substitute two countries for the two animals, and suppose that the countries are simultaneously choosing whether to be aggressive or passive in their foreign policy. Each country hopes to gain through being aggressive, but if both act aggressively they risk actually going to war, which would be disastrous for both. So in equilibrium, we can expect that one will be aggressive and one will be passive, but we can't predict who will follow which strategy. Again we would need to know more about the countries to predict which equilibrium will be played.

Hawk–Dove is another example of a game that can arise from a small change to the payoffs in the exam-or-presentation game from Section 6.1. Let's again recall the setup from that section; now we vary things so that if neither you nor your partner prepares for the presentation, you will get a very low joint grade of 60. (If one or both of you prepare, the grades for the presentation are the same as before.) If we compute the average grades received for different choices of strategies in this version of the game, we have the payoffs shown in Figure 6.13.

In this version of the game, there are two equilibria: (Presentation, Exam) and (Exam, Presentation). Essentially, one of you must behave passively and prepare for the presentation, while the other achieves the higher payoff by studying for the exam. If you both try to avoid the role of the passive player, you end up with very low payoffs, but we cannot predict from the structure of the game alone who will play this passive role.

The Hawk–Dove game is also known by a number of other names in the game theory literature. For example, it is frequently referred to as the game of *Chicken*, to evoke the

Your Partner

		Presentation	Exam
You	Presentation	90, 90	86, 92
	Exam	92, 86	76, 76

Figure 6.13. Exam or presentation (Hawk–Dove version)?

Player 2

		H	T
Player 1	H	−1, +1	+1, −1
	T	+1, −1	−1, +1

Figure 6.14. Matching Pennies game.

image of two teenagers racing their cars toward each other, daring each other to be the one to swerve out of the way. The two strategies here are *Swerve* and *Don't Swerve*: the one who swerves first suffers humiliation from his friends, but if neither swerves, then both suffer an actual collision.

6.7 Mixed Strategies

In the previous two sections, we have been discussing games whose conceptual complexity comes from the existence of multiple equilibria. However, there are also games that have no Nash equilibria at all. For such games, we will make predictions about players' behavior by enlarging the set of strategies to include the possibility of randomization; once players are allowed to behave randomly, one of John Nash's main results establishes that equilibria always exist [313, 314].

Probably the simplest class of games to expose this phenomenon are what might be called "attack–defense" games. In such games, one player behaves as the attacker while the other behaves as the defender. The attacker can use one of two strategies – let's call them A and B – while the defender's two strategies are "defend against A" or "defend against B." If the defender defends against the attack the attacker is using, then the defender gets the higher payoff; but if the defender defends against the wrong attack, then the attacker gets the higher payoff.

Matching Pennies. A simple attack–defense game is called *Matching Pennies*. It is based on a game in which two people each hold a penny and simultaneously choose whether to show heads (H) or tails (T) on their penny. Player 1 loses his penny to Player 2 if they match; Player 1 wins Player 2's penny if they don't match. This story produces the payoff matrix shown in Figure 6.14.

Matching Pennies is a simple example of a large class of interesting games with the property that the payoffs of the players sum to zero in every outcome. Such games are called *zero-sum games*, and many attack–defense games – and more generally, games where the players' interests are in direct conflict – have this structure. Games like Matching Pennies have in fact been used as metaphorical descriptions of decisions made in combat; for example, the Allied landing in Europe on June 6, 1944 – one of the pivotal moments in World War II – involved a decision by the Allies whether to cross the English Channel at Normandy or at Calais, and a corresponding decision by the German army whether to mass its defensive forces at Normandy or Calais. This situation has an attack–defense structure that closely resembles the Matching Pennies game [123].

The first thing to notice about Matching Pennies is that there is no pair of strategies that are best responses to each other. To see this, observe that, for any pair of strategies, one of the players gets a payoff of -1, and this player would improve his or her payoff to $+1$ by switching strategies. So for any pair of strategies, one of the players wants to switch what they're doing.[2]

Therefore, if we treat each player as simply having the two strategies H or T, then there is no Nash equilibrium for this game. This is not so surprising if we consider how Matching Pennies works. A pair of strategies, one for each player, forms a Nash equilibrium if even given knowledge of each other's strategies, neither player would have an incentive to switch to an alternate strategy. But in Matching Pennies, if Player 1 knows that Player 2 is going to play a particular choice of H or T, then Player 1 can exploit this by choosing the opposite and receiving a payoff of $+1$. Analogous reasoning holds for Player 2.

When we think intuitively about how games of this type are played in real life, we see that players generally try to make it difficult for their opponents to predict what they will play. This suggests that, in our modeling of a game like Matching Pennies, we shouldn't treat the strategies as simply H or T, but as ways of randomizing one's behavior between H and T. We now explore how to introduce randomization into our model for the play of this kind of game.

Mixed Strategies. The simplest way to introduce randomized behavior is to say that each player is not actually choosing H or T directly, but rather is choosing a *probability* with which he or she will play H. So in this model, the possible strategies for Player 1 are numbers p between 0 and 1; a given number p means that Player 1 is committing to play H with probability p, and T with probability $1 - p$. Similarly, the possible strategies for Player 2 are numbers q between 0 and 1, representing the probability that Player 2 will play H.

Since a game consists of a set of players, strategies, and payoffs, we should notice that, by allowing randomization, we have actually changed the game. It no longer consists of two strategies by each player, but instead a set of strategies corresponding to the interval of numbers between 0 and 1. We will refer to these as *mixed strategies*, since they involve "mixing" between the options H and T. Notice that the set of mixed strategies still includes the original two options of committing to definitely play H or T; these two choices correspond to selecting probabilities of 1 or 0, respectively, and we will refer to them as the two *pure strategies* in the game. To make things more informal notationally, we sometimes refer to the choice of $p = 1$ by Player 1 equivalently as the "pure strategy H," and similarly for $p = 0$ and $q = 1$ or 0.

---

[2] Incidentally, although it's not crucial for the discussion here, it's interesting to note that the three-client game used as an example in Section 6.4 can be viewed intuitively as a kind of hybrid of the Matching Pennies game and the Stag Hunt game. If we look just at how the two players evaluate the options of approaching clients B and C, we have Matching Pennies: firm 1 wants to match, whereas firm 2 wants to not match. However, if they coordinate on approaching client A, then they both get even higher payoffs – analogously to the two hunters coordinating to hunt stag.

Payoffs from Mixed Strategies. With this new set of strategies, we also need to determine the new set of payoffs. The subtlety in defining payoffs is that they are now random quantities: each player gets $+1$ with some probability and -1 with the remaining probability. When payoffs were numbers, it was obvious how to rank them: bigger was better. Now that payoffs are random, it is not immediately obvious how to rank them: we want a principled way to say that one random outcome is better than another.

To think about this issue, let's start by considering the Matching Pennies game from Player 1's point of view; we focus first on how she evaluates her two pure strategies of definitely playing H or definitely playing T. Suppose that Player 2 chooses the strategy q; that is, he commits to playing H with probability q and T with probability $1 - q$. Then if Player 1 chooses pure strategy H, she receives a payoff of -1 with probability q (since the two pennies match with probability q, in which event she loses), and she receives a payoff of $+1$ with probability $1 - q$ (since the two pennies don't match with probability $1 - q$). Alternatively, if Player 1 chooses pure strategy T, she receives $+1$ with probability q, and -1 with probability $1 - q$. So even if Player 1 uses a pure strategy, her payoffs can still be random due to the randomization employed by Player 2. How should we decide which of H or T is more appealing to Player 1 in this case?

To rank random payoffs numerically, we attach a number to each distribution that represents how attractive this distribution is to the player. Once numbers have been assigned to distributions, we can then rank them according to their associated number. The number we will use for this purpose is the *expected value* of the payoff. For example, if Player 1 chooses the pure strategy H while Player 2 chooses a probability of q, as before, then the expected payoff to Player 1 is

$$(-1)(q) + (1)(1 - q) = 1 - 2q.$$

Similarly, if Player 1 chooses the pure strategy T while Player 2 chooses a probability of q, then the expected payoff to Player 1 is

$$(1)(q) + (-1)(1 - q) = 2q - 1.$$

We will assume that each player is seeking to maximize the expected payoff they get from the choice of a mixed strategy. Although the expectation is a natural quantity, it is a subtle question whether maximizing expectation is a reasonable modeling assumption about the behavior of players. By now, however, there is a well-established foundation for the assumption that players rank distributions over payoffs (where these payoffs appropriately represent each player's satisfaction with the outcome of the game) according to their expected values [288, 363, 398], and so we will follow this assumption here.

We have now defined the mixed-strategy version of the Matching Pennies game: strategies are probabilities of playing H, and payoffs are the expectations of the payoffs from the four pure outcomes (H, H), (H, T), (T, H), and (T, T). We can now ask whether a Nash equilibrium exists for this richer version of the game.

Equilibrium with Mixed Strategies. We define a Nash equilibrium for the mixed-strategy version just as we did for the pure-strategy version: it is a pair of strategies (now probabilities) such that each is a best response to the other.

First, let's observe that in the Matching Pennies game, no pure strategy can be part of a Nash equilibrium. This reasoning is equivalent to what we did at the outset of this section. Suppose, for example, that the pure strategy H (i.e., probability $p = 1$) by Player 1 were part of a Nash equilibrium. Then Player 2's unique best response would be the pure strategy H as well (since Player 2 gets $+1$ whenever he matches). But H by Player 1 is not a best response to H by Player 2, so in fact this couldn't be a Nash equilibrium. Analogous reasoning applies to the other possible pure strategies followed by the two players. So we reach the natural conclusion that, in any Nash equilibrium, both players must be using probabilities that are strictly between 0 and 1.

Next, let's ask what Player 1's best response should be to strategy q used by Player 2. Earlier we determined that the expected payoff to Player 1 from the pure strategy H in this case is

$$1 - 2q,$$

while the expected payoff to Player 1 from the pure strategy T is

$$2q - 1.$$

Now here's the key point: if $1 - 2q \neq 2q - 1$, then one of the pure strategies H or T is in fact the unique best response by Player 1 to a play of q by Player 2. This holds simply because one of $1 - 2q$ or $2q - 1$ is larger in this case, and so there is no point for Player 1 to put any probability on her weaker pure strategy. But we have already established that pure strategies cannot be part of any Nash equilibrium for Matching Pennies, and because pure strategies are the best responses whenever $1 - 2q \neq 2q - 1$, probabilities that make these two expectations unequal cannot be part of a Nash equilibrium either.

So we've concluded that, in any Nash equilibrium for the mixed-strategy version of the Matching Pennies game, we must have

$$1 - 2q = 2q - 1,$$

or, in other words, $q = 1/2$. The situation is symmetric when we consider things from Player 2's point of view and evaluate the payoffs from a play of probability p by Player 1. We conclude from this that in any Nash equilibrium we must also have $p = 1/2$.

Thus, the pair of strategies $p = 1/2$ and $q = 1/2$ is the only possibility for a Nash equilibrium. We can check that the strategies in this pair are in fact best responses to each other. As a result, this is the unique Nash equilibrium for the mixed-strategy version of Matching Pennies.

Interpreting the Mixed-Strategy Equilibrium for Matching Pennies. Having derived the Nash equilibrium for this game, it's useful to think about what it means and how we can apply this reasoning to games in general.

First, let's picture a concrete setting in which two people actually sit down to play Matching Pennies, and each of them actually commits to behaving randomly according to probabilities p and q, respectively. If Player 1 believes that Player 2 will play H strictly more than half the time, then she should definitely play T – in which case Player 2 should not be playing H more than half the time. The symmetric reasoning applies if Player 1 believes that Player 2 will play T strictly more than half the time. In neither case would we have a Nash equilibrium. So the point is that the choice of

$q = 1/2$ by Player 2 makes Player 1 *indifferent* between playing H or T: the strategy $q = 1/2$ is effectively "nonexploitable" by Player 1. This reasoning was in fact our original intuition for introducing randomization: each player wants their behavior to be unpredictable to the other, so that their behavior can't be taken advantage of. We should note that the fact that both probabilities turned out to be $1/2$ is a result of the highly symmetric structure of Matching Pennies; as we will see in subsequent examples in the next section, when the payoffs are less symmetric, the Nash equilibrium can consist of unequal probabilities.

This notion of indifference is a general principle behind the computation of mixed-strategy equilibria in two-player, two-strategy games when there are no equilibria involving pure strategies: each player should randomize so as to make the other player indifferent between their two alternatives. This way, neither player's behavior can be exploited by a pure strategy, and the two choices of probabilities are best responses to each other. And although we won't pursue the details of it here, a generalization of this principle applies to games with any finite number of players and any finite number of strategies: Nash's main mathematical result accompanying his definition of equilibrium was to prove that *every* such game has at least one mixed-strategy equilibrium [313, 314].

It's also worth thinking about how to interpret mixed-strategy equilibria in real-world situations. In fact there are several possible interpretations, which are appropriate in different situations:

- Sometimes, particularly when the participants are genuinely playing a sport or game, the players may be actively randomizing their actions [107, 337, 405]: a tennis player may be randomly deciding whether to serve the ball up the center or out to the side of the court; a card player may be randomly deciding whether to bluff or not; two children may be randomizing among rock, paper, and scissors in the perennial elementary-school contest of the same name. We will look at some examples of this type of behavior in the next section.

- Sometimes the mixed strategies are better viewed as proportions within a population. Suppose, for example, that two species of animals, in the process of foraging for food, regularly engage in one-on-one attack–defense games with the structure of Matching Pennies. Here, a single member of the first species always plays the role of attacker, and a single member of the second species always plays the role of defender.

  Let's suppose that each individual animal is genetically hard-wired to always play H or always play T; and suppose further that the population of each species consists half of animals hard-wired to play H and half of animals hard-wired to play T. Then with this population mixture, H-animals in each species do exactly as well on average, over many random interactions, as T-animals. Hence, the population as a whole is in a kind of mixed equilibrium, even though each individual is playing a pure strategy. This story suggests an important link with evolutionary biology, which has in fact been developed through a long line of research [375, 376]; this topic is the focus of Chapter 7.

- Maybe the most subtle interpretation is based on recalling, from Section 6.4, that a Nash equilibrium is often best thought of as an equilibrium in beliefs. If each player

Defense

		Defend Pass	Defend Run
Offense	Pass	0, 0	10, −10
	Run	5, −5	0, 0

Figure 6.15. Run–pass game.

believes that her partner will play according to a particular Nash equilibrium, then she too will want to play according to it. In the case of Matching Pennies, with its unique mixed equilibrium, this means that it is enough for you to expect that when you meet an arbitrary person, they will play their side of Matching Pennies with a probability of 1/2. In this case, playing a probability of 1/2 makes sense for you too; hence, this choice of probabilities is self-reinforcing – it is in equilibrium – across the entire population.

6.8 Mixed Strategies: Examples and Empirical Analysis

Because mixed-strategy equilibrium is a subtle concept, it's useful to think about it through further examples. We will focus on two main examples, both drawn from the realm of sports, and both with attack–defense structures. The first is stylized and partly metaphorical, while the second represents a striking empirical test of whether people in high-stakes situations actually follow the predictions of mixed-strategy equilibrium. We conclude the section with a general discussion of how to identify all the equilibria of a two-player, two-strategy game.

The Run–Pass Game. First, let's consider a streamlined version of the problem faced by two American football teams as they plan their next play in a football game. The offense can choose either to run or to pass, and the defense can choose either to defend against the run or to defend against the pass. Here is how the payoffs work:

- If the defense correctly matches the offense's play, then the offense gains 0 yards.
- If the offense runs while the defense defends against the pass, the offense gains 5 yards.
- If the offense passes while the defense defends against the run, the offense gains 10 yards.

Hence, we have the payoff matrix shown in Figure 6.15.

[If you don't know the rules of American football, you can follow the discussion simply by taking the payoff matrix as self-contained. Intuitively, the point is simply that we have an attack–defense game with two players named "offense" and "defense," respectively, and where the attacker has a stronger option (pass) and a weaker option (run).]

Just as in Matching Pennies, it's easy to check that there is no Nash equilibrium in which either player uses a pure strategy: both have to make their behavior unpredictable by randomizing. So let's work out a mixed-strategy equilibrium for this game: let p

be the probability that the offense passes, and let q be the probability that the defense defends against the pass. (We know from Nash's result that at least one mixed-strategy equilibrium must exist, but not what the actual values of p and q should be.)

We use the principle that a mixed equilibrium arises when the probabilities used by each player make his opponent indifferent between his two options.

- First, suppose the defense chooses a probability of q for defending against the pass. Then the expected payoff to the offense from passing is

$$(0)(q) + (10)(1 - q) = 10 - 10q,$$

  while the expected payoff to the offense from running is

$$(5)(q) + (0)(1 - q) = 5q.$$

  To make the offense indifferent between its two strategies, we need to set $10 - 10q = 5q$; hence, $q = 2/3$.
- Second, suppose the offense chooses a probability of p for passing. Then the expected payoff to the defense from defending against the pass is

$$(0)(p) + (-5)(1 - p) = 5p - 5,$$

  and the expected payoff to the defense from defending against the run is

$$(-10)(p) + (0)(1 - p) = -10p.$$

  To make the defense indifferent between its two strategies, we need $5p - 5 = -10p$; hence, $p = 1/3$.

Thus, the only possible probability values that can appear in a mixed-strategy equilibrium are $p = 1/3$ for the offense and $q = 2/3$ for the defense, which in fact forms an equilibrium. Notice also that the expected payoff to the offense with these probabilities is $10/3$, and the corresponding expected payoff to the defense is $-10/3$. Also, in contrast to the Matching Pennies game, notice that because of the asymmetric structure of the payoffs here, the probabilities that appear in the mixed-strategy equilibrium are unbalanced as well.

Strategic Interpretation of the Run–Pass Game. There are several things to notice about this equilibrium. First, the strategic implications of the equilibrium probabilities are intriguing and a bit subtle. Specifically, although passing is the offense's more powerful weapon, it is used less than half the time: the offense places only probability $p = 1/3$ on passing. This initially seems counterintuitive: why not spend more time using your more powerful option? But the calculation that gave us the equilibrium probabilities also supplies the answer to this question. If the offense placed any higher probability on passing, then the defense's best response would be to always defend against the pass, and the offense would actually do worse in expectation.

We can see how this works by trying a larger value for p, like $p = 1/2$. In this case, the defense will always defend against the pass, and so the offense's expected payoff will be 5/2, since it gains 5 half the time and 0 the other half the time:

$$(1/2)(0) + (1/2)(5) = 5/2.$$

Above, we saw that, with the equilibrium probabilities, the offense has an expected payoff of $10/3 > 5/2$. Moreover, because $p = 1/3$ makes the defense indifferent between its two strategies, an offense that uses $p = 1/3$ is guaranteed to get $10/3 > 5/2$ no matter what the defense does.

One way to think about the real power of passing as a strategy is to notice that, in equilibrium, the defense is defending against the pass 2/3 of the time, even though the offense is using it only 1/3 of the time. So somehow the *threat* of passing is helping the offense, even though it uses it relatively rarely.

This example clearly oversimplifies the strategic issues at work in American football: there are many more than just two strategies, and teams are concerned with more than just their yardage on the very next play. Nevertheless, this type of analysis has been applied to statistics from American football, verifying some of the main qualitative conclusions at a broad level – that teams generally run more than they pass, and that the expected yardage gained per play from running is close to the expected yardage gained per play from passing for most teams [82, 84, 355].

The Penalty-Kick Game. The complexity of American football makes it hard to cast it truly accurately as a two-person, two-strategy game. We now focus on a different setting, also from professional sports, in which such a formalization can be done much more exactly: the modeling of penalty kicks in soccer as a two-player game.

In 2002, Ignacio Palacios-Huerta undertook a large study of penalty kicks from the perspective of game theory [337], and we focus on his analysis here. As he observed, penalty kicks capture the ingredients of two-player, two-strategy games remarkably faithfully. The kicker can aim the ball to the left or the right of the goal, and the goalie can dive to either the left or right as well.[3] The ball moves to the goal fast enough that the decisions of the kicker and goalie are effectively being made simultaneously; based on these decisions, the kicker is likely to score or not. Indeed, the structure of the game is very much like Matching Pennies: if the goalie dives in the direction where the ball is aimed, he has a good chance of blocking it; if the goalie dives in the wrong direction, it is very likely to go in the goal.

Based on an analysis of roughly 1,400 penalty kicks in professional soccer, Palacios-Huerta determined the empirical probability of scoring for each of the four basic outcomes: whether the kicker aims left or right, and whether the goalie dives left or right. This led to a payoff matrix as shown in Figure 6.16.

There are a few contrasts to note in relation to the basic Matching Pennies game. First, a kicker has a reasonably good chance of scoring even when the goalie dives in the correct direction (although a correct choice by the goalie still greatly reduces this

---

[3] Kicks up the center, and decisions by the goalie to remain in the center, are very rare and can be ignored in a simple version of the analysis.

Goalie

		L	R
Kicker	L	0.58, −0.58	0.95, −0.95
	R	0.93, −0.93	0.70, −0.70

Figure 6.16. Penalty-kick games (from empirical data; Palacios-Huerta, [337]).

probability). Second, kickers are generally right-footed, and so their chance of scoring is not completely symmetric between aiming left and aiming right.[4]

Despite these caveats, the basic premise of Matching Pennies is still present here: there is no equilibrium in pure strategies, and so we need to consider how players should randomize their behavior in playing this game. Using the principle of indifference as in previous examples, we see that if q is the probability that a goalie chooses L, we must set q so as to make the kicker indifferent between his two options:

$$(.58)(q) + (.95)(1 - q) = (.93)(q) + (.70)(1 - q).$$

Solving for q, we get $q = .42$. We can perform the analogous calculation to obtain the value of p that makes the goalie indifferent, obtaining $p = .39$.

The striking punchline to this study is that, in the data drawn from real penalty kicks, the goalies dive left a .42 fraction of the time (matching the prediction to two decimal places), and the kickers aim left a .40 fraction of the time (coming within .01 of the prediction). It is particularly nice to find the theory's predictions borne out in a setting such as professional soccer, since the two-player game under study is being played by experts, and the outcome is important enough to the participants that they are investing significant attention to their choice of strategies.

Finding All Nash Equilibria. To conclude our discussion of mixed-strategy equilibria, we consider the general question of how to find all Nash equilibria of a two-player, two-strategy game.

First, it is important to note that a game may have both pure-strategy and mixed-strategy equilibria. As a result, one should first check all four pure outcomes (given by pairs of pure strategies) to see which, if any, form equilibria. Then, to check for any mixed-strategy equilibria, we need to look for mixing probabilities p and q that are best responses to each other. If there is a mixed-strategy equilibrium, we can determine Player 2's strategy (q) from the requirement that Player 1 randomizes. Player 1 will only randomize if his pure strategies have equal expected payoff. This equality of expected payoffs for Player 1 gives us one equation that we can solve to determine q. The same process gives an equation to solve for determining Player 2's strategy p. If both of the obtained values, p and q, are strictly between 0 and 1, and are thus legitimate mixed strategies, then we have a mixed-strategy equilibrium.

Thus far, our examples of mixed-strategy equilibria have been restricted to games with an attack–defense structure, and so we have not seen an example exhibiting both

---

[4] For purposes of the analysis, we take all the left-footed kickers in the data and apply a left-right reflection to all their actions, so that R always denotes the "natural side" for each kicker.

	Your Partner	
	PowerPoint	*Keynote*
You *PowerPoint*	1, 1	0, 0
Keynote	0, 0	2, 2

Figure 6.17. Unbalanced coordination game.

pure and mixed equilibria. However, it is not hard to find such examples: in particular, coordination and Hawk–Dove games with two pure equilibria will each also have a third mixed equilibrium in which each player randomizes. As an example, let's consider the unbalanced coordination game from Section 6.5 (shown in Figure 6.17).

Suppose that you place a probability of p strictly between 0 and 1 on PowerPoint, and your partner places a probability of q strictly between 0 and 1 on PowerPoint. Then you'll be indifferent between PowerPoint and Keynote if

$$(1)(q) + (0)(1 - q) = (0)(q) + (2)(1 - q),$$

or, in other words, if $q = 2/3$. Since the situation is symmetric from your partner's point of view, we also get $p = 2/3$. Thus, in addition to the two pure equilibria, we also get an equilibrium in which each of you chooses PowerPoint with probability 2/3. Note that, unlike the two pure equilibria, this mixed equilibrium comes with a positive probability that the two of you will miscoordinate, but this is still an equilibrium, since if you truly believe that your partner is choosing PowerPoint with probability 2/3 and Keynote with probability 1/3, then you'll be indifferent between the two options and will get the same expected payoff however you choose.

6.9 Pareto Optimality and Social Optimality

In a Nash equilibrium, each player's strategy is a best response to the other player's strategy. In other words, the players are optimizing individually. But this doesn't mean that, as a group, the players will necessarily reach an outcome that is in any sense good. The exam-or-presentation game from the opening section, and related games like the Prisoner's Dilemma, serve as examples of this possibility. (We redraw the payoff matrix for the basic exam-or-presentation game in Figure 6.18.)

It is interesting to classify outcomes in a game not just by their strategic or equilibrium properties, but also by whether they are "good for society." To reason about this latter issue, we first need a way of making it precise. We now discuss two useful candidates for such a definition.

	Your Partner	
	Presentation	Exam
You Presentation	90, 90	86, 92
Exam	92, 86	88, 88

Figure 6.18. Exam or presentation?

Pareto Optimality. The first definition is *Pareto-optimality*, named after the Italian economist Vilfredo Pareto who worked in the late 1800s and early 1900s.

> A choice of strategies – one by each player – is *Pareto-optimal* if there is no other choice of strategies in which all players receive payoffs at least as high, and at least one player receives a strictly higher payoff.

To see the intuitive appeal of Pareto-optimality, let's consider a choice of strategies that is *not* Pareto-optimal. In this case, there's an alternate choice of strategies that makes at least one player better off without harming any player. In basically any reasonable sense, this alternate choice is superior to what's currently being played. If the players could jointly agree on what to do, and make this agreement binding, then surely they would prefer to move to this superior choice of strategies.

The motivation here relies crucially on the idea that the players can construct a binding agreement to actually play the superior pair of strategies: if this alternate choice is not a Nash equilibrium, then, absent a binding agreement, at least one player would want to switch to a different strategy. As an illustration of why this is a crucial point, consider the outcomes in the exam-or-presentation game. The outcome in which you and your partner both study for the exam is not Pareto-optimal, because the outcome in which you both prepare for the presentation is strictly better for both of you. This is the central difficulty at the heart of this example, now phrased in terms of Pareto-optimality. It shows that, even though you and your partner realize a superior solution is possible, there is no way to maintain it without a binding agreement between the two of you.

In this example, the two outcomes in which exactly one of you prepares for the presentation are also Pareto-optimal. In this case, although one of you is doing badly, there is no alternate choice of strategies in which *everyone* is doing at least as well. So in fact, the exam-or-presentation game, and the Prisoner's Dilemma, are examples of games in which the *only* outcome that is not Pareto-optimal is the one corresponding to the unique Nash equilibrium.

Social Optimality. A stronger condition that is even simpler to state is *social optimality.*

> A choice of strategies – one by each player – is a *social welfare maximizer* (or *socially optimal*) if it maximizes the sum of the players' payoffs.

In the exam-or-presentation game, the social optimum is achieved by the outcome in which both you and your partner prepare for the presentation, which produces a combined payoff of $90 + 90 = 180$. Of course, this definition is only appropriate to the extent that it makes sense to add the payoffs of different players together – it's not always clear that we can meaningfully combine my satisfaction with an outcome and your satisfaction by simply adding them up.

Outcomes that are socially optimal must also be Pareto-optimal: if such an outcome weren't Pareto-optimal, there would be a different outcome in which all payoffs were at least as large, and one was larger – and this would be an outcome with a larger sum of payoffs. However, a Pareto-optimal outcome need not be socially optimal.

For example, the exam-or-presentation game has three outcomes that are Pareto-optimal, but only one of these is the social optimum.

Finally, of course, it's not the case that Nash equilibria are at odds with the goal of social optimality in every game. For example, in the version of the exam-or-presentation game with an easier exam, yielding the payoff matrix that we saw earlier in Figure 6.4, the unique Nash equilibrium is also the unique social optimum.

6.10 Advanced Material: Dominated Strategies and Dynamic Games

In this final section, we consider two further issues that arise in the analysis of games. First, we study the role of *dominated strategies* in reasoning about behavior in a game; we find that the analysis of this type of strategy can provide a way to make predictions about play based on rationality, even when no player has a dominant strategy. Second, we discuss how to reinterpret the strategies and payoffs in a game to deal with situations in which play actually occurs sequentially through time.

Before doing this, however, we begin with a formal definition for games that have more than two players.

A. Multiplayer Games

A multiplayer game consists, as in the two-player case, of a set of players, a set of strategies for each player, and a payoff to each player for each possible outcome.

Specifically, suppose that a game has n players named $1, 2, \ldots, n$. Each player has a set of possible strategies. An *outcome* (or *joint strategy*) of the game is a choice of a strategy for each player. Finally, each player i has a *payoff function* P_i that maps outcomes of the game to a numerical payoff for i: for each outcome consisting of strategies $(S_1, S_2, \ldots, S_n)$, there is a payoff $P_i(S_1, S_2, \ldots, S_n)$ to player i.

Now we can say that a strategy S_i is a *best response* by Player i to a choice of strategies $(S_1, S_2, \ldots, S_{i-1}, S_{i+1}, \ldots, S_n)$ by all the other players if

$$P_i(S_1, S_2, \ldots, S_{i-1}, S_i, S_{i+1}, \ldots, S_n) \geq P_i(S_1, S_2, \ldots, S_{i-1}, S_i', S_{i+1}, \ldots, S_n)$$

for all other possible strategies S_i' available to player i.

Finally, an outcome consisting of strategies $(S_1, S_2, \ldots, S_n)$ is a *Nash equilibrium* if each strategy it contains is a best response to all the others.

B. Dominated Strategies and Their Role in Strategic Reasoning

In Sections 6.2 and 6.3, we discussed (strictly) dominant strategies – strategies that are a (strict) best response to every possible choice of strategies by the other players. Clearly if a player has a strictly dominant strategy then this is the strategy she should employ. But we also saw that, even for two-player, two-strategy games, it is common to have no dominant strategies. This fact holds even more strongly for larger games: although dominant and strictly dominant strategies can exist in games with many players and many strategies, they are rare.

Figure 6.19. In the Facility Location game on this six-node path, each player has strictly dominated strategies but no dominant strategy.

However, even if a player does not have a dominant strategy, she may still have strategies that are dominated by other strategies. In this section, we consider the role that such dominated strategies play in reasoning about behavior in games.

We begin with a formal definition: a strategy is *strictly dominated* if there is some other strategy available to the same player that produces a strictly higher payoff in response to *every* choice of strategies by the other players. In the notation we've just developed, strategy S_i for player i is strictly dominated if there is another strategy S_i' for player i such that

$$P_i(S_1, S_2, \ldots, S_{i-1}, S_i', S_{i+1}, \ldots, S_n) > P_i(S_1, S_2, \ldots, S_{i-1}, S_i, S_{i+1}, \ldots, S_n)$$

for all choices of strategies $(S_1, S_2, \ldots, S_{i-1}, S_{i+1}, \ldots, S_n)$ by the other players.

Now, in the two-player, two-strategy games we've been considering thus far, a strategy is strictly dominated precisely when the other strategy available to the same player is strictly dominant. In this context, it wouldn't make sense to study strictly dominated strategies as a separate concept. However, if a player has many strategies, then it's possible for a strategy to be strictly dominated without any strategy being dominant. In such cases, strictly dominated strategies can play a very useful role in reasoning about play in a game. In particular, we will see that there are games in which there are no dominant strategies, but where the outcome of the game can still be uniquely predicted using the structure of the dominated strategies. In this way, reasoning based on dominated strategies forms an intriguing intermediate approach between dominant strategies and Nash equilibrium: on the one hand, it can be more powerful than reasoning based solely on dominant strategies; but on the other hand, it still relies only on the premise that players seek to maximize payoffs and doesn't require the introduction of an equilibrium notion.

To see how this approach works, it's useful to introduce it in the context of a basic example.

Example: The Facility Location Game. Our example is a game in which two firms compete through their choice of locations. Suppose that two firms are each planning to open a store in one of six towns located along six consecutive exits on a highway. We can represent the arrangement of these towns using a six-node graph as in Figure 6.19.

Now, based on leasing agreements, Firm 1 has the option of opening its store in any of towns A, C, or E, while Firm 2 has the option of opening its store in any of towns B, D, or F. These decisions will be executed simultaneously. Once the two stores are opened, customers from the towns will go to the store that is closer to them. For example, if Firm 1 opens its store in town C and Firm 2 opens its store in town B, then the store in town B will attract customers from A and B, while the store in town C will attract customers from C, D, E, and F. If we assume that the towns contain an equal number of customers, and that payoffs are directly proportional to the number of

Firm 2

		B	D	F
	A	1, 5	2, 4	3, 3
Firm 1	C	4, 2	3, 3	4, 2
	E	3, 3	2, 4	5, 1

Figure 6.20. Facility location game.

customers, this would result in a payoff of 4 for Firm 1 and 2 for Firm 2, since Firm 1 claims customers from four towns while Firm 2 claims customers from the remaining two towns. Reasoning in this way about the number of towns claimed by each store, based on proximity to their locations, we get the payoff matrix shown in Figure 6.20.

We refer to this as the *Facility Location game*. The competitive location of facilities is a topic that has been the subject of considerable study in operations research and other areas [135]. Moreover, closely related models have been used when the entities being "located" are not stores along a one-dimensional highway but the positions of political candidates along a one-dimensional ideological spectrum – here too, choosing a certain position relative to one's electoral opponent can attract certain voters while alienating others [350]. We will return to issues related to political competition, though in a slightly different form, in Chapter 23.

We can verify that neither player has a dominant strategy in this game. For example, if Firm 1 locates at node A, then the strict best response of Firm 2 is B, while if Firm 1 locates at node E, then the strict best response of Firm 2 is D. The situation is symmetric if we interchange the roles of the two firms (and read the graph from the other direction).

Dominated Strategies in the Facility Location Game. We can make progress in reasoning about the behavior of the two players in the Facility Location game by thinking about their dominated strategies. First, notice that A is a strictly dominated strategy for Firm 1: in any situation where Firm 1 has the option of choosing A, it would receive a strictly higher payoff by choosing C. Similarly, F is a strictly dominated strategy for Firm 2: in any situation where Firm 1 has the option of choosing F, it would receive a strictly higher payoff by choosing D.

It is never in a player's interest to use a strictly dominated strategy; some strategy dominates it. Therefore, Firm 1 isn't going to use strategy A. Moreover, since Firm 2 knows the structure of the game, including Firm 1's payoffs, Firm 2 knows that Firm 1 won't use strategy A. It can be effectively eliminated from the game. The same reasoning shows that F can be eliminated from the game.

We now have a smaller instance of the Facility Location game, involving only the four nodes B, C, D, and E and the payoff matrix shown in Figure 6.21.

Now something interesting happens. Strategies B and E weren't previously strictly dominated: they were useful in case the other player used A or F, respectively. But with A and F eliminated, strategies B and E now *are* strictly dominated – by the same reasoning, both players know they won't be used, and so we can eliminate them from the game. This gives us the even smaller game shown in Figure 6.22.

Firm 2

		B	D
Firm 1	C	4, 2	3, 3
	E	3, 3	2, 4

Figure 6.21. Smaller Facility Location game.

At this point, there is a very clear prediction for the play of the game: Firm 1 will play C, and Firm 2 will play D. And the reasoning that led to this outcome is clear: after repeatedly removing strategies that were (or became) strictly dominated, we were left with only a single plausible option for each player.

The process that led us to this reduced game is called the *iterated deletion of strictly dominated strategies*, and we will next describe it in its full generality. Before doing this, however, it's worth making some observations about the example of the Facility Location game.

First, the pair of strategies (C,D) is indeed the unique Nash equilibrium in the game, and when we later discuss the iterated deletion of strictly dominated strategies in general, we will see that the process is an effective way to search for Nash equilibria. But beyond this, it is also an effective way to *justify* the Nash equilibria that one finds. When we first introduced the concept of Nash equilibrium, we observed that it couldn't be derived purely from an assumption of rationality on the part of the players; rather, we had to assume further that play of the game would be found at an equilibrium from which neither player had an incentive to deviate. On the other hand, when a unique Nash equilibrium emerges from the iterated deletion of strictly dominated strategies, it is in fact a prediction based purely on the assumptions of the players' rationality and their knowledge of the game, since all the steps that led to it were based simply on removing strategies that were strictly inferior to others from the perspective of payoff maximization.

A final observation is that iterated deletion can in principle be carried out for a very large number of steps, a fact that can be illustrated by a simple modification of the Facility Location game. Suppose that instead of a path of length 6, we had a path of length 1,000, with the options for the two firms still strictly alternating along this path (constituting 500 possible strategies for each player). Then it would still be the case that only the outer two nodes would be strictly dominated; after their removal, we'd have a path of length 998 in which the two new outer nodes had now become strictly dominated. We can continue removing nodes in this way and, after 499 steps of such reasoning, we have a game in which only the 500th and 501st nodes have survived as strategies. This is the unique Nash equilibrium for the game, and this unique prediction can be justified by a very long sequence of deletions of dominated strategies.

Firm 2

D

		D
Firm 1	C	3, 3

Figure 6.22. Even smaller Facility Location game.

It's also interesting how this prediction is intuitively natural, and one that is often borne out in real life: two competing stores staking out positions next to each other near the center of the population, or two political candidates gravitating toward the ideological middle ground as they compete for voters in a general election. In each case, this move toward the center is the unique way to maximize the territory that you can claim at the expense of your competitor.

Iterated Deletion of Dominated Strategies: The General Principle. In general, for a game with an arbitrary number of players, the process of *iterated deletion of strictly dominated strategies* proceeds as follows:

- We start with any n-player game, find all the strictly dominated strategies, and delete them.
- We then consider the reduced game in which these strategies have been removed. In this reduced game there may be strategies that are now strictly dominated, despite not having been strictly dominated in the full game. We find these strategies and delete them.
- We continue this process, repeatedly finding and removing strictly dominated strategies until none can be found.

An important general fact is that the set of Nash equilibria of the original game coincides with the set of Nash equilibria for the final reduced game, consisting only of strategies that survive iterated deletion. To prove this fact, it is enough to show that the set of Nash equilibria does not change when we perform one round of deleting strictly dominated strategies; if this is true, then we have established that the Nash equilibria continue to remain unchanged through an arbitrary finite sequence of deletions.

To prove that the set of Nash equilibria remains the same through one round of deletion, we need to show two things. First, any Nash equilibrium of the original game is a Nash equilibrium of the reduced game. To see this, note that otherwise there would be a Nash equilibrium of the original game involving a strategy S that was deleted. But in this case, S is strictly dominated by some other strategy S'. Hence, S cannot be part of a Nash equilibrium of the original game: it is not a best response to the strategies of the other players, since the strategy S' that dominates it is a better response. This argument establishes that no Nash equilibrium of the original game can be removed by the deletion process. Second, we need to show that any Nash equilibrium of the reduced game is also a Nash equilibrium of the original game. For this not to be the case, there would have to be a Nash equilibrium $E = (S_1, S_2, \ldots, S_n)$ of the reduced game, and a strategy S_i' that was deleted from the original game, such that player i has an incentive to deviate from its strategy S_i in E to the strategy S_i'. But strategy S_i' was deleted because it was strictly dominated by at least one other strategy; we can therefore find a strategy S_i'' that strictly dominated it and was not deleted. Then player i also has an incentive to deviate from S_i to S_i'', and S_i'' is still present in the reduced game, contradicting our assumption that E is a Nash equilibrium of the reduced game.

Therefore, we have established that the game we end up with, after iterated deletion of strictly dominated strategies, still has all the Nash equilibria of the original game. Hence, this process can be a powerful way to restrict the search for Nash equilibria. Moreover, although we described the process as operating in rounds, with all currently

Hunter 2

		Hunt Stag	Hunt Hare
Hunter 1	Hunt Stag	3, 3	0, 3
	Hunt Hare	3, 0	3, 3

Figure 6.23. Stag Hunt: a version with a weakly dominated strategy.

strictly dominated strategies being removed in each round, this approach is not essential. One can show that eliminating strictly dominated strategies in any order results in the same set of surviving strategies.

Weakly Dominated Strategies. It is also natural to ask about notions that are slightly weaker than our definition of strictly dominated strategies. One fundamental definition in this spirit is that of a weakly dominated strategy. We say that a strategy is *weakly dominated* if there is another strategy that does at least as well no matter what the other players do, and does strictly better against some joint strategy of the other players. In our notation from earlier, we say that a strategy S_i for player i is weakly dominated if there is another strategy S_i' for player i such that

$$P_i(S_1, S_2, \ldots, S_{i-1}, S_i', S_{i+1}, \ldots, S_n) \geq P_i(S_1, S_2, \ldots, S_{i-1}, S_i, S_{i+1}, \ldots, S_n)$$

for all choices of strategies $(S_1, S_2, \ldots, S_{i-1}, S_{i+1}, \ldots, S_n)$ by the other players, and

$$P_i(S_1, S_2, \ldots, S_{i-1}, S_i', S_{i+1}, \ldots, S_n) > P_i(S_1, S_2, \ldots, S_{i-1}, S_i, S_{i+1}, \ldots, S_n)$$

for at least one choice of strategies $(S_1, S_2, \ldots, S_{i-1}, S_{i+1}, \ldots, S_n)$ by the other players.

For strictly dominated strategies, the argument for deleting them was compelling: they are never best responses. For weakly dominated strategies, the issue is more subtle. Such strategies could be best responses to some joint strategy by the other players. So a rational player could play a weakly dominated strategy, and in fact Nash equilibria can involve weakly dominated strategies.

There are simple examples that make this clear even in two-player, two-strategy games. Consider, for example, a version of the Stag Hunt game in which the payoff from successfully catching a stag is the same as the payoff from catching a hare, as shown in Figure 6.23.

In this case, Hunt Stag is a weakly dominated strategy, since each player always does at least as well, and sometimes strictly better, by playing Hunt Hare. Nevertheless, the outcome in which both players choose Hunt Stag is a Nash equilibrium, since each is playing a best response to the other's strategy. Thus, deleting weakly dominated strategies is not generally a safe thing to do if one wants to preserve the essential structure of the game: such deletion operations can destroy Nash equilibria.

Of course, it might seem reasonable to suppose that a player should not play according to equilibrium involving a weakly dominated strategy – such as (Hunt Stag, Hunt Stag) – if he had any uncertainty about what the other players would do; after all, why not use an alternate strategy that is at least as good in every eventuality? But Nash equilibrium does not take into account this idea of uncertainty about the behavior of others, and hence has no way to rule out such outcomes. In the next chapter, we discuss an alternative equilibrium concept known as evolutionary stability that in fact does eliminate weakly dominated strategies in a principled way. The relationship between Nash equilibrium, evolutionary stability, and weakly dominated strategies is considered in the exercises at the end of the next chapter.

C. Dynamic Games

Our focus in this chapter has been on games in which all players choose their strategies simultaneously and then receive payoffs based on this joint decision. Of course, actual simultaneity is not crucial for the model, but it has been central to our discussions so far that each player is choosing a strategy without knowledge of the actual choices made by the other players.

Many games, however, are played over time: some player or set of players moves first, other players observe the choice(s) made, and then they respond, perhaps according to a predetermined order of governing who moves when. Such games are called *dynamic games*, and there are many basic examples: board games and card games in which players alternate turns; negotiations, which usually involve a sequence of offers and counteroffers; and bidding in an auction or pricing competing goods where participants must make decisions over time. Here we discuss an adaptation of the theory of games that incorporates this dynamic aspect.

Normal and Extensive Forms of a Game. To begin with, specifying a dynamic game is going to require a new kind of notation. Thus far, we've worked with something called the *normal-form* representation of a game, which specifies the list of players, their possible strategies, and the payoffs arising from every possible (simultaneous) choice of strategies by the players. (For two-player games, the payoff matrices we've seen in this chapter encode the normal-form representation of a game in a compact way.)

To describe a dynamic game, we require a richer representation; we need to specify who moves when, what each player knows at any opportunity they have to move, what they can do when it is their turn to move, and what the payoffs are at the end of the game. We refer to this specification as the *extensive-form* representation of the game.

Let's start with a very simple example of a dynamic game so that we can discuss what its extensive-form representation looks like. This game is simple enough that it avoids some of the subtleties that arise in the analysis of dynamic games, but it is useful as a first illustration; we'll proceed to a more complex second example afterward.

In our first example, we imagine two firms – Firm 1 and Firm 2 – each of whom is trying to decide whether to focus its advertising and marketing on two possible regions, named A and B. Firm 1 gets to choose first. If Firm 2 follows Firm 1 into the same region, then Firm 1's "first-mover advantage" gives it 2/3 of the profit obtainable from the market in that region, while Firm 2 will only get 1/3. If Firm 2 moves into the other region, then each firm gets all the profit obtainable in their respective region. Finally, Region A has twice as large a market as Region B: the total profit obtainable in region A is equal to 12, while in Region B it's 6.

We write the extensive-form representation as a "game tree," depicted in Figure 6.24. This tree is designed to be read downward from the top. The top node represents Firm

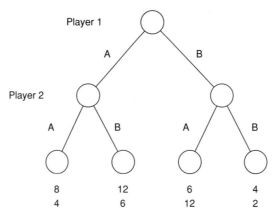

Figure 6.24. A simple game in extensive form.

1's initial move, and the two edges descending from this node represent its two options, A or B. Once a branch is taken, this leads to a node representing Firm 2's subsequent move. Firm 2 can then also choose option A or B, again represented by edges descending from the node. This choice leads to a terminal node representing the end of play in the game; each terminal node is labeled with the payoffs to the two players.

Thus, a specific play – determined by a sequence of choices by Firm 1 and Firm 2 – corresponds to a path from the top node in the tree down to some terminal node. First Firm 1 chooses A or B, then Firm 2 chooses A or B, and then the two players receive their payoffs. In a more general model of dynamic games, each node could contain an annotation saying what information about the previous moves is known to the player currently making a move; however, for our purposes here, we will focus on the case in which each player knows the complete history of past moves when he or she goes to make the current move.

Reasoning about Behavior in a Dynamic Game. As with simultaneous-move games, we'd like to make predictions about what players will do in dynamic games. One way is to reason from the game tree. In our current example, we can start by considering how Firm 2 will behave after each of the two possible opening moves by Firm 1. If Firm 1 chooses A, then Firm 2 maximizes its payoff by choosing B; on the other hand, if Firm 1 chooses B, then Firm 2 maximizes its payoff by choosing A. Now let's consider Firm 1's opening move, given what we've just concluded about Firm 2's subsequent behavior. If Firm 1 chooses A, then it expects Firm 2 to choose B, yielding a payoff of 12 for Firm 1. If Firm 1 chooses B, then it expects Firm 2 to choose A, yielding a payoff of 6 for Firm 1. Since we expect the firms to try to maximize their payoffs, we predict that Firm 1 should choose A, after which Firm 2 should choose B.

This approach is a useful way to analyze dynamic games. We start one step above the terminal nodes, where the last player to move has complete control over the outcome of the payoffs. This lets us predict what the last player will do in all cases. Having established this prediction, we then move one more level up the game tree, using these predictions to reason about what the player at that level will do. We continue in this way up the tree, eventually making predictions for play all the way up to the top node.

Firm 2

Firm 1		AA,AB	AA,BB	BA,AB	BA,BB
	A	8, 4	8, 4	12, 6	12, 6
	B	6, 12	4, 2	6, 12	4, 2

Figure 6.25. Conversion to normal form.

A different style of analysis exploits an interesting connection between normal and extensive forms, allowing us to write a normal-form representation for a dynamic game as follows. Suppose that, before the game is played, each player makes up a plan for how to play the entire game, covering every possible eventuality. This plan will serve as the player's strategy. One way to think about such strategies, and a useful way to be sure that they include a complete description of every possibility, is to imagine that each player has to provide all of the information necessary to write a computer program that will actually play the game in their place.

For the game in Figure 6.24, Firm 1 only has two possible strategies: A or B. Since Firm 2 moves after observing what Firm 1 did, and Firm 2 has two possible choices for each of the two options by Firm 1, Firm 2 has four possible plans for playing the game. They can be written as contingencies, specifying what Firm 2 will do in response to each possible move by Firm 1:

(A if A, A if B), (A if A, B if B), (B if A, A if B), and (B if A, B if B),

or in abbreviated form as

(AA, AB), (AA, BB), (BA, AB), and (BA, BB).

If each player chooses a complete plan for playing the game as its strategy, then we can determine the payoffs directly from this pair of chosen strategies via the payoff matrix in Figure 6.25.

Because the plans describe everything about how a player will behave, we have managed to describe this dynamic game in normal form: each player chooses a strategy (consisting of a complete plan) in advance, and from this joint choice of strategies we can determine payoffs. Later we will see that some important subtleties are involved in using this interpretation of the underlying dynamic game; in particular the translation from extensive to normal form sometimes does not preserve the full structure implicit in the game. But the translation is a useful tool for analysis, and the subtle lack of fidelity that can arise in the translation is in itself a revealing notion to develop and explore.

With this in mind, we first finish our simple example – where the translation works perfectly – and then move on to a second example where the complications begin to arise. For the normal-form payoff matrix corresponding to our first example, the payoff matrix has eight cells, while the extensive-form representation only has four terminal nodes with payoffs. This occurs because each terminal node can be reached with two different pairs of strategies, with each pair forming a cell of the payoff matrix. Both pairs of strategies dictate the same actions in the path of the game tree that actually occurs, but they describe different hypothetical actions in other unrealized paths. For example, the payoffs in the entries for (A, (AA, AB)) and for (A, (AA, BB)) are the same because both strategy combinations lead to the same terminal node. In both cases, Firm 2 chooses A in response to what Firm 1 actually does; Firm 2's plan for what to do in the event Firm 1 chose B is not realized by the actual play.

Now, using the normal-form representation, we can quickly see that, for Firm 1, strategy A is strictly dominant. Firm 2 does not have a strictly dominant strategy, but it should play a best response to Firm 1, which would be either (BA, AB) or (BA, BB). Notice that this prediction of play by Firm 1 and Firm 2 based on the normal-form representation is the same as our prediction based on direct analysis of the game tree, where we reasoned upward from the terminal nodes: Firm 1 will play A, and in response Firm 2 will play B.

A More Complex Example: The Market Entry Game. In our first dynamic game, reasoning based on the extensive- and normal-form representations led to essentially identical conclusions. As games get larger, extensive forms are representationally more streamlined than normal forms for dynamic games, but if this were the only distinction, it would be hard to argue that dynamic games truly add much to the overall theory of games. In fact, however, the dynamic aspect leads to new subtleties, which can be exposed by considering a case in which the translation from extensive to normal form ends up obscuring some of the structure that is implicit in the dynamic game.

To illustrate these subtleties we consider a second example of a dynamic game, also played between two competing firms. We call this the *Market Entry game*, and it's motivated by the following scenario. Consider a region where Firm 2 is currently the only serious participant in a given line of business, and Firm 1 is considering whether to enter the market.

- The first move in this game is made by Firm 1, which must decide whether to stay out of the market or to enter it.
- If Firm 1 chooses to stay out, then the game ends, with Firm 1 getting a payoff of 0 and Firm 2 keeping the payoff from the entire market.
- If Firm 1 chooses to enter, then the game continues to a second move by Firm 2, who must choose whether to cooperate and divide the market evenly with Firm 1 or retaliate and engage in a price war.
  - If Firm 2 cooperates, then each firm gets a payoff corresponding to half the market.
  - If Firm 2 retaliates, then each firm gets a negative payoff.

Choosing numerical payoffs to fill in this story, we can write the extensive-form representation of the Market Entry game as in Figure 6.26.

Subtle Distinctions Between Extensive- and Normal-Form Representations. Let's take the two ways we developed to analyze our previous dynamic game and apply them here. First, we can work our way up the game tree starting at the terminal nodes, as follows. If Firm 1 chooses to enter the market, then Firm 2 achieves a higher payoff by cooperating than by retaliating, so we should predict cooperation in the event the game reaches this point. Given this, when Firm 1 goes to make its first move, it can expect a

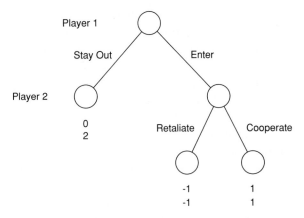

Figure 6.26. Extensive-form representation of the Market Entry game.

payoff of 0 by staying out, and a payoff of 1 by entering, so it should choose to enter the market. We can therefore predict that Firm 1 will enter the market, and then Firm 2 will cooperate.

Now let's consider the normal-form representation. Firm 1's possible plans for playing the game are just to choose Stay Out (S) or Enter (E). Firm 2's possible plans are to choose retaliation in the event of entry, or cooperation in the event of entry. We'll denote these two plans by R and C, respectively. This gives us the payoff matrix in Figure 6.27.

Here's the surprise: when we look at this game in normal form, we discover two distinct (pure-strategy) Nash equilibria: (E, C) and (S, R). The first corresponds to the prediction for play that we obtained by analyzing the extensive-form representation. What does the second one correspond to?

To answer this question, it helps to recall our view of the normal-form representation as capturing the idea that each player commits in advance to a computer program that will play the game in its place. Viewed this way, the equilibrium (S, R) corresponds to an outcome in which Firm 2 commits in advance to a computer program that will automatically retaliate in the event that Firm 1 enters the market. Firm 1, meanwhile, commits to a program that stays out of the market. Given this pair of choices, neither firm has an incentive to change the computer program they're using: for example, if Firm 1 were to switch to a program that entered the market, it would trigger retaliation by the program that Firm 2 is using.

This contrast between the prediction from the extensive and normal forms highlights some important points. First, it shows that the premise behind our translation from

		Firm 2	
		R	C
Firm 1	S	0, 2	0, 2
	E	−1, −1	1, 1

Figure 6.27. Normal form of the Market Entry game.

extensive to normal form – that each player commits ahead of time to a complete plan for playing the game – is not really equivalent to our initial premise in defining dynamic games – namely that each player makes an optimal decision at each intermediate point in the game, based on what has already happened up to that point. Firm 2's decision to retaliate on entry highlights this point clearly. If Firm 2 can truly precommit to this plan, then the equilibrium (S, R) makes sense, since Firm 1 will not want to provoke the retaliation that is encoded in Firm 2's plan. But if we take the dynamic game as originally defined in extensive form, then precommitment to a plan is not part of the model: rather, Firm 2 only gets to evaluate its decision to cooperate or retaliate once Firm 1 has already entered the market, and at that point its payoff is better if it cooperates. Given this, Firm 1 can predict that it is safe to enter.

In game theory, the standard model for dynamic games in extensive form assumes that players seek to maximize their payoff at any intermediate stage of play that can be reached in the game. In this interpretation, there is a unique prediction for play in the Market Entry game, corresponding to the equilibrium (E, C) in normal form. However, the issues surrounding the other equilibrium, (S, R), are not simply notational or representational; they are deeper. For any given scenario, it is really a question of what we believe is being modeled by the underlying dynamic game in extensive form. It is a question of whether we are in a setting in which a player can irrevocably precommit to a certain plan, to the extent that other players will believe the commitment as a credible threat – or not.

Further, the Market Entry game shows how the ability to commit to a particular course of action – when possible – can in fact be a valuable thing for an individual player, even if that course of action would be bad for everyone if it were actually carried out. In particular, if Firm 2 could make Firm 1 believe that it really would retaliate in the event of entry, then Firm 1 would choose to stay out, resulting in a higher payoff for Firm 2. In practice, this suggests particular courses of action that Firm 2 could take before the game even starts. For example, suppose that before Firm 1 had decided whether to enter the market, Firm 2 were to publically advertise an offer to beat any competitor's price by 10%. This would be a safe thing to do as long as Firm 2 is the only serious participant in the market, but it becomes dangerous to both firms if Firm 1 actually enters. The fact that the plan has been publicly announced means that it would be very costly (reputationally, and possibly legally) for Firm 2 to back away from it. In this way, the announcement can serve as a way of switching the underlying model from one in which Firm 2's threat to retaliate is not credible to one in which Firm 2 can actually precommit to a plan for retaliation.

Relationship to Weakly Dominated Strategies. In discussing these distinctions, it is also interesting to note the role played here by weakly dominated strategies. Notice that in the normal-form representation in Figure 6.27, the strategy R for Firm 2 is weakly dominated, and for a simple reason: it yields the same payoff if Firm 1 chooses S (since then Firm 2 doesn't actually get to move), and it yields a lower payoff if Firm 1 chooses E. So our translation from extensive form to normal form for dynamic games provides another reason to be careful about predictions of play in a normal-form game that rely on weakly dominated strategies: if the structure actually arises from a dynamic game in extensive form, then information about the dynamic game that is lost in the translation to normal form could potentially be sufficient to eliminate such equilibria.

However, we can't simply fix up the translation by eliminating weakly dominated strategies. We saw earlier that iterated deletion of strictly dominated strategies can be done in any order: all orders yield the same final result. But this is not true for the iterated deletion of weakly dominated strategies. To see this, suppose we vary the Market Entry game slightly so that the payoff from the joint strategy (E, C) is (0, 0). (In this version, both firms know they will fail to gain a positive payoff even if Firm 2 cooperates on entry, although they still don't do as badly as when Firm 2 retaliates.) Strategy R is a weakly dominated strategy as before, but now so is E. (E and S produce the same payoff for Firm 1 when Firm 2 chooses C, and S produces a strictly higher payoff when Firm 2 chooses R.)

In this version of the game, there are now three (pure-strategy) Nash equilibria: (S, C), (E, C), and (S, R). If we first eliminate the weakly dominated strategy R, then we are left with (S, C) and (E, C) as equilibria. Alternately, if we first eliminate the weakly dominated strategy E, then we are left with (S, C) and (S, R) as equilibria. In both cases, no further elimination of weakly dominated strategies is possible, so the order of deletion affects the final set of equilibria. We can ask which of these equilibria actually make sense as predictions of play in this game. If this normal form actually arose from the dynamic version of the Market Entry game, then C is still the only reasonable strategy for Firm 2, while Firm 1 could now play either S or E.

Final Comments. The style of analysis we developed for most of this chapter is based on games in normal form. One approach to analyzing dynamic games in extensive form is to first find all Nash equilibria of the translation to normal form, treating each as a candidate prediction of play in the dynamic game, and then to go back to the extensive-form version to see which make sense as actual predictions.

There is an alternate theory that works directly with the extensive-form representation. The simplest technique used in this theory is the style of analysis we employed to analyze an extensive-form representation from the terminal nodes upward. But the theory involves more complex components as well, allowing for richer structure such as the possibility that players at any given point have only partial information about the history of play up to that point. Although we will not go further into this theory here, it is developed in a number of books on game theory and microeconomic theory [263, 288, 336, 398].

6.11 Exercises

1. Say whether the following claim is true or false, and provide a brief (one- to three-sentence) explanation for your answer.

   Claim: If player A in a two-person game has a dominant strategy s_A, then there is a pure-strategy Nash equilibrium in which player A plays s_A and player B plays a best response to s_A.

2. Consider the following statement:

> In a Nash equilibrium of a two-player game, each player is playing an optimal strategy, so the two players' strategies are social-welfare maximizing.

Is this statement correct or incorrect? If you think it is correct, give a brief (one- to three-sentence) explanation why. If you think it is incorrect, give an example of a game discussed in Chapter 6 that shows it to be incorrect (you do not have to spell out all the details of the game, provided you make it clear what you are referring to), together with a brief (one- to three-sentence) explanation.

3. Find all pure-strategy Nash equilibria in the game that follows. In the payoff matrix of Figure 6.28, the rows correspond to player A's strategies and the columns correspond to player B's strategies. The first entry in each box is player A's payoff and the second entry is player B's payoff.

		Player B	
		L	R
Player A	U	1, 2	3, 2
	D	2, 4	0, 2

Figure 6.28. A two-player game for Exercise 3.

4. Consider the two-player game with players, strategies, and payoffs described in the game matrix of Figure 6.29.

		Player B		
		L	M	R
	t	0, 3	6, 2	1, 1
Player A	m	2, 3	0, 1	7, 0
	b	5, 3	4, 2	3, 1

Figure 6.29. A two-player game for Exercise 4.

(a) Does either player have a dominant strategy? Explain briefly (one to three sentences).

(b) Find all pure-strategy Nash equilibria for this game.

5. Consider the two-player game in Figure 6.30 in which each player has three strategies.

		Player B		
		L	M	R
	U	1, 1	2, 3	1, 6
Player A	M	3, 4	5, 5	2, 2
	D	1, 10	4, 7	0, 4

Figure 6.30. A two-player game for Exercise 5.

Find all the pure strategy Nash equilibria for this game.

6. In this question we consider several two-player games. In each payoff matrix that follows, the rows correspond to player A's strategies and the columns correspond to player B's strategies. The first entry in each box is player A's payoff and the second entry is player B's payoff.

   (a) Find all pure-strategy (nonrandomized) Nash equilibria for the game described in the payoff matrix of Figure 6.31:

   Player B

	L	R
U	2, 15	4, 20
D	6, 6	10, 8

   Player A U / D

   Figure 6.31. A two-player game for Exercise 6(a).

   (b) Find all pure-strategy Nash equilibria for the game described in the payoff matrix of Figure 6.32:

   Player B

	L	R
U	3, 5	4, 3
D	2, 1	1, 6

   Player A U / D

   Figure 6.32. A two-player game for Exercise 6(b).

   (c) Find *all* Nash equilibria for the game described in the payoff matrix of Figure 6.33:

   Player B

	L	R
U	1, 1	4, 2
D	3, 3	2, 2

   Player A U / D

   Figure 6.33. A two-player game for Exercise 6(c).

   [Hint: This game has both a pure-strategy equilibrium and a mixed-strategy equilibrium. To find the mixed-strategy equilibrium, let the probability that player A uses strategy U be p and the probability that player B uses strategy L be q. As we learned in our analysis of Matching Pennies, if a player uses a mixed strategy (one that is not really just some pure strategy played with probability 1) then the player must be indifferent between two pure strategies; that is, the strategies must have equal expected payoffs. So, for example, if p is not 0 or 1 then it must be the case that $q + 4(1 - q) = 3q + 2(1 - q)$ because these are the expected payoffs to player A from U and D when player B uses probability q.]

7. In this question we consider several two-player games. In each payoff matrix, the rows correspond to player A's strategies and the columns correspond to player B's

strategies. The first entry in each box is player A's payoff and the second entry is player B's payoff.

(a) Find all Nash equilibria for the game described in the payoff matrix of Figure 6.34:

Player B

		L	R
	U	1, 1	3, 2
Player A	D	0, 3	4, 4

Figure 6.34. A two-player game for Exercise 7(a).

(b) Find all Nash equilibria for the game described in the payoff matrix of Figure 6.35 (include an explanation for your answer):

Player B

		L	R
	U	5, 6	0, 10
Player A	D	4, 4	2, 2

Figure 6.35. A two-player game for Exercise 7(b).

[Hint: This game has a mixed-strategy equilibrium. To find the equilibrium, let the probability that player A uses strategy U be p and the probability that player B uses strategy L be q. As we learned in our analysis of Matching Pennies, if a player uses a mixed strategy (one that is not really just some pure strategy played with probability 1) then the player must be indifferent between two pure strategies; that is, the strategies must have equal expected payoffs. So, for example, if p is not 0 or 1 then it must be the case that $5q + 0(1 - q) = 4q + 2(1 - q)$ because these are the expected payoffs to player A from U and D when player B uses probability q.]

8. Consider the two-player game described in the payoff matrix of Figure 6.36:

Player B

		L	R
	U	1, 1	0, 0
Player A	D	0, 0	4, 4

Figure 6.36. A two-player game for Exercise 8.

(a) Find all pure-strategy Nash equilibria for this game.
(b) This game also has a mixed-strategy Nash equilibrium; find the probabilities the players use in this equilibrium, together with an explanation for your answer.
(c) Keeping in mind Schelling's focal point idea from this chapter, what equilibrium do you think is the best prediction of how the game will be played? Explain.

9. For each of the following two-player games, find all Nash equilibria. In each of the payoff matrices of Figures 6.37 and 6.38, the rows correspond to player A's strategies and the columns correspond to player B's strategies. The first entry in each box is player A's payoff and the second entry is player B's payoff.

(a)

Player B

		L	R
Player A	U	8, 4	5, 5
	D	3, 3	4, 8

Figure 6.37. A two-player game for Exercise 9(a).

(b)

Player B

		L	R
Player A	U	0, 0	−1, 1
	D	−1, 1	2, −2

Figure 6.38. A two-player game for Exercise 9(b).

10. In the payoff matrix of Figure 6.39, the rows correspond to player A's strategies and the columns correspond to player B's strategies. The first entry in each box is player A's payoff and the second entry is player B's payoff.

Player B

		L	R
Player A	U	3, 3	1, 2
	D	2, 1	3, 0

Figure 6.39. A two-player game for Exercise 10.

(a) Find all pure-strategy Nash equilibria of this game.
(b) Notice from the payoff matrix that Player A's payoff from the pair of strategies (U, L) is 3. Can you change player A's payoff from this pair of strategies to some nonnegative number in such a way that the resulting game has *no* pure-strategy Nash equilibrium? Give a brief (one- to three-sentence) explanation for your answer.

[Note that in answering this question you should only change Player A's payoff for this one pair of strategies (U, L). In particular, leave the rest of the structure of the game unchanged: the players, their strategies, the payoff from strategies other than (U, L), and B's payoff from (U, L).]

(c) Now let's go back to the original payoff matrix from part (a) and ask an analogous question about player B. So we're back to the payoff matrix in which players A and B each get a payoff of 3 from the pair of strategies (U, L).

Can you change player B's payoff from the pair of strategies (U, L) to some nonnegative number in such a way that the resulting game has *no* pure-strategy Nash equilibrium? Give a brief (one- to three-sentence) explanation for your answer.

[Again, in answering this question, you should only change Player B's payoff for this one pair of strategies (U, L). In particular, leave the rest of the structure of the game unchanged: the players, their strategies, the payoff from strategies other than (U, L), and A's payoff from (U, L).]

11. In the text we discussed dominant strategies and noted that if a player has a dominant strategy we would expect it to be used. The opposite of a dominant strategy is a strategy that is dominated. There are several possible notions of what it means for a strategy to be dominated. In this problem we focus on strict domination. The following is the definition of *strictly dominated*:

A strategy s_i^* is strictly dominated if player i has another strategy s_i' with the property that player i's payoff is strictly greater from s_i' than from s_i^* no matter what the other players in the game do.

We do not expect a player to use a strategy that is strictly dominated, and this can help in finding Nash equilibria. Here is an example of this idea. In the game with payoff matrix given by Figure 6.40, M is a strictly dominated strategy (it is strictly dominated by R), and player B will not use it:

Player B

		L	M	R
Player A	U	2, 4	2, 1	3, 2
	D	1, 2	3, 3	2, 4

Figure 6.40. A two-player game for Exercise 11.

Therefore, in analyzing the game we can delete M and look at the remaining game with payoff matrix given by Figure 6.41:

Player B

		L	R
Player A	U	2, 4	3, 2
	D	1, 2	2, 4

Figure 6.41. The game with strategy M deleted, for use in Exercise 11.

Now player A has a dominant strategy (U) and it is easy to see that the Nash equilibrium of the 2 × 2 game is (U, L). You can check the original game to see that (U, L) is a Nash equilibrium. Of course, using this procedure requires that we know that a strictly dominated strategy cannot be used in a Nash equilibrium.[5]

---

[5] This is actually true for any number of players. It would also help to know that if we iteratively remove strictly dominated strategies (in any order) and analyze the reduced games we still find the Nash equilibria of the original game. This is also true and it is discussed in the Advanced Material section of this chapter, Section 6.10.

Consider any two-player game that has at least one (pure-strategy) Nash equilibrium. Explain why the strategies used in an equilibrium of this game are not strictly dominated strategies.

12. In this chapter we discussed dominant strategies and noted that if a player has a dominant strategy we would expect it to be used. The opposite of a dominant strategy is a strategy that is dominated. There are several possible notions of what it means for a strategy to be dominated. In this problem we focus on weak domination.

    A strategy s_i^* is *weakly dominated* if player i has another strategy s_i' with the property that:

    - No matter what the other player does, player i's payoff from s_i' is at least as large as the payoff from s_i^*, and
    - Some strategy exists for the other player such that player i's payoff from s_i' is strictly greater than the payoff from s_i^*.

    (a) It seems unlikely that a player would use a weakly dominated strategy, but these strategies can occur in a Nash equilibrium. Find all pure-strategy (nonrandomized) Nash equilibria for the game with payoff matrix given by Figure 6.42. Do any of them use weakly dominated strategies?

		Player B	
		L	R
Player A	U	1, 1	1, 1
	D	0, 0	2, 1

Figure 6.42. A two-player game for Exercise 12.

    (b) One way to reason about weakly dominated strategies that you should have found in answering the preceding question is to consider the following sequential game. Suppose that the players actually move sequentially, but the player to move second does not know what the player moving first chose. Player A moves first and, if he chooses U, player B's choice does not matter. Effectively the game is over if A chooses U because no matter what B does the payoff is (1, 1). If player A chooses D, then player B's move matters, and the payoff is (0, 0) if B chooses L or (2, 1) if B chooses R. [Note that, because B does not observe A's move, the simultaneous-move game with the preceding payoff matrix is equivalent to this sequential-move game.]

    In this game, how would you expect the players to behave? Explain your reasoning. [The players are not allowed to change the game. They play it once just as it is given above. You may reason from the payoff matrix or the story behind the game, but if you use the story remember that B does not observe A's move until after the game is over.]

13. Here we consider a game with three players, named A, B, and C. To define the game we must specify the sets of strategies available to each player; also, when each of the three players chooses a strategy, a triple of strategies is given and we must specify the payoff each player receives from any possible triple of strategies played. Let's suppose that Player A's strategy set is {U, D}, Player B's strategy set is {L, R}, and Player C's strategy set is {l, r}.

One way to specify the payoffs would be to write down every possible triple of strategies and the payoffs for each. A different but equivalent way to interpret triples of strategies, which makes it easier to specify the payoffs, is to imagine that Player C chooses which of two distinct two-player games Players A and B will play. If Player C chooses *l* then the payoff matrix is given by Figure 6.43.

Player B

		L	R
Player A U		4, 4, 4	0, 0, 1
D		0, 2, 1	2, 1, 0

Figure 6.43. The two-player game between A and B if player C chooses l, for Exercise 13.

where the first entry in each cell is the payoff to Player A, the second entry is the payoff to Player B and the third entry is the payoff to Player C.

If Player C chooses *r* then the payoff matrix is given by Figure 6.44.

Player B

		L	R
Player A U		2, 0, 0	1, 1, 1
D		1, 1, 1	2, 2, 2

Figure 6.44. The two-player game between A and B if player C chooses r, for Exercise 13.

So, for example, if Player A chooses U, Player B chooses R, and player C chooses *r*, the payoffs are 1 for each player.

(a) First suppose the players all move simultaneously. That is, Players A and B do not observe which game Player C has selected until after they each choose a strategy. Find all of the (pure-strategy) Nash equilibria for this game.

(b) Now suppose that Player C gets to move first and that Players A and B observe Player C's move before they decide how to play. That is, if Player C chooses the strategy *r* then Players A and B play the game determined by C's choice of *r* and they both know that they are playing this game. Similarly, if Player C chooses strategy *l* then Players A and B play the game determined by C's choice of *l* and they both know that they are playing this game.

Let's also suppose that if Players A and B play the game determined by C's choice of *r*, they play a (pure-strategy) Nash equilibrium for that game; similarly, if Players A and B play the game determined by C's choice of *l* they play a (pure-strategy) Nash equilibrium for that game. Finally, let's suppose that Player C understands that this is how Players A and B will behave.

What do you expect Player C to do and why? What triple of strategies would you expect to see played? Is this list of strategies a Nash equilibrium of the simultaneous-move game between the three players?

14. Consider the two-player game with players, strategies, and payoffs described in the payoff matrix given in Figure 6.45.

Player 2

		L	R
Player 1	U	1, 1	4, 0
	D	4, 0	3, 3

Figure 6.45. A two-player game for Exercise 14.

(a) Find all of the Nash equilibria of this game.

(b) In the mixed strategy equilibrium you found in part (a), you should notice that Player 1 plays strategy U more often than strategy D. One of your friends remarks that your answer to part (a) must be wrong because clearly for Player 1 strategy D is a more attractive strategy than strategy U. Both U and D give Player 1 a payoff of 4 on the off-diagonal elements of the payoff matrix, but D gives Player 1 a payoff of 3 on the diagonal while U only gives Player 1 a payoff of 1 on the diagonal. Explain what is wrong with this reasoning.

15. Two identical firms – let's call them Firm 1 and Firm 2 – must decide simultaneously and independently whether to enter a new market and what product to produce if they do enter the market. Each firm, if it enters, can develop and produce either product A or product B. If both firms enter and produce product A they each lose ten million dollars. If both firms enter and both produce product B, they each make a profit of five million dollars. If both enter and one produces A while the other produces B, then they each make a profit of ten million dollars. Any firm that does not enter makes a profit of zero. Finally, if one firm does not enter and the other firm produces A it makes a profit of fifteen million dollars, while if the single entering firm produces B it makes a profit of thirty million dollars.

You are the manager of firm 1 and you have to choose a strategy for your firm.

(a) Set this situation up as a game with two players, Firms 1 and 2, and three strategies for each firm: produce A, produce B, or do not enter.

(b) One of your employees argues that you should enter the market (although he is not sure what product you should produce) because no matter what Firm 2 does, entering and producing product B is better than not entering. Evaluate this argument.

(c) Another employee agrees with the person in part (b) and argues that as strategy A could result in a loss (if the other firm also produces A) you should enter and produce B. If both firms reason this way, and thus enter and produce product B, will their play of the game form a Nash equilibrium? Explain.

(d) Find all the pure-strategy Nash equilibria of this game.

(e) Another employee of your firm suggests merging the two firms and deciding cooperatively on strategies so as to maximize the sum of profits. Ignoring whether this merger would be allowed by the regulators, do you think it's a good idea? Explain.

CHAPTER 7

Evolutionary Game Theory

In Chapter 6, we developed the basic ideas of game theory, in which individual players make decisions and the payoff to each player depends on the decisions made by all. As we saw there, a key question in game theory is to reason about the behavior we should expect to see when players take part in a given game.

The discussion in Chapter 6 was based on considering how players simultaneously reason about what the other players may do. In this chapter, on the other hand, we explore the notion of *evolutionary game theory*, which shows that the basic ideas of game theory can be applied even to situations in which no individual is overtly reasoning or even making explicit decisions. Instead, game-theoretic analysis will be applied here to settings in which individuals can exhibit different forms of behavior (including those that may not be the result of conscious choices), and we will consider which forms of behavior have the ability to persist in the population and which forms of behavior have a tendency to be driven out by others.

As its name suggests, evolutionary game theory has been applied most widely in the area of evolutionary biology, the domain in which the idea was first articulated by John Maynard Smith and G. R. Price [375, 376]. Evolutionary biology is based on the idea that an organism's genes largely determine its observable characteristics, and hence its fitness, in a given environment. Organisms that are more fit will tend to produce more offspring, causing genes that provide greater fitness to increase their representation in the population. In this way, fitter genes tend to win over time, because they provide higher rates of reproduction.

The key insight of evolutionary game theory is that many behaviors involve the *interaction* of multiple organisms in a population, and the success of any one of these organisms depends on how its behavior interacts with that of others. So the fitness of an individual organism can't be measured in isolation; rather it has to be evaluated in the context of the full population in which it lives. This approach opens the door to a natural game-theoretic analogy: an organism's genetically determined characteristics and behaviors are like its strategy in a game, its fitness is like its payoff, and this payoff depends on the strategies (characteristics) of the organisms with which it interacts.

189

Written this way, it is hard to tell in advance whether this analogy will turn out to be superficial or deep, but in fact the connections turn out to run very deeply: game-theoretic ideas like equilibrium turn out to be a useful way to make predictions about the results of evolution on a population.

7.1 Fitness as a Result of Interaction

To make this idea concrete, we now describe a first simple example of how game-theoretic ideas can be applied in evolutionary settings. This example is designed for ease of explanation rather than perfect fidelity to the underlying biology, but after this we will discuss instances in which the phenomena at the heart of this first example have been empirically observed in a variety of natural settings.

For the example, let's consider a particular species of beetle and suppose that each beetle's fitness in a given environment is determined largely by the extent to which it can find food and use the nutrients from the food effectively. Now, suppose a particular mutation is introduced into the population, causing beetles with the mutation to grow a significantly larger body size. Thus, we now have two distinct kinds of beetles in the population – small ones and large ones. It is actually difficult for the large beetles to maintain the metabolic requirements of their larger body size – it requires diverting more nutrients from the food they eat – and so this has a negative effect on fitness.

If this were the full story, we'd conclude that the large-body-size mutation is fitness-decreasing, and so it will likely be driven out of the population over time, through multiple generations. But in fact, there's more to the story, as we'll now see.

Interaction Among Organisms. The beetles in this population compete with each other for food; when they come upon a food source, there's crowding among the beetles as they each try to get as much of the food as they can. And, not surprisingly, the beetles with large body sizes are more effective at claiming an above-average share of the food.

Let's assume for simplicity that food competition in this population involves pairs of beetles interacting with each other at any given point in time. (This assumption makes the ideas easier to describe, but the principles we develop can also be applied to interactions that occur simultaneously among many individuals.) When two beetles compete for some food, we have the following possible outcomes:

- When beetles of the same size compete, they get equal shares of the food.
- When a large beetle competes with a small beetle, the large beetle gets the majority of the food.
- In all cases, large beetles experience less of a fitness benefit from a given quantity of food, since some of it is diverted into maintaining their expensive metabolism.

Thus, the fitness that each beetle gets from a given food-related interaction can be thought of as a numerical payoff in a two-player game between a first beetle and a second beetle, as follows. The first beetle plays one of the two strategies *Small* or *Large*, depending on its body size, and the second beetle plays one of these two strategies

Beetle 2

		Small	Large
Beetle 1	Small	5, 5	1, 8
	Large	8, 1	3, 3

Figure 7.1. The body-size game.

as well. Based on the two strategies used, the payoffs to the beetles are described by Figure 7.1.

Notice how the numerical payoffs satisfy the principles just outlined: when two small beetles meet, they share the fitness from the food source equally; large beetles do well at the expense of small beetles; but large beetles cannot extract the full amount of fitness from the food source. (In this payoff matrix, the reduced fitness when two large beetles meet is particularly pronounced, since a large beetle has to expend extra energy in competing with another large beetle.)

This payoff matrix is a nice way to summarize what happens when two beetles meet, but compared with the game in Chapter 6, there is something fundamentally different in what's being described here. The beetles in this game aren't asking themselves, "What do I want my body size to be in this interaction?" Rather, each is genetically hard-wired to play one of these two strategies through its whole lifetime. Given this important difference, the idea of choosing strategies – which was central to our formulation of game theory – is missing from the biological side of the analogy. As a result, in place of the idea of Nash equilibrium – which was based fundamentally on the relative benefit of changing one's own personal strategy – we will need to think about strategy changes that operate over longer time scales, taking place as shifts in a population under evolutionary forces. We develop the fundamental definitions for this in the next section.

7.2 Evolutionarily Stable Strategies

In Chapter 6, the notion of Nash equilibrium was central in reasoning about the outcome of a game. In a Nash equilibrium for a two-player game, neither player has an incentive to deviate from the strategy they are currently using; the equilibrium is a choice of strategies that tends to persist once the players are using it. The analogous notion for evolutionary settings is that of an *evolutionarily stable strategy* – a genetically determined strategy that tends to persist once it is prevalent in a population.

We formulate this notion as follows. Suppose, in our example, that each beetle is repeatedly paired off with other beetles in food competitions over the course of its lifetime. We assume the population is large enough that no two particular beetles have a significant probability of interacting with each other repeatedly. A beetle's overall fitness will be equal to the average fitness it experiences from each of its many pairwise interactions with others, and this overall fitness determines its reproductive success – the number of offspring that carry its genes (and hence its strategy) into the next generation.

In this setting, we say that a given strategy is *evolutionarily stable* if, when the whole population is using this strategy, any small group of invaders using a different strategy will eventually die off over multiple generations. (We can think of these invaders either as migrants who move to join the population, or as mutants who were born with the new behavior directly into the population.) We capture this idea in terms of numerical payoffs by saying that, when the whole population is using a strategy S, then a small group of invaders using any alternate strategy T should have strictly lower fitness than the users of the majority strategy S. Since fitness translates into reproductive success, evolutionary principles posit that strictly lower fitness is the condition that causes a subpopulation (like the users of strategy T) to shrink over time, through multiple generations, and eventually die off with high probability.

More formally, we phrase the basic definitions as follows:

- The *fitness* of an organism in a population is the expected payoff it receives from an interaction with a random member of the population.
- A strategy T *invades* a strategy S at level x, for some small positive number x, if an x fraction of the underlying population uses T and a $1 - x$ fraction of the underlying population uses S.
- Finally, a strategy S is *evolutionarily stable* if there is a (small) positive number y such that, when any other strategy T invades S at any level $x < y$, the fitness of an organism playing S is strictly greater than the fitness of an organism playing T.

Evolutionarily Stable Strategies in the First Example. Let's see what happens when we apply this definition to our example involving beetles competing for food. We first check whether the strategy Small is evolutionarily stable, and then we do the same for the strategy Large.

Following the definition, let's suppose that, for some small positive number x, a $1 - x$ fraction of the population uses Small and an x fraction of the population uses Large. (This is what the picture would look like just after a small invader population of large beetles arrives.)

- What is the expected payoff to a small beetle in a random interaction in this population? With probability $1 - x$, it meets another small beetle, receiving a payoff of 5, while with probability x, it meets a large beetle, receiving a payoff of 1. Therefore, its expected payoff is

$$5(1 - x) + 1x = 5 - 4x.$$

- What is the expected payoff to a large beetle in a random interaction in this population? With probability $1 - x$, it meets a small beetle, receiving a payoff of 8, while with probability x, it meets another large beetle, receiving a payoff of 3. Therefore, its expected payoff is

$$8(1 - x) + 3x = 8 - 5x.$$

It's easy to check that, for small enough values of x (and even for reasonably large ones in this case), the expected fitness of large beetles in this population exceeds the expected fitness of small beetles. Therefore, Small is not evolutionarily stable.

Now let's check whether Large is evolutionarily stable. For this, we suppose that, for some very small positive number x, a $1 - x$ fraction of the population uses Large and an x fraction of the population uses Small.

- What is the expected payoff to a large beetle in a random interaction in this population? With probability $1 - x$, it meets another large beetle, receiving a payoff of 3, while with probability x, it meets a small beetle, receiving a payoff of 8. Therefore, its expected payoff is

$$3(1 - x) + 8x = 3 + 5x.$$

- What is the expected payoff to a small beetle in a random interaction in this population? With probability $1 - x$, it meets a large beetle, receiving a payoff of 1, while with probability x, it meets another small beetle, receiving a payoff of 5. Therefore, its expected payoff is

$$(1 - x) + 5x = 1 + 4x.$$

In this case, the expected fitness of large beetles in this population exceeds the expected fitness of small beetles, and so Large is evolutionarily stable.

Interpreting the Evolutionarily Stable Strategy in the Body-Size Game. Intuitively, this analysis can be summarized by saying that if a few large beetles are introduced into a population consisting of small beetles, then the large beetles do extremely well; since they rarely meet each other, they get most of the food in almost every competition they experience. As a result, the population of small beetles cannot drive out the large ones, and so Small is not evolutionarily stable.

On the other hand, in a population of large beetles, a few small beetles will do very badly, losing almost every competition for food. As a result, the population of large beetles resists the invasion of small beetles, and so Large is evolutionarily stable.

Therefore, if we know that the large-body-size mutation is possible, we should expect to see populations of large beetles in the wild, rather than populations of small ones. In this way, our notion of evolutionary stability has predicted a strategy for the population – as we predicted outcomes for games among rational players in Chapter 6, but by different means.

What's striking about this particular predicted outcome, though, is the fact that the fitness of each organism in a population of small beetles is 5, which is larger than the fitness of each organism in a population of large beetles. In fact, the game between small and large beetles has precisely the structure of a Prisoner's Dilemma game; the motivating scenario based on competition for food makes it clear that the beetles are engaged in an arms race, like the game from Chapter 6 in which two competing athletes must decide whether to use performance-enhancing drugs. In that earlier game from Chapter 6, it was a dominant strategy to use drugs, even though both athletes understand that they are better off in an outcome where neither of them uses drugs – it's simply that this mutually better joint outcome is not sustainable. In the present case, the beetles individually don't understand anything, nor could they change their body sizes even if they wanted to. Nevertheless, evolutionary forces over multiple generations are achieving a completely analogous effect, as the large beetles benefit at the expense of the small ones. Later in this chapter, we will see that this similarity in the conclusions of two different styles of analysis is in fact part of a broader principle.

Here is a different way to summarize the striking feature of our example: Starting from a population of small beetles, evolution by natural selection is causing the fitness of the organisms to decrease over time. This may seem troubling initially, since we think of natural selection as being fitness-increasing. But in fact, it's not hard to reconcile what's happening with this general principle of natural selection. Natural selection increases the fitness of individual organisms in a fixed environment; if the environment changes to become more hostile to the organisms, then clearly this could cause their fitness to go down. This is what is happening to the population of beetles. Each beetle's environment includes all the other beetles, since these other beetles determine its success in food competitions; therefore, the increasing fraction of large beetles can be viewed, in a sense, as a shift to an environment that is more hostile for everyone.

Empirical Evidence for Evolutionary Arms Races. Biologists have offered recent evidence for the presence of evolutionary games in nature with the Prisoner's Dilemma structure we've just seen. It is very difficult to truly determine payoffs in any real-world setting, and so all of these studies are the subject of ongoing investigation and debate. For our purposes in this discussion, they are perhaps most usefully phrased as deliberately streamlined examples, illustrating how game-theoretic reasoning can help provide qualitative insight into different forms of biological interaction.

It has been argued that the heights of trees can obey Prisoner's Dilemma payoffs [156, 226]. If two neighboring trees both grow short, then they share the sunlight equally. They also share the sunlight equally if they both grow tall, but in this case their payoffs are each lower because they have to invest a lot of resources in achieving the additional height. The trouble is that if one tree is short while its neighbor is tall, then the tall tree gets most of the sunlight. As a result, we can easily end up with payoffs just like the body-size game among beetles, with the trees' evolutionary strategies Short and Tall serving as analogues to the beetles' strategies Small and Large. Of course, the real situation is more complex, since genetic variation among trees can lead to a wide range of different heights, and hence a range of different strategies (rather than just two strategies labeled Short and Tall). Within this continuum, Prisoner's Dilemma payoffs can only apply to a certain range of tree heights: there is some height beyond which further height-increasing mutations no longer provide the same payoff structure, because the additional sunlight is more than offset by the fitness downside of sustaining an enormous height.

Similar kinds of competition take place in the root systems of plants [181]. Suppose you grow two soybean plants at opposite ends of a large pot of soil; then their root systems will each fill out the available soil and intermingle with each other as they try to claim as many resources as they can. In doing so, they divide the resources in the soil equally. Now, suppose that instead you partition the same quantity of soil using a wall down the middle, so that the two plants are on opposite sides of the wall. Then each still gets half the resources present in the soil, but each invests less of its energy in producing roots and consequently has greater reproductive success through seed production.

Virus 2

		Φ6	ΦH2
Virus 1	Φ6	1.00, 1.00	0.65, 1.99
	ΦH2	1.99, 0.65	0.83, 0.83

Figure 7.2. The virus game.

This observation has implications for the following simplified evolutionary game involving root systems. Imagine that instead of a wall, we have two kinds of root-development strategies available to soybean plants: Conserve, in which a plant's roots only grow into its own share of the soil, and Explore, in which the roots grow everywhere they can reach. Then we again have the scenario and payoffs from the body-size game, with the same conclusion: all plants are better off in a population where everyone plays Conserve, but only Explore is evolutionarily stable.

As a third example, there was recent excitement over the discovery that virus populations can also play an evolutionary version of the Prisoner's Dilemma [326, 392, 393]. Turner and Chao studied a virus called Phage Φ6, which infects cells and manufactures products needed for its own replication. A mutational variant of this virus called Phage ΦH2 is also able to replicate in bacterial hosts, though less effectively on its own. However, ΦH2 is able to take advantage of chemical products produced by Φ6, which gives ΦH2 a fitness advantage when it is in the presence of Φ6. This turns out to yield the structure of the Prisoner's Dilemma: viruses have the two evolutionary strategies Φ6 and ΦH2; in a pure Φ6 population, all viruses are doing better than they would be in a pure ΦH2 population; and regardless of what the other viruses are doing, you (as a virus) are better off playing ΦH2. Thus, only ΦH2 is evolutionarily stable.

The virus system under study was so simple that Turner and Chao were able to infer an actual payoff matrix based on measuring the relative rates at which the two viral variants were able to replicate under different conditions. Using an estimation procedure derived from these measurements, they obtained the payoffs in Figure 7.2. The payoffs are re-scaled so that the payoffs in upper-left box are (1.00, 1.00).[1]

Whereas our earlier examples had an underlying story very much like the use of performance-enhancing drugs, this game among phages is actually reminiscent of a different story that also motivates the Prisoner's Dilemma payoff structure: the scenario behind the exam-or-presentation game with which we began Chapter 6. There, two college students would both be better off if they jointly prepared for a presentation, but the payoffs led them to each think selfishly and study for an exam instead. What the virus game shows here is that shirking a shared responsibility isn't just something that rational decision makers do; evolutionary forces can induce viruses to play this strategy as well.

---

[1] It should be noted that even in a system this simple, there are many other biological factors at work, and hence this payoff matrix is still just an approximation to the performance of Φ6 and ΦH2 populations under real experimental and natural conditions. Other factors appear to affect these populations, including the density of the population and the potential presence of additional mutant forms of the virus [393].

Organism 2

		S	T
	S	a, a	b, c
Organism 1			
	T	c, b	d, d

Figure 7.3. General symmetric game.

7.3 A General Description of Evolutionarily Stable Strategies

The connections between evolutionary games and games played by rational participants are suggestive enough that it makes sense to understand how the relationship works in general. We will focus here, as we have thus far, on two-player, two-strategy games. We will also restrict our attention to symmetric games, as in the previous sections of this chapter, in which the roles of the two players are interchangeable.

The payoff matrix for a completely general two-player, two-strategy game that is symmetric can be written as in Figure 7.3.

Let's check how to write the condition that S is evolutionarily stable in terms of the four variables a, b, c, and d. As before, we start by supposing that, for some very small positive number x, a $1 - x$ fraction of the population uses S and an x fraction of the population uses T.

- What is the expected payoff to an organism playing S in a random interaction in this population? With probability $1 - x$ it meets another player of S, receiving a payoff of a, while with probability x, it meets a player of T, receiving a payoff of b. Therefore, its expected payoff is

$$a(1 - x) + bx.$$

- What is the expected payoff to an organism playing T in a random interaction in this population? With probability $1 - x$ it meets a player of S, receiving a payoff of c, while with probability x it meets another player of T, receiving a payoff of d. Therefore, its expected payoff is

$$c(1 - x) + dx.$$

Therefore, S is evolutionarily stable if, for all sufficiently small values of $x > 0$, the inequality

$$a(1 - x) + bx > c(1 - x) + dx$$

holds. As x goes to 0, the left-hand side becomes a and the right-hand side becomes c. Hence, if $a > c$, then the left-hand side is larger once x is sufficiently small, while if $a < c$ then the left-hand side is smaller once x is sufficiently small. Finally, if $a = c$, then the left-hand side is larger precisely when $b > d$. Therefore, we have a simple way to express the condition that S is evolutionarily stable:

In a two-player, two-strategy, symmetric game, S is evolutionarily stable precisely when either (i) $a > c$ or (ii) $a = c$ and $b > d$.

Hunter 2

		Hunt Stag	Hunt Hare
Hunter 1	Hunt Stag	4, 4	0, 3
	Hunt Hare	3, 0	3, 3

Figure 7.4. Stag Hunt game.

It is easy to see the intuition behind our calculations that translates into this condition, as follows.

- First, for S to be evolutionarily stable, the payoff of using strategy S against S must be at least as large as the payoff of using strategy T against S. Otherwise, an invader who uses T would have a higher fitness than the rest of population, and the fraction of the population who are invaders would grow over time.
- Second, if S and T are equally good responses to S, then for S to be evolutionarily stable, players of S must do better in their interactions with T than players of T do with each other. Otherwise, players of T would do as well against the S part of the population as players of S, and at least as well against the T part of the population, so their overall fitness would be at least as high as the fitness of players of S.

7.4 Relationship between Evolutionary and Nash Equilibria

Using our general way of characterizing evolutionarily stable strategies, we can now understand how they relate to Nash equilibria. If we go back to the general symmetric game from the previous section, we can write down the condition for (S, S) (i.e., the choice of S by both players) to be a Nash equilibrium: (S, S) is a Nash equilibrium when S is a best response to the choice of S by the other player. This translates into the simple condition

$$a \geq c.$$

If we compare this to the conditions for S to be evolutionarily stable,

$$\text{(i) } a > c \text{ or (ii) } a = c \text{ and } b > d,$$

we immediately get the following conclusion:

If strategy S is evolutionarily stable, then (S, S) is a Nash equilibrium.

We can also see that the other direction does not hold: it is possible to have a game where (S, S) is a Nash equilibrium, but S is not evolutionarily stable. The difference in the respective conditions for evolutionary stability and Nash equilibrium tells us how to construct such a game: we should have $a = c$ and $b < d$.

To get a sense for where such a game might come from, let's recall the Stag Hunt game from Chapter 6. In this game each player can hunt stag or hunt hare; hunting hare successfully just requires your own effort, whereas hunting the more valuable stag requires that you both do so. This produces payoffs as shown in Figure 7.4.

Hunter 2

		Hunt Stag	Hunt Hare
Hunter 1	Hunt Stag	4, 4	0, 4
	Hunt Hare	4, 0	3, 3

Figure 7.5. Stag hunt: a version with added benefit from hunting hare alone.

In this game, as written, Hunt Stag and Hunt Hare are both evolutionarily stable, which we can check from the conditions on a, b, c, and d. (To check the condition for Hunt Hare, we simply interchange the rows and columns of the payoff matrix, to put Hunt Hare in the first row and first column.)

However, suppose we make up a modification of the Stag Hunt game by shifting the payoffs as follows. In this new version, when the players miscoordinate, so that one hunts stag while the other hunts hare, then the hare hunter gets an extra benefit due to the lack of competition for hare. In this way, we get a payoff matrix as in Figure 7.5.

In this case, the choice of strategies (Hunt Stag, Hunt Stag) is still a Nash equilibrium: if each player expects the other to hunt stag, then hunting stag is a best response. But Hunt Stag is not an evolutionarily stable strategy for this version of the game, because (in the notation from our general symmetric game) we have $a = c$ and $b < d$. Informally, the problem is that a hare hunter and a stag hunter do equally well when each is paired with a stag hunter; but hare hunters do better than stag hunters when each is paired with a hare hunter.

There is also a relationship between evolutionarily stable strategies and the concept of a *strict Nash equilibrium*. We say that a choice of strategies is a strict Nash equilibrium if each player is using the unique best response to what the other player is doing. We can check that, for symmetric two-player, two-strategy games, the condition for (S, S) to be a strict Nash equilibrium is that $a > c$. So we see that in fact these different notions of equilibrium naturally *refine* each other. The concept of an evolutionarily stable strategy can be viewed as a refinement of the concept of a Nash equilibrium: the set of evolutionarily stable strategies S is a subset of the set of strategies S for which (S, S) is a Nash equilibrium. Similarly, the concept of a strict Nash equilibrium (when the players use the same strategy) is a refinement of evolutionary stability: if (S, S) is a strict Nash equilibrium, then S is evolutionarily stable.

It is intriguing that, despite the extremely close similarities between the conclusions of evolutionary stability and Nash equilibrium, they are built on very different underlying stories. In a Nash equilibrium, we consider players choosing mutual best responses to each other's strategy. This equilibrium concept places great demands on the ability of the players to choose optimally and to coordinate on strategies that are best responses to each other. Evolutionary stability, on the other hand, supposes no intelligence or coordination on the part of the players. Instead, strategies are viewed as being hard-wired into the players, perhaps because their behavior is encoded in their genes. According to this concept, strategies that are more successful in producing offspring are selected for.

Although this evolutionary approach to analyzing games originated in biology, it can be applied in many other contexts. For example, suppose people belonging to a large group are being matched repeatedly over time to play the general symmetric

Animal 2

		D	H
Animal 1	D	3, 3	1, 5
	H	5, 1	0, 0

Figure 7.6. Hawk–Dove game.

game from Figure 7.3. Now the payoffs should be interpreted as reflecting the welfare of the players and not their number of offspring. If any player can look back at how others have played and can observe their payoffs, then imitation of the strategies that have been most successful may induce an evolutionary dynamic. Alternatively, if a player can observe his own past successes and failures then his learning may induce an evolutionary dynamic. In either case, strategies that have done relatively well in the past will tend to be used by more people in the future. This approach can lead to the same behavior that underlies the concept of evolutionarily stable strategies, and hence can promote the play of such strategies.

7.5 Evolutionarily Stable Mixed Strategies

As a further step in developing an evolutionary theory of games, we now consider how to handle cases in which no strategy is evolutionarily stable.

In fact, it is not hard to see how this can happen, even in two-player games that have pure-strategy Nash equilibria.[2] Perhaps the most natural example is the Hawk–Dove game from Chapter 6, and we use this to introduce the basic ideas of this section. Recall that in the Hawk–Dove game, two animals compete for a piece of food; an animal that plays the strategy Hawk (H) behaves aggressively, while an animal that plays the strategy Dove (D) behaves passively. If one animal is aggressive while the other is passive, then the aggressive animal benefits by getting most of the food, but if both animals are aggressive, then they risk destroying the food and injuring each other. This type of interaction to the payoff matrix shown in Figure 7.6.

In Chapter 6, we considered this game in contexts where the two players were making choices about how to behave. Now let's consider the same game in a setting where each animal is genetically hard-wired to play a particular strategy. How does it look from this perspective, when we consider evolutionary stability?

Neither D nor H is a best response to itself, and so using the general principles from the last two sections, we see that neither is evolutionarily stable. Intuitively, a hawk does very well in a population consisting of doves; but in a population of all hawks, a dove actually has an advantage by staying out of the way while the hawks fight with each other.

As a two-player game in which players are actually choosing strategies, the Hawk–Dove game has two pure Nash equilibria: (D, H) and (H, D). But this doesn't directly help us identify an evolutionarily stable strategy, since thus far our definition of

---

[2] Recall that a player is using a *pure strategy* if she always plays a particular one of the strategies in the game, as opposed to a *mixed strategy*, in which she chooses at random from among several possible strategies.

evolutionary stability has been restricted to populations in which (almost) all members play the same pure strategy. To reason about what happens in the Hawk–Dove game under evolutionary forces, we need to generalize the notion of evolutionary stability by allowing some notion of "mixing" between strategies.

Defining Mixed Strategies in Evolutionary Game Theory. There are at least two natural ways to introduce the idea of mixing into the evolutionary framework. First, it could be that each individual is hard-wired to play a pure strategy, but some portion of the population plays one strategy while the rest of the population plays another. If the fitness of individuals in each part of the population is the same, and if invaders eventually die off, this situation could be considered to exhibit a kind of evolutionary stability. Second, it could be that each individual is hard-wired to play a particular mixed strategy; that is, they are genetically configured to choose randomly from among certain options with certain probabilities. If invaders using any other mixed strategy eventually die off, then this too could be considered a kind of evolutionary stability. We will see that for our purposes, these two concepts are actually equivalent to each other, and we will focus initially on the second idea, in which individuals use mixed strategies. Essentially, we will find that in situations like the Hawk–Dove game, the individuals or the population as a whole must display a mixture of the two behaviors in order to have any chance of being stable against invasion by other forms of behavior.

The definition of an evolutionarily stable mixed strategy is in fact completely parallel to the definition of evolutionary stability we have seen thus far – we are simply greatly enlarging the set of possible strategies so that each strategy corresponds to a particular randomized choice over pure strategies.

Specifically, let's consider the general symmetric game from Figure 7.3. A mixed strategy here corresponds to a probability p between 0 and 1, indicating that the organism plays S with probability p and plays T with probability $1 - p$. As in our discussion of mixed strategies from Chapter 6, this includes the possibility of playing the pure strategies S or T by simply setting $p = 1$ or $p = 0$. When Organism 1 uses the mixed strategy p and Organism 2 uses the mixed strategy q, the expected payoff to Organism 1 can be computed as follows. There is a probability pq of an (X, X) pairing, yielding a for the first player; a probability $p(1 - q)$ of an (X, Y) pairing, yielding b for the first player; a probability $(1 - p)q$ of a (Y, X) pairing, yielding c for the first player; and a probability $(1 - p)(1 - q)$ of a (Y, Y) pairing, yielding d for the first player. So the expected payoff for this first player is

$$V(p, q) = pqa + p(1 - q)b + (1 - p)qc + (1 - p)(1 - q)d.$$

As before, the *fitness* of an organism is its expected payoff in an interaction with a random member of the population. We can now give the precise definition of an evolutionarily stable mixed strategy.

> In the general symmetric game, p is an evolutionarily stable mixed strategy if there is a (small) positive number y such that, when any other mixed strategy q invades p at any level $x < y$, the fitness of an organism playing p is strictly greater than the fitness of an organism playing q.

This definition is just like our previous formulation of evolutionarily stable (pure) strategies, except that we allow the strategy to be mixed *and* we allow the invaders to use a mixed strategy. An evolutionarily stable mixed strategy with $p = 1$ or $p = 0$ is evolutionarily stable under our original definition for pure strategies as well. However, note the subtle point that even if S were an evolutionarily stable strategy under our previous definition, it is not necessarily an evolutionarily stable mixed strategy under this new definition with $p = 1$. The problem is that it is possible to construct games in which no pure strategy can successfully invade a population playing S, but a mixed strategy can. As a result, it is important to be clear in any discussion of evolutionary stability on what kinds of behavior an invader can employ.

Directly from the definition, we can write the condition for p to be an evolutionarily stable mixed strategy as follows. For some y and any $x < y$, the following inequality must hold for all mixed strategies $q \neq p$:

$$(1 - x)V(p, p) + xV(p, q) > (1 - x)V(q, p) + xV(q, q). \qquad (7.1)$$

This inequality also makes it clear that there is a relationship between mixed Nash equilibria and evolutionarily stable mixed strategies, and this relationship parallels the one we saw earlier for pure strategies. In particular, if p is an evolutionarily stable mixed strategy, then we must have $V(p, p) \geq V(q, p)$, and so p is a best response to p. As a result, the pair of strategies (p, p) is a mixed Nash equilibrium. However, because of the strict inequality in Equation (7.1), it is possible for (p, p) to be a mixed Nash equilibrium without p being evolutionarily stable. So again, evolutionary stability serves as a refinement of the concept of mixed Nash equilibrium.

Evolutionarily Stable Mixed Strategies in the Hawk–Dove Game. Now let's see how to apply these ideas to the Hawk–Dove game. First, since any evolutionarily stable mixed strategy must correspond to a mixed Nash equilibrium of the game, we have a way to search for possible evolutionarily stable strategies: we first work out the mixed Nash equilibria for the Hawk–Dove game, and then we check if they are evolutionarily stable.

As we saw in Chapter 6, in order for (p, p) to be a mixed Nash equilibrium, it must make the two players indifferent between their two pure strategies. When the other player is using the strategy p (as the probability of playing Dove), the expected payoff from playing D is $3p + (1 - p) = 1 + 2p$, while the expected payoff from playing H is $5p$. Setting these two quantities equal (to capture the indifference between the two strategies), we get $p = 1/3$. Therefore, $(1/3, 1/3)$ is a mixed Nash equilibrium. In this case, both pure strategies, as well as any mixture between them, produce an expected payoff of $5/3$ when played against the strategy $p = 1/3$.

To see whether $p = 1/3$ is evolutionarily stable, we must check Inequality (7.1) when some other mixed strategy q invades at a small level x. Here is a first observation that makes evaluating this inequality a bit easier. Since (p, p) is a mixed Nash equilibrium that uses both pure strategies, we have just argued that all mixed strategies q have the same payoff when played against p. As a result, we have $V(p, p) = V(q, p)$ for all q. Subtracting these terms from the left and right of Inequality (7.1), and then dividing by x, we get the following inequality to check:

$$V(p, q) > V(q, q). \tag{7.2}$$

The point is that because (p, p) is a mixed equilibrium, the strategy p can't be a strict best response to itself – all other mixed strategies are just as good against it. Therefore, for p to be evolutionarily stable, it must be a strictly better response to every other mixed strategy q than q is to itself; that is what causes it to have higher fitness when q invades.

In fact, it is true that $V(p, q) > V(q, q)$ for all mixed strategies $q \neq p$, and we can check this as follows. Using the fact that $p = 1/3$, we have

$$V(p, q) = 1/3 \times q \times 3 + 1/3(1 - q) \times 1 + 2/3 \times q \times 5 = 4q + 1/3$$

while

$$V(q, q) = q^2 \times 3 + q(1 - q) \times 1 + (1 - q) \times q \times 5 = 6q - 3q^2.$$

Now we have

$$V(p, q) - V(q, q) = 3q^2 - 2q + 1/3 = \frac{1}{3}(9q^2 - 6q + 1) = \frac{1}{3}(3q - 1)^2.$$

This last way of writing $V(p, q) - V(q, q)$ shows that it is a perfect square, and so it is positive whenever $q \neq 1/3$. This observation is just what we want for showing that $V(p, q) > V(q, q)$ whenever $q \neq p$, and so it follows that p is indeed an evolutionarily stable mixed strategy.

Interpretations of Evolutionarily Stable Mixed Strategies. The kind of mixed equilibrium that we see here in the Hawk–Dove game is typical of biological situations in which organisms must break the symmetry between two distinct behaviors, when consistently adopting just one of these behaviors is evolutionarily unsustainable.

We can interpret the result of this example in two possible ways. First, all participants in the population may actually be mixing over the two possible pure strategies with the given probability. In this case, all members of the population are genetically the same, but whenever two of them are matched up to play, any combination of D and H could potentially be played. We know the empirical frequency with which any pair of strategies will be played, but not what any two animals will actually do. A second interpretation is that the mixture is taking place at the population level: it could be that 1/3 of the animals are hard-wired to always play D, and 2/3 are hard-wired to always play H. In this case, no individual is actually mixing, but as long as it is not possible to tell in advance which animal will play D and which will play H, the interaction of two randomly selected animals results in the same frequency of outcomes that we see when each animal is actually mixing. Notice also that in this case the fitnesses of both kinds of animals are the same, because both D and H are best responses to the mixed strategy $p = 1/3$. Thus, these two different interpretations of the evolutionarily stable mixed strategy lead to the same calculations and the same observed behavior in the population.

This type of mixing between pure strategies has been discussed in a number of other settings in biology. A common scenario is that there is an undesirable, fitness-lowering role in a population of organisms, but if some organisms don't choose to play this

Virus 2

		Φ6	ΦH2
Virus 1	Φ6	1.00, 1.00	0.65, 1.99
	ΦH2	1.99, 0.65	0.50, 0.50

Figure 7.7. The virus game: hypothetical payoffs with stronger fitness penalties to ΦH2.

role, then everyone suffers considerably. For example, let's think back to the virus game in Figure 7.2 and suppose (purely hypothetically, for the sake of this example) that the payoff when both viruses use the strategy ΦH2 was (0.50, 0.50), as shown in Figure 7.7.

In this event, rather than having a Prisoner's Dilemma type of payoff structure, we'd have a Hawk–Dove payoff structure: having both viruses play ΦH2 is sufficiently bad that one of them needs to play the role of Φ6. The two pure equilibria of the resulting two-player game – viewed as a game among rational players, rather than a biological interaction – would be (Φ6,ΦH2) and (ΦH2,Φ6). In a virus population, we'd expect to find an evolutionarily stable mixed strategy in which both kinds of virus behavior were observed.

This example, like the examples from our earlier discussion of the Hawk–Dove game in Section 6.6, suggests the delicate boundary that exists between Prisoner's Dilemma and Hawk–Dove. In both cases, a player can choose to be "helpful" to the other player or "selfish." In Prisoner's Dilemma, however, the payoff penalties from selfishness are mild enough that selfishness by both players is the unique equilibrium, whereas in Hawk–Dove, selfishness is sufficiently harmful that at least one player should try to avoid it.

There has been research into how this boundary between the two games manifests itself in other biological settings as well. One example is the implicit game played by female lions in defending their territory [218, 327]. When two female lions encounter an attacker on the edge of their territory, each can choose to play the strategy Confront, in which she confronts the attacker, or Lag, in which she lags behind and tries to let the other lioness confront the attacker first. If you're one of the lionesses, and your fellow defender chooses the strategy Confront, then you get a higher payoff by choosing Lag, because you're less likely to get injured. What's harder to determine in empirical studies is what a lioness's best response should be to a play of Lag by her partner. Choosing *Confront* risks injury, but joining your partner in *Lag* risks a successful assault on the territory by the attacker. Understanding which is the best response is important for understanding whether this game is more like Prisoner's Dilemma or Hawk–Dove, and what the evolutionary consequences might be for the observed behavior within a lion population.

In this example, as in many from evolutionary game theory, it is beyond the power of current empirical studies to work out detailed fitness values for particular strategies. However, even in situations where exact payoffs are not known, the evolutionary framework can provide an illuminating perspective on the interactions between different forms of behavior in an underlying population, and how these interactions shape the composition of the population.

7.6 Exercises

1. In the payoff matrix that follows, the rows correspond to player A's strategies and the columns correspond to player B's strategies. The first entry in each box is player A's payoff and the second entry is player B's payoff.

Player B

	x	y
x	2, 2	0, 0
y	0, 0	1, 1

Player A

Figure 7.8. A two-player game for Exercise 1.

(a) Find all pure-strategy Nash equilibria.
(b) Find all evolutionarily stable strategies. Give a brief explanation for your answer.
(c) Briefly explain how the answers to parts (a) and (b) relate to each other.

2. In the payoff matrix that follows, the rows correspond to player A's strategies and the columns correspond to player B's strategies. The first entry in each box is player A's payoff and the second entry is player B's payoff.

Player B

	x	y
x	4, 4	3, 5
y	5, 3	5, 5

Player A

Figure 7.9. A two-player game for Exercise 2.

(a) Find all pure-strategy Nash equilibria.
(b) Find all evolutionarily stable strategies. Give a brief explanation for your answer.
(c) Briefly explain how the answers to parts (a) and (b) relate to each other.

3. In this problem we consider the relationship between Nash equilibria and evolutionarily stable strategies for games with a strictly dominant strategy. First, let's define what we mean by *strictly dominant*. In a two-player game, strategy X is said to be a strictly dominant strategy for a player i if, no matter what strategy the other player j uses, player i's payoff from using strategy X is strictly greater than his payoff from any other strategy. Consider the following game in which $a, b, c,$ and d are nonnegative numbers.

Player B

	X	Y
X	a, a	b, c
Y	c, b	d, d

Player A

Figure 7.10. A two-player game for Exercise 3.

Suppose that strategy X is a strictly dominant strategy for each player; that is, $a > c$ and $b > d$.

(a) Find all of the pure-strategy Nash equilibria of this game.
(b) Find all of the evolutionarily stable strategies of this game.
(c) How would your answers to parts (a) and (b) change if we change the assumption on payoffs to $a > c$ and $b = d$?

4. Consider following the two-player, symmetric game where x can be 0, 1, or 2.

Player B

		X	Y
Player A	X	1, 1	2, x
	Y	x, 2	3, 3

Figure 7.11. A two-player game for Exercise 4(a).

(a) For each of the possible values of x, find all (pure-strategy) Nash equilibria and all evolutionarily stable strategies.
(b) Your answers to part (a) should suggest that the difference between the predictions of evolutionary stability and Nash equilibrium arises when a Nash equilibrium uses a *weakly dominated strategy*. We say that a strategy s_i^* is weakly dominated if player i has another strategy s_i' with the following properties.

  i. No matter what the other player does, player i's payoff from s_i' is at least as large as the payoff from s_i^*, and
  ii. There is some strategy for the other player so that player i's payoff from s_i' is strictly greater than the payoff from s_i^*.

Now consider the following claim that makes a connection between evolutionarily stable strategies and weakly dominated strategies.

Claim: Suppose that, in the following game below, (X, X) is a Nash equilibrium and that strategy X is weakly dominated. Then X is not an evolutionarily stable strategy.

Player B

		X	Y
Player A	X	a, a	b, c
	Y	c, b	d, d

Figure 7.12. A two-player game for Exercise 4(b).

Explain why this claim is true. (You do not have to write a formal proof; a careful explanation is fine.)

CHAPTER 8

Modeling Network Traffic Using Game Theory

Among the initial examples in our discussion of game theory in Chapter 6, we noted that traveling through a transportation network, or sending packets through the Internet, involves fundamentally game-theoretic reasoning: rather than simply choosing a route in isolation, individuals must evaluate routes in the presence of the congestion resulting from the decisions made by themselves and everyone else. In this chapter, we develop models for network traffic using the game-theoretic ideas developed thus far. In the process, we will discover a rather unexpected result – known as *Braess's Paradox* [76] – which shows that adding capacity to a network can sometimes actually slow down the traffic.

8.1 Traffic at Equilibrium

Let's begin by developing a model of a transportation network and how it responds to traffic congestion; with this model in place, we can then introduce the game-theoretic aspects of the problem.

We represent a transportation network by a directed graph: we consider the edges to be highways, and the nodes to be exits where you can get on or off a particular highway. There are two particular nodes, which we call A and B, and we assume everyone wants to drive from A to B. For example, we can imagine that A is an exit in the suburbs, B is an exit downtown, and we're looking at a large collection of morning commuters. Finally, each edge has a designated travel time that depends on the amount of traffic it contains.

To make this concrete, consider the graph in Figure 8.1. The label on each edge gives the travel time (in minutes) when there are x cars using the edge. In this simplified example, the A-D and C-B edges are insensitive to congestion: each takes 45 minutes to traverse regardless of the number of cars traveling on them. On the other hand, the

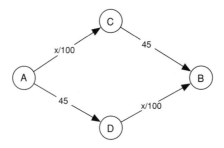

Figure 8.1. A highway network, with each edge labeled by its travel time (in minutes) when there are x cars using it. When 4,000 cars need to get from A to B, they divide evenly over the two routes at equilibrium, and the travel time is 65 minutes.

A-C and D-B edges are highly sensitive to congestion: for each one, it takes $x/100$ minutes to traverse when there are x cars using the edge.[1]

Now, suppose that 4,000 cars want to get from A to B as part of the morning commute. There are two possible routes that each car can choose: the upper route through C or the lower route through D. For example, if each car takes the upper route (through C), then the total travel time for everyone is 85 minutes, since $4,000/100 + 45 = 85$. The same is true if everyone takes the lower route. However, if the cars divide up evenly between the two routes, so that each carries 2,000 cars, then the total travel time for people on both routes is $2,000/100 + 45 = 65$.

Equilibrium Traffic. So what do we expect will happen? The traffic model we've described is really a game in which the players correspond to the drivers, and each player's possible strategies consist of the possible routes from A to B. In our example, each player only has two strategies; however, larger networks could contain many strategies for each player. The payoff for a player is the negative of his or her travel time (we use the negative since large travel times are bad).

This all fits very naturally into the framework we've been using. One thing to notice, of course, is that in the two previous chapters we have focused primarily on games with two players, whereas the current traffic game will generally have an enormous number of players (4,000 in our example). But this poses no direct problem for applying any of the ideas we've developed. A game can have any number of players, each of whom can have any number of available strategies, and the payoff to each player depends on the strategies chosen by all. A Nash equilibrium is still a list of strategies, one for each player, so that each player's strategy is a best response to all the others. The notions of dominant strategies, mixed strategies, and Nash equilibrium with mixed strategies all have direct parallels with their definitions for two-player games.

In this traffic game, there is generally not a dominant strategy; for example, in Figure 8.1 either route has the potential to be the best choice for a player if all the other players are using the other route. The game does have Nash equilibria, however; as we

[1] The travel times here are simplified to make the reasoning clearer: in any real application, each road would have both some minimum travel time and also some sensitivity to the number of cars, x, that are using it. However, the analysis here adapts directly to more intricate functions specifying the travel times on edges.

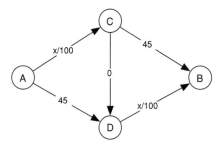

Figure 8.2. The highway network from the previous figure, after a very fast edge has been added from C to D. Although the highway system has been "upgraded," the travel time at equilibrium is now 80 minutes, since all cars use the route through C and D.

will now argue, any list of strategies in which the drivers balance themselves evenly between the two routes (2,000 on each) is a Nash equilibrium, and these are the only Nash equilibria.

Why does equal balance yield a Nash equilibrium, and why do all Nash equilibria have equal balance? To answer the first question, we just observe that, with an even balance between the two routes, no driver has an incentive to switch over to the other route. For the second question, consider a list of strategies in which x drivers use the upper route and the remaining $4,000 - x$ drivers use the lower route. Then if x is not equal to 2,000, the two routes will have unequal travel times, and any driver on the slower route would have an incentive to switch to the faster one. Hence, any list of strategies in which x is not equal to 2,000 cannot be a Nash equilibrium, and any list of strategies in which $x = 2,000$ is a Nash equilibrium.

8.2 Braess's Paradox

In Figure 8.1, everything works out very cleanly: self-interested behavior by all drivers causes them – at equilibrium – to balance perfectly between the available routes. But with only a small change to the network, we can quickly find ourselves in truly counterintuitive territory.

The change is as follows: suppose that the city government decides to build a new, very fast highway from C to D, as indicated in Figure 8.2. To keep things simple, we model its travel time as 0, regardless of the number of cars on it, although the resulting effect would happen even with more realistic (but small) travel times. It would stand to reason that people's travel time from A to B ought to get better after this edge from C to D is added. Does it?

Here's the surprise: there is a unique Nash equilibrium in this new highway network, but it leads to a worse travel time for everyone. At equilibrium, every driver uses the route through both C and D; as a result, the travel time for every driver is 80 (since $4,000/100 + 0 + 4,000/100 = 80$). To see why this is an equilibrium, note that no driver can benefit by changing their route: with traffic snaking through C and D the way it is, any other route would now take 85 minutes. And to see why it's the only equilibrium, you can check that the creation of the edge from C to D has in fact made the route through C and D a dominant strategy for all drivers: regardless of the current traffic pattern, you gain by switching your route to go through C and D.

In other words, once the fast highway from C to D is built, the route through C and D acts like a "vortex" that draws all drivers into it – to the detriment of all. In the new network there is no way, given individually self-interested behavior by the drivers, to get back to the even-balance solution that was better for everyone.

This phenomenon – that adding resources to a transportation network can sometimes hurt performance at equilibrium – was first articulated by Dietrich Braess in 1968 [76], and it has become known as Braess's Paradox. Like many counterintuitive anomalies, it requires the correct combination of conditions to actually pop up in real life; but it has been observed empirically in real transportation networks – including in Seoul, Korea, where the destruction of a six-lane highway to build a public park actually improved travel time into and out of the city (even though traffic volume stayed roughly the same before and after the change [37]).

Some Reflections on Braess's Paradox. Having now seen how Braess's Paradox works, we can also appreciate that there is actually nothing really "paradoxical" about it. There are many settings in which adding a new strategy to a game makes things worse for everyone. For example, the Prisoner's Dilemma from Chapter 6 can be used to illustrate this point: if the only strategy for each player were Not-Confess (an admittedly very simple game), then both players would be better off compared with the game where Confess is added as an option. (Indeed, that's why the police offer Confess as an option in the first place.)

Still, it's reasonable to view the analogous phenomenon at the heart of the Braess Paradox as more paradoxical, at an intuitive level. We all have an informal sense that "upgrading" a network has to be a good thing, and so it is surprising when it turns out to make things worse.

The example in this section is actually the starting point for a large body of work on game-theoretic analysis of network traffic. For example, we could ask how bad Braess's Paradox can be for networks in general: how much larger can the equilibrium travel time be after the addition of an edge, relative to what it was before? Suppose in particular that we allow the graph to be arbitrary, and we assume that the travel time on each edge depends in a linear way on the number of cars traversing it; that is, all travel times across edges have the form $ax + b$, where each of a and b is either zero or a positive number. In this case, elegant results of Tim Roughgarden and Éva Tardos can be used to show that, if we add edges to a network with an equilibrium pattern of traffic, there is always an equilibrium in the new network whose travel time is no more than 4/3 times as large [18, 353]. Moreover, 4/3 is the factor increase that we'd get in the example from Figures 8.1 and 8.2 if we replace the two travel times of 45 with 40. (In that case, the travel time at equilibrium would jump from 60 to 80 when we add the edge from C to D.) So the Roughgarden–Tardos result shows that this simple example is as bad as the Braess Paradox can get, in a quantitative sense, when edges respond linearly to traffic. (When edges can respond nonlinearly, things can be much worse.)

Many other types of questions can be pursued as well. For example, we could think about ways of designing networks to prevent bad equilibria from arising, or to avoid

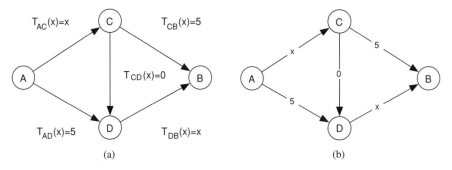

Figure 8.3. A network annotated with the travel-time function on each edge. Travel times are written as (a) explicit functions of x and (b) annotations on the edges.

bad equilibria through the judicious use of tolls on certain parts of the network. Many of these extensions, as well as others, are discussed by Tim Roughgarden [352] in his book on game-theoretic models of network traffic.

8.3 Advanced Material: The Social Cost of Traffic at Equilibrium

The Braess Paradox is one aspect of a larger phenomenon, which is that network traffic at equilibrium may not be socially optimal. In this section, we try to quantify how *far* from optimal traffic can be at equilibrium.

We would like our analysis to apply to any network, and so we introduce the following general definitions. The network can be any directed graph. There is a set of drivers, and different drivers may have different starting points and destinations. Now, each edge e has a *travel-time function* $T_e(x)$, which gives the time it takes all drivers to cross the edge when there are x drivers using it. These travel times are simply the functions that we drew as labels inside the edges in the figures in Section 8.1. We will assume that all travel-time functions are linear in the amount of traffic, so that $T_e(x) = a_e x + b_e$ for some choice of numbers a_e and b_e that are either positive or zero. For example, in Figure 8.3 we draw another network on which Braess's Paradox arises, with the travel-time functions scaled down to involve smaller numbers. The version of the drawing in Figure 8.3(a) has the travel-time functions explicitly written out, while the version of the drawing in Figure 8.3(b) has the travel-time functions written as labels inside the edges.

Finally, we say that a *traffic pattern* is simply a choice of a path by each driver, and the *social cost* of a given traffic pattern is the sum of the travel times incurred by all drivers when they use this traffic pattern. For example, Figure 8.4 shows two different traffic patterns in the network from Figure 8.3, when there are four drivers, each with starting node A and destination node B. The first of these traffic patterns, in Figure 8.4(a), achieves the minimum possible social cost – each driver requires 7 units of time to get to their destination, and so the social cost is 28. We refer to such a traffic pattern, which achieves the minimum possible social cost, as *socially optimal*. (Other traffic patterns in this network also achieve a social cost of 28; that is, there are multiple

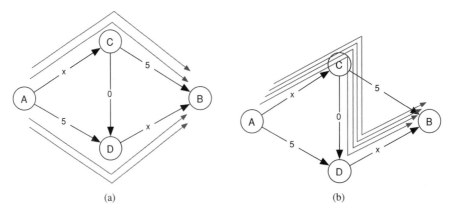

(a)   (b)

Figure 8.4. A version of Braess's Paradox. In the socially optimal traffic pattern (a) the social cost is 28, while in the unique Nash equilibrium (b), the social cost is 32.

traffic patterns for this network that are socially optimal.) Note that socially optimal traffic patterns are simply the social welfare maximizers of this traffic game, since the sum of the drivers' payoffs is the negative of the social cost. The second traffic pattern, Figure 8.4(b), is the unique Nash equilibrium, and it has a larger social cost of 32.

The main two questions we consider in the remainder of this chapter are the following. First, in any network (with linear travel-time functions), is there always an equilibrium traffic pattern? We have seen examples in Chapter 6 of games where equilibria do not exist using pure strategies, and it is not a priori clear that they should always exist for the traffic game we've defined here. However, we will find in fact that equilibria always do exist. The second main question is whether there always exists an equilibrium traffic pattern whose social cost is not much more than the social optimum. We will find that this is in fact the case: we will show a result due to Roughgarden and Tardos [353] that there is always an equilibrium whose social cost is at most *twice* that of the optimum.[2]

A. How to Find a Traffic Pattern at Equilibrium

We prove that an equilibrium exists by analyzing the following procedure that explicitly searches for one. The procedure starts from any traffic pattern. If it is an equilibrium, we are done. Otherwise, there is at least one driver whose best response, given what everyone else is doing, is some alternate path providing a strictly lower travel time. We pick one such driver and have him switch to this alternate path. We now have a new traffic pattern and we again check whether it is an equilibrium. If it isn't, then we have some driver switch to his best response, and we continue in this fashion.

---

[2] In fact, stronger results of Roughgarden and Tardos, supplemented by subsequent results of Anshelevich et al. [18], establish that in fact every equilibrium traffic pattern has social cost at most 4/3 times the optimum. (One can show that this implies their result on the Braess Paradox cited in the previous section – with linear travel times, adding edges cannot make things worse by a factor of more than 4/3.) However, since it is harder to prove the bound of 4/3, we limit ourselves here to proving the easier but weaker factor of 2 between the social optimum and some equilibrium traffic pattern.

This procedure is called *best-response dynamics*, because it dynamically reconfigures the players' strategies by constantly having some player perform his or her best response to the current situation. If the procedure ever stops, in a state where everyone is in fact playing their best response to the current situation, then we have an equilibrium. So the key is to show that, in any instance of our traffic game, best-response dynamics must eventually stop at an equilibrium.

But why should it? Certainly for games that lack an equilibrium, best-response dynamics will run forever: for example, in the Matching Pennies game from Chapter 6, when only pure strategies are allowed, best-response dynamics simply consists of the two players endlessly switching their strategies between H and T. It seems plausible that for some network this could happen in the traffic game as well: one at a time, drivers shift their routes to ones that are better for them, thus increasing the delay for another driver who then switches and continues the cascade.

In fact, however, this cannot happen in the traffic game. We now show that best-response dynamics must always terminate in an equilibrium, thus proving not only that equilibria exist but also that they can be reached by a simple process in which drivers constantly update what they're doing according to best responses.

Analyzing Best-Response Dynamics via Potential Energy. How should we go about proving that best-response dynamics must come to a halt? When you have a process that runs according to some set of instructions like, "Do the following ten things and then stop," it's generally obvious that the process will eventually come to an end: the process essentially comes with its own guarantee of termination. But we have a process that runs according to a different kind of rule, one that says, "Keep doing something until a particular condition happens to hold." In this case, there is no a priori reason to believe it will ever stop.

In such cases, a useful analysis technique is to define some kind of *progress measure* that tracks the process as it operates and to show that eventually enough "progress" is made that the process must stop. For the traffic game, it's natural to think of the social cost of the current traffic pattern as a possible progress measure, but in fact the social cost is not so useful for this purpose. Some best-response updates by drivers can make the social cost better (for example, if a driver leaves a congested road for a relatively empty one), but others can make it worse (as in the sequence of best-response updates that shifts the traffic pattern from the social optimum to the inferior equilibrium in the Braess Paradox). So in general, as best-response dynamics runs, the social cost of the current traffic pattern can oscillate between going up and going down, and it's not clear how this is related to our progress toward an equilibrium.

Instead, we're going to define an alternate quantity that initially seems a bit mysterious. However, we will see that it has the property that it strictly decreases with each best-response update, and so it can be used to track the progress of best-response dynamics [303]. We will refer to this quantity as the *potential energy* of a traffic pattern.

The potential energy of a traffic pattern is defined edge-by-edge, as follows. If an edge e currently has x drivers on it, then we define the potential energy of this edge to be

$$\text{Energy}(e) = T_e(1) + T_e(2) + \cdots + T_e(x).$$

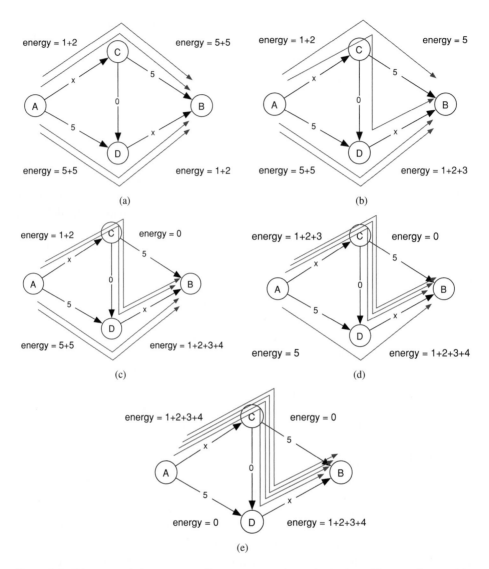

Figure 8.5. We can track the progress of best-response dynamics in the traffic game by watching how the potential energy changes: (a) initial traffic pattern (potential energy is 26); (b) after one step of best-response dynamics (potential energy is 24); (c) after two steps (potential energy is 23); (d) after three steps (potential energy is 21); and (e) after four steps, when equilibrium is reached (potential energy is 20).

If an edge has no drivers on it, its potential energy is defined to be zero. The potential energy of a traffic pattern is then simply the sum of the potential energies of all the edges, with their current numbers of drivers in this traffic pattern. Figure 8.5 shows the potential energy of each edge for the five traffic patterns that best-response dynamics produces as it moves from the social optimum to the unique equilibrium in the Braess Paradox network from Figure 8.4.

Notice that the potential energy of an edge e with x drivers is not the total travel time experienced by the drivers that cross it. Because the x drivers on this edge are each experiencing a travel time of $T_e(x)$, their total travel time is $xT_e(x)$, which is a different number. The potential energy, instead, is a sort of "cumulative" quantity in which we imagine drivers crossing the edge one by one, and each driver only "feels" the delay caused by himself and the drivers crossing the edge in front of him.

Of course, the potential energy is only useful for our purpose if it lets us analyze the progress of best-response dynamics. We show how to do this next.

Proving That Best-Response Dynamics Comes to an End. Our main claim is the following: Each step of best-response dynamics causes the potential energy of the current traffic pattern to strictly decrease. Proving this will be enough to show that best-response dynamics must come to an end, for the following reason. The potential energy can only take a finite number of possible values – one for each possible traffic pattern. If it is strictly decreasing with each step of best-response dynamics, this means that it is "consuming" this finite supply of possible values, because it can never revisit a value once it drops below it. So best-response dynamics must come to a stop by the time the potential energy reaches its minimum possible value (if not sooner). And once best-response dynamics comes to a stop, we must be at an equilibrium – otherwise, the dynamics would have a way to continue. Thus, showing that the potential energy strictly decreases in every step of best-response dynamics is enough to show the existence of an equilibrium traffic pattern.

As an example, let's return to the sequence of best-response steps from Figure 8.5. Although the social cost is rising through the five traffic patterns (increasing from 28 to 32), the potential energy decreases strictly in each step (in the sequence 26, 24, 23, 21, and 20). In fact, it is easy to track the change in potential energy through this sequence as follows. From one traffic pattern to the next, the only change is that one driver abandons his current path and switches to a new one. Suppose we really view this switch as a two-step process: first the driver abandons his current path, temporarily leaving the system; then the driver returns to the system by adopting a new path. This first step releases potential energy as the driver leaves the system, and the second step adds potential energy as he rejoins. What's the net change?

For example, the transition from Figure 8.5(a) to 8.5(b) occurs because one driver abandons the upper path and adopts the zigzag path. As shown in Figure 8.6, abandoning the upper path releases $2 + 5 = 7$ units of potential energy, while adopting the zigzag path puts $2 + 0 + 3$ units of potential energy back into the system. The resulting change is a decrease of 2.

Notice that the decrease of 7 is simply the travel time the driver was experiencing on the path he abandoned, and the subsequent increase of 5 is the travel time the driver now experiences on the path he has adopted. This relationship is in fact true for any network and any best response by a driver, and it holds for a simple reason. Specifically, the potential energy of edge e with x drivers is

$$T_e(1) + T_e(2) + \cdots + T_e(x - 1) + T_e(x),$$

and when one of these drivers leaves it drops to

$$T_e(1) + T_e(2) + \cdots + T_e(x - 1).$$

Hence, the change in potential energy on edge e is $T_e(x)$, exactly the travel time that the driver was experiencing on e. Summing this value over all edges used by the driver,

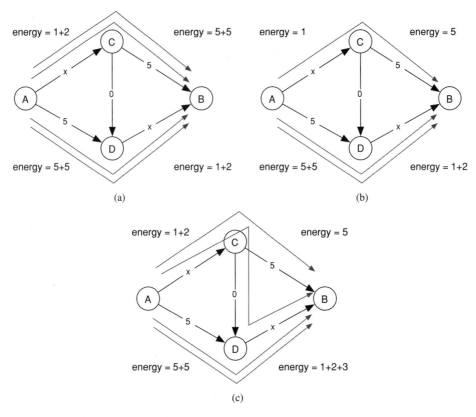

Figure 8.6. When a driver abandons one path in favor of another, the change in potential energy is exactly the improvement in the driver's travel time: (a) potential energy of a traffic pattern not in equilibrium, (b) potential energy released when a driver abandons his current path, and (c) potential energy put back into the system when the driver chooses a new path.

we see that the potential energy released when a driver abandons his current path is *exactly equal* to the travel time the driver was experiencing. By the same reasoning, when a driver adopts a new path, the potential energy on each edge e he joins increases from

$$T_e(1) + T_e(2) + \cdots + T_e(x)$$

to

$$T_e(1) + T_e(2) + \cdots + T_e(x) + T_e(x + 1),$$

and the increase of $T_e(x + 1)$ is exactly the new travel time the driver experiences on this edge. Hence, the potential energy added to the system when a driver adopts a new path is exactly equal to the travel time the driver now experiences.

It follows that when a driver switches paths, the net change in potential energy is simply his new travel time minus his old travel time. But in best-response dynamics, a driver only changes paths when it causes his travel time to decrease; hence, the change in potential energy is negative for any best-response move. We have therefore established what we wanted to show: that the potential energy in the system strictly decreases throughout best-response dynamics. As argued earlier, because the potential energy cannot decrease forever, best-response dynamics must therefore eventually come to an end, at a traffic pattern in equilibrium.

B. Comparing Equilibrium Traffic to the Social Optimum

Having shown that an equilibrium traffic pattern always exists, we now consider how its travel time compares to that of a socially optimal traffic pattern. We will see that the potential energy we've defined is very useful for making this comparison. The basic idea is to establish a relationship between the potential energy of an edge and the total travel time of all drivers crossing the edge. Once this relationship is established, we will sum these two quantities over all the edges to compare travel times at equilibrium and at social optimality.

Relating Potential Energy to Travel Time for a Single Edge. We denote the potential energy of an edge by Energy(e), and we recall that, when there are x drivers, this potential energy is defined by

$$\text{Energy}(e) = T_e(1) + T_e(2) + \cdots + T_e(x).$$

On the other hand, each of the x drivers experiences a travel time of $T_e(x)$, and so the total travel time experienced by all drivers on the edge is

$$\text{Total-Travel-Time}(e) = x T_e(x).$$

For purposes of comparison with the potential energy, it is useful to write this as follows:

$$\text{Total-Travel-Time}(e) = \underbrace{T_e(x) + T_e(x) + \cdots + T_e(x)}_{x \text{ terms}}.$$

Since the potential energy and the total travel time each have x terms, but the terms in the latter expression are at least as large as the terms in the former, we have

$$\text{Energy}(e) \leq \text{Total-Travel-Time}(e).$$

Figure 8.7 shows how the potential energy and the total travel time compare when T_e is a linear function: the total travel time is the shaded area under the horizontal line with y-value $T_e(x)$, while the potential energy is the total area under all the unit-width rectangles of heights $T_e(1), T_e(2), \ldots, T_e(x)$. As this figure makes clear geometrically, since T_e is a linear function, we have

$$T_e(1) + T_e(2) + \cdots + T_e(x) \geq \frac{1}{2} x T_e(x).$$

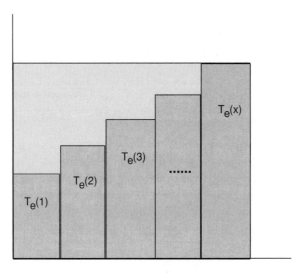

Figure 8.7. The potential energy is the area under the shaded rectangles; it is always at least half the total travel time, which is the area inside the enclosing rectangle.

Alternately, we can see this by a bit of simple algebra, recalling that $T_e(x) = a_e x + b_e$:

$$T_e(1) + T_e(2) + \cdots + T_e(x) = a_e(1 + 2 + \cdots + x) + b_e x$$
$$= \frac{a_e x(x + 1)}{2} + b_e x$$
$$= x \left[\frac{a_e(x + 1)}{2} + b_e \right]$$
$$\geq \frac{1}{2} x(a_e x + b_e)$$
$$= \frac{1}{2} x T_e(x).$$

In terms of energies and total travel times, this says

$$\text{Energy}(e) \geq \frac{1}{2}[\text{Total-Travel-Time}(e)].$$

So the conclusion is that the potential energy of an edge is never far from the total travel time: it is sandwiched between the total travel time and half the total travel time.

Relating the Travel Time at Equilibrium and Social Optimality. We now use this relationship between potential energy and total travel time to relate the equilibrium and socially optimal traffic patterns.

Let Z be a traffic pattern; we define Energy(Z) to be the total potential energy of all edges when drivers follow the traffic pattern Z. We write Social-Cost(Z) to denote the social cost of the traffic pattern; recall that this is the sum of the travel times experienced by all drivers. Equivalently, summing the social cost edge-by-edge, Social-Cost(Z) is the sum of the total travel times on all the edges. So applying our relationships between potential energy and travel time on an edge-by-edge basis, we see that the same relationships govern the potential energy and social cost of a traffic pattern:

$$\frac{1}{2}[\text{Social-Cost}(Z)] \le \text{Energy}(Z) \le \text{Social-Cost}(Z).$$

Now, suppose that we start from a socially optimal traffic pattern Z, and we then allow best-response dynamics to run until it stops at an equilibrium traffic pattern Z'. The social cost may start increasing as we run best-response dynamics, but the potential energy can only go down. And because the social cost can never be more than twice the potential energy, this shrinking potential energy keeps the social cost from ever getting more than twice as high as where it started. Therefore, the social cost of the equilibrium we reach is at most twice the cost of the social optimum we started with; hence, we have an equilibrium with at most twice the socially optimal cost, as we wanted to show.

Let's write this argument out in terms of the inequalities on energies and social costs. First, we saw in the previous section that the potential energy decreases as best-response dynamics moves from Z to Z', and so

$$\text{Energy}(Z') \le \text{Energy}(Z).$$

Second, the quantitative relationships between energies and social cost say that

$$\text{Social-Cost}(Z') \le 2[\text{Energy}(Z')]$$

and

$$\text{Energy}(Z) \le \text{Social-Cost}(Z).$$

Now we just chain these inequalities together, concluding that

$$\text{Social-Cost}(Z') \le 2[\text{Energy}(Z')] \le 2[\text{Energy}(Z)] \le 2[\text{Social-Cost}(Z)].$$

Note that this really is the same argument that we made in words in the previous paragraph: the potential energy decreases during best-response dynamics, and this decrease prevents the social cost from ever increasing by more than a factor of 2.

Thus, tracking potential energy is not only useful for showing that best-response dynamics must reach an equilibrium; by relating this potential energy to the social cost, we can use it to put a bound on the social cost of the equilibrium that is reached.

8.4 Exercises

1. There are 1,000 cars that must travel from town A to town B. There are two possible routes that each car can take: the upper route through town C or the lower route through town D. Let x be the number of cars traveling on the edge A-C and let y be the number of cars traveling on the edge D-B. The directed graph in Figure 8.8 indicates that travel time per car on edge A-C is $x/100$ if x cars use edge A-C, and similarly the travel time per car on edge D-B is $y/100$ if y cars use edge D-B. The travel time per car on each of edges C-B and A-D is 12 regardless of the number of cars on these edges. Each driver wants to select a route to minimize his travel time. The drivers make simultaneous choices.

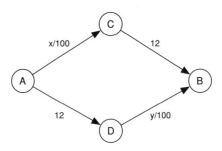

Figure 8.8. The traffic network for Exercise 1.

(a) Find Nash equilibrium values of x and y.

(b) Now the government builds a new (one-way) road from town C to town D. The new road adds the path A-C-D-B to the network. This new road from C to D has a travel time of 0 per car regardless of the number of cars that use it. Find a Nash equilibrium for the game played on the new network. What are the equilibrium values of x and y? What happens to total cost of travel (the sum of total travel times for the 1,000 cars) as a result of the availability of the new road?

(c) Suppose now that conditions on edges C-B and A-D are improved so that the travel times on each edge are reduced to 5. The road from C to D that was constructed in part (b) is still available. Find a Nash equilibrium for the game played on the network with the smaller travel times for C-B and A-D. What are the equilibrium values of x and y? What is the total cost of travel? What would happen to the total cost of travel if the government closed the road from C to D?

2. There are two cities A and B joined by two routes. There are 80 travelers who begin in city A and must travel to city B. There are two routes between A and B. Route 1 begins with a highway leaving city A; this highway takes one hour of travel time per traveler regardless of how many travelers use it, and it ends with a local street leading into city B. This local street near city B requires a travel time per traveler in minutes equal to 10 plus the number of travelers who use the street. Route 2 begins with a local street leaving city A, which requires a travel time per traveler in minutes equal to 10 plus the number of travelers who use this street and ends with a highway into city B that requires one hour of travel time per traveler regardless of the number of travelers who use this highway.

(a) Draw the network described above and label each edge with the travel time needed to move along the edge. Let x be the number of travelers who use Route 1. The network should be a directed graph because all roads are oneway.

(b) Travelers simultaneously choose which route to use. Find the Nash equilibrium value of x.

(c) Now the government builds a new (two-way) road connecting the nodes where local streets and highways meet. This connection adds two new routes. One new route consists of the local street leaving city A (on Route 2), the new road, and the local street into city B (on Route 1). The second new route consists of the highway leaving city A (on Route 1), the new road, and the highway leading into city B (on Route 2). The new road

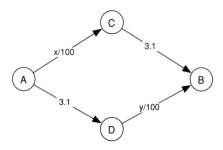

Figure 8.9. The traffic network for Exercise 3.

is very short and takes no travel time. Find the new Nash equilibrium. [Hint: There is an equilibrium in which no one chooses to use the second new route described above.]

(d) What happens to the total travel time as a result of the availability of the new road?

(e) If you can assign travelers to routes, then in fact it's possible to reduce total travel time relative to what it was before the new road was built. That is, the total travel time of the population can be reduced [below that in the original Nash equilibrium from part (b)] by assigning travelers to routes. There are many assignments of routes that can accomplish this outcome. Find one. Explain why your reassignment reduces total travel time. [Hint: Remember that travel on the new road can go in either direction. You do not need to find the assignment of travelers that minimizes the total travel time. One approach to this question is to start with the Nash equilibrium from part (b) and look for a way to assign some travelers to different routes to reduce total travel time.]

3. There are 300 cars which must travel from city A to city B. There are two possible routes that each car can take: the upper route through city C or the lower route through city D. Let x be the number of cars traveling on edge A-C and let y be the number of cars traveling on edge D-B. The directed graph in Figure 8.9 indicates that total travel time per car along the upper route is $(x/100) + 3.1$ if x cars use the upper route, and similarly the total travel time per car along the lower route is $3.1 + (y/100)$ if y cars take the lower route. Each driver wants to select a route to minimize his total travel time. The drivers make simultaneous choices.

(a) Find Nash equilibrium values of x and y.

(b) Now the government builds a new (one-way) road from city A to city B. The new route has a travel time of 5 minutes per car regardless of the number of cars that use it. Draw the new network and label the edges with the cost of travel needed to move along the edge. The network should be a directed graph because all roads are one way. Find a Nash equilibrium for the game played on the new network. What happens to total cost of travel (the sum of total travel times for the 300 cars) as a result of the availability of the new road?

(c) Now the government closes the direct route between city A and city B and builds a new one-way road that links city C to city D. This new road between C and D is very short and has a travel time of 0 regardless of the number of cars that use it. Draw the new network and label the edges with the cost of travel needed to move along the edge. The network should be a directed graph because all roads are one way. Find a Nash equilibrium for the game played on the new network. What happens to total cost of travel as a result of the availability of the new road?

(d) The government is unhappy with the outcome in part (c) and decides to reopen the road directly linking city A and city B [the road that was built in part (b) and closed in part (c)]. The route between C and D that was constructed in part (c) remains open. This direct A-B road still has a travel time of 5 minutes per car regardless of the number of cars that use it. Draw the new network and label the edges with the cost of travel needed to move along the edge. The network should be a directed graph because all roads are one way. Find a Nash equilibrium for the game played on the new network. What happens to total cost of travel as a result of reopening the direct route between A and B?

4. There are two cities, A and B, joined by two routes, 1 and 2. All roads are oneway roads. There are 100 travelers who begin in city A and must travel to city B. Route 1 links city A to city B through city C. This route begins with a road linking city A to city C, which has a cost of travel for each traveler equal to $0.5 + x/200$, where x is the number of travelers on this road. Route 1 ends with a highway from city C to city B which has a cost of travel for each traveler of 1 regardless of the number of travelers who use it. Route 2 links city A to city B through city D. This route begins with a highway linking city A to city D, which has a cost of travel for each traveler of 1 regardless of the number of travelers who use it. Route 2 ends with a road linking city D to city B, which has a cost of travel for each traveler equal to $0.5 + y/200$, where y is the number of travelers on this road.

These costs of travel correspond to the value that travelers put on the time lost due to travel plus the cost of gasoline for the trip. Currently there are no tolls on these roads, so the government collects no revenue from travel on them.

(a) Draw the network described above and label the edges with the cost of travel needed to move along the edge. The network should be a directed graph because all roads are one way.

(b) Travelers simultaneously choose which route to use. Find Nash equilibrium values of x and y.

(c) Now the government builds a new (one-way) road from city C to city D. The new road is very short and has zero cost of travel. Find a Nash equilibrium for the game played on the new network.

(d) What happens to total cost of travel as a result of the availability of the new road?

(e) The government is unhappy with the outcome in part (c) and decides to impose a toll on users of the road from city A to city C and to simultaneously subsidize users of the highway from city A to city D. They charge a toll of 0.125 to each user, thus increasing the cost of travel by this amount for users of the road from city A to city C. They also subsidize travel, and thus reduce the cost of travel by this amount, for each user of the highway from city A to city D by 0.125. Find a new Nash equilibrium. [If you are curious about how a subsidy could work, you can think of it as a negative toll. In this economy all tolls are collected electronically, much as New

York State attempts to do with its E-ZPass system. A subsidy just reduces the total amount that highway users owe.]

(f) As you will observe in solving part (e), the toll and subsidy in part (e) were designed so that there is a Nash equilibrium in which the amount the government collects from the toll just equals the amount it loses on the subsidy. So the government is breaking even on this policy. What happens to total cost of travel between parts (c) and (e)? Can you explain why this occurs? Can you think of any break-even tolls and subsidies that could be placed on the roads from city C to city B, and from city D to city B, that would lower the total cost of travel even more?

CHAPTER 9

Auctions

In Chapter 8, we considered a first extended application of game-theoretic ideas in our analysis of traffic flow through a network. Here we consider a second major application – the behavior of buyers and sellers in an auction.

An auction is a kind of economic activity that has been brought into many people's everyday lives by the Internet, through sites such as eBay. But auctions also have a long history that spans many different domains. For example, the U.S. government uses auctions to sell Treasury bills and timber and oil leases; Christie's and Sotheby's use them to sell art; and Morrell & Company and the Chicago Wine Company use them to sell wine.

Auctions will also play an important and recurring role in this book, since the simplified form of buyer–seller interaction they embody is closely related to more complex forms of economic interaction as well. In particular, in the next part of the book, when we discuss markets in which multiple buyers and sellers are connected by an underlying network structure, we'll use ideas initially developed in this chapter for understanding simpler auction formats. Similarly, in Chapter 15, we'll study a more complex kind of auction in the context of a Web search application, analyzing the ways in which search companies like Google, Yahoo!, and Microsoft use an auction format to sell advertising rights for keywords.

9.1 Types of Auctions

In this chapter we focus on different simple types of auctions and how they promote different kinds of behavior among bidders. We consider the case of a seller auctioning one item to a set of buyers. We could symmetrically think of a situation in which a buyer tries to purchase a single item and runs an auction among a set of multiple sellers, each of whom is able to provide the item. Such *procurement auctions* are frequently run by governments to purchase goods. But here we'll focus on the case in which the seller runs the auction.

There are many different ways of defining auctions that are much more complex than what we consider here. The subsequent chapters will generalize our analysis to the case in which multiple goods are being sold, and the buyers assign different values to these goods. Other variations, which fall outside the scope of the book, include auctions in which goods are sold sequentially over time. These more complex variations can also be analyzed using extensions of the ideas discussed here, and there is a large literature in economics that considers auctions at this broad level of generality [256, 292].

The underlying assumption we make when modeling auctions is that each bidder has an *intrinsic value* for the item being auctioned; she is willing to purchase the item for a price up to this value, but not for any higher price. We will also refer to this intrinsic value as the bidder's *true value* for the item. There are four main types of auctions in which a single item is sold (and many variants of these types).

1. *Ascending-bid auctions*, also called *English auctions*. These auctions are carried out interactively in real time, with bidders present either physically or electronically. The seller gradually raises the price, bidders drop out until finally only one bidder remains, and that bidder wins the object at this final price. Oral auctions in which bidders shout out prices, or submit them electronically, are forms of ascending-bid auctions.

2. *Descending-bid auctions*, also called *Dutch auctions*. This is also an interactive auction format, in which the seller gradually lowers the price from some high initial value until the first moment when some bidder accepts and pays the current price. These auctions are called Dutch auctions because flowers have long been sold in the Netherlands using this procedure.

3. *First-price sealed-bid auctions*. In this kind of auction, bidders submit simultaneous "sealed bids" to the seller. The terminology comes from the original format for such auctions, in which bids were written down and provided in sealed envelopes to the seller, who would then open them all together. The highest bidder wins the object and pays the value of her bid.

4. *Second-price sealed-bid auctions*, also called *Vickrey auctions*. Bidders submit simultaneous sealed bids to the sellers; the highest bidder wins the object and pays the value of the second-highest bid. These auctions are called Vickrey auctions in honor of William Vickrey, who wrote the first game-theoretic analysis of auctions (including the second-price auction [400]). Vickery won the Nobel Memorial Prize in Economics in 1996 for this body of work.

9.2 When Are Auctions Appropriate?

Auctions are generally used by sellers in situations where they do not have a good estimate of the buyers' true values for an item, and where buyers do not know each other's values. In this case, as we will see, some of the main auction formats can be used to elicit bids from buyers that reveal these values.

Known Values. To motivate the setting in which buyers' true values are unknown, let's start by considering the case in which the seller and buyers know each other's values for an item; we'll see that an auction is unnecessary in this scenario. In particular, suppose that a seller is trying to sell an item that he values at x, and suppose that the maximum value held by any potential buyer of the item is some larger number y. In this case, we say there is a *surplus* of $y - x$ that can be generated by the sale of the item: it can go from someone who values it less (x) to someone who values it more (y).

If the seller knows the true values that the potential buyers assign to the item, then he can simply announce that the item is for sale at a fixed price just below y, and that he would not accept any lower price. In this case, the buyer with value y will buy the item, and the full value of the surplus will go to the seller. In other words, the seller has no need for an auction in this case: he gets as much as he could reasonably expect just by announcing the right price.

Notice the asymmetry in the formulation of this example: we gave the seller the ability to commit to the mechanism that was used for selling the object. This ability of the seller to "tie his hands" by committing to a fixed price is in fact very valuable to him: assuming the buyers believe this commitment, the item is sold for a price just below y, and the seller makes all the surplus. In contrast, consider what would happen if we gave the buyer with maximum value y the ability to commit to the mechanism. In this case, this buyer could announce that she is willing to purchase the item for a price just above the larger of x and the values held by all other buyers. With this announcement, the seller would still be willing to sell – since the price would be above x – but now at least some of the surplus would go to the buyer. As with the seller's commitment, this commitment by the buyer also requires knowledge of everyone else's values.

These examples show how commitment to a mechanism can shift the power in the transaction in favor of the seller or the buyer. One can also imagine more complex scenarios in which the seller and buyers know each other's values, but neither has the power to unilaterally commit to a mechanism. In this case, one may see some kind of bargaining take place over the price; we will discuss the topic of bargaining further in Chapter 12. As we will see in the current chapter, the issue of commitment is also crucial in the context of auctions – specifically, it is important that a seller be able to reliably commit in advance to a given auction format.

Unknown Values. Thus far we've discussed how sellers and buyers might interact when everyone knows each other's true values for the item. Beginning in the next section, we'll see how auctions come into play when the participants do not know each other's values.

For most of this chapter we will restrict our attention to the case in which the buyers have *independent, private values* for the item. That is, each buyer knows how much she values the item, but she does not know how much others value it, and her value for it does not depend on others' values. For example, the buyers could be interested in consuming the item, and their values reflect how much they each would enjoy it.

Later we will also consider the polar opposite of this setting – the case of *common values*. Suppose that an item is being auctioned and, instead of consuming the item, each buyer plans to resell the item if she gets it. In this case (assuming the buyers would do a comparably good job of reselling it), the item has an unknown but common value regardless of who acquires it: it is equal to how much revenue this future reselling of the item will generate. Buyers' estimates of this revenue may differ if they have some private information about the common value, and so their valuations of the item may differ. In this setting, the value each buyer assigns to the object would be affected by knowledge of the other buyers' valuations, since the buyers could use this knowledge to further refine their estimates of the common value.

9.3 Relationships between Different Auction Formats

Our main goal will be to consider how bidders behave in different types of auctions. We begin in this section with some simple, informal observations that relate behavior in interactive auctions (ascending-bid and descending-bid auctions, which play out in real time) with behavior in sealed-bid auctions. These observations can be made mathematically rigorous, but for the discussion here we will stick to an informal description.

Descending-Bid and First-Price Auctions. First, consider a descending-bid auction. As the seller lowers the price from its high initial starting point, no bidder says anything until finally someone actually accepts the bid and pays the current price. Bidders therefore learn nothing while the auction is running, other than the fact that no one has yet accepted the current price. For each bidder i, there's a first price b_i at which she would be willing to break the silence and accept the item at price b_i. So with this view, the process is equivalent to a sealed-bid first-price auction: this price b_i plays the role of bidder i's bid, the item goes to the bidder with the highest bid value, and this bidder pays the value of her bid in exchange for the item.

Ascending-Bid and Second-Price Auctions. Now let's think about an ascending-bid auction, in which bidders gradually drop out as the seller steadily raises the price. The winner of the auction is the last bidder remaining, and she pays the price at which the second-to-last bidder drops out.[1]

Suppose that you're a bidder in such an auction; let's consider how long you should stay in the auction before dropping out. First, does it ever make sense to stay in the auction after the price reaches your true value? No: by staying in, you either lose and get nothing, or else you win and have to pay more than your value for the item. Second, does it ever make sense to drop out before the price reaches your true value for the item? Again, no: if you drop out early (before your true value is reached), then you get nothing, whereas by staying in you might win the item at a price below your true value.

So this informal argument indicates that you should stay in an ascending-bid auction up to the exact moment at which the price reaches your true value. If we think of each

---

[1] It's conceptually simplest to think of three things happening simultaneously at the end of an ascending-bid auction: (i) the second-to-last bidder drops out; (ii) the last remaining bidder sees that she is alone and stops agreeing to any higher prices; and (iii) the seller awards the item to this last remaining bidder at the current price. Of course, in practice we might well expect that there is some very small increment by which the bid is raised in each step, and that the last remaining bidder actually wins only after one more raising of the bid by this tiny increment. But keeping track of this small increment makes for a more cumbersome analysis without changing the underlying ideas, and so we will assume that the auction ends at precisely the moment when the second-highest bidder drops out.

bidder i's "drop-out price" as her bid b_i, this says that people should use their true values as their bids.

Moreover, with this definition of bids, the rule for determining the outcome of an ascending-bid auction can be reformulated as follows. The person with the highest bid is the one who stays in the longest, thus winning the item, and she pays the price at which the second-to-last person dropped out – in other words, she pays the bid of this second-to-last person. Thus, the item goes to the highest bidder at a price equal to the second-highest bid. This is precisely the rule used in the sealed-bid second-price auction, with the difference that the ascending-bid auction involves real-time interaction between the buyers and the seller, while the sealed-bid version takes place purely through sealed bids that the seller opens and evaluates. But the close similarity in rules helps to motivate the initially counterintuitive pricing rule for the second-price auction: it can be viewed as a simulation, using sealed bids, of an ascending-bid auction. Moreover, the fact that bidders want to remain in an ascending-bid auction up to exactly the point at which their true value is reached provides the intuition for our main result in the next section: after formulating the sealed-bid second-price auction in terms of game theory, we will find that bidding one's true value is a dominant strategy.

Comparing Auction Formats. In the next two sections we will consider the two main formats for sealed-bid auctions in more detail. However, before doing this, it's worth making two points. First, the discussion in this section shows that, when we analyze bidder behavior in sealed-bid auctions, we also learn about their interactive analogues, with the descending-bid auction as the analogue of the sealed-bid first-price auction, and the ascending-bid auction as the analogue of the sealed-bid second-price auction.

Second, a purely superficial comparison of the first- and second-price sealed-bid auctions might suggest that the seller would get more money for the item if he ran a first-price auction: after all, he'll get paid the highest bid rather than the second-highest bid. It may seem strange that in a second-price auction the seller is intentionally undercharging the bidders. But such reasoning ignores one of the main messages from our study of game theory – that when you make up rules to govern people's behavior, you have to assume that they'll adapt their behavior in light of the rules. Here, the point is that bidders in a first-price auction will tend to bid *lower* than they do in a second-price auction, and in fact this lowering of bids will tend to offset what would otherwise look like a difference in the size of the winning bid. This consideration will come up as a central issue at various points later in the chapter.

9.4 Second-Price Auctions

The sealed-bid second-price auction is particularly interesting, and there are a number of examples of it in widespread use. The auction form used on eBay is essentially a second-price auction. The pricing mechanism that search engines use to sell keyword-based advertising is a generalization of the second-price auction, as we will see in Chapter 15. One of the most important results in auction theory is the fact we mentioned toward the end of the previous section: with independent, private values, bidding your true value is a dominant strategy in a second-price sealed-bid auction. That is, the best choice of bid is exactly what the object is worth to you.

Formulating the Second-Price Auction as a Game. To see why this is true, we set things up using the language of game theory, defining the auction in terms of players, strategies, and payoffs. The bidders correspond to the players. Let v_i be bidder i's true value for the object. Bidder i's strategy is an amount b_i to bid as a function of her true value v_i. In a second-price sealed-bid auction, the payoff to bidder i with value v_i and bid b_i is defined as follows.

> If b_i is not the winning bid, then the payoff to i is 0. If b_i is the winning bid, and some other b_j is the second-place bid, then the payoff to i is $v_i - b_j$.

To make this completely well-defined, we need to handle the possibility of ties: what do we do if two people submit the same bid, and it's tied for the largest? One way to handle the case of a tie is to assume that a fixed ordering on the bidders is agreed on in advance, and if a set of bidders ties for the numerically largest bid, then the winning bid is the one submitted by the bidder in this set that comes first in this order. Our formulation of the payoffs works with this more refined definition of "winning bid" and "second-place bid." (And note that in the case of a tie, the winning bidder receives the item but pays the full value of her own bid, for a payoff of zero, since in the event of a tie the first-place and second-place bids are equal.)

There is one further point worth noting about our formulation of auctions in the language of game theory. When we defined games in Chapter 6, we assumed that each player knew the payoffs of all players in the game. Here this isn't the case, since the bidders don't know each other's values, and so strictly speaking we need to use a slight generalization of the notions from Chapter 6 to handle this lack of knowledge. For our analysis here, however, since we focus on dominant strategies in which a player has an optimal strategy regardless of the other players' behavior, we will be able to disregard this subtlety.

Truthful Bidding in Second-Price Auctions. The precise statement of our claim about second-price auctions is as follows.

> *Claim:* In a sealed-bid second-price auction, it is a dominant strategy for each bidder i to choose a bid $b_i = v_i$.

To prove this claim, we need to show that if bidder i bids $b_i = v_i$ then no deviation from this bid would improve her payoff, regardless of which strategy everyone else is using. There are two cases to consider: deviations in which i raises her bid, and deviations in which i lowers her bid. The key point in both cases is that the value of i's bid only affects whether i wins or loses, but it never affects how much i pays in the event that she wins. The amount paid by the winner is determined entirely by the other bids, and in particular by the largest among the other bids. Since all other bids remain the same when i changes her bid, a change to i's bid only affects her payoff if it changes her win/loss outcome. This argument is summarized in Figure 9.1.

With this in mind, let's consider the two cases. First, suppose that instead of bidding v_i, bidder i chooses a bid $b_i' > v_i$. This only affects bidder i's payoff if i would lose

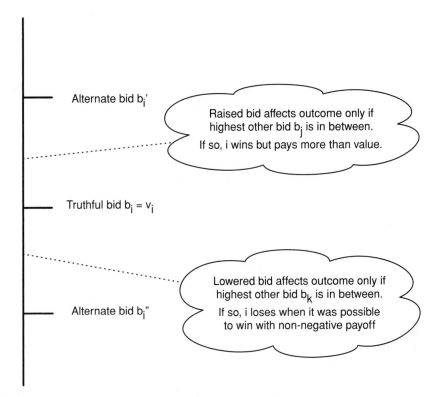

Figure 9.1. If bidder i deviates from a truthful bid in a second-price auction, the payoff is only affected if the change in bid changes the win/loss outcome.

with bid v_i but would win with bid b_i'. In order for this to happen, the highest other bid b_j must be between b_i and b_i'. In this case, the payoff to i from deviating would be at most $v_i - b_j \leq 0$, and so this deviation to bid b_i' does not improve i's payoff.

Next, suppose that instead of bidding v_i, bidder i chooses a bid $b_i'' < v_i$. This only affects bidder i's payoff if i would win with bid v_i but would lose with bid b_i''. So before deviating, v_i was the winning bid, and the second-place bid b_k was between v_i and b_i''. In this case, i's payoff before deviating was $v_i - b_k \geq 0$, and after deviating it is 0 (since i loses), so again this deviation does not improve i's payoff.

This completes the argument that truthful bidding is a dominant strategy in a sealed-bid second-price auction. The heart of the argument is the fact noted at the outset: in a second-price auction, your bid determines whether you win or lose, but not how much you pay in the event that you win. Therefore, you need to evaluate changes to your bid in light of this fact. This also further highlights the parallels to the ascending-bid auction. There too, the analogue of your bid – the point up to which you're willing to stay in the auction – determines whether you'll stay in long enough to win; however, the amount you pay in the event that you win is determined by the point at which the second-place bidder drops out.

The fact that truthfulness is a dominant strategy also makes second-price auctions conceptually very clean. Because truthful bidding is a dominant strategy, it is the best thing to do regardless of what the other bidders are doing. So, in a second-price auction, it makes sense to bid your true value even if other bidders are overbidding, underbidding, colluding, or behaving in other unpredictable ways. In other words, truthful bidding is a good idea even if the competing bidders in the auction don't know that they ought to be bidding truthfully as well.

We now turn to first-price auctions, where we'll find that the situation is much more complex. In particular, each bidder now has to reason about the behavior of her competitors in order to arrive at an optimal choice for her own bid.

9.5 First-Price Auctions and Other Formats

In a sealed-bid first-price auction, the value of your bid affects not only whether you win but also how much you pay. As a result, most of the reasoning from the previous section has to be redone, and the conclusions are now different.

To begin with, we can set up the first-price auction as a game in essentially the same way that we did for second-price auctions. As before, bidders are players, and each bidder's strategy is an amount to bid as a function of her true value. The payoff to bidder i with value v_i and bid b_i is simply the following.

> If b_i is not the winning bid, then the payoff to i is 0. If b_i is the winning bid, then the payoff to i is $v_i - b_i$.

The first thing we notice is that bidding your true value is no longer a dominant strategy. By bidding your true value, you would get a payoff of 0 if you lose (as usual), and you would also get a payoff of 0 if you win, since you'd pay exactly what the item was worth to you.

As a result, the optimal way to bid in a first-price auction is to "shade" your bid slightly downward, so that if you win you will get a positive payoff. Determining how much to shade your bid involves balancing a trade-off between two opposing forces. If you bid too close to your true value, then your payoff won't be very large in the event that you win. But if you bid too far below your true value, so as to increase your payoff in the event of winning, then you reduce your chance of being the high bid, and hence your chance of winning at all.

Finding the optimal trade-off between these two factors is a complex problem that depends on knowledge of the other bidders and their distribution of possible values. For example, it is intuitively natural that your bid should be higher – shaded less, closer to your true value – in a first-price auction with many competing bidders than in a first-price auction with only a few competing bidders (keeping other properties of the bidders the same). This is simply because, with a large pool of other bidders, the highest competing bid is likely to be larger, and hence you need to bid higher to get above this and be the highest bid. We will discuss how to determine the optimal bid for a first-price auction in Section 9.7.

All-Pay Auctions. There are other sealed-bid auction formats that arise in different settings. One that initially seems counterintuitive in its formulation is the *all-pay auction*: each bidder submits a bid; the highest bidder receives the item; and *all* bidders pay their bids, regardless of whether they win or lose. That is, the payoffs are now as follows.

> If b_i is not the winning bid, then the payoff to i is $-b_i$. If b_i is the winning bid, then the payoff to i is $v_i - b_i$.

Games with this type of payoff arise in a number of situations, usually where the notion of "bidding" is implicit. Political lobbying can be modeled in this way: each side must spend money on lobbying, but only the successful side receives anything of value for this expenditure. While it is not true that the side spending more on lobbying always wins, there is a clear analogy between the amount spent on lobbying and a bid, with all parties paying their bid regardless of whether they win or lose. One can picture similar considerations arising in settings such as design competitions, in which competing architectural firms spend money on preliminary designs to try to win a contract from a client. This money must be spent before the client makes a decision.

The determination of an optimal bid in an all-pay auction shares a number of qualitative features with the reasoning in a first-price auction: in general you want to bid below your true value, and you must balance the trade-off between bidding high (increasing your probability of winning) and bidding low (decreasing your expenditure if you lose and increasing your payoff if you win). In general, the fact that everyone must pay in this auction format means that bids are typically shaded much lower than in a first-price auction. The framework we develop for determining optimal bids in first-price auctions will also apply to all-pay auctions, as we will see in Section 9.7.

9.6 Common Values and the Winner's Curse

Thus far, we have assumed that bidders' values for the item being auctioned are independent: each bidder knows her own value for the item and is not concerned with how much it is worth to anyone else. This makes sense in a lot of situations, but it clearly doesn't apply to a setting in which the bidders intend to resell the object. In this case, there is a common eventual value for the object – the amount it will generate on resale – but it is not necessarily known. Each bidder i may have some private information about the common value, leading to an estimate v_i of this value. Individual bidder estimates will typically be slightly wrong, and they also will typically not be independent of each other. One possible model for such estimates is to suppose that the true value is v and that each bidder i's estimate v_i is defined by $v_i = v + x_i$, where x_i is a random number with a mean of 0, representing the error in i's estimate.

Auctions with common values introduce new sources of complexity. To see this, let's start by supposing that an item with a common value is sold using a sealed-bid second-price auction. Is it still a dominant strategy for bidder i to bid v_i? In fact, it's not. To get a sense for why this is true, we can use the model with random errors $v + x_i$. Suppose there are many bidders and that each bids her estimate of the true value. Then, from the result of the auction, the winning bidder not only receives the object, she also learns something about her estimate of the common value – that it was the highest of all the estimates. So in particular, her estimate is more likely to be an overestimate of the common value than an underestimate. Moreover, with many bidders, the second-place bid – which is what she paid – is also likely to be an overestimate. As a result, she will likely lose money on the resale relative to what she paid.

This is known as the *winner's curse*, and it is a phenomenon that has a rich history in the study of auctions. Richard Thaler's review of this history [387] notes that the winner's curse appears to have been first articulated by researchers in the petroleum industry [95]. In this domain, firms bid on oil-drilling rights for tracts of land that have a common value, equal to the value of the oil contained in the tract. The winner's curse has also been studied in the context of competitive contract offers to baseball free agents [98] – with the unknown common value corresponding to the future performance of the baseball player being courted.[2]

Rational bidders should take the winner's curse into account in deciding on their bids: a bidder should bid her best estimate of the value of the object conditional both on her private estimate v_i and on winning the object at her bid. That is, it must be the case that, at an optimal bid, it is better to win the object than not to win it. This means in a common-value auction that bidders will shade their bids downward even when the second-price format is used; with the first-price format, bids will be reduced even further. Determining the optimal bid is fairly complex, and we will not pursue the details of it here. It is also worth noting that in practice, the winner's curse can lead to outright losses on the part of the winning bidder [387], since in a large pool of bidders, anyone who in fact makes an error and overbids is more likely to be the winner of the auction.

9.7 Advanced Material: Bidding Strategies in First-Price and All-Pay Auctions

In the previous two sections we offered some intuition about the way to bid in first-price auctions and in all-pay auctions, but we did not derive optimal bids. We now develop models of bidder behavior that we can use to derive equilibrium bidding strategies in these auctions. We then explore how optimal behavior varies depending on the number of bidders and on the distribution of values. Finally, we analyze how much revenue the seller can expect to obtain from various auctions. The analysis in this section uses elementary calculus and probability theory.

A. Equilibrium Bidding in First-Price Auctions

As the basis for the model, we want to capture a setting in which bidders know how many competitors they have, and they have partial information about their competitors' values for the item. However, they do not know their competitors' values exactly.

---

[2] In these cases as well as others, one could argue that the model of common values is not entirely accurate. One oil company could in principle be more successful than another at extracting oil from a tract of land, and a baseball free agent may flourish if he joins one team but fail if he joins another. But common values are a reasonable approximation in both settings, as in any case where the purpose of bidding is to obtain an item that has some intrinsic but unknown future value. Moreover, the reasoning behind the winner's curse arises even when the item being auctioned has related but nonidentical values to the different bidders.

Let's start with a simple case first and then move on to a more general formulation. In the simple case, suppose there are two bidders, each with a private value that is independently and uniformly distributed between 0 and 1.[3] This information is common knowledge among the two bidders. A *strategy* for a bidder is a function $s(v) = b$ that maps her true value v to a nonnegative bid b. We will make the following simple assumptions about the strategies the bidders are using:

(i) $s(\cdot)$ is a strictly increasing, differentiable function; so in particular, if two bidders have different values, then they produce different bids.

(ii) $s(v) \leq v$ for all v: bidders can shade their bids down, but they never bid above their true values. Notice that, since bids are always non-negative, we have $s(0) = 0$.

These two assumptions permit a wide range of strategies. For example, the strategy of bidding your true value is represented by the function $s(v) = v$, while the strategy of shading your bid downward by a factor of $c < 1$ is represented by $s(v) = cv$. More complex strategies such as $s(v) = v^2$ are also allowed, although we will see later that they are not optimal in first-price auctions.

The two assumptions help us narrow the search for equilibrium strategies. The second of our assumptions only rules out strategies (based on overbidding) that are nonoptimal. The first assumption restricts the scope of possible equilibrium strategies, but it makes the analysis easier while still allowing us to study the important issues.

Finally, because the two bidders are identical in all ways except the actual value they draw from the distribution, we narrow the search for equilibria in one further way: we will consider the case in which the two bidders follow the same strategy $s(\cdot)$.

Equilibrium with Two Bidders: The Revelation Principle. Let's consider what such an equilibrium strategy should look like. First, assumption (i) says that the bidder with the higher value will also produce the higher bid. If bidder i has a value of v_i, the probability that this value is higher than the value of i's competitor in the interval $[0, 1]$ is exactly v_i. Therefore, i will win the auction with probability v_i. If i does win, i receives a payoff of $v_i - s(v_i)$. Putting all this together, we see that i's expected payoff is

$$g(v_i) = v_i(v_i - s(v_i)). \tag{9.1}$$

Now, what does it mean for $s(\cdot)$ to be an equilibrium strategy? It means that, for each bidder i, there is no incentive for i to deviate from strategy $s(\cdot)$ if i's competitor is also using strategy $s(\cdot)$. It's not immediately clear how to analyze deviations to an arbitrary strategy satisfying assumptions (i) and (ii). Fortunately, there is an elegant device that lets us reason about deviations as follows: rather than actually switching to a different strategy, bidder i can implement her deviation by keeping the strategy $s(\cdot)$ but supplying a different "true value" to it.

Here is how this works. First, if i's competitor is also using strategy $s(\cdot)$, then i should never announce a bid above $s(1)$, since i can win with bid $s(1)$ and get a higher payoff with bid $s(1)$ than with any bid $b > s(1)$. So in any possible deviation by

---

[3] The fact that the 0 and 1 are the lowest and highest possible values is not crucial; by shifting and rescaling these quantities, we could equally well consider values that are uniformly distributed between any other pair of endpoints.

i, the bid she will actually report is between $s(0) = 0$ and $s(1)$. Therefore, for the purposes of the auction, she can simulate her deviation to an alternate strategy by first pretending that her true value is v_i' rather than v_i and then applying the existing function $s(\cdot)$ to v_i' instead of v_i. This is a special case of a much broader idea known as the *Revelation Principle* [124, 207, 310]; for our purposes, we can think of it as saying that deviations in the bidding strategy function can instead be viewed as deviations in the "true value" that bidder i supplies to her current strategy $s(\cdot)$.

With this in mind, we can write the condition that i does not want to deviate from strategy $s(\cdot)$ as follows:

$$v_i(v_i - s(v_i)) \geq v(v_i - s(v)) \tag{9.2}$$

for all possible "fake" values v between 0 and 1 that bidder i might want to supply to the function $s(\cdot)$.

Is there a function that satisfies this property? In fact, it is not hard to check that $s(v) = v/2$ satisfies it. To see why, notice that, with this choice of $s(\cdot)$, the left-hand side of Inequality (9.2) becomes $v_i(v_i - v_i/2) = v_i^2/2$ while the right-hand side becomes $v(v_i - v/2) = vv_i - v^2/2$. Collecting all the terms on the left, the inequality simply becomes

$$\frac{1}{2}(v^2 - 2vv_i + v_i^2) \geq 0,$$

which holds because the left-hand side is the square $\frac{1}{2}(v - v_i)^2$.

Thus, the conclusion in this case is quite simple to state. If two bidders know they are competing against each other, and they know that each has a private value drawn uniformly at random from the interval $[0, 1]$, then it is an equilibrium for each to shade their bid down by a factor of 2. Bidding half your true value is optimal if the other bidder is doing this as well.

Note that unlike the case of the second-price auction, we have not identified a dominant strategy, only an equilibrium. In solving for a bidder's optimal strategy, we used each bidder's expectation about her competitor's bidding strategy. In an equilibrium, these expectations are correct. But if other bidders for some reason use nonequilibrium strategies, then any bidder should optimally respond and potentially also play some other bidding strategy.

Deriving the Two-Bidder Equilibrium. In our discussion of the equilibrium $s(v) = v/2$, we initially conjectured the form of the function $s(\cdot)$ and then checked that it satisfied Inequality (9.2). But this approach does not suggest how to discover a function $s(\cdot)$ to use as a conjecture.

An alternate approach is to derive $s(\cdot)$ directly by reasoning about the condition in Inequality (9.2). Here is how we can do this. In order for $s(\cdot)$ to satisfy Inequality (9.2), it must have the property that, for any true value v_i, the expected payoff function $g(v) = v(v_i - s(v))$ is maximized by setting $v = v_i$. Therefore, v_i should satisfy $g'(v_i) = 0$, where g' is the first derivative of $g(\cdot)$ with respect to v. Since

$$g'(v) = v_i - s(v) - vs'(v)$$

by the Product Rule for derivatives, we see that $s(\cdot)$ must solve the differential equation

$$s'(v_i) = 1 - \frac{s(v_i)}{v_i}$$

for all v_i in the interval $[0, 1]$. This differential equation is solved by the function $s(v_i) = v_i/2$.

Equilibrium with Many Bidders. Now let's suppose that there are n bidders, where n can be larger than 2. To start with, we'll continue to assume that each bidder i draws her true value v_i independently and uniformly at random from the interval between 0 and 1.

Much of the reasoning for the case of two bidders still works here, although the basic formula for the expected payoff changes. Specifically, assumption (i) still implies that the bidder with the highest true value will produce the highest bid and hence win the auction. For a given bidder i with true value v_i, what is the probability that her bid is the highest? This requires each other bidder to have a value below v_i; since the values are chosen independently, this event has a probability of v_i^{n-1}. Therefore, bidder i's expected payoff is

$$G(v_i) = v_i^{n-1}(v_i - s(v_i)). \tag{9.3}$$

The condition for $s(\cdot)$ to be an equilibrium strategy remains the same as it was in the case of two bidders. Using the Revelation Principle, we view a deviation from the bidding strategy as supplying a "fake" value v to the function $s(\cdot)$; given this, we require that the true value v_i produces an expected payoff at least as high as the payoff from any deviation:

$$v_i^{n-1}(v_i - s(v_i)) \geq v^{n-1}(v_i - s(v)) \tag{9.4}$$

for all v between 0 and 1.

From this, we can derive the form of the bidding function $s(\cdot)$ using the differential-equation approach that worked for two bidders. The expected payoff function $G(v) = v^{n-1}(v_i - s(v))$ must be maximized by setting $v = v_i$. Setting the derivative $G'(v_i) = 0$ and applying the Product Rule to differentiate G, we get

$$(n-1)v^{n-2}v_i - (n-1)v^{n-2}s(v_i) - v_i^{n-1}s'(v_i) = 0$$

for all v_i between 0 and 1. Dividing through by $(n-1)v^{n-2}$ and solving for $s'(v_i)$, we get the equivalent but typographically simpler equation

$$s'(v_i) = (n-1)\left(1 - \frac{s(v_i)}{v_i}\right) \tag{9.5}$$

for all v_i between 0 and 1. This differential equation is solved by the function

$$s(v_i) = \left(\frac{n-1}{n}\right)v_i.$$

So if each bidder shades her bid down by a factor of $(n-1)/n$, then this behavior is optimal given what everyone else is doing. Notice that when $n = 2$ this is our two-bidder strategy. The form of this strategy highlights an important principle that we discussed in Section 9.5 about strategic bidding in first-price auctions: as the number of bidders increases, you generally have to bid more "aggressively" – shading your bid down less – in order to win. For the simple case of values drawn independently from the uniform distribution, our analysis here quantifies exactly how this increased aggressiveness should depend on the number of bidders, n.

General Distributions. In addition to considering larger numbers of bidders, we can also relax the assumption that bidders' values are drawn from the uniform distribution on an interval.

Suppose that each bidder has her value drawn from a probability distribution over the nonnegative real numbers. We can represent the probability distribution by its *cumulative distribution function* $F(\cdot)$: for any x, the value $F(x)$ is the probability that a number drawn from the distribution is at most x. We will assume that F is a differentiable function.

Most of the earlier analysis continues to hold at a general level. The probability that a bidder i with true value v_i wins the auction is the probability that no other bidder has a larger value, so it is equal to $F(v_i)^{n-1}$. Therefore, the expected payoff to v_i is

$$F(v_i)^{n-1}(v_i - s(v_i)).$$

Then the requirement that the bidder does not want to deviate from this strategy becomes

$$F(v_i)^{n-1}(v_i - s(v_i)) \geq F(v)^{n-1}(v_i - s(v)) \tag{9.6}$$

for all v between 0 and 1.

Finally, this equilibrium condition can be used to write a differential equation just as before, using the fact that the function of v on the right-hand side of Inequality (9.6) should be maximized when $v = v_i$. We apply the Product Rule, and also the Chain Rule for derivatives, keeping in mind that the derivative of the cumulative distribution function $F(\cdot)$ is the probability density function $f(\cdot)$ for the distribution. Proceeding by analogy with the analysis for the uniform distribution, we get the differential equation

$$s'(v_i) = (n - 1)\left(\frac{f(v_i)v_i - f(v_i)s(v_i)}{F(v_i)}\right). \tag{9.7}$$

Notice that, for the uniform distribution on the interval [0, 1], the cumulative distribution function is $F(v) = v$ and the density is $f(v) = 1$, which applied to Equation (9.7) gives us back Equation (9.5).

Finding an explicit solution to Equation (9.7) isn't possible unless we have an explicit form for the distribution of values, but it provides a framework for taking arbitrary distributions and solving for equilibrium bidding strategies.

B. Seller Revenue

Now that we've analyzed bidding strategies for first-price auctions, we can return to an issue that came up at the end of Section 9.3: how to compare the revenue a seller should expect to make in first- and second-price auctions.

There are two competing forces at work here. On the one hand, in a second-price auction, the seller explicitly commits to collecting less given any fixed set of bids, since he only charges the second-highest bid. On the other hand, in a first-price auction, the bidders reduce their bids, which also reduces what the seller can collect.

To understand how these opposing factors trade off against each other, suppose we have n bidders with values drawn independently from the uniform distribution on the interval [0, 1]. Since the seller's revenue is based on the values of the highest and second-highest bids, which in turn depend on the highest and second-highest values, we need to know the expectations of these quantities.[4] Computing these expectations is a bit complicated, but the form of the answer is very simple. Here is the basic statement:

> Suppose n numbers are drawn independently from the uniform distribution on the interval [0, 1] and then sorted from smallest to largest. The expected value of the number in the kth position on this sorted list is $\frac{k}{n+1}$.

Now, if the seller runs a second-price auction, and the bidders follow their dominant strategies and bid truthfully, the seller's expected revenue is the expectation of the second-highest value. Since this will be the value in position $n - 1$ in the sorted order of the n random values from smallest to largest, the expected value is $(n - 1)/(n + 1)$, by the formula just described. On the other hand, if the seller instead runs a first-price auction, then in equilibrium we expect the winning bidder to submit a bid that is $(n - 1)/n$ times her true value. Her true value has an expectation of $n/(n + 1)$ (since it is the largest of n numbers drawn independently from the unit interval), and so the seller's expected revenue is

$$\left(\frac{n - 1}{n}\right)\left(\frac{n}{n + 1}\right) = \frac{n - 1}{n + 1}.$$

The two auctions provide exactly the same expected revenue to the seller!

Revenue Equivalence. As far as seller revenue is concerned, this calculation is in a sense the tip of the iceberg: it is a reflection of a much broader and deeper principle known in the auction literature as *revenue equivalence* [256, 288, 311]. Roughly speaking, revenue equivalence asserts that a seller's revenue will be the same across a broad class of auctions and arbitrary independent distributions of bidder values, when bidders follow equilibrium strategies. A formalization and proof of the revenue equivalence principle can be found in the book on auctions by Paul Klemperer [256].

From the discussion here, it is easy to see how the ability to commit to a selling mechanism is valuable for a seller. Consider, for example, a seller using a second-price auction. If the bidders bid truthfully and the seller does not sell the object as promised, then the seller knows the bidders' values and can bargain with them from this advantaged position. At worst, the seller should be able to sell the object to the bidder with the highest value at a price equal to the second-highest value. (The bidder with the highest value knows that if she turns down the trade at this price then the bidder with the second-highest value will take it.) But the seller may be able to

---

[4] In the language of probability theory, these are known as the expectations of the *order statistics*.

do better than this in the negotiation, and so overall the bidders lose relative to the originally promised second-price auction. If bidders suspect that this scenario may occur with some probability, then they may no longer find it optimal to bid truthfully in the auction, and so it is not clear what the seller receives.

Reserve Prices. In our discussion of how a seller should choose an auction format, we have implicitly assumed that the seller must sell the object. Let's briefly consider how the seller's expected revenue changes if he has the option of holding onto the item and choosing not to sell it. To be able to reason about the seller's payoff in the event that this happens, let's assume that the seller values the item at $u \geq 0$, which is thus the payoff he gets from keeping the item rather than selling it.

It's clear that if $u > 0$ then the seller should not use a simple first- or second-price auction. In either case, the winning bid may be less than u, and the seller would not want to sell the object. If the seller refuses to sell after having specified a first- or second-price auction, then we are back to the case of a seller who might break his initial commitment to the format.

Instead, it is better for the seller to announce a *reserve price* of r before running the auction. With a reserve price, the item is sold to the highest bidder *if* the highest bid is above r; otherwise, the item is not sold. In a first-price auction with a reserve price, the winning bidder (if there is one) still pays her bid. In a second-price auction with a reserve price, the winning bidder (if there is one) pays the maximum of the second-place bid and the reserve price r. As we will see, it is in fact useful for the seller to declare a reserve price even if his value for the item is $u = 0$.

Let's consider how to reason about the optimal value for the reserve price in the case of a second-price auction. First, it is not difficult to go back over the argument that truthful bidding is a dominant strategy in second-price auctions and to check that it still holds in the presence of a reserve price. Essentially, it is as if the seller were another "simulated" bidder who always bids r; since truthful bidding is optimal regardless of how other bidders behave, the presence of this additional simulated bidder has no effect on how any of the real bidders should behave.

Now, what value should the seller choose for the reserve price? If the item is worth u to the seller, then clearly he should set $r \geq u$. But in fact the reserve price that maximizes the seller's expected revenue is strictly greater than u. To see why this is true, let's first consider a very simple case: a second-price auction with a single bidder, whose value is uniformly distributed on $[0, 1]$, and a seller whose value for the item is $u = 0$. With only one bidder, the second-price auction with no reserve price will sell the item to the bidder at a price of 0. On the other hand, suppose the seller sets a reserve price of $r > 0$. In this case, with probability $1 - r$, the bidder's value is above r, and the object will be sold to the bidder at a price of r. With probability r, the bidder's value is below r, and so the seller keeps the item, receiving a payoff of $u = 0$. Therefore, the seller's expected revenue is $r(1 - r)$, which is maximized at $r = 1/2$. If the seller's value u is greater than 0, then his expected payoff is $r(1 - r) + ru$ (since he receives a payoff of u when the item is not sold), and this payoff is maximized by setting $r = (1 + u)/2$. So with a single bidder, the optimal reserve price is halfway between the value of the object to the seller and the maximum possible bidder value. With more intricate analyses, one can similarly determine the optimal reserve price for a second-price auction with multiple bidders, as well as for a first-price auction with equilibrium bidding strategies of the form we derived earlier.

C. Equilibrium Bidding in All-Pay Auctions

The style of analysis we've been using for first-price auctions can be adapted without much difficulty to other formats as well. Here we will show how this works for the analysis of all-pay auctions: recall from Section 9.5 that this is an auction format – designed to model activities such as lobbying – where the highest bidder wins the item but everyone pays their bid.

We keep the general framework we used earlier in this section for first-price auctions with n bidders, each with a value drawn independently and uniformly at random from between 0 and 1. As before, we want to find a function $s(\cdot)$ mapping values to bids, so that using $s(\cdot)$ is optimal if all other bidders are using it.

With an all-pay auction, the expected payoff for bidder i has a negative term if i does not win. The formula is now

$$v_i^{n-1}(v_i - s(v_i)) + (1 - v_i^{n-1})(-s(v_i)),$$

where the first term corresponds to the payoff in the event that i wins, and the second term corresponds to the payoff in the event that i loses. As before, we can think of a deviation from this bidding strategy as supplying a fake value v to the function $s(\cdot)$; so if $s(\cdot)$ is an equilibrium choice of strategies by the bidders, then

$$v_i^{n-1}(v_i - s(v_i)) + (1 - v_i^{n-1})(-s(v_i)) \geq v^{n-1}(v_i - s(v)) + (1 - v^{n-1})(-s(v)) \quad (9.8)$$

for all v in the interval $[0, 1]$.

Notice that the expected payoff consists of a fixed cost $s(v)$ that is paid regardless of the win/loss outcome, plus a value of v_i in the event that i wins. Canceling the common terms in Inequality (9.8), we can rewrite it as

$$v_i^n - s(v_i) \geq v^{n-1}v_i - s(v) \quad (9.9)$$

for all v in the interval $[0, 1]$. Now, writing the right-hand side as a function $g(v) = v^{n-1}v_i - s(v)$, we can view Inequality (9.9) as requiring that $v = v_i$ maximizes the function $g(\cdot)$. The resulting equation $g'(v_i) = 0$ then gives us a differential equation that specifies $s(\cdot)$ quite simply:

$$s'(v_i) = (n - 1)v_i^{n-1}$$

and hence $s(v) = \left(\dfrac{n - 1}{n}\right) v_i^n$.

Since $v_i < 1$, raising it to the nth power (as specified by the function $s(\cdot)$) reduces it exponentially in the number of bidders. This shows that bidders will shade their bids downward significantly as the number of bidders in an all-pay auction increases.

We can also work out the seller's expected revenue. The seller collects money from everyone in an all-pay auction; however, the bidders all submit low bids. The expected value of a single bidder's contribution to seller revenue is simply

$$\int_0^1 s(v)\,dv = \left(\frac{n - 1}{n}\right) \int_0^1 v^n\,dv = \left(\frac{n - 1}{n}\right)\left(\frac{1}{n + 1}\right).$$

Since the seller collects this much in expectation from each bidder, the seller's overall expected revenue is

$$n \left(\frac{n-1}{n} \right) \left(\frac{1}{n+1} \right) = \frac{n-1}{n+1}.$$

This is exactly the same as the seller's expected revenue in the first- and second-price auctions with the same assumptions about bidder values. Again, this is a reflection of the much broader revenue equivalence principle, which includes all-pay auctions in the general set of auction formats it covers.

9.8 Exercises

1. In this question we consider an auction in which there is one seller who wants to sell one unit of a good and a group of bidders who are each interested in purchasing the good. The seller will run a sealed-bid, second-price auction. Your firm will bid in the auction, but it does not know for sure how many other bidders will participate in the auction. There will be either two or three other bidders in addition to your firm. All bidders have independent, private values for the good. Your firm's value for the good is c. What bid should your firm submit, and how does it depend on the number of other bidders who show up? Give a brief (one- to three-sentence) explanation for your answer.

2. In this problem we ask how the number of bidders in a second-price, sealed-bid auction affects how much the seller can expect to receive for his object. Assume that there are two bidders who have independent, private values v_i that are either 1 or 3. For each bidder, the probabilities of 1 and 3 are both $\frac{1}{2}$. (If there is a tie at a bid of x for the highest bid, the winner is selected at random from among the highest bidders and the price is x.)

    (a) Show that the seller's expected revenue is $\frac{6}{4}$.
    (b) Now let's suppose that there are three bidders who have independent, private values v_i that are either 1 or 3. For each bidder, the probabilities of 1 and 3 are both $\frac{1}{2}$. What is the seller's expected revenue in this case?
    (c) Briefly explain why changing the number of bidders affects the seller's expected revenue.

3. In this problem we ask how much a seller can expect to receive for his object in a second-price, sealed-bid auction. Assume that all bidders have independent, private values v_i that are either 0 or 1. The probability of 0 and 1 are both $\frac{1}{2}$.

    (a) Suppose there are two bidders. Then there are four possible pairs of their values (v_1, v_2): $(0, 0), (1, 0), (0, 1),$ and $(1, 1)$. Each pair of values has probability 1/4. Show that the seller's expected revenue is 1/4. (Assume that if there is a tie at a bid of x for the highest bid the winner is selected at random from among the highest bidders and the price is x.)
    (b) What is the seller's expected revenue if there are three bidders?
    (c) This suggests a conjecture that, as the number of bidders increases, the seller's expected revenue also increases. In the example we consider that the seller's expected revenue actually converges to 1 as the number of

bidders grows. Explain why this should occur. You do not need to write a proof; an intuitive explanation is fine.

4. A seller intends to run a second-price, sealed-bid auction for an object. There are two bidders, a and b, who have independent, private values v_i that are either 0 or 1. For both bidders the probabilities of $v_i = 0$ and $v_i = 1$ are each $\frac{1}{2}$. Both bidders understand the auction, but bidder b sometimes makes a mistake about his value for the object. Half of the time his value is 1 and he is aware that it is 1; the other half of the time his value is 0 but occasionally he mistakenly believes that his value is 1. Let's suppose that when b's value is 0 he acts as if it is 1 with probability $\frac{1}{2}$ and as if it is 0 with probability $\frac{1}{2}$. So in effect bidder b sees value 0 with probability $\frac{1}{4}$ and value 1 with probability $\frac{3}{4}$. Bidder a never makes mistakes about his value for the object, but he is aware of the mistakes that bidder b makes. Both bidders bid optimally given their perceptions of the value of the object. Assume that if there is a tie at a bid of x for the highest bid the winner is selected at random from among the highest bidders and the price is x.

    (a) Is bidding his true value still a dominant strategy for bidder a? Explain briefly.
    (b) What is the seller's expected revenue? Explain briefly.

5. Consider a second-price, sealed-bid auction with one seller who has one unit of the object, which he values at s, and two buyers, 1 and 2, who have values of v_1 and v_2 for the object. The values s, v_1, and v_2 are all independent, private values. Suppose that both buyers know that the seller will submit his own sealed bid of s, but they do not know the value of s. Is it optimal for the buyers to bid truthfully? That is, should they each bid their true value? Give an explanation for your answer.

6. In this question we consider the effect of collusion between bidders in a second-price, sealed-bid auction. There is one seller who will sell one object using a second-price, sealed-bid auction. The bidders have independent, private values drawn from a distribution on $[0, 1]$. If a bidder with value v gets the object at price p, his payoff is $v - p$; if a bidder does not get the object his payoff is 0. We consider the possibility of collusion between two bidders who know each other's value for the object. Suppose that the objective of these two colluding bidders is to choose their two bids to maximize the sum of their payoffs. The bidders can submit any bids they like as long as the bids are in $[0, 1]$.

    (a) Let's first consider the case in which there are only two bidders. What two bids should they submit? Explain.
    (b) Now suppose that there is a third bidder who is not part of the collusion. Does the existence of this bidder change the optimal bids for the two bidders who are colluding? Explain.

7. A seller announces that he will sell a case of rare wine using a sealed-bid, second-price auction. A group of I individuals plans to bid on this case of wine. Each bidder is interested in the wine for his or her personal consumption; the bidders' consumption values for the wine may differ, but they don't plan to resell the wine. So we view their values for the wine as independent, private values (as earlier in this chapter). You are one of these bidders; in particular, you are bidder number i and your value for the wine is v_i.

How should you bid in each of the following situations? In each case, provide an explanation for your answer; a formal proof is not necessary.

(a) You know that a group of the bidders will collude on bids. This group will choose one bidder to submit a "real bid" of v and the others will all submit bids of 0. You are not a member of this collusive group, and you cannot collude with any other bidder.

(b) You, and all of the other bidders, have just learned that this seller will collect bids but won't actually sell the wine according to the rules of a second-price auction. Instead, after collecting the bids the seller will tell all of the bidders that some other fictional bidder actually submitted the highest bid and so won the auction. This bidder, of course, doesn't exist, so the seller will still have the wine after the auction is over. The seller plans to privately contact the highest actual bidder and tell him or her that the fictional high bidder defaulted (he didn't buy the wine after all) and that this bidder can buy the wine for the price he or she bid in the auction. You cannot collude with any bidder. (You do not have to derive an optimal bidding strategy. It is enough to explain whether your bid would differ from your value and if so in what direction.)

8. In this problem we ask how irrational behavior on the part of one bidder affects optimal behavior for the other bidders in an auction. In this auction the seller has one unit of a good which will be sold using a second-price, sealed-bid auction. Assume that there are three bidders who have independent, private values for the good, v_1, v_2, and v_3, which are uniformly distributed on the interval $[0, 1]$.

(a) Suppose first that all bidders behave rationally; that is, they submit optimal bids. Which bidder (in terms of values) wins the auction and how much does this bidder pay (again in terms of the bidder's values)?

(b) Suppose now that bidder 3 irrationally bids more than his true value for the object; in particular, bidder 3's bid is $(v_3 + 1)/2$. All other bidders know that bidder 3 is irrational in this way, although they do not know bidder 3's actual value for the object. How does this affect the behavior of the other bidders?

(c) What effect does bidder 3's irrational behavior have on the expected pay-offs of bidder 1? Here the expectation is over the values of v_2 and v_3, which bidder 1 does not know. You do not have to provide an explicit solution or write a proof for your answer; an intuitive explanation of the effect is fine. (Remember that a bidder's payoff is the bidder's value for the object minus the price, if the bidder wins the auction, or 0, if the bidder does not win the auction.)

9. In this problem we ask how much a seller can expect to receive for his object in a second-price, sealed-bid auction. Assume that there are two bidders who have independent, private values v_i, which are either 1 or 2. For each bidder, the probabilities of $v_i = 1$ and $v_i = 2$ are each $\frac{1}{2}$. Assume that if there is a tie at a bid of x for the highest bid the winner is selected at random from among the highest bidders and the price is x. We also assume that the value of the object to the seller is 0.

(a) Show that the seller's expected revenue is $\frac{5}{4}$.

(b) Now let's suppose that the seller sets a reserve price of R, where $1 < R < 2$; that is, the object is sold to the highest bidder if her bid is at least R, and the price this bidder pays is the maximum of the second-highest bid and R. If no bid is at least R, then the object is not sold, and the seller receives zero revenue. Suppose that all bidders know R. What is the seller's expected revenue as a function of R?

(c) Using the previous part, show that a seller who wants to maximize expected revenue would never set a reserve price, R, that is more than 1 and less than 1.5.

10. In this problem we examine a second-price, sealed-bid auction. Assume that there are two bidders who have independent, private values v_i, which are either 1 or 7. For each bidder, the probabilities of $v_i = 1$ and $v_i = 7$ are each $\frac{1}{2}$. So there are four possible pairs of the bidders' values (v_1, v_2): $(1, 1), (1, 7), (7, 1),$ and $(7, 7)$. Each pair of values has probability $\frac{1}{4}$.

Assume that if there is a tie at a bid of x for the highest bid the winner is selected at random from among the highest bidders and the price is x.

(a) For each pair of values, what bid will each bidder submit, what price will the winning bidder pay, and how much profit (the difference between the winning bidder's value and price he pays) will the winning bidder earn?

(b) Now let's examine how much revenue the seller can expect to earn and how much profit the bidders can expect to make in the second-price auction. Both revenue and profit depend on the values, so let's calculate the average of each of these numbers across all four of the possible pairs of values. (Note that in doing this we are computing each bidder's expected profit before the bidder knows his value for the object.) What is the seller's expected revenue in the second-price auction? What is the expected profit for each bidder?

(c) The seller now decides to charge an entry fee of 1. Any bidder who wants to participate in the auction must pay this fee to the seller before bidding begins and, in fact, this fee is imposed before each bidder knows his or her own value for the object. The bidders know only the distribution of values and that anyone who pays the fee will be allowed to participate in a second-price auction for the object. This adds a new first stage to the game in which bidders decide simultaneously whether to pay the fee and enter the auction, or to not pay the fee and stay out of the auction. This first stage is then followed by a second stage in which anyone who pays the fee participates in the auction. We assume that after the first stage is over, both potential bidders learn their own value for the object (but not the other potential bidder's value for the object) and that they both learn whether or not the other potential bidder decided to enter the auction.

Let's assume that any potential bidder who does not participate in the auction has a profit of 0; if no one chooses to participate, then the seller keeps the object and does not run an auction; if only one bidder chooses to participate in the auction then the seller runs a second-price auction with only this one bidder (and treats the second highest bid as 0); and finally, if both bidders participate, the second-price auction is the one you solved in part (a).

Is there an equilibrium in which each bidder pays the fee and participates in the auction? Give an explanation for your answer.

11. In this question we will examine a second-price, sealed-bid auction for a single item. We'll consider a case in which true values for the item may differ across bidders, and it requires extensive research by a bidder to determine her own true value for an item – maybe this is because the bidder needs to determine her ability to extract value from the item after purchasing it (and this ability may differ from bidder to bidder).

There are three bidders. Bidders 1 and 2 have values v_1 and v_2, each of which is a random number independently and uniformly distributed on the interval $[0,1]$. Through having performed the requisite level of research, bidders 1 and 2 know their own values for the item, v_1 and v_2, respectively, but they do not know each other's value for item.

Bidder 3 has not performed enough research to know his own true value for the item. He does know that he and bidder 2 are extremely similar, and therefore that his true value v_3 is exactly equal to the true value v_2 of bidder 2. The problem is that bidder 3 does not know this value v_2 (nor does he know v_1).

(a) How should bidder 1 bid in this auction?
How should bidder 2 bid?

(b) How should bidder 3 behave in this auction?
Provide an explanation for your answer; a formal proof is not necessary.

PART THREE

Markets and Strategic Interaction in Networks

CHAPTER 10

Matching Markets

We have now seen a number of ways of thinking both about network structure and about the behavior of agents as they interact with each other. A few of our examples have brought these together directly – such as the issue of traffic in a network, including Braess's Paradox – and in the next few chapters we explore this convergence of network structure and strategic interaction more fully, and in a range of different settings.

First, we think about markets as a prime example of network-structured interaction between many agents. When we consider markets creating opportunities for interaction among buyers and sellers, there is an implicit network that encodes the access between these buyers and sellers. In fact, there are a number of ways of using networks to model interactions among market participants, and we will discuss several of these models. Later, in Chapter 12 on *network exchange theory*, we will discuss how market-style interactions become a metaphor for the broad notion of *social exchange*, in which the social dynamics within a group can be modeled by the power imbalances of the interactions within the group's social network.

10.1 Bipartite Graphs and Perfect Matchings

Matching markets form the first class of models we consider, as the focus of the current chapter. Matching markets have a long history of study in economics, operations research, and other areas because they embody, in a very clean and stylized way, a number of basic principles: the way in which people may have different preferences for different kinds of goods, the way in which prices can decentralize the allocation of goods to people, and the way in which such prices can in fact lead to allocations that are socially optimal.

We will introduce these various ingredients gradually, by progressing through a succession of increasingly rich models. We begin with a setting in which goods are allocated to people based on preferences, and these preferences are expressed in network form, but there is no explicit buying, selling, or price setting. This first setting will also be a crucial component of the more complex ones that follow.

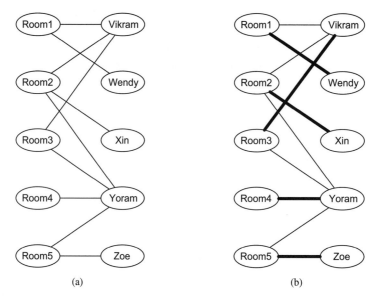

Figure 10.1. (a) An example of a bipartite graph and (b) a perfect matching in this graph, indicated via the dark edges.

Bipartite Graphs. The model we start with is called the *bipartite matching problem*, and we can motivate it via the following scenario. Suppose that the administrators of a college dormitory are assigning rooms to returning students for a new academic year; each room is designed for a single student, and each student is asked to list several acceptable options for the room they'd like to get. Students can have different preferences over rooms; some people might want larger rooms, quieter rooms, sunnier rooms, and so forth – and so the lists provided by the students may overlap in complex ways.

We can model the lists provided by the students using a graph, as follows. There is a node for each student, a node for each room, and an edge connecting a student to a room if the student has listed the room as an acceptable option. Figure 10.1(a) shows an example with five students and five rooms (indicating, for instance, that the student named Vikram has listed each of rooms 1, 2, and 3 as acceptable options, while the student named Wendy only listed room 1).

This type of graph is *bipartite*, an important property that we saw earlier, in a different context, in talking about affiliation networks in Chapter 4. In a bipartite graph the nodes are divided into two categories, and each edge connects a node in one category to a node in the other category. In this case, the two categories are students and rooms. Just as bipartite graphs were useful in Chapter 4 to represent the participation of people in different activities, here they are useful for modeling situations in which individuals or objects of one type are being assigned or matched up with individuals or objects of another type. As in Chapter 4, we generally draw bipartite graphs as in Figure 10.1(a), with the two different categories of nodes drawn as two parallel vertical columns, and the edges crossing between the two columns.

Perfect Matchings. Let's return to the task that the college dorm administrators were trying to solve: assigning each student a room that they'd be happy to accept. This task has a natural interpretation in terms of the graph we've just drawn: because the edges represent acceptable options for students, we want to assign a distinct room to each student, so that each student is assigned a room to which he or she is connected by an edge. Figure 10.1(b) shows such an assignment, with the darkened edges indicating who gets which room.

We will refer to such an assignment as a *perfect matching*:

> When there are an equal number of nodes on each side of a bipartite graph, a *perfect matching* is an assignment of nodes on the left to nodes on the right, in such a way that
>
> (i) each node is connected by an edge to the node it is assigned to, and
> (ii) no two nodes on the left are assigned to the same node on the right.

As Figure 10.1(b) makes clear, there is an equivalent way to think about perfect matchings in terms of the *edges* that form the assignment: a perfect matching can also be viewed as a choice of edges in the bipartite graph so that each node is the endpoint of *exactly one* of the chosen edges.

Constricted Sets. If a bipartite graph has a perfect matching, it's easy to demonstrate this fact: you just indicate the edges that form the perfect matching. But what if a bipartite graph has no perfect matching? What could you show someone to convince them that there isn't one?

At first glance, this is not clear; one naturally worries that the only way to convince someone that there is no perfect matching is to plow through all the possibilities and show that no pairing works. But in fact there is a clean way to demonstrate that no perfect matching exists, based on the idea illustrated in Figure 10.2. First, Figure 10.2(a) shows a bipartite graph that contains no perfect matching. In Figure 10.2(b) we show a succinct reason why there is no perfect matching in this graph: the set consisting of Vikram, Wendy, and Xin, taken together, has collectively provided only two options for rooms that would be acceptable to any of them. With three people and only two acceptable rooms, there is clearly no way to construct a perfect matching – one of these three people would have to get an option they didn't want in any assignment of rooms.

We call the set of three students in this example a *constricted set*, because their edges to the other side of the bipartite graph "constrict" the formation of a perfect matching. This example points to a general phenomenon, which we can make precise by defining in general what it means for a set to be constricted, as follows. First, for any set of nodes, S, on the right-hand side of a bipartite graph, we say that a node on the left-hand side is a *neighbor* of S if it has an edge to some node in S. We define the *neighbor set* of S, denoted $N(S)$, to be the collection of all neighbors of S. Finally, we say that a set S on the right-hand side is *constricted* if S is strictly larger than $N(S)$; that is, S contains strictly more nodes than $N(S)$ does.

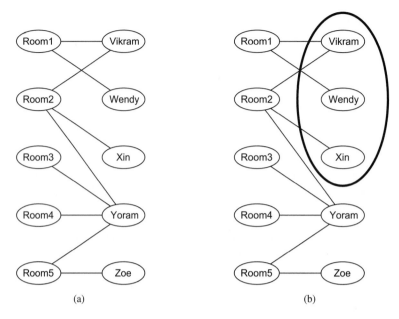

Figure 10.2. (a) A bipartite graph with no perfect matching and (b) a constricted set demonstrating there is no perfect matching.

If there's a constricted set S in a bipartite graph, it immediately shows that there can be no perfect matching: each node in S would have to be matched to a different node in $N(S)$, but there are more nodes in S than there are in $N(S)$, so this is not possible.

So it's fairly easy to see that constricted sets form one kind of obstacle to the presence of perfect matchings. What's also true, though far from obvious, is that constricted sets are in fact the *only* kind of obstacle. This is the crux of the following fact, known as the *Matching Theorem.*

> *Matching Theorem:* If a bipartite graph (with equal numbers of nodes on the left and right) has no perfect matching, then it must contain a constricted set.

The Matching Theorem was independently discovered by Denes König in 1931 and Phillip Hall in 1935 [280]. Without the theorem, one might have imagined that a bipartite graph could fail to have a perfect matching for all sorts of reasons, some of them perhaps even too complicated to explain. But what the theorem says is that the simple notion of a constricted set is in fact the *only* obstacle to having a perfect matching. For our purposes in this chapter, we will only need to use the fact that the Matching Theorem is true, without having to go into the details of its proof. However, its proof is elegant as well, and we describe a proof of the theorem in Section 10.6 at the end of this chapter.

One way to think about the Matching Theorem, using our example of students and rooms, is as follows. After the students submit their lists of acceptable rooms, it's easy for the dormitory administrators to explain to the students what happened, regardless of the outcome. Either they can announce the perfect matching giving the assignment of students to rooms, or they can explain that no assignment is possible by indicating a

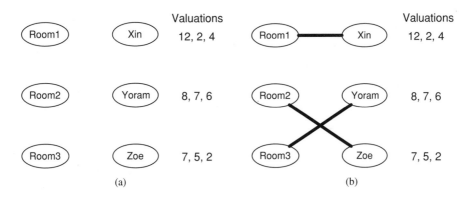

Figure 10.3. (a) A set of valuations. Each person's valuations for the objects appear as a list next to him or her. (b) An optimal assignment with respect to these valuations.

set of students who collectively gave too small a set of acceptable options. This latter case is a constricted set.

10.2 Valuations and Optimal Assignments

The problem of bipartite matching from the previous section illustrates some aspects of a market in a very simple form: individuals express preferences in the form of acceptable options; a perfect matching then solves the problem of allocating objects to individuals according to these preferences; and if there is no perfect matching, it is because of a "constriction" in the system that blocks it.

We now want to extend this model to introduce some additional features. First, rather than expressing preferences simply as binary "acceptable-or-not" choices, we allow each individual to express *how much* they'd like each object, in numerical form. In our example of students and dorm rooms from Section 10.1, suppose that, rather than specifying a list of acceptable rooms, each student provides a numerical score for each room, indicating how happy they'd be with it. We will refer to these numbers as the students' *valuations* for the respective rooms. Figure 10.3(a) shows an example of this with three students and three rooms; for instance, Xin's valuations for rooms 1, 2, and 3 are 12, 2, and 4, respectively (while Yoram's valuations for rooms 1, 2, and 3 are 8, 7, and 6, respectively). Notice that students may disagree on which rooms are better, and by how much.

We can define valuations whenever we have a collection of individuals evaluating a collection of objects. And using these valuations, we can evaluate the *quality* of an assignment of objects to individuals, as follows: it is the sum of each individual's valuation for what they get.[1] Thus, for example, the quality of the assignment illustrated in Figure 10.3(b) is $12 + 6 + 5 = 23$.

---

[1] Of course, this notion of the quality of an assignment is appropriate only if adding individual's valuations makes sense. We can interpret individual valuations here as the maximum amount the individuals are willing to pay for items, so the sum of their valuations for the items they are assigned is just the maximum amount the group would be willing to pay in total for the assignment. The issue of adding individuals' payoffs was also discussed in Chapter 6, where we defined social optimality using the sum of payoffs in a game.

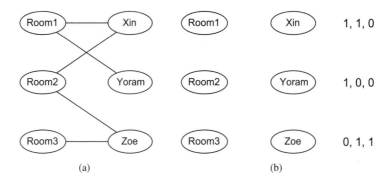

Figure 10.4. (a) A bipartite graph in which we want to search for a perfect matching and (b) a corresponding set of valuations for the same nodes so that finding the optimal assignment lets us determine whether there is a perfect matching in the original graph.

If the dorm administrators had accurate data on each student's valuations for each room, then a reasonable way to assign rooms to students would be to choose the assignment of maximum possible quality. We refer to this as the *optimal assignment*, because it maximizes the total happiness of everyone for what they get. You can check that the assignment in Figure 10.3(b) is in fact the optimal assignment for this set of valuations. Of course, although the optimal assignment maximizes total happiness, it does not necessarily give everyone their favorite item; for example, in Figure 10.3(b), all the students think room 1 is the best, but it can only go to one of them.

In a very concrete sense, the problem of finding an optimal assignment also forms a natural generalization of the bipartite matching problem from Section 10.1. Specifically, it contains the bipartite matching problem as a special case. Here is why. Suppose, as in Section 10.1, that there are an equal number of students and rooms, and each student simply submits a list of acceptable rooms without providing a numerical valuation; this gives us a bipartite graph as in Figure 10.4(a). We would like to know if this bipartite graph contains a perfect matching, and we can express precisely this question in the language of valuations and optimal assignments as follows. We give each student a valuation of 1 for each room they included on their acceptable list, and a valuation of 0 for each room they omitted from their list. Applying this translation to the graph in Figure 10.4(a), for example, we get the valuations shown in Figure 10.4(b). Now, there is a perfect matching precisely when we can find an assignment that gives each student a room that he or she values at 1 rather than 0 – that is, precisely when the optimal assignment has a total valuation equal to the number of students. This simple translation shows how the problem of bipartite matching is implicit in the broader problem of finding an optimal assignment.

While the definition of an optimal assignment is quite natural and general, it is far from obvious whether there is a comparably natural way to find or characterize the optimal assignment for a given set of valuations. This is in fact a bit subtle; we will describe a way to determine an optimal assignment, in the context of a broader market interpretation of this problem, in the two next sections.

10.3 Prices and the Market-Clearing Property

Thus far, we have been using the metaphor of a central "administrator" who determines a perfect matching, or an optimal assignment, by collecting data from everyone and then performing a centralized computation. And while there are clearly instances of market-like activity that function this way (such as our example of students and dorm rooms), a more standard picture of a market involves much less central coordination, with individuals making decisions based on prices and their own valuations.

Capturing this latter idea brings us to the crucial step in our formulation of matching markets: understanding the way in which prices can serve to decentralize the market. We will see that if we replace the role of the central administrator by a particular scheme for pricing items, then allowing individuals to follow their own self-interest based on valuations and prices can still produce optimal assignments.

To describe this, let's change the housing metaphor slightly, from students and dorm rooms to one where the role of prices is more natural. Suppose that we have a collection of *sellers*, each with a house for sale, and an equal-sized collection of *buyers*, each of whom wants a house. By analogy with the previous section, each buyer has a *valuation* for each house and, as before, two different buyers may have very different valuations for the same houses. The valuation that a buyer j has for the house held by seller i will be denoted v_{ij}, with the subscripts i and j indicating that the valuation depends on the identities of both the seller i and the buyer j. We also assume that each valuation is a nonnegative whole number $(0, 1, 2, \ldots)$. We assume that sellers have a valuation of 0 for each house; they care only about receiving payment from buyers, which we define next.[2]

Prices and Payoffs. Suppose that each seller i puts his house up for sale, offering to sell it for a price $p_i \geq 0$. If a buyer j buys the house from seller i at this price, we say that the buyer's *payoff* is her valuation for this house, minus the amount of money she had to pay: $v_{ij} - p_i$. So given a set of prices, if buyer j wants to maximize her payoff, she will buy from the seller i for which this quantity $v_{ij} - p_i$ is maximized, with the following caveats. First, if this quantity is maximized in a tie between several sellers, then the buyer can maximize her payoff by choosing any one of them. Second, if her payoff $v_{ij} - p_i$ is negative for every choice of seller i, then the buyer would prefer not to buy any house: we assume she can obtain a payoff of 0 by simply not transacting.

We will call the seller or sellers that maximize the payoff for buyer j the *preferred sellers* of buyer j, provided the payoff from these sellers is not negative. We say that buyer j has no preferred seller if the payoffs $v_{ij} - p_i$ are negative for all choices of i.

---

[2] Our assumption that sellers all have valuations of 0 for their houses is done for the sake of simplicity; if we wanted, we could directly adapt the arguments here to the case in which "zero" is really some minimum base level, and all other valuations and prices represent amounts above this base level. It is also not hard to adapt our analysis to the case in which sellers each might have different valuations for their houses. Since none of these more general models adds much to the underlying set of ideas, we will stick with the simple assumption that sellers have valuations of 0 for their houses.

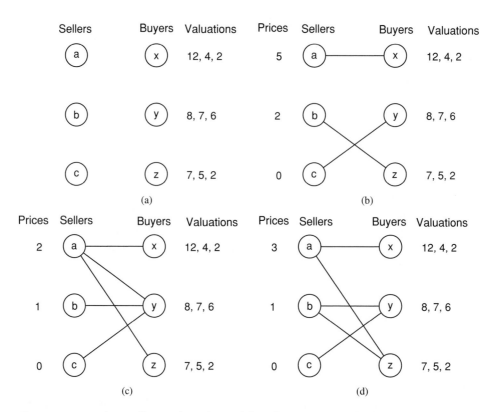

Figure 10.5. (a) Three sellers (*a*, *b*, and *c*) and three buyers (*x*, *y*, and *z*). For each buyer node, the valuations for the houses of the respective sellers appear in a list next to the node. (b) Each buyer creates a link to her preferred seller. The resulting set of edges is the preferred-seller graph for this set of market-clearing prices. (c) The preferred-seller graph for prices 2, 1, and 0 (prices that don't clear the market). (d) The preferred-seller graph for prices 3, 1, and 0 (market-clearing prices, where tie-breaking is required).

In Figures 10.5(b)–10.5(d), we show the results of three different sets of prices for the same set of buyer valuations. Note how the sets of preferred sellers for each buyer change depending on what the prices are. For example, in Figure 10.5(b), buyer *x* would receive a payoff of $12 - 5 = 7$ if she buys from *a*, a payoff of $4 - 2 = 2$ if she buys from *b*, and $2 - 0 = 2$ if she buys from *c*. This is why *a* is her unique preferred seller. We can similarly determine the payoffs for buyers *y* (3, 5, and 6) and *z* (2, 3, and 2) for transacting with sellers *a*, *b*, and *c*, respectively.

Market-Clearing Prices. Figure 10.5(b) has the particularly nice property that, if each buyer simply claims the house that she likes best, each buyer ends up with a different house: somehow the prices have perfectly resolved the contention for houses. And this happens despite the fact that each buyer values the house of seller *a* the highest; it is the high price of 5 that dissuades buyers *y* and *z* from pursuing this house.

We will call such a set of prices *market clearing*, since they cause each house to get bought by a different buyer. In contrast, Figure 10.5(c) shows an example of prices that are not market clearing, because buyers *x* and *z* both want the house offered by seller *a*. In this case, when each buyer pursues the house that maximizes her payoff, the contention for houses is not resolved. (Notice that although each of a, b, and c is a preferred seller for y, because they all give y equal payoffs, this does not help with the contention between x and z.)

Figure 10.5(d) illustrates one further subtlety in the notion of market-clearing prices. Here, if the buyers coordinate so that each chooses the appropriate preferred seller, then each buyer gets a different house. (This requires that y take c's house and z take b's house.) Because it is possible to eliminate contention using preferred sellers, we say that this set of prices is market clearing as well, even though a bit of coordination is required due to ties in the maximum payoffs. In some cases, ties like this may be inevitable: for example, if all buyers have the same valuations for everything, then no choice of prices will break this symmetry.

Given the possibility of ties, we will think about market-clearing prices more generally as follows. For a set of prices, we define the *preferred-seller graph* on buyers and sellers by simply constructing an edge between each buyer and her preferred seller or sellers. (There is no edge out of a buyer if she has no preferred seller.) So in fact, Figures 10.5(b)–10.5(d) are just drawings of preferred-seller graphs for each of the three indicated sets of prices. Now we simply say: a set of prices is *market clearing* if the resulting preferred-seller graph has a perfect matching.

Properties of Market-Clearing Prices. In a way, market-clearing prices feel a bit too good to be true: if sellers set prices the right way, then self-interest runs its course and (potentially with a bit of coordination over tie-breaking) all the buyers get out of each other's way and claim different houses. We've seen that such prices can be achieved in one very small example; but in fact, something much more general is true:

> *Existence of Market-Clearing Prices:* For any set of buyer valuations, there exists a set of market-clearing prices.

So market-clearing prices are not just a fortuitous outcome in certain cases; they are always present. This is far from obvious, and we will turn shortly to a method for constructing market-clearing prices that, in the process, proves they always exist.

Before doing this, we consider another natural question: the relationship between market-clearing prices and social welfare. Just because market-clearing prices resolve the contention among buyers, causing them to get different houses, does this mean that the total valuation of the resulting assignment will be good? In fact, there is something very strong that can be said here as well: market-clearing prices (for this buyer–seller matching problem) always provide socially optimal outcomes:

> *Optimality of Market-Clearing Prices:* For any set of market-clearing prices, a perfect matching in the resulting preferred-seller graph has the maximum total valuation of any assignment of sellers to buyers.

Compared with the previous claim on the existence of market-clearing prices, this fact about optimality can be justified by a much shorter, if somewhat subtle, argument.

The argument is as follows. Consider a set of market-clearing prices, and let M be a perfect matching in the preferred-seller graph. Now, consider the *total payoff* of this matching, defined simply as the sum of each buyer's payoff for what she gets. Since each buyer is grabbing a house that maximizes her payoff individually, M has the maximum total *payoff* of any assignment of houses to buyers. Now how does total payoff relate to total valuation, which is what we're hoping that M maximizes? If buyer j chooses house i, then her valuation is v_{ij} and her payoff is $v_{ij} - p_i$. Thus, the total payoff to all buyers is simply the total valuation, minus the sum of all prices:

$$\text{Total Payoff of } M = \text{Total Valuation of } M - \text{Sum of all prices.}$$

But the sum of all prices is something that doesn't depend on which matching we choose (it's just the sum of everything the sellers are asking for, regardless of how they get paired up with buyers). So a matching M that maximizes the total payoff is also one that maximizes the total valuation. This completes the argument.

There is another important way of thinking about the optimality of market-clearing prices, which turns out to be essentially equivalent to the formulation we've just described. Suppose that, instead of thinking about the total valuation of the matching, we think about the total of the payoffs received by all participants in the market – both the sellers and the buyers. For a buyer, her payoff is defined as above: it is her valuation for the house she gets minus the price she pays. A seller's payoff is simply the amount of money he receives in payment for his house. Therefore, in any matching, the total of the payoffs to all the sellers is simply equal to the sum of the prices (since they all get paid, and it doesn't matter which buyer pays which seller). Above, we just argued that the total of the payoffs to all the buyers is equal to the total valuation of the matching M, minus the sum of all prices. Therefore, the total of the payoffs to all participants – both the sellers and the buyers – is exactly equal to the total valuation of the matching M; the point is that the prices detract from the total buyer payoff by exactly the amount that they contribute to the total seller payoff; hence, the sum of the prices cancels out completely from this calculation. Therefore, to maximize the total payoffs to all participants, we want prices and a matching that lead to the maximum total valuation, and this is achieved by using market-clearing prices and a perfect matching in the resulting preferred-seller graph. We can summarize this as follows.

> *Optimality of Market-Clearing Prices (equivalent version):* A set of market-clearing prices, and a perfect matching in the resulting preferred-seller graph, produces the maximum possible sum of payoffs to all sellers and buyers.

10.4 Constructing a Set of Market-Clearing Prices

Now let's turn to the harder challenge: understanding why market-clearing prices must always exist. We're going to do this by taking an arbitrary set of buyer valuations and describing a procedure that arrives at market-clearing prices. The procedure will in fact be a kind of auction – not a single-item auction of the type we discussed in Chapter 9, but a more general kind that takes into account the fact that there are multiple things being auctioned and multiple buyers with different valuations. This particular auction procedure was described by the economists Demange, Gale, and Sotomayor in 1986 [129], but it's actually equivalent to a construction of market-clearing prices discovered by the Hungarian mathematician Egerváry seventy years earlier, in 1916 [280].

Here's how the auction works. Initially all sellers set their prices to 0. Buyers react by choosing their preferred seller(s), and we look at the resulting preferred-seller graph. If this graph has a perfect matching we're done. Otherwise – and this is the key point – there is a constricted set of buyers, S. Consider the set of neighbors $N(S)$, which is a set of sellers. The buyers in S only want what the sellers in $N(S)$ have to sell, but there are fewer sellers in $N(S)$ than there are buyers in S. So the sellers in $N(S)$ are in "high demand" – too many buyers are interested in them. These sellers respond by each simultaneously raising their prices by one unit, and the auction then continues.

There's one more ingredient, which is a *reduction* operation on the prices defined as follows. It will be useful to have our prices scaled so that the smallest one is 0. Thus, if we ever reach a point where all prices are strictly greater than 0 – suppose the smallest price has value $p > 0$ – then we reduce the prices by subtracting p from each one. This drops the lowest price to 0 and shifts all other prices by the same relative amount.

A general round of the auction looks like what we've just described:

(i) At the start of each round, there is a current set of prices, with the smallest one equal to 0.

(ii) We construct the preferred-seller graph and check whether there is a perfect matching.

(iii) If there is, we're done: the current prices are market-clearing.

(iv) If not, we find a constricted set of buyers, S, and their neighbors $N(S)$.

(v) Each seller in $N(S)$ (simultaneously) raises his price by one unit.

(vi) If necessary, we reduce the prices: The same amount is subtracted from each price so that the smallest price becomes zero.

(vii) We now begin the next round of the auction, using these new prices.

Figure 10.6 shows what happens when we apply the auction procedure to the example from Figure 10.5.

The example in Figure 10.6 illustrates two aspects of this auction that should be emphasized. First, in any round where the set of "overdemanded" sellers $N(S)$ consists of more than one individual, all the sellers in this set raise their prices simultaneously. For example, in the third round in Figure 10.6, the set $N(S)$ consists of both a and b, and so they both raise their prices to produce the prices used for the start of the fourth round. Second, while the auction procedure shown in Figure 10.6 produces the market-clearing prices shown in Figure 10.5(d), we know from Figure 10.5(b) that there can be other market-clearing prices for the same set of buyer valuations.

Showing That the Auction Must Come to an End. Here is a key property of the auction procedure we've defined: the only way it can come to end is if it reaches a set of market-clearing prices; otherwise, the rounds continue. So if we can show that the auction must come to an end for any set of buyer valuations – in other words, that the rounds cannot go on forever – then we've shown that market-clearing prices always exist.

It's not immediately clear, however, why the auction must always come to an end. Consider, for example, the sequence of steps the auction follows in Figure 10.6: prices

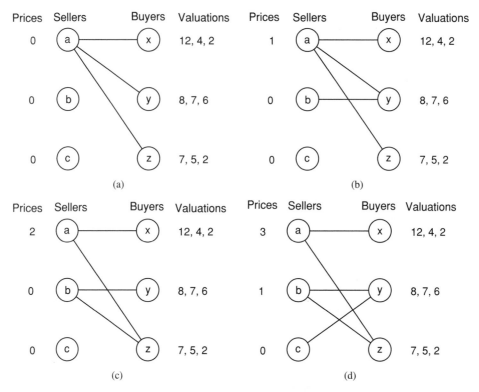

Figure 10.6. The auction procedure applied to the example from Figure 10.5. Each separate picture shows steps (i) and (ii) of successive rounds, in which the preferred-seller graph for that round is constructed. (a) In the first round, all prices start at 0. The set of all buyers forms a constricted set S, with $N(S)$ equal to the seller a. So a raises his price by one unit and the auction continues to the second round. (b) In the second round, the set of buyers consisting of x and z forms a constricted set S, with $N(S)$ again equal to seller a. Seller a again raises his price by one unit and the auction continues to the third round. (Notice that in this round, we could have alternatively identified the set of all buyers as a different constricted set S, in which case $N(S)$ would have been the set of sellers a and b. There is no problem with this – it just means that there can be multiple options for how to run the auction procedure in certain rounds, with any of these options leading to market-clearing prices when the auction comes to an end.) (c) In the third round, the set of all buyers forms a constricted set S, with $N(S)$ equal to the set of two sellers a and b. So a and b simultaneously raise their prices by one unit each, and the auction continues to the fourth round. (d) In the fourth round, when we build the preferred-seller graph, we find it contains a perfect matching. Hence, the current prices are market clearing, and the auction comes to an end.

change, different constricted sets form at different points in time, and eventually the auction stops with a set of market-clearing prices. But why should this happen in general? Why couldn't there be a set of valuations that cause the prices to constantly shift around so that some set of buyers is always constricted, and the auction never stops?

In fact, the prices can't shift forever without stopping; the auction must always come to an end. The way we're going to show this is by identifying a precise sense in which a certain kind of "potential energy" is draining out of the auction as it runs; since the auction starts with only a bounded supply of this potential energy at the beginning, it must eventually run out.

Here is how we precisely define this notion of potential energy. For any current set of prices, define the *potential of a buyer* to be the maximum payoff she can currently get from any seller. This is the buyer's potential payoff; the buyer will actually get this payoff if the current prices are market-clearing prices. We also define the *potential of a seller* to be the current price he is charging. This is the seller's potential payoff; the seller will actually get this payoff if the current prices are market-clearing prices. Finally, we define the *potential energy of the auction* to be the sum of the potential of all participants, both buyers and sellers.

How does the potential energy of the auction behave as we run it? It begins with all sellers having potential 0, and each buyer having a potential equal to her maximum valuation for any house – so the potential energy of the auction at the start is some whole number $P_0 \geq 0$. Also, notice that at the start of each round of the auction, everyone has potential at least 0. The sellers always have potential at least 0 since the prices are always at least 0. Because of the price-reduction step in every round, the lowest price is always 0, and therefore each buyer is always doing at least as well as the option of buying a zero-cost item, which gives a payoff of at least 0. (This also means that each buyer has at least one preferred seller at the start of each round.) Finally, since the potentials of the sellers and buyers are all at least 0 at the start of each round, so is the potential energy of the auction.

Now, the potential only changes when the prices change, and this only happens in steps (v) and (vi). Notice that the reduction of prices, as defined earlier, does not change the potential energy of the auction: if we subtract p from each price, then the potential of each seller drops by p, but the potential of each buyer goes up by p – it all cancels out. Finally, what happens to the potential energy of the auction in step (v), when the sellers in $N(S)$ all raise their prices by one unit? Each of these sellers' potentials goes up by one unit. But the potential of each buyer in S goes down by one unit, since all their preferred houses just got more expensive. Since S has strictly more nodes than $N(S)$ does, the potential energy of the auction goes down by at least one unit more than it goes up, so it strictly decreases by at least one unit.

So what we've shown is that, in each step that the auction runs, the potential energy of the auction decreases by at least one unit. It starts at some fixed value P_0, and it can't drop below 0, so the auction must come to an end within P_0 steps – and when it comes to an end, we have our market-clearing prices.

10.5 How Does This Relate to Single-Item Auctions?

We talked in Chapter 9 about single-item auctions, and we've now seen a more complex type of auction based on bipartite graphs. It makes sense to ask how these different kinds of auctions relate to each other. In fact, there is a very natural way to view the single-item auction – both the outcome and the procedure itself – as a special case of the bipartite graph auction we've just defined. We can do this as follows.

Suppose we have a set of n buyers and a single seller auctioning an item; let buyer j have valuation v_j for the item. To map this to our model based on perfect matchings,

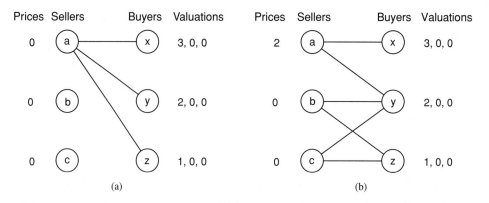

Figure 10.7. A single-item auction can be represented by the bipartite graph model: the item is represented by one seller node, and then there are additional seller nodes for which all buyers have 0 valuation. (a) The start of the bipartite graph auction. (b) The end of the bipartite graph auction, when buyer x gets the item at the valuation of buyer y.

we must have an equal number of buyers and sellers, but this is easily dealt with: we create $n - 1$ "fake" additional sellers (who conceptually represent $n - 1$ different ways to fail to acquire the item), and we give buyer j a valuation of 0 for the item offered by each of these fake sellers. With the real seller labeled 1, this means we have $v_{1j} = v_j$, the valuation of buyer j for the real item; and $v_{ij} = 0$ for larger values of i.

Now we have a genuine instance of our bipartite graph model: from a perfect matching of buyers to sellers, we can see which buyer ends up paired with the real seller (this is the buyer who gets the item), and from a set of market-clearing prices, we can see what the real item sells for.

Moreover, the price-raising procedure to produce market-clearing prices – based on finding constricted sets – has a natural meaning here as well. The execution of the procedure on a simple example is shown in Figure 10.7. Initially, all buyers will identify the real seller as their preferred seller (assuming that they all have positive valuations for the item). The first constricted set S we find is the set of all buyers, and $N(S)$ is just the single real seller. Thus, the seller raises his price by one unit. This continues as long as at least two buyers have the real seller as their unique preferred seller: they form a constricted set S with $N(S)$ equal to the real seller, and this seller raises his price by one unit. The prices of the fake items remain fixed at 0 throughout the auction. Finally, when all but one buyer has identified other sellers as preferred sellers, the graph has a perfect matching. This happens at precisely the moment that the buyer with the second-highest valuation drops out – in other words, the buyer with the highest valuation gets the item and pays the second-highest valuation. So the bipartite graph procedure precisely implements an ascending-bid (English) auction.

10.6 Advanced Material: A Proof of the Matching Theorem

The discussion in this chapter has provided a complete proof that market-clearing prices exist, omitting the details in only one place: we deferred the proof of the Matching

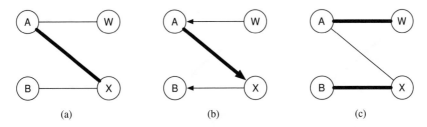

Figure 10.8. (a) A matching that does not have maximum size. (b) When a matching does not have maximum size, we can try to find an *augmenting path* that connects unmatched nodes on opposite sides while alternating between nonmatching and matching edges. (c) If we then swap the edges on this path – taking out the matching edges on the path and replacing them with the nonmatching edges – then we obtain a larger (in this case, perfect) matching.

Theorem in Section 10.1, because it was enough for our purposes to use it in a "black-box" fashion. However, the standard proof of the Matching Theorem in fact provides important insights into the structure of bipartite graphs, and so we present it here.

Recall that the statement is the following.

> *Claim:* If a bipartite graph (with equal numbers of nodes on the left and right) has no perfect matching, then it must contain a constricted set.

The tricky part of proving this is to come up with some means of identifying a constricted set in a bipartite graph, knowing only that it contains no perfect matching. Our general plan for doing this is as follows. We will take a bipartite graph, with equal numbers of nodes on the left and right but no perfect matching, and consider a matching that includes as many nodes as possible; we will call this a *maximum matching*. We then try to enlarge it by searching for a way to include one more node from each side in the matching. This search must fail (since the matching is already as large as possible for the given graph), and we show that, when this search for a larger matching fails, it produces a constricted set.

Naturally, there is a lot that needs to be fleshed out in this strategy, and the first step is to consider how one goes about "enlarging" a matching in a bipartite graph. This will turn out to be the key issue in the whole proof.

Alternating and Augmenting Paths. With this in mind, let's forget about constricted sets for a little while and simply think about matchings and how they can be enlarged. As a first example, consider the bipartite graph in Figure 10.8(a), with a matching indicated using bold edges. (We'll say that the *matching edges* are the edges used in a given matching, and the *nonmatching edges* are the other, unused ones.) The matching shown in Figure 10.8(a) is not a maximum matching – we could clearly pair up W with A and X with B to get a larger one, as in Figure 10.8(c).

For examples this small, it's easy just to look at the picture of the graph and see how to find a larger matching. But for bipartite graphs that are more complicated, it's useful to have a more principled way of growing a smaller matching into a larger one. Here's how we can do this in Figure 10.8(a). We start at node W, looking for a matching that would include it while still including everyone who's currently matched. It's not immediately obvious whether we can pair up W with A, since A is already

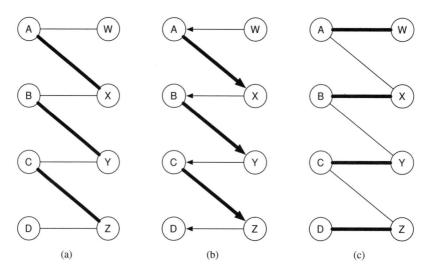

Figure 10.9. The principle used in Figure 10.8 can be applied to larger bipartite graphs as well, sometimes producing long augmenting paths: (a) a matching that is not of maximum size, (b) an augmenting path, and (c) a larger (perfect) matching.

matched to X. So we try "undoing" the pairing of A and X, which would let W and A be matched. This in turn frees up X, which can then be matched with B, and we've enlarged the matching.

This process is depicted in Figure 10.8(b). We followed a zigzag path through the bipartite graph, alternately adding unused edges to the matching while removing currently used edges from the matching: in particular, we added the edges A-W and B-X to the matching, while removing the edge A-X. It was also important that the path was *simple* – it did not repeat any nodes. We call a simple path that alternates between nonmatching and matching edges in this way an *alternating path*.

This example illustrates a principle that's true in general. In any bipartite graph with a matching, if we can find an alternating path that begins and ends at an unmatched node, then we can swap the roles of all edges on this path: each nonmatching edge gets put into the matching, and each edge on the path that is currently in the matching gets removed from it. In this way, all the nodes in the path become paired up: we have managed to include the two formerly unmatched endpoints in the matching, thereby enlarging it. We can summarize this as follows.

> *Claim:* In a bipartite graph with a matching, if there is an alternating path whose endpoints are unmatched nodes, then the matching can be enlarged.

In view of this, we call an alternating path with unmatched endpoints an *augmenting path*, since it gives us a way to augment the matching.

Augmenting paths can get much longer than what we see in Figure 10.8. For example, in Figure 10.9, we show an augmenting path that includes a total of eight nodes, and it succeeds in including its two endpoints W and D in the matching. It's also the case that augmenting paths can be harder to find than these two simple examples might suggest. In each of these examples, looking for the augmenting path never

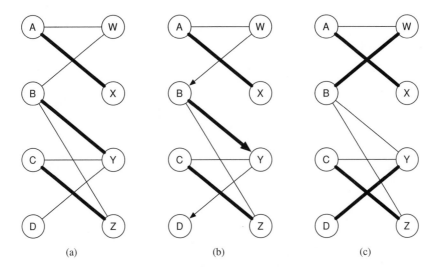

Figure 10.10. In more complex graphs, finding an augmenting path can require a more careful search, in which some choices lead to "dead ends" while others connect two unmatched nodes: (a) a matching that is not of maximum size, (b) an augmenting path, and (c) a larger (perfect) matching.

involves any real choices – we just keep following the only edge available at each step. But in more complicated bipartite graphs, there can be lots of dead ends in the search for an augmenting path. Consider, for example, the graph with a matching in Figure 10.10(a). There is in fact an augmenting path that succeeds in including W and D in the matching, but even on this relatively small example one must check a bit carefully to find it. Moreover, there are other alternating paths starting from W – such as W-A-X and W-B-Y-C-Z – that don't make it to the other unmatched node D, as well as paths from W to D – such as W-B-Z-C-Y-D – that are not alternating.

Searching for an Augmenting Path. Fortunately, however, there is a natural procedure we can use to search for an augmenting path in a bipartite graph with a matching. It works by simply adapting the breadth-first search (BFS) procedure to include the requirement of alternation – as a result, we will refer to this new procedure as *alternating BFS*.

Here is how it works. We start at any unmatched node on the right. Then, as in traditional BFS, we explore the rest of the graph layer by layer, adding new nodes to the next layer when they are connected by an edge to a node in the current layer. Because the graph is bipartite, these layers alternate between consisting of nodes on the left and nodes on the right. Now, here is the difference from traditional BFS: because we are searching specifically for an augmenting path, we want the paths that move downward layer-by-layer to all be alternating. Thus, when we build a new layer of nodes from the left-hand side, we should only use nonmatching edges to discover new nodes, and when we build a new layer of nodes from the right-hand side, we should only use matching edges to discover new nodes.

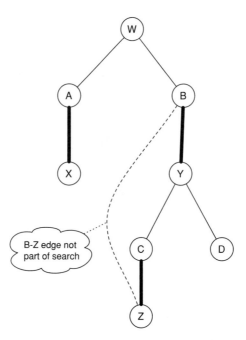

Figure 10.11. In an alternating breadth-first search, we construct layers that alternately use non-matching and matching edges; if an unmatched node is ever reached, this results in an augmenting path.

Figure 10.11 shows how this works on the example from Figure 10.10(a). Starting at W (which we think of as layer 0), we build the first layer by following nonmatching edges to A and B. We then build the second layer by following only matching edges, which leads us to nodes X and Y. Following nonmatching edges from this layer to new nodes not already discovered, we get a third layer consisting of C and D. Finally, taking the matching edge from C brings us to Z in the fourth layer. Notice that in this process we never used the edge B-Z: we couldn't use it out of B in the first layer, because we were only allowed to follow matching edges at that point, and we couldn't use it out of Z in the fourth layer, because by then B had already been discovered.

Now, the crucial thing to observe is that if this alternating BFS procedure ever produces a layer containing an unmatched node from the left-hand side of the graph, we have found an augmenting path (and can thus enlarge the matching). We simply move downward in a path from the unmatched node in layer 0 to the unmatched node from the left-hand side, proceeding one layer at a time. The edges on this path will alternate between being nonmatching and matching, and so this serves as an augmenting path.

Augmenting Paths and Constricted Sets. We now have a systematic procedure to search for an augmenting path. However, it leaves a basic question unresolved: if this search procedure fails to find an augmenting path, can we necessarily conclude that there is no perfect matching? This is certainly not a priori clear: why couldn't it be that there is a perfect matching hidden somewhere in the graph, and we just need a more powerful way to find it? But in fact, alternating BFS is all that we need: what

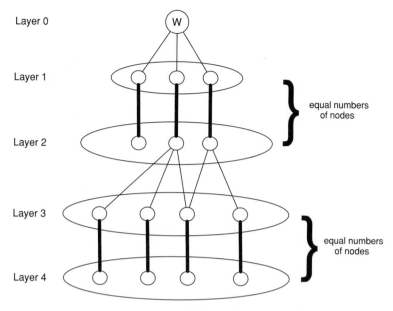

Figure 10.12. A schematic view of alternating breadth-first search, which produces pairs of layers of equal size.

we show next is that, when alternating BFS fails to find an augmenting path, we can in fact extract from this failed search a constricted set that proves there is no perfect matching.

Here is how we show this fact. Consider any bipartite graph, and suppose we are currently looking at a matching in it that is not perfect. Suppose further that we perform an alternating BFS from an unmatched node W on the right-hand side, and we fail to reach any unmatched node on the left-hand side. The resulting set of layers at the end of the search will look schematically like what's depicted in Figure 10.12. More concretely, Figure 10.13(a) shows a specific example of a graph with no perfect matching, and Figure 10.13(b) shows a set of layers from a failed alternating BFS for this example.

Let's make some observations about the structure after a failed search.

1. First, the even-numbered layers consist of nodes from the right-hand side, while the odd-numbered layers consist of nodes from the left-hand side.
2. Moreover, each odd layer contains exactly the same number of nodes as the subsequent even layer. This is because we never reach an unmatched node in an odd layer, and so, in every odd layer, the nodes are all connected by their matching edges to distinct nodes in the next layer, as illustrated in Figure 10.12.
3. So, not counting node W in layer 0, there are exactly the same number of nodes in even layers (numbered 2 and higher) as there are in odd layers. Counting the one extra node in layer 0, there are strictly more nodes in even layers overall than there are in odd layers.
4. Finally, every node in an even layer has all of its neighbors in the graph present in some layer. This is because each even-layer node other than W has its matched

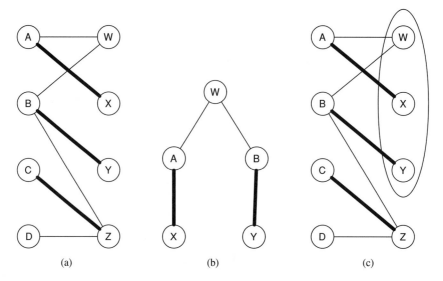

Figure 10.13. (a) A matching that has maximum size, but is not perfect. (b) For such a matching, the search for an augmenting path using alternating breadth-first search must fail. (c) The failure of this search exposes a constricted set – the set of nodes belonging to the even layers.

partner just above it in the previous layer, and if any of its other neighbors were not already present in a higher layer, they would be added to the next layer down, when we're allowed to explore using nonmatching edges.

(Notice that it's not necessarily true that every node in an odd layer has all of its neighbors in the graph present in some layer. For example, in Figure 10.13(b), node B's neighbor Z is not present in any layer. This is because we were not allowed to add Z when we got to B in the search, since we could only follow the matching edge out of B.)

Putting these observations together, we discover the following fact: *the set of nodes in all even layers, at the end of a failed alternating BFS, forms a constricted set.* This is simply because it's a set of nodes S on the right-hand side whose set of neighbors – because they're contained among the nodes in the odd layers – is strictly smaller than S. Figures 10.13(b) and 10.13(c) show how this works in one specific example.

This completes our plan: to extract a constricted set from the failure of alternating BFS. Here is one way to summarize the conclusion.

Claim: Consider any bipartite graph with a matching, and let W be any unmatched node on the right-hand side. Then either there is an augmenting path beginning at W, or there is a constricted set containing W.

The Matching Theorem. The fact we've just discovered is the crucial step in proving the Matching Theorem; from here it's easy, as follows.

Consider a bipartite graph with an equal number of nodes on the left and right, and suppose it has no perfect matching. Let's take a maximum matching in it – one that includes as many edges as possible. Since this matching is not perfect, and since there are an equal number of nodes on the two sides of the bipartite graph, there must be a node W on the right-hand side that is unmatched. We know there cannot be an augmenting path containing W, since then we'd be able to enlarge the matching – and this isn't possible because we chose a matching of maximum size. Now, by our previous claim, since there is no augmenting path beginning at W, there must be a constricted set containing W. Because we've deduced the existence of a constricted set from the fact that the graph has no perfect matching, this completes the proof of the Matching Theorem.

Computing a Perfect Matching. One final dividend from this analysis is that we actually have a reasonably efficient method to determine whether a graph has a perfect matching – enormously more efficient than the brute-force approach of trying all ways to pair up the nodes on the left and right.

The method works as follows. Given a bipartite graph with an equal number of nodes on the left and right, we will progress through a sequence of matchings, and each matching in the sequence will be one edge larger than the previous one. We can start from the empty matching – the trivial one in which no nodes at all are paired. Now in general, we look at our current matching and find an unmatched node W. We use alternating BFS to search for an augmenting path beginning at W. If we find one, we use this augmenting path to enlarge the matching, and we continue with this new matching. If we don't find one, we can stop with a constricted set that proves the graph has no perfect matching.

Because the matchings get larger at every step while the process is running, the number of matchings we pass through can be at most the number of nodes on each side of the graph. By then, we will either have reached a perfect matching or have stopped earlier with a constricted set.

An interesting question is the following. When the procedure stops with a constricted set, are we guaranteed to have a maximum matching? As we've described the procedure so far, the answer is no. Consider for example Figure 10.14. If we try to find an augmenting path starting at W, then we will fail (producing the constricted set consisting of W and X). This is indeed enough to prove there is no perfect matching. However, it does not mean that the current matching has maximum size: if we instead had searched for an augmenting path starting from Y, we would have succeeded, producing the path Y-B-Z-D. In other words, if we're looking for a maximum matching and not just a perfect matching, it can matter where we start our search for an augmenting path; certain parts of the graph can become "wedged," while other parts still contain the potential for enlarging the matching.

However, there is a variation on our procedure that is guaranteed to produce a maximum matching. We won't go through all the details of this (see, e.g., Kozen [260] for more), but the idea is as follows. By revisiting the analysis we've used thus far, and adapting it a little bit, one can show that if there is no augmenting path beginning at *any* node on the right-hand side then in fact the current matching has maximum size. This shows that if, as we progress through larger and larger matchings, we always search for an augmenting path from every node on the right-hand side, then either one of these searches will succeed, or else we can conclude that the current matching has maximum size. And although this sounds like an expensive thing to do – having

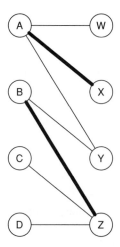

Figure 10.14. If the alternating breadth-first search fails from any one node on the right-hand side, this is enough to expose a constricted set and hence prove there is no perfect matching. However, it is still possible that an alternating breadth-first search could still succeed from some other node. (In this case, the search from W would fail, but the search from Y would succeed.)

to search separately from each node on the right – in fact it can be done efficiently by making *all* the unmatched nodes on the right constitute layer 0 in the alternating BFS, and otherwise running it as before. Then if an unmatched node on the left is ever reached in some layer, we can follow the path from the appropriate node in layer 0 down to it, producing an augmenting path.

A lot of work has gone into the design of efficient methods for finding maximum matchings in bipartite graphs, and a number of further improvements are possible, including versions of alternating BFS that try to find many augmenting paths simultaneously, thereby cutting down the number of intermediate matchings one must pass through on the way to the maximum. Determining how efficiently maximum matchings can be found remains an open area of research.

10.7 Exercises

1. Suppose we have a set of two sellers, labeled *a* and *b*, and a set of two buyers, labeled *x* and *y*. Each seller is offering a distinct house for sale, and the valuations of the buyers for the houses are as follows.

Buyer	Value for *a*'s house	Value for *b*'s house
x	2	4
y	3	6

Suppose that *a* charges a price of 0 for his house, and *b* charges a price of 1 for his house. Is this set of prices market clearing? Give a brief (one- to three-sentence) explanation; as part of your answer, say what the preferred-seller graph is with this given set of prices, and use this in your explanation.

2. Suppose we have a set of three sellers, labeled *a*, *b*, and *c*, and a set of three buyers, labeled *x*, *y*, and *z*. Each seller is offering a distinct house for sale, and the valuations of the buyers for the houses are as follows.

Buyer	Value for *a*'s house	Value for *b*'s house	Value for *c*'s house
x	5	7	1
y	2	3	1
z	5	4	4

Suppose that sellers *a* and *b* each charge 2, and seller *c* charges 1. Is this set of prices market clearing? Give a brief explanation.

3. Suppose we have a set of three sellers, labeled *a*, *b*, and *c*, and a set of three buyers, labeled *x*, *y*, and *z*. Each seller is offering a distinct house for sale, and the valuations of the buyers for the houses are as follows.

Buyer	Value for *a*'s house	Value for *b*'s house	Value for *c*'s house
x	2	4	6
y	3	5	1
z	4	7	5

Suppose that sellers *a* and *c* each charge 1, and seller *b* charges 3. Is this set of prices market clearing? Give a brief explanation.

4. Suppose we have a set of three sellers, labeled *a*, *b*, and *c*, and a set of three buyers, labeled *x*, *y*, and *z*. Each seller is offering a distinct house for sale, and the valuations of the buyers for the houses are as follows.

Buyer	Value for *a*'s house	Value for *b*'s house	Value for *c*'s house
x	12	9	8
y	10	3	6
z	8	6	5

Suppose that *a* charges a price of 3 for his house, *b* charges a price of 1 for his house, and *c* charges a price of 0. Is this set of prices market clearing? If so, explain which buyer you would expect to get which house; if not, say which seller or sellers should raise their price(s) in the next round of the bipartite-graph auction procedure from Chapter 10.

5. Suppose we have a set of three sellers, labeled *a*, *b*, and *c*, and a set of three buyers, labeled *x*, *y*, and *z*. Each seller is offering a distinct house for sale, and the valuations of the buyers for the houses are as follows.

Buyer	Value for *a*'s house	Value for *b*'s house	Value for *c*'s house
x	7	7	4
y	7	6	3
z	5	4	3

Suppose that a charges a price of 4 for his house, b charges a price of 3 for his house, and c charges a price of 1. Is this set of prices market clearing? Give an explanation for your answer, using the relevant definitions from Chapter 10.

6. Suppose we have a set of three sellers, labeled a, b, and c, and a set of three buyers, labeled x, y, and z. Each seller is offering a distinct house for sale, and the valuations of the buyers for the houses are as follows.

Buyer	Value for a's house	Value for b's house	Value for c's house
x	6	3	2
y	10	5	4
z	7	8	6

Suppose that a charges a price of 4 for his house, b charges a price of 1 for his house, and c charges a price of 0. Is this set of prices market clearing? If so, explain which buyer you would expect to get which house; if not, say which seller or sellers should raise their price(s) in the next round of the bipartite-graph auction procedure from Chapter 10.

7. Suppose we have a set of three sellers, labeled a, b, and c, and a set of three buyers, labeled x, y, and z. Each seller is offering a distinct house for sale, and the valuations of the buyers for the houses are as follows.

Buyer	Value for a's house	Value for b's house	Value for c's house
x	6	8	7
y	5	6	6
z	3	6	5

Suppose that a charges a price of 2 for his house, b charges a price of 5 for his house, and c charges a price of 4. Is this set of prices market clearing? If so, explain which buyer you would expect to get which house; if not, say which seller or sellers should raise their price(s) in the next round of the bipartite-graph auction procedure from Chapter 10.

8. Suppose we have a set of two sellers, labeled a and b, and a set of two buyers, labeled x and y. Each seller is offering a distinct house for sale, and the valuations of the buyers for the houses are as follows.

Buyer	Value for a's house	Value for b's house
x	7	5
y	4	1

Describe what happens, if we run the bipartite-graph auction procedure to determine market-clearing prices, by saying what the prices are at the end of each round of the auction, including what the final market-clearing prices are when the auction comes to an end.

9. Suppose we have a set of three sellers, labeled *a*, *b*, and *c*, and a set of three buyers, labeled *x*, *y*, and *z*. Each seller is offering a distinct house for sale, and the valuations of the buyers for the houses are as follows.

Buyer	Value for *a*'s house	Value for *b*'s house	Value for *c*'s house
x	3	6	4
y	2	8	1
z	1	2	3

Describe what happens, if we run the bipartite-graph auction procedure from Chapter 10, by saying what the prices are at the end of each round of the auction, including what the final market-clearing prices are when the auction comes to an end.

[Note: In some rounds, you may notice that there are multiple choices for the constricted set of buyers, *A*. Under the rules of the auction, you can choose any such constricted set. It's interesting to consider – though not necessary for this question – how the eventual set of market-clearing prices depends on how one chooses among the possible constricted sets.]

10. Suppose we have a set of three sellers, labeled *a*, *b*, and *c*, and a set of three buyers, labeled *x*, *y*, and *z*. Each seller is offering a distinct house for sale, and the valuations of the buyers for the houses are as follows.

Buyer	Value for *a*'s house	Value for *b*'s house	Value for *c*'s house
x	9	7	4
y	5	9	7
z	11	10	8

Describe what happens, if we run the bipartite graph auction procedure from Chapter 10, by saying what the prices are at the end of each round of the auction, including what the final market-clearing prices are when the auction comes to an end.

[Note: In some rounds, you may notice that there are multiple choices for the constricted set of buyers, *A*. Under the rules of the auction, you can choose any such constricted set. It's interesting to consider – though not necessary for this question – how the eventual set of market-clearing prices depends on how one chooses among the possible constricted sets.]

11. Figure 10.15 shows a map of part of the Back Bay section of Boston. Suppose that the dark circles labeled *x*, *y*, and *z* represent people living in apartments in Back Bay who want to rent parking spaces by the month for parking their cars. (Due to the density of buildings, these parking spaces may be a short walk from where they live, rather than right at their apartment.) The dark circles labeled *a*, *b*, and *c* represent parking spaces available for rent.

Let's define the *distance* between a person and a parking space to be the number of blocks the person would have to walk from their apartment to the parking space.

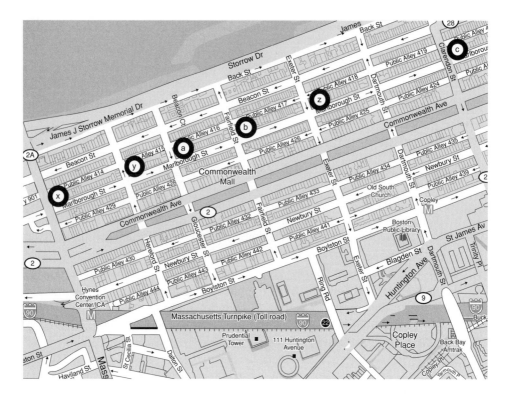

Figure 10.15. The map for a parking-space market described in Exercise 11. (Image from Google Maps, http://maps.google.com/)

Thus, for example, z is at a distance of 2 from space c, whereas y is at a distance of 5 from c and x is at a distance of 6 from c. (We ignore the fact that the block between Gloucester and Hereford is a bit shorter than the others; all blocks are treated as the same in counting distance.)

Suppose that a person has a valuation for a potential parking space equal to

$$8 - \text{(their distance to the parking space)}.$$

(Notice that this formula gives higher valuations to closer parking spaces.) In terms of these valuations, we'd like to think about prices that could be charged for the parking spaces.

(a) Describe how you would set up this question as a matching market in the style of Chapter 10. Say who the sellers and buyers would be in your setup, as well as the valuation each buyer has for the item offered by each seller.

(b) Describe what happens if we run the bipartite-graph auction procedure from Chapter 10 on the matching market you set up in part (a) by saying what the prices are at the end of each round of the auction, including what the final market-clearing prices are when the auction comes to an end.

[Note: In some rounds, you may notice that there are multiple choices for the constricted set of buyers. Under the rules of the auction, you can choose any such constricted set. It's interesting to consider – though not necessary for this question – how the eventual set of market-clearing prices depends on how one chooses among the possible constricted sets.]

(c) At a more informal level, how do the prices you determined for the parking spaces in part (b) relate to the intuitive "attractiveness" these spaces would have for the people in apartments x, y, and z? Explain.

12. Suppose we have a set of two sellers, labeled a and b, and a set of two buyers, labeled x and y. Each seller is offering a distinct house for sale, and the valuations of the buyers for the houses are as follows.

Buyer	Value for a's house	Value for b's house
x	4	1
y	3	2

In general, there are multiple sets of market-clearing prices for a given set of sellers, buyers, and valuations: any set of prices that produces a preferred-seller graph with a perfect matching is market clearing.

As a way of exploring this issue in the context of the preceding example, give three *different* sets of market-clearing prices for this matching market. The prices should be whole numbers (i.e., they should be numbers from 0, 1, 2, 3, 4, 5, 6, . . .). (Note that for two sets of market-clearing prices to be different it is enough that they not consist of exactly the same set of numbers.) Explain your answer.

13. Suppose you want to design an auction for the following type of situation: you have two identical copies of a valuable object, and there are four potential buyers for the object. Each potential buyer j wants at most one copy and has a value v_j for either copy.

You decide to design the auction by analogy with the way in which we derived the single-item ascending-bid (English) auction from the general procedure for matching markets. In the present case, as there, you want to create a bipartite graph that encodes the situation and then see what prices the bipartite-graph auction procedure comes up with.

(a) Describe how this construction would work using an example with four potential buyers. In creating your example, first choose specific valuations for the potential buyers, and then show how the auction proceeds and what the market-clearing prices are.

(b) In the case of the single-item auction, the bipartite-graph procedure yielded the simple rule from the ascending-bid (English) auction: sell to the highest bidder at the second-highest price. Describe in comparably simple terms what the rule is for the current case of two identical items (i.e., your description should not involve the terms "bipartite," "graph," or "matching").

14. In Chapter 10, we discussed the notion of social-welfare maximization for matching markets: finding a matching M that maximizes the sum of buyers' valuations for what they get, over all possible perfect matchings. We say such a matching is *social-welfare maximizing*. However, the sum of buyers' valuations is not the only quantity one may want to maximize; another natural goal might be to make sure that no individual buyer gets a valuation that is too small.

With this in mind, let's define the *baseline* of a perfect matching M to be the minimum valuation that any buyer has for the item she gets in M. We could then seek a perfect matching M whose baseline is as large as possible, over all possible perfect matchings. We say such a matching is *baseline-maximizing*.

For example, in the following set of valuations,

Buyer	Value for a's house	Value for b's house	Value for c's house
x	9	7	4
y	5	9	7
z	11	10	8

the matching M consisting of the pairs a-x, b-y, and c-z has a baseline of 8 (this is the valuation of z for what she gets, which is lower than the valuations of x and y for what they get), while the matching M' consisting of the pairs b-x, c-y, and a-z has a baseline of 7. In fact the first of these example matchings, M, is baseline-maximizing for this sample set of valuations.

Now, finding a perfect matching that is baseline-maximizing is grounded in a kind of "egalitarian" motivation – no one should be left too badly off. This may sometimes be at odds with the goal of social-welfare maximization. We now explore this tension further.

(a) Give an example of equal-sized sets of sellers and buyers, with valuations on the buyers, so that there is no perfect matching that is both social-welfare maximizing and baseline-maximizing. (In other words, in your example, social-welfare maximization and baseline maximization should only occur with different matchings.)

(b) It is also natural to ask whether a baseline-maximizing matching can always be supported by market-clearing prices. Here is a precise way to ask the question.

> For any equal-sized sets of sellers and buyers, with valuations on the buyers, is there always a set of market-clearing prices so that the resulting preferred-seller graph contains a baseline-maximizing perfect matching M?

Give a yes/no answer to this question, together with a justification of your answer. (If you answer "yes," you should explain why there must always exist such a set of market-clearing prices; if you answer "no," you should explain why there can be examples in which a baseline-maximizing matching cannot be found in the preferred-seller graph resulting from market-clearing prices.)

15. Consider again the setup for the bipartite-graph auction, with an equal number of buyers and sellers and with each buyer having a valuation for the object being sold by any other seller. Suppose that we have an instance of this problem in which there is a particular seller i who is the *favorite*: every buyer j has a higher valuation for seller i's object than for the object being sold by any other seller k. (In notation, we have $v_{ij} > v_{kj}$ for all buyers j and all sellers $k \neq i$.)

Consider a set of market-clearing prices in this situation. Must it be the case that the price charged by seller i is at least as high as the price charged by any other seller? Give an explanation for your answer.

CHAPTER 11

Network Models of Markets with Intermediaries

11.1 Price Setting in Markets

In Chapter 10 we developed an analysis of trade and prices on a bipartite graph consisting of buyers, sellers, and the edges connecting them. Most importantly, we showed that market-clearing prices exist and that trade at these prices results in maximal total valuation among the buyers and sellers, and we found a procedure that allowed us to construct market-clearing prices. This analysis shows in a striking way how prices have the power to direct the allocation of goods in a desirable way. What it doesn't do is provide a clear picture of where prices in real markets tend to come from. That is, who sets the prices in real markets, and why do they choose the particular prices they do?

Auctions, which we discussed in Chapter 9, provide a concrete example of price determination in a controlled setting. In our discussion of auctions, we found that if a seller with a single object runs a second-price sealed-bid auction – or equivalently an ascending-bid auction – then buyers bid their true values for the seller's object. In that discussion, the buyers were choosing prices (via their bids) in a procedure selected by the seller. We could also consider a *procurement auction* in which the roles of buyers and sellers are reversed, and a single buyer is interested in purchasing an object from one of several sellers. Here, our auction results imply that if the buyer runs a second-price sealed-bid auction (buying from the lowest bidder at the second-lowest price), or equivalently a descending-offer auction, then the sellers will offer to sell at their true costs. In this case, the sellers are choosing prices (their offers) in a procedure selected by the buyer.

But who sets prices, and who trades with whom, if there are many buyers and many sellers? To get a feel for what happens, let's look first at how trade takes place in an actual market.

Trade with Intermediaries. In a wide range of markets, individual buyers and sellers do not interact directly with each other, but instead trade through intermediaries – brokers, market makers, or middlemen who set the prices. This is true in settings that

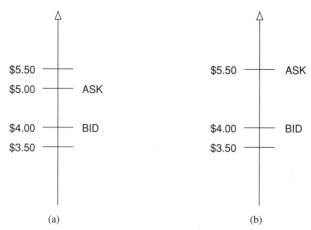

(a)   (b)

Figure 11.1. (a) A book of limit orders for a stock with a bid of $4 and an ask of $5. (b) A book of limit orders for a stock with a bid of $4 and an ask of $5.50.

range from the trade of agricultural goods in developing countries to the trade of assets in financial markets.

To get a sense for how markets with intermediaries typically work, let's focus on the latter example and consider how buyers and sellers interact in the stock market. In the United States, buyers and sellers trade more than a billion shares of stock daily. But there is no single market for trade in stocks in the United States. Instead, trade occurs on multiple exchanges such as the New York Stock Exchange (NYSE) or the NASDAQ-OMX, as well as on alternative trading systems, such as those run by Direct Edge, Goldman Sachs, or Investment Technologies Group (ITG), which arrange trades in stocks for their clients. These markets operate in various ways: some (such as the NYSE or the NASDAQ-OMX) determine prices that look very much like our market-clearing prices from Chapter 10, while others (like Direct Edge, Goldman Sachs, or ITG) simply match up orders to buy and sell stocks at prices determined in other markets. Some have people (called specialists in the NYSE) directly involved in setting prices, while others are purely electronic markets with prices set by algorithms; some trade continuously throughout the day, while others trade less frequently as they wait for batches of buy and sell orders to arrive; and some allow anyone at least indirect access to the market, while others restrict the group of buyers and sellers that they will deal with (often to large institutional traders).

Many of these markets create something called an *order book* for each stock that they trade. An order book is simply a list of the orders that buyers and sellers have submitted for that stock. A trader may, for instance, submit an order to sell 100 shares if the price is at $5.00 or more per share; another trader may submit an order to sell 100 shares if the price is at $5.50 or more per share. Two other traders may submit orders to buy 100 shares if the price is no more than $4.00 per share, and to buy 100 shares if the price is no more than $3.50 per share. Orders of this type are called *limit orders*, because they are commitments to buy or sell only once the price reaches some limit set by the trader. If these were the only orders that existed, then the order book for this stock would look like Figure 11.1(a).

The highest outstanding offer to buy the stock is referred to as the current *bid* for the stock, while the lowest outstanding offer to sell it is referred to as the *ask*. If the market uses a specialist then this person knows the book of orders and may choose to submit his or her own better offer to buy or sell out of inventory of the stock, which becomes the bid or ask, respectively. For example, if Figure 11.1(a) describes the order book, then the specialist may choose to display a bid of $4.25, based on his or her own better offer, and an ask of $5.00. These are the prices displayed to the trading public.

Retail traders (small traders who buy and sell stocks using their own assets) most often do not submit limit orders; instead they typically submit orders to buy or sell at the existing quotes – the current bid and ask. This type of order to trade immediately at market prices is called a *market order*. For example, if a trader submits a market order to buy 100 shares of a stock with the order book described by Figure 11.1(a), then the seller whose limit order was placed at $5.00 sells 100 shares and the buyer who submitted the market order buys 100 shares at $5.00. (Note that the seller can be either a member of the public or the specialist.) The new order book would then be as displayed in Figure 11.1(b), and the new ask would be $5.50. This process continues throughout the trading day with new limit orders, specialist offers, and market orders arriving over time, and transactions being performed.

Of course, orders to buy or sell are not always for 100 shares, and in fact order sizes vary greatly. For example, if the order book is as depicted in Figure 11.1(a), and a market order to buy 200 shares arrives, then both sellers on the book sell at their ask prices. The buyer will buy 100 shares at $5.00 and 100 shares at $5.50. We can think of this order as "walking up the book," since executing it exposes multiple orders at different prices.

Large mutual funds such as Fidelity or Vanguard, and other institutional traders such as banks, pension funds, insurance companies, and hedge funds, buy and sell a very large number of shares each day. They don't really want to trade many small lots of shares with retail traders and, as in our 200-share example, walk up or down the book. They also don't want to submit a single large limit order to the market, as then other market participants would know their trading desires and could take advantage of them.[1] Instead of submitting a single large market or limit order, these traders use a variety of orders and trading venues. They typically split their order into many pieces and trade these pieces over the trading day, or over several days, in order to minimize the impact of their trading desire on the price. One way in which large traders hide their trading desires is to submit pieces of it to many different trading systems to which they have access. One particularly interesting group of trading systems are called *dark pools*. Examples of these alternative trading systems are Goldman Sachs's Sigma-X and the systems run by ITG. Access to these systems is limited, and orders submitted to these systems are not displayed to the public. Instead these systems simply match

---

[1] A large order to buy, for example, may provide information to other market participants suggesting that the stock is currently undervalued and its price is likely to increase. These other market participants may then jump into the market, perhaps getting ahead of the execution of some part of the large order, and drive the price up quickly. This would harm the trader who submitted the large order as he may then have to pay more than expected for his order. This is related to broader questions about the role of information in markets, a topic we discuss in Chapter 22.

orders submitted by their clients at prices established in the public market and charge their clients a fee for the service. This is a relatively new, but growing, segment of the market; in April 2009, for example, approximately 9% of the trade in U.S. equities was done on dark pools.

As one might imagine, the actual structure of the stock market is very complex and rapidly evolving. There are many trading systems, many types of orders that buyers and sellers can use, and a wide variety of market participants. The questions of how prices evolve over time and how they relate to the underlying fundamental value of the assets being traded are also important, and we have ignored these issues so far. We will discuss some aspects of the evolution of prices and their relation to the underlying values in Chapter 22; more detailed analyses of the stock market are carried out in a number of books [206, 209, 332].

The collection of different trading venues for stocks ultimately results in a variety of markets with restricted participation. So when we take into account the full set of trading options for all market participants, both large and small, we see a network structure emerge that connects buyers and sellers to different possible intermediaries. A fundamental question is how to determine equilibrium trading behavior when there are multiple markets connected by a network in this way. In the next section, we develop a network model for trade which abstracts away the specific details of the stock market, focusing on the general issue of how the underlying structure constrains who can trade with whom and how prices are set by market participants.

11.2 A Model of Trade on Networks

Our network model will be based on three fundamental principles that we saw in discussing the stock market: individual buyers and sellers often trade through intermediaries, not all buyers and sellers have access to the same intermediaries, and not all buyers and sellers trade at the same price. Rather, the prices that each buyer and seller commands are determined in part by the range of alternatives that their respective network positions provide.

Before specifying the model, let's first look at another example of trade, in a very different setting, that exhibits these properties. This is the market for agricultural goods between local producers and consumers in a developing country. In many cases there are middlemen, or traders, who buy from farmers and then resell to consumers. Given the often poor transportation networks, the perishability of the products, and limited access to capital by farmers, individual farmers can sell only to a limited number of intermediaries [46, 153]. Similarly, consumers can buy from only a limited number of intermediaries. A developing country may have many such partially overlapping local markets existing alongside modern, more global markets.

We can use a graph to describe the trading opportunities available to sellers, buyers, and middlemen (traders). Figure 11.2 depicts a simple example of such a trading network, superimposed on its geographic setting. Here we've labeled seller nodes with S, buyer nodes with B, and trader nodes with T, and we've placed an edge between any two agents who can trade with each other. Notice in this example that the seller and buyer on the right-hand margin of the picture only have access to the trader on

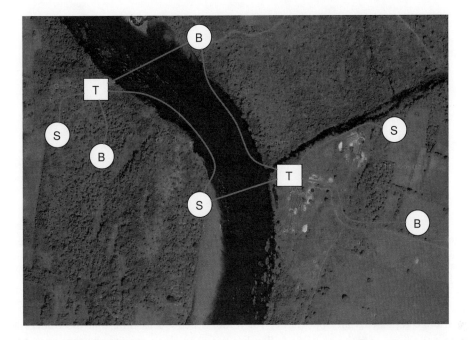

Figure 11.2. Trading networks for agricultural markets can be based on geographic constraints, giving certain buyers (nodes labeled B) and sellers (nodes labeled S) greater access to traders (nodes labeled T).

their side of the river. The buyer at the top of the figure has access to both traders – perhaps he has a boat. You might imagine that the extra trading opportunities available to this buyer, and the similar extra trading opportunities available to the seller on the west bank of the river, would result in better prices for them. We will see that this is exactly what happens in the trading outcomes determined by our model in networks of this type.

Network Structure. We now describe a simple model of trade on a network that is general enough to incorporate important features of the trading and price-setting process for commodities as varied as financial assets traded in developed countries and agricultural goods in developing countries [63].

For the simplest form of the model, we don't try to address the issue of multiple goods for sale, or multiple possible quantities; instead, we assume there is a single type of good that comes in indivisible units. Each seller i initially holds one unit of the good, which he values at v_i; he is willing to sell it at any price that is at least v_i. Each buyer j values one copy of the good at v_j and will try to obtain a copy of the good if she can do it by paying no more than v_j. No individual wants more than one copy of the good, so additional copies are valued at 0. All buyers, sellers, and traders are assumed to know these valuations. As a result, this model is best thought of as describing interaction between individuals who have a history of trade with each other, and hence know each other's willingness to pay for goods.

Trade takes place on a network that represents who can trade with whom. As in the example depicted in Figure 11.2, the nodes consist of buyers, sellers, and traders, and

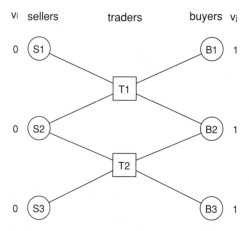

Figure 11.3. A standardized view of the trading network from Figure 11.2. Sellers are represented by circles on the left, buyers are represented by circles on the right, and traders are represented by squares in the middle. The value that each seller and buyer places on a copy of the good is written next to the respective node.

each edge represents an opportunity for trade. Since we assume that the traders act as intermediaries for the possible seller–buyer transactions, we require that each edge connects a buyer or seller to a trader. In Figure 11.3, we depict the same graph from Figure 11.2, but redrawn to emphasize these features of the network model. (In all of our figures depicting trading networks we will use the following conventions. Sellers are represented by circles on the left, buyers are represented by circles on the right, and traders are represented by squares in the middle. The value that each seller and buyer places on a copy of the good is written next to the respective node that represents them.)

Beyond the fact that we now have intermediaries, there are a few other differences between this model and our model of matching markets from Chapter 10. First, we assume that buyers have the same valuation for all copies of a good, whereas in matching markets we allowed buyers to have different valuations for the goods offered by different sellers. The model in this chapter can be extended to allow for valuations that vary across different copies of the good; things become more complicated, but the basic structure of the model and its conclusions remain largely the same. A second difference is that the network here is fixed and externally imposed by constraints such as geography (in agricultural markets) or eligibility to participate (in different financial markets). In matching markets, we began the chapter with fixed graphs, but then focused the core of the analysis on preferred-seller graphs that were determined not by external forces but by the preferences of buyers with respect to an evolving set of prices.

Prices and the Flow of Goods. The flow of goods from sellers to buyers is determined by a game in which traders first set prices, and then sellers and buyers react to these prices.

Specifically, each trader t offers a *bid price* to each seller i that he is connected to; we will denote this bid price by b_{ti}. (The notation indicates that this is a price for a transaction between t and i). This bid price is an offer by t to buy i's copy of the good at a value of b_{ti}. Similarly, each trader t offers an *ask price* to each buyer j to which he

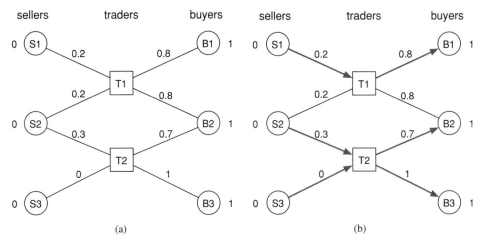

Figure 11.4. (a) Each trader posts bid prices to the sellers to which he is connected, and ask prices to the buyers to which he is connected. (b) These prices determine a flow of goods as sellers and buyers each choose the offer that is most favorable to them.

is connected. This ask price, denoted a_{tj}, is an offer by t to sell a copy of the good to buyer j at a value of a_{tj}. In Figure 11.4(a), we show an example of bid and ask prices on the graph from Figure 11.3.

Once traders announce prices, each seller and buyer chooses at most one trader to deal with; each seller sells his copy of the good to the trader he selects (or keeps his copy of the good if he chooses not to sell it), and each buyer purchases a copy of the good from the trader she selects (or receives no copy of the good if she does not select a trader). This determines a flow of goods from sellers, through traders, to buyers; Figure 11.4(b) depicts such a flow of goods, with the sellers' and buyers' choices of traders indicated by the edges with arrows on them.

Because each seller has only one copy of the good, and each buyer only wants one copy, at most one copy of the good moves along any edge in the network. On the other hand, there is no limit on the number of copies of the good that can pass through a single trader node. Note that a trader can only sell as many goods to buyers as he receives from sellers; we will include in the model a large penalty imposed on a trader who defaults on an offer to sell to a buyer as a result of not having enough goods on hand. Therefore, a trader has strong incentives not to produce bid and ask prices that cause more buyers than sellers to accept his offers. There are also incentives for a trader not to be caught in the reverse difficulty, with more sellers than buyers accepting his offers; in this case, he ends up with excess inventory that he cannot sell. We will find that neither of these outcomes happens in the solutions we consider; traders will choose bid and ask prices such that the number of goods they receive from sellers is equal to the number of goods they pass on to buyers.

Finally, notice something else about the flow of goods in this example: seller S3 accepts the bid even though it is equal to his value, and likewise buyer B3 accepts the ask even though it is equal to his value. In fact, each of S3 and B3 is *indifferent* between accepting and rejecting the offer. Our assumption in this model is that, when a seller or buyer is indifferent between accepting or rejecting, then we (as the modelers) can choose either alternative as the outcome that actually happens. Finding a way to handle indifference is an important aspect in most market models, since transactions will typically take place right at the boundary of an individual's willingness to trade. This is similar to the tie-breaking issue inherent in the formulation of market-clearing prices in Chapter 10 as well. An alternate way to handle indifference in the present case is to assume a miniscule positive amount of payoff (e.g., a penny) that is required for an agent to be willing to trade, in which case we would see bid and ask values like 0.01 and 0.99. Although this makes the tie-breaking decision more explicit, the model becomes much messier and ultimately harder to reason about. As a result, we will stick to the approach where we allow trades at zero payoff, with ties broken as needed; in doing so, we will remember that this is essentially a formal way to represent the idea of a price or a profit margin being driven to (almost) zero. And if it makes things simpler to think about, whenever you see an indifferent seller or buyer choosing to transact or not, you can imagine the price being shifted either upward or downward by 0.01 to account for this decision by the seller or buyer.

Payoffs. Recall that specifying a game requires a description of the strategies and the payoffs. We have already discussed the strategies: a trader's strategy is a choice of bid and ask prices to propose to each neighboring seller and buyer; a seller or buyer's strategy is a choice of a neighboring trader to deal with, or the decision not to take part in a transaction.

The payoffs follow naturally from the discussion thus far.

- A trader's payoff is the profit he makes from all his transactions: it is the sum of the ask prices of his accepted offers to buyers minus the sum of the bid prices of his accepted offers to sellers. (As discussed earlier, we also subtract a large penalty if the trader has more accepted asks than bids, the effect of which is primarily to ensure that traders will never expose themselves to this situation in the solutions we consider.)
- For a seller i, the payoff from selecting trader t is b_{ti}, while the payoff from selecting no trader is v_i. In the former case, the seller receives b_{ti} units of money, while in the latter he keeps his copy of the good, which he values at v_i. (We will consider only cases in which all the seller v_i's are 0.)
- For each buyer j, the payoff from selecting trader t is $v_j - a_{tj}$, while the payoff from selecting no trader is 0. In the former case, the buyer receives the good but gives up a_{tj} units of money.

For example, with prices and the flow of goods as in Figure 11.4(b), the payoff to the first trader is $(0.8 - 0.2) = 0.6$ while the payoff to the second trader is $(0.7 + 1 - 0.3 - 0) = 1.4$. The payoffs to the three sellers are 0.2, 0.3, and 0, respectively, while the payoffs to the three buyers are $1 - 0.8 = 0.2$, $1 - 0.7 = 0.3$, and $1 - 1 = 0$, respectively.

The game we've defined here has a further important feature, which forms a contrast with other games we discussed earlier. In earlier games, all players moved (i.e., executed their chosen strategies) simultaneously, while in this game the moves happen in two stages. In the first stage, all the traders simultaneously choose bid and ask prices. In the second stage, all the sellers and buyers then simultaneously choose traders to deal

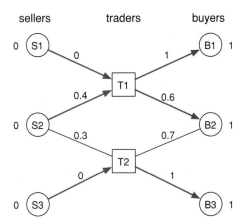

Figure 11.5. Relative to the choice of strategies in Figure 11.4(b), trader T1 has a way to improve his payoff by undercutting T2 and performing the transaction that moves S2's copy of the good to B2.

with. For us, this two-stage structure will not make things too complicated, particularly because the second stage is extremely simple: the best response for each seller and buyer is always simply to choose the trader with the best offer, and so we can essentially view the sellers and buyers as "drones" who are hard-wired to follow this rule. Still, we will have to take the two-stage structure into account when we consider the equilibria for this game, which we do next.

Best Responses and Equilibrium. Let's think about the strategies that the two traders have chosen in Figure 11.4(b). The upper trader, T1, is making several bad decisions. First, because of the offers he is making to seller S2 and buyer B2, he is losing out on this deal to the lower trader, T2. If, for example, he were to raise his bid to seller S2 to 0.4, and lower his ask to buyer B2 to 0.6, then he'd take the trade away from trader T2: seller S2 and buyer B2 would both choose him, and he'd make a profit of 0.2.

Second, and even more simply, there is no reason for trader T1 not to lower his bid to seller S1 and raise his ask to buyer B1. Even with worse offers, S1 and B1 will still want to deal with T1, since they have no other options aside from choosing not to transact. Given this, T1 will make more money with a lower bid to S1 and a higher ask to B1. Figure 11.5 shows the results of a deviation by the upper trader that takes both of these points into account; his payoff has now increased to $(1 + 0.6 - 0 - 0.4) = 1.2$. Note that seller S1 and buyer B1 are now indifferent between performing the transaction or not, and as discussed earlier, we give ourselves (as the modelers) the power to break ties in determining the equilibrium for such situations.

This discussion motivates the equilibrium concept we will use for this game, which is a generalization of Nash equilibrium. As in the standard notion of Nash equilibrium from Chapter 6, it is based on a set of strategies such that each player is choosing a best response to what all the other players are doing. However, the definition also needs to take the two-stage structure of the game into account.

To do this, we first think about the problem faced by the buyers and sellers in the second stage, after traders have already posted prices. Here, we have a standard game among the buyers and sellers, and each of them chooses a strategy that is a best response to what all other players are doing. Next, we think about the problem faced by the traders in deciding what prices to post in the first stage. Here, each trader chooses a strategy that is a best response to both the strategies the sellers and buyers will use (what bids and asks they will accept) and to the strategies the other traders use (what bids and asks they post). So everyone is employing a best response just as in any Nash equilibrium. The one difference here is that since the sellers and buyers move second they are required to choose optimally given *whatever* prices the traders have posted, and the traders know this. This equilibrium is called a *subgame perfect Nash equilibrium*; in this chapter, we will simply refer to it as an *equilibrium*.[2]

The two-stage nature of our game here is particularly easy to think about, since the behavior of sellers and buyers is very simple. Thus, for purposes of reasoning about equilibria, we can mainly think about the strategies of the traders in the first stage, just as in a simultaneous-move game, knowing that sellers and buyers will simply choose the best offers (possibly with tie-breaking) once the traders post prices.

In the next section, we'll work out the set of possible equilibria for the trading network in Figures 11.3–11.5 by first dissecting the network into simpler "building blocks." In particular, these building blocks will correspond to two of the basic structures contained within the network in Figures 11.3–11.5: buyers and sellers who are *monopolized* by having only a single trader they can deal with, and buyers and sellers who benefit from *perfect competition* between multiple traders. In the process, we'll see that network structure and access to alternatives can significantly affect the power of participants in the market.

11.3 Equilibria in Trading Networks

We now discuss the process of analyzing equilibria in trading networks. We begin with simple network structures and build up to the example from the previous section. Following our plan, we'll begin by considering simple networks corresponding to monopoly and perfect competition.

Monopoly. Buyers and sellers are subject to monopoly in our model when they have access to only a single trader. Perhaps the simplest example of this situation is depicted in Figure 11.6. Here we have one seller who values the good at 0, one trader, and one buyer who values the good at 1.

In this trading network the trader is in a monopoly position relative to both the seller and the buyer (there is only one trader available to each of them). The only equilibrium is for the trader to set a bid of 0 to the seller and an ask of 1 to the buyer; the seller and buyer will accept these prices and so the good will flow from the seller to the trader

---

[2] "Subgame" refers to the fact that, once traders post prices, the buyers and sellers are faced with a new free-standing game in the second stage. "Perfect" refers to the requirement that in the subgame, the players who have choices remaining are required to behave optimally given the choices that have already been made. This concept is considered at a general level, although without this particular terminology, in the discussion of games with sequential moves in Section 6.10.

Figure 11.6. A simple example of a trading network in which the trader has a monopoly and extracts all of the surplus from trade.

and then on to the buyer. Note that we are using the indifference of the seller and buyer as in the example from the previous section: since the seller and buyer are indifferent between engaging in a transaction or not, we as the modelers are choosing the outcome and having them perform the transaction.

To see why this is the only equilibrium, we simply notice that, for any other bid and ask between 0 and 1, the trader could slightly lower the bid or raise the ask, thereby performing the transaction at a higher profit.

Perfect Competition. Now let's look at a basic example showing perfect competition between two traders, as depicted in Figure 11.7.

In Figure 11.7 there is competition between traders T1 and T2 to buy the copy of the good from S1 and sell it to B1. To help in thinking about what would form an equilibrium, let's first think about things that are out of equilibrium, in a manner similar to what we saw in Figure 11.5. In particular, suppose trader T1 is performing the trade and making a positive profit: suppose his bid to the seller is some number b, and his ask to the buyer is a number $a > b$. Since T2 is not performing the trade, he currently has a payoff of zero. But then it must be that T2's current strategy is not a best response to what T1 is doing: T2 could instead offer a bid slightly above b and an ask slightly below a, thereby taking the trade away from T1 and receiving a positive payoff instead of zero.

So it follows that whichever trader is performing the trade at equilibrium must have a payoff of 0: he must be offering the same value x as his bid and ask. Suppose that trader T1 is performing the trade. Notice that this equilibrium involves indifference on his part: he is indifferent between performing the trade at zero profit and not performing the trade. As in the earlier case of indifference by sellers and buyers, we assume that we (the modelers) can choose an outcome in this case, and we will assume that the transaction is performed. Here too, we could handle indifference by assuming a minimum increment of money (e.g., 0.01) and having the transaction take place with

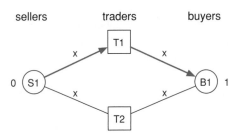

Figure 11.7. A trading network in which there is perfect competition between the two traders, T1 and T2. The equilibrium has a common bid and ask of x, where x can be any real number between 0 and 1.

a bid and ask of $x - 0.01$ and x, respectively, but again handling indifference via zero payoffs (and keeping in mind that they are designed to model profits that come arbitrarily close to 0) makes the analysis simpler without affecting the outcome.

Next we want to argue that the trader not performing the trade at equilibrium (T2 in this case) must also have bid and ask values of x. First, notice that in equilibrium we cannot have a trader buy the good from the seller without also selling it to the buyer; therefore, T2 must be offering a bid $b \leq x$ (or else the seller would sell to T2) and an ask $a \geq x$ (or else the buyer would buy from T2). But if this bid and ask were not the same (i.e., if $a > b$), then T1 could lower his bid or raise his ask so that they still lie strictly between a and b. In that case T1 could perform the trade while making a positive profit, and hence his current strategy of bidding and asking x would not be a best response to what T2 is doing.

So the equilibrium occurs at a common bid and ask of x. What can we say about the value of x? It clearly has to be between 0 and 1: otherwise either the seller wants to sell but the buyer wouldn't want to buy, or conversely the buyer wants to buy but the seller wouldn't want to sell. In fact this is all that we can say about x. Any equilibrium consists of a common bid and ask by each trader, and a flow of goods from the seller to the buyer through one of the traders. A key feature of the equilibrium is that the seller sells to the same trader that the buyer buys from: this is another kind of coordination in the face of indifference that is reminiscent of the tie-breaking issues in market-clearing prices from Chapter 10. It is also interesting that, although traders make no profit in any equilibrium, the choice of equilibrium – captured in the value of x – determines which of the seller or the buyer receives a higher payoff. It ranges from the extreme cases of $x = 0$ (where the buyer consumes all the available payoff) and $x = 1$ (where the seller consumes it) to the intermediate value of $x = \frac{1}{2}$ (where the seller and buyer receive equal payoffs). In the end, the choice of equilibrium reflects something about the relative power of the seller and buyer that can only be inferred by looking outside the formulation of the trading game – the game itself can determine only the range of possible equilibria.

The Network from Section 11.2. Using the networks in Figures 11.6 and 11.7 as building blocks, it is not hard to work out the equilibria in the example from Section 11.2. The possible equilibria for this example are illustrated in Figure 11.8. Sellers S1 and S3, and buyers B1 and B3, are monopolized by their respective traders, and so in any equilibrium these traders will drive the bids and asks all the way to 0 and 1, respectively.

Seller S2 and buyer B2, on the other hand, benefit from perfect competition between the two traders. Here the argument follows what we used in analyzing the simpler network in Figure 11.7: the trader performing the transaction must have bid and ask values equal to the same number x (for some real number x between 0 and 1), or else the other trader could take the trade away from him; given this, the other trader must also have bid and ask values equal to x.

These types of reasoning are useful in analyzing other more complex networks as well. When you see a seller or buyer connected to only a single trader, they will receive zero payoff in any equilibrium, since the trader will drive the bid or ask to as extreme a value as possible. On the other hand, when two traders both connect the same seller

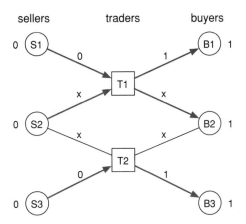

Figure 11.8. The equilibria for the trading network from Section 11.2. This network can be analyzed using the ideas from the simpler networks representing monopoly and perfect competition.

and buyer, then neither can make a positive profit in conveying a good from this seller to this buyer: if one trader performed the trade at a positive profit, the other could undercut them.

We now consider a further example that illustrates how the network structure can also produce more complex effects that are not explained by these two principles.

Implicit Perfect Competition. In our examples so far, when a trader makes no profit from a transaction, it is always because there is another trader who can precisely replicate the transaction – a trader who is connected to the same seller and buyer. However, it turns out that traders can make zero profit for reasons based more on the global structure of the network, rather than on direct competition with any one trader.

The network in Figure 11.9 illustrates how this can arise. In this trading network there is no direct competition for any one "trade route" from a seller to a buyer.

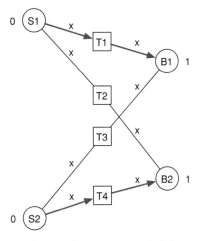

Figure 11.9. A form of *implicit perfect competition*: all bid/ask spreads will be zero in equilibrium, even though no trader directly "competes" with any other trader for the same buyer–seller pair.

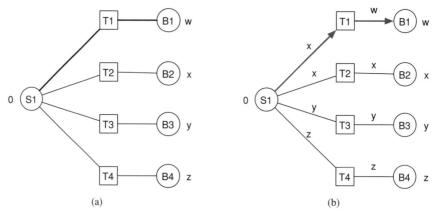

Figure 11.10. (a) A single-item auction can be represented using a trading network. (b) Equilibrium prices and flow of goods. The resulting equilibrium implements the second-price rule from Chapter 9.

However, in any equilibrium, all bid and ask prices take on some common value x between 0 and 1, and the goods flow from the sellers to the buyers. So all traders again make zero profit.

It is easy to see that this is an equilibrium: we can simply check that each trader is using a best response to all the other traders' strategies. It takes a bit more work to verify that in every equilibrium all bid and ask prices are the same value x: this is most easily done by checking alternatives in which some trader posts a bid that is less than the corresponding ask, and by identifying a deviation that arises.

11.4 Further Equilibrium Phenomena: Auctions and Ripple Effects

The network model we've been considering is expressive enough that it can represent a diverse set of other phenomena. Here we consider two distinct examples: the first shows how the second-price auction for a single item arises from a trading network equilibrium, and the second explores how small changes to a network can produce effects that ripple to other nodes.

Second-Price Auctions. Figure 11.10 shows how we can represent the structure of a single-item auction using a trading network. Suppose there is a single individual S1 with an item to sell, and four potential buyers who value the item at values w, x, y, and z, listed in descending order: $w > x > y > z$. We use four buyers in this example but our analysis would work for an arbitrary number of buyers.

In keeping with our model in which trading happens through intermediaries, we assume that each buyer is represented by a distinct trader – essentially, someone who serves as the buyer's "proxy" for the transaction. This gives us a trading network as depicted in Figure 11.10(a).

Now let's consider a possible equilibrium for this network. Trader T1 has the ability to outbid all the other traders, since he has the ability to sell to his buyer for an ask up to w. In equilibrium, he will outbid them by the minimum needed to make the trade, which he can do by offering x to outbid T2. Here we use indifference to assume that the sale at x will go to T1 rather than T2, that buyer B1 will buy from T1 at a price of w, and that buyers B2 through B4 will choose not to buy the good from their respective traders.

We therefore get the equilibrium depicted in Figure 11.10(b). Notice how this equilibrium has exactly the form of a second-price auction, in which the item goes to the highest bidder, with the seller receiving the second-highest valuation in payment.[3] What's interesting is that the second-price rule wasn't in any sense "built into" the formulation of the auction; it emerged naturally as an equilibrium in our network representation.

Ripple Effects from Changes to a Network. Our network model also allows us to explore how small changes to the network structure can affect the payoffs of nodes that are not directly involved in the change. This suggests a way of reasoning about how "shocks" to highly interconnected trading networks can ripple to more distant parts of the network.

This is a very general issue; we consider it here in a specific example where we can see concretely how such effects can arise. Consider the pair of networks in Figure 11.11: the second network is obtained from the first simply by adding a link from S2 to T2. We first work out the equilibria for each of these networks, and then we consider how they differ.

In Figure 11.11(a), all sellers and buyers are monopolized except for B2, so their payoffs will all be zero; we use indifference to assume that B3 will not buy the good but B1 and B4 will. (As in all our examples, we can view this as modeling the fact that T2 can charge a price very slightly higher than 3 to B3, dissuading B3 from purchasing.) The one part that requires additional analysis is the pair of asks charged to B2. In equilibrium, these must be the same (otherwise, the trader making the sale could slightly raise his ask), and this common value x can be anything between 0 and 2. We exploit indifference here to assume that B2 buys from trader T1. Note that there cannot be an equilibrium in which buyer B2 buys from trader T2, since B2 can pay only 2 while trader T2 can sell the unit of the good he is able to buy at a price of 4.

---

[3] With a little more work, we can describe the full set of equilibria for this network, and show that the second-price rule is unique over equilibria that avoid a certain "pathological" structure, as follows. In any equilibrium, the good flows from the seller to buyer B1, and each trader offers to sell the good to his monopolized buyer for the buyer's value. In the equilibrium we consider, T1 and T2 both bid x. However, there are other bids that can be part of an equilibrium: essentially, as long as one of traders T2, T3, or T4 bids between x and w, and T1 matches this bid, we have an equilibrium. If the highest bid among T2, T3, and T4 is strictly greater than x, then we have a situation in which this high-bidding trader among T2 through T4 has a *crossing* pair of bid and ask values: his bid is higher than his corresponding ask. This is an equilibrium, since T1 still makes the trade, the trader with the crossing bid–ask pair doesn't lose money, and no one has an incentive to deviate. However, it is a pathological kind of equilibrium since there is a trader who is offering to buy for more than he is offering to sell [63]. Thus, if we consider only equilibria without such crossing pairs of bid–ask values, then T2 bids the "second-price value" x, and this is what the good sells for. So the second-price rule is unique over equilibria without crossing pairs.

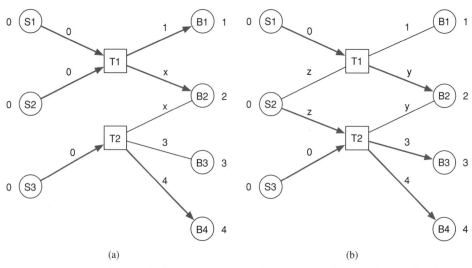

(a)   (b)

Figure 11.11. (a) Equilibrium before the new S2-T2 link is added. (b) Equilibrium after the S2-T2 edge is added. A number of changes take place in the equilibrium. Among these changes is the fact that buyer B1 no longer gets a copy of the good, and B3 gets one instead.

In Figure 11.11(b), once the edge from S2 to T2 has been added, we need to work out the equilibrium bids and asks charged to S2 and B2, and the flow of goods. Reasoning about these bids and asks requires a bit more work than we've seen in previous examples, so we build up to it in a sequence of steps.

- The two bids to S2 must be the same as each other; otherwise the trader getting the good could slightly lower his bid. For a similar reason, the two asks to B2 must also be the same as each other. Let's call the common bid z and the common ask y.
- We can next determine how the seller–trader transactions work out in equilibrium. Seller S2 will sell to T2 rather than T1 in equilibrium: if S2 were selling to T1, and T1 were receiving a nonnegative payoff from this transaction, then S2 would be selling for at most 2. In this case, T2 could slightly outbid T1 and sell S2's copy of the good to B3. So in equilibrium, T2 buys two copies of the good, while T1 buys only one.
- Now let's figure out the possible values for the ask y. The ask y must be at least 1: otherwise, one of the traders is selling to B2 for a low price, and the trader performing this sale has an alternate trader whom he monopolizes and from whom he would get a higher payoff. This can't happen in equilibrium, so y is at least 1.

    Also, the ask y cannot be greater than 2 in equilibrium: in this case, B2 would not buy, and so T1 could perform a payoff-improving change in strategy by lowering his ask to B2, thereby getting B2 to buy from T1 for a price between 1 and 2.
- Next, we determine how the trader–buyer transactions work out in equilibrium. We've already concluded that T2 is buying two copies of the good, and so he maximizes his payoff by selling them to B3 and B4. Therefore, T2 is not selling

to B2 in equilibrium. Since the ask y is at least 1, trader T1 will buy from S1 and sell to B2.

- Finally, what do we know about the value of z? It has to be at least 1, or else T1 could outbid T2 for S2's copy of the good and receive a positive payoff by selling it to B1. It also has to be at most 3, or else T2 would prefer not to buy it from S2.

This sums up the analysis: in equilibrium, the bid z can be anything between 1 and 3, the ask y can be anything between 1 and 2, and the goods flow from S1 through T1 to B2, and from S2 and S3 through T2 to B3 and B4. Notice that this flow of goods maximizes the total valuation of the buyers who obtain the good, given the constraints on trade imposed by the network. Later in this chapter we will see that any equilibrium has this efficiency property.

Let's consider at a high level what's going on in this pair of examples. In Figure 11.11(a), trader T2 has access to a set of buyers who want copies of the good very badly (they value it highly), but his access to sellers is very limited. Trader T1, on the other hand, is able to use all his available trading opportunities. The market in this respect has a "bottleneck" that is restricting the flow of goods.

Once S2 and T2 form a link, creating the network in Figure 11.11(b), a number of things change. First, and most noticeably, buyer B3 now gets a copy of the good while B1 doesn't. Essentially, the bottleneck in the market has been broken open, so the high-value buyers can now obtain the good at the expense of the low-value buyers. From B1's perspective, this is a "nonlocal" effect: a link formed between two nodes, neither of which are neighbors of hers, has caused her to no longer be able to obtain the good.

There are other changes as well. Seller S2 is now in a much more powerful position and will command a significantly higher price (since y is at least 1 in any equilibrium). Moreover, the range of possible equilibrium asks to B2 has been reduced from the interval $[0, 2]$ to the interval $[1, 2]$. So in particular, if we were previously in an equilibrium where the ask to B2 was a value $x < 1$, then this equilibrium gets disrupted and replaced by one in which the ask is a higher number, $y \geq 1$. This indicates a subtle way in which B2 was implicitly benefitting from the weak position of the sellers, which has now been strengthened by the creation of the edge between S2 and T2.

This is a simple example, but it already illustrates some of the complexities that can arise when the structure of a trading network changes to alleviate (or create) bottlenecks for the flow of goods. With more work, one can create examples where the effects of changes in the network ripple much farther through the structure.

This style of reasoning also points to a line of questions in which we view the network as something malleable, and partially under the control of the market participants. For example, how much should S2 and T2 be willing to spend to create a link between each other, shifting the network structure from the one in Figure 11.11(a) to the one in Figure 11.11(b)? More generally, how should different nodes evaluate the trade-offs between investing resources to create and maintain links, and the benefits they get in terms of increased payoffs? This is a question that has been considered in other models of trading networks [150, 261], and it is part of a much broader research activity that investigates the formation of networks as a game-theoretic activity under a variety of different kinds of payoffs [19, 39, 121, 152, 227, 385].

11.5 Social Welfare in Trading Networks

When we've looked at games in earlier settings, we've considered not just equilibrium solutions but also the question of whether these solutions are *socially optimal*. That is, do they maximize *social welfare*, the sum of the payoffs of all players?

In the context of our game, each good that moves from a seller i to a buyer j contributes $v_j - v_i$ to the social welfare. This is how much more j values the good than i, and the money that is spent in moving the good from i to j is simply transferred from one player to another, creating a net effect of zero to the total payoff. In more detail, if the good moves through trader t, who offers a bid of b_{ti} to i and an ask of a_{tj} to j, then the sum of the payoffs of i and j, plus the portion of t's payoffs arising from this transaction, is equal to

$$(b_{ti} - v_i) + (a_{tj} - b_{ti}) + (v_j - a_{tj}) = v_j - v_i.$$

Thus, the social welfare is simply the sum of $v_j - v_i$ over all goods that move from a seller i to a buyer j. This makes sense, because it reflects how much happier, in total, the new owners of the goods are compared to the original owners of the goods. The maximum value of this quantity over all possible flows of goods – the socially optimal value – depends not just on the valuations of the sellers and buyers but also on the network structure. Networks that are more richly connected can potentially allow a flow of goods achieving a higher social welfare than networks that are more sparsely connected, with bottlenecks that prevent a desirable flow of goods.

For example, let's go back to the pair of networks in Figure 11.11. In each case, the equilibrium yields a flow of goods that achieves the social optimum. In Figure 11.11(a), the best possible value of the social welfare is $1 + 2 + 4 = 7$, since there is no way to use the network to get copies of the goods to both B3 and B4. However, when the single edge from S2 to T2 is added, it suddenly becomes possible for both of these buyers to receive copies of the good, and so the value of the social welfare increases to $2 + 3 + 4 = 9$. This provides a simple illustration of how a more richly connected network structure can enable greater social welfare from trade.

In our discussion of social optimality, we count the gains to traders as part of the social welfare (since they are part of the society of players, along with sellers and buyers). In the next section, we will consider how the total payoff is divided between sellers, buyers, and traders, and how it depends on the network structure.

Equilibria and Social Welfare. In both the networks in Figure 11.11, the flow of goods that maximizes social welfare can be achieved by an equilibrium.

In fact, this holds for all the examples we've seen thus far, and it's a fact that's true in general: it can be shown that, in every trading network, there is always at least one equilibrium, and every equilibrium produces a flow of goods that achieves the social optimum [63]. Although we won't go into the details of the proof here, it is similar in structure to the existence and optimality of market-clearing prices that we discussed in the previous chapter. There too, without intermediaries present, we were able to show that prices achieving a certain type of equilibrium always exist (in that case the market-clearing property) and that all such prices produce an allocation that maximize social welfare.

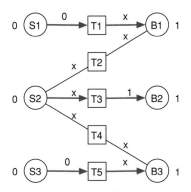

Figure 11.12. Whether a trader can make a profit may depend on the choice of equilibrium. In this trading network, when $x = 1$, traders T1 and T5 make a profit, while when $x = 0$, only trader T3 makes a profit.

11.6 Trader Profits

We now consider the question of how the social welfare in an equilibrium is divided up as payoffs among the sellers, buyers, and traders. In particular, the examples we've studied so far suggest the informal principle that, as the network becomes more richly connected, individual traders have less and less power, and their payoffs go down. Understanding this more precisely points to a basic question that can be expressed in terms of our network model: what is the structural basis of perfect competition?

Our examples suggest that, in order to make a profit (i.e., a positive payoff), a trader must in some way be "essential" to the functioning of the trading network. Certainly, if there is another trader who can replicate his function completely, then he cannot make a profit, nor can he make a profit in more complex settings like the implicit perfect competition in Figure 11.9. In fact, it turns out that a version of this "essentiality" principle is true in general, but it is a bit more subtle than it might initially appear. To motivate it, we start with two illuminating examples.

First, whether a trader makes a profit can depend on the equilibrium: in some networks, it can be possible for a trader to make a profit in some equilibria but not others. Figure 11.12 shows how this can occur. Any choice of x between 0 and 1 will result in an equilibrium, with the traders T2 and T4 who are left out of trades serving to "lock" the value of x in place. However, when $x = 1$, traders T1 and T5 make a profit, while when $x = 0$, only trader T3 makes a profit. Furthermore, while every equilibrium produces a flow of goods to all three sellers, for a social welfare of 3, the amount of this social welfare that goes to the buyers and sellers – rather than the traders – varies between 1 and 2 as x ranges from 1 to 0.

The second example, in Figure 11.13, is even more counterintuitive. Here, traders T1 and T2 both have monopoly power over their respective sellers, and yet their profits are zero in *every* equilibrium. We can verify this fact as follows. First, we notice that any equilibrium must look like one of the solutions in Figure 11.13(b) or Figure 11.13(c). The sellers are monopolized and will get bids of 0. For each buyer, the two asks must be the same; otherwise, the trader making the sale could slightly raise his ask. Now, finally, notice that if the common ask to either buyer were positive, then the trader left

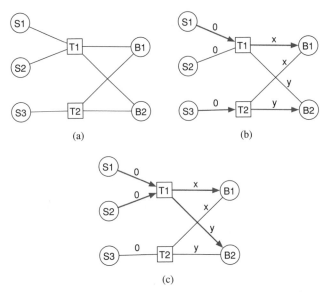

Figure 11.13. Despite a form of monopoly power in this network, neither trader can make a profit in any equilibrium: (a) a network in which trader T1 is essential, (b) an equilibrium where T1 trades one unit of the good, or (c) an equilibrium where T1 trades two units of the good.

out of the trade on the higher one has a profitable deviation by slightly undercutting this ask.

Therefore, in this example, all bids and asks equal 0 in any equilibrium, and so neither trader profits. This happens despite the monopoly power of the traders; moreover, T1 fails to make a profit despite the fact that T2 can only perform one trade on his own. We can interpret this as a situation in which a small trader competes with a larger trader across his full set of potential buyers, despite having access to an insufficient set of sellers to actually perform all the available trades – a situation in which "the threat is stronger than its execution." While this fits naturally within the scope of the model, examples such as this one also suggest natural extensions to the model, in which each trader has an intrinsic limit on the number of trades he can perform, and this affects the behavior of competing traders. While the possibility of such intrinsic limits haven't played a role in our earlier examples, Figure 11.13 suggests that allowing for such limits could change the outcome in certain settings.

With these examples in mind, let's return to the question of when, for a given trader T in a network, there exists an equilibrium in which T receives a positive payoff. It turns out that there exists such an equilibrium precisely when T has an edge e to a seller or buyer such that deleting e would change the value of the social optimum. In such a situation, we say that e is an *essential edge* from T to the other node. The proof of this statement is somewhat involved, and we refer the reader to [63] for the details. Figures 11.6 and 11.8 are examples of trading networks in which each trader has an essential edge and thus makes a profit in equilibrium, while Figures 11.7 and 11.9 are examples in which no trader has an essential edge and no trader makes a profit.

This essential-edge condition is a stronger form of monopoly power than we saw in Figure 11.13(a). There, although deleting node T1 would change the value of the social optimum, there is no single edge whose deletion would reduce the value of the social optimum below 2; rather, after the removal of any one edge, there would still be a flow of goods to both buyers. This is the crux of why T1 is not able to make a profit in Figure 11.13(a), despite his powerful position.

The example in Figure 11.12 also shows that this condition only implies a profit in *some* equilibrium, as opposed to every equilibrium. In Figure 11.12, the available profit essentially "slides" smoothly from one trader to another as we vary the value of x in the equilibrium.

11.7 Reflections on Trade with Intermediaries

In closing, it is useful to reflect on how our analysis of trade on networks relates to the motivating examples from the beginning of this chapter: trade in the stock market and the trade of agricultural goods in developing countries. The network model we analyzed in this chapter is an abstraction that captures some essential features of these real markets but leaves out other features. Our trade model reflects the constraint that trade takes place through intermediaries and that there is differential access to these intermediaries. Equilibria in our trading networks reflect the fact that buyers and sellers in intermediated markets, such as the stock market, face a bid–ask spread. In our model, as in actual intermediated markets, the size of this spread, and how much profit intermediaries make, depends on the amount of competition between intermediaries for the trade flow.

However, there are other interesting aspects of trade in intermediated markets that are not captured by our simple network model. In particular, we do not ask where buyers' and sellers' values come from, nor do we ask about how they might use information revealed by bids, asks, or trades to update these values. We discuss the role of beliefs and information in markets in Chapter 22.

11.8 Exercises

1. Consider a trading network with intermediaries in which there is one seller S, two buyers B1 and B2, and two traders (intermediaries) T1 and T2. The seller is allowed to trade with either trader. The buyers can each trade with only one of the traders: buyer B1 can only trade with trader T1, and buyer B2 can only trade with trader T2. The seller has one unit of the object and values it at 0; the buyers are not endowed with the object. Buyer B1 values a unit at 1 and buyer B2 values a unit at 2.

    (a) Draw the trading network, with the traders as squares, the buyers and the seller as circles, and edges representing pairs of people who are able to trade with each other. Label each node as S, B1, B2, T1, or T2.

    (b) Suppose the traders offer prices as follows:
    - Trader T1 offers a bid price of $\frac{1}{3}$ to S and an ask price of 1 to B1.
    - Trader T2 offers a bid price of $\frac{2}{3}$ to S and an ask price of 2 to B2.

    Are these bids and asks Nash equilibrium prices? If you think the answer is yes, give a brief (one- to three-sentence) explanation. If you think the answer is no, describe a way in which one of the traders could change its prices so as to increase its profit.

2. Consider a trading network in which there are two buyers (B1 and B2), two sellers (S1 and S2), and one trader (T1). All of the buyers and the sellers are allowed to trade with the trader. The sellers each have one unit of the object and value it at 0; the buyers are not endowed with the object, but they each want one unit; buyer B1 attaches a value of 1 to one unit, while buyer B2 attaches a value of 2 to one unit.

   (a) Draw the trading network, with the trader as a square, the buyers and the sellers as circles, and edges representing pairs of people who are able to trade with each other. Label the nodes as T1, B1, B2, S1, and S2. Find Nash equilibrium bid and ask prices. (You do not have to provide an explanation for your answer.)

   (b) Suppose now that we add a second trader (T2) who can trade with each seller and each buyer. In the new network, is there a Nash equilibrium in which each trader's bid price to each seller is 1, each trader's ask price to buyer B1 is 1, each trader's ask price to buyer B2 is 2, one unit of the good flows from S1 to B1 through trader T1, and one unit of the good flows from S2 to B2 through trader T2? Draw the new trading network and give a brief (one- to three-sentence) explanation for your answer.

3. Consider a trading network with intermediaries in which there are two sellers S1 and S2, three buyers B1, B2, and B3, and two traders (intermediaries) T1 and T2. Each seller can trade with either trader. Buyer B1 can only trade with trader T1. Buyer B2 can trade with either trader. Buyer B3 can only trade with trader T2. The sellers each have one unit of the object and value it at 0; the buyers are not endowed with the object. Buyer B1 values a unit at 1, buyer B2 values a unit at 2, and buyer B3 values a unit at 3.

   (a) Draw the trading network, with the traders as squares, the buyers and the sellers as circles, and edges representing pairs of people who are able to trade with each other. Label each node as S1, S2, B1, B2, B3, T1, or T2.

   (b) Suppose the prices and the flow of goods are as follows:
   - Trader T1 offers a bid price of 1 to each seller, an ask price of 1 to B1, and an ask price of 2 to B2.
   - Trader T2 offers a bid price of 1 to each seller, an ask price of 2 to B2, and an ask price of 3 to B3.
   - One unit of the good flows from seller S1 to buyer B2 through trader T1 and one unit of the good flows from seller S2 to buyer B3 through trader T2.

   (If it is useful, it is okay to write these prices and this flow of goods on the picture you drew for part (a), provided the picture itself is still clear.) Do these prices and this flow of goods form a Nash equilibrium? If you think the answer is yes, give a brief (one- to three-sentence) explanation. If you think the answer is no, describe a way in which one of the traders could change its prices so as to increase its profit.

4. Consider a trading network with intermediaries in which there is one buyer, one seller, and two traders (intermediaries). The buyer and the seller each are allowed to trade with either trader. The seller has one unit of the object and values it at 0; the buyer is not endowed with the object but attaches a value of 1 to one unit of it.

   Draw the trading network, with traders as squares, the buyer and the seller as circles, and edges representing pairs of people who are able to transact directly.

Then describe what the possible Nash equilibrium outcomes are, together with an explanation for your answer.

5. Consider a trading network with intermediaries in which there is one seller S, two buyers B1 and B2, and two traders (intermediaries) T1 and T2. The seller is allowed to trade with either trader. The buyers can each trade with only one of the traders: buyer B1 can only trade with trader T1, and buyer B2 can only trade with trader T2. The seller has one unit of the object and values it at 0; the buyers are not endowed with the object. Buyer B1 values a unit at 3 and buyer B2 values a unit at 1.

    (a) Draw the trading network, with the traders as squares, the buyers and the seller as circles, and edges connecting people who are able to trade with each other. Label each node as S, B1, B2, T1, or T2.
    (b) Find Nash equilibrium bid and ask prices for this trading network. How much profit do the traders make?
    (c) Suppose now that we add edges representing the idea that each buyer can trade with each trader. Find a Nash equilibrium in this new trading game. What happens to trader profits? Why?

6. Consider a trading network with intermediaries in which there are three sellers S1, S2, and S3, two buyers B1 and B2, and two traders (intermediaries) T1 and T2. Sellers S1 and S2 can trade only with trader T1, and seller S3 can trade only with trader T2. The buyers can each trade with only one of the traders: buyer B1 can only trade with trader T1, and buyer B2 can only trade with trader T2. The sellers each have one unit of the object and value it at 0. The buyers are not endowed with the object and they each value a unit at 1.

    (a) Draw the trading network, with the traders as squares, the buyers and sellers as circles, and edges connecting nodes that are able to trade with each other. Label each node as S1, S2, S3, B1, B2, T1, or T2.
    (b) Find a Nash equilibrium of this trading game, including both prices and the flow of goods. Give an explanation for your answer.
    (c) Suppose now that we add an edge between buyer B2 and trader T1. We want to examine whether this new edge changes the outcome in the game. To do this, take the equilibrium from your answer to part (b), keep the prices and the flow of goods on the edges from part (b) the same as before, and then suppose that the ask price on the new B2-T1 edge is 1, and that no good flows on this new edge. Do these prices and this flow of goods still form an equilibrium? If you think that the answer is yes, give a brief (one- to three-sentence) explanation. If you think the answer is no, describe a way in which one of the participants in the game would deviate.

7. Consider a trading network in which there are two buyers (B1 and B2), two sellers (S1 and S2), and two traders (T1 and T2). The sellers each have one unit of the object and value it at 0; the buyers are not endowed with the object, but they each want one unit and attach a value of 1 to one unit. Seller S1 and buyer B1 can trade only with trader T1; seller S2 and buyer B2 can each trade with either trader.

    (a) Draw the trading network, with the traders as squares, the buyers and the sellers as circles, and edges representing pairs of people who are able to trade with each other. Label the nodes as T1, T2, B1, B2, S1, and S2.

(b) Consider the following prices and flow of goods:

- T1's bid price to seller S1 is 0, his bid price to seller S2 is $\frac{1}{2}$, his ask price to buyer B1 is 1, and his ask price to buyer B2 is $\frac{1}{2}$.
- T2's bid price to seller S2 is $\frac{1}{2}$ and his ask price to buyer B2 is $\frac{1}{2}$.
- One unit of the good flows from seller S1 to buyer B1 through trader T1, and one unit of the good flows from seller S2 to buyer B2 through trader T2.

Do these prices and this flow of goods describe an equilibrium of the trading game? If you think that the answer is no, then briefly describe how someone should deviate. If you think that the answer is yes, then briefly explain (in one to three sentences) why the answer is yes.

(c) Suppose now that we add a third trader (T3) who can trade with seller S1 and buyer B1. This trader cannot trade with the other seller or buyer, and the rest of the trading network remains unchanged. Consider the following prices and flow of goods:

- The prices on the old edges are unchanged from those in part (b).
- The prices on the new edges are a bid of $\frac{1}{2}$ to seller S1 by trader T3 and an ask of $\frac{1}{2}$ to buyer B1 by trader T3.
- The flow of goods is the same as in part (b).

Do these prices and this flow of goods describe an equilibrium of the trading game? If you think that the answer is no, then briefly describe how someone should deviate. If you think that the answer is yes, then briefly explain (in one to three sentences) why the answer is yes.

CHAPTER 12

Bargaining and Power
in Networks

In our analysis of economic transactions on networks, particularly the model in Chapter 11, we considered how a node's position in a network affects its power in the market. In some cases, we were able to come up with precise predictions about prices and power, but in others the analysis left open a range of possibilities. For example, in the case of perfect competition between traders, we could conclude that the traders would make no profit, but it was not possible to say whether the resulting situation would favor particular buyers or sellers – different divisions of the available surplus were possible. This is an instance of a broader phenomenon that we discussed earlier, in Chapter 6: when there are multiple equilibria, some of which favor one player and some of which favor another, we may need to look for additional sources of information to predict how things will turn out.

In this chapter, we formulate a perspective on power in networks that can help us further refine our predictions for the outcomes of different participants. This perspective arises dominantly from research in sociology, and it addresses not just economic transactions but also a range of social interactions more generally that are mediated by networks. We will develop a set of formal principles that aim to capture some subtle distinctions in how a node's network position affects its power. The goal will be to create a succinct mathematical framework enabling predictions of which nodes have power, and how much power they have, for arbitrary networks.

12.1 Power in Social Networks

The notion of *power* is a central issue in sociology, and it has been studied in many forms. Like many related notions, a fundamental question is the extent to which power is a property of individuals (i.e., someone is particularly powerful because of his own exceptional attributes) and the extent to which it is a property of network structure (i.e., someone is particularly powerful because he holds a pivotal position in the underlying social structure).

The goal here is to understand power not just as a property of agents in economic settings, or in legal or political settings, but in social interaction more generally – in the roles people play in groups of friends, in communities, or in organizations. A particular focus is on the way in which power is manifested between pairs of people linked by edges in a larger social network. Indeed, as Richard Emerson [148] has observed in his fundamental work on this subject, power is not so much a property of an individual as it is a property of a relation between two individuals; it makes more sense to study the conditions under which one person has power over another, rather than simply asserting that a particular person is "powerful."

A common theme in this line of work is to view a social relation between two individuals as producing value for both of them. We will be deliberately vague in specifying what this value is, since it clearly depends on the type of social relation we are discussing, but the idea adapts naturally to many contexts. In an economic setting, it could be the revenue that two people can produce by working together; in a political setting, it could be the ability of each person in the relationship to do useful favors for the other; and in the context of friendship, it could be the social or psychological value that the two people derive from being friends with one another. In any of these examples, the value may be divided equally or unequally between the two parties. For example, one of the two parties in the relationship may get more benefit from it than the other – they may get more than half the profits in a joint business relationship, or in the context of a friendship they may be the center of attention, or get their way more often in the case of disagreements. The way in which the value in the relationship is divided between the two parties can be viewed as a kind of *social exchange*, and *power* then corresponds to the imbalance in this division – with the powerful party in the relationship getting the majority of the value.

In some cases, this imbalance in a relationship may be almost entirely the result of the personalities of the two people involved. But in other cases, it may also be a function of the larger social network in which the two people are embedded: one person may be more powerful in a relationship because they occupy a more dominant position in the social network, with greater access to social opportunities outside this single relationship. In this latter case, the imbalance in the relationship may be rooted in considerations of network structure and may transcend the individual characteristics of the two people involved. The ways in which social imbalances and power can be partly rooted in the structure of the social network has motivated the growth of a research area in sociology known as *network exchange theory* [417].

An Example of a Powerful Network Position. It is useful to discuss this in the context of a simple example. Consider the group of five friends depicted in Figure 12.1, with strong friendships indicated by the social network links. Intuitively, node B appears to hold a powerful position in the network, and in particular to be powerful relative to two of her three neighbors, A and C. What general principle or principles should lead us to this conclusion? Here are several proposals, which we state informally here but make more precise in what follows.

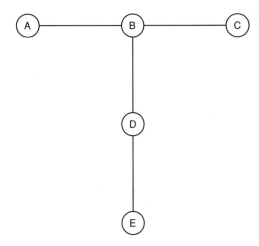

Figure 12.1. A social network on five people, with node B occupying an intuitively powerful position.

(i) *Dependence.* Recalling that social relations confer value, nodes A and C are completely dependent on B as a source of such value; B, on the other hand, has multiple sources.

(ii) *Exclusion.* Related to proposal (i), B has the ability to exclude A and C. In particular, suppose each person were to choose a "best friend" in the group; then B has the unilateral power to choose one of A and C, excluding the other. (However, B does not have the analogous power over D.)

(iii) *Satiation.* A somewhat different basis for B's power may be implicit in the psychological principle of *satiation* – having diminishing rewards for increased amounts of something. Again, viewing social relations as conferring value, B will acquire value at a greater rate than the other members of the group; having thus become satiated, B may be interested in maintaining these social relations only if she can receive an unequal share of their value.

(iv) *Betweenness.* If we believe that the value generated in social relations flows not just across single edges but more generally along paths, then we are led to consider notions such as *betweenness*. Betweenness was considered extensively in Section 3.6; for our purposes here, it is enough to think informally of a node as having high betweenness if it lies on paths (and particularly short paths) between many pairs of other nodes. In our example, B has high betweenness because she is the unique access point between multiple different pairs of nodes in the network, and this potentially confers power. More generally, betweenness is one example of a *centrality measure* that tries to find the "central" points in a network. We saw in our discussion of structural holes in Section 3.5 that evaluating a node's power in terms of its role as an access point between different parts of the network makes sense in contexts where we are concerned about issues like the flow of information. Here, however, where we are concerned about power arising from the asymmetries in pairwise relations, we will see some concrete cases where a simple application of ideas about centrality can in fact be misleading.

12.2 Experimental Studies of Power and Exchange

While all of these principles are presumably at work in many situations, it is difficult to make precise or quantify their effects in most real-world settings. As a result, researchers have turned to laboratory experiments in which they ask test subjects to take part in stylized forms of social exchange under controlled conditions. This style of research grew into an active experimental program carried out by a number of research groups in network exchange theory [417]. The basic idea underlying the experiments is to take the notion of "social value" and represent it under laboratory conditions using a concrete economic framework, of the type that we have seen in Chapters 10 and 11. In these experiments, the value that relationships produce is represented by an amount of money that the participants in a relationship get to share. This does not mean, however, that an individual necessarily cares only about the amount of money that he receives. As we shall see, it's clear from the results that even subjects in the experiments may also care about other aspects of the relationship, such as the fairness of the sharing.

While the details vary across experiments, here is the setup for a typical one. Roughly, people are placed at the nodes of a small graph representing a social network, a fixed sum of money is placed on each edge of a graph, and nodes joined by an edge negotiate over how the money placed between them should be divided up. The final, crucial part of the setup is that each node can take part in a division with only one neighbor, and so is faced with the choice not just of how large a share to seek, but also with whom. The experiment is run over multiple periods to allow for repeated interaction by the participants, and we study the divisions of money after many rounds.

Here are the mechanics in more detail.

1. A small graph (such as the one in Figure 12.1) is chosen, and a distinct volunteer test subject is chosen to represent each node. Each person, representing a node, sits at a computer and can exchange instant messages with the people representing the neighboring nodes.

2. The value in each social relation is made concrete by placing a *resource pool* on each edge. Let's imagine this as a fixed sum of money, say $1, which can be divided between the two endpoints of the edge. We will refer to a division of this money between the endpoints as an *exchange*. Whether this division ends up equal or unequal will be taken as a sign of the asymmetric amounts of power in the relationship that the edge represents.

3. Each node is given a limit on the number of neighbors with whom she can perform an exchange. The most common variant is to impose the extreme restriction that each node can be involved in a successful exchange with only *one* of her neighbors; this is called the *one-exchange rule*. Thus, for example, in Figure 12.1, node B can ultimately make money from an exchange with only one of her three neighbors. Given this restriction, the set of exchanges that take place in a given round of the experiment can be viewed as a *matching* in the graph – a set of edges that have no endpoints in common. However, it will not necessarily be a *perfect matching*, because some nodes may not take part in any exchange. For example, in the graph in Figure 12.1, the exchanges will definitely not form a perfect matching, since there are an odd number of nodes.

4. Here is how the money on each edge is divided. A given node takes part in simultaneous sessions of instant messaging separately with each of her neighbors in the network. In each, she engages in relatively free-form negotiation, proposing splits of the money on the edge, and potentially reaching an agreement on a proposed split. These negotiations must be concluded by a fixed time limit, and to enforce the one-exchange rule defined above, as soon as a node reaches an agreement with one neighbor, her negotiations with all other neighbors are immediately terminated.

5. Finally, the experiment is run for multiple rounds. The graph and the assignment of subjects to nodes as described in point 1 are kept fixed across rounds. In each round, new money is placed on each edge as in point 2, each node can take part in an exchange as in point 3, and the money is divided as in point 4. The experiment is run for multiple rounds to allow for repeated interactions among the nodes, and we study the exchange values that occur after many rounds.

Thus, the general notion of "social value" on edges is implemented using a specific economic metaphor: the value is represented using money, and people are negotiating explicitly over how to divide it up. We will mainly focus on the one-exchange rule, unless noted otherwise. We can view the one-exchange rule as encoding the notion of choosing "best friends," which we discussed earlier when we talked about exclusion. That is, the one-exchange rule models a setting in which the nodes are trying to form partnerships: each node wants to be in a partnership and, subject to this condition, the node wants to get a reasonable share of the value implicit in this partnership. Later in this chapter we will see that varying the number of successful exchanges in which a node can participate has effects on which nodes hold power, often in interesting ways.

There are many variations in the precise way these experiments are implemented. One particularly interesting dimension is the amount of information provided to the participants about the exchanges made by other participants. This has ranged in experiments from a *high-information* version – in which each person sees not just what is happening on their edges, but also what is happening on every edge in the network, in real time – to a *low-information* version – in which each person is told only what is happening on the edges she is directly involved in; for example, she may have no idea how many other potential partners each of her neighbors has. An interesting finding from this body of work is that the experimental results do not change much with the amount of information available [389]; this suggests a certain robustness to the results and allows us to draw some conclusions about the kinds of reasoning that participants are engaging in as they take part in these experiments.

12.3 Results of Network Exchange Experiments

Let's start by discussing what happens when one runs this type of experiment on some simple graphs using human test subjects. Since the results are intuitively reasonable and fairly robust, we'll then consider – in increasing levels of detail – what sorts of principles can be inferred about power in these types of exchange situations.

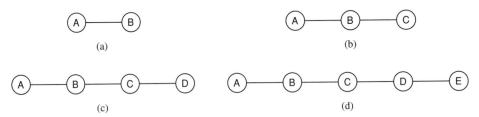

Figure 12.2. Paths of lengths (a) 2, (b) 3, (c) 4, and (d) 5 form instructive examples of different phenomena in exchange networks.

Figure 12.2 depicts four basic networks that have been used in experiments. Notice that these are just paths of lengths 2, 3, 4, and 5. Despite their simplicity, however, each introduces novel issues, which we discuss in order.

The Two-Node Path. The two-node path is as simple as it gets: two people are given a fixed amount of time in which to agree on a way to split $1. Yet even this simple setting introduces a lot of conceptual complexity. A large amount of work in game theory has been devoted precisely to the problem of reasoning about outcomes when two parties with oppositely aligned interests sit down to negotiate. As we will discuss more fully later in this chapter, most of the standard theoretical treatments predict an equal split. This seems to be a reasonable prediction, and it is indeed approximately what happens in network exchange experiments on a two-node graph.

The Three-Node Path. On a three-node path with nodes labeled A, B, and C in order, node B intuitively has power over both A and C. For example, as B negotiates with A, she has the ability to fall back on her alternative with C, whereas A has no other alternatives. The same reasoning applies to B's negotiations with C.

Moreover, at least one of A or C must be excluded from an exchange in each round. In experiments, one finds that subjects who are excluded tend to ask for less in the next round in the hope of becoming included. Thus, the repeated exclusion of A and C tends to drive down what they ask for, and one finds in practice that B indeed receives the overwhelming majority of the money in her exchanges (roughly $\frac{5}{6}$ in one recent set of experiments [281]).

An interesting variation on this experiment is to modify the one-exchange rule to allow B to take part in *two* exchanges in each round. One now finds that B negotiates on roughly equal footing with both A and C. This is consistent with the notions of dependence and exclusion discussed earlier: for B to achieve half the value from each exchange in each round, she needs A and C as much as they need her.

This result for the version in which B is allowed two exchanges is less consistent with satiation, however: if B were becoming satiated by money twice as quickly as A and C, one could expect to start seeing an effect in which A and C have to offer unequal splits to B in order to keep B interested. But this is not what actually happens.

The Four-Node Path. The four-node path is already significantly more subtle than the previous two examples. There is an outcome in which all nodes take part in an exchange – A exchanges with B and C exchanges with D – but there is also an outcome in which B and C exchange with each other while excluding A and D.

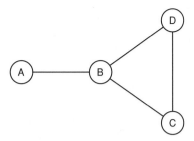

Figure 12.3. An exchange network with a weak power advantage for node B.

Thus, B should have some amount of power over A, but it is a weaker kind of power than in the three-node path. In the three-node path, B could exclude A and seek an exchange with C, who has no other options. In the four-node path, however, if B excludes A, then B herself pays a price by having to seek an exchange with C, who already has an attractive alternative in D. In other words, B's threat to exclude A is a costly one to actually execute. Experiments bear out this notion of *weak power*: in A–B exchanges, B gets roughly between $\frac{7}{12}$ and $\frac{2}{3}$ of the money, but not more [281, 373].

The Five-Node Path. Paths of length 5 introduce a further subtlety: node C, which intuitively occupies the "central" position in the network, is in fact weak when the one-exchange rule is used. This is because C's only opportunities for exchange are with B and D, and each of these nodes have very attractive alternatives in A and E, respectively. Thus, C can be excluded from exchange almost as easily as A and E. Put succinctly, C's partners for negotiation all have access to very weak nodes as alternatives, and this makes C weak as well.

In experiments, one finds that C does slightly better than A and E, but only slightly. Thus, the five-node path shows that simple centrality notions like betweenness can be misleading measures of power in some kinds of exchange networks.

Note that the weakness of C really does depend on the fact that the one-exchange rule is used. Suppose, for example, that we instead allowed A, C, and E to take part in one exchange each, but allowed B and D to take part in two exchanges each. Then suddenly each of B and D need C to make full use of their exchange opportunities, and C is now the node with the ability to exclude some of his exchange partners.

Other Networks. Many other networks have been studied experimentally. In a number of cases, the outcomes can be understood by combining ideas from the four basic networks in Figure 12.2.

For example, the graph in Figure 12.1 has been extensively studied by network exchange theorists. Since B has the ability to exclude both A and C, she tends to achieve highly favorable exchanges with them. Given these two alternatives, B and D almost never exchange; as a result, D doesn't have a realistic second option besides E, and hence D and E tend to exchange on roughly equal footing. All these observations are borne out by the experimental results.

Another interesting example that has been extensively studied is the "stem graph" shown in Figure 12.3. Here, C and D typically exchange with each other, while B

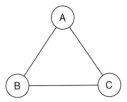

Figure 12.4. An exchange network in which negotiations never stabilize.

exchanges with A, obtaining favorable terms. The position of node B in this network is conceptually similar to the position of B in the four-node path: in the stem graph, B has a power advantage in her dealings with A, but it is a weak power advantage, since to exclude A she has to exchange with C or D, who each have exchange options in each other. Experiments have shown that node B in the stem graph makes slightly more money than node B in the four-node path, and there is an intuitive, if somewhat subtle, reason for this: B's threat over A in the four-node path is to negotiate with the comparably powerful node C, while B's threat in the stem graph is to negotiate with people who are slightly weaker.

An Unstable Network. A common theme in all the networks we have discussed thus far is that the negotiations among participants tend to wrap up reliably by the time limit, with fairly consistent outcomes. But there exist pathological networks in which negotiations tend to drag out until the very end, with unpredictable individual outcomes for the participants.

To see how this might happen, we consider the simplest of these pathological examples, depicted in Figure 12.4: three nodes each connected to each other. It is not hard to see what happens when an exchange experiment is run on the triangle. Only one exchange can be completed among the three nodes, and so as time is running out, two of the nodes – say, A and B – will be wrapping up negotiations, while the third node (C in this case) is completely left out and stands to get nothing. This means that C will be willing to break into the A-B negotiations up to the very end, offering an exchange to either of these nodes in which they get almost everything as long as C can get a small amount. If this happens – say that C breaks up the A-B negotiations by offering highly favorable terms to A – then there will be a different node left out (B in this case), who will in turn be willing to offer highly favorable terms to get back in on an exchange.

This process, by itself, would cycle indefinitely – with some node always left out and trying anything to get back in – and it is only brought to a halt by the arbitrary arrival of the time limit. Under these conditions, you have nodes "playing for the last shot," with the outcome for any one node correspondingly hard to predict.

Again, this is not an issue that comes up in any of the earlier examples we discussed; what's different in the triangle network is that, no matter what tentative exchanges are being planned, excluded nodes have a natural way to "break into" the negotiations. This prevents the outcome from ever stabilizing across the network. It is also worth noting that the mere presence of a triangle in a larger network does not necessarily cause problems: for example, the stem graph in Figure 12.3 contains a triangle, but the

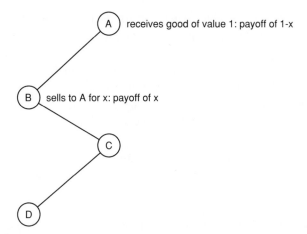

Figure 12.5. An exchange network built from the four-node path can also be viewed as a buyer–seller network with two sellers and two buyers.

exchange possibilities provided by the additional node A allow for robust outcomes in which A exchanges with B, and C and D exchange with each other. The problem with a "free-standing" triangle as in Figure 12.4 is fundamentally different: here, there is always a node who is left out and yet has the ability to do something about it.

12.4 A Connection to Buyer–Seller Networks

When we discussed matching markets in Chapter 10, we considered bipartite graphs consisting of buyers and sellers. Here, on the other hand, we have been talking about graphs in which the participants all play the same role (there is no division into buyers and sellers); rather than conducting trade, they negotiate over the division of money on the edges.

Despite these surface-level differences, there is a close connection between the two settings. To see this connection, let's consider the four-node path as an example. Suppose we declare nodes A and C to be buyers, and nodes B and D to be sellers. We give one unit of a good to each of B and D, and one unit of money to each of A and C; we assume that A and C each have a valuation of 1 for one copy of the good, and that B and D have no valuation for the good. We now consider the prices at which sales of the good will take place.

It takes a bit of thought, but this is completely equivalent to the exchange network experiment on the four-node path, as indicated in Figure 12.5. For example, if B sells to A for a price of x, then B gets a payoff of x (from the x units of money) and A gets a payoff of $1 - x$ (from the one unit of value for the good, minus the x units of money he has to pay). Thus, the negotiation between A and B over a price x in the buyer–seller network is just like the negotiation between A and B over the division of $1 into x and $1 - x$ in an exchange network. Furthermore, the one-exchange rule corresponds to the requirement that each seller can only sell a single unit of the good, and each buyer only wants one unit of the good.

One can perform a comparable translation for all the graphs in Figures 12.1 and 12.2. However, it is important to note two caveats about this general observation on the relationship between exchange networks and buyer–seller networks. First, the translation is only possible for graphs that are bipartite (as all the graphs in Figures 12.1 and 12.2 are), even if they are not drawn with the nodes in two parallel columns. The triangle graph in Figure 12.4 is not bipartite, and although we can still talk about the exchange network experiment, it is not possible to label the nodes as buyers and sellers in such a way that all edges join a seller to a buyer. We can make one node a seller, and another node a buyer, but then we have no options for what to label the third node. Similarly, the stem graph in Figure 12.3 is not bipartite, and so the analogy to buyer–seller networks cannot be applied there either.

A second caveat is that, for bipartite graphs, the two formulations are equivalent only at a mathematical level. It is not at all clear that human subjects placed in a buyer–seller experiment would behave in the same way as human subjects in a network-exchange experiment, even on the very same graph. Indeed, there is recent empirical evidence suggesting that one may in fact see different outcomes from these two ways of describing the same process to test subjects [397].

12.5 Modeling Two-Person Interaction: The Nash Bargaining Solution

Thus far, we have seen a range of networks on which exchange experiments have been carried out, and we have developed some of the informal reasons why the outcomes turn out the way they do. We'd now like to develop a more mathematical framework allowing us to express predictions about what will happen when network exchange takes place in an arbitrary network. Among the phenomena we'd like to be able to explain are the distinctions between equal and asymmetric division of value across an edge; between strong power (when imbalances go to extremes) and weak power (as in the four-node path, when the imbalance remains moderate); and between networks where outcomes stabilize and networks (like the triangle in Figure 12.4) where they don't.

In fact, we will be able to achieve this goal to a surprising extent, capturing each of these phenomena in a model based on simple principles. We begin the formulation of this model here and in the next section by developing two important ingredients, each based on a different type of two-person interaction. The first ingredient – the Nash bargaining solution – has a more mathematical flavor, while the second – the Ultimatum Game – is based primarily on human-subject experiments.

The Nash Bargaining Solution. Let's start with a simple formulation of two-person bargaining. Suppose, as in network exchange on a two-node path, that two people, A and B, are negotiating over how to split $1 between them. Now, however, we extend the story to assume that A also has an outside option of x, and B has an outside option of y (see Figure 12.6). By this we mean that if A doesn't like his share of the $1 arising from the negotiations with B, he can leave and take x instead. This will presumably happen, for instance, if A is going to get less than x from the negotiations.

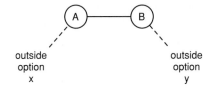

Figure 12.6. Two nodes bargaining with outside options.

Similarly, B has the option of abandoning the negotiation at any time and taking her outside option of y. Notice that if $x + y > 1$, then no agreement between A and B is possible, since they can't divide a dollar so that one gets at least x and the other gets at least y. Consequently, we will assume $x + y \leq 1$ when we consider this type of situation.

Given these conditions, A requires at least x from the negotiations over splitting the dollar, and B requires at least y. Consequently, the negotiation is really over how to split the *surplus* $s = 1 - x - y$ (which is at least 0, given our assumption that $x + y \leq 1$ in the previous paragraph). A natural prediction is that if the two people A and B have equal bargaining power, then they will agree on the division that splits this surplus evenly: A gets $x + \frac{1}{2}s$, and B gets $y + \frac{1}{2}s$. This is the prediction of a number of general theories including the *Nash bargaining solution* [312], and we use this as our term for the outcome:

> *Nash Bargaining Solution:* When A and B negotiate over splitting a dollar, with an outside option of x for A and an outside option of y for B (and $x + y \leq 1$), the Nash bargaining outcome is
>
> - $x + \dfrac{1}{2}s = \dfrac{x + 1 - y}{2}$ to A, and
>
> - $y + \dfrac{1}{2}s = \dfrac{y + 1 - x}{2}$ to B.

In the literature on network exchange theory, this division is sometimes referred as the *equidependent* outcome [120], since each person is depending equally on the other for concessions to make the negotiation work. At a high level, the formulation of the Nash bargaining solution emphasizes an important point about the process of negotiation in general: trying to ensure that you have as strong an outside option as possible, before the negotiations even begin, can be very important for achieving a favorable outcome. For most of this chapter, it is enough to take the Nash bargaining solution as a self-contained principle supported by the results of experiments. In the final section of the chapter, however, we ask whether it can be derived from more fundamental models of behavior. We show there that in fact it can – it arises naturally as an equilibrium when we formulate the process of bargaining as a game.

Experiments on Status Effects. When we think about bargaining in the context of experiments with human subjects, we of course need to consider the assumption that the two people have equal bargaining power. While in our models we will make use of this assumption, it is interesting to think about how external information could affect relative bargaining power in settings such as these.

The effects of perceived social status on bargaining power have been explored experimentally by sociologists. In these experiments, two people are asked to divide money in situations where they are led to believe that one person is "higher status" and the other is "lower status." For example, in a recent set of these experiments, pairs of people A and B, both female college sophomores, negotiated in the presence of outside options using instant messaging. However, each was given false information about the other: A was told that B was a high school student with low grades, while B was told that A was a graduate student with very high grades [390]. Thus, A believed B to be of low status, while B believed A to be of high status.

The results of these experiments illustrate interesting ways in which beliefs about differential status can lead to deviations from theoretical predictions in bargaining. First, each subject had to communicate information about her own outside options to her partner as part of the negotiation (this information was not provided by the experimenters). It was found that people tended to inflate the size of their outside option when they believed their negotiating partner was of lower status, and they tended to reduce the size of their outside option when they believed their negotiating partner was of higher status. Compounding this effect, people tended to partially discount a negotiating partner's claims about outside options when they believed this partner to be of lower status. (In other words, lower-status people tended to underreport the value of their outside options, and even these underreported values were discounted by their partners.) Overall, for these and other reasons, the subject who was believed to be of higher status by her partner tended to achieve significantly better bargaining outcomes than the theoretical predictions.

Naturally, these status effects are interesting additional factors to incorporate into models of exchange. For developing the most basic family of models, however, we will focus on the case of interaction in the absence of additional status effects, using the Nash bargaining outcome as a building block.

12.6 Modeling Two-Person Interaction: The Ultimatum Game

The Nash bargaining outcome provides us with a way of reasoning about two people whose power differences arise through differences in their outside options. In principle, this applies even to situations with extreme power imbalances. For example, in network exchange on a three-node path, we saw that the center node holds all the power, because it can exclude either of the two other nodes. However, in exchange experiments on this network, the center node is not generally able to drive its partners' shares all the way down to 0; rather one sees splits like $\frac{5}{6}$–$\frac{1}{6}$.

What causes the negotiations to "pull back" from a completely unbalanced outcome? This is in fact a recurring effect in exchange experiments: human subjects placed in bargaining situations with strong power imbalances will systematically deviate from the extreme predictions of simple theoretical models. One of the most basic experimental frameworks for exploring this effect is called the *Ultimatum Game* [203, 386], and it works as follows.

Like the bargaining framework discussed in the previous section, the Ultimatum Game also involves two people dividing a dollar, but following a very different procedure than what we saw before:

  (i) Person A is given a dollar and is told to propose a division of it to person B. That is, A should propose how much he keeps for himself, and how much he gives to B.
 (ii) Person B is then given the option of approving or rejecting the proposed division.
(iii) If B approves, each person keeps the proposed amount. If B rejects, then each person gets nothing.

Moreover, let's assume that A and B are communicating by instant messaging from different rooms; they are told at the outset that they have never met each other before, and quite possibly will never meet again. For all intents and purposes, this is a one-shot interaction.

Suppose first that both people are strictly interested in maximizing the amount of money they walk away with; how should they behave? This is not hard to work out. First, let's consider how B should behave. If A proposes a division that gives any positive amount to B, then B's choice is between getting this positive amount of money (by accepting) and getting nothing (by rejecting). Hence, B should accept any positive offer.

Given that this is how B is going to behave, how should A behave? Since B will accept any positive offer, A should pick the division that gives B something and otherwise maximizes A's own earnings. Thus, A should propose $0.99 for himself and $0.01 for B, knowing that B will accept this offer. A could alternately propose $1.00 for himself and $0.00 for B, gambling that B – who would then be indifferent between accepting and rejecting – would still accept. But for this discussion we'll stick with the division in which A offers B a penny.

This, then, is a prediction of how purely money-maximizing individuals would behave in a situation of extreme power imbalance: the one holding all the power (A) will offer as little as possible, and the one with essentially no power will accept anything offered. Intuition – and, as we will see next, experimental results – suggests that this is not how human beings will typically behave.

The Results of Experiments on the Ultimatum Game. In 1982, Güth, Schmittberger, and Schwarze [203] performed a series of influential experiments in which they studied how people would actually play the Ultimatum Game. They found that people playing the role of A tended to offer fairly balanced divisions of the money – on average, about a third of the total, with a significant number of people playing A in fact offering an even split. Moreover, they found that very unbalanced offers were often rejected by the person playing the role of B.

A large amount of follow-up work has shown these findings to be highly robust [386], even when relatively large amounts of money are at stake. The experiment has also been carried out in a number of different countries, and there are interesting cultural variations, although again the tendency toward relatively balanced divisions is consistent [93].

Can these observation of relatively balanced offers in the Ultimatum Game, and rejections of positive amounts of money, be reconciled with the game-theoretic framework we've used in previous chapters? There are in fact a number of ways to do so.

Perhaps the most natural is to keep in mind one of the basic principles we discussed when defining payoffs in game-theoretic situations: a player's payoff should reflect his or her complete evaluation of a given outcome. So when a player B evaluates an outcome in which she walks away with only 10% of the total, one interpretation is that there is a significant negative emotional payoff to being treated unfairly; hence, when we consider B's complete evaluation of the options, B finds a a greater overall benefit to rejecting the low offer and feeling good about it than accepting the low offer and feeling cheated. Moreover, because people playing the role of A understand that this is the likely evaluation that their partner B will bring to the situation, they tend to offer relatively balanced divisions to avoid rejection, because rejection results in A getting nothing as well.

It remains true that if you find yourself playing the role of A in an instance of the Ultimatum Game where player B is a money-maximizing robot, you should offer as little as possible. What the line of experiments on this topic have shown is simply that real people's payoffs are not well modeled by strict money maximization. Even a robot will reject low offers if you instruct it to care about feeling cheated.

All these observations are useful when we think about network exchange experiments where there are strong power imbalances between adjacent nodes – in these situations, we should expect to see wide asymmetries in the division of resources, but not necessarily as wide as the basic models might predict.

12.7 Modeling Network Exchange: Stable Outcomes

Having now built up some principles – both theoretical and empirical – that govern two-person interactions, we apply these to build a model that can approximately predict the outcomes of network exchange on arbitrary graphs.

Outcomes. Let's begin by making precise what we mean by an *outcome*. We say that an outcome of network exchange on a given graph consists of two things:

(i) A matching on the set of nodes, specifying who exchanges with whom. Recall that a matching, as discussed in Chapter 10, is a set of edges in which each node is the endpoint of at most one edge. This corresponds to the one-exchange rule, in which each node can complete at most one exchange, and some nodes may be left out.

(ii) A number associated with each node, called its *value*, indicating how much this node gets from its exchange. If two nodes are matched in the outcome, then the sum of their values should equal 1, indicating that they split the one unit of money in some fashion between them. If a node is not part of any matching in the outcome, then its value should equal 0, indicating that it does not take part in an exchange.

Figure 12.7 depicts examples of outcomes on the three- and four-node paths.

Stable Outcomes. For any network, there is almost always a wide range of possible outcomes. Our goal is to identify the outcome or outcomes that we should expect in a network when an exchange experiment is actually performed.

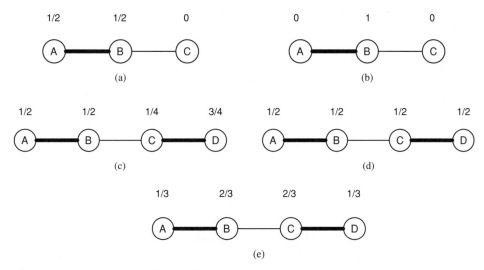

Figure 12.7. Some examples of stable and unstable outcomes of network exchange on the three-node path and the four-node path: (a) unstable and (b) stable outcomes on the three-node path, (c) unstable and (d, e) stable outcomes on the four-node path. The darkened edges constitute matchings showing who exchanges with whom, and the numbers above the nodes represent the values.

A basic property we'd expect an outcome to have is *stability*: no node X can propose an offer to some other node Y that makes both X and Y better off – thus "stealing" node Y away from an existing agreement. For example, consider Figure 12.7(a). In addition to C feeling left out by the outcome, there is something that C can do to improve the situation: for example, C can offer $\frac{2}{3}$ to B (keeping $\frac{1}{3}$ for himself), if B will break her agreement with A and exchange with C instead. This offer from C to B would make B better off (as she would get $\frac{2}{3}$ instead of her current $\frac{1}{2}$) and it would also make C better off (as he would get $\frac{1}{3}$ instead of 0). There is nothing to prevent this from happening, so the current situation is unstable. (Although we've described this trade as having been initiated by C, it could equally well be initiated by B in an attempt to improve on her current value of $\frac{1}{2}$.)

Compare this to the situation in Figure 12.7(b). Here too C is doing badly, but now there is nothing he can do to remedy the situation. B is already getting 1 – the most she possibly can – and so there is nothing that C can offer to B to break the current A–B exchange. The situation, even though it is bad for some parties, is stable.

We can make this idea precise for any network, defining an *instability* in an outcome to be a situation in which two nodes have both the opportunity and the incentive to disrupt the existing pattern of exchanges. Specifically, we have the following definition:

> *Instability:* Given an outcome consisting of a matching and values for the nodes, an *instability* in this outcome is an edge not in the matching, joining two nodes X and Y, such that the sum of X's value and Y's value is less than 1.

Notice how this captures the kind of situation we're been discussing: in an instability, the two nodes X and Y have the *opportunity* to disrupt the status quo (because they're connected by an edge, and hence allowed to exchange), and they also have the *incentive* – since the sum of their values is less than 1, they can find a way to divide the dollar between them and each end up better than they currently are doing.

In the example we discussed from Figure 12.7(a), the instability is the edge connecting B and C – the sum of the values is $\frac{1}{2}$, and so both B and C can end up better off by exchanging with each other. On the other hand, Figure 12.7(b) has no instabilities; there are no inherent stresses that could disrupt the status quo in Figure 12.7(b). Thus, we introduce a further definition, which we call *stability*.

> *Stability:* An outcome of network exchange is *stable* if and only if it contains no instabilities.

Given the inherent fragility of outcomes with instabilities, we expect to see stable outcomes in practice; for networks that have stable outcomes, we in fact typically do see results that are close to stable outcomes.

Figures 12.7(c)–12.7(e) provide some further opportunities to test these definitions using examples. There is an instability in Figure 12.7(c), since nodes B and C are connected by an edge and collectively making less than the one unit of money they could split by exchanging with each other. On the other hand, the outcomes in Figures 12.7(d) and 12.7(e) are both stable, since on the one edge not in the matching, the two nodes are collectively making at least one unit of money from the current situation.

Applications of Stable Outcomes. In addition to being intuitively natural, the notion of a stable outcome helps to explain some of the general principles observed in network exchange experiments.

First, stable outcomes are good at approximately capturing what's going on in situations with extreme power imbalances. If we think a bit about Figures 12.7(a) and 12.7(b), we can convince ourselves that the only stable outcomes on the three-node path are those in which B exchanges with one of A or C and gets the full one unit of value for herself. Indeed, if B got anything less than one unit, the unmatched edge would form an instability. Hence, stability shows why B occupies the dominant position in this network. In fact, with a bit of analysis, we can see on the five-node path from Figure 12.2(d) that the only stable outcomes give values of 1 to the "off-center" nodes B and D. So stable outcomes are also able to pick up on the subtlety that the central node C on the five-node path is in fact very weak.

Now we know that in fact human subjects on the three- or five-node paths will not push things all the way to 0–1 outcomes; rather, the powerful nodes tend to get amounts more like $\frac{5}{6}$. But our discussion surrounding the Ultimatum Game shows that this is, in a sense, the most extreme kind of outcome that we would see from real people. Because the notion of stability isn't designed to avoid extremes, we view this mismatch between theory and experiment as something that is relatively easy to explain and account for: when we see strong-power outcomes in practice like $\frac{1}{6}$–$\frac{5}{6}$, we can think of this as being as close to 0–1 as human players will get.[1]

Our current framework is also good at identifying situations that have no stable outcome. In particular, recall the pathological behavior of network exchange on the

---

[1] In fact, one can extend the theory of stability fairly easily to be able to handle this effect explicitly. For the discussion here, however, we'll stick with the simpler version that allows things to go to extremes.

triangle network in Figure 12.4, which never settles down to a predictable result. We can now explain what's going on by observing that *there is no stable outcome for the triangle network.* To see why, notice first that in any outcome, some node will be unmatched and get a value of 0. Let's suppose this is node C. (Due to the symmetry of the situation, it doesn't matter which node we choose for this argument.) This unmatched node C has edges to both other nodes and, no matter how these other two nodes divide the money, at least one of them (say B) will get less than 1. But now the edge connecting B and C is an instability, since they collectively are getting less than 1 and yet have the ability to perform an exchange.

The fact that there is no stable outcome provides us with a way to think about the dynamics of negotiation on the triangle – no matter what tentative agreement is reached, the system necessarily contains internal stress that will disrupt it.

Limitations of Stable Outcomes. The explanatory power of stability also has significant limitations, however. One source of limitations lies in the fact that it allows outcomes to go to extremes that people will not actually follow in real life. But, as we've already observed, this difficulty is something where the theory is approximately accurate, and the discrepancies can be recognized and dealt with relatively easily.

A more fundamental difficulty with the notion of a stable outcome is that it is too ambiguous in situations where there is a weak power imbalance between individuals. For example, let's go back to Figures 12.7(d) and 12.7(e). Both of these represent stable outcomes on the four-node path, but the first of these gives equal values to all the nodes, despite the power advantages of the middle nodes. In fact, there is a large range of possible stable outcomes on the four-node path: when the matching consists of the two outer edges, then any way of dividing the value on these edges so that B and C cumulatively get at least 1 will be stable.

To summarize, while stability is an important concept for reasoning about outcomes of exchange, it is too weak in networks that exhibit subtle power differences. On these networks, it is not restrictive enough, since it permits too many outcomes that don't actually occur. Is there a way to strengthen the notion of stability so as to focus on the outcomes that are most typical in real life? There is, and this will be the focus of the next section.

12.8 Modeling Network Exchange: Balanced Outcomes

In cases where there are many possible stable outcomes for a given network, we will show in this section how to select a particularly natural set of outcomes that we call *balanced*.

The idea behind balanced outcomes is perhaps best illustrated by considering the four-node path. In particular, Figure 12.7(d) is a stable outcome, but it doesn't correspond to what one sees in real experiments. Moreover, there is something clearly "not right" about it: nodes B and C are being severely outnegotiated. Despite the fact that each of them has an alternate option, they are splitting the money evenly with A and D, respectively, even though A and D have nowhere else to go.

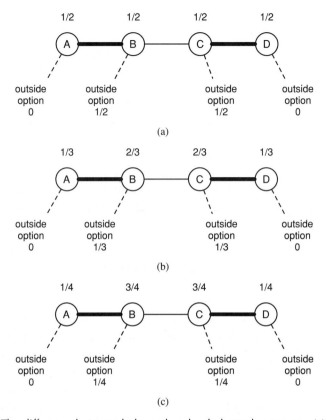

Figure 12.8. The difference between balanced and unbalanced outcomes: (a) not balanced, (b) balanced, and (c) not balanced.

We can think about this issue by noticing that network exchange can be viewed as a type of bargaining in which the "outside options" – in the sense of the Nash bargaining solution from Section 12.5 – are provided by the other nodes in the network. Figure 12.8(a) depicts this for the all-$\frac{1}{2}$ outcome we've been considering. Given the values for each node, we observe that B in effect has an outside option of $\frac{1}{2}$, because she can offer $\frac{1}{2}$ to C (or an amount very slightly higher than $\frac{1}{2}$) and steal C away from his current agreement with D. For the same reason, C also has an outside option of $\frac{1}{2}$, by considering what he would have to offer B to steal her away from her current agreement with A. On the other hand, the network with its current node values provides A and D with outside options of 0 – they have no alternatives to their current agreements.

Defining Balanced Outcomes. The preceding discussion suggests a useful way to view the problem with the all-$\frac{1}{2}$ outcome: the exchanges that are happening do not represent the Nash bargaining outcomes with respect to the nodes' outside options. And it is in this context that the outcome in Figure 12.8(b) starts to look particularly natural. With these values, B has an outside option of $\frac{1}{3}$, because to steal C away from his current partnership B would have to offer C a value of $\frac{2}{3}$, keeping $\frac{1}{3}$ for herself. Thus, B's $\frac{2}{3}$–$\frac{1}{3}$ split with A represents the Nash bargaining solution for B and A with outside options provided by the values in the rest of the network. The same

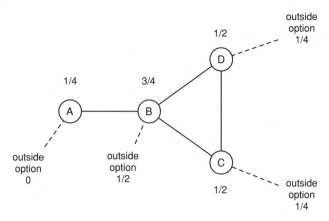

Figure 12.9. A balanced outcome on the stem graph.

reasoning holds for the C–D exchange. Hence, this set of values on the four-node path has an elegant self-supporting property: each exchange represents the Nash bargaining outcome, given the exchanges and values elsewhere in the network.

We can define this notion of balance in general for any network as follows [120, 349]. First, for any outcome in a network, we can identify each node's best outside option just as we did in the four-node path: it is the most money the node can make by stealing a neighbor away from his or her current partnership. Now we define a *balanced outcome* as follows:

> *Balanced Outcome:* An outcome (consisting of a matching and node values) is *balanced* if, for each edge in the matching, the split of the money represents the Nash bargaining outcome for the two nodes involved, given the best outside options for each node provided by the values in the rest of the network.

Notice how this type of outcome really is "balanced" between different extremes. On the one hand, it prevents B and C from getting too little, as in Figure 12.8(a); on the other hand, it also prevents B and C from getting too much. For example, the outcome in Figure 12.8(c) is not balanced either, because B and C are each getting more than their share under the Nash bargaining outcome.

Notice also that all of the outcomes in Figure 12.8 are stable. So in this example it's reasonable to think of balance as a refinement of stability. In fact, for any network, every balanced outcome is stable. In a balanced outcome each node in the matching gets at least its best outside option, which is the most the node could get on any unused edge. So no two nodes have an incentive to disrupt a balanced outcome by using a currently unused edge, and therefore the outcome is stable. But balance is more restrictive than stability, in that there can be many stable outcomes that are not balanced.

Applications and Interpretations of Balanced Outcomes. In addition to its elegant definition, the balanced outcome corresponds approximately to the results of experiments with human subjects. We have seen this already for the four-node path. The results for the stem graph provide another basic example.

Figure 12.9 shows the unique balanced outcome for the stem graph: C and D exchange on even terms, providing B with an outside option of $\frac{1}{2}$ and hence leading to a Nash bargaining outcome of $\frac{1}{4}$–$\frac{3}{4}$ between A and B. The balanced outcome thus captures not just weak power advantages but also subtle differences in these advantages across networks – in this case, the idea that B's advantage in the stem graph is slightly greater than in the four-node path.

Given the delicate self-reference in the definition of a balanced outcome – with values defined by determining outside options in terms of the values themselves – it is natural to ask whether balanced outcomes even exist for all networks. Of course, since any balanced outcome is stable, a balanced outcome can only exist when a stable outcome exists, and we know from the previous section that for certain graphs (such as the triangle) there is no stable outcome. But it can be shown that, in any network with a stable outcome, there is also a balanced outcome, and there are also methods to compute the set of all balanced outcomes for a given network [31, 242, 254, 349, 378].

In fact, the concepts of stability and balance from this and the previous sections can be framed in terms of ideas from an area known as *cooperative game theory*, which studies how a collection of players will divide up the value arising from a collective activity (such as network exchange in the present case). In this framework, stability can be formulated using a central notion in cooperative game theory known as the *core solution*, and balance can be formulated as a combination of the core solution and a second notion known as the *kernel solution* [234, 289, 349].

Finally, we note that balance is one of several definitions proposed for refining stable outcomes to produce reasonable alignment with experiments. There are competing theories, including one called *equiresistance*, that achieve similar results [373]. It remains an open research question to understand how closely the predictions of all these theories match up with human-subject experiments when we move to significantly larger and more complex networks.

12.9 Advanced Material: A Game-Theoretic Approach to Bargaining

In Section 12.5 we considered a basic setting in which two people, each with outside options, bargain over a shared resource. We argued that the Nash bargaining solution provides a natural prediction for how the surplus available in the bargaining will be divided. When John Nash [312] originally formulated this notion, he motivated it by first writing down a set of axioms he believed the outcome of any bargaining solution should satisfy, and then showing that these axioms characterize his bargaining solution. But one can also ask whether the same solution can be motivated through a model that takes into account the strategic behavior of the people performing the bargaining – that is, whether we can formulate a game that captures the essentials of bargaining as an activity and in which the Nash bargaining outcome emerges as an equilibrium. This was done in the 1980s by Binmore, Rubinstein, and Wolinsky [60] using a game-theoretic formulation of bargaining due to Rubinstein [356].

Here we describe how this strategic approach to the Nash bargaining solution works. It is based on the notion of a dynamic game as formulated in Section 6.10. In our formulation of bargaining, we will use the basic setup from Section 12.5. There are two individuals, A and B, who negotiate over how to split $1 between them. Person A has an outside option of x and person B has an outside option of y. We assume that $x + y < 1$ because otherwise there is no way to split the \$1 that would be beneficial to both people.

Formulating Bargaining as a Dynamic Game. The first step is to formulate bargaining as a game. To do this, we imagine a stylized picture for how two people, A and B, might negotiate over the division of a dollar, as suggested by the following hypothetical conversation (in which A presumably has the stronger outside option):

A: I'll give you 30% of the dollar.
B: No, I want 40%.
A: How about 34%?
B: I'll take 36%.
A: Agreed.

To capture the intuition suggested by this conversation, we define a dynamic *bargaining game* that proceeds over a sequence of *periods* that can continue indefinitely.

- In the first period, A proposes a split of the dollar in which he gets a_1 and B gets b_1. (The subscript "1" indicates that this is the split proposed in the first period.) We denote this split by (a_1, b_1).
- B can then either accept A's proposal or reject it. If B accepts, the game ends and each player gets their respective portion. Otherwise, the game continues to period 2.
- In the second period, B proposes a split (a_2, b_2) in which she gets b_2 and A gets a_2. Now A can either accept or reject; again, the game ends if A accepts, and it continues if A rejects.
- The periods continue indefinitely in this fashion, with A proposing a split in each odd-numbered period, and B proposing a split in each even-numbered period. Any accepted offer ends the game immediately.

The preceding conversation between A and B fits the structure of this game, if we rewrite it using our notation as follows:

(Period 1) A: (.70, .30)? B: Reject.
(Period 2) B: (.60, .40)? A: Reject.
(Period 3) A: (.66, .34)? B: Reject.
(Period 4) B: (.64, .36)? A: Accept.

There is one more important part to the game, which models the idea that the two parties experience some pressure to actually reach a deal. At the end of each round, and before the next round begins, there is a fixed probability $p > 0$ that negotiations abruptly break down. In the event of such a breakdown, there will be no further periods, and the players will be forced to take their respective outside options.

This describes the full game: it proceeds through a sequence of alternating offers, and it continues until someone accepts an offer or negotiations break down. At its conclusion, each player receives a payoff – either the accepted split of the dollar or the outside options in the event of a breakdown.

The possibility of a breakdown in negotiations means that if B decides to reject the proposed split in the first period, for example, she is risking the possibility that there won't be a second round, and she will have to fall back to her outside option. Each player has to take this risk into account each time they reject an offer. This breakdown probability is necessary for the results we derive on bargaining, and we can view it as reflecting the idea that each player believes there is some chance the game will end before they reach an agreement. Perhaps the other player will give up on the negotiation or will abruptly be drawn away by some unexpected better opportunity that comes along, or perhaps there is simply some outside reason that the game itself suddenly ends.

Analyzing the Game: An Overview. The game we have just defined is a dynamic game in the sense of Section 6.10, but with two differences worth noting. The first difference is that each time a player makes a proposal, the set of available strategies is infinite rather than finite: he or she can propose to keep a portion of the dollar equal to any real number between 0 and 1. For our purposes, this difference ends up being relatively minor, and it doesn't cause any trouble in the analysis. The second difference is more significant. In Section 6.10, we considered *finite-horizon games* that ran for at most a finite number of periods, whereas here we have an *infinite-horizon game* in which the sequence of periods can in principle go on forever. This poses a problem for the style of analysis we used in Section 6.10, where we reasoned from the final period of the game (with just a single move left to make) backward to the beginning. Here there is no final period, so we will need a different way to analyze the game.

Despite this, the type of reasoning that we employed in Section 6.10 will help us to solve this game. The equilibrium we will look for is a *subgame perfect equilibrium* – a notion that we also saw in Chapter 11 associated with the trading game in which traders post prices, and buyers and sellers subsequently react. A subgame perfect equilibrium is simply a Nash equilibrium with the property that the strategies, beginning from any intermediate point in the game, still form a Nash equilibrium for the play proceeding from that point onward.

Our main result is twofold. First, the bargaining game has a subgame perfect equilibrium with a simple structure in which A's initial offer is accepted. Second, for this equilibrium, we can work out the values in the initial split (a_1, b_1) that is proposed and accepted. The quantities a_1 and b_1 depend on the underlying value of the breakdown probability p, and, as p goes to 0, the split (a_1, b_1) converges to the Nash bargaining outcome. The point, therefore, is that when two strategic bargainers interact through negotiations that are unlikely to break down quickly, the Nash bargaining solution is a good approximate prediction for the outcome.

It is also worth considering how our formulation of bargaining here relates to the experimental work in network-exchange theory from earlier in this chapter. There are a few differences. First, of course, the experiments discussed earlier involve multiple interlinked negotiations that take place concurrently – one negotiation for each edge in a network. It is an interesting but largely open question to adapt the kind of bargaining game formulated here to a setting where negotiations take place simultaneously across all the edges of a network. But beyond this consideration, there are still differences between our game-theoretic model here and the exchange-theory experiments even when we look at just a single edge of the network. First, the experiments generally allowed for free-form discussion between the two endpoints of an edge, whereas we have a specified a fixed format in which the two bargainers take turns proposing splits, beginning with A. The fact that A gets to move first in our game gives him some advantage, but in the case we are mainly interested in for our results – as the breakdown probability p becomes small – this advantage becomes negligible. Second, the experiments generally imposed a fixed time limit to ensure that negotiations would eventually end, whereas we are using a breakdown probability that applies to each round. It is not clear exactly how these two sources of time pressure in a negotiation relate to each other; even with a fixed time limit, the fact that nodes may have multiple network neighbors in the exchange-theory experiments makes it difficult to reason about how long the negotiation on any particular edge is likely to last.

A First Step: Analyzing a Two-Period Version of Bargaining. Because of the complexity introduced by the infinite nature of the game, it is useful to get some initial insight by first analyzing a finite version of it.

In particular, let's take our earlier version of the game and assume that it ends for sure at the end of the second period. (As before, it may also end with probability p at the end of the first period.) Since this is now a game with a finite number of periods, we can solve it backward through time as follows.

- First, A will accept B's proposal (a_2, b_2) in period 2 provided that a_2 is at least as large as A's outside option x. (Since negotiations are guaranteed to end after this round, A is simply choosing at this point between a_2 and x.)
- Given this, there is no reason for B to offer A more than x, so B's proposal in period 2 will be $(x, 1 - x)$. Since we have assumed $x + y < 1$, we have $1 - x > y$, and so B prefers this split to the outcome in which negotiations end and B gets only y.[2]
- Now, when B considers whether to accept or reject A's offer in the first round, she should compare it to the expected payoff she'd get by rejecting it and allowing the game to continue. If she rejects the offer, then, with probability p, negotiations break down immediately and she gets y. Otherwise, the game continues to its second and final round, where we've already concluded that B will get $1 - x$. Therefore, B's expected payoff if she rejects the offer is

$$py + (1 - p)(1 - x).$$

Let's call this quantity z; our conclusion is that, in the first round, B will accept any offer of at least z.

- Finally, we need to determine what A will propose in the first round. There is no point in A's offering to B anything more generous than $(1 - z, z)$, since B will accept this proposal, so the question is simply whether A prefers this split to his

---

[2] We exploit indifference, as in many of our previous models, to assume that A accepts the proposed split $(x, 1 - x)$ rather than letting negotiations end. Alternately, as usual, we could imagine that B proposes an amount very slightly above x to A, to make sure A accepts.

outside option x. In fact he does: since $y < 1 - x$, and z is a weighted average of y and $1 - x$, it follows that $z < 1 - x$, and so $1 - z > x$.

Therefore, A will propose $(1 - z, z)$ in the first round, and it will be immediately accepted.

This describes the complete solution to the two-period bargaining game, and it's interesting to consider how the outcome for each player depends on the value of the breakdown probability p. On the one hand, when p is close to 1, so that negotiations are very likely to break down in the first round, B's payoff $z = py + (1 - p)(1 - x)$ is very close to her outside option y; correspondingly, A gets almost all the surplus. On the other hand, when p is close to zero, so that negotiations are very likely to continue to the second round, B's payoff is very close to $1 - x$, and so A is driven down almost to his outside option.

This makes sense intuitively. When p is close to 1, A has most of the leverage in the negotiations because his offer is probably the only one that will be made. When p is close to 0, B has most of the leverage in the negotiations because she will probably get to make the final offer and can therefore safely ignore an undesirable initial offer from A. Notice also that, when p is exactly equal to $\frac{1}{2}$, the payoffs correspond to the Nash bargaining outcome: each player gets an amount halfway between their outside option and their outside option plus the full surplus. So this in fact provides us with a first way to obtain the Nash bargaining solution from a two-player game – when the players take part in a two-round negotiation that ends with probability $\frac{1}{2}$ after the first round. As a reasonable model of bargaining, however, this structure is a bit artificial: why only two rounds and, moreover, why a breakdown probability of exactly $\frac{1}{2}$? It feels more reasonable to consider negotiations that are allowed to go on for a long time, with the small underlying breakdown probability imposing a mild form of pressure to reach an agreement. This is the infinite-horizon version that we formulated initially and which we will analyze next.

Back to the Infinite-Horizon Bargaining Game. One way to build up to the analysis of the infinite-horizon game would be to consider finite-horizon bargaining games that are allowed to last for a larger and larger number of rounds and to try to argue that these games eventually approximate the infinite-horizon version. Finite-horizon games of even length give B the last offer, while those of odd length give A the last offer. However, as the length increases, the chance decreases that the last round is ever reached. It is possible to carry out this analysis, but in fact it's easier to use what we learned in the two-round version of the game to directly conjecture the structure of an equilibrium for the infinite-horizon game.

In particular, we saw in the analysis of the two-round bargaining game that offers are not rejected in equilibrium. There are two reasons for this. First, both players stand to gain from splitting the surplus $1 - x - y$ in some fashion, and delaying by rejecting offers makes it possible that negotiations will break down and this surplus will be lost. Second, each player can reason about the minimum amount that the other is willing to accept, and so he or she can offer exactly this amount when given the opportunity to make an offer. At a general level, these considerations still apply to the infinite-horizon game, and so it is natural to conjecture there is an equilibrium in which A's initial offer is accepted. We will search for such an equilibrium – and in fact, more strongly for an equilibrium where from any intermediate point in the game, the next offer to be made would be accepted.

There is another issue to consider: there is at least one sense in which the finite-horizon bargaining games actually have a more complicated structure than the infinite-horizon game. For a finite-horizon bargaining game, the reasoning in each period is slightly different – you have to evaluate the expected payoff a bit differently with ten rounds left to go than you do with nine rounds or eight rounds left to go. This means that the splits being proposed will also change slightly in value as the time until the end of the game changes. The infinite-horizon game, on the other hand, is fundamentally different: after a back-and-forth pair of offers by A and B, there is another copy of exactly the same infinite-horizon game left to be played. The structure and payoffs in the game don't change over time. Of course, the players do observe offers being made and rejected if the game actually continues past the first period, and they could condition their behavior on this history of offers. But given the stationary nature of the game's structure over time, it's natural to look for an equilibrium among the set of *stationary strategies*: those in which each of A and B plans to propose the same split in every period in which they are scheduled to propose, and each of A and B also has a fixed amount that they require in order to accept a proposal. An equilibrium that uses stationary strategies is called a *stationary equilibrium*.

Analyzing the Game: A Stationary Equilibrium. A nice feature of stationary strategies is that they're very easy to describe and work with. Although the game is complex, any pair of stationary strategies for A and B can be represented by just a few numbers, as follows:

- the split (a_1, b_1) that A will offer whenever he is scheduled to propose a split;
- the split (a_2, b_2) that B will offer whenever she is scheduled to propose a split; and
- reservation amounts $\overline{a}$ and $\overline{b}$, constituting the minimum offers that A and B will accept from the other, respectively.

Moreover, because the offers constitute proposed splits of one dollar, the two parts of each split sum to 1, so we have $b_1 = 1 - a_1$ and $a_2 = 1 - b_2$.

Our plan is to write a set of equations on the values describing the stationary strategies such that any pair of stationary strategies satisfying these equations constitutes an equilibrium. We will then solve these equations, obtaining a stationary equilibrium, and show that as the breakdown probability p converges to 0, the payoffs to A and B converge to the Nash bargaining outcome.

The equations are as follows. First, as in the two-period version of the game, A will offer B the least he can to get B to accept his offer, so we set

$$b_1 = \overline{b}. \tag{12.1}$$

Similarly, B will offer the least she can to get A to accept her offer, so

$$a_2 = \overline{a}. \tag{12.2}$$

Again following the reasoning from the two-period version, B will set her reservation amount $\overline{b}$ right at the level where she is indifferent between accepting A's offer and rejecting it. If she accepts, she gets b_1; if she rejects, she gets the expected payoff that comes from allowing the game to continue. We can determine this expected value as follows. With probability p, the game ends immediately after her rejection, in which case she receives y. Otherwise, the game continues with an offer by B to A, and this offer will be accepted because, by Equation (12.2), we've set $a_2 = \overline{a}$. In this case, B receives b_2, so her overall expected payoff from allowing the game to continue would be $py + (1 - p)b_2$. For B to be indifferent between accepting and rejecting, we need

$$b_1 = py + (1 - p)b_2. \tag{12.3}$$

Similar reasoning applies to A's reservation amount: if he rejects an offer from B and allows the game to continue, his expected payoff is $px + (1 - p)a_1$, and so for him to be indifferent between accepting and rejecting B's offer we have

$$a_2 = px + (1 - p)a_1. \tag{12.4}$$

Following the earlier reasoning, we can check that Equations (12.1)–(12.4) are enough to ensure that the pair of stationary strategies forms an equilibrium.

Since $b_1 = 1 - a_1$ and $a_2 = 1 - b_2$, this gives us two linear equation in two unknowns:

$$1 - a_1 = py + (1 - p)b_2,$$
$$1 - b_2 = px + (1 - p)a_1.$$

Solving these, we get

$$a_1 = \frac{(1 - p)x + 1 - y}{2 - p}$$

$$b_2 = \frac{(1 - p)y + 1 - x}{2 - p}.$$

In this equilibrium, A's initial offer is accepted, so A gets a payoff of a_1, and B gets a payoff of

$$b_1 = 1 - a_1 = \frac{y + (1 - p)(1 - x)}{2 - p}.$$

We can check how these values for a_1 and b_1 behave as a function of p. When p is close to 1, they are approximately $1 - y$ and y, respectively. A gets almost all the surplus and B gets very close to her outside option, because the negotiations are likely to break down after the opening offer by A, and A is taking advantage of this fact.

More interestingly, as p converges to 0, so that the players can expect the negotiations to continue for a long time, the opening offer is still accepted in this stationary equilibrium, but the payoffs converge to

$$\left(\frac{x + 1 - y}{2}, \frac{y + 1 - x}{2} \right),$$

which are the values for the Nash bargaining solution. This completes the analysis; we have shown how the Nash bargaining outcome arises very naturally from a game-theoretic model in which the two bargainers behave strategically, following a simple model of negotiations.

12.10 Exercises

1. Suppose a network-exchange theory experiment is run on the graph depicted in Figure 12.10 using the one-exchange rule. Which node or nodes you would expect to make the most money (i.e., receive the most favorable exchanges)? Provide a brief (one- to three-sentence) explanation for your answer.

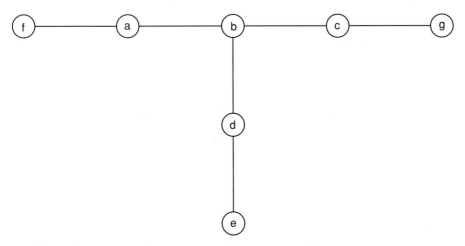

Figure 12.10. The graph used for the network-exchange theory experiment in Exercise 1.

2. Suppose a network-exchange theory experiment is run on the graph depicted in Figure 12.11 (i.e., a graph that is a three-node path), using the one-exchange rule.

    Now you, playing the role of a fourth node, d, are told to attach by a single edge to one of the nodes in the network. How should you attach to the network to put yourself in as powerful a position as possible, where power will be determined by the result of a network-exchange theory experiment run on the resulting four-node network? Give a brief explanation for your answer.

Figure 12.11. The three-node graph used as the starting point for the network-exchange theory experiment in Exercise 2.

3. Suppose a network-exchange theory experiment is run on the graph depicted in Figure 12.12 using the one-exchange rule with $10 placed on each edge.

    (a) Which node or nodes you would expect to make the most money (i.e., receive the most favorable exchanges)? Provide a brief (one- to three-sentence) explanation for your answer. You do not have to give actual numbers for the amounts of money the nodes would receive.

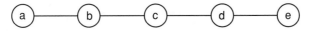

Figure 12.12. The five-node graph used as the starting point for the network-exchange theory experiment in Exercise 3.

(b) Now the experimenters vary the network: they introduce a sixth node, f, which is attached by a single edge to just the node c. A new person is brought in to play the role of f, and a new round of experiments is performed with this new six-node network.

   Explain what you think will happen to the relative power of the participants, compared to the situation in part (a), and give a brief (one- to three-sentence) explanation for your answer. Again, you do not have to give actual numbers for the amounts of money the nodes would receive.

4. Suppose a network-exchange theory experiment is run on the graph depicted in Figure 12.13 using the one-exchange rule with $10 placed on each edge.

   (a) Which node or nodes you would expect to make the most money (i.e., receive the most favorable exchanges)? Provide a brief (one- to three-sentence) explanation for your answer. You do not have to give actual numbers for the amounts of money the nodes would receive.

   (b) Now the experimenters vary the conditions slightly: instead of placing $10 on the b-c edge, they place only $2. Otherwise, the experiment is run exactly as before.

      Explain what you think will happen to the relative power of each of the participants, compared to the situation in part (a), and give a brief (one- to three-sentence) explanation for your answer. Again, you do not have to give actual numbers for the amounts of money the nodes would receive.

Figure 12.13. The four-node graph used for the network-exchange theory experiment in Exercise 4.

5. Suppose a network-exchange theory experiment is run on the graph depicted in Figure 12.14 using the one-exchange rule with $10 placed on each edge.

   (a) After running the experiment for awhile, the experimenters vary the network: they introduce two further nodes, e and f, and bring in additional people to play the roles of these nodes. Node e is attached by a single edge to node b, while node f is attached by a single edge to node c.

      A new round of experiments is performed with this new six-node network. Explain what you think will happen to the relative power of the participants, compared to the situation in the original four-node network. Give a brief (one- to three-sentence) explanation for your answer. You do not have to give actual numbers for the amounts of money the nodes would receive.

   (b) The experimenters now decide to vary the network again. They keep the same set of nodes, but now they add an edge linking node e directly to node f. (The existing edges continue to remain in place as well.)

Figure 12.14. The four-node graph used as the starting point for the network-exchange theory experiment in Exercise 5.

A new round of experiments is performed with this modified six-node network. Explain what you think will happen to the relative power of the participants, compared to the situation in the previous six-node network in part (a). Give a brief (one- to three-sentence) explanation for your answer. You do not have to give actual numbers for the amounts of money the nodes would receive.

6.   (a) Suppose that two different network-exchange theory experiments are run, using the one-exchange rule – one on the three-node path depicted in Figure 12.15, and the other on the four-node path depicted in Figure 12.15. In which set of experiments do you expect node b to receive more money (i.e., receive more favorable exchanges)? Give a brief (one- to three-sentence) explanation for your answer. (You do not have to give actual numbers for the amounts of money the nodes would receive.)

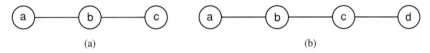

(a)   (b)

Figure 12.15. (a) A three-node path and (b) a four-node path.

   (b) Suppose a network-exchange theory experiment is run on the graph depicted in Figure 12.16 using the one-exchange rule. Which node or nodes you would expect to make the most money (i.e., receive the most favorable exchanges)?

Also, do you think the advantage experienced by the most powerful nodes in Figure 12.16 will be more similar to the advantage experienced by node b on the three-node path from part (a), or more similar to the advantage experienced by node b on the four-node path from part (a)?

Give a brief (one- to three-sentence) explanation for your answers. (Again, you do not have to give actual numbers for the amounts of money the nodes would receive.)

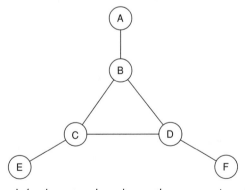

Figure 12.16. The graph for the network-exchange theory experiment in part (b) of Exercise 6.

PART FOUR

Information Networks and the World Wide Web

CHAPTER 13

The Structure of the Web

Up to this point in the book, we've considered networks in which the basic units being connected were people or other social entities, like firms or organizations. The links connecting them have generally corresponded to opportunities for some kind of social or economic interaction.

In the next several chapters, we consider a different type of network, in which the basic units being connected are pieces of information, and links join pieces of information that are related to each other in some fashion. We will call such a network an *information network*. As we will see, the World Wide Web is arguably the most prominent current example of such a network, and while the use of information networks has a long history, it was really the growth of the Web that brought such networks to wide public awareness.

While there are basic differences between information networks and the kinds of social and economic networks that we've discussed earlier, many of the central ideas developed earlier in the book turn out to be fundamental here as well: we'll be using the same basic ideas from graph theory, including short paths and giant components; formulating notions of power in terms of the underlying graph structure; and even drawing connections to matching markets when we consider some of the ways in which search companies on the Web have designed their businesses.

Because the Web plays such a central role in the modern version of this topic, we begin with some context about the Web, and then look further back into the history of information networks that led up to the Web.

13.1 The World Wide Web

If you're reading this book, it's likely that you use the Web on a daily basis. But because the Web is so enmeshed in the broader information infrastructure of the world (including the Internet, wireless communication systems, and the global media industry), it's actually useful to think a bit about what the Web is and how it came about, starting from first principles.

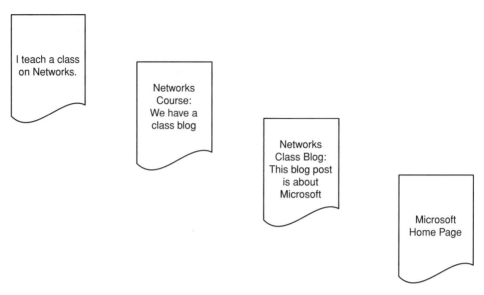

Figure 13.1. A set of four Web pages.

At a basic level, the Web is an application developed to let people share information over the Internet; it was created by Tim Berners-Lee during the period 1989–1991 [54, 55]. Although it is a simplification, we can view the original conception and design of the Web as involving two central features. First, it provided a way to make documents easily available to anyone on the Internet, in the form of *Web pages* that you could create and store on a publicly accessible part of your computer. Second, it provided a way for others to easily access such Web pages, using a *browser* that could connect to the public spaces on computers across the Internet and retrieve the Web pages stored there.

To a first approximation, this is still how we experience the Web today: as a sequence of Web pages rendered inside a browser. For example, Figure 13.1 shows a set of four separate Web pages: the home page of a college instructor who teaches a class on networks; the home page of the networks class he teaches; the blog for the class, with a post about Microsoft listed at the top; and the corporate home page for Microsoft. Because of the underlying design, we can think of these pages both as part of a single coherent system (the Web), but also as files that likely reside on four separate computers, controlled by several different and completely independent organizations, and made publicly accessible by a now-universal consensus to participate in the protocols of the Web.

Hypertext. Beyond these basic features, there is a crucial design principle embedded in the Web – the decision to organize the information using a network metaphor. This is what turns the set of Web pages from Figure 13.1 into the "web" of Web pages in Figure 13.2. In writing a Web page, you can annotate any portion of the document with a virtual link to another Web page, allowing a reader to move directly from your page to this other one. The set of pages on the Web thereby becomes a graph, and in fact a directed graph: the nodes are the pages themselves, and the directed edges are the links that lead from one page to another.

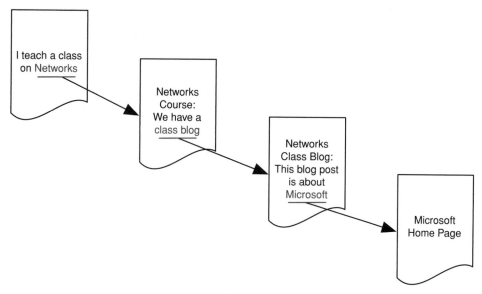

Figure 13.2. Information on the Web is organized using a network metaphor: the links among Web pages turn the Web into a directed graph.

Much as we're familiar with the idea of links among Web pages, we should appreciate that the idea to organize Web pages as a network was both inspired and nonobvious. There are many ways to arrange information – according to a classification system, like books in a library; as a series of folders, like the files on your computer; or even purely alphabetically, like the terms in an index or the names in a phone directory. Each of these organizational systems can make sense in different contexts, and any of them could in principle have been used for the Web. But the use of a network structure truly brings forth the globalizing power of the Web, by allowing anyone authoring a Web page to highlight a relationship with any other existing page, anywhere in the world.

The decision to use this network metaphor also didn't arise out of thin air; it's an application of a computer-assisted style of authoring known as *hypertext* that had been explored and refined since the middle of the twentieth century [316, 324]. The motivating idea behind hypertext is to replace the traditional linear structure of text with a network structure, in which any portion of the text can link directly to any other part. In this way, logical relationships within the text that are traditionally implicit become first-class objects, foregrounded by the use of explicit links. In its early years, hypertext was a cause passionately advocated by a relatively small group of technologists; the Web subsequently brought hypertext to a global audience, at a scale that no one could have anticipated.

13.2 Information Networks, Hypertext, and Associative Memory

The hypertextual structure of the Web provides us with a familiar and important example of an information network – nodes (Web pages in this case) containing information,

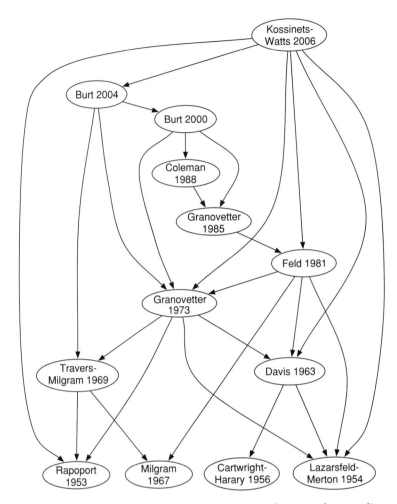

Figure 13.3. The network of citations among a set of research papers forms a directed graph that, like the Web, is a kind of information network. In contrast to the Web, however, the passage of time is much more evident in citation networks, since their links tend to point strictly backward in time.

with explicit links encoding relationships between the nodes. But the notion of an information network significantly predates the development of computer technology, and the creators of hypertext were in their own right motivated by earlier networks that wove together large amounts of information.

Intellectual Precursors of Hypertext. A first important intellectual precursor of hypertext is the concept of *citation* among scholarly books and articles. When the author or authors of a scholarly work wish to credit the source of an idea they are invoking, they include a citation to the earlier paper that provides the source of this idea. For example, Figure 13.3 shows the citations among a set of sociology papers that provided some of the key ideas in the first part of this book. (At the bottom of this figure are seminal papers on – from left to right – triadic closure, the small-world phenomenon, structural balance, and homophily.) We can see how work in this field – as in any academic discipline – builds on earlier work, with the dependence represented by a citation structure. We can also see how this citation structure naturally forms a directed graph, with nodes representing books and articles, and directed edges representing citations from one work to another. The same structure arises among patents, which provide citations to prior work and earlier inventions, and among legal decisions, which provide citations to earlier decisions that are being used as precedents or are being distinguished from the present case. Of course, the example in Figure 13.3 is a tiny piece of a much larger directed graph; for instance, Mark Granovetter's 1973 paper on the strength of weak ties has been cited several thousand times in the academic literature, so in the full citation structure we should imagine thousands of arrows all pointing to this single node.

One distinction between citation networks and the Web is that citations are governed much more strongly by an underlying "arrow of time." A book, article, patent, or legal decision is written at a specific point in time, and the citations it contains – the edges pointing outward to other nodes – are effectively "frozen" at the point when it is written. In other words, citations lead back into the past: if paper X cites paper Y, then we generally won't find a citation from Y back to X for the simple reason that Y was written at a time before X existed. Of course, there are exceptions to this principle – two papers that were written concurrently, with each citing the other, or a work that is revised to include more recent citations – but this flow backward in time is a dominant pattern in citation networks. On the Web, in contrast, while some pages are written once and then frozen forever, a significant portion of them are evolving works in progress where the links are updated over long periods of time. Although links on the Web are directed, there is no strong sense of "flow" from the present into the past.

Citation networks are not the only earlier form of information network. The cross-references within a printed encyclopedia or similar reference work form another important example; one article often includes pointers to other related articles. An online reference work like Wikipedia (even when viewed simply as a collection of linked articles, independent of the fact that it exists on the Web) is structured in the same way. This organizing principle is a clear precursor of hypertext, in that the cross-referencing links make relationships among the articles explicit. It is possible to browse a printed or online encyclopedia through its cross references, pursuing serendipitous leads from one topic to another.

For example, Figure 13.4 shows the cross-references among Wikipedia articles on certain topics in game theory, together with connections to related topics.[1] We can see, for example, how it's possible to get from the article on Nash equilibrium to the article on NASA (the U.S. National Aeronautics and Space Administration) by passing through articles on John Nash (the creator of Nash equilibrium), *A Beautiful Mind* (a film about John Nash's life), Ron Howard (the director of *A Beautiful Mind*), *Apollo 13* (another film directed by Ron Howard), and finally on to the article about NASA (the U.S. government agency that managed the real Apollo 13 space mission). In short: Nash equilibrium was created by someone whose life was the subject of a movie by

---

[1] Because Wikipedia changes constantly, Figure 13.4 necessarily represents the state of the links among these articles only at the time of this writing. The need to stress this point reinforces the contrast with the frozen nature of the citations in a collection of papers such as those in Figure 13.3.

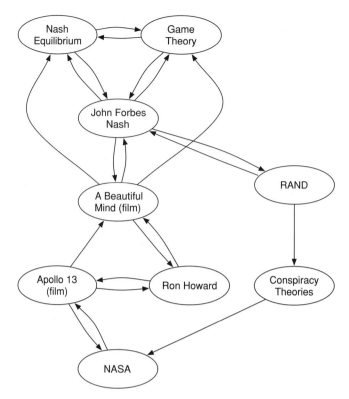

Figure 13.4. The cross-references among a set of articles in an encyclopedia form another kind of information network that can be represented as a directed graph. The figure shows the cross-references among a set of Wikipedia articles on topics in game theory and their connections to related topics, including popular culture and government agencies.

a director who also made a movie about NASA. Nor is this the only short chain of articles from Nash equilibrium to NASA. Figure 13.4 also contains a sequence of cross-references based on the fact that John Nash worked for a period of time at RAND, and RAND is the subject of several conspiracy theories, as is NASA. These short paths between seemingly distant concepts reflect an analogue, for information networks, of the "six degrees of separation" phenomenon in social networks from Chapter 2, where similarly short paths link apparently distant pairs of people.

Indeed, browsing through chains of cross-references is closely related to the stream-of-consciousness way in which one mentally free-associates between different ideas. For example, suppose you've just been reading about Nash equilibrium in a book, and while thinking about it during a walk home your mind wanders, and you suddenly notice that you've shifted to thinking about NASA. It may take a bit of reflection to figure out how this happened, and to reconstruct a chain of free association like the one pictured in Figure 13.4, carried out entirely among the existing associations in your mind. This idea has been formalized in another kind of information network, a *semantic network*, in which nodes literally represent concepts, and edges represent some kind of logical or perceived relationship between the concepts. Researchers have used techniques like *word association studies* (e.g., "Tell me what you think of when

I say the word 'cold' ") as a way to probe the otherwise implicit structure of semantic networks as they exist in people's minds [381].

Vannevar Bush and the Memex. Thus, information networks date back into much earlier periods in our history; for centuries, they were associated with libraries and scholarly literature rather than with computer technology and the Internet. The idea that they could assume a strongly technological incarnation, in the form of something like the Web, is generally credited to Vannevar Bush and his seminal 1945 article in the *Atlantic Monthly*, entitled "As We May Think" [89]. Written at the end of World War II, it imagined with eerie prescience the ways in which nascent computing and communication technology might revolutionize the ways we store, exchange, and access information.

In particular, Bush observed that traditional methods for storing information in a book, a library, or a computer memory are highly *linear* – they consist of a collection of items sorted in some sequential order. Our conscious experience of thinking, on the other hand, exhibits what might be called an *associative memory*, the kind that a semantic network represents – you think of one thing; it reminds you of another; you see a novel connection; some new insight is formed. Bush therefore called for the creation of information systems that mimicked this style of memory; he imagined a hypothetical prototype called the *Memex* that functioned very much like the Web, consisting of digitized versions of all human knowledge connected by associative links, and he imagined a range of commercial applications and knowledge-sharing activities that could take place around such a device. In this way, Bush's article foreshadowed not only the Web itself, but also many of the dominant metaphors that are now used to think about the Web: the Web as universal encyclopedia; the Web as giant socioeconomic system; the Web as global brain.

The fact that Vannever Bush's vision was so accurate is not in any sense coincidental; Bush occupied a prominent position in the U.S. government's scientific funding establishment, and his ideas about future directions had considerable reach. Indeed, the creators of early hypertext systems explicitly invoked Bush's ideas, as did Tim Berners-Lee when he set out to develop the Web.

The Web and Its Evolution. This brings us back to the 1990s, the first decade of the Web, during which it grew rapidly from a modest research project to a vast new medium with global reach. In the early phase of this period, the simple picture in Figure 13.2 captured the Web's essential nature: most pages were relatively static documents, and most links served primarily *navigational* functions – to transport you from one page to another according to the relational premise of hypertext.

This is still a reasonable working approximation for large portions of the Web, but the Web has also increasingly outgrown the simple model of documents connected by navigational links, and it is important to understand how this has happened in order to be able to interpret any analysis of the Web's structure. In the earliest days of the Web, the computers hosting the content played a relatively passive role: they mainly just served up pages in response to requests for them. Now, on the other hand, the powerful computation available at the other end of a link is often brought more directly into play: links now often trigger complex programs on the computer hosting the page. Links with labels like "Add to Shopping Cart," "Submit my Query," "Update my Calendar," or "Upload my Image," are not intended by their authors primarily to transport you to a new page (though they may do that incidentally as part of their function); such links exist to activate computational transactions on the machine that runs the site. Here's an example to make this concrete. If we continued to follow links from the Microsoft home page in the example from Figure 13.2, we could imagine taking a next step to the online shopping site that Microsoft hosts for its products. From this page, clicking on a link labeled "Buy Now" next to one of the featured products would result in a charge to your credit card and the delivery of the product to your home in the physical, offline world. There would also be a new page providing a receipt, but the purpose of this last "Buy Now" link was not primarily to transport you, hypertextually, to a "receipt page"; rather, it was to perform the indicated transaction.

In view of these considerations, it is useful to think of a coarse division of links on the Web into *navigational* and *transactional*, with the former serving the traditional hypertextual functions of the Web and the latter primarily existing to perform transactions on the computers hosting the content. This is not a perfect or clear-cut distinction, since many links on the Web have both navigational and transactional functions, but it is a useful dichotomy to keep in mind when evaluating the function of the Web's pages and links.

While a lot of content on the Web now has a primarily transactional nature, this content still remains largely linked together by a navigational "backbone" – it is reachable via relatively stable Web pages connected to each other by more traditional navigational links. This is the portion of the Web we will focus on in our analysis of its global structure. Sorting out what should and shouldn't belong to this navigational backbone is ultimately a type of judgment call, but fortunately there is a lot of experience in making and even codifying such judgments. This is because distinguishing between navigational and transactional links has long been essential to Web search engines when they build their indexes of the available content on the Web. It's clearly not in a search engine's interest to index, for the general public, every receipt from an online purchase that every user of the Web has ever made, or every query result for available airline flight times or product specifications that every Web user ever has made. As a result, search engines have developed and refined automated rules that try to assess whether the content they are collecting is relatively stable and intended for public consumption, and they tend to collect content that is reachable via navigational links. We will implicitly be following such working definitions when we talk about the structure of the Web, and when we discuss empirical data on large sets of Web pages in Section 13.4, the discussion will be based on collections assembled by search engines according to such rules.

13.3 The Web as a Directed Graph

Viewing social and economic networks in terms of their graph structures provides significant insights, and the same is true for information networks such as the Web. When we view the Web as a graph, it allows us to better understand the logical relationships expressed by its links; to break its structure into smaller, cohesive units;

and – as we will see in Chapter 14 – to identify important pages as a step in organizing the results of Web searches.

To begin with, it is important to note two things. First, in discussing the graph structure of the Web, we will follow the plan outlined at the end of Section 13.2 and focus on the Web's navigational links. As we observed in that discussion, the navigational links still form the bulk of the Web's structural backbone, despite the increasing richness of Web content as a whole.

Second, we need to appreciate that the fundamentally *directed* nature of the Web makes it different from many of the networks we've considered thus far. Recall that in a directed graph, the edges don't simply connect pairs of nodes in a symmetric way – they point *from* one node *to* another. This is clearly true on the Web: just because you write a blog post and include a link to the Web page of a company or organization, there is no reason to believe that they will necessarily reciprocate and include a link back to the blog post.

This distinction between directedness and undirectedness is an important aspect of the difference between social and information networks; an analogy here is to the difference between the global friendship network that we discussed in Chapter 2, showing who is friends with whom, and the *global name-recognition network*, in which there is a link from person A to person B if A has heard of B. This latter network is directed and in fact quite asymmetric – famous celebrities are recognizable to millions of people, and in fact millions closely track the goings-on in their lives, but one doesn't expect that such celebrities are in any sense aware of the names or identities of all these fans. In other words, the global name-recognition network is structurally more similar to an information network like the Web than it is to a traditional social network defined by friendship.

Paths and Strong Connectivity. The connectivity of undirected graphs was defined in terms of paths: two nodes are linked by a *path* if we can follow a sequence of edges from one to the other; a graph is *connected* if every pair of nodes is linked by a path; and we can break up a disconnected graph into its connected *components*. Now that we're dealing with a directed graph, we're going to try following the same general strategy for talking about connectivity; but to do this, we first need to rework the definition of a path to take directions into account, and this will necessarily make the subsequent definitions more subtle.

First, a *path* from a node A to a node B in a directed graph is a sequence of nodes, beginning with A and ending with B, with the property that each consecutive pair of nodes in the sequence is connected by an edge pointing in the forward direction. This "pointing in the forward direction" condition makes the definition of a path in a directed graph different from the corresponding definition for undirected graphs, where edges have no direction. On the Web, this notion of following links only in the forward direction corresponds naturally to the notion of viewing Web pages with a browser: we can follow a link when it's emanating from the page we're on, but we aren't in general aware of all the links that point *to* the page we're currently visiting.

We can try out this definition on the example in Figure 13.5, which shows the directed graph formed by the links among a small set of Web pages; it depicts some of the people and classes associated with the hypothetical University of X, which we

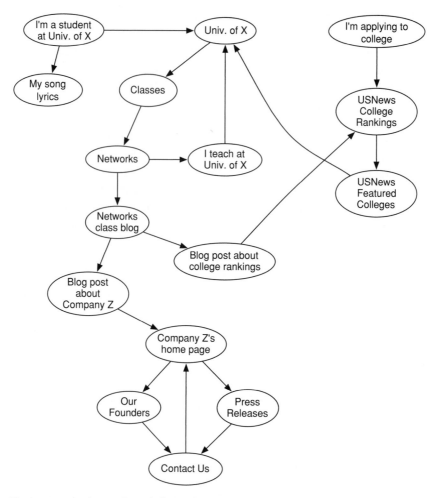

Figure 13.5. A directed graph formed by the links among a small set of Web pages.

imagine to have once been a featured college in a national magazine. By following a sequence of links in this example (all in the forward direction), we can discover that there's a path from the node labeled "Univ. of X" to the node labeled "US News College Rankings": we can follow a link from "Univ. of X" to its "Classes" page, then to the home page of its class entitled "Networks," then to the "Networks class blog," then to a class blog post about college rankings, and finally via a link from this blog post to the page "US News College Rankings." In contrast, there's no path from the node labeled "Company Z's home page" to the node labeled "US News College Rankings" – there would be if we were allowed to follow directed edges in the reverse direction, but following edges forward from "Company Z's home page" we can only reach "Our Founders," "Press Releases," and "Contact Us."

With the definition of a path in hand, we can adapt the notion of connectivity to the setting of directed graphs. We say that a directed graph is *strongly connected* if there is a path from every node to every other node. So, for example, the directed graph of

Web pages in Figure 13.5 is not strongly connected because, as we've just observed, there are certain pairs of nodes for which there's no path from the first to the second.

Strongly Connected Components. When a directed graph is not strongly connected, it's important to be able to describe its *reachability* properties: identifying which nodes are "reachable" from which others using paths. To define this notion precisely, it's again useful to draw an analogy to the simpler case of undirected graphs, and try to start from there. For an undirected graph, its connected components serve as a very effective summary of reachability: if two nodes belong to the same component, then they can reach each other by paths, and if two nodes belong to different components, then they can't.

But reachability in a directed graph is a harder thing to summarize. In a directed graph, we can have pairs of nodes for which each can reach the other (like "Univ. of X" and "US News College Rankings"), pairs for which one can reach the other but not vice versa (like "US News College Rankings" and "Company Z's home page"), and pairs for which neither can reach the other (like "I'm a student at Univ. of X" and "I'm applying to college"). Moreover, the conceptual complexity of reachability in a directed graph corresponds to a kind of "visual" complexity as well: whereas the components of an undirected graph naturally correspond to separate chunks of the graph with no edges between them, a directed graph that is not strongly connected does not break equally obviously into noninteracting pieces. How then should we describe its reachability properties?

The key is to find the right notion of a "component" for directed graphs, and in fact one can do this with a definition that strictly mirrors the formal definition of a component in an undirected graph.

> We say that a *strongly connected component* (SCC) in a directed graph is a subset of the nodes such that (i) every node in the subset has a path to every other and (ii) the subset is not part of some larger set with the property that every node can reach every other.

As in the undirected case, part (i) of this definition says that all nodes within a strongly connected component can reach each other, and part (ii) of this definition says that the strongly connected components correspond as much as possible to separate "pieces," not smaller portions of larger pieces.

It helps to consider an example: in Figure 13.6 we show the strongly connected components for the directed graph from Figure 13.5. Notice the role that part (ii) of the definition plays in producing the separate pieces of the graph in this picture: the set of four nodes consisting of "Univ. of X," "Classes," "Networks," and "I teach at Univ. of X" collectively satisfy part (i) of the definition, but they do not form a strongly connected component because they belong to a larger set that also satisfies part (i).

Looking at this picture, one can see how the SCCs serve as a compact summary of the reachability properties of the directed graph. Given two nodes A and B, we can tell if there is a path from A to B as follows. First, we find the SCCs containing A and B, respectively. If A and B belong to the same SCC, then they can each reach each other by paths. Otherwise, viewing the SCCs themselves as larger "supernodes," we see if there is a way to walk from the SCC of A to the SCC of B, following edges between

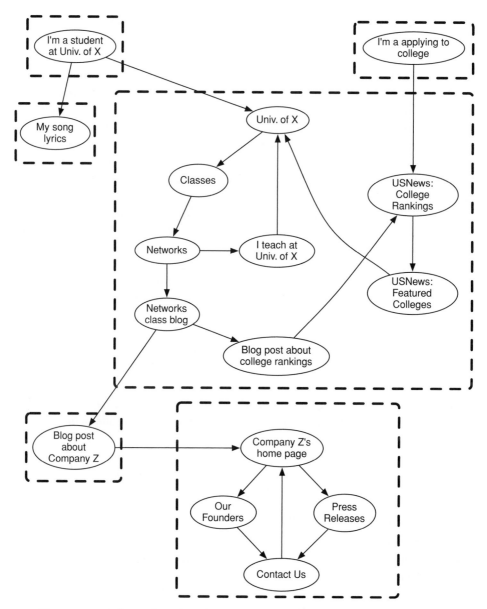

Figure 13.6. A directed graph with its strongly connected components identified.

SCCs in the forward direction. If there is a way to do this, then this walk can be opened up into a path from A to B in the graph; if there is no way to do this, then there is no path from A to B.

13.4 The Bow-Tie Structure of the Web

In 1999, after the Web had been growing for the better part of a decade, Andrei Broder and his colleagues [80] set out to build a global map of the Web, using strongly connected components as the basic building blocks. For their raw data, they used the index of pages and links from one of the largest commercial search engines at the time, AltaVista. Their influential study has since been replicated on other, even larger snapshots of the Web, including an early index of Google's search engine [56] and large research collections of Web pages [133]. Similar analyses have been carried out for particular well-defined pieces of the Web, including the links among articles on Wikipedia [83], and even for complex directed graph structures arising in other domains, such as the network of interbank loans depicted in Figure 1.3 from Chapter 1 [50]. In this way, although the actual snapshot of the Web used by Broder et al. in their original study comes from an earlier time in the Web's history, the mapping paradigm they proposed continues to be a useful way of thinking about giant directed graphs in the context of the Web and more generally.

A Giant Strongly Connected Component. A "map" of the Web clearly can't resemble a map of the physical world in any serious sense, given the scale and complexity of the network being analyzed. Rather, what Broder et al. wanted was something more conceptual – an abstract map dividing the Web into a few large pieces, and showing in a stylized way how these pieces fit together.

Their first finding was that the Web contains a giant strongly connected component. Recall from our discussions in Chapter 2 that many naturally occuring undirected graphs have a giant connected component – a single component containing a significant fraction of all the nodes. The fact that the directed analogue of this phenomenon holds for the Web is not hard to believe based on analogous thought experiments. Roughly, the point is that a number of major search engines and other "starting page" sites have links leading to directory-type pages from which one can, in turn, reach the home pages of major educational institutions, large companies, and governmental agencies. From here one can reach most of the pages within each of these large sites. Furthermore, many of the pages within these sites link back to the search engines and starting pages themselves. (The path from "US News College Rankings" to a class blog and back in Figures 13.5 and 13.6 suggests a concrete example for how this happens.) Thus, all these pages can mutually reach one another, and hence they all belong to the same SCC. Given that this SCC contains (at least) the home pages of many of the major commercial, governmental, and nonprofit organizations in the world, it is easy to believe that it is a giant SCC.

From here, we can invoke an argument – familiar from the undirected case as well – that there is almost surely at most one giant SCC. For if there were two giant SCCs – call them X and Y – all it would take is a single link from any node in X to any node Y, and another link from any node in Y to any node in X, and X and Y would merge to become part of a single SCC.

The Bow-Tie Structure. The second step in the analysis by Broder et al. was to position all the remaining SCCs in relation to the giant one. This involves classifying nodes by their ability to reach and be reached from the giant SCC. The first two sets in this classification are the following.

1. *IN*: nodes that can reach the giant SCC but cannot be reached from it – in other words, nodes that are "upstream" of it.

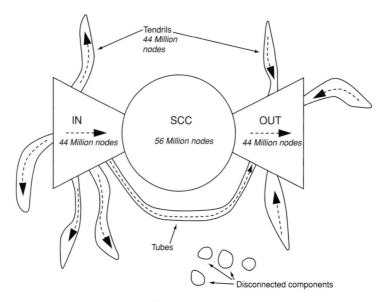

Figure 13.7. A schematic picture of the bow-tie structure of the Web (image from Broder et al., [80]). Although the numbers are now outdated, the structure has persisted.

2. *OUT*: nodes that can be reached from the giant SCC but cannot reach it – in other words, nodes that are "downstream" of it.

Figure 13.6 forms a useful example for trying out these definitions. Although the network in Figure 13.6 is much too small for any of its SCCs to be considered "giant," we can imagine its largest SCC as the giant one and consider how the other nodes are positioned in relation to it. In this case, the pages "I'm a student at Univ. of X" and "I'm applying to college" constitute IN, and the pages "Blog post about Company Z" and the whole SCC involving Company Z constitute OUT. And this is roughly what one intuitively expects to find in these sets: IN contains pages that have not been "discovered" by members of the giant SCC, whereas OUT contains pages that may receive links from the giant SCC, but which choose not to link back.

Figure 13.7 shows the original schematic image from Broder et al., depicting the relation of IN, OUT, and the giant SCC. Because of the visual effect of IN and OUT as large lobes hanging off the central SCC, Broder et al. termed this the "bow-tie picture" of the Web, with the giant SCC as the "knot" in the middle. The actual sizes of the different pieces shown in the figure come from the 1999 AltaVista data, and are long since obsolete – the main point, which has remained true over time and across different domains, is that each of these three pieces accounts for a significant fraction of the total number of nodes.

As Figure 13.7 also makes clear, there are pages that belong to none of IN, OUT, or the giant SCC – that is, they can neither reach the giant SCC nor be reached from it. These can be further classified as

3. *Tendrils:* The "tendrils" of the bow-tie consist of (a) the nodes reachable from IN that cannot reach the giant SCC, and (b) the nodes that can reach OUT but cannot be reached from the giant SCC. For example, the page "My song lyrics" in

Figure 13.6 is an example of a tendril page, since it's reachable from IN but has no path to the giant SCC. It's possible for a tendril node to satisfy both (a) and (b), in which case it's part of a "tube" that travels from IN to OUT without touching the giant SCC. (For example, if the page "My song lyrics" happened to link to "Blog post about Company Z" in Figure 13.6, it would be part of a tube.)

4. *Disconnected:* Finally, there are nodes that would not have a path to the giant SCC even if we completely ignored the directions of the edges. These belong to none of the preceding categories.

Taken as a whole, then, the bow-tie picture of the Web provides a high-level view of the Web's structure, based on its reachability properties and how its strongly connected components fit together. From it, we see that the Web has a central "core" containing many of its most prominent pages, with many other nodes that lie upstream, downstream, or "off to the side" relative to this core. It is also a highly dynamic picture: as people create pages and links, the constituent pieces of the bow tie are constantly shifting their boundaries, with nodes entering (and also leaving) the giant SCC over time. But subsequent studies suggest that the aggregate picture remains relatively stable over time, even as the detailed structure changes continuously.

While the bow-tie picture gives us a global view of the Web, it doesn't give us insight into the more fine-grained patterns of connections within the constituent parts – connections that could serve to highlight important Web pages or communities of thematically related pages. Addressing these latter issues requires more detailed network analysis, which we undertake in Chapter 14; as we will see, this requires us to think about what it means for a Web page to occupy a "powerful" position, and it leads to methods that bear directly on the design of Web search engines. More generally, network analysis of the Web forms one ingredient in a broader emerging research agenda that aims to understand the structure, behavior, and evolution of the Web as a phenomenon in itself [220].

13.5 The Emergence of Web 2.0

The increasing richness of Web content, which we've encountered through the distinction between navigational and transactional links, fueled a series of further significant changes in the Web during its second decade of existence, between 2000 and 2009. Three major forces behind these changes were

(i) the growth of Web authoring styles that enabled many people to collectively create and maintain shared content;

(ii) the movement of people's personal online data (including e-mail, calendars, photos, and videos) from their own computers to services offered and hosted by large companies; and

(iii) the growth of linking styles that emphasize online connections between people, not just between documents.

Taken together, this set of changes altered user experience on the Web sufficiently that technologists led by Tim O'Reilly and others began speaking in 2004 and 2005 about the emergence of *Web 2.0* [335]. While the term evokes images of a new software release, there is agreement that Web 2.0 is principally "an attitude, not a technology" [125]. There has never been perfect consensus on the meaning of the term, but it has generally connoted a major next step in the evolution of the Web, driven by versions of principles (i), (ii), and (iii) above (as well as others), and arising from a confluence of factors rather than any one organization's centralized decisions.

Indeed, there was an explosion of prominent new sites during the period 2004–2006 that exemplified the preceding three principles, sometimes in combination. To name just a few examples, Wikipedia grew rapidly during this period as people embraced the idea of collectively editing articles to create an open encyclopedia on the Web [principle (i)]; Gmail and other online e-mail services encouraged individuals to let companies like Google host their archives of e-mail [principle (ii)]; and MySpace and Facebook achieved widespread adoption with a set of features that primarily emphasized the creation of online social networks [principle (iii)].

Many sites during this period combined versions of all three principles. For example, the photo-sharing site Flickr and subsequently the video-sharing site YouTube provided users with a centralized place to store their own photos and videos [principle (ii)], simultaneously enriched this content by allowing a large user community to tag and comment on it [principle (i)], and allowed users to form social connections to others whose content they followed [principle (iii)]. The microblogging service Twitter extended principle (ii) further by creating an online forum for personal data (in the form of short real-time descriptions of one's experiences, thoughts, and questions) that would otherwise never have been recorded at all. Because many people all comment at roughly the same time on a current event in the news, Twitter also creates collective summaries of worldwide reactions to such events [principle (i)] and allows users to construct links by which they follow the writings of other users [principle (iii)].

Even if some (or many) of these specific sites are replaced by others in the coming years, the principles they embody have clearly brought about a lasting change in perspective on Web content. These principles have also led to a point that we discussed early in Chapter 1: designers of Web sites today need to think not just about organizing information but also about the social feedback effects inherent in maintaining an audience of millions of users – users who are able to interact directly not just with the site itself but with one another.

This helps to explain why many of the central concepts in this book relate to phenomena that surround this current phase of the Web's evolution. For example, many of the key rallying cries that accompanied the emergence of Web 2.0 are in a sense shorthand for social phenomena that we discuss in other chapters:

- *"Software that gets better the more people use it."* A core principle of Web 2.0 is that online Web sites and services can become more appealing to users – and in fact, often genuinely more valuable to them – as their audiences grow larger. When and how this process takes place forms a central focus in chapters from the next two parts of the book, particularly Chapters 16, 17, and 19.
- *"The wisdom of crowds."* The collaborative authoring of an encyclopedia by millions on Wikipedia, the elevation of news content by group evaluation on Digg, the fact that photos of breaking news now often appear on Flickr before they do

in the mainstream news, and many similar developments highlighted the ways in which the audience of a Web 2.0 site – each contributing specific expertise and sometimes misinformation – can produce a collective artifact of significant value. But the "wisdom of the crowds," as this process is now often called, is a subtle phenomenon that can fail as easily as it can succeed. In Chapter 22 we discuss some of the basic work in the theory of markets that helps explain how collective information residing in a large group can be synthesized successfully, and in Chapter 16 we describe ways in which this process can also lead to unexpected and sometimes undesirable outcomes.

- *The "Long Tail."* With many people contributing content to a Web 2.0 site, the system will generally reach a balance between a small amount of hugely popular content and a "long tail" of content with various levels of niche appeal. Such distributions of popularity have important consequences; they are the topic of Chapter 18.

In addition to the ideas suggested by such mantras, the premises underlying Web 2.0 appear in many other contexts in the book as well. The social-networking aspects of Web 2.0 sites provide rich data for large studies of social network structure, as discussed in Chapter 2. They offer a basis for empirical investigations of the ideas of triadic closure and group affiliation from Chapters 3 and 4, and have been used to evaluate the theories underlying the small-world phenomenon in Chapter 20.

Moreover, many of the features that are common to Web 2.0 sites are designed to explicitly steer some of the underlying social feedback mechanisms in desirable directions. For example, *reputation systems* and *trust systems* enable users to provide signals about the behavior – and misbehavior – of other users. We discussed such systems in the context of structural balance in Chapter 5, and we will see their role in providing information essential to the functioning of online markets in Chapter 22. Web 2.0 sites also make use of *recommendation systems* to guide users toward items that they may not know about. In addition to serving as helpful features for a site's users, such recommendation systems interact in complex but important ways with distributions of popularity and the long tail of niche content, as we will see in Chapter 18.

The development of the current generation of Web search engines, led by Google, is sometimes seen as a crucial step in the pivot from the early days of the Web to the era of Web 2.0. In the next two chapters we will discuss how thinking of the Web as a network helped form the foundation for these search engines, and how models based on matching markets helped turn search into a profitable business.

13.6 Exercises

1. Consider the set of eighteen Web pages drawn in Figure 13.8, with links forming a directed graph. Which set of nodes constitutes the largest strongly connected component (SCC) in this graph? Taking this as the *giant SCC*, which nodes then belong to the sets IN and OUT defined in Section 13.4? Which nodes belong to the *tendrils* of the graph?

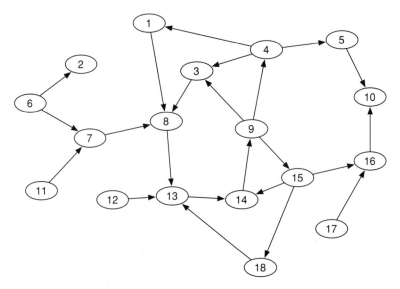

Figure 13.8. A directed graph of Web pages.

2. As new links are created and old ones are removed among an existing set of Web pages, the pages move between different parts of the bow-tie structure.

   (a) Name an edge you could add or delete from the graph in Figure 13.8 so as to increase the size of the largest SCC.

   (b) Name an edge you could add or delete from the graph in Figure 13.8 so as to increase the size of the set IN.

   (c) Name an edge you could add or delete from the graph in Figure 13.8 so as to increase the size of the set OUT.

3. In Exercise 2, we considered how the consistuent parts of the bow-tie structure change as edges are added to or removed from the graph. It's also interesting to ask about the magnitude of these changes.

   (a) Describe an example of a graph where removing a single edge can reduce the size of the largest SCC by at least 1000 nodes. (Clearly you shouldn't attempt to draw the full graph; rather, you can describe it in words, and also draw a schematic picture if it's useful.)

   (b) Describe an example of a graph where adding a single edge can reduce the size of the set OUT by at least 1000 nodes. (Again, you should describe the graph rather than actually drawing it.)

CHAPTER 14

Link Analysis and Web Search

14.1 Searching the Web: The Problem of Ranking

When you go to Google and type the word "Cornell," the first result it shows you is www. cornell.edu, the home page of Cornell University. It's certainly hard to argue with this as a first choice, but how did Google "know" that this was the best answer? Search engines determine how to rank pages using automated methods that look at the Web itself, not some external source of knowledge, so the conclusion is that there must be enough information *intrinsic* to the Web and its structure to figure this out.

Before discussing some of the ideas behind the ranking of pages, let's begin by considering a few basic reasons why it's a hard problem. First, search is a hard problem for computers to solve in any setting, not just on the Web. Indeed, the field of *information retrieval* [36, 360] dealt with this problem for decades before the creation of the Web: automated information retrieval systems starting in the 1960s were designed to search repositories of newspaper articles, scientific papers, patents, legal abstracts, and other document collections in reponse to keyword queries. Information retrieval systems have always had to deal with the problem that keywords are a very limited way to express a complex information need. In addition to the fact that a list of keywords is short and inexpressive, it suffers from the problems of *synonymy* (multiple ways to say the same thing, so that your search for recipes involving scallions fails because the recipe you wanted called them "green onions") and *polysemy* (multiple meanings for the same term, so that your search for information about the animal called a jaguar instead produces results primarily about automobiles, football players, and an operating system for the Apple Macintosh.)

For a long time, up through the 1980s, information retrieval was the province of reference librarians, patent attorneys, and other people whose jobs consisted of searching collections of documents. Such people were trained in how to formulate effective queries, and the documents they were searching tended to be written by professionals, using a controlled style and vocabulary. With the arrival of the Web, where everyone is an author and everyone is a searcher, the problems surrounding information retrieval exploded in scale and complexity.

351

To begin with, the diversity in authoring styles makes it much harder to rank documents according to a common criterion: on a single topic, one can easily find pages written by experts, novices, children, or conspiracy theorists, and not necessarily be able to tell which is which. Once upon a time, the fact that someone had the money and resources to produce a professional-looking, typeset, bound document meant that they were very likely (even if not always) someone who could be taken seriously. Today, anyone can create a Web page with high production values.

There is a correspondingly rich diversity in the set of people issuing queries, and the problem of multiple meanings becomes particularly severe. For example, when someone issues the single-word query "Cornell," a search engine doesn't have very much to go on. Did the searcher want information about the university? The university's hockey team? The Lab of Ornithology run by the university? Cornell College in Iowa? The Nobel Prize–winning physicist Eric Cornell? The same ranking of search results can't be right for everyone.

These represent problems that were already present in traditional information retrieval systems, just taken to new extremes. But the Web also introduces new kinds of problems. One is the dynamic and constantly changing nature of Web content. On September 11, 2001, many people ran to Google and typed "World Trade Center." But there was a mismatch between what people thought they could get from Google and what they really got: at the time, Google was built on a model in which it periodically collected Web pages and indexed them, so the results were all based on pages that were gathered days or weeks earlier, and the top results were all descriptive pages about the building itself, not about what had occurred that morning. In response to such events, Google and the other main search engines built specialized "News Search" features, which collect articles more or less continuously from a relatively fixed number of news sources, so as to be able to answer queries about news stories minutes after they appear. Even today, such news search features are only partly integrated into the core parts of the search engine interface, and emerging Web sites such as Twitter continue to fill in the spaces that exist between static content and real-time awareness.

More fundamental still, and at the heart of many of these issues, is the fact that the Web has shifted much of the information retrieval question from a problem of *scarcity* to a problem of *abundance*. The prototypical applications of information retrieval in the pre-Web era had a "needle-in-a-haystack" flavor. For example, an intellectual-property attorney might express the information need, "find me any patents that have dealt with the design of elevator speed regulators based on fuzzy-logic controllers." Such issues still arise today, but the hard part for most Web searches carried out by the general public is in a sense the opposite: to filter, from among an enormous number of relevant documents, the few that are most important. In other words, a search engine has no problem finding and indexing literally millions of documents that are genuinely relevant to the one-word query "Cornell"; the problem is that the human being performing the search is going to want to look at only a few of these. Which few should the search engine recommend?

An understanding of the network structure of Web pages is crucial for addressing these questions, as we now discuss.

14.2 Link Analysis Using Hubs and Authorities

So we're back to our question from the beginning of the chapter: in response to the one-word query "Cornell," what are the clues that suggest Cornell's home page, www.cornell.edu, is a good answer?

Voting by In-Links. In fact, there is a natural way to address this question, provided we start from the right perspective. This perspective is to note that there is not really any way to use features purely internal to the page www.cornell.edu to solve this problem: it does not use the word "Cornell" more frequently or more prominently than thousands of other pages, and so there is nothing on the page itself that makes it stand out. Rather, it stands out because of features on other Web pages: when a page is relevant to the query "Cornell," very often www.cornell.edu is among the pages it links to.

This is the first part of the argument that links are essential to ranking: that we can use them to assess the authority of a page on a topic, through the implicit endorsements that other pages on the topic confer through their links to it. Of course, each individual link may have many possible meanings: it may be off-topic; it may convey criticism rather than endorsement; it may be a paid advertisement. It is difficult for search engines to automatically assess the intent of each link. But we hope that, in aggregate, if a page receives many links from other relevant pages, then it is receiving a kind of collective endorsement.

In the case of the query "Cornell," we could operationalize this by first collecting a large sample of pages that are relevant to the query, as determined by a classical, text-only, information retrieval approach. We could then let pages in this sample "vote" through their links: which page on the Web receives the greatest number of in-links from pages that are relevant to Cornell? Even this simple measure of link-counting works quite well for queries such as "Cornell," where, ultimately, there is a single page that most people agree should be ranked first.

A List-Finding Technique. It's possible to make deeper use of the network structure than just counting in-links, and this brings us to the second part of the argument that links are essential. Consider, as a typical example, the one-word query "newspapers." Unlike the query "Cornell," there is not necessarily a single, intuitively "best" answer here; there are a number of prominent newspapers on the Web, and an ideal answer would consist of a list of the most prominent among them. With the query "Cornell," we discussed collecting a sample of pages relevant to the query and then letting them vote using their links. What happens if we try this for the query "newspapers"?

What you will typically observe, if you try this experiment, is that you get high scores for a mix of prominent newspapers (i.e., the results you'd want) along with pages that are going to receive a lot of in-links no matter what the query is – pages like Yahoo!, Facebook, Amazon, and others. In other words, to make up a very simple hyperlink structure for purposes of this example, we'd see something like Figure 14.1: the unlabeled circles represent our sample of pages relevant to the query "newspapers," and among the four pages receiving the most votes from them, two are newspapers (*New York Times* and *USA Today*) and two are not (Yahoo! and Amazon). This example

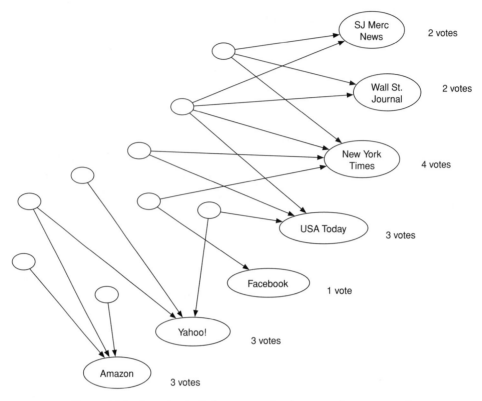

Figure 14.1. Counting in-links to pages for the query "newspapers."

is designed to be small enough to try by hand; in a real setting, of course, there would be many plausible newspaper pages and many more off-topic pages.

But votes are only a very simple kind of measure that we can get from the link structure; there is much more to be discovered if we look more closely. To try getting more, we ask a different question. In addition to the newspapers themselves, there is another kind of useful answer to our query: pages that compile lists of resources relevant to the topic. Such pages exist for most broad enough queries: for "newspapers," they would correspond to lists of links to online newspapers; for "Cornell," one can find many alumni who maintain pages with links to the University, its hockey team, its Medical School, its Art Museum, and so forth. If we could find good list pages for newspapers, we would have another approach to the problem of finding the newspapers themselves.

In fact, the example in Figure 14.1 suggests a useful technique for finding good lists. Among the pages casting votes, we notice that a few of them in fact voted for *many* of the pages that received a lot of votes. It would be natural, therefore, to suspect that these pages have some sense of where the good answers are, and to score them highly as lists. Concretely, we could say that a page's value as a list is equal to the sum of the votes received by all pages for which it voted. Figure 14.2 shows the result of applying this rule to the pages casting votes in our example.

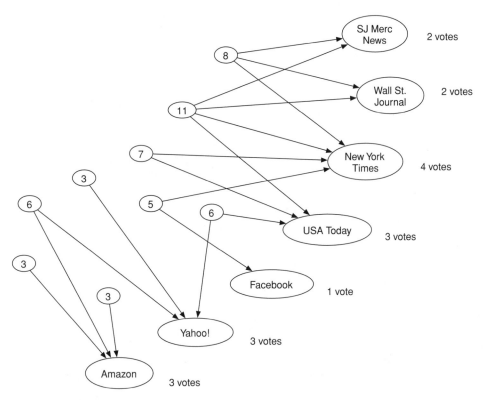

Figure 14.2. Finding good lists for the query "newspapers": each page's value as a list is written as a number inside it.

The Principle of Repeated Improvement. If we believe that pages scoring well as lists actually have a better sense for where the good results are, then we should weight their votes more heavily. So, in particular, we could tabulate the votes again, but this time giving each page's vote a weight equal to its value as a list. Figure 14.3 shows what happens when we do this on our example: now the other newspapers have surpassed the initially high-scoring Yahoo! and Amazon, because these other newspapers were endorsed by pages that were estimated to be good lists.

In fact, you can recognize the intuition behind this reweighting of votes in the way we evaluate endorsements in our everyday lives. Suppose you move to a new town and hear restaurant recommendations from a lot of people. After discovering that certain restaurants get mentioned by a lot of people, you realize that certain *people* in fact had mentioned most of these highly recommended restaurants when you asked them. These people play the role of the high-value lists on the Web, and it's only natural to go back and take more seriously the more obscure restaurants that they recommended, because you now particularly trust their judgment. This last step is exactly what we are doing in reweighting the votes for Web pages.

The final part of the argument for link analysis is then the following: Why stop here? If we have better votes on the right-hand side of the figure, we can use these to get still more refined values for the quality of the lists on the left-hand side of the figure. And

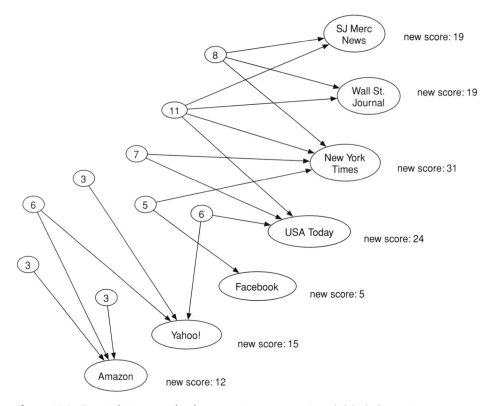

Figure 14.3. Reweighting votes for the query "newspapers": each labeled page's new score is equal to the sum of the values of all lists that point to it.

with more refined estimates for the high-value lists, we can reweight the votes that we apply to the right-hand side once again. The process can go back and forth forever: it can be viewed as a *principle of repeated improvement*, in which each refinement to one side of the figure enables a further refinement to the other.

Hubs and Authorities. This suggests a ranking procedure that we can try to make precise, as follows [247]. First, we'll call the kinds of pages we were originally seeking – the prominent, highly endorsed answers to the queries – the *authorities* for the query. We'll call the high-value lists the *hubs* for the query. Now, for each page p, we're trying to estimate its value as a potential authority and as a potential hub, and so we assign it two numerical scores: $auth(p)$ and $hub(p)$. Each of these starts out with a value equal to 1, indicating that we're initially agnostic as to which is the best in either of these categories.

Now, voting – in which we use the quality of the hubs to refine our estimates for the quality of the authorities – is simply the following:

> *Authority Update Rule:* For each page p, update $auth(p)$ to be the sum of the hub scores of all pages that point to it.

On the other hand, the list-finding technique – in which we use the quality of the authorities to refine our estimates for the quality of the hubs – is the following:

Hub Update Rule: For each page p, update $hub(p)$ to be the sum of the authority scores of all pages that it points to.

Notice how a single application of the Authority Update Rule (starting from a setting in which all scores are initially 1) is simply the original casting of votes by in-links. A single application of the Authority Update Rule followed by a single application of the Hub Update Rule produces the results of the original list-finding technique. In general, the principle of repeated improvement says that, to obtain better estimates, we should simply apply these rules in alternating fashion, as follows:

- We start with all hub scores and all authority scores equal to 1.
- We choose a number of steps, k.
- We then perform a sequence of k hub–authority updates. Each update works as follows:
  - First apply the Authority Update Rule to the current set of scores.
  - Then apply the Hub Update Rule to the resulting set of scores.
- At the end, the hub and authority scores may involve numbers that are very large. However, we only care about their relative sizes, so we can *normalize* to make them smaller: we divide down each authority score by the sum of all authority scores, and divide down each hub score by the sum of all hub scores. (For example, Figure 14.4 shows the result of normalizing the authority scores that we determined in Figure 14.3.)

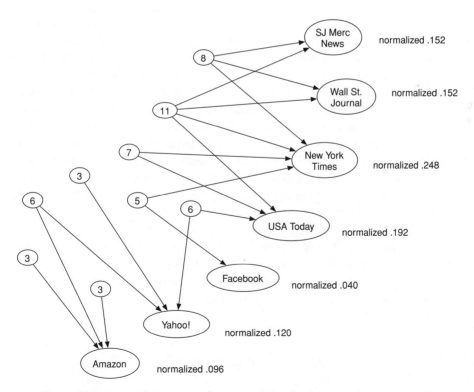

Figure 14.4. Reweighting votes after normalizing for the query "newspapers."

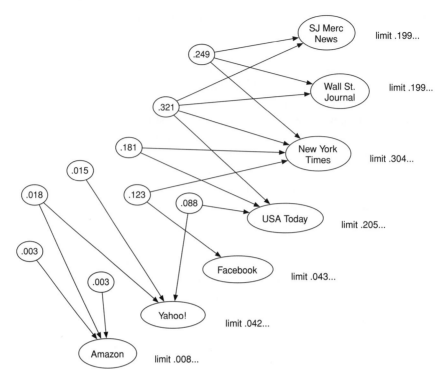

Figure 14.5. Limiting hub and authority values for the query "newspapers."

What happens if we do this for larger and larger values of k? It turns out that the normalized values actually converge to limits as k goes to infinity: in other words, the results stabilize so that continued improvement leads to smaller and smaller changes in the values we observe. We won't prove this right now, but we provide a proof in Section 14.6 at the end of this chapter. Moreover, the analysis in that section shows that something even deeper is going on: except for a few rare cases (characterized by a certain kind of degenerate property of the link structure), we reach the same limiting values no matter what we choose as the *initial* hub and authority values, provided only that all of them are positive. In other words, the limiting hub and authority values are purely a property of the link structure, not of the initial estimates we use to start the process of computing them. (For the record, the limiting values for our "newspapers" example are shown, to three decimal places, in Figure 14.5.)

Ultimately, what these limiting values correspond to is a kind of equilibrium: their relative sizes remain unchanged if we apply the Authority Update Rule or the Hub Update Rule. As such, they reflect the balance between hubs and authorities that provided the initial intuition for them: your authority score is proportional to the hub scores of the pages that point to you, and your hub score is proportional to the authority scores of the pages you point to.

14.3 PageRank

The intuition behind hubs and authorities is based on the idea that pages play multiple roles in the network, and in particular that pages can play a powerful endorsement role without themselves being heavily endorsed. For queries with a commercial aspect – such as our query for newspapers in the previous section, or searches for particular products to purchase, or more generally searches that are designed to yield corporate pages of any type – there is a natural basis for this intuition. Competing firms do not link to each other, except in unusual circumstances, and so they can't be viewed as directly endorsing each other; rather, the only way to conceptually pull them together is through a set of hub pages that link to all of them at once.

In other settings on the Web, however, endorsement is best viewed as passing directly from one prominent page to another – a page is important if it is cited by other important pages. This is often the dominant mode of endorsement, for example, among academic or governmental pages, among bloggers, or among personal pages more generally. It is also the dominant mode in the scientific literature. And it is this mode of endorsement that forms the basis for the PageRank measure of importance [79].

As with hubs and authorities, the intuition behind PageRank starts with simple voting based on in-links, and refines it using the principle of repeated improvement. In particular, the principle is applied here by having nodes repeatedly pass endorsements across their outgoing links, with the weight of a node's endorsement based on the current estimate of its PageRank: nodes that are currently viewed as more important get to make stronger endorsements.

The Basic Definition of PageRank. Intuitively, we can think of PageRank as a kind of "fluid" that circulates through the network, passing from node to node across edges and pooling at the nodes that are the most important. Specifically, PageRank is computed as follows.

- In a network with n nodes, we assign all nodes the same initial PageRank, $1/n$.
- We choose a number of steps, k.
- We then perform a sequence of k *updates* to the PageRank values, using the following rule for each update:

> *Basic PageRank Update Rule:* Each page divides its current PageRank equally across its outgoing links and passes these equal shares to the pages it points to. (If a page has no outgoing links, it passes all its current PageRank to itself.) Each page updates its new PageRank to be the sum of the shares it receives.

Notice that the total PageRank in the network will remain constant as we apply these steps: since each page takes its PageRank, divides it up, and passes it along links, PageRank is neither created nor destroyed, just moved around from one node to another. As a result, we don't need to do any normalizing of the numbers to prevent them from growing, the way we had to with hub and authority scores.

As an example, let's consider how this computation works on the collection of 8 Web pages in Figure 14.6. All pages start out with a PageRank of $\frac{1}{8}$, and their PageRank values after the first two updates are given by the following table:

Step	A	B	C	D	E	F	G	H
1	$\frac{1}{2}$	$\frac{1}{16}$	$\frac{1}{16}$	$\frac{1}{16}$	$\frac{1}{16}$	$\frac{1}{16}$	$\frac{1}{16}$	$\frac{1}{8}$
2	$\frac{3}{16}$	$\frac{1}{4}$	$\frac{1}{4}$	$\frac{1}{32}$	$\frac{1}{32}$	$\frac{1}{32}$	$\frac{1}{32}$	$\frac{1}{16}$

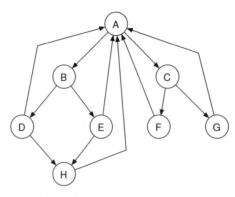

Figure 14.6. A collection of eight pages: page A has the largest PageRank, followed by pages B and C (which collect endorsements from A).

For example, A gets a PageRank of $\frac{1}{2}$ after the first update because it gets all of F's, G's, and H's PageRank, and half each of D's and E's. On the other hand, B and C each get half of A's PageRank, so they only get $\frac{1}{16}$ each in the first step. But once A acquires a lot of PageRank, B and C benefit in the next step. This is in keeping with the principle of repeated improvement: after the first update causes us to estimate that A is an important page, we weigh its endorsement more highly in the next update.

Equilibrium Values of PageRank. As with hub–authority computations, one can prove that, except in certain degenerate special cases, the PageRank values of all nodes converge to limiting values as the number of update steps, k, goes to infinity.

Because PageRank is conserved throughout the computation – with the total Page-Rank in the network equal to 1 – the limit of the process has a simple interpretation. We can think of the limiting PageRank values, one value for each node, as exhibiting the following kind of *equilibrium*: if we take the limiting PageRank values and apply one step of the Basic PageRank Update Rule, then the values at every node remain the same. In other words, the limiting PageRank values regenerate themselves exactly when they are updated. This description gives a simple way to check whether an assignment of numbers to a set of Web pages forms such an equilibrium set of PageRank values: we check that they sum to 1, and we check that when we apply the Basic PageRank Update Rule, we get the same values back.

For example, on the network of Web pages from Figure 14.6, we can check that the values shown in Figure 14.7 have the desired equilibrium property: assigning a PageRank of $\frac{4}{13}$ to page A, $\frac{2}{13}$ to each of B and C, and $\frac{1}{13}$ to the five other pages achieves this equilibrium.

Now, depending on the network structure, the set of limiting values may not be the only values that exhibit this kind of equilibrium. However, one can show that if the network is strongly connected – that is, each node can reach each other node by a directed path, following the definition from Chapter 13 – then there is a unique set of equilibrium values, and so whenever limiting PageRank values exist, they are the only values that satisfy this equilibrium.

Scaling the Definition of PageRank. There is a difficulty with the basic definition of PageRank, however: in many networks, the "wrong" nodes can end up with all the

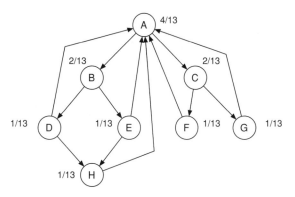

Figure 14.7. Equilibrium PageRank values for the network of eight Web pages from Figure 14.6.

PageRank. Fortunately, there is a simple and natural way to fix this problem, yielding the actual definition of PageRank that is used in practice. Let's first describe the problem and then its solution.

To trigger the problem, suppose we take the network in Figure 14.6 and make a small change, so that F and G now point to each other rather than pointing to A. The result is shown in Figure 14.8. Clearly this ought to weaken A somewhat, but in fact a much more extreme thing happens: PageRank that flows from C to F and G can never circulate back into the rest of the network, and so the links out of C function as a kind of "slow leak" that eventually causes all the PageRank to end up at F and G. We can indeed check that by repeatedly running the Basic PageRank Update Rule, we converge to PageRank values of $\frac{1}{2}$ for each of F and G, and 0 for all other nodes.

This is clearly not what we wanted, but it's an inevitable consequence of the definition. And it becomes a problem in almost any real network to which PageRank is applied: as long as there are small sets of nodes that can be reached from the rest of the graph, but have no paths back, then PageRank will accumulate there.[1] Fortunately, there is a simple and natural way to modify the definition of PageRank to get around this problem, and it follows from the "fluid" intuition for PageRank. Specifically, if we think about the (admittedly simplistic) question of why all the water on earth doesn't inexorably run downhill and reside exclusively at the lowest points, it's because there's a counterbalancing process at work: water also evaporates and gets rained back down at higher elevations.

We can use this idea here. We pick a *scaling factor s* that should be strictly between 0 and 1. We then replace the Basic PageRank Update Rule with the following:

> *Scaled PageRank Update Rule:* First apply the Basic PageRank Update Rule. Then scale down all PageRank values by a factor of *s*. This means that the total PageRank in the network has shrunk from 1 to *s*. We divide the residual $1 - s$ units of PageRank equally over all nodes, giving $(1 - s)/n$ to each.

---

[1] If we think back to the bow-tie structure of the Web from Chapter 13, there is a way to describe the problem in those terms as well: there are many "slow leaks" out of the giant strongly connected component (SCC), and so in the limit, all nodes in the giant SCC will get PageRank values of 0; instead, all the PageRank will end up in the set OUT of downstream nodes.

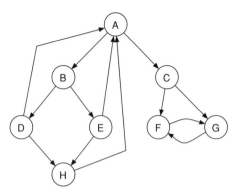

Figure 14.8. The same collection of eight pages, but F and G have changed their links to point to each other instead of to A. Without a smoothing effect, all the PageRank would go to F and G.

This rule also preserves the total PageRank in the network, since it is just based on redistribution according to a different "water cycle" that evaporates $1 - s$ units of PageRank in each step and rains it down uniformly across all nodes.

The Limit of the Scaled PageRank Update Rule. One can show that repeated application of the Scaled PageRank Update Rule converges to a set of limiting PageRank values as the number of updates, k, goes to infinity. Moreover, for any network, these limiting values form the unique equilibrium for the Scaled PageRank Update Rule: they are the unique set of values that remain unchanged under the application of this update rule. Notice, of course, that these values depend on our choice of the scaling factor s: in effect, there is really a different update rule for each possible value of s.

This is the version of PageRank that is used in practice, with a scaling factor s that is usually chosen to be between 0.8 and 0.9.[2] The use of the scaling factor also turns out to make the PageRank measure less sensitive to the addition or deletion of small numbers of nodes or links [268, 422].

Random Walks: An Equivalent Definition of PageRank. To conclude our discussion in this section, we now describe an equivalent formulation of PageRank that looks quite different on the surface, but in fact leads to exactly the same definition.

It works as follows. Consider someone who is randomly browsing a network of Web pages, such as the one in Figure 14.6. They start by choosing a page at random, picking each page with equal probability. They then follow links for a sequence of k steps: in each step, they pick a random outgoing link from their current page and follow it to where it leads. (If their current page has no outgoing links, they just stay where they

---

[2] As an aside about our earlier motivating example, one can check that using a value of s in this range doesn't completely fix the problem with Figure 14.8: nodes F and G still get most (though no longer all) of the PageRank under the scaled update rule with such values of s. The problem is that an eight-node example is simply too small for the redistribution of the PageRank to truly offset the problem of a slow leak into a dead-end region of the network: on only eight nodes, a "slow leak" isn't actually so slow. However, on large networks such as are used in real applications, the redistribution of PageRank works well to give very small limiting PageRank values to most nodes outside the giant strongly connected component of the network.

are.) Such an exploration of nodes performed by randomly following links is called a *random walk* on the network. We should stress that this is not meant to be an accurate model of an actual person exploring the Web; rather it is a thought experiment that leads to a particular definition.

In Section 14.6, we analyze this random walk and show the following fact.

> *Claim:* The probability of being at a page X after k steps of this random walk is precisely the PageRank of X after k applications of the Basic PageRank Update Rule.

Given that the two formulations of PageRank – based on repeated improvement and random walks, respectively – are equivalent, we do not strictly speaking gain anything at a formal level by having this new definition. But the analysis in terms of random walks provides some additional intuition for PageRank as a measure of importance: the PageRank of a page X is the limiting probability that a random walk across hyperlinks will end up at X as we run the walk for larger and larger numbers of steps.

This equivalent definition using random walks also provides a new and sometimes useful perspective for thinking about some of the issues that came up earlier in the section. For example, the "leakage" of PageRank to nodes F and G in Figure 14.8 has a natural interpretation in terms of the random walk on the network. In the limit, as the walk runs for more and more steps, the probability of the walk reaching F or G is converging to 1, and once it reaches either F or G, it is stuck at these two nodes forever. Thus, the limiting probabilities of being at F and G are converging to $\frac{1}{2}$ each, and the limiting probabilities are converging to 0 for all other nodes.

We will also show in Section 14.6 how to formulate the Scaled PageRank Update Rule in terms of random walks. Rather than simply following a random edge in each step, the walker performs a "scaled" version of the walk as follows. With probability s, the walker follows a random edge as before; with probability $1 - s$, the walker jumps to a random node anywhere in the network, choosing each node with equal probability.

14.4 Applying Link Analysis in Modern Web Search

The link analysis ideas described in Sections 14.2 and 14.3 have played an integral role in the ranking functions of the current generation of Web search engines, including Google, Yahoo!, Microsoft's search engine Bing, and Ask. In the late 1990s, it was possible to produce reasonable rankings using these link analysis methods almost directly on top of conventional search techniques, but with the growth and enormously expanding diversity of Web content since then, link analysis ideas have been extended and generalized considerably, so that they are now used in a wide range of different ways inside the ranking functions of modern search engines.

It is difficult to say anything completely concrete about the current ranking functions of the main search engines, given that they are constantly evolving in complexity, and given that the search engine companies themselves are extremely secretive about what goes into their ranking functions. (There are good reasons for this secrecy, as we will discuss later.) But we can make general observations coupled with sentiments that represent the conventional wisdom of the search community. In particular, PageRank was one of the original and central ingredients of Google, and it has always been a core component of Google's methodology. The importance of PageRank as a feature in Google's ranking function has long been claimed to be declining over time, however. For example, in 2003 and 2004, a significant overhaul of Google's ranking function was generally believed to involve non-PageRank styles of link analysis, including a method called Hilltop developed by Krishna Bharat and George Mihaila [58] as an extension of the two-sided form of endorsement behind hubs and authorities. Around a similar time period, the search engine Ask rebuilt its ranking function around hubs and authorities, though its recent extensions have increasingly blended this with many other features as well.

Combining Links, Text, and Usage Data. While our emphasis on link analysis in this chapter is meant to motivate the ideas in a clean setting, in practice one clearly needs to closely integrate information from both network structure and textual content in order to produce the highest-quality search results. One particularly effective way to combine text and links for ranking is through the analysis of *anchor text*, the highlighted bits of clickable text that activate a hyperlink leading to another page [102]. Anchor text can be a highly succinct and effective description of the page residing at the other end of a link; for example, if you read "I am a student at Cornell University" on someone's Web page, it's a good guess that clicking on the highlighted link associated with the text "Cornell University" will take you to a page that is in some way about Cornell.[3]

In fact, the link analysis methods we have been describing can be easily extended to incorporate textual features such as anchor text. In particular, the basic forms of both hubs and authorities and PageRank perform updates simply by adding up values across links. But if certain links have highly relevant anchor text while others don't, we can weight the contributions of the relevant links more heavily than the others; for example, as we pass hub or authority scores, or PageRank values, across a link, we can multiply them by a factor that indicates the quality of the anchor text on the link [57, 102].

In addition to text and links, search engines use many other features as well. For example, the way in which users choose to click or not click on a search result conveys a lot of information: if, among a search engine's ranked results for the query "Cornell," most users skip the first result and click on the second, it suggests that the first two results should potentially be reordered. There is ongoing research on methods for tuning search results based on this type of feedback [228].

A Moving Target. A final important aspect of Web search serves to illustrate a basic game-theoretic principle that we have encountered many times already – that you should always expect the world to react to what you do. As search grew into the dominant means of accessing information on the Web, it mattered to a lot of people whether they ranked highly in search engine results. For example, many small companies had business models that increasingly depended on showing up among the first screen of

---

[3] Of course, not all anchor text is useful; consider the ubiquitous bit of Web page text, "For more information, click here." Such examples make you realize that creating useful anchor text is an aspect of hypertext authoring style worth paying attention to.

Google's results for common queries ranging from "Caribbean vacations" to "vintage records." An update to Google's ranking function that pushed them off the first screen could spell financial ruin. Indeed, search-industry publications began naming some of Google's more significant updates to its core ranking function in the alphabetic style usually reserved for hurricanes; the analogy was an apt one, since each of these updates was an unpredictable act of nature (in this case, Google) that inflicted millions of dollars of economic damage.

With this in mind, people who depended on the success of their Web sites increasingly began modifying their Web-page authoring styles to score highly in search engine rankings. For people who had conceived of Web search as a kind of classical information retrieval application, this was something novel. Back in the 1970s and 1980s, when people designed information retrieval tools for scientific papers or newspaper articles, authors were not overtly writing their papers or abstracts with these search tools in mind.[4] From the relatively early days of the Web, however, people have written Web pages with search engines quite explicitly in mind. At first, this was often done using over-the-top tricks that aroused the ire of the search industry; as the digital librarian Cliff Lynch noted at the time, "Web search is a new kind of information retrieval application in that the documents are actively behaving badly."

Over time, though, the use of focused techniques to improve a page's performance in search engine rankings became regularized and accepted, and guidelines for designing these techniques emerged; a fairly large industry known as *search engine optimization* (SEO) came into being, consisting of search experts who advise companies on how to create pages and sites that rank highly. And so, to return to the game-theoretic view, the growth of SEO followed naturally once search became such a widespread application on the Web; it simply mattered too much to too many people that they be easily findable through search.

These developements have had several consequences. First, for search engines, the "perfect" ranking function will always be a moving target: if a search engine maintains the same method of ranking for too long, Web-page authors and their consultants become too effective at reverse-engineering the important features, and the search engine is in effect no longer in control of what ranks highly. Second, search engines are incredibly secretive about the internals of their ranking functions – not just to prevent competing search engines from finding out what they're doing, but also to prevent designers of Web sites from finding out.

And finally, with so much money at stake, the search industry turned these developments into a very successful business model based on advertising. Rather than simply showing results computed by a ranking function, the search engine offered additional slots on the main results page through a market in which sites could pay for placement. Thus, when you look at a search results page today, you see the results computed by the ranking function alongside the paid results. We have just seen some of the ideas behind ranking functions; the paid results, as we will see in the next chapter, are allocated using the kinds of matching markets discussed in Chapter 10.

---

[4] Of course, one can argue that, at a much less overt level, the development of standard authoring styles in these domains has been motivated by the goal of making these kinds of documents easier to classify and organize.

14.5 Applications beyond the Web

Link analysis techniques of the kind we've been discussing have been applied to a wide range of other settings, both before and after their use on the Web. In essentially any domain where information is connected by a network structure, it becomes natural to infer measures of authority from the patterns of links.

Citation Analysis. As we discussed in Chapters 2 and 13, the study of citations among scientific papers and journals has a long history that significantly predates the Web [145]. A standard measure in this field is Garfield's *impact factor* for a scientific journal [177], defined to be the average number of citations received by a paper in the given journal over the past two years. This type of voting by in-links can thus serve as a proxy for the collective attention that the scientific community pays to papers published in the journal.

In the 1970s, Pinski and Narin [341] extended the impact factor by taking into account the idea that not all citations should be counted equally; rather, citations from journals that are themselves of high impact should be viewed as more important. This can be viewed as a use of the principle of repeated improvement, in the context of the scientific literature, just as we've seen it used for Web-page ranking. Pinski and Narin used this to formulate a notion of *influence weights* for journals [180, 341] that is defined very similarly to the notion of PageRank for Web pages.

Link Analysis of U.S. Supreme Court Citations. Recently, researchers have adapted link analysis techniques from the Web to study the network of citations among legal decisions by U.S. courts [166, 377]. Citations are crucial in legal writing – to ground a decision in precedent and to explain the relation of a new decision to what has come before. Using link analysis in this context can help in identifying cases that play especially important roles in the overall citation structure.

In one example of this style of research, Fowler and Jeon [166] applied hub and authority measures to the set of all U.S. Supreme Court decisions, a collection of documents that spans more than two centuries. They found that the set of Supreme Court decisions with high authority scores in the citation network align well with the more qualitative judgments of legal experts about the Court's most important decisions. This set includes some cases that acquired significant authority according to numerical measures shortly after they appeared, but which took much longer to gain recognition from the legal community.

Supreme Court decisions also provide a rich setting for looking at how authority can change over long time periods. For example, Fowler and Jeon analyzed the rising and falling authority of some of the key Fifth Amendment cases from the twentieth century, as illustrated in Figure 14.9. In particular, *Brown v. Mississippi* – a 1936 case concerning confessions obtained under torture – began rising rapidly in authority in the early 1960s as the Warren Court forcefully took on a range of issues surrounding due process and self-incrimination. This development ultimately led to the landmark case *Miranda v. Arizona* in 1966 and – with this clear precedent established – the need for citations to *Brown v. Mississippi* quickly declined as the authority of *Miranda* shot upward.

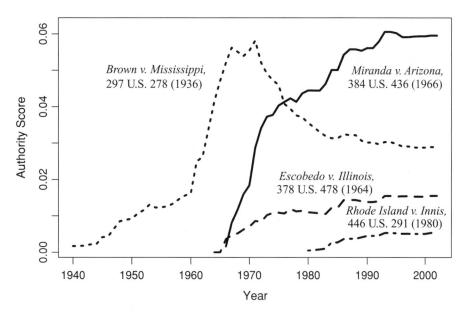

Figure 14.9. The rising and falling authority of key Fifth Amendment cases from the twentieth century illustrates some of the relationships among them. (Image from [166], courtesy of Elsevier Science and Technology Journals)

The analysis of Supreme Court citations also shows that significant decisions can vary widely in the rate at which they acquire authority. For example, Figure 14.10 (also from [166]) shows that *Roe v. Wade* – like *Miranda* – grew in authority very rapidly from the time it was first issued. On the other hand, the equally consequential *Brown v. Board of Education* only began acquiring significant authority in the citation network roughly a decade after it was issued. Fowler and Jeon argue that this trajectory aligns with legal scholars' views of the case, writing, "Judicial specialists often point

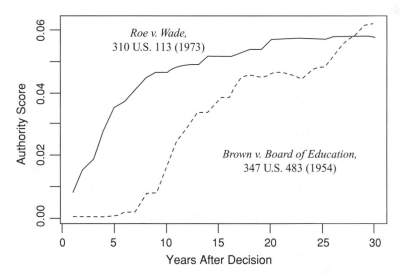

Figure 14.10. *Roe v. Wade* and *Brown v. Board of Education* acquired authority at very different speeds. (Image from [166], courtesy of Elsevier Science and Technology Journals)

towards the ruling issued in *Brown* as an example of a precedent that was legally weak when first issued, and was strengthened through the Civil Rights Act of 1964 and its application in subsequent civil rights cases" [166].

This style of analysis thus shows how a strictly network-based analysis of a topic as intricate as legal precedent can reveal subtleties that align well with the views of the scholarly community. It also indicates some of the interesting effects that emerge when one tries to track the rising and falling pattern of authority in a complex domain – an activity that stands to provide important insights in many other settings as well.

14.6 Advanced Material: Spectral Analysis, Random Walks, and Web Search

We now discuss how to analyze the methods for computing hub, authority, and Page-Rank values. This analysis will require some basic familiarity with matrices and vectors. Building on this, we will show that the limiting values of these link-analysis measures can be interpreted as coordinates in eigenvectors of certain matrices derived from the underlying networks. The use of eigenvalues and eigenvectors to study the structure of networks is often referred to as the *spectral analysis* of graphs, and we will see that this theory forms a natural language for discussing the outcome of methods based on repeated improvement.

A. Spectral Analysis of Hubs and Authorities

Our first main goal is to show why the hub–authority computation converges to limiting values for the hub and authority scores, as claimed in Section 14.2. As a first important step in this process, we show how to write the Authority Update and Hub Update Rules from that section as matrix–vector multiplications.

Adjacency Matrices and Hub–Authority Vectors. We will view a set of n pages as a set of nodes in a directed graph. Given this set of nodes, labeled $1, 2, 3, \ldots, n$, let's encode the links among them in an $n \times n$ matrix M as follows: the entry in the ith row and jth column of M, denoted M_{ij}, is equal to 1 if there is a link from node i to node j, and it is equal to 0 otherwise. We call this the *adjacency matrix* of the network. Figure 14.11 shows an example of a directed graph and its adjacency matrix. Given a large set of pages, we expect that most of them will have very few out-links relative to the total number of pages, and so most entries in the adjacency matrix will be equal to 0. As a result, the adjacency matrix is not necessarily a very efficient way to represent the network, but as we will see, it is conceptually very useful.

Now, since the hub and authority scores are lists of numbers – one associated with each of the n nodes of the network – we can represent them simply as vectors in n dimensions, where the ith coordinate gives the hub or authority score of node i. Specifically, we write h for the vector of hub scores, where h_i is equal to the hub score of node i, and we similarly write a for the vector of authority scores.

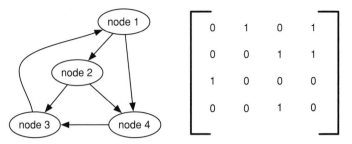

Figure 14.11. The directed hyperlinks among Web pages can be represented using an *adjacency matrix* M: the entry M_{ij} is equal to 1 if there is a link from node i to node j; otherwise, $M_{ij} = 0$.

Hub and Authority Update Rules as Matrix–Vector Multiplication. Let's consider the Hub Update Rule in terms of the notation we've just defined. For a node i, its hub score h_i is updated to be the sum of a_j over all nodes j to which i has an edge. Note that these nodes j are precisely the ones for which $M_{ij} = 1$. Thus, we can write the update rule as

$$h_i \leftarrow M_{i1}a_1 + M_{i2}a_2 + \cdots + M_{in}a_n, \tag{14.1}$$

where we use the notation "$\leftarrow$" to mean that the quantity on the left-hand side is updated to become the quantity on the right-hand side. This is a correct way to write the update rule, since the values M_{ij} as multipliers select out precisely the authority values that we wish to sum.

But Equation (14.1) corresponds exactly to the definition of matrix-vector multiplication, so we can write it in the following equivalent way:

$$h \leftarrow Ma.$$

Figure 14.12 shows this for the example from Figure 14.11: the authority scores (2, 6, 4, 3) lead to the hub scores (9, 7, 2, 4) via the Hub Update Rule. Indeed, this is an example of a general principle: if you're updating a collection of variables according to a rule that selects out certain ones to add up, you can often write this update rule as a matrix–vector multiplication for a suitably chosen matrix and vector.

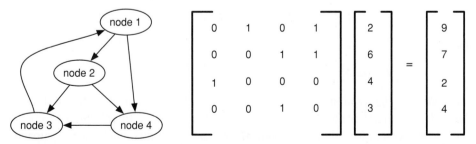

Figure 14.12. By representing the link structure using an adjacency matrix, the Hub and Authority Update Rules become matrix-vector multiplication. In this example, we show how multiplication by a vector of authority scores produces a new vector of hub scores.

Specifying the Authority Update Rule in this style is strictly analogous, except that the scores flow in the other direction across the edges. That is, a_i is updated to be the sum of h_j over all nodes j that have an edge to i, so

$$a_i \leftarrow M_{1i}h_1 + M_{2i}h_2 + \cdots + M_{ni}h_n. \tag{14.2}$$

This too corresponds to a matrix–vector multiplication, but using a matrix where the entries have all been "reflected" so that the roles of rows and columns are interchanged. This can be specified using the *transpose* of the matrix M, denoted M^T and defined by the property that the (i, j) entry of M^T is the (j, i) entry of M; that is, $M_{ij}^T = M_{ji}$. Then Equation (14.2) corresponds to the update rule

$$a \leftarrow M^T h.$$

Unwinding the k-Step Hub–Authority Computation. Thus far we have discussed a single application of each of the update rules. What happens when we perform the k-step hub–authority computation for some large value of k?

We start with initial vectors of authority and hub scores that we denote $a^{(0)}$ and $h^{(0)}$, each of them equal to the vector whose coordinates are all 1. Now, let $a^{(k)}$ and $h^{(k)}$ denote the vectors of authority and hub scores after k applications of the Authority and then Hub Update Rules in order, as in Section 14.2. If we simply follow the preceding formulas, we first find that

$$a^{(1)} = M^T h^{(0)}$$

and

$$h^{(1)} = Ma^{(1)} = MM^T h^{(0)}.$$

That's the result of the one-step hub–authority computation. In the second step, we therefore get

$$a^{(2)} = M^T h^{(1)} = M^T MM^T h^{(0)}$$

and

$$h^{(2)} = Ma^{(2)} = MM^T MM^T h^{(0)} = (MM^T)^2 h^{(0)}.$$

One more step makes the pattern clear:

$$a^{(3)} = M^T h^{(2)} = M^T MM^T MM^T h^{(0)} = (M^T M)^2 M^T h^{(0)}$$

and

$$h^{(3)} = Ma^{(3)} = MM^T MM^T MM^T h^{(0)} = (MM^T)^3 h^{(0)}.$$

Proceeding for larger numbers of steps, then, we find that $a^{(k)}$ and $h^{(k)}$ are products of the terms M and M^T in alternating order, where the expression for $a^{(k)}$ begins with M^T and the expression for $h^{(k)}$ begins with M. We can write this much more compactly as

$$a^{(k)} = (M^T M)^{k-1} M^T h^{(0)}$$

and

$$h^{(k)} = (MM^T)^k h^{(0)}.$$

So that's a direct picture of what's happening in the k-step hub–authority computation: the authority and hub vectors are the results of multiplying an initial vector by larger and larger powers of $M^T M$ and MM^T, respectively. We now consider why this process converges to stable values.

Thinking About Multiplication in Terms of Eigenvectors. Let's keep in mind that, because the actual magnitudes of the hub and authority values tend to grow with each update, they only converge when we take normalization into account. To put it another way, it is the *directions* of the hub and authority vectors that are converging. Concretely, what we will show is that there are constants c and d such that the sequences of vectors $\dfrac{h^{(k)}}{c^k}$ and $\dfrac{a^{(k)}}{d^k}$ converge to limits as k goes to infinity.

We talk first about the sequence of hub vectors, and then we consider the authority vectors largely by pursuing a direct analogy to the analysis of hub vectors. If

$$\frac{h^{(k)}}{c^k} = \frac{(MM^T)^k h^{(0)}}{c^k}$$

is going to converge to a limit $h^{(*)}$, what properties do we expect $h^{(*)}$ to have? Because the direction is converging, we expect at the limit that the direction of $h^{(*)}$ shouldn't change when it is multiplied by (MM^T), although its length may grow by a factor of c. That is, we expect that $h^{(*)}$ should satisfy the equation

$$(MM^T)h^{(*)} = ch^{(*)}.$$

Any vector satisfying this property – that it doesn't change direction when multiplied by a given matrix – is called an *eigenvector* of the matrix, and the scaling constant c is called the *eigenvalue* corresponding to the eigenvector. So we expect that $h^{(*)}$ should be an eigenvector of the matrix MM^T, with c a corresponding eigenvalue. We now prove that the sequence of vectors $\dfrac{h^{(k)}}{c^k}$ indeed converges to an eigenvector of MM^T.

To prove this, we use the following basic fact about matrices. We say that a square matrix A is *symmetric* if it remains the same after transposing it: $A_{ij} = A_{ji}$ for each choice of i and j, or in other words $A = A^T$. The fact we will use is the following [268]:

> Any symmetric matrix A with n rows and n columns has a set of n eigenvectors that are all unit vectors and all mutually orthogonal; that is, they form a *basis* for the space $\mathbf{R}^n$.

Since MM^T is symmetric, we can apply this fact to it. Let's write the resulting mutually orthogonal eigenvectors as $z_1, z_2, \ldots, z_n$, with corresponding eigenvalues $c_1, c_2, \ldots, c_n$, respectively, and let's order the eigenvalues so that $|c_1| \geq |c_2| \geq \cdots \geq |c_n|$. Furthermore, to make things simpler in this explanation, let's suppose that $|c_1| > |c_2|$. (This essentially always happens in link analysis applications; later we explain the small changes that need to be made in the discussion if this assumption does not hold.) Now, given any vector x, a good way to think about the matrix–vector product

$(MM^T)x$ is to first write x as a linear combination of the vectors $z_1, \ldots, z_n$. That is, with $x = p_1 z_1 + p_2 z_2 + \cdots + p_n z_n$ for coefficients $p_1, \ldots, p_n$, we have

$$(MM^T)x = (MM^T)(p_1 z_1 + p_2 z_2 + \cdots + p_n z_n)$$
$$= p_1 MM^T z_1 + p_2 MM^T z_2 + \cdots + p_n MM^T z_n$$
$$= p_1 c_1 z_1 + p_2 c_2 z_2 + \cdots + p_n c_n z_n,$$

where the third equality follows from the fact that each z_i is an eigenvector.

What this says is that $z_1, z_2, \ldots, z_n$ is a very useful set of coordinate axes for representing x: multiplication by MM^T consists simply of replacing each term $p_i z_i$ in the representation of x by $c_i p_i z_i$. We now see how this makes it easy to analyze multiplication by larger powers of MM^T, which will be the last step we need for showing convergence.

Convergence of the Hub–Authority Computation. We've seen that, when we take any vector x and write it in the form $p_1 z_1 + \cdots + p_n z_n$, multiplication by MM^T produces $c_1 p_1 z_1 + \cdots + c_n p_n z_n$. When we multiply repeatedly by MM^T, each successive multiplication introduces an additional factor of c_i in front of the ith term. Therefore, we have

$$(MM^T)^k x = c_1^k p_1 z_1 + c_2^k p_2 z_2 + \cdots + c_n^k p_n z_n.$$

Now let's think of this in the context of the vectors of hub scores, where $h^{(k)} = (MM)^T h^{(0)}$. Recall that $h^{(0)}$ is just the fixed starting vector in which each coordinate is equal to 1; it can be represented in terms of the basis vectors $z_1, \ldots, z_n$ as some linear combination $h^{(0)} = q_1 z_1 + q_2 z_2 \cdots + q_n z_n$. So

$$h^{(k)} = (MM^T)^k h^{(0)} = c_1^k q_1 z_1 + c_2^k q_2 z_2 + \cdots + c_n^k q_n z_n, \qquad (14.3)$$

and if we divide both sides by c_1^k, then we get

$$\frac{h^{(k)}}{c_1^k} = q_1 z_1 + \left(\frac{c_2}{c_1}\right)^k q_2 z_2 + \cdots + \left(\frac{c_n}{c_1}\right)^k q_n z_n. \qquad (14.4)$$

Recalling our assumption that $|c_1| > |c_2|$ (which we'll relax shortly), we see that, as k goes to infinity, every term but the first on the right-hand side is going to 0. As a result, the sequence of vectors $\dfrac{h^{(k)}}{c_1^k}$ is converging to the limit $q_1 z_1$ as k goes to infinity.

Wrapping Up. We're essentially done at this point, but to round out the picture of convergence, we show two important things. First, we need to make sure that the coefficient q_1 in the preceding argument is not zero, to ensure that the limit $q_1 z_1$ is in fact a nonzero vector in the direction of z_1. Second, we will find that in fact a limit in the direction of z_1 is reached essentially *regardless* of our choice of starting hub scores $h^{(0)}$: it is in this sense that the limiting hub weights are really a function of the network structure, not the starting estimates. We show these two facts in reverse order, considering the second point first.

To begin with, then, let's suppose we initiated the computation of the hub vector from a different starting point: rather than having $h^{(0)}$ be the vector with all coordinates equal to 1, we picked some other starting vector x. Let's suppose only that x has a positive number in each coordinate – we call such a vector a *positive vector*. As we noted before, any vector x can be written as $x = p_1 z_1 + \cdots + p_n z_n$, for some choice of multipliers $p_1, \ldots, p_n$, and so $(MM^T)^k x = c_1^k p_1 z_1 + \cdots + c_n^k p_n z_n$. Then $h^{(k)}/c_1^k$ is converging to $p_1 z_1$ – in other words, it is still converging to a vector in the direction of z_1 even with this new choice for the starting vector $h^{(0)} = x$.

Now, let's show why q_1 and p_1 above are not zero (and, hence, that the limits are nonzero vectors). Given any vector x, there is an easy way to think about the value of p_1 in its representation as $x = p_1 z_1 + \cdots + p_n z_n$: we just compute the inner product of z_1 and x. Indeed, since the vectors $z_1, \ldots, z_n$ are all mutually orthogonal, we have

$$z_1 \cdot x = z_1 \cdot (p_1 z_1 + \cdots p_n z_n) = p_1(z_1 \cdot z_1) + p_2(z_1 \cdot z_2) + \cdots + p_n(z_1 \cdot z_n) = p_1,$$

since all terms in the last sum are 0 except for $p_1(z_1 \cdot z_1) = p_1$. Because p_1 is just the inner product of x and z_1, we see that our sequence of hub vectors converges to a nonzero vector in the direction of z_1 provided only that our starting hub vector $h^{(0)} = x$ is not orthogonal to z_1.

We now argue that no positive vector can be orthogonal to z_1, which will conclude the picture of convergence that we've been seeking to establish. The argument works via the following steps.

1. It is not possible for every positive vector to be orthogonal to z_1, and so there is some positive vector x for which $(MM^T)^k x/c_1^k$ converges to a nonzero vector $p_1 z_1$.
2. Since the expressions for $(MM^T)^k x/c_1^k$ only involve nonnegative numbers, and their values converge to $p_1 z_1$, it must be that $p_1 z_1$ has only nonnegative coordinates, and $p_1 z_1$ must have at least one positive coordinate, because it is not equal to zero.
3. So if we consider the inner product of any positive vector with $p_1 z_1$, the result must be positive. Hence, we conclude that *no* positive vector can be orthogonal to z_1. This establishes that in fact the sequence of hub vectors converges to a vector in the direction of z_1 when we start from *any* positive vector (including the all-ones vector), which is what we wanted to show.

This is pretty much the complete story, with the only loose end being our assumption that $|c_1| > |c_2|$. Let's now relax this assumption. In general, there may be $\ell > 1$ eigenvalues that are tied for the largest absolute value: we can have $|c_1| = \cdots = |c_\ell|$, and then eigenvalues $c_{\ell+1}, \ldots, c_n$ are all smaller in absolute value. Although we won't go through all the details here, it is not hard to show that all the eigenvalues of MM^T are nonnegative, so in fact we have $c_1 = \cdots = c_\ell > c_{\ell+1} \geq \cdots \geq c_n \geq 0$. In this case, going back to Equations (14.3) and (14.4), we have

$$\frac{h^{(k)}}{c_1^k} = \frac{c_1^k q_1 z_1 + \cdots + c_n^k q_n z_n}{c_1^k}$$

$$= q_1 z_1 + \cdots + q_\ell z_\ell + \left(\frac{c_{\ell+1}}{c_1}\right)^k q_{\ell+1} z_{\ell+1} + \cdots + \left(\frac{c_n}{c_1}\right)^k q_n z_n.$$

Terms $\ell + 1$ through n of this sum go to zero, and so the sequence converges to $q_1 z_1 + \cdots + q_\ell z_\ell$. Thus, when $c_1 = c_2$, we still have convergence, but the limit to which

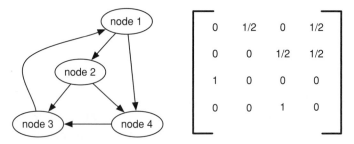

Figure 14.13. The flow of PageRank under the Basic PageRank Update Rule can be represented using a matrix N derived from the adjacency matrix M: the entry N_{ij} specifies the portion of i's PageRank that should be passed to j in one update step.

the sequence converges may now depend on the choice of the initial vector $h^{(0)}$ (and particularly its inner product with each of $z_1, \ldots, z_\ell$). We should emphasize, though, that in practice, with real and sufficiently large hyperlink structures, one essentially always gets a matrix M with the property that MM^T has $|c_1| > |c_2|$.

Finally, we observe that even though this whole discussion has been in terms of the sequence of hub vectors, it can be adapted directly to analyze the sequence of authority vectors as well. For the authority vectors, we are looking at powers of $(M^T M)$, and so the basic result is that the vector of authority scores converges to an eigenvector of the matrix $M^T M$ associated with its largest eigenvalue.

B. Spectral Analysis of PageRank

The analysis we've just seen emphasizes how eigenvectors arise naturally as the limits of repeated improvement. We now discuss how PageRank can be similarly analyzed using matrix–vector multiplication and eigenvectors.

Recall that, like hub and authority scores, the PageRank of a node is a numerical quantity that is repeatedly refined using an update rule. Let's start by thinking about the Basic PageRank Update Rule from Section 14.3 and then move on to the scaled version. Under the basic rule, each node takes its current PageRank and divides it equally over all the nodes to which it points. This suggests that the "flow" of PageRank specified by the update rule can be naturally represented using a matrix N as depicted in Figure 14.13: we define N_{ij} to be the share of i's PageRank that j should get in one update step. This means that $N_{ij} = 0$ if i doesn't link to j, and otherwise N_{ij} is the reciprocal of the number of nodes that i points to. In other words, when i links to j, then $N_{ij} = 1/\ell_i$, where ℓ_i is the number of links out of i. (If i has no outgoing links, then we define $N_{ii} = 1$, in keeping with the rule that a node with no outgoing links passes all its PageRank to itself.) In this way, N is similar in spirit to the adjacency matrix M, but with a different definition when i links to j.

Now, let's represent the PageRanks of all nodes using a vector r, where the coordinate r_i is the PageRank of node i. Using this notation, we can write the Basic PageRank Update Rule as

$$r_i \leftarrow N_{1i}r_1 + N_{2i}r_2 + \cdots + N_{ni}r_n. \tag{14.5}$$

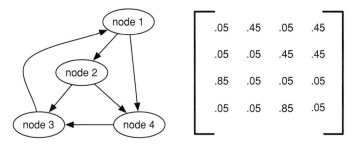

$$\begin{bmatrix} .05 & .45 & .05 & .45 \\ .05 & .05 & .45 & .45 \\ .85 & .05 & .05 & .05 \\ .05 & .05 & .85 & .05 \end{bmatrix}$$

Figure 14.14. The flow of PageRank under the Scaled PageRank Update Rule can also be represented using a matrix derived from the adjacency matrix M (shown here with scaling factor $s = 0.8$). We denote this matrix by $\tilde{N}$; the entry $\tilde{N}_{ij}$ specifies the portion of i's PageRank that should be passed to j in one update step.

This corresponds to multiplication by the transpose of the matrix, just as we saw for the Authority Update Rule; thus, Equation (14.5) can be written as

$$r \leftarrow N^T r. \tag{14.6}$$

The Scaled PageRank Update Rule can be represented in essentially the same way, but with a different matrix $\tilde{N}$ to represent the different flow of PageRank, as indicated in Figure 14.14. Recall that, in the scaled version of the update rule, the updated PageRank is scaled down by a factor of s, and the residual $1 - s$ units are divided equally over all nodes. Thus, we can simply define $\tilde{N}_{ij}$ to be $sN_{ij} + (1 - s)/n$, and then the scaled update rule can be written as

$$r_i \leftarrow \tilde{N}_{1i}r_1 + \tilde{N}_{2i}r_2 + \cdots + \tilde{N}_{ni}r_n \tag{14.7}$$

or equivalently

$$r \leftarrow \tilde{N}^T r. \tag{14.8}$$

Repeated Improvement Using the Scaled PageRank Update Rule. As we apply the scaled update rule repeatedly, starting from an initial PageRank vector $r^{(0)}$, we produce a sequence of vectors $r^{(1)}, r^{(2)}, \ldots$ where each vector is obtained from the preceding one via multiplication by $\tilde{N}^T$. Thus, unwinding this process, we see that

$$r^{(k)} = (\tilde{N}^T)^k r^{(0)}.$$

Moreover, since PageRank is conserved as it is updated – that is, the sum of the PageRanks at all nodes remains constant through the application of the scaled update rule – we don't have to worry about normalizing these vectors as we proceed.

So by analogy with the limiting values of the hub–authority computation (but with the added fact that normalization isn't needed), one expects that if the Scaled PageRank Update Rule converges to a limiting vector $r^{(*)}$, this limit should satisfy $\tilde{N}^T r^{(*)} = r^{(*)}$; that is, we should expect $r^{(*)}$ to be an eigenvector of $\tilde{N}^T$ with corresponding eigenvalue 1. Such an $r^{(*)}$ has the property that it does not change under further refinements by the Scaled PageRank Update Rule.

In fact, all this turns out to be true: repeated application of the Scaled PageRank Update Rule converges to precisely such an $r^{(*)}$. To prove this, however, we can't use the same approach that we applied in the case of the hub–authority computation: there, the matrices involved (MM^T and $M^T M$) were symmetric, and so they had eigenvalues that were real numbers and orthogonal eigenvectors that formed a basis. In general, for matrices such as $\tilde{N}$ that are not symmetric, the eigenvalues can be complex numbers, and the eigenvectors may have less clean relationships to one another.

Convergence of the Scaled PageRank Update Rule. Fortunately, for matrices such as $\tilde{N}$ in which all entries are positive (i.e., $\tilde{N}_{ij} > 0$ for all entries $\tilde{N}_{ij}$), we can use a powerful result known as *Perron's Theorem* [268]. For our purposes, Perron's Theorem says that any matrix P in which all entries are positive has the following properties.

  (i) P has a real eigenvalue $c > 0$ such that $c > |c'|$ for all other eigenvalues c'.
  (ii) There is an eigenvector y with positive real coordinates corresponding to the largest eigenvalue c, and y is unique up to multiplication by a constant.
  (iii) If the largest eigenvalue c is equal to 1, then, for any starting vector $x \neq 0$ with nonnegative coordinates, the sequence of vectors $P^k x$ converges to a vector in the direction of y as k goes to infinity.

Interpreted in terms of the scaled version of PageRank, Perron's Theorem tells us that there is a unique vector y that remains fixed under the application of the scaled update rule, and that repeated application of the update rule from any starting point converges to y. This vector y thus corresponds to the limiting PageRank values we have been seeking.

C. Formulation of PageRank Using Random Walks

To close this chapter, we consider how to formulate PageRank in terms of a random walk on the nodes of the network, following the discussion at the end of Section 14.3.

First let's make the description of the random walk precise. A walker chooses a starting node at random, picking each node with equal probability. (When a random choice is made with equal probability over the options, we will say it is made *uniformly at random*.) Then, in each step, the walker follows an outgoing link selected uniformly at random from its current node, and it moves to the node that this link points to. In this way, a random path through the graph is constructed one node at a time.

Let's ask the following question: if $b_1, b_2, \ldots, b_n$ denote the probabilities of the walk being at nodes $1, 2, \ldots, n$, respectively, in a given step, what is the probability it will be at node i in the next step? We can answer this by reasoning as follows.

  1. For each node j that links to i, if we are given that the walk is currently at node j, then there is a $1/\ell_j$ chance that it moves from j to i in the next step, where ℓ_j is the number of links out of j.
  2. The walk has to actually be at node j for this to happen, so node j contributes $b_j(1/\ell_j) = b_j/\ell_j$ to the probability of being at i in the next step.
  3. Therefore, summing b_j/ℓ_j over all nodes j that link to i gives the probability that the walk is at b_i in the next step.

So the overall probability that the walk is at i in the next step is the sum of b_j/ℓ_j over all nodes that link to i. We can use the matrix N defined in the analysis of PageRank to write this update to the probability b_i as follows:

$$b_i \leftarrow N_{1i}b_1 + N_{2i}b_2 + \cdots + N_{ni}b_n. \tag{14.9}$$

If we represent the probabilities of being at different nodes using a vector b, where the coordinate b_i is the probability of being at node i, then this update rule can be written using matrix–vector multiplication by analogy with what we did in our earlier analyses:

$$b \leftarrow N^T b. \tag{14.10}$$

What we discover is that this is exactly the same as the Basic PageRank Update Rule from Equation (14.6). Since both PageRank values and random-walk probabilities start out the same (they are initially $1/n$ for all nodes), and they then evolve according to exactly the same rule, they remain the same forever. This justifies the claim that we made in Section 14.3.

> *Claim:* The probability of being at a page X after k steps of this random walk is precisely the PageRank of X after k applications of the Basic PageRank Update Rule.

And this claim makes intuitive sense. Like PageRank, the probability of being at a given node in a random walk is something that gets divided up evenly over all the outgoing links from a given node and then passed on to the nodes at the other ends of these links. In other words, probability and PageRank both flow through the graph according to the same process.

A Scaled Version of the Random Walk. We can also formulate an interpretation of the Scaled PageRank Update Rule in terms of random walks. As suggested at the end of Section 14.3, this modified walk works as follows, for a number $s > 0$: with probability s, the walk follows a random edge as before, and with probability $1 - s$, it jumps to a node chosen uniformly at random.

Again, let's ask the following question: if $b_1, b_2, \ldots, b_n$ denote the probabilities of the walk being at nodes $1, 2, \ldots, n$, respectively, in a given step, what is the probability it will be at node i in the next step? The probability of being at node i is now the sum of sb_j/ℓ_j, over all nodes j that link to i, plus $(1 - s)/n$. If we use the matrix $\tilde{N}$ from our analysis of the Scaled PageRank Update Rule, then we can write the probability update as

$$b_i \leftarrow \tilde{N}_{1i}b_1 + \tilde{N}_{2i}b_2 + \cdots + \tilde{N}_{ni}b_n \tag{14.11}$$

or equivalently

$$b \leftarrow \tilde{N}^T b. \tag{14.12}$$

This is the same as the update rule from Equation (14.8) for the scaled PageRank values. The random-walk probabilities and the scaled PageRank values start at the same initial values, and then they evolve according to the same update, so they remain the same forever. This argument justifies the following claim.

Claim: The probability of being at a page X after k steps of the scaled random walk is precisely the PageRank of X after k applications of the Scaled PageRank Update Rule.

It also establishes that, as we let the number of these scaled random-walk steps go to infinity, the limiting probability of being at a node X is equal to the limiting scaled PageRank value of X.

14.7 Exercises

1. Show the values that you get if you run two rounds of computing hub and authority values on the network of Web pages in Figure 14.15 (i.e., the values computed by the k-step hub–authority computation when we choose the number of steps k to be 2).

   Show the values both before and after the final *normalization* step, in which we divide each authority score by the sum of all authority scores and divide each hub score by the sum of all hub scores. (It's fine to write the normalized scores as fractions rather than decimals.)

2.   (a) Show the values that you get if you run two rounds of computing hub and authority values on the network of Web pages in Figure 14.16 (i.e., the values computed by the k-step hub–authority computation when we choose the number of steps k to be 2).

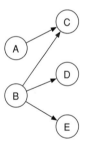

Figure 14.15. A network of Web pages.

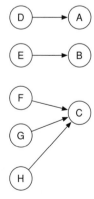

Figure 14.16. A network of Web pages.

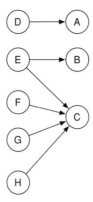

Figure 14.17. A network of Web pages.

Show the values both before and after the final *normalization* step, in which we divide each authority score by the sum of all authority scores and divide each hub score by the sum of all hub scores. (We call the scores obtained after this dividing-down step the *normalized scores*. It's fine to write the normalized scores as fractions rather than decimals.)

(b) Due to the symmetry of nodes A and B in part (a), you should have seen that they get the same authority scores. Now let's look at what happens to the scores when node E, which links to B, decides to link to C as well. This produces the new network of Web pages shown in Figure 14.17.

Similarly to part (a), show the normalized hub and authority values that each node gets when you run the two-step hub–authority computation on the new network in Figure 14.17.

(c) In part (b), which of nodes A or B now has the higher authority score? Give a brief explanation in which you provide some intuition for why the difference in authority scores between A and B in part (b) turned out the way it did.

3. In Chapter 14, we discussed the fact that designers of Web content often reason explicitly about how to create pages that will score highly on search engine rankings. In a scaled-down setting, this question explores some reasoning in that style.

(a) Show the values that you get if you run two rounds of computing hub and authority values on the network of Web pages in Figure 14.18 (i.e., the values computed by the *k*-step hub–authority computation when we choose the number of steps *k* to be 2).

Show the values both before and after the final *normalization* step, in which we divide each authority score by the sum of all authority scores and divide each hub score by the sum of all hub scores. (We call the scores obtained after this dividing-down step the *normalized scores*. It's fine to write the normalized scores as fractions rather than decimals.)

(b) Now we come to the issue of creating pages to achieve large authority scores, given an existing hyperlink structure.

In particular, suppose you wanted to create a new Web page X and add it to the network in Figure 14.18, so that it could achieve a (normalized) authority score that is as large as possible. One thing you might try is

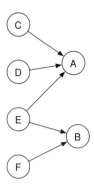

Figure 14.18. A network of Web pages.

to create a second page *Y* as well, so that Y links to X and thus confers authority on it. In doing this, it's natural to wonder whether it helps or hurts X's authority to have Y link to other nodes as well.

Specifically, suppose you add X and Y to the network in Figure 14.18. To add X and Y to this network, one must specify what links they will have. Here are two options; in the first option, Y links only to X, whereas in the second option, Y links to other strong authorities in addition to X.

- *Option 1:* Add new nodes X and Y to Figure 14.18, create a single link from Y to X, and create no links out of X.
- *Option 2:* Add new nodes X and Y to Figure 14.18; create links from Y to each of A, B, and X; and create no links out of X.

For each of these two options, we'd like to know how X fares in terms of its authority score. So, for each option, show the normalized authority values that each of A, B, and X get when you run the two-step hub–authority computation on the resulting network [as in part (a)]. (That is, you should perform the normalization step in which you divide each authority value down by the total.)

For which of options 1 or 2 does page X get a higher authority score (taking normalization into account)? Give a brief explanation in which you provide some intuition for why this option gives X a higher score.

(c) Suppose, instead of creating two pages, you create three pages, X, Y, and Z, and again try to strategically create links out of them so that X gets ranked as well as possible.

Describe a strategy for adding three nodes X, Y, and Z to the network in Figure 14.18, with choices of links out of each, so that when you run the two-step hub–authority computation [as in parts (a) and (b)], and then rank all pages by their authority score, node X shows up in second place.

[Hint: Note that there's no way to do this so that X shows up in first place, so second place is the best one can hope for using only three nodes X, Y, and Z.]

4. Let's consider the limiting values that result from the Basic PageRank Update Rule (i.e., the version where we don't introduce a scaling factor *s*). In Chapter 14, these limiting values are described as capturing "a kind of equilibrium based on direct endorsement: they are values that remain unchanged when everyone divides up their PageRank and passes it forward across their outgoing links."

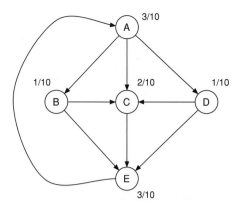

Figure 14.19. A network of Web pages.

This description gives a way to check whether an assignment of numbers to a set of Web pages forms an equilibrium set of PageRank values: the numbers should add up to 1, and they should remain unchanged when we apply the Basic PageRank Update Rule. For example, this is illustrated in Chapter 14 via Figure 14.6: you can check that if we assign a PageRank of $\frac{4}{13}$ to page A, $\frac{2}{13}$ to each of B and C, and $\frac{1}{13}$ to the five other pages, then these numbers add up to 1 and they remain unchanged when we apply the Basic PageRank Update Rule. Hence, they form an equilibrium set of PageRank values.

For each of the following two networks, use this approach to check whether the numbers indicated in the figure form an equilibrium set of PageRank values. (In cases where the numbers do not form an equilibrium set of PageRank values, you do not have to give numbers that do; you simply have to explain why the given numbers do not.)

(a) Does the assignment of numbers to the nodes in Figure 14.19 form an equilibrium set of PageRank values for this network of Web pages? Give an explanation for your answer.

(b) Does the assignment of numbers to the nodes in Figure 14.20 form an equilibrium set of PageRank values for this network of Web pages? Give an explanation for your answer.

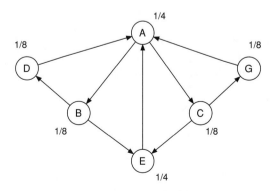

Figure 14.20. A network of Web pages.

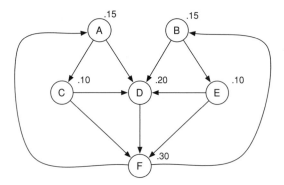

Figure 14.21. A collection of six Web pages, with possible PageRank values.

5. Figure 14.21 depicts the links among six Web pages, and also a proposed PageRank value for each one, expressed as a decimal next to the node.

    Are these correct equilibrium values for the Basic PageRank Update Rule? Give a brief (one- to three-sentence) explanation for your answer.

6. One of the basic ideas behind the computation of hubs and authorities is to distinguish between pages that have multiple reinforcing endorsements and those that simply have high in-degree. (Recall that the in-degree of a node is the number of links coming into it.)

    Consider, for example, the graph shown in Figure 14.22. (Despite the fact that it has two separate pieces, keep in mind that it is a single graph.) The contrast described above can be seen by comparing node D to nodes B1, B2, and B3: whereas D has many in-links from nodes that only point to D, nodes B1, B2, and B3 have fewer in-links each, but from a mutually reinforcing set of nodes.

    Let's explore how this contrast plays out in the context of this stylized example.

    (a) Show the values you get from running the two-step hub–authority computation from the chapter on link analysis. (If you want, you can omit the final step in which the values are normalized; i.e., you can just leave the values as large numbers.)

    (b) Give formulas, in terms of k, for the values at each node that you get from running the k-step hub–authority computation. (Again, if you want, you can omit the final step in which the values are normalized and give the formulas in terms of k without normalization.)

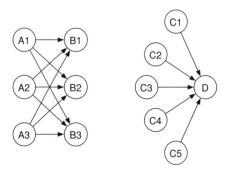

Figure 14.22. A network of Web pages.

(c) As k goes to infinity, what do the normalized values at each node converge to? Give an explanation for your answer; this explanation does not have to constitute a formal proof, but it should argue at least informally why the process is converging to the values you claim. In addition to your explanation of what's happening in the computation, briefly discuss (in one or two sentences) how this relates to the intuition suggested in the opening paragraph of this problem about the difference between pages that have multiple reinforcing endorsements and those that simply have a high in-degree.

CHAPTER 15

Sponsored Search Markets

15.1 Advertising Tied to Search Behavior

The problem of Web search, as traditionally formulated, has a very "pure" motivation: it seeks to take the content people produce on the Web and find the pages that are most relevant, useful, or authoritative for any given query. However, it soon became clear that a lucrative market existed within this framework for combining search with advertising, targeted to the queries that users were issuing.

The basic idea behind this is simple. Early Web advertising was sold on the basis of "impressions," by analogy with the print ads one sees in newspapers or magazines: a company like Yahoo! would negotiate a rate with an advertiser, agreeing on a price for showing its ad a fixed number of times. But if the ad you're showing a user isn't tied in some intrinsic way to their behavior, then you're missing one of the main benefits of the Internet as an advertising venue, compared to print or television. Suppose, for example, that you're a very small retailer who's trying to sell a specialized product; say, for example, that you run a business that sells calligraphy pens over the Web. Then paying to display ads to the full Internet-using population seems like a very inefficient way to find customers; instead, you might want to work out an agreement with a search engine that said, "Show my ad to any user who enters the query 'calligraphy pens'." After all, search engine queries are a potent way to get users to express their *intent* – what it is that they're interested in at the moment they issue their query – and an ad that is based on the query catches a user at precisely this receptive moment.

Originally pioneered by the company Overture, this style of *keyword-based advertising* has turned out to be an enormously successful way for search engines to make money. At present it's a business that generates tens of billions of dollars per year in revenue, and it is responsible, for example, for nearly all of Google's revenue. From our perspective, it's also a very nice blend of ideas that have come up earlier in this book: it creates markets out of the information-seeking behavior of hundreds of millions of people traversing the Web, and we will see shortly that it has surprisingly deep connections to the kinds of auctions and matching markets that we discussed in Chapters 9 and 10.

Figure 15.1. Search engines display paid advertisements (shown on the right-hand side of the page in this example) that match the query issued by a user. These appear alongside the results determined by the search engine's own ranking method (shown on the left-hand side). An auction procedure determines the selection and ordering of the ads. (Courtesy of Google Image.)

Keyword-based ads show up on search engine results pages alongside the unpaid ("organic" or "algorithmic") results. Figure 15.1 shows an example of how this currently looks on Google for the query "Keuka Lake," one of the Finger Lakes in upstate New York. The algorithmic results generated by the search engine's internal ranking procedure are on the left, while the paid results (in this case for real estate and vacation rentals) are ordered on the right. There can be multiple paid results for a single query term, which simply means that the search engine has sold an ad on the query to multiple advertisers. Among the multiple slots for displaying ads on a single page, the slots higher up on the page are more expensive, since users click on these at a higher rate.

The search industry has developed certain conventions in the way it sells keyword-based ads, and for thinking about this market it's worth highlighting two of these at the outset.

Paying per Click. Ads such as those shown in Figure 15.1 are based on a *cost-per-click* model. This means that if you create an ad that is shown to users entering the query "Keuka Lake," it will contain a link to your company's Web site – and you only pay when a user actually clicks on the ad. Clicking on an ad represents an even stronger indication of intent than simply issuing a query; it corresponds to a user who issued the query, read your ad, and is now visiting your site. As a result, the amount that advertisers are willing to pay per click is often surprisingly high. For example, to occupy the most prominent spot for "calligraphy pens" costs about $1.70 per click on Google as of this writing; occupying the top spot for "Keuka Lake" costs about $1.50 per click. (For the misspelling "calligaphy pens," the cost is still about $0.60 per click – after all, advertisers are still interested in potential customers even if their query contains a small but frequent typo.)

For some queries, the cost per click can be positively stratospheric. Queries like "loan consolidation," "mortgage refinancing," and "mesothelioma" often reach $50 per click or more. One can take this as an advertiser's estimate that it stands to gain an expected value of $50 for every user who clicks through such an ad to its site.[1]

Setting Prices Through an Auction. There is still the question of how a search engine should set the prices per click for different queries. One possibility is simply to post prices, the way that products in a store are sold. But with so many possible keywords and combinations of keywords, each appealing to a relatively small number of potential advertisers, it would be extremely difficult for the search engine to maintain reasonable prices for each query in the face of changing demand from advertisers.

Instead, search engines determine prices using an auction procedure, in which they solicit bids from the advertisers. If there were just a single slot in which an ad could be displayed, then this would be just a single-item auction such as we saw in Chapter 9, and there we found that the sealed-bid second-price auction has many appealing features. The problem is more complicated in the present case, however, since there are multiple slots for displaying ads, and some are more valuable than others.

We will consider how to design an auction for this setting in several stages.

1. First, if the search engine knew all the advertisers' valuations for clicks, the situation could be represented directly as a matching market in the style that we discussed in Chapter 10: essentially, the slots are the items being sold, and they're being matched with the advertisers as buyers.

2. If we assume that the advertisers' valuations are not known, however, then we need to think about ways of encouraging truthful bidding, or to deal with the consequences of untruthful bidding. This leads us directly to an interesting general question that long predates the specific problem of keyword-based advertising: how do you design a price-setting procedure for matching markets in which truthful bidding is a dominant strategy for the buyers? We will resolve this question using an elegant procedure called the *Vickrey–Clarke–Groves* (VCG) *mechanism* [112, 199, 400], which can be viewed as a far-reaching generalization of the second-price rule for single-item auctions that we discussed in Chapter 9.

3. The VCG mechanism provides a natural way to set prices in matching markets, including those arising from keyword-based advertising. For various reasons, however, it is not the procedure that the search industry adopted. As a result, our third topic will be an exploration of the auction procedure that is used to sell search advertising in practice, the *generalized second-price auction* (GSP). Although GSP has a simple description, the bidding behavior it leads to is very complex, with untruthful bidding and socially nonoptimal outcomes. Trying to understand bidder behavior under this auction turns out to be an interesting case study in the intricacies of a complex auction procedure as it is implemented in a real application.

---

[1] Naturally, you may be wondering at this point what mesothelioma is. As a quick check on Google reveals, it's a rare form of lung cancer that is believed to be caused by exposure to asbestos in the workplace. So if you know enough to be querying this term, you may well have been diagnosed with mesothelioma, and are considering suing your employer. Most of the top ads for this query link to law firms.

15.2 Advertising as a Matching Market

Clickthrough Rates and Revenues per Click. To begin formulating a precise description of how search advertising is sold, let's consider the set of available "slots" that the search engine has for selling ads on a given query, like the three advertising slots shown in Figure 15.1. The slots are numbered $1, 2, 3, \ldots$, starting from the top of the page, and users are more likely to click on the higher slots. We will assume that each slot has a specific *clickthrough rate* associated with it, which is the number of clicks per hour that an ad placed in that slot will receive.

In the models we discuss, we will make a few simplifying assumptions about the clickthrough rates. First, we assume that advertisers know the clickthrough rates. Second, we assume that the clickthrough rate depends only on the slot itself and not on the ad that is placed there. Third, we assume that the clickthrough rate of a slot also doesn't depend on the ads that are in *other* slots. In practice, the first of these assumptions is not particularly problematic since advertisers have a number of means (including tools provided by the search engine itself) for estimating clickthrough rates. The second assumption is an important issue: a relevant, high-quality ad in a high slot will receive more clicks than an off-topic ad, and in fact we will describe how to extend the basic models to deal with ad relevance and ad quality at the end of the chapter. The third assumption – interaction among the different ads being shown – is a more complex issue, and it is still not well understood even within the search industry.

This is the full picture from the search engine's side: the slots are the inventory that it is trying to sell. Now, from the advertisers' side, we assume that each advertiser has a *revenue per click*: the expected amount of revenue it receives per user who clicks on the ad. Here too, we will assume that this value is intrinsic to the advertiser and does not depend on what was being shown on the page when the user clicked on the ad. We will also assume that if an advertiser wants to be shown in a given slot, it wants to be shown there for every single search on the given query. (In practice, advertisers can specify more complex arrangements with the search engine, such as being shown for only a fraction of the queries issued, but we will not consider this here.)

This is all the information we need to understand the market for a particular keyword: the clickthrough rates of the slots, and the revenues per click of the advertisers. Figure 15.2 shows a small example with three slots and three advertisers: the slots have clickthrough rates of 10, 5, and 2, respectively, while the advertisers have revenues per click of 3, 2, and 1, respectively.

Constructing a Matching Market. We now show how to represent the market for a particular keyword as a matching market of the type we studied in Chapter 10. To do this, it is useful to first review the basic ingredients of a matching market from Chapter 10:

- The participants in a matching market consist of a set of buyers and a set of sellers.
- Each buyer j has a *valuation* for the item offered by each seller i. This valuation can depend on the identities of both the buyer and the seller, and we denote it v_{ij}.
- The goal is to match up buyers with sellers, in such a way that no buyer purchases two different items and the same item isn't sold to two different buyers.

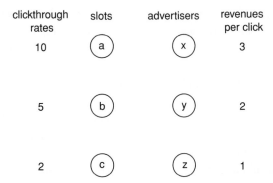

Figure 15.2. In the basic setup of a search engine's market for advertising, there are a certain number of advertising slots to be sold to a population of potential advertisers. Each slot has a *clickthrough rate*: the number of clicks per hour it will receive, with higher slots generally getting higher clickthrough rates. Each advertiser has a *revenue per click*, the amount of money it expects to receive, on average, each time a user clicks on one of its ads and arrives at its site. We draw the advertisers in descending order of their revenue per click; for now, this is purely a pictorial convention, but in Section 15.2 we show that the market in fact generally allocates slots to the advertisers in this order.

To cast the search engine's advertising market for a particular keyword in this framework, we use r_i to denote the clickthrough rate of slot i, and v_j to denote the revenue per click of advertiser j. The benefit that advertiser j receives from being shown in slot i is then just $r_i v_j$, the product of the number of clicks and the revenue per click.

In the language of matching markets, this is advertiser j's valuation v_{ij} for slot i – the value it receives from acquiring slot i. So by declaring the slots to be the sellers, the advertisers to be the buyers, and the buyers' valuations to be $v_{ij} = r_i v_j$, the problem of assigning slots to advertisers is precisely the problem of assigning sellers to buyers in a matching market. In Figure 15.3(a), we show how this conversion is applied to

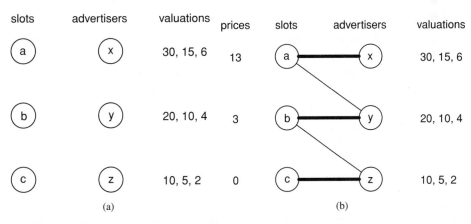

Figure 15.3. The allocation of advertising slots to advertisers can be represented as a matching market, in which the slots are the items to be sold, and the advertisers are the buyers. (a) An advertiser's valuation for a slot is simply the product of its own revenue per click and the clickthrough rate of the slot; these can be used to determine (b) market-clearing prices for the slots.

the example in Figure 15.2, yielding the buyer valuations shown. As this figure makes clear, the advertising setup produces a matching market with a special structure: since the valuations are obtained by multiplying rates by revenues, we have a situation where all the buyers agree on their preferences for the items being sold and where, in fact, the valuations of one buyer simply form a multiple of the valuations of any other buyer.

When we considered matching markets in Chapter 10, we focused on the special case in which the number of sellers and the number of buyers were the same. This made the discussion simpler in a number of respects; in particular, it meant that the buyers and sellers could be perfectly matched, so that each item is sold and each buyer purchases exactly one item. We will make the analogous assumption here: with slots playing the role of sellers and advertisers playing the role of buyers, we will focus on the case in which the numbers of slots and advertisers are the same. But it is important to note that this assumption is not at all essential, because for purposes of analysis we can always translate a scenario with unequal numbers of slots and advertisers into an equivalent one with equal numbers, as follows. If there are more advertisers than slots, we simply create additional "fictitious" slots of clickthrough rate 0 (i.e., of valuation 0 to all buyers) until the number of slots is equal to the number of advertisers. The advertisers who are matched with the slots of clickthrough rate 0 are then simply the ones who don't get assigned a (real) slot for advertising. Similarly, if there are more slots than advertisers, we just create additional "fictitious" advertisers who have a valuation of 0 for all slots.

Obtaining Market-Clearing Prices. With the connection to matching markets in place, we can use the framework from Chapter 10 to determine *market-clearing prices*. Again, it is worth reviewing this notion from Chapter 10 in a bit of detail as well, since we will use it heavily in what follows. Recall, roughly speaking, that the prices charged by the sellers are market clearing if, with these prices, each buyer prefers a different seller's item. More precisely, the basic ingredients of market-clearing prices are as follows:

- Each seller i announces a price p_i for his item. (In our case, the items are the slots.)
- Each buyer j evaluates her payoff for choosing a particular seller i: it is equal to the valuation minus the price for this seller's item, $v_{ij} - p_i$.
- We then build a *preferred-seller graph* as in Figure 15.3(b) by linking each buyer to the seller or sellers from which she gets the highest payoff.
- The prices are *market-clearing* if this graph has a perfect matching: in this case, we can assign distinct items to all the buyers in such a way that each buyer gets an item that maximizes her payoff.

In Chapter 10, we showed that market-clearing prices exist for every matching market, and we gave a procedure to construct them. We also showed in Chapter 10 that the assignment of buyers to sellers achieved by market-clearing prices always maximizes the buyers' total valuations for the items they get.

Returning to the specific context of advertising markets, market-clearing prices for the search engine's advertising slots have the desirable property that advertisers prefer different slots, and the resulting assignment of advertisers to slots maximizes the total valuations of each advertiser for what they get. [Again, see Figure 15.3(b).] In fact, it is not hard to work out that when valuations have the special form that we see in advertising markets – each consisting of a clickthrough rate times a revenue per click – then the maximum valuation is always obtained by giving the slot with the highest clickthrough rate to the advertiser with maximum revenue per click, the slot with the second-highest rate to the advertiser with the second-highest revenue per click, and so forth.

The connection with matching markets shows that we can in fact think about advertising prices in the more general case where different advertisers can have arbitrary valuations for slots – they need not be the product of a clickthrough rate and a revenue per click. This allows advertisers, for example, to express how they feel about users who arrive via an ad in the third slot compared with those who arrive via an ad in the first slot. (And indeed, it is reasonable to believe that these two populations of users might have different behavioral characteristics.)

Finally, however, this construction of prices can only be carried out by a search engine if it actually knows the valuations of the advertisers. In the next section we consider how to set prices in a setting where the search engine doesn't know these valuations; it must rely on advertisers to report them without being able to know whether this reporting is truthful.

15.3 Encouraging Truthful Bidding in Matching Markets: The VCG Principle

What would be a good price-setting procedure when the search engine doesn't know the advertisers' valuations? In the early days of the search industry, variants of the first-price auction were used: advertisers were simply asked to report their revenues per click in the form of bids, and then they were assigned slots in decreasing order of these bids, and charged a price per click equal to the full value of their respective bids. Recall from Chapter 9 that when bidders are charged the full value of their bids, they will generally underreport, and this is what happened here. Bids were shaded downward, below their true values. More problematically, because the auctions were running continuously over time, advertisers constantly adjusted their bids by small increments to experiment with the outcome and to try to slightly outbid competitors. This resulted in a highly turbulent market and a huge resource expenditure on the part of both the advertisers and the search engines, as the constant price experimentation led to prices for most queries being updated extremely frequently.

In the case of a single-item auction, we saw in Chapter 9 that these problems are handled by running a second-price auction, in which the single item is awarded to the highest bidder at a price equal to the second-highest bid. As we showed there, truthful bidding is a *dominant strategy* for second-price auctions – it is at least as good as any other strategy, regardless of what the other participants are doing. This dominant-strategy result means that second-price auctions avoid many of the pathologies associated with more complex auctions.

But what is the analogue of the second-price auction for advertising markets with multiple slots? Given the connections to matching markets in the previous section, this turns out to be a special case of an interesting and fundamental question: how can we define a price-setting procedure for matching markets so that truthful reporting of valuations is a dominant strategy for the buyers? Such a procedure would be a massive generalization of the second-price auction, which – though already fairly subtle – only applies to the case of single items.

The VCG Principle. Since a matching market contains many items, it is hard to directly generalize the literal description of the second-price single-item auction, in which we assign the item to the highest bidder at the second-highest price. However, by viewing the second-price auction in a somewhat less obvious way, we get a principle that does generalize.

This view is the following. First, the second-price auction produces an allocation that maximizes social welfare: the bidder who values the item the most gets it. Second, the winner of the auction is charged an amount equal to the "harm" he causes the other bidders by receiving the item. That is, suppose the bidders' values for the item are $v_1, v_2, v_3, \ldots, v_n$ in decreasing order. Then if bidder 1 were not present, the item would have gone to bidder 2, who values it at v_2. The other bidders still would not get the item, even if bidder 1 weren't there. Thus, bidders 2 through n collectively experience a harm of v_2 because bidder 1 is there – since bidder 2 loses this much value, and bidders 3 through n are unaffected. This harm of v_2 is exactly what bidder 1 is charged. Indeed, the other bidders are also charged an amount equal to the harm they cause to others – in this case zero, since no bidder is affected by the presence of any of bidders 2 through n in the single-item auction.

Again, this approach is a nonobvious way to think about single-item auctions, but it is a principle that turns out to encourage truthful reporting of values in much more general situations: each individual is charged the harm they cause to the rest of the world. To put it another way, each individual is charged a price equal to the total amount everyone would be better off if this individual weren't there. We will refer to this as the Vickrey-Clarke-Groves (VCG) principle, after the work of Clarke and Groves, who generalized the central idea behind Vickrey's second-price auction for single items [112, 199, 400]. For matching markets, we will describe an application of this principle due to Herman Leonard [270] and Gabrielle Demange [128]; it develops a pricing mechanism in this context that causes buyers to reveal their valuations truthfully.

Applying the VCG Principle to Matching Markets. In a matching market, we have a set of buyers and a set of sellers – with equal numbers of each – and buyer j has a valuation of v_{ij} for the item being sold by seller i.[2] We assume here that each buyer knows her own valuations, but that these valuations are not known to the other buyers or to the sellers. Also, we assume that each buyer only cares which item she receives, not about how the remaining goods are allocated to the other buyers. Thus, in the language of auctions, the buyers have *independent, private values*.

Under the VCG principle, we first assign items to buyers so as to maximize total valuation. Then, the price buyer j should pay for seller i's item – in the event she

---

[2] As always, we can handle unequal numbers of buyers and sellers by creating "fictitious" individuals and valuations of 0, as in Section 15.2.

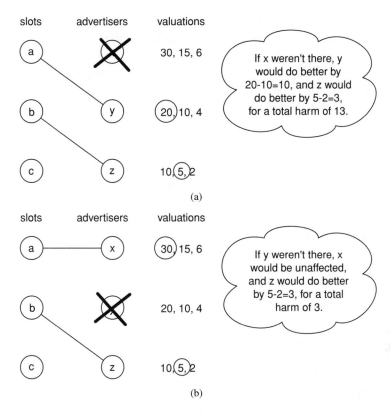

Figure 15.4. The VCG price an individual buyer pays for an item can be determined by working out how much better off all other buyers would be if this individual buyer were not present: (a) determining how much better off y and z would be if x were not present and (b) determining how much better off x and z would be if y were not present.

receives it – is the harm she causes to the remaining buyers through her acquisition of this item. This value is equal to the total boost in valuation everyone else would get if we computed the optimal matching without buyer j present. To give a better sense of how this principle works for matching markets, we first walk through how it would apply to the example in Figure 15.3. We then define the VCG price-setting mechanism in general, and in the next section we show that it yields truth-telling as a dominant strategy: for each buyer, truth-telling is at least as good as any other option, regardless of what the other buyers are doing.

In Figure 15.3, where the buyers are advertisers and the items are advertising slots, suppose we assign items to maximize total valuation: item a to buyer x, item b to buyer y, and item c to buyer z. What prices does the VCG principle dictate for each buyer? We show the reasoning in Figure 15.4.

- First, in the optimal matching without buyer x present, buyer y gets item a and buyer z gets item b. This outcome improves the respective valuations of y and z for their assigned items by $20 - 10 = 10$ and $5 - 2 = 3$, respectively. The total harm caused by x is therefore $10 + 3 = 13$, and so this is the price that x should pay.

- In the optimal matching without buyer y present, buyer x still gets a (so she is unaffected), while buyer z gets item b, for an improved valuation of 3. The total harm caused by y is $0 + 3 = 3$, and so this is the price that y should pay.
- Finally, in the optimal matching without buyer z present, buyers x and y each get the same items they would have gotten had z been there; buyer z causes no harm to the rest of the world, and so her VCG price is 0.

With this example in mind, we now describe the VCG prices for a general matching market. This follows exactly from the principle we've been discussing, but it requires a bit of notation due to the multiple items and valuations. First, let S denote the set of sellers and B denote the set of buyers. Let V_B^S denote the maximum total valuation over all possible perfect matchings of sellers and buyers – simply the value of the socially optimal outcome with all buyers and sellers present.

Now, let $S–i$ denote the set of sellers with seller i removed, and let $B–j$ denote the set of buyers with buyer j removed. So if we give item i to seller j, then the best total valuation the rest of the buyers could get is V_{B-j}^{S-i}: this is the value of the optimal matching of sellers and buyers when we've taken item i and buyer j out of consideration. On the other hand, if buyer j simply didn't exist but item i were still an option for everyone else, then the best total valuation the rest of the buyers could get is V_{B-j}^S. Thus, the total harm caused by buyer j to the rest of the buyers is the difference between how they'd do without j present and how they do with j present; in other words, it is the difference $V_{B-j}^S - V_{B-j}^{S-i}$. This is the VCG price p_{ij} that we charge to buyer j for item i, so we have the equation

$$p_{ij} = V_{B-j}^S - V_{B-j}^{S-i}. \tag{15.1}$$

The VCG Price-Setting Mechanism. Using the ideas developed so far, we can now define the complete VCG price-setting mechanism for matching markets. We assume that there is a single price-setting authority (an "auctioneer") who can collect information from buyers, assign items to them, and charge prices. Fortunately, this framework works very well for selling advertising slots, where all the items (the slots) are under the control of a single agent (the search engine).

The mechanism works as follows:

1. Ask buyers to announce valuations for the items. (These announcements need not be truthful.)
2. Choose a socially optimal assignment of items to buyers – that is, a perfect matching that maximizes the total valuation of each buyer for what they get. This assignment is based on the announced valuations (since that's all we have access to.)
3. Charge each buyer the appropriate VCG price; that is, if buyer j receives item i under the optimal matching, then charge buyer j a price p_{ij} determined according to Equation (15.1).

Essentially, what the auctioneer has done is to define a game that the buyers play. They must choose a strategy (a set of valuations to announce), and they receive a payoff – their valuation for the item they get, minus the price they pay. What turns out to be true, though it is far from obvious, is that this game has been designed to make truth-telling – in which a buyer announces her true valuations – a dominant strategy. We will prove this in the next section; but before this, we make a few observations.

First, notice that there's a crucial difference between the VCG prices defined here and the market-clearing prices arising from the auction procedure in Chapter 10. The market-clearing prices defined there were *posted prices*, in that the seller simply announced a price and was willing to charge it to any buyer who was interested. The VCG prices here, on the other hand, are *personalized prices*: they depend on both the item being sold and the buyer to whom it is being sold. The VCG price p_{ij} paid by buyer j for item i may well differ, under Equation (15.1), from the VCG price p_{ik} that buyer k would pay if it were assigned item i.[3]

Another way to think about the relationship between the market-clearing prices from Chapter 10 and the VCG prices here is to observe how each is designed to generalize a different single-item auction format. The market-clearing prices in Chapter 10 were defined by a significant generalization of the ascending (English) auction: prices were raised step-by-step until each buyer favored a different item, and we saw in Section 10.5 that one could encode the single-item ascending auction as a special case of the general construction of market-clearing prices.

The VCG prices, on the other hand, are defined by an analogous and equally substantial generalization of the sealed-bid second-price auction. At a qualitative level, we can see that the "harm-done-to-others" principle is behind both the second-price auction and the VCG prices, but in fact we can also see fairly directly that the second-price auction is a special case of the VCG mechanism. Specifically, suppose there are n buyers who each want a single item, and buyer i has valuation v_i for it, where the numbers v_i are sorted in descending order so that v_1 is the largest. Let's turn this into a matching market with n buyers and n sellers by simply adding $n - 1$ fictitious items; all buyers have valuation 0 for each fictitious item. Now, if everyone reports their values truthfully, then the VCG mechanism would assign item 1 (the real item and the only one with any value) to buyer 1 (who has the highest valuation), and all the rest of the buyers would get fictitious items of zero value. What price should buyer 1 pay? According to Equation (15.1), she should pay $V_{B-1}^{S} - V_{B-1}^{S-1}$. The first term is buyer 2's valuation, since with buyer 1 gone the socially optimal matching gives item 1 to buyer 2. The second term is 0 since, with both buyer 1 and item 1 gone, there are no remaining items of any value. Thus, buyer 1 pays buyer 2's valuation, and so we have precisely the pricing rule for second-price sealed-bid auctions.

15.4 Analyzing the VCG Mechanism: Truth-Telling as a Dominant Strategy

We now show that the VCG mechanism encourages truth-telling in a matching market. Concretely, we will prove the following claim.

> *Claim:* If items are assigned and prices computed according to the VCG mechanism, then truthfully announcing valuations is a dominant strategy for each buyer, and the resulting assignment maximizes the total valuation of any perfect matching of items and buyers.

---

[3] Despite this, there are deep and subtle connections between the two kinds of prices; we explore this issue further in the final section of this chapter.

The second part of this claim (that the total valuation is maximized) is easy to justify: if buyers report their valuations truthfully, then the assignment of items is designed to maximize the total valuation by definition.

The first part of the claim is more subtle: why is truth-telling a dominant strategy? Suppose that buyer j announces her valuations truthfully, and in the matching we assign her item i. Then her payoff is $v_{ij} - p_{ij}$. We want to show that buyer j has no incentive to deviate from a truthful announcement.

If buyer j decides to lie about her valuations, then one of two things can happen: either this lie affects the item she gets, or it doesn't. If buyer j lies but still gets the same item i, then her payoff remains exactly the same, because the price p_{ij} is computed only using announcements by buyers other than j. So if a deviation from truth-telling is going to be beneficial for buyer j, it has to affect the item she receives.

Suppose, therefore, that buyer j lies about her valuations and gets item h instead of item i. In this case, her payoff would be $v_{hj} - p_{hj}$. Notice again that the price p_{hj} is determined only by the announcements of buyers other than j. To show that there is no incentive to lie and receive item h instead of i, we need to show that

$$v_{ij} - p_{ij} \geq v_{hj} - p_{hj}.$$

If we expand out the definitions of p_{ij} and p_{hj} using Equation (15.1), this is equivalent to showing

$$v_{ij} - \left(V_{B-j}^{S} - V_{B-j}^{S-i}\right) \geq v_{hj} - \left(V_{B-j}^{S} - V_{B-j}^{S-h}\right).$$

Both sides of this inequality contain the term V_{B-j}^{S}, so we can add this to both sides; in this way, the previous inequality is equivalent to showing

$$v_{ij} + V_{B-j}^{S-i} \geq v_{hj} + V_{B-j}^{S-h}. \tag{15.2}$$

We now argue why this last inequality holds. In fact, the left- and right-hand sides each describe the total valuation of different matchings, as shown in Figure 15.5. The matching on the left-hand side is constructed by pairing j with the item i she would get in an optimal matching and then optimally matching the remaining buyers and items. In other words, it is a matching that achieves the maximum total valuation over all possible perfect matchings, so we can write the left-hand side as

$$v_{ij} + V_{B-j}^{S-i} = V_{B}^{S}. \tag{15.3}$$

In contrast, the matching on the right-hand side of Inequality (15.2) is constructed by pairing j with some other item h and then optimally matching the remaining buyers and items. So it is a matching that achieves the maximum total valuation *only over those matchings that pair j with h*. Therefore,

$$v_{hj} + V_{B-j}^{S-h} \leq V_{B}^{S}.$$

The left-hand side of Inequality (15.2) – the maximum valuation with no restrictions on who gets any slot – must be at least as large as the right-hand side – the maximum with a restriction. And this is what we wanted to show.

Nothing in this argument depends on the decisions made by other buyers about what to announce. For example, it doesn't require them to announce their true values; the arguments comparing different matchings can be applied to whatever valuations are

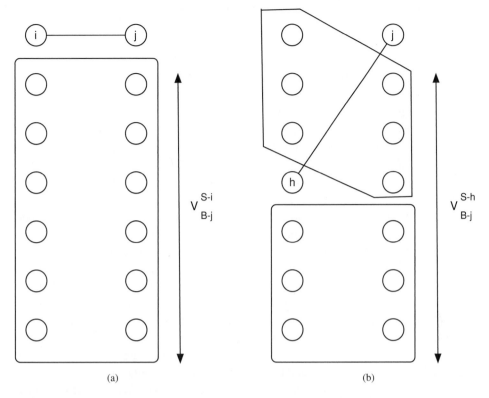

Figure 15.5. The heart of the proof that the VCG mechanism encourages truthful bidding comes down to a comparison of the value of two matchings: (a) $v_{ij} + V_{B-j}^{S-i}$ is the maximum valuation of any matching and (b) $v_{hj} + V_{B-j}^{S-h}$ is the maximum valuation only over matchings constrained to assign h to j.

announced by the other buyers, with the same consequences. Thus, we have shown that truthfully announcing valuations is a dominant strategy in the VCG mechanism.

To close this section, let's go back to the specific case of keyword-based advertising, in which the buyers correspond to advertisers and the items for sale correspond to advertising slots. Our discussion so far has focused on finding and achieving an assignment of advertisers to slots that maximizes the total valuation obtained by advertisers. But of course, this is not what the search engine selling the advertising slots directly cares about. Instead it cares about its revenue: the sum of the prices that it can charge for slots. It is not clear that the VCG mechanism is the best way to generate revenue for the search engine. Determining which procedure maximizes seller revenue is a current topic of research. It could be that the best a seller can do is to use some procedure that generates an optimal matching, and potentially one that is better than VCG at converting more of the total valuation into seller revenue. Or it could be that the seller is better off using a procedure that does not always yield an optimal matching. And it may be that some version of a revenue-equivalence principle – such as we saw for single-item auctions in Chapter 9 – holds here as well, showing that certain classes of auction provide equivalent amounts of revenue to the seller when buyers behave strategically.

In the next sections, we sample the general flavor of some of these revenue issues by considering the alternative to VCG that the search industry has adopted in practice – a simple-to-describe auction, called the generalized second-price auction, that induces complex bidding behavior.

15.5 The Generalized Second-Price Auction

After some initial experiments with other formats, the main search engines have adopted a procedure for selling advertising slots called the generalized second-price (GSP) auction. At some level, GSP – like VCG – is a generalization of the second-price auction for a single item. However, as we will see, GSP is a generalization only in a superficial sense, since it doesn't retain the nice properties of the second-price auction and VCG.

In the GSP procedure, each advertiser j announces a *bid* consisting of a single number b_j – the price it is willing to pay per click. (This would correspond, for example, to the $1.70 for "calligraphy pens" or $1.50 for "Keuka Lake" that we saw at the beginning of the chapter.) As usual, it is up to the advertiser whether or not its bid is equal to its true valuation per click, v_j. Then, after each advertiser submits a bid, the GSP procedure awards each slot i to the ith highest bidder, at a price per click equal to the $(i + 1)$st highest bid. In other words, each advertiser shown on the results page is paying a price per click equal to the bid of the advertiser just below them.

So GSP and VCG can be viewed in parallel terms, in that each asks for announced valuations from the advertisers, and then each uses these announcements to determine an assignment of slots to advertisers, as well as prices to charge. When there is a single slot, both are equivalent to the second-price auction. But when there are multiple slots, their rules for producing prices are different. VCG's rule is given by Equation (15.1). GSP's rule, when the bids per click are $b_1, b_2, b_3, \ldots$ in descending order, is to charge a cumulative price of $r_i b_{i+1}$ for slot i. This is because the ith highest bidder will get slot i at a price per click of b_{i+1}; multiplying by the clickthrough rate of r_i gives a total price of $r_i b_{i+1}$ for all the clicks associated with slot i.

In the version of GSP we consider here, there is no minimum bid, just as we did not have a minimum bid (or reserve price) when we first introduced second-price auctions in Chapter 9. In practice, search engines do impose a minimum bid, and this minimum bid may increase the revenue generated by the auction, particularly if the smallest clickthrough rate is very low. This minimum bid plays a role similar to that played by the reserve price in a second price auction (as discussed in the final section of Chapter 9).

Analyzing GSP. GSP was originally developed at Google; once it had been in use for a while in the search industry, researchers including Varian [399] and Edelman, Ostrovsky, and Schwarz [144] began working out some of its basic properties. Their analysis formulates the problem as a game, using the definitions from Chapter 6. Each advertiser is a player, its bid is its strategy, and its payoff is its revenue minus the price it pays. In this game, we will consider Nash equilibria: we seek sets of bids so that, given these bids, no advertiser has an incentive to change how it is behaving.[4]

---

[4] In order to fit our Nash equilibrium analysis here into the framework defined in Chapter 6, we will assume that each advertiser knows the values of all other advertisers, so that each player (i.e., advertiser) in the bidding

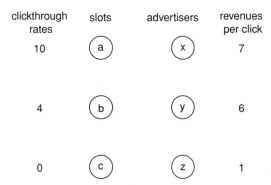

clickthrough rates	slots	advertisers	revenues per click
10	a	x	7
4	b	y	6
0	c	z	1

Figure 15.6. An example of a set of advertisers and slots for which truthful bidding is not an equilibrium in the GSP auction. Moreover, this example possesses multiple equilibria, some of which are not socially optimal.

First, we'll see that GSP has a number of pathologies that VCG was designed to avoid: truth-telling may not constitute a Nash equilibrium, there can in fact be multiple possible equilibria, and some of these may produce assignments of advertisers to slots that do not maximize total advertiser valuation. On the positive side, we show in the next section that there is always at least one Nash equilibrium set of bids for GSP, and that among the (possibly multiple) equilibria, there is always one that does maximize total advertiser valuation. The analysis leading to these positive results about equilibria builds directly on the market-clearing prices for the matching market of advertisers and slots, thus establishing a connection between GSP and market-clearing prices.

Hence, while GSP possesses Nash equilibria, it lacks some of the main nice properties of the VCG mechanism from Sections 15.3 and 15.4. However, in keeping with our discussion from the end of the previous section, the search engines ultimately have an interest in choosing a procedure that maximizes their revenue (given the behavior of the advertisers in response to it). Viewed in this light, it is not clear that GSP is the wrong choice, though it is also far from clear that it is the right choice. As mentioned at the end of Section 15.4, understanding the revenue trade-offs among different procedures for selling keyword-based advertising is largely an open question, and the subject of current research.

Truth-Telling May Not Be an Equilibrium. It is not hard to construct an example to show that truth-telling may not be an equilibrium when the GSP procedure is used. One example of this is depicted in Figure 15.6:

- There are two slots for ads, with clickthrough rates of 10 and 4. In the figure, we also show a third fictitious slot of clickthrough rate 0, so as to equalize the number of advertisers and slots.
- There are three advertisers, x, y, and z, with values per click of 7, 6, and 1, respectively.

game knows the full set of payoffs to all players. It is also interesting to consider how this game works when the players do not know each other's payoffs, but only their own; however, we do not consider this version here.

Now, if each advertiser bids its true valuation, then advertiser x gets the top slot at a price per click of 6; since there are 10 clicks associated with this slot, x pays a cumulative price of $6 \times 10 = 60$ for the slot. Advertiser x's valuation for the top slot is $7 \times 10 = 70$, so its payoff is $70 - 60 = 10$. Now, if x were to lower its bid to 5, then it would get the second slot for a price per click of 1, implying a cumulative price of 4 for the slot. Because its valuation for the second slot is $7 \times 4 = 28$, this is a payoff of $28 - 4 = 24$, which is an improvement over the result of bidding truthfully.

Multiple and Nonoptimal Equilibria. The example in Figure 15.6 turns out to illustrate some other complex properties of bidding behavior in GSP auctions. In particular, there is more than one equilibrium set of bids for this example, and among these equilibria are some that produce a socially nonoptimal assignment of advertisers to slots.

First, suppose that advertiser x bids 5, advertiser y bids 4, and advertiser z bids 2. With a little effort, we can check that this forms an equilibrium: checking the condition for z is easy, and the main further things to observe are that x doesn't want to lower its bid below 4 so as to move to the second slot, and y doesn't want to raise its bid above 5 to get the first slot. This is an equilibrium that produces a socially optimal allocation of advertisers to slots, since x gets slot a while y gets b and z gets c.

But one can also check that if advertiser x bids 3, advertiser y bids 5, and advertiser z bids 1, then we also get a set of bids in Nash equilibrium. Again, the main thing to verify is that x doesn't want to raise its bid above y's, and that y doesn't want to lower its bid below x's. This equilibrium is not socially optimal, since it assigns y to the highest slot and x to the second highest.

There is much that is not understood in general about the structure of the suboptimal equilibria arising from the GSP procedure. For example, it is an interesting question to try to quantify how far from social optimality a Nash equilibrium of GSP can be.

The Revenue of GSP and VCG. The existence of multiple equilibria also adds to the difficulty in reasoning about the search engine revenue generated by GSP, since it depends on which equilibrium is selected (potentially from among many) by the bidders. In the example we've been working with, we'll show that, depending on which equilibrium of GSP the advertisers actually use, the revenue to the search engine can be either higher or lower than the revenue it would collect by charging the VCG prices.

Let's start by determining the revenue to the search engine from the two GSP equilibria that we worked out earlier.

- With bids of 5, 4, and 2, the 10 clicks in the top slot are sold for 4 per click, and the 4 clicks in the second slot are sold for 2 per click, for a total revenue to the search engine of 48.
- On the other hand, with bids of 3, 5, and 1, the 10 clicks in the top slot are sold for 3 per click, and the 4 clicks in the second slot are sold for 1 per click, for a total revenue to the search engine of 34.

Now, how do these compare with the revenue generated by the VCG mechanism? To work out the VCG prices, we first need to convert the example from Figure 15.6

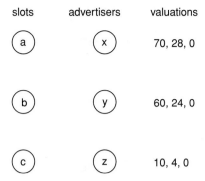

slots	advertisers	valuations
a	x	70, 28, 0
b	y	60, 24, 0
c	z	10, 4, 0

Figure 15.7. The example from Figure 15.6 as a matching market, with advertiser valuations for the full set of clicks associated with each slot.

into a matching market, just as we did in Section 15.2: for each advertiser and each slot, we work out the advertiser's valuation for the full set of clicks associated with that slot. We show these valuations in Figure 15.7.

The matching used by the VCG mechanism is the one that maximizes the total valuation of all advertisers for the slot they get; this is achieved by assigning slot a to x, slot b to y, and slot c to z. Now, we work out a price to charge each advertiser for the full set of clicks in the slot it gets, by determining the harm each advertiser causes to all others. The harm x causes to y and z can be computed as follows: without x present, y would move up one slot, obtaining an increased valuation of $60 - 24 = 36$, and z would move up one slot, obtaining an increased valuation of $4 - 0 = 4$. Therefore, x should pay 40 for the full set of clicks in the first slot. Similarly, without y present, z would get 4 instead of 0, so y should pay 4 for the set of clicks in the second slot. Finally, since z causes no harm to anyone, it pays 0. Thus, the total revenue collected by the search engine is 44.

So in this example we find that the answer to the question, "Does GSP or VCG provide more revenue to the search engine?" is indeed that it depends on which equilibrium of GSP the advertisers use. With the first equilibrium of GSP that we identified, the revenue is 48, while with the second, the revenue is 34. The revenue from the VCG mechanism is in between these two values, at 44.

15.6 Equilibria of the Generalized Second-Price Auction

The examples in the previous section give a sense for some of the complex behavior of GSP auctions. Here, we show that there is nonetheless a natural connection between GSP and market-clearing prices: from a set of market-clearing prices for the matching market of advertisers and slots, one can always construct a set of bids in Nash equilibrium – and moreover, one that produces a socially optimal assignment of advertisers to slots. As a consequence, there always exists a set of socially optimal equilibrium bids for the GSP procedure.

To give the basic idea for how to construct an equilibrium, we do it first for the example from Figure 15.6. In fact, we've just seen two equilibria for this example in

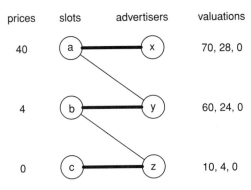

Figure 15.8. Determining market-clearing prices for the example in Figure 15.6, starting with its representation as a matching market.

the previous section, but the point here is to see how a socially optimal one can be easily constructed by following a few simple principles, rather than by trial-and-error or guesswork. We'll then identify the principles from this example that carry over to construct equilibria in general.

An Equilibrium for Figure 15.6. The basic idea is to use market-clearing prices to guide us to a set of bids that produce these prices. To construct market-clearing prices, we first convert the example from Figure 15.6 into a matching market by determining advertisers' valuations for each slot, as we did at the end of the previous section (in Figure 15.7). We then determine market-clearing prices for this matching market, as shown in Figure 15.8.

These market-clearing prices are cumulative prices for each slot – single prices that cover all the clicks associated with that slot. We can easily translate back to prices per click by simply dividing by the clickthrough rate; this produces a price per click of $40/10 = 4$ for the first slot, and $4/4 = 1$ for the second slot. It turns out not to be important how we price the fictitious third slot per click, but it is fine to give it a price of 0.

Next, we find bids that result in these prices per click. This is not hard to do: the prices per click are 4 and 1 for the two slots, so these should be the bids of y and z, respectively. Then the bid of x can be anything as long as it's more than 4. With these bids, x pays 4 per click for the first slot, y pays 1 per click for the second slot, and z pays 0 per click for the (fake) third slot – and the allocation of advertisers to slots is socially optimal.

Having used the market-clearing prices to guide us toward a set of bids, we now use the market-clearing property to verify that these bids form a Nash equilibrium. There are several cases to consider, but the overall reasoning will form the general principles that extend beyond just this example. First, let's argue that x doesn't want to lower its bid. If it drops down to match y's bid, then it can get the second slot at the price that y is currently paying. Similarly, it could match z's bid and get the third slot at the price that z is currently paying. But, since the prices are market clearing, x doesn't want to do either of these things. For similar reasons, y doesn't want to drop its bid to get the third slot at the price z is currently paying.

Next, let's argue that y doesn't want to raise its bid. Indeed, suppose that it raised its bid to get the first slot; to do this, it would need to match x's current bid. But in this case, x becomes the second-highest bidder, and so y would get the first slot at a price per click equal to x's current bid, which is above 4. Because the prices are market clearing, y doesn't prefer the first slot to its current slot at a price per click of 4, so it certainly doesn't prefer the first slot to its current slot at a higher price per click. Thus, y doesn't want to raise its bid. Similar reasoning shows that z doesn't want to raise its bid.

This concludes the analysis: no advertiser wants to raise or lower its current bid, and so the set of bids in this example forms a Nash equilibrium.

It is not hard to carry out the construction and the reasoning used here in general; we show how to do this next.

GSP Always Has a Nash Equilibrium: The General Argument. Now let's consider a general instance in which we have a set of advertisers and a set of slots. By adding fake slots of 0 value if necessary, we will assume that these two sets have the same size.

Let's suppose that the advertisers are labeled $1, 2, \ldots, n$ in decreasing order of their valuations per click, and let's suppose that the slots are labeled $1, 2, \ldots, n$ in decreasing order of their clickthrough rates. We first represent the set of advertisers and slots using a matching market, and we consider any set of market-clearing prices for the slots, denoted $p_1, p_2, \ldots, p_n$, in order. Again, these are prices for the full set of clicks in each slot; we will consider the price per click of each slot below. In Section 15.2, we argued that because a perfect matching in the resulting preferred-seller graph maximizes the total valuation of each advertiser for the slot it gets, it follows that the advertiser with the highest valuation per click gets the top slot, the advertiser with next-highest valuation gets the second slot, and so forth, with advertiser i getting slot i.

We now show how to get this outcome from an equilibrium set of bids in a GSP auction. Our plan is first to construct a set of bids that produces this same set of market-clearing prices, together with the same socially optimal matching of advertisers to slots. Then we will show that these bids form a Nash equilibrium.

Constructing the Bids. For the first step, we start by considering the prices per click that we get from the market-clearing prices: $p_j^* = p_j/r_j$. We start by arguing that these prices per click decrease as we move down the slots: $p_1^* \geq p_2^* \geq \cdots \geq p_n^*$. To see why this is true, let's compare two slots j and k, where j is numbered lower than k, and show that $p_j^* \geq p_k^*$.

Since the prices are market clearing, advertiser k prefers slot k to slot j. In slot k, its total payoff is the product of its payoff per click, $v_k - p_k^*$, times the clickthrough rate r_k. In slot j, its total payoff would be the product of its payoff per click there, $v_k - p_j^*$, times the clickthrough rate r_j. Now, the clickthrough rate is higher in slot j, yet slot k is preferred; so it must be that the payoff per click is smaller in slot j. That is, $v_k - p_j^*$ is smaller than $v_k - p_k^*$, or equivalently, $p_j^* \geq p_k^*$. This inequality is precisely the fact we were looking for.

Now that we have decreasing prices per click, we can construct the bids we're looking for. We simply have advertiser j place a bid of p_{j-1}^* for each $j > 1$, and we have advertiser 1 place any bid larger than p_1^*. Notice that this is exactly what happened when we constructed an equilibrium for the example in Figure 15.6. With these bids, we have all the desired properties: for each j, advertiser j is assigned to slot j and pays a price per click of p_j^*.

Why Do the Bids Form a Nash Equilibrium?   To show why these bids form a Nash equilibrium, we adapt the principles that we used in analyzing the equilibrium for Figure 15.6. We first argue that no advertiser will want to lower its bid, and then that no advertiser will want to raise its bid either.

Consider an advertiser j, currently in slot j. If it were to lower its bid, the best it could do is to pick some lower slot k, bid just under the current bid of advertiser k, and thereby get slot k at the price that advertiser k is currently paying. But because the prices are market clearing, j is at least as happy with its current slot at its current price as it would be with k's current slot at k's current price. So in fact, this shows that no advertiser will want to lower its bid.

How about raising a bid? The best advertiser j could do here is to pick some higher slot i, bid just above the current bid of advertiser i, and thereby get slot i. What price would j pay for slot i if it did this? It's forcing advertiser i one slot down, and so it would pay the current *bid* of advertiser i. This is actually larger than what advertiser i is currently paying for slot i: advertiser i is currently paying the bid of advertiser $i + 1$, which is lower. So the upshot is that j would get slot i at a price *higher* than the current price of slot i. Since the market-clearing condition says that j doesn't even prefer slot i at the current price, it certainly wouldn't prefer it at a higher price. This shows that no advertiser wants to raise its bid either, and so the set of bids indeed forms a Nash equilibrium.

15.7 Ad Quality

What we've discussed thus far forms part of the basic framework for thinking about search advertising markets. Of course, there are numerous further issues that come up in the use of this framework by the major search engines, and in this section and the next we briefly discuss a few of these issues. We begin with the issue of ad quality.

The Assumption of a Fixed Clickthrough Rate.   One of the assumptions we've made throughout the analysis is that a fixed clickthrough rate r_j is associated with each slot j – in other words, that the number of clicks this slot receives is independent of which ad you place there. But in general this is not likely to be true: users will look at the thumbnail description of an ad placed in a given slot (evaluating, for example, whether they recognize the name of the company placing the ad), and this will affect whether they click on the ad. And *this*, in turn, affects how much money the search engine makes, since it's charging per click, not per impression.

So from the search engine's point of view, the worrisome scenario is that a low-quality advertiser bids very highly, thus obtaining the first slot under the GSP procedure.

Users are then not interested in clicking through on this ad (maybe they don't trust the company, or the ad is only minimally relevant to the query term). As a result, it sits at the top of the list as the high bidder, but the search engine makes almost no money from it because users rarely click on the ad. If the search engine could somehow expel this ad and promote the higher-quality ads, it could potentially make more money.

Again, our model as described can't really address this problem, since it starts from the assumption that an ad in position i will get clicks at rate r_i, regardless of which ad it is. This "pure" version of GSP, using the model from Sections 15.5 and 15.6, is essentially what the company Overture used at the time it was acquired by Yahoo!, and hence what Yahoo! used initially as well. And indeed, it suffers from exactly this problem – advertisers can sometimes occupy high slots without generating much money for the search engine.

The Role of Ad Quality. When Google developed its system for advertising, it addressed this problem as follows. For each ad submitted by an advertiser j, they determine an estimated *quality factor* q_j. This is intended as a "fudge factor" on the clickthrough rate: if advertiser j appears in slot i, then the clickthrough rate is estimated to be not r_i but the product $q_j r_i$. The introduction of ad quality is simply a generalization of the model we've been studying all along. In particular, if we assume that all factors q_i are equal to 1, then we get back the model that we've been using thus far in the chapter.

From the perspective of our matching market formulation, it's easy to incorporate these quality factors: we simply change the valuation of advertiser j for slot i, from $v_{ij} = r_i v_j$ to $v_{ij} = q_j r_i v_j$. The rest of the analysis remains the same, using these new valuations.

Google has adapted the GSP procedure analogously. Rather than assigning advertisers to slots in decreasing order of their bids b_j, it assigns them in decreasing order of the product of their bid and quality factor, $q_j b_j$. This makes sense, since this is the ordering of advertisers by expected revenue to the search engine. The payments change correspondingly. The previous rule – paying the bid of the advertiser just below you – can, in retrospect, be interpreted more generally as paying the minimum bid you would need in order to hold your current position. This rule carries over to the version with quality factors: each advertiser pays the minimum amount it would need to keep its current position, when ranked according to $q_j b_j$.

With these changes, it's possible to go back and perform the analysis of GSP at this more general level. Close analogues of all the previous findings still hold here; although the introduction of quality factors makes the analysis a little bit more complicated, the basic ideas remain largely the same [144, 399].

The Mysterious Nature of Ad Quality. How is ad quality computed? To a significant extent, it's estimated by actually observing the clickthrough rate of the ad when shown on search results pages; this makes sense, since the goal of the quality factor is to act as a modifier on the clickthrough rate. But other factors are taken into account, including the relevance of the ad text and the "landing page" to which the ad links. Just as with the unpaid organic search engine results on the left-hand side of the screen, search engines are very secretive about how they compute ad quality, and do not reveal the details of this ad-quality computation to the advertisers who are bidding.

One consequence is that the introduction of ad quality factors makes the keyword-based advertising market much more opaque to the advertisers. With pure GSP, the rules were very simple: for a given set of bids, it was clear how the advertisers would be allocated to slots. But because the ad quality factor is under the search engine's control, it gives the search engine nearly unlimited power to affect the actual ordering of the advertisers for a given set of bids.

How does the behavior of a matching market such as this one change when the precise rules of the allocation procedure are being kept secret from the bidders? This is an issue that is actively discussed in the search industry, and a topic for potential research.

15.8 Complex Queries and Interactions among Keywords

At the outset, we observed that markets are being conducted simultaneously for millions of query words and phrases. In our analysis, we've focused the model on what goes on in a single one of these markets, for a single keyword; but in reality, of course, there are complex interactions among the markets for different keywords.

In particular, consider the perspective of a company that's trying to advertise a product using keyword-based advertising. Suppose, for example, that the company is selling ski vacation packages to Switzerland. There are a lot of different keywords and phrases on which the company might want to place bids: "Switzerland," "Swiss vacation," "Swiss hotels," "Alps," "ski vacation," "European ski vacation," and many others (including grammatical permutations of these). With a fixed advertising budget, and some estimates about user behavior and the behavior of other advertisers, how should the company go about dividing its budget across different keywords? This is a challenging problem, and one that is the subject of current research [357].

There's an analogous problem from the search engine's perspective. Suppose advertisers have placed bids on many queries relevant to Swiss ski vacations, and then a user comes and issues the query, "Zurich ski vacation trip December." It's quite likely that very few users have ever issued this exact query before, and also very likely that no advertiser has placed a bid on this exact phrase. If the rules of the keyword-based advertising market are defined too strictly – that the search engine can only show ads for words or phrases that have been explicitly bid on – then it seems as though both the search engine and the advertisers are losing money: there clearly are advertisers who would be happy to be displayed for this query.

The question of which ads to show, however, is quite a difficult problem. A simple rule, such as showing the advertisers that placed the maximum bid for any of the words in the query, seems like a bad idea: probably there are advertisers who have placed very high bids on "vacation" (e.g., companies that sell generic vacation packages) and "ski" (e.g., companies that sell skis), and neither of these seems like the right match to the query. It seems important to take into account the fact that the query, through its choice of terms, is specifying something fairly narrow.

Furthermore, even if relevant advertisers can be identified, how much should they be charged for a click, given that they never expressed a bid on exactly this query? The main search engines tend to get agreements from advertisers that they'll extrapolate from their bids on certain queries to implied bids on more complex queries, such as in this example, but working out the best way to do this is not fully understood. These issues are the subject of active work at search engine companies, and again the subject of some very interesting potential further research.

15.9 Advanced Material: VCG Prices and the Market-Clearing Property

At the end of Section 15.3, we noted some of the differences between the two main ways we've seen to assign prices to items in matching markets: the VCG prices defined in this chapter, and the construction of market-clearing prices from Chapter 10. In particular, we observed that the difference reflected a contrast between *personalized* and *posted* prices. VCG prices are selected only after a matching between buyers and sellers has been determined – the matching that maximizes the total valuation of buyers for what they get. The VCG price of an item thus makes use of information not just about the item itself but also about who is buying it in the matching. Market-clearing prices, in a sense, work the other way around: the prices are chosen first, and they are posted prices that are offered to any buyer who is interested. The prices then cause certain buyers to select certain items, resulting in a matching.[5]

Given these significant differences, one might expect the prices to look different as well. But a comparison of simple examples suggests that something intriguing may be going on. Consider, for instance, the matching market shown in Figures 15.3 and 15.4. In Figure 15.3 we see a set of market-clearing prices constructed using the procedure from Chapter 10. In Figure 15.4, we see that these same prices also arise as the VCG prices.

Nor is it the special structure of prices arising from clickthrough rates and revenues per click that causes this. For instance, let's go back to the example used in Figure 10.6 from Chapter 10, which has valuations with a much more "scrambled" structure. We've redrawn the final preferred-seller graph arising from the auction procedure in Figure 15.9, with the (unique) perfect matching in this graph indicated by bold edges. This is the matching that maximizes the total valuation of buyers for the item they get, so we apply the definitions from earlier in the current chapter to determine the VCG prices. For example, to determine the price that should be charged for seller a's item, we observe the following:

- If neither a nor x were present, the maximum total valuation of a matching between the remaining sellers and buyers would be 11, by matching y to c and z to b.
- If x wasn't present but a was, then the maximum total valuation possible would be 14, by matching y to b and z to a.
- The difference between these two quantities is the definition of the VCG price for item a; it is $14 - 11 = 3$.

---

[5] In the discussion that follows, we'll refer to nodes on the left-hand side of the bipartite graph sometimes as "items" and sometimes as "sellers"; for our purposes here, they mean the same thing.

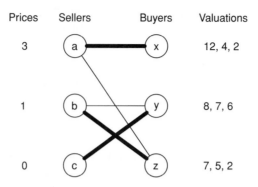

Figure 15.9. A matching market, with valuations and market-clearing prices specified, and a perfect matching in the preferred-seller graph indicated by the bold edges.

We could perform the corresponding analysis to get the VCG prices for items b and c, and we'd see that the values are 1 and 0, respectively. In other words, we again find that the VCG prices are also market-clearing prices.

In this section, we show that the relationship suggested by these examples holds in general. Our main result is that, despite their definition as personalized prices, VCG prices are always market clearing. That is, suppose we were to compute the VCG prices for a given matching market, first determining a matching of maximum total valuation and then assigning each buyer the item they receive in this matching, with a price tailored for this buyer–seller match. Then, however, suppose we go on to post the prices publicly: rather than requiring buyers to follow the matching used in the VCG construction, we allow any buyer to purchase any item at the indicated price. We will see that despite this greater freedom, each buyer will in fact achieve the highest payoff by selecting the item she was assigned when the VCG prices were constructed. This will establish that the prices are market clearing under the definition from Chapter 10.

First Steps Toward a Proof. Let's think for a minute about how you might prove such a fact, once you start to suspect from simple examples that it might be true. It's tempting to start with the very compact formula defining the VCG prices – Equation (15.1) – and then to somehow reason about this formula to show that it has the market-clearing property.

In fact, it's tricky to make this approach work, and it's useful to understand why. Recall that Equation (15.1) says that if item i is assigned to buyer j in the optimal matching then we should charge a price of

$$V^S_{B-j} - V^{S-i}_{B-j},$$

where V^S_{B-j} is the total valuation of an optimal matching with j removed, and V^{S-i}_{B-j} is the total valuation of an optimal matching with both i and j removed. Now, the term V^S_{B-j} is in fact a sum of many smaller terms, each consisting of the valuation of a distinct buyer for the item she is assigned in an optimal matching. Similarly, V^{S-i}_{B-j} is a sum of many terms, but the key conceptual difficulty is the following: V^S_{B-j} and V^{S-i}_{B-j} arise from different matchings – potentially very different matchings – and so there is no direct way to compare the sums that they represent and easily subtract the terms of one from the other.

To make progress, we need to actually understand how the matchings that define these two terms V_{B-j}^S and V_{B-j}^{S-i} relate to each other at a structural level. To do this, we will show that matchings achieving these respective quantities can in fact arise from a common set of market-clearing prices: there is a single set of market-clearing prices on the set of items S so that matchings achieving each of V_{B-j}^S and V_{B-j}^{S-i} arise as perfect matchings in the preferred-seller graphs of related but slightly different matching markets. This fact will enable us to see how the two matchings relate to each other – and in particular how to build one from the other – in a way that lets us subtract the relevant terms from each other and thus analyze the right-hand side of Equation (15.1).

For all this to work, we need to first understand *which* set of market-clearing prices actually correspond to the VCG prices. There are many possible sets of market-clearing prices, but with some checking, we can see that in our examples the VCG prices have corresponded to prices that are as small as possible, subject to having the market-clearing property. So let's consider the following way to make this precise. Over all possible sets of market-clearing prices, consider the ones that minimize the total sum of the prices. (For example, in Figure 15.9, the total sum of prices is $3 + 1 + 0 = 4$.) We will refer to such prices as a set of *minimum market-clearing prices*. In principle, there could be multiple sets of minimum market-clearing prices, but in fact we will see that there is only one such set of these prices, and they form the VCG prices. This is the crux of the following result, proved by Leonard [270] and Demange [128].

> *Claim:* In any matching market, the VCG prices form the unique set of market-clearing prices of minimum total sum.

This is the statement we will prove in this section.

The proof of this statement is quite elegant, but it is also arguably the most intricate piece of analysis in the book; it has a level of complexity that involves bringing together several non-trivial lines of argument as part of the overall proof. In approaching a proof with this type of structure, it helps to proceed in two stages. First, we will outline a sequence of two key facts that illuminate the structure of the underlying matchings. Each of these two facts needs a proof, but we will first simply state the facts and show how the overall proof of the claim follows directly from them. This provides a high-level overview of how the proof works, in a way that is self-contained and contains the central ideas. After this high-level overview, we will describe how to prove the two facts themselves, which will fill in the remaining details of the proof.

Finally, here is one more point to note before beginning: as in a number of previous places when we discussed matching markets, we will assume that all valuations are whole numbers $(0, 1, 2, \ldots)$ and that all prices are whole numbers as well.

A. High-Level Overview of the Proof

Recall that our basic plan is to understand how matchings defining the quantities V_{B-j}^S and V_{B-j}^{S-i} relate to each other, by showing how they arise from a common structure. The

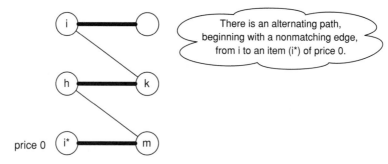

Figure 15.10. The key property of the preferred-seller graph for minimum market-clearing prices: for each item of price greater than 0, there is an alternating path, beginning with a nonmatching edge, to an item of price 0.

first step in doing this to show that the preferred-seller graph for the minimum market-clearing prices contains not only the edges of a perfect matching but also enough extra edges that we can easily assemble other matchings once we begin removing buyers in the ways suggested by the VCG formula.

The First Fact: The Preferred-Seller Graph for Minimum Market-Clearing Prices. The first of our two facts talks about the structure of the preferred-seller graph in the case when a set of market-clearing prices has minimum total sum. As a first step, let's go back to the initial example of market-clearing prices from Chapter 10, and in particular compare preferred-seller graphs for two different sets of market-clearing prices on the same set of valuations, shown in Figures 10.5(b) and 10.5(d). (This latter preferred-seller graph is the one we've redrawn in Figure 15.9.) Notice that the prices in the first of these, Figure 10.5(b), are larger and more "spread out," while the prices in Figure 10.5(d) in fact have minimum total sum. This corresponds to a difference in the structures of the preferred-seller graphs as well. The preferred-seller graph in Figure 10.5(b) is very sparse, with just three separate edges that constitute a perfect matching. The preferred-seller graph in Figure 10.5(d) is much denser: although it too contains only one perfect matching, it has additional edges that seem to serve as supports, "anchoring" the matching in place.

We now show that this anchoring effect is a general one: essentially, whenever a set of market-clearing prices has minimum total sum, the preferred-seller graph must contain not only a perfect matching but also enough other edges to form a path linking each item to an item of price 0. In fact, the paths we construct will be *alternating paths* in the sense defined in Section 10.6: for a given perfect matching in the graph, the edges on the paths will alternate between being part of the matching and not being part of the matching. We refer to these two kinds of edges as *matching edges* and *nonmatching edges*, respectively.

Here is the exact statement of the first fact, shown schematically in Figure 15.10.

> *Fact 1:* Consider the preferred-seller graph for a set of market-clearing prices of minimum total sum, fix a particular perfect matching in this graph, and let *i* be any item whose price is greater than 0. Then there is an alternating path, beginning with a nonmatching edge, that connects *i* to some item of price 0.

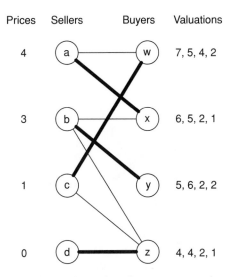

Prices Sellers Buyers Valuations

4 a — w 7, 5, 4, 2

3 b — x 6, 5, 2, 1

1 c — y 5, 6, 2, 2

0 d — z 4, 4, 2, 1

Figure 15.11. A matching market with market-clearing prices of minimum total sum. Note how there is an alternating path from each item, beginning with a nonmatching edge, that leads to the item of zero price.

For example, in Figure 15.9, with the matching indicated in bold, there is an alternating path from b to y to c; this path begins with the nonmatching b-y edge and ends at the zero-priced item c. Similarly, there is a longer alternating path from a through z, b, and y, ending at c. Figure 15.11 shows a larger example, also with market-clearing prices of minimum-total sum, and also with the matching indicated in bold; here too one can find alternating paths from each of items a, b, and c down to the zero-priced item d.

Following our plan, we defer the proof of Fact 1 until later in the section. However, we can give some intuition for the proof as follows. Roughly speaking, if there weren't alternating paths anchoring all the items to items of price 0, then we could find a set of items that were "floating" free of any relation to the zero-priced items. In this case, we could push the prices of these free-floating items down slightly while still preserving the market-clearing property. This would yield a set of market-clearing prices of smaller total sum, contradicting our assumption that we already have the minimum market-clearing prices. This contradiction will show that the minimum market-clearing prices are all anchored via alternating paths to zero-priced items.

The Second Fact: Zeroing Out a Buyer. Our second main fact relates the minimum market-clearing prices to a matching that achieves the value V_{B-j}^S, the first term on the right-hand side of Equation (15.1).

To explain how this fact works, we start with a useful way to think about the quantity V_{B-j}^S. Formally, V_{B-j}^S is the maximum total valuation of any matching in the market where j has been removed, but where all items have been kept. But here's a different, equivalent way to define V_{B-j}^S. Suppose that we were to change j's valuations for every item to 0; we'll call this the version of the matching market in which j has been *zeroed out*. To find an optimal matching in this market with j zeroed out, we note that it doesn't matter which item j gets (since j values them all at zero); therefore, we can

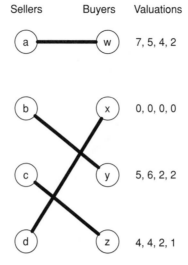

Figure 15.12. If we start with the example in Figure 15.11 and zero out buyer x, the structure of the optimal matching changes significantly.

first optimally match all the other buyers with items and then give j whatever is left over. The value of the resulting matching is V_{B-j}^S. In other words, V_{B-j}^S is the value of the optimal matching in the market where j is zeroed out: she is still present, but all her valuations are now equal to 0.

Now, an optimal matching in the market with j zeroed out may have a structure very different from that of an optimal matching in the original market; different buyers may get completely different items. For example, Figure 15.12 shows the unique optimal matching in the market from Figure 15.11 after we zero out x: other than buyer y, who still gets item b, the assignment of items to all other buyers has changed completely. This is another reflection of the difficulty in reasoning about Equation (15.1): when we remove buyers or items, the matchings can rearrange themselves in complex ways.

Despite this difficulty, there is an important connection between the original market and the zeroed-out market: *the minimum market-clearing prices for the original market are also market-clearing for the zeroed-out market.* We illustrate this for our example in Figure 15.13. Keeping the same prices that were used in Figure 15.11, we see that the preferred-seller graph still has a perfect matching even after x has been zeroed out, which means that the prices are still market clearing. Moreover, we can observe some additional features of this example. First, x now receives an item of price 0. Second, consider the *payoff* of each other buyer, defined as the valuation minus the price of the item she gets. For each other buyer, the payoff is the same in Figures 15.11 and 15.13.

Our second fact shows that all these observations hold in general.

> *Fact 2:* Consider any matching market with minimum market-clearing prices p, and let j be any buyer.
>
> (i) The prices p are also market clearing for the market in which j is zeroed out.

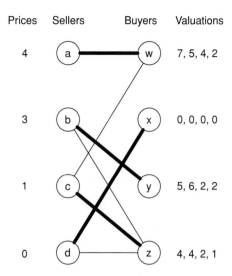

Prices   Sellers   Buyers   Valuations

4   a   w   7, 5, 4, 2

3   b   x   0, 0, 0, 0

1   c   y   5, 6, 2, 2

0   d   z   4, 4, 2, 1

Figure 15.13. However, even after we zero out buyer x, the same set of prices remains market clearing. This principle is true not just for this example, but in general.

Moreover, for any perfect matching in the preferred-seller graph of the zeroed-out market,

(ii) buyer j receives a zero-priced item, and
(iii) each buyer other than j obtains the same payoff that she did in the original market.

Again, we defer the proof of Fact 2 to later in the section, but it is not difficult to establish the proof using Fact 1. Essentially, when we zero out j, we look at the item i that j formerly got in the original market, before she was zeroed out. We follow the alternating path provided by Fact 1 from i down to an item i^* of price 0. We then show that assigning item i^* to j, and shifting the assignment to all other buyers using the edges on this alternating path gives us a perfect matching in the preferred-seller graph of the zeroed-out market at the same prices. This shows that the same prices are in fact market clearing for the zeroed-out market and will establish parts (ii) and (iii) of the claim as well.

Proving the Claim Using Facts 1 and 2. With Facts 1 and 2 in place, we can finish the proof of our main claim – that the minimum market-clearing prices are defined by the VCG formula.

To start, let's review some notation. As before, let v_{ij} denote the valuation that a buyer j has for an item i. Let p_i be the price charged for item i in our market-clearing prices (for the original market, before any buyers are zeroed out), and let P be the sum of the prices of all items. Suppose that buyer j is matched to item i in the perfect matching in the preferred-seller graph. Buyer j receives a payoff of $v_{ij} - p_i$ from this item i; we will use z_j to denote this payoff,

$$z_j = v_{ij} - p_i, \tag{15.4}$$

and Z to denote the sum of the payoffs of all buyers from the items they are matched with.

Next, let's recall two basic observations that were made in earlier sections. First, each buyer j achieves a payoff of $v_{ij} - p_i$ from the item to which she is matched. As we noted in Chapter 10, if we add these expressions up over all buyers, we get the following relationship for the matching M of buyers to items:

Total Payoff of M = Total Valuation of M − Sum of All Prices.

In our current notation, this is

$$Z = V_B^S - P. \tag{15.5}$$

Second, we argued in Section 15.4 that, if i is matched to j in an optimal matching, then

$$v_{ij} + V_{B-j}^{S-i} = V_B^S. \tag{15.6}$$

This is Equation (15.3) from Section 15.4, and it follows simply because one way to achieve an optimal matching is to first pair i with j (obtaining a valuation of v_{ij}) and then optimally match all the remaining buyers and items.

Finally, let's consider this same formula,

Total Payoff of M = Total Valuation of M − Sum of All Prices,

for the market in which j has been zeroed out, using the same set of market-clearing prices and a perfect matching in the preferred-seller graph that Fact 2 provides. The total valuation of this matching is V_{B-j}^S, as we argued earlier. The prices haven't changed, so their total sum is still P. Finally, what's the total payoff? By part (ii) of Fact 2, the payoff for buyer j has dropped from z_j, which it was in the original market, to 0. By part (iii) of Fact 2, the payoff for every other buyer has remained the same. Therefore, the total payoff in the zeroed-out market is $Z - z_i$. Putting all these together, we have the equation

$$Z - z_i = V_{B-j}^S - P. \tag{15.7}$$

Since we now have equations that relate the two terms on the right-hand side of Equation (15.1) to a common set of quantities, we can finish the proof using a small amount of algebraic manipulation. Let's first subtract Equation (15.7) from Equation (15.5), which gives us

$$z_i = V_B^S - V_{B-j}^S.$$

Next, let's expand z_i using Equation (15.4) and expand V_B^S using Equation (15.6), which gives us

$$v_{ij} - p_i = v_{ij} + V_{B-j}^{S-i} - V_{B-j}^S.$$

Canceling the common term of v_{ij} and negating everything, we get

$$p_i = V_{B-j}^S - V_{B-j}^{S-i},$$

which is the VCG formula we were seeking. This shows that the market-clearing prices of minimum total sum are defined by the VCG formula, and hence proves the claim.

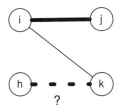

Figure 15.14. In order for a matching edge from a buyer k to an item h to leave the preferred-seller graph when the price of i is reduced by 1, it must be that k now strictly prefers i. In this case, k must have previously viewed i as comparable in payoff to h, resulting in a nonmatching edge to i.

B. Details of the Proof

The discussion so far provides a complete proof, assuming that we take Facts 1 and 2 as given. To finish the proof, therefore, we need to provide proofs of Facts 1 and 2. The crux of this is proving Fact 1, which will consist of an analysis of alternating paths in the style of Section 10.6. After this analysis, establishing Fact 2 is relatively quick using Fact 1.

A First Step Toward Fact 1. To prove Fact 1, we consider a set of minimum market-clearing prices and an item i whose price is greater than 0, and we try to construct an alternating path (beginning with a nonmatching edge) from i to some zero-priced item.

As a first step, to convey the idea at the heart of the argument, let's show something simpler: that this item i, of price $p_i > 0$, is connected to at least one nonmatching edge (in addition to its matching edge to the buyer j that obtains it). Clearly it is necessary to establish the presence of such a nonmatching edge in any case, if we want ultimately to show that i has an alternating path all the way down to a zero-priced item.

So suppose, by way of contradiction, that i is not connected to a nonmatching edge: its only edge is the matching edge to buyer j. In this case, we claim that we can subtract 1 from the price p_i, and the resulting modified prices would still be market clearing. This would be a contradiction, since we assumed our market-clearing prices have minimum total sum.

Clearly if we subtract 1 from p_i, it is still nonnegative, so we just need to show that the preferred-seller graph still contains a perfect matching. In fact, we'll show the stronger fact that the preferred-seller graph still contains all the matching edges that it used to have. Indeed, how could a matching edge leave the preferred-seller graph after the price reduction? The only item that became more attractive was item i, so for a matching edge to leave the preferred-seller graph, it must be that some buyer k other than j, who used to be matched to an item h, drops its edge to h because it now strictly prefers i. This situation is pictured in Figure 15.14. Now, since i's price was only reduced by 1, and since all prices and valuations are whole numbers, if k now strictly prefers to i to h after the price reduction, it must have formerly viewed them as tied. But this means that, before the reduction in i's price, k had a preferred-seller edge to i. Since k was matched to h, this k-i edge would be a nonmatching edge in the preferred-seller graph, which is not possible since we assumed at the outset that i's only edge in the preferred-seller graph was its matching edge to j. This

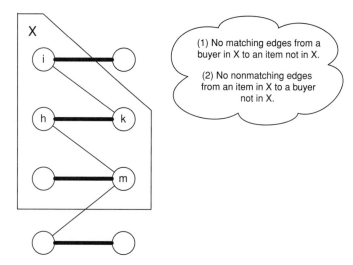

Figure 15.15. Consider the set X of all nodes that can be reached from i using an alternating path that begins with a nonmatching edge. As we argue in the text, if k is a buyer in X, then the item to which she is matched must also be in X. Also, if h is an item in X, then any buyer to which h is connected by a nonmatching edge must also be in X. An equivalent way to phrase this is as follows: there cannot be a matching edge connecting a buyer in X to an item not in X, or a nonmatching edge connecting an item in X to a buyer not in X.

completes the chain of conclusions we need: no matching edge can leave the preferred-seller graph when i's price is reduced by 1, so the reduced prices are still market clearing, and this contradicts the assumption that we had minimum market-clearing prices.

A Proof of Fact 1. The preceding argument is the key to proving Fact 1; for the complete proof, we need to move from simply showing the existence of a nonmatching edge out of i to a full alternating path, beginning with such an edge, all the way to a zero-priced item.

To do this, we start at the item i, and we consider the set X of all nodes in the bipartite graph (both items and buyers) that can be reached from i, using an alternating path that begins with a nonmatching edge. Here are two simple observations about the set X.

(a) For any buyer k who is in X, the item h to which she is matched is also in X. Figure 15.15 helps make clear why this must be true. The alternating path that reached k from i must have ended on a nonmatching edge, so by adding the matching edge to h to the end of this path, we see that h must also be in X.

(b) For any item h that is in X, and any buyer m connected to h by a nonmatching edge in the preferred-seller graph, the buyer m must also be in X. This is a direct companion to the previous fact and is also illustrated by Figure 15.15: the alternating path that reached h from i must have ended on a matching edge, so by adding the nonmatching edge to m to the end of this path, we see that m must also be in X.

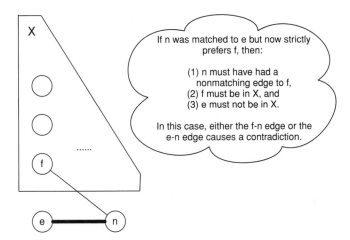

Figure 15.16. We can reduce the prices of all items in X by 1 and still retain the market-clearing property. As argued in the text, the only way this can fail is if some matching edge connects a buyer in X to an item not in X, or some nonmatching edge connects an item in X to a buyer not in X. Either of these possibilities would contradict the facts in Figure 15.15.

If this set X contains an item of price 0, we are done; we have the path we want. If this set X doesn't contain an item of price 0, then we complete the proof using the same price-reduction idea we saw earlier, in our warmup to the proof of Fact 1: we will reduce the price of each item in X by 1, show that the resulting prices are still market clearing, and thereby contradict our assumption that we had the minimum market-clearing prices. It will follow that X must contain a zero-priced item.

Here is the main thing we need to show.

> Suppose we reduce the price of each item in X by 1. Then all matching edges that were in the preferred-seller graph before the price reduction remain in the preferred-seller graph after the price reduction.

The argument is essentially the same as the one we used earlier when reducing the price of just item i. We ask: how could a matching edge leave the preferred-seller graph after the reduction? Figure 15.16 shows what must happen for this to be possible: a buyer n was formerly matched to an item e, and now some other item f has strictly higher payoff after the price reduction. Because all valuations, prices, and payoffs are whole numbers, and no price changed by more than 1, it must be that e and f used to be tied for the highest payoff to n (so n had edges to both of them in the preferred-seller graph before the reduction) and f is in the set X while e is not (so f had its price reduced while e's price remained the same).

Now we get a contradiction to one of our basic observations (a) and (b) about the set X. Since n was matched to e, and e is not in X, observation (a) says that n must not be in X, but since n was not matched to f, and f is in X, observation (b) says that n must be in X. This contradiction – n must be both in X and not in X – shows that no matching edge can leave the preferred-seller graph after the price reduction. And this in turn establishes that the reduced prices are still market clearing after the price

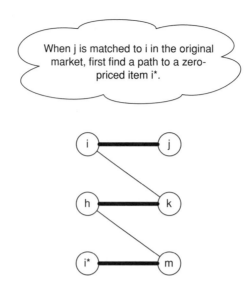

Figure 15.17. The first step in analyzing the market with j zeroed out: find an alternating path from item i – to which buyer j was matched in the original market – to a zero-priced item i^*.

reduction, contradicting our assumption that they were the minimum market-clearing prices.

This concludes the proof; if we look back at how it worked, we can see that it bears out our intuition for how the nonmatching edges serve to anchor all the items via alternating paths to the items of price 0. Specifically, if this anchoring did not happen, then there would be a set X that was floating free of any connections to zero-priced items, and in this case the prices of all items in X could be pushed further downward. This can't happen if the market-clearing prices are already as low as possible.

A Proof of Fact 2. To prove Fact 2, we start with a matching market with minimum market-clearing prices p, and we consider the preferred-seller graph for these prices. Now, suppose that we zero out a buyer j but keep the prices the same. The resulting preferred-seller graph is now different, but we'd like to show that it still contains a perfect matching.

How does the preferred-seller graph change when we zero out j, keeping the prices fixed? For buyers other than j, their edges remain the same, since they have the same valuations and observe the same prices. For j, on the other hand, the zero-priced items are now the only items that give her a nonnegative payoff, so her edges in the preferred-seller graph now go to precisely this set of zero-priced items. Notice, for example, that this is what happens to the preferred-seller graph as we move from Figure 15.11 to Figure 15.13: the zeroed-out buyer x has its preferred-seller edge shift from item b to the zero-priced item d.

Because we know that the preferred-seller graph in the original market has the structure guaranteed by Fact 1, we can view this change to the preferred-seller graph in the way suggested by Figures 15.17 and 15.18. Before zeroing out j, when it is matched to some item i, there is an alternating path in the preferred-seller graph, beginning with

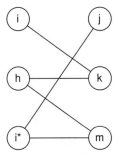

Figure 15.18. The second step in analyzing the market with j zeroed out: build the new preferred-seller graph by rewiring j's preferred-seller edges to point to the zero-priced items.

a nonmatching edge, from i to a zero-priced item i^*. After zeroing out j, there is a preferred-seller edge from j directly to i^* (and to any other zero-priced items as well).

It is easy to see from this pair of pictures how to find a perfect matching in the preferred-seller graph after this change to its structure. This is shown in Figure 15.19: for each buyer other than j who is involved in the alternating path from i to i^*, we simply shift her edge "upward" along the alternating path. This shift makes room for j to match with i^*, restoring the perfect matching.

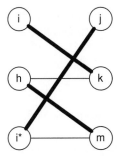

Figure 15.19. The third and final step in analyzing the market with j zeroed out: observe that the rewired preferred-seller graph still contains a perfect matching, in which j is now paired with i^*.

Since the preferred-seller graph has a perfect matching, this establishes that the prices are still market clearing for the zeroed-out market. We can also establish parts (ii) and (iii) of Fact 2 directly from our construction. Part (ii) follows simply from the fact that j only has edges to zero-priced items in the preferred-seller graph. For part (iii), note first of all that it is a statement about the payoffs that buyers receive. Even when there are potentially multiple perfect matchings in a preferred-seller graph, any given buyer obtains the same payoff in every one of these perfect matchings, since all of her edges in the preferred-seller graph yield the same payoff. As a result, it is enough to establish part (iii) for the perfect matching we just constructed, and it then applies to the payoff properties of every perfect matching in the preferred-seller graph. So consider the matching we just constructed, and let k be any buyer other than j. Either k gets the same item she had in the perfect matching for the original market – in which case she gets the same payoff – or else k shifts from one item to another along the alternating path. In this latter case, since k had edges to both of these items in the preferred-seller graph of the original market, she receives the same payoff from each of them, and so again k's payoff remains the same. This completes the proof of Fact 2, and hence fills in the final details needed to complete the proof of the overall claim.

15.10 Exercises

1. Suppose a search engine has two ad slots that it can sell. Slot a has a clickthrough rate of 10 and slot b has a clickthrough rate of 5. There are three advertisers who are interested in these slots. Advertiser x values clicks at 3 per click, advertiser y values clicks at 2 per click, and advertiser z values clicks at 1 per click.

   Compute the socially optimal allocation and the VCG prices for it. Give a brief explanation for your answer.

2. Suppose a search engine has three ad slots that it can sell. Slot a has a clickthrough rate of 6, slot b has a clickthrough rate of 5, and slot c has a clickthrough rate of 1. There are three advertisers who are interested in these slots. Advertiser x values clicks at 4 per click, advertiser y values clicks at 2 per click, and advertiser z values clicks at 1 per click. Compute the socially optimal allocation and the VCG prices for it. Give a brief explanation for your answer.

3. Suppose a search engine has three ad slots that it can sell. Slot a has a clickthrough rate of 5, slot b has a clickthrough rate of 2, and slot c has a clickthrough rate of 1. There are three advertisers who are interested in these slots. Advertiser x values clicks at 3 per click, advertiser y values clicks at 2 per click, and advertiser z values clicks at 1 per click.

   Compute the socially optimal allocation and the VCG prices for it. Give a brief explanation for your answer.

4. Suppose a search engine has two ad slots that it can sell. Slot a has a clickthrough rate of 4 and slot b has a clickthrough rate of 3. There are three advertisers who are interested in these slots. Advertiser x values clicks at 4 per click, advertiser y values clicks at 3 per click, and advertiser z values clicks at 1 per click.

   (a) Suppose that the search engine runs the VCG mechanism to allocate slots. What assignment of slots will occur and what prices will the advertisers pay? Give an explanation for your answer.

(b) Now the search engine is considering the creation of a third ad slot which will have a clickthrough rate of 2. Let's call this new ad slot c. Suppose that search engine does create this slot and again uses the VCG mechanism to allocate slots. What assignment of slots will occur and what prices will the advertisers pay? Give an explanation for your answer.

(c) What revenue will the search engine receive from the VCG mechanism in parts (a) and (b)? If you were running the search engine, given this set of advertisers and slots, and could choose whether to create slot c, what would you do? Why? (In answering this question, assume that you have to use the VCG mechanism to allocate any slots you create.)

5. Suppose a search engine has two ad slots that it can sell. Slot a has a clickthrough rate of 12 and slot b has a clickthrough rate of 5. There are two advertisers who are interested in these slots. Advertiser x values clicks at 5 per click and advertiser y values clicks at 4 per click.

(a) Compute the socially optimal allocation and the VCG prices for it.

(b) Suppose the search engine decides not to sell slot b. Instead, it sells only slot a using a sealed-bid, second-price auction. What bids will the advertisers submit for slot a, who will win, and what price will they pay?

(c) Which of these two possible procedures, (a) or (b), generates the greater revenue for the search engine? By how much?

(d) Now let's see if the result in part (c) is general or not. That is, does it depend on the clickthrough rates and values? Suppose there are two slots and two advertisers; the clickthrough rates are r_a for slot a and r_b for slot b, with $r_a > r_b > 0$; and the advertisers' values are v_x and v_y, with $v_x > v_y > 0$. Can you determine which of the two procedures generates the greater revenue for the search engine? Explain.

6. Chapter 15 discusses the relationship between the VCG principle and second-price auctions. In particular, we saw that the VCG principle is a generalization of the idea behind second-price auctions to a setting in which there is more than one object being sold. In this problem we explore this relationship in an example. Suppose that a seller has one item, which we call item x. There are three buyers, whom we call a, b, and c. The values that these buyers (a, b, and c) have for the item are 6, 3, and 1, respectively.

(a) Suppose that the seller runs a second-price auction for the item. Which buyer will win the auction and how much will this buyer pay?

(b) Now let's suppose that the seller uses the VCG mechanism to allocate the item. Remember that the first step in the running the VCG mechanism when there are more buyers than items is to create fictional items, which each buyer values at 0, so that the number of items to be allocated is the same as the number of bidders. Let's call these additional (fictional) items y and z. Find the allocation that results from running the VCG mechanism. What are the prices charged to each buyer for the item that they receive? Explain why the price that buyer a pays is the harm that he causes to the remaining bidders by taking the item he is assigned.

PART FIVE

Network Dynamics: Population Models

CHAPTER 16

Information Cascades

16.1 Following the Crowd

When people are connected by a network, it becomes possible for them to influence each other's behavior and decisions. In the next several chapters, we will explore how this basic principle gives rise to a range of social processes in which networks serve to aggregate individual behavior and thus produce population-wide, collective outcomes.

There is a nearly limitless set of situations in which people are influenced by others: in the opinions they hold, the products they buy, the political positions they support, the activities they pursue, the technologies they use, and many other things. What we'd like to do here is to go beyond this observation and consider some of the reasons why such influence occurs. We'll see that there are many settings in which it may in fact be rational for an individual to imitate the choices of others even if the individual's own information suggests an alternative choice.

As a first example, suppose that you are choosing a restaurant in an unfamiliar town, and based on your own research about restaurants, you intend to go to restaurant A. However, when you arrive you see that no one is eating in restaurant A, whereas restaurant B next door is nearly full. If you believe that other diners have tastes similar to yours, and that they too have some information about where to eat, it may be rational to join the crowd at B rather than to follow your own information. To see how this is possible, suppose that each diner has obtained independent but imperfect information about which of the two restaurants is better. Then if there are already many diners in restaurant B, the information that you can infer from their choices may be more powerful than your own private information, in which case it would in fact make sense for you to join them regardless of your own private information. In this case, we say that *herding*, or an *information cascade*, has occurred. This terminology, as well as this example, comes from the work of Banerjee [40]; the concept was also developed in other work around the same time by Bikhchandani, Hirshleifer, and Welch [59, 412].

Roughly, then, an information cascade has the potential to occur when people make decisions sequentially, with later people watching the actions of earlier people and from these actions inferring something about what the earlier people know. In our restaurant

425

example, when the first diners to arrive chose restaurant B, they conveyed information to later diners about what they knew. A cascade then develops when people abandon their own information in favor of inferences based on earlier people's actions.

What is interesting here is that individuals in a cascade are imitating the behavior of others, but it is not mindless imitation. Rather, it is the result of drawing rational inferences from limited information. Of course, imitation may also occur due to social pressure to conform, without any underlying informational cause, and it is not always easy to tell these two phenomena apart. Consider, for example, the following experiment performed by Milgram, Bickman, and Berkowitz in the 1960s [298]. The experimenters had groups of people, ranging in size from just one person to as many as fifteen people, stand on a street corner and stare up into the sky. They then observed how many passersby stopped and also looked up at the sky. They found that with only one person looking up, very few passersby stopped. If five people were staring up into the sky, then more passersby stopped, but most still ignored them. Finally, with fifteen people looking up, they found that 45% of passersby stopped and also stared up into the sky.

The experimenters interpreted this result as demonstrating a social force for conformity that grows stronger as the group conforming to the activity becomes larger. But another possible explanation – essentially, a possible mechanism giving rise to the conformity observed in this kind of situation – is rooted in the idea of information cascades. It could be that initially the passersby saw no reason to look up (they had no private or public information that suggested it was necessary), but with more and more people looking up, future passersby may have rationally decided that there was good reason to also look up (since perhaps those looking up knew something that the passersby didn't know).

Ultimately, information cascades may be at least part of the explanation for many types of imitation in social settings. Fashions and fads, voting for popular candidates, the self-reinforcing success of books placed highly on best-seller lists, the spread of a technological choice by consumers and by firms, and the localized nature of crime and political movements can all be seen as examples of herding, in which people make decisions based on inferences from what earlier people have done.

Informational Effects Versus Direct-Benefit Effects. There is also a fundamentally different class of rational reasons why you may want to imitate what other people are doing. You may want to copy the behavior of others if there is a direct benefit to you from aligning your behavior with their behavior. For example, consider the first fax machines to be sold. A fax machine is useless if no one else owns one, and so in evaluating whether to buy one, it's very important to know whether there are other people who own one as well – not just because their purchase decisions convey information, but because they directly affect the fax machine's value to you as a product. A similar argument can be made for computer operating systems, social networking sites, and other kinds of technology where you directly benefit from choosing an option that has a large user population.

This type of direct-benefit effect is different from the informational effects we discussed previously: here, the actions of others affect your payoffs directly, rather than indirectly by changing your information. Many decisions exhibit both information and direct-benefit effects. For example, in the technology-adoption decisions just discussed, you potentially learn from others' decisions in addition to benefiting from compatibility with them. In some cases, the two effects are even in conflict: if you have to wait in a long line to get into a popular restaurant, you are choosing to let the informational benefits of imitating others outweigh the direct inconvenience (from waiting) that this imitation causes you.

In this chapter, we develop some simple models of information cascades; in the next chapter, we do this for direct-benefit effects. One reason to develop minimal, stylized models for these effects is to see whether the stories we've been telling can have a simple basis, and we will see that much of what we've been discussing at an informal level can indeed be represented in very basic models of decision-making by individuals.

16.2 A Simple Herding Experiment

Before delving into the mathematical models for information cascades [40, 59, 412], we start with a simple herding experiment created by Anderson and Holt [14, 15] to illustrate how these models work.

The experiment is designed to capture situations with the basic ingredients from our discussion in the previous section:

(a) There is a decision to be made – for example, whether to adopt a new technology, wear a new style of clothing, eat in a new restaurant, or support a particular political position.
(b) People make the decision sequentially, and each person can observe the choices made by those who acted earlier.
(c) Each person has some private information that helps guide their decision.
(d) A person can't directly observe the private information that other people *know*, but he or she can make inferences about this private information from what they *do*.

We imagine the experiment taking place in a classroom, with a large group of students as participants. The experimenter puts an urn at the front of the room with three marbles hidden in it; she announces that there is a 50% chance that the urn contains two red marbles and one blue marble, and a 50% chance the urn contains two blue marbles and one red marble. In the former case, we say that it is a "majority-red" urn, and in the latter case, we say that it is a "majority-blue" urn.[1]

Now, one by one, each student comes to the front of the room and draws a marble from the urn; he looks at the color and then places it back in the urn without showing it to the rest of the class. The student then guesses whether the urn is majority-red or majority-blue and publicly announces this guess to the class. (We assume that, at

---

[1] It's important that the students believe this statement about probabilities. So you can imagine, if you like, that the experimenter has actually filled two urns with marbles. One has two red marbles and one blue marble, and the other urn contains two blue marbles and one red marble. One of these urns is selected at random, with equal probability for each urn, and this is the urn used in the experiment.

the very end of the experiment, each student who has guessed correctly receives a monetary reward, while students who have guessed incorrectly receive nothing.) The public announcement is the key part of the setup: the students who have not yet had their turn don't get to see which colors the earlier students draw, but they do get to hear the guesses that are being made. This parallels our original example with the two restaurants: one by one, each diner needs to guess which is the better restaurant, and while they don't get to see the reviews read by the earlier diners, they do get to see which restaurant these earlier diners chose.

Let's now consider what we should expect to happen when this experiment is performed. We will assume that all the students reason correctly about what to do when it is their turn to guess, using everything they have heard so far. We will keep the analysis of the experiment informal; later we will use a mathematical model to justify it more precisely.

We organize the discussion by considering what happens with each student in order. Things are fairly straightforward for the first two students; they become interesting once we reach the third student.

- *The First Student.* The first student should follow a simple decision rule for making a guess: if he sees a red marble, it is better to guess that the urn is majority-red; and if he sees a blue marble, it is better to guess that the urn is majority-blue. (This is an intuitively natural rule, and – as with the other conclusions we draw here – we will justify it later mathematically using the model we develop in the subsequent sections.) This means the first student's guess conveys perfect information about what he has seen.
- *The Second Student.* If the second student sees the same color that the first student announced, then her choice is simple: she should guess this color as well.

  However, suppose she sees the opposite color – say that she sees red while the first guess was blue. Since the first guess was exactly what the first student saw, the second student can essentially reason as though she got to draw twice from the urn, seeing blue once and red once. In this case, she is indifferent about which guess to make; we will assume in this case that she breaks the tie by guessing the color she saw. Thus, whichever color the second student draws, her guess too conveys perfect information about what she has seen.
- *The Third Student.* Things start to get interesting here. If the first two students have guessed opposite colors, then the third student should just guess the color he sees, since it will effectively break the tie between the first two guesses.

  But suppose the first two guesses have been the same – say they've both been blue – and the third student draws red. Since we've decided that the first two guesses convey perfect information, the third student can reason in this case as though he saw three draws from the urn: two blue, and one red. Given this information, he should guess that the urn is majority-blue, ignoring his own private information (which, taken by itself, suggested that the urn is majority-red).

  More generally, the point is that when the first two guesses are the same, the third student should guess this color as well, *regardless* of which color he draws from the urn. And the rest of class will only hear his guess; they don't get to see which color he's drawn. In this case, an information cascade has begun. The third student makes the same guess as the first two, regardless of which color he draws from the urn, and hence regardless of his own private information.

- *The Fourth Student and Onward.* For purposes of this informal discussion, let's consider just the "interesting" case of the third student discussed above, in which the first two guesses were the same – suppose they were both blue. In this case, we've argued that the third student will also announce a guess of blue, regardless of what he actually saw.

  Now consider the situation faced by the fourth student, getting ready to make a guess having heard three guesses of "blue" in a row. She knows that the first two guesses conveyed perfect information about what the first two students saw. She also knows that, given this, the third student was going to guess "blue" no matter what he saw – so his guess conveys no information.

  As a result, the fourth student is in exactly the same situation – from the point of view of making a decision – as the third student. Whichever color she draws, it will be outweighed by the two draws of blue by the first two students, and so she should guess "blue" regardless of what she sees.

  This will continue with all the subsequent students: if the first two guesses are "blue," then everyone in order will guess "blue" as well. (Of course, a completely symmetric thing happens if the first two guesses are "red.") An information cascade has taken hold: no one is under the illusion that every single person is drawing a blue marble, but once the first two guesses turn out "blue," the future announced guesses become worthless and so everyone's best strategy is to rely on the limited genuine information they have available.

In the next section, we'll discuss a model of decision making under uncertainty that justifies the guesses made by the students. More generally, our discussion hasn't considered every possible eventuality (for example, what should you do if you're the sixth student and you've heard the guesses "blue, red, red, blue, blue"?), but our subsequent model will actually predict an outcome for any sequence of guesses.

For now, though, let's think about the particular scenario discussed here – the way in which a cascade takes place as long as the first two guesses are the same. Although the setting is very stylized, it teaches us a number of general principles about information cascades. First, it shows how easily they can occur, given the right structural conditions. It also shows how a bizarre pattern of decisions – each of a large group of students making exactly the same guess – can take place even when all the decision makers are being completely rational.

Second, it shows that information cascades can lead to nonoptimal outcomes. Suppose, for example, that we have an urn that is majority-red. There is a $\frac{1}{3}$ chance that the first student draws a blue marble and a $\frac{1}{3}$ chance that the second student draws a blue marble; since these draws are independent, there is a $\frac{1}{3} \times \frac{1}{3} = \frac{1}{9}$ chance that both draw a blue marble. In this case, both of the first two guesses will be "blue"; therefore, as we have just argued, all subsequent guesses will be "blue" and all of these guesses will be wrong, because the urn is majority-red. This $\frac{1}{9}$ chance of a population-wide error is not ameliorated by having many people participate, since under rational decision making, everyone will guess blue if the first two guesses are blue, no matter how large the group.

Third, this experiment illustrates that cascades – despite their potential to produce long runs of conformity – can be fundamentally very fragile. For example, suppose that, in a class of 100 students, the first two guesses are "blue," and all subsequent guesses are proceeding – as predicted – to be "blue" as well. Now, suppose that students 50 and 51 both draw red marbles, and they each "cheat" by showing their marbles directly to the rest of the class. In this case, the cascade has been broken: when student 52 gets up to make a guess, she has four pieces of genuine information to go on: the colors observed by students 1, 2, 50, and 51. Since two of these colors are blue and two are red, she should make the guess based on her own draw, which will break the tie.

The point is that everyone knew the initial run of 49 "blue" guesses had very little information supporting it, and so it was easy for a fresh infusion of new information to overturn it. This is the essential fragility of information cascades: even after they have persisted for a long time, they can be overturned with comparatively little effort.[2]

This style of experiment has generated a significant amount of subsequent research in its own right, and understanding the extent to which human subjects follow this type of behavior under real experimental conditions is a subtle issue [100, 223]. For our purposes, however, the simple description of the experiment is intended to serve mainly as a vivid illustration of some of the basic properties of information cascades in a controlled setting. Having now developed some of these basic properties, we turn to the formulation of a model that lets us reason precisely about the decision making that takes place during a cascade.

16.3 Bayes's Rule: A Model of Decision Making under Uncertainty

If we want to build a mathematical model for how information cascades occur, it will necessarily involve people asking themselves questions like, "What is the probability this is the better restaurant, given the reviews I've read and the crowds I see in each one?" Or, "What is the probability this urn is majority-red, given the marble I just drew and the guesses I've heard?" In other words, we need a way to determine probabilities of events given information that is observed.

Conditional Probability and Bayes' Rule. We will compute the probabilities of various *events*, and use these probabilities to reason about decision making. In the context of the experiment from Section 16.2, an event could be "the urn is majority-blue," or "the first student draws a blue marble." Given any event A, we will denote its probability of occurring by $\Pr[A]$. Whether an event occurs or not is the result of certain random outcomes (which urn was placed at the front of the room, which marble a particular student grabbed when he reached in, and so forth). Therefore, we imagine a large *sample space* in which each point in the sample space consists of a particular realization for each of these random outcomes.

---

[2] It is important to note that not all imitative effects are so easy to overturn. As we will see in the next chapter, for example, imitation based on direct-benefit effects can be very difficult to reverse once it is under way.

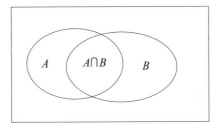

Figure 16.1. Two events A and B in a sample space, and the joint event A ∩ B.

Given a sample space, events can be pictured graphically as in Figure 16.1: the unit-area rectangle in the figure represents the sample space of all possible outcomes, and the event A is then a region within this sample space – the set of all outcomes where event A occurs. In the figure, the probability of A corresponds to the area of this region. The relationship between two events can be illustrated graphically as well. In Figure 16.1 we see two events, A and B. The area where they overlap corresponds to the joint event when both A and B occur. This event is the intersection of A and B, and it's denoted by A ∩ B.

If we think about the examples of questions at the start of this section, we see that it is not enough to talk about the probability of an event A; rather, we need to consider the probability of A *given that some other event B has occurred*. For example, A may be the event that the urn in the experiment from Section 16.2 is majority-blue, and B may be the event that the ball you've drawn is blue. We will refer to this quantity as the *conditional probability of A given B* and denote it by $\Pr[A \mid B]$. Again, the graphical depiction in Figure 16.1 is useful: to determine the conditional probability of A given B, we assume that we are in the part of the sample space corresponding to B, and we want to know the probability that we are also in A (that is, in the intersection A ∩ B). We can think of this as the fraction of the area of region B occupied by A ∩ B, and so we define

$$\Pr[A \mid B] = \frac{\Pr[A \cap B]}{\Pr[B]}. \tag{16.1}$$

Similarly, the conditional probability of B given A is

$$\Pr[B \mid A] = \frac{\Pr[B \cap A]}{\Pr[A]} = \frac{\Pr[A \cap B]}{\Pr[A]}, \tag{16.2}$$

where the second equality follows simply because A ∩ B and B ∩ A are the same set.

Rewriting Equations (16.1) and (16.2), we have

$$\Pr[A \mid B] \times \Pr[B] = \Pr[A \cap B] = \Pr[B \mid A] \times \Pr[A], \tag{16.3}$$

and therefore, dividing through by $\Pr[B]$,

$$\Pr[A \mid B] = \frac{\Pr[A] \times \Pr[B \mid A]}{\Pr[B]}. \tag{16.4}$$

Equation (16.4) is called *Bayes' rule*. There is also a bit of extra useful terminology surrounding Bayes' rule. When we want to make explicit that we're interested in the effect of event B on the probability of an event A, we refer to $\Pr[A]$ as the *prior probability* of A, since it reflects our understanding of the probability of A without knowing anything about whether B has occurred. Correspondingly, we refer to Pr [A | B] as the *posterior probability* of A given B, since it reflects our new understanding of the probability of A now that we know B has occurred. The effect of knowing B is thus captured in the change from the prior probability of A to the posterior probability of A, using Equation (16.4).

An Example of Bayes' Rule. As noted earlier, we will apply Bayes' rule when a decision maker is assessing the probability that a particular choice is the best one, *given* the event that he has received certain private information, observed certain other decisions, or both. To get used to Bayes' rule, we first work through a basic example that illustrates how it is typically applied.

The example involves eyewitness testimony. Suppose that in some city 80% of taxi cabs are black and the remaining 20% are yellow. A witness to a hit-and-run accident involving a taxi states that the cab involved was yellow. Suppose that eyewitness testimony is imperfect in the sense that witnesses sometimes misidentify the colors of cabs. In particular, let's suppose that if a taxi is yellow then a witness will claim it is yellow after the fact 80% of the time; if it is black, they will claim it is black 80% of the time.

Interpreting eyewitness testimony, therefore, is at some level a question of conditional probability: what is the probability the cab is yellow (or black), given that the witness says it is yellow? Introducing some notation, let "true" denote the true color of the cab, and let "report" denote the reported color of the cab; let Y denote yellow and B denote black. We are looking for the value of Pr [*true* = Y | *report* = Y].

The information we have does not directly include the answer to this question, but we can determine the answer using Bayes' rule. Applying Equation (16.4) with A equal to the event *true* = Y and B equal to the event *report* = Y, we have

$$\Pr[true = Y \mid report = Y] = \frac{\Pr[true = Y] \times \Pr[report = Y \mid true = Y]}{\Pr[report = Y]}. \quad (16.5)$$

Now, we've been told that Pr [*report* = Y | *true* = Y] is 0.8 (this is the accuracy of eyewitness testimony) and that Pr [*true* = Y] is 0.2 (this is the frequency of yellow taxi cabs and hence provides the prior probability of the event *true* = Y). We can also figure out the denominator with a little work, as follows. There are two ways for a witness to report that a cab is yellow: one is for the cab to actually be yellow, and the other is for it to actually be black. The probability of getting a report of yellow via the former option is

$$\Pr[true = Y] \times \Pr[report = Y \mid true = Y] = 0.2 \times 0.8 = 0.16,$$

and the probability of getting a report of yellow via the latter option is

$$\Pr[true = B] \times \Pr[report = Y \mid true = B] = 0.8 \times 0.2 = 0.16.$$

The probability of a report of yellow is the sum of these two probabilities,

$$\Pr[report = Y] = \Pr[true = Y] \times \Pr[report = Y \mid true = Y]$$
$$+ \Pr[true = B] \times \Pr[report = Y \mid true = B]$$
$$= 0.2 \times 0.8 + 0.8 \times 0.2 = 0.32.$$

We can now put everything together via Equation (16.5) to get

$$\Pr[\mathit{true} = \mathrm{Y} \mid \mathit{report} = \mathrm{Y}] = \frac{\Pr[\mathit{true} = \mathrm{Y}] \times \Pr[\mathit{report} = \mathrm{Y} \mid \mathit{true} = \mathrm{Y}]}{\Pr[\mathit{report} = \mathrm{Y}]}$$

$$= \frac{0.2 \times 0.8}{0.32}$$

$$= 0.5.$$

So if the witness says the cab was yellow, the conclusion is that it is in fact equally likely to have been yellow or black. Because the frequency of black and yellow cabs makes black substantially more likely in the absence of any other information (0.8 versus 0.2), the witness's report had a substantial effect on our beliefs about the color of the particular cab involved. But the report should not lead us to believe that the cab was in fact more likely to have been yellow than black.[3]

A Second Example: Spam Filtering. As the example with taxi cabs illustrates, Bayes' rule is a fundamental way to make inferences from observations, and as such it is used in a wide variety of settings. One application where it has been very influential is in e-mail spam detection – automatically filtering unwanted e-mail out of a user's incoming e-mail stream. Bayes' rule was a crucial conceptual ingredient in the first generation of e-mail spam filters, and it continues to form part of the foundation for many spam filters [187].

We can appreciate the connection between Bayes' rule and spam filtering through the following example. Suppose that you receive a piece of e-mail whose subject line contains the phrase "check this out" (a popular phrase among spammers). Based just on this (and without looking at the sender or the message content), what is the chance the message is spam?

This is already a question about conditional probability: we're asking for the value of

$$\Pr[\mathit{message\ is\ spam} \mid \mathit{subject\ contains\ ``check\ this\ out"}].$$

To make this equation and the ones that follow a bit simpler to read, let's abbreviate *message is spam* to just *spam*, and abbreviate *subject contains "check this out"* to just *"check this out"*; so we want the value of

$$\Pr[\mathit{spam} \mid \mathit{``check\ this\ out"}].$$

To determine this value, we need to know some facts about your e-mail and the general use of the phrase "check this out" in subject lines. Suppose that 40% of all your e-mail is spam and the remaining 60% is e-mail you want to receive. Also, suppose that 1% of all spam messages contain the phrase "check this out" in their subject lines, while 0.4% of all nonspam messages contain this phrase. Writing these in terms of probabilities, it says that $\Pr[\mathit{spam}] = 0.4$; this is the prior probability that an incoming message is

---

[3] Kahneman and Tversky have run an experiment with a similar example which shows that people sometimes do not make predictions according to Bayes' rule [231]. In their experiment, subjects place too much weight on their observations and too little weight on prior probabilities. The effect of errors in predictions on actions, and the subsequent effect on cascades is an interesting topic, but we do not address it here.

spam (without conditioning on events based on the message itself). Also, we have

$$\Pr[\textit{"check this out"} \mid spam] = 0.01$$

and

$$\Pr[\textit{"check this out"} \mid not\ spam] = 0.004.$$

We're now in a situation completely analogous to the calculations involving eyewitness testimony: we can use Bayes' rule to write

$$\Pr[spam \mid \textit{"check this out"}] = \frac{\Pr[spam] \times \Pr[\textit{"check this out"} \mid spam]}{\Pr[\textit{"check this out"}]}.$$

Based on what we know, we can determine that the numerator is $0.4 \times 0.01 = 0.004$. For the denominator, as in the taxi cab example, we note that there are two ways for a message to contain "check this out" – either by being spam or by not being spam. As in that calculation,

$$\Pr[\textit{"check this out"}] = \Pr[spam] \times \Pr[\textit{"check this out"} \mid spam]$$
$$+ \Pr[not\ spam] \times \Pr[\textit{"check this out"} \mid not\ spam]$$
$$= 0.4 \times 0.01 + 0.6 \times 0.004 = 0.0064.$$

Dividing numerator by denominator, we get our answer:

$$\Pr[spam \mid \textit{"check this out"}] = \frac{0.004}{0.0064} = \frac{5}{8} = 0.625.$$

In other words, although spam (in this example) forms less than half of your incoming e-mail, a message whose subject line contains the phrase "check this out" is – in the absence of any other information – more likely to be spam than not.

We can therefore view the presence of this phrase in the subject line as a weak "signal" about the message, providing us with evidence about whether it's spam. In practice, spam filters built on Bayes' rule look for a wide range of different signals in each message – the words in the message body, the words in the subject, properties of the sender (do you know them? what kind of an e-mail address are they using?), properties of the mail program used to compose the message, and other features. Each signal provides its own estimate for whether the message is spam or not, and spam filters then combine these estimates to arrive at an overall guess about whether the message is spam. For example, if we also knew that the message came from someone you send mail to every day, then presumably this competing signal – strongly indicating that the message is not spam – should outweigh the presence of the phrase "check this out" in the subject.

16.4 Bayes's Rule in the Herding Experiment

Let's now use Bayes' rule to justify the reasoning used by the students in the simple herding experiment from Section 16.2. First, notice that each student's decision is intrinsically based on determining a conditional probability: each student is trying to estimate the conditional probability that the urn is majority-blue or majority-red, given what she has seen and heard. To maximize her chance of winning the monetary reward for guessing correctly, she should guess majority-blue if

$$\Pr[\text{majority-blue} \mid \text{what she has seen and heard}] > \frac{1}{2}$$

and guess majority-red otherwise. If the two conditional probabilities are both exactly 0.5, then it doesn't matter what she guesses.

We know the following facts from the setup of the experiment, before anyone has drawn any marbles. First, the prior probabilities of majority-blue and majority-red are each $\frac{1}{2}$:

$$\Pr[\text{majority-blue}] = \Pr[\text{majority-red}] = \frac{1}{2}.$$

Also, based on the composition of the two kinds of urns,

$$\Pr[\text{blue} \mid \text{majority-blue}] = \Pr[\text{red} \mid \text{majority-red}] = \frac{2}{3}.$$

Now, following the scenario from Section 16.2, let's suppose that the first student draws a blue marble. He therefore wants to determine $\Pr[\text{majority-blue} \mid \text{blue}]$ and, just as in the examples from Section 16.3, he can use Bayes' rule to calculate

$$\Pr[\text{majority-blue} \mid \text{blue}] = \frac{\Pr[\text{majority-blue}] \times \Pr[\text{blue} \mid \text{majority-blue}]}{\Pr[\text{blue}]}. \quad (16.6)$$

The numerator is $\frac{1}{2} \times \frac{2}{3} = \frac{1}{3}$. For the denominator, we reason just as in Section 16.3 by noting that there are two possible ways to get a blue marble – if the urn is majority-blue or if it is majority-red:

$$\Pr[\text{blue}] = \Pr[\text{majority-blue}] \times \Pr[\text{blue} \mid \text{majority-blue}]$$
$$+ \Pr[\text{majority-red}] \times \Pr[\text{blue} \mid \text{majority-red}]$$
$$= \frac{1}{2} \times \frac{2}{3} + \frac{1}{2} \times \frac{1}{3} = \frac{1}{2}.$$

The answer $\Pr[\text{blue}] = \frac{1}{2}$ makes sense, given that the roles of blue and red in this experiment are completely symmetric.

Dividing numerator by denominator, we get

$$\Pr[\text{majority-blue} \mid \text{blue}] = \frac{1/3}{1/2} = \frac{2}{3}.$$

Since this conditional probability is greater than $\frac{1}{2}$, we get the intuitive result that the first student should guess majority-blue when he sees a blue marble. Note that in addition to providing the basis for the guess, Bayes' rule provides a probability, namely $\frac{2}{3}$, that the guess will be correct.

The calculation is very similar for the second student, and we skip it so as to move on to the calculation for the third student, where a cascade begins to form. Let's suppose, as in the scenario from Section 16.2, that the first two students have announced guesses of blue, and the third student draws a red marble. As we discussed there, the first two guesses convey genuine information, so the third student knows that there have been three draws from the urn, consisting of the sequence of colors blue, blue, and red. What he wants to know is

$$\Pr[\textit{majority-blue} \mid \textit{blue, blue, red}]$$

so as to make a guess about the urn. Using Bayes' rule we get

$$\Pr[\textit{majority-blue} \mid \textit{blue, blue, red}]$$
$$= \frac{\Pr[\textit{majority-blue}] \times \Pr[\textit{blue, blue, red} \mid \textit{majority-blue}]}{\Pr[\textit{blue, blue, red}]}. \qquad (16.7)$$

Since the draws from the urn are independent, the probability $\Pr[\textit{blue, blue, red} \mid \textit{majority-blue}]$ is determined by multiplying the probabilities of the three respective draws together:

$$\Pr[\textit{blue, blue, red} \mid \textit{majority-blue}] = \frac{2}{3} \times \frac{2}{3} \times \frac{1}{3} = \frac{4}{27}.$$

To determine $\Pr[\textit{blue, blue, red}]$, as usual we consider the two different ways this sequence could have happened – if the urn is majority-blue or if it is majority-red:

$$\Pr[\textit{blue, blue, red}] = \Pr[\textit{majority-blue}] \times \Pr[\textit{blue, blue, red} \mid \textit{majority-blue}]$$
$$+ \Pr[\textit{majority-red}] \times \Pr[\textit{blue, blue, red} \mid \textit{majority-red}]$$
$$= \frac{1}{2} \times \frac{2}{3} \times \frac{2}{3} \times \frac{1}{3} + \frac{1}{2} \times \frac{1}{3} \times \frac{1}{3} \times \frac{2}{3} = \frac{6}{54} = \frac{1}{9}.$$

Plugging all this back into Equation (16.7), we get

$$\Pr[\textit{majority-blue} \mid \textit{blue, blue, red}] = \frac{\frac{4}{27} \times \frac{1}{2}}{\frac{1}{9}} = \frac{2}{3}.$$

Therefore, the third student should guess majority-blue (from which he will have a $\frac{2}{3}$ chance of being correct). This outcome confirms our intuitive observation in Section 16.2 that the student should ignore what he sees (red) in favor of the two guesses he's already heard (both blue).

Finally, once these three draws from the urn have taken place, all future students will have the same information as the third student, and so they will all perform the same calculation, resulting in an information cascade of blue guesses.

16.5 A Simple, General Cascade Model

Let's return to the motivation for the herding experiment in Section 16.2: the experiment served as a stylized metaphor for any situation in which people make decisions sequentially, basing these decisions on a combination of their own private information and observations of what earlier people have done. We now formulate a model that covers such situations in general. We will see that Bayes' rule predicts in this general model that cascades will form, with probability tending to 1 as the number of people goes to infinity.

Formulating the Model. Consider a group of people (numbered 1, 2, 3, . . .) who will sequentially make decisions; that is, individual 1 will decide first, then individual 2 will decide, and so on. We will describe the decision as a choice between *accepting* or *rejecting* some option. This decision could be about whether to adopt a new technology, wear a new fashion, eat in a new restaurant, commit a crime, vote for a particular political candidate, or choose one route to a common destination rather than an alternative route.

First Model Ingredient: States of the World. At the start of everything, before any individual has made a decision, we assume that the world is randomly placed into one of two possible *states*: it is placed in either a state in which the option is actually a good idea or a state in which the option is actually a bad idea. We imagine that the state of the world is determined by some initial random event that the individuals can't observe, but they will try to use what they observe to make inferences about this state. For example, the world is either in a state where the new restaurant is good or a state where it is bad; the individuals in the model know that it was randomly placed in one of these two states, and they're trying to figure out which.

We write the two possible states of the world as G, which represents the state where the option is a good idea, and B, which represents the state where the option is a bad idea. We suppose that each individual knows the following fact: the initial random event that placed the world into state G or B placed it into state G with probability p, and into state B with probability $1 - p$. This will serve as the prior probabilities of G and B; in other words, $\Pr[G] = p$, and hence $\Pr[B] = 1 - \Pr[G] = 1 - p$.

Second Model Ingredient: Payoffs. Each individual receives a payoff based on her decision to accept or reject the option. If the individual chooses to reject the option, she receives a payoff of 0. The payoff for accepting depends on whether the option is a good idea or a bad idea. Let's suppose that if the option is a good idea then the payoff obtained from accepting it is a positive number $v_g > 0$. If the option is a bad idea, then the payoff is a negative number $v_b < 0$. We will also assume that the expected payoff from accepting in the absence of other information is equal to 0; in other words, $v_g p + v_b (1 - p) = 0$. That is, before an individual gets any additional information, the expected payoff from accepting is the same as the payoff from rejecting.

Third Model Ingredient: Signals. In addition to the payoffs, we also want to model the effect of private information. We assume that, before any decisions are made, each individual gets a *private signal* that provides information about whether accepting is a good idea or a bad idea. The private signal is designed to model private information that the person happens to know, beyond just the prior probability p that accepting the option is a good idea.

The private signal does not convey perfect certainty about what to do (since we want to model individual uncertainty even after the signal comes in), but it does convey useful information. Specifically, there are two possible signals: a *high signal* (denoted H), which suggests that accepting is a good idea, and a *low signal* (denoted L), which suggests that accepting is a bad idea. We can make this precise by saying that if accepting is in fact a good idea then high signals are more frequent than low signals: $\Pr[H \mid G] = q > \frac{1}{2}$, while $\Pr[L \mid G] = 1 - q < \frac{1}{2}$. Similarly, if accepting the option is a bad idea, then low signals are more frequent: $\Pr[L \mid B] = q$ and $\Pr[H \mid B] = 1 - q$, for this same value of $q > \frac{1}{2}$. This is summarized in Figure 16.2.

Notice how the herding experiment from Section 16.2 fits the properties of this more abstract model. The two possible states of the world are that the urn placed at the front of the room was majority-blue or that it was majority-red. We can think of "accepting"

States

		B	G
Signals	L	q	$1 - q$
	H	$1 - q$	q

Figure 16.2. The probability of receiving a low or high signal, as a function of the two possible states of the world (G or B).

as guessing "majority-blue"; this is a good idea (G) if the true urn really is majority-blue and a bad idea (B) otherwise. The prior probability of accepting being a good idea is $p = \frac{1}{2}$. The private information in the experiment is the color of the ball the individual draws; it's a "high" signal if it is blue, and so $\Pr[\text{H} \mid \text{G}] = \Pr[blue \mid majority\text{-}blue] = q = \frac{2}{3}$.

Similarly, to return to the two-restaurant example from the opening section, "accepting" could correspond to choosing the first restaurant, A; it's a good idea if restaurant A is actually better than the second restaurant, B. The private information could be a review that you read of the first restaurant, with a high signal corresponding to a review comparing it favorably to restaurant B next door. If choosing the first restaurant is actually good, there should be a higher number of such reviews, so $\Pr[\text{H} \mid \text{G}] = q > \frac{1}{2}$.

Individual Decisions. We now want to model how people should make decisions about accepting or rejecting. First, let's consider how someone should do this based only on their own private signal, and then consider the effect of observing the earlier decisions of others.

Suppose that a person gets a high signal. This shifts their expected payoff from $v_g \Pr[\text{G}] + v_b \Pr[\text{B}] = 0$ to $v_g \Pr[\text{G} \mid \text{H}] + v_b \Pr[\text{B} \mid \text{H}]$. To determine this new expected payoff, we use Bayes' rule; the calculation is just like the ones from the previous sections:

$$\Pr[\text{G} \mid \text{H}] = \frac{\Pr[\text{G}] \times \Pr[\text{H} \mid \text{G}]}{\Pr[\text{H}]}$$

$$= \frac{\Pr[\text{G}] \times \Pr[\text{H} \mid \text{G}]}{\Pr[\text{G}] \times \Pr[\text{H} \mid \text{G}] + \Pr[\text{B}] \cdot \Pr[\text{H} \mid \text{B}]}$$

$$= \frac{pq}{pq + (1 - p)(1 - q)}$$

$$> p,$$

where in the second line we compute the denominator $\Pr[\text{H}]$ as usual by expanding out the two possible ways of getting a high signal (if the option is a good idea or a bad idea). The final inequality follows since we have $pq + (1 - p)(1 - q) < pq + (1 - p)q = q$ in the denominator.

This result makes sense. A high signal is more likely to occur if the option is good than if it is bad, so if an individual observes a high signal they raise their estimate of the probability that the option is good. As a result, the expected payoff shifts from zero to a positive number, and so they should accept the option.

A completely analogous calculation shows that if the individual receives a low signal, they should reject the option.

Multiple Signals. We know from the herding experiment that an important step in reasoning about how people make decisions in sequence is to understand how an individual should use the evidence of multiple signals. Using Bayes' rule, it's not hard to reason directly about an individual's decision when they get a sequence S of independently generated signals consisting of a high signals and b low signals, interleaved in some fashion. We do this by deriving the following facts:

(i) The posterior probability $\Pr[G \mid S]$ is greater than the prior probability $\Pr[G]$ when $a > b$.
(ii) The posterior probability $\Pr[G \mid S]$ is less than the prior probability $\Pr[G]$ when $a < b$.
(iii) The two probabilities $\Pr[G \mid S]$ and $\Pr[G]$ are equal when $a = b$.

As a result, individuals should accept the option when they get more high signals than low signals, and reject it when they get more low signals than high signals; they are indifferent when they get the same number of each. In other words, in this simple setting with a sequence of signals, individuals can decide according to a majority vote over the signals they receive.

In the remainder of this section, we justify facts (i)–(iii), using Bayes' rule and a bit of algebra. In the next section, we then explore the consequences of these facts for sequential decision-making in the cascade model. To apply Bayes' rule, we write

$$\Pr[G \mid S] = \frac{\Pr[G] \times \Pr[S \mid G]}{\Pr[S]}, \tag{16.8}$$

where S is a sequence with a high signals and b low signals. To compute $\Pr[S \mid G]$ in the numerator, we note that because the signals are generated independently, we can simply multiply their probabilities, which gives us a factors of q and b factors of $(1 - q)$, and so $\Pr[S \mid G] = q^a(1 - q)^b$.

To compute $\Pr[S]$, we consider that S can arise if the option is a good idea or a bad idea, so

$$\Pr[S] = \Pr[G] \times \Pr[S \mid G] + \Pr[B] \times \Pr[S \mid B]$$
$$= pq^a(1 - q)^b + (1 - p)(1 - q)^a q^b.$$

Plugging this back into Equation (16.8), we get

$$\Pr[G \mid S] = \frac{pq^a(1 - q)^b}{pq^a(1 - q)^b + (1 - p)(1 - q)^a q^b}.$$

What we want to know is how this expression compares to p. One way to answer this question is as follows. If we were to replace the second term in the denominator by $(1 - p)q^a(1 - q)^b$, then the denominator would become $pq^a(1 - q)^b + (1 - p)q^a(1 - q)^b = q^a(1 - q)^b$, and so the whole expression would become

$$\frac{pq^a(1 - q)^b}{q^a(1 - q)^b} = p.$$

So the question is: does this replacement make the denominator smaller or larger?

(i) If $a > b$, then this replacement makes the denominator larger, since $q > \frac{1}{2}$ and we now have more factors of q and fewer factors of $1 - q$. Since the denominator gets larger, the overall expression gets smaller as it is converted to a value of p, and therefore $\Pr[G \mid S] > p = \Pr[G]$.

(ii) If $a < b$, the argument is symmetric: this replacement makes the denominator smaller, and hence the overall expression larger. So $\Pr[G \mid S] < p = \Pr[G]$.

(iii) Finally, if $a = b$, then this replacement keeps the value of the denominator the same, and so $\Pr[G \mid S] = p = \Pr[G]$.

16.6 Sequential Decision Making and Cascades

Let's now consider what happens when individuals make decisions in sequence. As before, we want to capture situations in which each person can see what earlier people *do*, but not what they *know*. In our model, this means that when a given person decides whether to accept or reject the option, they have access to their own private signal and also the accept/reject decisions of all earlier people. Crucially, however, they do not see the actual private signals of any of these earlier people.

The reasoning is now very similar to what we did for the sequence of students in the herding experiment from Section 16.2. To start, let's note the close parallels to our discussion there.

- Person 1 will follow his own private signal, as we just saw in Section 16.5.
- Person 2 will know that person 1's decision reveals their private signal, and so it is as though person 2 gets two signals. If these signals are the same, person 2's decision is easy. If they are different, then as we saw at the end of Section 16.5, person 2 will be indifferent between accepting and rejecting. Here we assume she follows her own private signal. Thus, either way, person 2 is following her own signal.
- As a result, person 3 knows that person 1 and person 2 both acted on their private signals, so it is as though person 3 has received three independent signals (the two he infers, and his own observation). We know from the argument in Section 16.5 that person 3 will follow the majority signal (high or low) in choosing whether to accept or reject.

  This means that if person 1 and person 2 have made opposite decisions (i.e., they received opposite signals), then person 3 will use his own signal as the tie-breaker. Hence, future people will know that person 3's decision was based on his own signal, and so they can use this information in their own decisions.

  On the other hand, if person 1 and person 2 have made the same decision (i.e., received the same signal), then person 3 will follow this regardless of what his own signal says. Hence, future people will know that person 3's decision conveys no information about his signal, and these future people will all be in the same position as person 3. In this case, a cascade has begun. That is, we are in a situation where no individual's decision can be influenced by his own signal. No matter what they see, every individual from person 3 on will make the same decision that persons 1 and 2 made.

Let's now consider how this process unfolds through future people beyond person 3. In particular, let's consider the perspective of a person numbered N. Suppose that

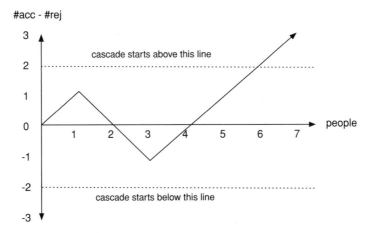

Figure 16.3. A cascade begins when the difference between the number of acceptances and rejections reaches two.

person N knows that everyone before her has followed their own signal; that is, suppose the accept/reject decisions of these earlier people exactly coincide with whether they received a high or low signal, and person N knows this. There are several possible cases to consider:

- If the number of acceptances among the people before N is equal to the number of rejections, then N's signal will be the tie-breaker, and so N will follow her own signal.
- If the number of acceptances among the people before N differs from the number of rejections by one, then either N's private signal will make her indifferent or it will reinforce the majority signal. Either way, N will follow her private signal (since we assume a person follows their own signal in the case of indifference).
- If the number of acceptances among the people before N differs from the number of rejections by two or more, then however N's private signal turns out, it won't outweigh this earlier majority. As a result, N will follow the earlier majority and ignore her own signal.

  Moreover, in this case, the people numbered $N + 1$, $N + 2$, and onward will know that person N ignored her own signal (whereas we've assumed that all earlier people were known to have followed their private signals). So they will each be in exactly the same position as N. This means that each of them will also ignore their own signals and follow the majority; hence, a cascade has begun.

We can therefore sum up the behavior of the decision-making process as follows. As long as the number of acceptances differs from the number of rejections by at most one, each person in sequence is simply following their own private signal in deciding what to do. But once the number of acceptances differs from the number of rejections by two or more, a cascade takes over, and everyone simply follows the majority decision forever. Figure 16.3 illustrates this for a sample outcome of the process, in which we plot the difference between the number of acceptances and the number of rejections over time as people make decisions. This plot moves up or down by one each time a new decision is made, since either the number of acceptances or the number of rejections grows by exactly one with each decision. Once the difference between the number of acceptances and the number of rejections escapes from the narrow horizontal ribbon around zero – that is, once the plot moves at least two steps away from the x-axis – a cascade begins and runs forever.

Finally, it is very difficult for this difference to remain in such a narrow interval (between -1 and $+1$) forever. For example, during the period of time when people are following their own signals, if three people in a row ever happen to get the same signal, a cascade will definitely have begun. (Note that a cascade can begin even without this happening, but you can check that three matching signals in a row are always enough to make one begin.) Now, let's argue that the probability of finding three matching signals in a row converges to 1 as the number of people, N, goes to infinity. To see why, suppose we divide the first N people into blocks of three consecutive people each (people 1, 2, 3; people 4, 5, 6; people 7, 8, 9; and so on). Then the people in any one block will receive identical signals with probability $q^3 + (1 - q)^3$. The probability that none of these blocks consists of identical signals is therefore $(1 - q^3 - (1 - q)^3)^{N/3}$. As N goes to infinity, this quantity goes to zero.

What this short argument shows is that, as the number of people goes to infinity, the probability that a cascade begins converges to 1. Thus, in the limit, a cascade takes place in this model almost surely.

Now that the analysis is complete, it is worth making a few final observations. First, this is ultimately an extremely simple model of individual decision making. In more general versions, for example, it could well be the case that people don't see *all* the decisions made earlier but only some of them; that not all private signals convey equal information, or that not everyone receives the same payoffs [2, 38, 186]. Many of these more general variants become much more complicated to analyze, and they can differ in their specifics (for example, the condition for a cascade to begin is clearly not always as simple as having the number of acceptances differ from the number of rejections by at least two). But the general conclusions from these models tend to be qualitatively similar. When people can see what others do but not what they know, there is an initial period when people rely on their own private information; but as time goes on, the population can tip into a situation where people – still behaving fully rationally – begin ignoring their own information and following the crowd.

We now turn to some of the general conclusions from these cascade models, relating them to more qualitative principles that have been observed about information cascades in different settings.

16.7 Lessons from Cascades

At the end of Section 16.2, we made some observations about the simple herding experiment that are reinforced by the general model we've just analyzed.

   (i) *Cascades can be wrong.* If, for example, accepting the option is in fact a bad idea but the first two people happen to get high signals, a cascade of acceptances will start immediately, even though it is the wrong choice for the population.

(ii) *Cascades can be based on very little information.* Because people ignore their private information once a cascade starts, only the pre-cascade information influences the behavior of the population. This means that if a cascade starts relatively quickly in a large population, most of the private information that is collectively available to the population (in the form of private signals to individuals) is not being used.

(iii) *Cascades are fragile.* The previous point – that cascades can be based on relatively little information – makes them easy to start, but it can also make them easy to stop. One manifestation of this fact is that people who receive slightly superior information can overturn even long-lived cascades.

Suppose, for example, that a cascade of acceptances is under way in our model; so we know that the number of high signals exceeded the number of low signals by two at the time the cascade began. Now suppose someone making a decision in the midst of this cascade happens to receive two private signals. If they are both low signals, then this person (taking into account the earlier signals he can infer) has now seen an equal number of high and low signals. Because he is indifferent, our assumption is that he will reject (since his own signals were low) despite the long run of acceptances that preceded him. A single public signal can have the same effect: if, in the midst of a cascade, there is a public signal that everyone sees, then the next person to decide in effect receives two signals (the public one and her own private one), with similar consequences.

More generally, perhaps the main lesson to be learned from studying cascades is to be careful in drawing conclusions about the best course of action from the behavior of a crowd. As we have just seen, the crowd can be wrong even if everyone is rational and everyone takes the same action.

This forms an interesting contrast with an argument made by popular general-audience books such as James Surowiecki's *The Wisdom of Crowds* [383] – that the aggregate behavior of many people with limited information can sometimes produce very accurate results. In his opening example, Surowiecki notes that, if many people are guessing independently, then the average of their guesses is often a surprisingly good estimate of whatever they are guessing about (perhaps the number of jelly beans in a jar, or the weight of a bull at a fair). The key to this argument of course is that the individuals each have private information (their signals), and they guess *independently*, without knowing what the others have guessed. If instead they guess sequentially, and can observe the earlier guesses of others, then we are back in the cascade setting and there would be no reason to expect the average guess to be good at all. Surowiecki also notes this possibility of cascades as a caution in following the crowd.

These observations suggest how the possibility of cascades can affect the behavior of individuals or groups in a range of different situations. One setting that is susceptible to cascades is the style of group decision making in which a committee of people sit around a table and discuss potential solutions to a problem. For example, consider a hiring committee that needs to decide whether to make a job offer to candidate A or candidate B. In these kinds of situations, a common strategy is to go around the table, asking people in sequence to express their support for option A or option B. But if the participants assume that they all have roughly equal insight into the problem, then a cascade can quickly develop: if a few people initially favor A, others may be led to conclude that they should favor A, even if they initially preferred B on their own. The cascade principles we've seen in this chapter suggest that this may not just be an issue of social pressure to conform to the majority, but in fact a rational approach to decision making, in which you assume that the people speaking before you have information about the problem that is comparable in quality to your own.

Such considerations suggest an inherent tension between getting a group of experts to work together and build on each other's ideas, on the one hand, and giving them the opportunity to form their own opinions, on the other. This in turn suggests strategies for balancing this tension, potentially by forcing experts to reach partial decisions independently before entering a phase of collaboration and consensus. It also suggests that if certain people are known to have particularly good information about a problem, it can matter whether they weigh in earlier in the process or later.

Marketers also use the idea of cascades to attempt to get a buying cascade started for a new product. If they can induce an initial set of people to adopt the new product, then those who make purchasing decisions later on may also adopt the product even it is no better than, or perhaps even worse than, competing products. This is most effective if these later consumers are able to observe the adoption decisions, but not how satisfied the early customers actually were with their choices; this is consistent with the idea that cascades arise naturally when people can see what others do but not what they know. If the payoffs (or statistics based on the payoffs) from earlier consumers are visible, this can help prevent a cascade of bad choices – another example of how changing the information available to a group of people can have an effect on their overall behavior.

16.8 Exercises

1. In this problem we ask whether an information cascade can occur if each individual sees only the action of his immediate neighbor rather than the actions of all those who have chosen previously. Let's keep the same setup as in Chapter 16, except than when individual i chooses he observes only his own signal and the action of individual $i - 1$.

   (a) Briefly explain why the decision problems faced by individuals 1 and 2 are unchanged by this modification to the information network.
   (b) Individual 3 observes the action of individual 2, but not the action of individual 1. What can 3 infer about 2's signal from 2's action?
   (c) Can 3 infer anything about 1's signal from 2's action? Explain.
   (d) What should 3 do if he observes a high signal and he knows that 2 accepted? What if 3's signal was low and 2 accepted?
   (e) Do you think that a cascade can form in this world? Explain why or why not. A formal proof is not necessary; a brief argument is sufficient.

2. In this question we consider a variation on the model of information cascades from Chapter 16. Suppose that there is a new technology that individuals sequentially decide to adopt or reject. Let's suppose that anyone who adopts the new technology receives either a positive or a negative payoff from using the new technology. Unlike the model used in Chapter 16, these payoffs are random and have the property that

the average payoff is positive if the technology is good, and negative if the technology is bad. Anyone who decides to reject the new technology always receives a payoff of exactly zero.

As in the model used in Chapter 16, each person receives a private signal about the technology and observes the actions of all who chose previously. However, unlike the model used in Chapter 16, each person is also told the payoffs received by everyone who moved previously. (One interpretation of this is that a government agency collects information about individuals' experiences and distributes it for free as a public service.)

(a) Suppose that the new technology is actually Bad. How does this new in-formation about payoffs (the payoffs received by each of those who moved previously) affect the potential for an information cascade of choices to adopt the new technology to form and persist? (You do not need to write a proof. A brief argument is sufficient.)

(b) Suppose that the new technology is actually Good. Can an information cascade of rejections of the new technology occur? Explain briefly.

3. In this problem we consider the information cascades model from Chapter 16 with specific values for the probabilities. Let's suppose that the probability that Accept (A) is a good idea is $p = 1/2$, and the probability of a High signal if Good is true (as well as the probability of a Low signal if Bad is true) is $q = 3/4$. Finally, let's assume that Good is actually true.

(a) What is the probability that the first person to decide will choose Accept? What's the probability that this person will choose Reject?

(b) What is the probability of observing each of the four possible pairs of choices by the first two people: (A,A), (A,R), (R,A), and (R,R)? [A pair of choices such as (A,R) means that the first person chose Accept and the second person chose Reject.]

(c) What is the probability of an Accept or a Reject cascade emerging with the decision by the third person to choose? Explain why a cascade emerges with this probability.

4. Let's consider the model of information cascades. Assume that the probability that the state is Good (G) is $p = 1/2$, and that the probability of a High signal given a Good state is $q = 2/3$. (The probability of a Low signal given a Bad state is also $q = 2/3$.) Remember that each person observes a signal and the choices (but not the signals) of all those who chose before him. Each person chooses between Accept (A) and Reject (R).

Suppose that you are the tenth person to make a choice and you have observed that everyone before you chose R. That is, we are in an R cascade.

(a) What is the probability that this is an incorrect cascade (the probability that the state is actually G given that we are in this R cascade)?

(b) Now let's suppose that before you (person 10) receive your signal, you decide to ask person 9 about the signal that they observed. Let's suppose that person 9 observed a High signal, that person 9 tells you that his signal was High, and that you know that person 9 is telling the truth. After this, you receive your own signal. What decision should you make, A or R, and how does it depend on which signal you receive?

(c) Now let's consider person 11. Person 11 observes only his own signal and the choices of those who decided before him (1 to 10). Person 11 knows that you have observed both your signal and person 9's signal. Person 11 cannot observe these signals; all he knows is the choices that have been made. The first nine people have chosen R. What should person 11 do if you choose R? What should he do if you choose A? Why? Remember that person 11 observes a signal, and so his choice can depend on his signal as well as the earlier choices.

5. Suppose you're working at a company, and your boss asks you to explain what went wrong in a recent hiring decision. The company decided to interview two candidates for a single job. Let's call the two candidates A and B. A hiring committee was formed to attend the interviews and decide which of the two candidates to hire. Everyone on the committee was interested in making the best possible hire, but after the interview it was clear that members of the committee had different ideas about which of the two candidates was the best choice. When the committee met to make the final decision they decided to go around the room and ask each person on the committee to announce which of the two candidates they believed to be the best choice for the company. In fact, everyone on the committee said that candidate A seemed to be the best choice, so the offer was made immediately to candidate A without additional discussion.

    Now that candidate A has worked for the firm for a while it is clear that candidate B would have been a better choice.

    (a) Your boss has asked you to explain how the committee members could have unanimously supported candidate A when she was reasonably certain that before the committee meeting at least some of the members of the committee thought that B was probably the best choice. What can you tell her?

    (b) Can you suggest another procedure that the committee could have used that would have revealed the initially differing opinions about the candidates and which may have resulted in the actually better choice of candidate B?

6. You have to make a choice between two alternatives. These alternatives might be, for example, whether to believe a rumor, which of two competing products to purchase, which of two competing political candidates to vote for, or which of two possible technologies to adopt for the new firm that you have just started. Unfortunately, you do not know much about the potential benefits of choosing either of the alternatives. We represent this formally by saying that you believe that each of the alternatives is equally likely to be the best choice. However, there are experts who do have information about the benefit (to you) from each of the alternatives. Experts are not perfect; they just know more than you do. We represent this formally by saying that each expert has some imperfect, private information about the benefit of each alternative and we assume that all experts are equally good in evaluating the two alternatives.

    The experts have made public recommendations about which of the alternatives is best. (The experts cannot convey their information directly. It's just too complex, and if they tried you would not know what to do with their statements anyhow.) Experts make recommendations sequentially, and each expert knows what all of those who have announced their recommendation earlier have chosen. (This is a bit extreme, but the opposite case in which they simultaneously choose is even more extreme.) You see the recommendations of all of the experts, but you do not know the order in which they made those recommendations. Finally, we assume that experts are honest; that is, they always make the recommendation that they believe is best (for you) given their private information and any inferences that they can draw from the recommendations of other experts.

(a) Suppose that the majority of the experts recommend alternative A. How confident should you be that A is in fact the best choice? Should you be more confident that A is the best choice if the fraction of experts who recommend A is even larger (i.e., not just more than one-half, but close to one)? Explain. (You can't provide a numerical answer to this question. Just discuss the inference that you can make from seeing recommendations.)

(b) Suppose now that experts do not make public recommendations. Instead, you have to hire a few experts to obtain their recommendations. Let's also suppose that experts don't talk to each other before you hire them; instead they privately obtain information and update their opinions about the alternatives. You know experts are not perfect so you plan to hire five of them in the hope that having more opinions is better. Consider two procedures for how to organize the process of obtaining the experts' recommendations. In the first procedure, bring all of the experts together in a room and ask them to announce their recommendations sequentially. In the second procedure, privately ask each expert to announce their recommendation. Which procedure provides you with the most information? Why?

CHAPTER 17

Network Effects

At the beginning of Chapter 16, we discussed two fundamentally different reasons why individuals might imitate the behavior of others. One reason was based on *informational effects*: since the behavior of other people conveys information about what they know, observing this behavior and copying it (even against the evidence of one's own private information) can sometimes be a rational decision. This was our focus in Chapter 16. The other reason was based on *direct-benefit effects*, also called *network effects*: for some kinds of decisions, you incur an explicit benefit when you align your behavior with the behavior of others. This is what we will consider in this chapter.

A natural setting where network effects arise is in the adoption of technologies for which interaction or compatibility with others is important. For example, when the fax machine was first introduced as a product, its value to a potential consumer depended on how many others were also using the same technology. The value of a social networking or media-sharing site exhibits the same properties: it's valuable to the extent that other people are using it as well. Similarly, a computer operating system can be more useful if many other people are using it: even if the primary purpose of the operating system itself is not to interact with others, an operating system with more users will tend to have a larger amount of software written for it and will use file formats (e.g., for documents, images, and movies) that more people can easily read.

Network Effects as Externalities. The effects we are describing here are called *positive externalities*. An *externality* is any situation in which the welfare of an individual is affected by the actions of other individuals, without a mutually agreed-upon compensation. For example, the benefit to you from a social networking site is directly related to the total number of people who use the site. When someone else joins the site, they have increased your welfare even though no explicit compensation accounts for this. This is an externality, and it is *positive* in the sense that your welfare increases. In this chapter, we consider the consequences of positive externalities due to network effects. In the settings we analyze here, payoffs depend on the number of others who use a good and not on the details of how they are connected. In Chapter 19, we will look at the details of network connectivity and ask how they affect the positive externalities that result.

Notice that earlier in the book we have also seen examples of *negative externalities* – cases where an externality causes a decrease in welfare. Traffic congestion as discussed in Chapter 8 is an example in which your use of a (transportation or communication) network decreases the payoff to other users of the network, again despite the lack of compensation among the affected parties. In the final section of this chapter, we will look at a direct comparison of positive and negative externalities in more detail.

It's important, also, to note that not everything is an externality; the key part is that the effect has to be *uncompensated*. For example, if you drink a can of Diet Coke then there is one less can of Diet Coke for the rest of the world to consume, so you decrease the welfare of others by your action. But in this case, in order to drink the can of Diet Coke you have to pay for it, and if you pay what it costs to make another can of Diet Coke, then you have exactly compensated the rest of the world for your action. That is, there is no uncompensated effect, and hence no externality. We explore the interaction of externalities and compensation further when we discuss property rights in Chapter 24.

17.1 The Economy without Network Effects

Our canonical setting in this chapter will be the market for a good: we will first consider how the market functions when there is no network effect – that is, when consumers do not care how many other users of the good there are – and then we will see how things change when a network effect is present.

We want to analyze markets with a huge number of potential purchasers, each of whom is small enough relative to the entire market that he or she can make individual decisions without affecting the aggregate behavior. For example, each individual considering the purchase of a loaf of bread does so without worrying about whether her individual decision – all else remaining the same – will affect the price of bread. (Note that this is different from worrying about whether decisions made by a large number of people will have an effect, which they certainly can.) Of course, in real markets the number of consumers is finite, and each individual decision does have a very, very small effect on the aggregate. But each purchaser's impact is so small relative to the market that we can model individuals as not taking this into account when they make a decision.

Formally, we model the lack of individual effects on the aggregate by representing the consumers as the set of all real numbers in the interval strictly between 0 and 1. That is, each consumer is named by a different real number, and the total mass of consumers is 1. This naming of the consumers by real numbers will be notationally useful. For example, the set of consumers with names between 0 and $x < 1$ represents an x fraction of the population. A good way to think of this model of consumers is as a continuous approximation to a market with a very large, but finite, number of consumers; the continuous model will be useful in various places to avoid having to deal with the explicit effect of any one individual on the overall population.

Each consumer wants at most one unit of the good; each consumer has a personal intrinsic interest in obtaining the good that can vary from one consumer to another. When there are no network effects at work, we model a consumer's willingness to pay as being determined entirely by this intrinsic interest. When network effects are present, a consumer's willingness to pay is determined by two things:

- intrinsic interest, and
- the number of other people using the good – the larger the user population, the more she is willing to pay.

Our study of network effects here can be viewed as an analysis of how things change once this second factor comes into play.

To start understanding this issue, we first consider how a market works when there are no network effects.

Reservation Prices. With no network effects, each consumer's interest in the good is specified by a single *reservation price*: the maximum amount she is willing to pay for one unit of the good. We'll assume that the individuals are arranged in the interval between 0 and 1 in order of decreasing reservation price, so that if consumer x has a higher reservation price than consumer y, then $x < y$. Let $r(x)$ denote the reservation price of consumer x. For the analysis in this chapter, we will assume that this function $r(\cdot)$ is continuous and that no two consumers have exactly the same reservation price: the function $r(\cdot)$ is strictly decreasing as it ranges over the interval from 0 to 1.

Suppose that the *market price* for a unit of the good is p: everyone who wants to buy the good can buy it at price p, and no units are offered for sale at a price above or below p. At price p, everyone whose reservation price is at least p will actually buy the good, and everyone whose reservation price is below p will not buy it. Clearly at a price of $r(0)$ or more, no one will buy the good; at a price of $r(1)$ or less, everyone will buy the good. So let's consider the interesting region for the price p, when it lies strictly between $r(1)$ and $r(0)$. In this region, there is some unique number x with the property that $r(x) = p$: as Figure 17.1 illustrates, because $r(\cdot)$ is a continuous function that strictly decreases, it must cross the horizontal line $y = p$ somewhere.

This means that all consumers between 0 and x buy the product, and all consumers above x don't, so an x fraction of the population buys the product. We can do this for every price p: there is an x depending on p that specifies the fraction of the population that will purchase at price p. This way of reading the relation between price and quantity (for any price the quantity that will be demanded) is usually called the (market) *demand* for the good, and it is a very useful way to think of the relation between the price and the number of units purchased.[1]

The Equilibrium Quantity of the Good. Let's suppose that this good can be produced at a constant cost of p^* per unit, and that, as is the case for consumers, there are many potential producers of the good so that none of them is large enough to be able to

---

[1] In the language of microeconomics, the function $r(\cdot)$ describes the *inverse demand function*. The inverse of $r(\cdot)$, giving x in terms of p, is the *demand function*.

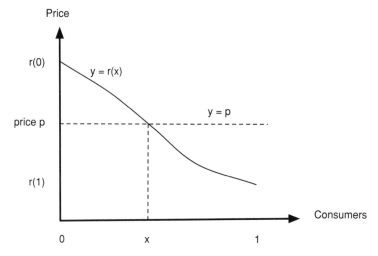

Figure 17.1. When there are no network efforts, the demand for a product at a fixed market price p can be found by locating the point where the curve $y = r(x)$ intersects the horizontal line $y = p$.

influence the market price of the good. Then, in aggregate, the producers will be willing to supply any amount of the good at a price of p^* per unit, and none of the good at any price below p^*. Moreover, the assumption of a large number of potential producers who can create new copies of the good at a constant cost of p^* implies that the price cannot remain above p^*, since any profit to a producer would be driven to zero by competition from other producers. Thus, we can assume a market price of p^*, regardless of the number of units of the good produced.[2] As mentioned earlier, cases in which p^* is above $r(0)$ or below $r(1)$ are not particularly interesting, since at such prices either everyone or no one buys the good. Therefore, we assume that $r(0) > p^* > r(1)$.

To complete the picture of how the market operates without network effects, we now determine the *supply* of the good. Since p^* is between the highest and lowest reservation prices, we can find a unique x^* between 0 and 1 so that $r(x^*) = p^*$. We call x^* the *equilibrium quantity* of the good, given the reservation prices and the cost p^*. Figure 17.2 revisits Figure 17.1, including the cost p^* and the equilibrium quantity x^*.

Notice the sense in which x^* represents an equilibrium in the population's consumption of the good. If less than an x^* fraction of the population purchased the good, there would be consumers who have not purchased but who would have an incentive to do so, because of reservation prices above p^*. In other words, there would be "upward pressure" on the consumption of the product, since there is a portion of the population that would not have purchased but wished they had. On the other hand, if more than an x^* fraction of the population purchased the good, there would be consumers who had purchased the good but wished they had not, because of reservation prices below p^*. In this case, we'd have "downward pressure" on the consumption of the good.

---

[2] Continuing with the microeconomic language, this is the long-run competitive supply for any good produced by a constant-cost industry.

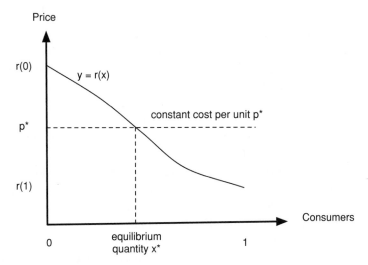

Figure 17.2. When copies of a good can be produced at a constant cost p^* per unit, the equilibrium quantity consumed will be the number x^* for which $r(x^*) = p^*$.

One attractive feature of this equilibrium is that it is socially optimal (as defined in Chapter 6). To see why, let's consider the social welfare of the allocation, which we can think of as the difference between the total reservation prices of the consumers who receive a copy of the good and the total cost of producing the corresponding quantity of the good. Now, if society were going to produce enough of the good to give it to an x fraction of the population, then social welfare would be maximized by giving it to all consumers between 0 and x, since they correspond to the x fraction of the population that values the good the most. Which value of x would be the best choice? Since the contribution of a consumer x' to the social welfare is the difference $r(x') - p^*$, we can think of the social welfare, when consumers 0 through x get copies of the good, as the (signed) area between the curve $y = r(x)$ and the horizontal line $y = p^*$. It's signed in the sense that portions of the curve $y = r(x)$ that drop below $y = p^*$ contribute negatively to the area. Given this, we'd want to choose x so that we collect all the positive area between $y = r(x)$ and $y = p^*$, and none of the negative area. This is achieved by choosing x to be the equilibrium x^*. Hence the equilibrium quantity x^* is socially optimal.

We now introduce network effects, which will cause several important features of the market to change in fundamental ways.

17.2 The Economy with Network Effects

In this section, we discuss a model for network effects in the market for a good. We will follow a general approach suggested by Katz, Shapiro, and Varian [235, 368]; see also the writings of Brian Arthur [25, 27] for influential early discussions of these ideas.

With network effects, a potential purchaser takes into account both her own reservation price and the total number of users of the good. A simple way to model this is to say that there are now two functions at work: when a z fraction of the population is using the good, the reservation price of consumer x is equal to $r(x)f(z)$, where $r(x)$ as before is the intrinsic interest of consumer x in the good, and $f(z)$ measures the benefit to each consumer from having a z fraction of the population use the good. This new function $f(z)$ is increasing in z: it controls how much more valuable a product is when more people are using it. The multiplicative form for reservation prices, $r(x)f(z)$, means that those who place a greater intrinsic value on the good benefit more from an increase in the fraction of the population using the good than do those who place a smaller intrinsic value on the good.

For now, in keeping with the motivation from communication technology and social media, we assume that $f(0) = 0$: if no one has purchased the good, no one is willing to pay anything for the good. In Section 17.6 we will consider versions of the model where $f(0)$ is not 0. We also assume that f is a continuous function. Finally, to make the discussion a bit simpler, we assume that $r(1) = 0$. This means that, as we consider consumers x tending to 1 (the part of the population least interested in purchasing), their willingness to pay is converging to 0.[3]

Since a consumer's willingness to pay depends on the fraction of the population using the good, each consumer needs to predict what this fraction will be in order to evaluate whether to purchase. Suppose that the price of the good is p^*, and that consumer x expects a z fraction of the population to use the good. Then x will want to purchase provided that $r(x)f(z) \geq p^*$.

We begin by considering what happens in the case when all consumers make perfect predictions about the number of users of the good; after this, we will then consider the population-level dynamics that are caused by imperfect predictions.

Equilibria with Network Effects. What do we have in mind, in the context of the current discussion, when we suppose that consumers' predictions are perfect? We mean that the consumers form a shared expectation that the fraction of the population using the product is z, and if each of them then makes a purchasing decision based on this expectation, then the fraction of people who actually purchase is in fact z. We call this a *self-fulfilling expectations equilibrium* for the quantity of purchasers z: if everyone expects that a z fraction of the population will purchase the product, then this expectation is in turn fulfilled by people's behavior.

Let's consider what such an equilibrium value of z looks like, in terms of the price $p^* > 0$. First of all, if everyone expects a fraction $z = 0$ of the population to purchase the good, then the reservation price of each consumer x is $r(x)f(0) = 0$, which is below p^*. Hence, no one will want to purchase, and the shared expectation of $z = 0$ has been fulfilled.

Now let's consider a value of z strictly between 0 and 1. If exactly a z fraction of the population purchases the good, which set of individuals does this correspond to? Clearly if consumer x' purchases the good and $x < x'$, then consumer x will purchase it as well. Therefore, the set of purchasers will be precisely the set of consumers between 0 and z. What is the price p^* at which these consumers want to purchase, and no one

---

[3] The assumption that $r(1) = 0$ isn't necessary for our qualitative results, but it avoids various additional steps later on.

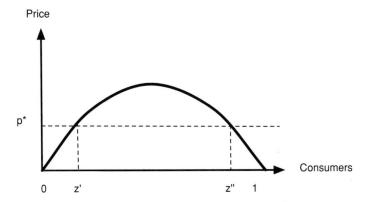

Figure 17.3. Suppose there are network effects and $f(0) = 0$, so that the good has no value to people when no one is using it. In this case, there can be multiple self-fulfilling expectations equilibria: at $z = 0$, and also at the points where the curve $r(z)f(z)$ crosses the horizontal line at height p^*.

else wants to purchase the good? The lowest reservation price in this set will belong to consumer z, who – because of the shared expectation that a z fraction of the population will purchase – has a reservation price of $r(z)f(z)$. In order for exactly this set of consumers, and no one else, to purchase the good, we must have $p^* = r(z)f(z)$.

We can summarize this as follows:

> If the price $p^* > 0$ together with the quantity z (strictly between 0 and 1) form a self-fulfilling expectations equilibrium, then $p^* = r(z)f(z)$.

This highlights a clear contrast with the model of the previous section, in which network effects were not present. There, we saw that to have more of the good sold, the price has to be lowered – or equivalently, at high prices the number of units of the good that can be sold is smaller. This follows directly from the fact that the equilibrium quantity x^* without network effects is governed by $p^* = r(x^*)$, and $r(x)$ is decreasing in x. The market for a good with network effects is more complicated, since the amount of the good demanded by consumers depends on how much they expect to be demanded, which leads to the more complex equation $p^* = r(z)f(z)$ for the equilibrium quantity z. Under our assumption that $f(0) = 0$, we've seen that one equilibrium with network effects occurs at price p^* and $z = 0$: producers are willing to supply a zero quantity of the good, and since no one expects the good to be used, none of it is demanded either.

A Concrete Example. To find whether other equilibria exist, we need to know the form of the functions $r(\cdot)$ and $f(\cdot)$ in order to analyze the equation $p^* = r(z)f(z)$. To show how this works, let's consider a concrete example in which $r(x) = 1 - x$ and $f(z) = z$. In this case, $r(z)f(z) = z(1 - z)$, which has a parabolic shape as shown in Figure 17.3: it is 0 at $z = 0$ and $z = 1$, and it has a maximum at $z = \frac{1}{2}$, when it takes the value $\frac{1}{4}$. Of course, in general the functions $r(\cdot)$ and $f(\cdot)$ need not look exactly like this example, but typically we expect to see something like the shape displayed in Figure 17.3.

Continuing with this concrete example, we can now work out the set of equilibria exactly. If $p^* > \frac{1}{4}$, then there is no solution to $p^* = r(z)f(z) = z(1 - z)$ (since the right-hand side has a maximum value of $\frac{1}{4}$ at $z = \frac{1}{2}$) and so the only equilibrium is when $z = 0$. This corresponds to a good that is simply too expensive, and so the only equilibrium is when everyone expects it not to be used.

On the other hand, when p^* is between 0 and $\frac{1}{4}$, there are two solutions to $p^* = z(1 - z)$: they are at points z' and z'', where the horizontal line $y = p^*$ slices through the parabola defined by $z(1 - z)$, as shown in Figure 17.3. Thus, there are three possible equilibria in this case: when z is equal to any of 0, z', or z''. For each of these three values of z, if people expect exactly a z fraction of the population to buy the good, then precisely the z fraction of the population between 0 and z will do so.

Two initial observations are worth making from this example. First, the notion of a self-fulfilling expectations equilibrium corresponds, in a general sense, to the effects of aggregate "consumer confidence." If the population has no confidence in the success of the good, then because of the network effects, no one will want it, and this lack of confidence will be borne out by the failure of people to purchase it. On the other hand – for the very same good, at the same price – if the population is confident of its success, then it is possible for a significant fraction of the population to decide to purchase it, thereby confirming its success. The possibility of multiple equilibria in this way is characteristic of markets in which network effects are at work.

A second observation concerns the nature of consumer demand in this case. Compared to the simple, decreasing curve in Figure 17.2, the curve in Figure 17.3 highlights the complicated relationship between the price and the equilibrium quantity. In particular, as the price p^* drops gradually below $\frac{1}{4}$, the "high" equilibrium z'' moves right (as in the simple model without network effects), but the "low" equilibrium z' moves left, toward smaller fractions of the population. To understand how these two equilibria relate to each other, we need to consider an important qualitative contrast between them, which we formulate in the next section.

17.3 Stability, Instability, and Tipping Points

Let's continue with the example in Figure 17.3 and explore the properties of its equilibria. To begin with, it's useful to work through the details of why values of z other than 0, z', or z'' do not constitute equilibria. In particular, suppose that a z fraction of the population were to purchase the good, where z is not one of these three equilibrium quantities.

- If z is between 0 and z', then there is "downward pressure" on the consumption of the good: since $r(z)f(z) < p^*$, the purchaser named z (and other purchasers just below z) will value the good at less than p, and hence will wish they hadn't bought it. This would push demand downward.
- If z is between z' and z'', then there is "upward pressure" on the consumption of the good: since $r(z)f(z) > p^*$, consumers with names slightly above z have not purchased the good but will wish they had. This would drive demand upward.

- Finally, if z is above z'', then there is again downward pressure: since $r(z)f(z) < p^*$, purchaser z and others just below will wish they hadn't bought the good, pushing demand down.

This set of three different possibilities for the nonequilibrium values of z has interesting consequences for the equilibria z' and z''. First, it shows that z'' has a strong *stability* property. If slightly more than a z'' fraction buys the good, then the demand gets pushed back toward z''; if slightly less than a z'' fraction buys the good, then the demand correspondingly gets pushed up toward z''. So in the event of a "near miss" in the population's expectations around z'', we would expect the outcome to settle down to z'' anyway.

The situation looks different – and highly unstable – in the vicinity of the equilibrium z'. If slightly more than a z' fraction buys the good, then upward pressure drives the demand away from z' toward the higher equilibrium at z''. And if slightly less than a z' fraction buys the good, then downward pressure drives the demand away from z' in the other direction, down toward the equilibrium at 0. Thus, if *exactly* a z' fraction of the population purchases the good, then we are at equilibrium, but if the fraction is even slightly off from this value, the system will tend to spiral up or spiral down to a significant extent.

Thus, z' is not just an unstable equilibrium; it is really a *critical point*, or a *tipping point*, in the success of the good. If the firm producing the good can get the population's expectations for the number of purchasers above z', then they can use the upward pressure of demand to get their market share to the stable equilibrium at z''. On the other hand, if the population's expectations are even slightly below z', then the downward pressure will tend to drive the market share to 0. The value z' is the hump the firm must get over in order to succeed.

This view of the equilibria suggests a way of thinking about the price p^*. If the firm were to price the good more cheaply – in other words, to lower the price p^* – then this would have two beneficial effects. First, since the parabola in Figure 17.3 would now be sliced by a *lower* horizontal line (reflecting the lower price), the low equilibrium z' would move to the left, which provides a critical point that is easier to get past. Moreover, the high equilibrium z'' would move to the right, so if the firm is able to get past the critical point, the eventual size of its user population z'' would be even larger. Of course, if p^* is set below the cost of production, the firm loses money. But as part of a pricing strategy over time, in which early losses may be offset by growth in the user population and later profits, this may be a viable strategy. Many firms do this by offering free trials for their products or by setting low introductory prices.

17.4 A Dynamic View of the Market

There is another way to view this critical point idea that is particularly illuminating. We have been focusing on an equilibrium in which consumers correctly predict the number of actual users of the good. Let's now ask what this would look like if consumers have common beliefs about how many users there will be, but we allow for the possibility that these beliefs are not correct.

This means that if everyone believes a z fraction of the population will use the product, then consumer x, based on this belief, will want to purchase if $r(x)f(z) \geq p^*$. Hence, if anyone at all wants to purchase, the set of people who will purchase will be between 0 and $\hat{z}$, where $\hat{z}$ solves the equation $r(\hat{z})f(z) = p^*$. Equivalently,

$$r(\hat{z}) = \frac{p^*}{f(z)}, \tag{17.1}$$

or, taking the inverse of the function $r(\cdot)$,

$$\hat{z} = r^{-1}\left(\frac{p^*}{f(z)}\right). \tag{17.2}$$

This equation provides a way of computing the outcome $\hat{z}$ from the shared expectation z, but we should keep in mind that we can only use this equation when there is in fact a value of $\hat{z}$ that solves Equation (17.1). Otherwise, the outcome is simply that no one purchases.

Since $r(\cdot)$ is a continuous function that decreases from $r(0)$ down to $r(1) = 0$, such a solution will exist and be unique precisely when $\dfrac{p^*}{f(z)} \leq r(0)$. Therefore, in general, we can define a function $g(\cdot)$ that gives the outcome $\hat{z}$ in terms of the shared expectation z as follows. When the shared expectation is $z \geq 0$, the outcome is $\hat{z} = g(z)$, where

$$g(z) = r^{-1}\left(\frac{p^*}{f(z)}\right) \text{ when the condition for a solution } \frac{p^*}{f(z)} \leq r(0) \text{ holds, and}$$
$$g(z) = 0 \text{ otherwise.}$$

Let's try this on the example illustrated in Figure 17.3, where $r(x) = 1 - x$ and $f(z) = z$. In this case, $r^{-1}(x)$ turns out to be $1 - x$. Also, $z(0) = 1$, so the condition for a solution $\dfrac{p^*}{f(z)} \leq r(0)$ is just $z \geq p^*$. Therefore, in this example,

$$g(z) = 1 - \frac{p^*}{z} \text{ when } z \geq p^*, \text{ and } g(z) = 0 \text{ otherwise.}$$

We can plot the function $\hat{z} = g(z)$ as shown in Figure 17.4. Beyond the simple shape of the curve, however, its relationship to the 45° line $\hat{z} = z$ provides a striking visual summary of the issues around equilibrium, stability, and instability that we've been discussing. Figure 17.5 illustrates this. To begin with, when the plots of the two functions $\hat{z} = g(z)$ and $\hat{z} = z$ cross, we have a self-fulfilling expectations equilibrium: here $g(z) = z$, and so if everyone expects a z fraction of the population to purchase, then in fact a z fraction will do so. When the curve $\hat{z} = g(z)$ lies below the line $\hat{z} = z$, we have downward pressure on the consumption of the good: if people expect a z fraction of the population to use the good, then the outcome will underperform these expectations, and we would expect a downward spiral in consumption. And correspondingly, when the curve $\hat{z} = g(z)$ lies above the line $\hat{z} = z$, we have upward pressure on the consumption of the good.

This gives a pictorial interpretation of the stability properties of the equilibria. Based on how the functions cross in the vicinity of the equilibrium z'', we see that it is stable: there is upward pressure from below and downward pressure from above. On the other hand, where the curves cross in the vicinity of the equilibrium z', there is

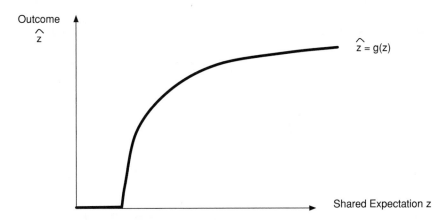

Figure 17.4. From a model with network effects, we can define a function $\hat{z} = g(z)$: if everyone expects a z fraction of the population to purchase the good, then in fact a $g(z)$ fraction will do so.

instability – downward pressure from below and upward pressure from above – causing the equilibrium to quickly unravel if it is perturbed in either direction.

The particular shape of the curve in Figure 17.5 depends on the functions we chose in our example, but the intuition behind this picture is much more general than the example. With network effects in general, we would expect to see a relation between the expected number of users and the actual number of purchasers that looks qualitatively like this curve, or more generally like the smoother version in Figure 17.6. Where the curve $\hat{z} = g(z)$ crosses the line $\hat{z} = z$, we have equilibria that can be either stable or unstable depending on whether the curve crosses from above or below the line.

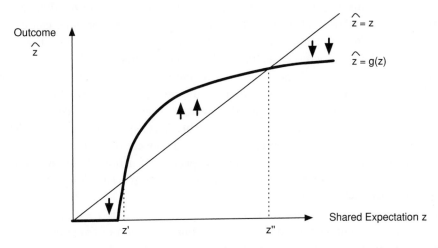

Figure 17.5. When $r(x) = 1 - x$ and $f(z) = z$, we get the curve for $g(z)$ shown in the plot: $g(z) = 1 - p^*/z$ if $z \geq p^*$ and $g(z) = 0$ if $z < p^*$. Where the curve $\hat{z} = g(z)$ crosses the line $\hat{z} = z$, we have self-fulfilling expectations equilibria. When $\hat{z} = g(z)$ lies below the line $\hat{z} = z$, we have downward pressure on the consumption of the good (indicated by the downward arrows); when $\hat{z} = g(z)$ lies above the line $\hat{z} = z$, we have upward pressure on the consumption of the good (indicated by the upward arrows). This indicates visually why the equilibrium at z' is unstable while the equilibrium at z'' is stable.

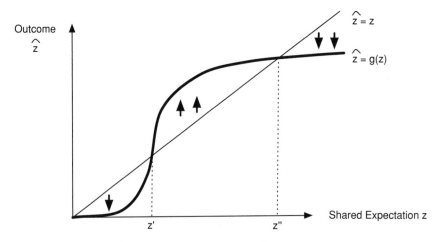

Figure 17.6. The curve $g(z)$, and its relation to the line $\hat{z} = z$, illustrates a pattern that we expect to see in settings more general than just the example used for Figure 17.5.

The Dynamic Behavior of the Population. In the 1970s, Mark Granovetter and Thomas Schelling used pictures like the ones in Figures 17.5 and 17.6 to model how a population might react dynamically to a network effect [192, 366]. Specifically, they were interested in how the number of people participating in a given activity with network effects would tend to grow or shrink over time.

To motivate the kind of question they formulated, let's imagine that, instead of evaluating the purchase of a discrete object like a fax machine, people in society are evaluating their participation in a large social media site – something where you chat with friends, share videos, or some similar activity. We are formulating the underlying story here in terms of participation rather than purchasing because the dynamics of participation are more fluid than the dynamics of purchasing: someone can change their mind about participation in a social media site from one day to the next, whereas purchasing a physical good is a step that isn't as naturally undone.

Despite the change in the motivating story, the model remains exactly the same. Each person x has an intrinsic interest in using the site, represented by a function $r(x)$, and the site is more attractive to people if it has more users, as governed by a function $f(z)$. Let's suppose that there is also a fixed level of effort required to use the site, which serves the role of a "price" p^* (except that the price may consist of the expenditure of effort rather than money). Thus, if person x expects a z fraction of the population to want to participate, then x will participate if $r(x)f(z) \geq p^*$. This is just the same as the criterion we saw before.

Let's suppose that time proceeds in a fixed set of periods $t = 0, 1, 2, \ldots$ (e.g., days, weeks, or months). At time $t = 0$, some initial fraction of the population z_0 is participating in the site – let's call this the initial *audience size*. Now, the audience size changes dynamically over time as follows. In each period t, people evaluate whether to participate based on a shared expectation that the audience size will be the same as what it was in the previous period. In terms of our function $g(\cdot)$, which maps shared expectations to outcomes, this means that $z_1 = g(z_0)$, since everyone acts in period $t = 1$ on the expectation that the audience size will be z_0. After this, $z_2 = g(z_1)$, since

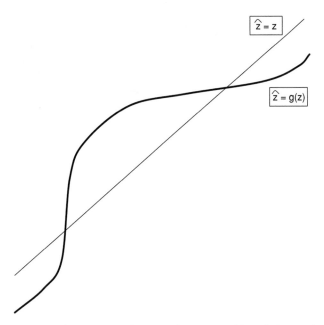

Figure 17.7. A "zoomed-in" region of a curve $\hat{z} = g(z)$ and its relation to the line $\hat{z} = z$.

in period $t = 2$ everyone will act based on the expectation that the audience size is now z_1; more generally, we have $z_t = g(z_{t-1})$ for each t.

This is clearly a model in which the population is behaving in a myopic way – they evaluate the benefits of participation as though the future will be the same as the present. However, it is an approximation that can be reasonable in settings where people have relatively limited information, and where they are behaving according to simple rules. Moreover, part of its value as an approximation in this case is that it produces dynamic behavior that closely corresponds to our notions of equilibrium: if the population follows this model, then it converges precisely to self-fulfilling expectations equilibria that are stable. We discuss the reasons for this next.

Analyzing the Dynamics. The dynamic behavior of the population can be analyzed in a way that is purely "pictorial" but nevertheless completely rigorous. Here is how this works, using a zoomed-in region of the curve $\hat{z} = g(z)$ in the vicinity of two equilibria as shown in Figure 17.7.

We have an initial audience size z_0, and we want to understand how the sequence of audience sizes $z_1 = g(z_0)$, $z_2 = g(z_1)$, $z_3 = g(z_2)$, ... behaves over time. We will do this by tracking the points (z_t, z_t), as t ranges over $t = 0, 1, 2, \ldots$; notice that all of these points lie on the diagonal line $\hat{z} = z$. The basic way we move from one of these points to the next one is shown in Figure 17.8. We start by locating the current audience size z_0 on the line $\hat{z} = z$. Now, to determine z_1, we simply move vertically until we reach the curve $\hat{z} = g(z)$, since this gives us the value of $z_1 = g(z_0)$. Then we again locate the audience size z_1 on the line $\hat{z} = z$; this involves moving horizontally from the point $(z_0, z_1 = g(z_0))$ until we reach the point (z_1, z_1). We have therefore gone from (z_0, z_0) to (z_1, z_1), following the evolution of the audience in the first time period.

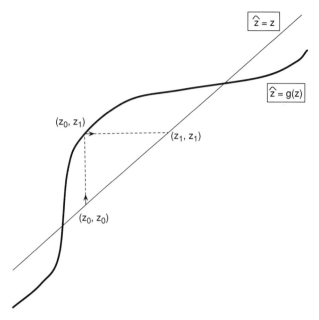

Figure 17.8. The audience size changes dynamically as people react to the current audience size. This effect can be tracked using the curve $\hat{z} = g(z)$ and the line $\hat{z} = z$.

This is the basic operation: for each time period t, we can determine the new audience size z_t from the current one, z_{t-1}, in the same way. We first move vertically from the point (z_{t-1}, z_{t-1}) to the point (z_{t-1}, z_t) (which lies on the curve $\hat{z} = g(z)$); we then move horizontally from the point (z_{t-1}, z_t) to the point (z_t, z_t).

Figure 17.9 now shows what happens as we track this sequence of points, following how the audience size changes. When we're following a part of the curve $\hat{z} = g(z)$ that lies above the diagonal line $\hat{z} = z$, the points move upward, converging to the nearest place where the two functions cross, which will be at a stable equilibrium point. On the left- and right-hand parts of the picture, we show what happens to two other trajectories that start out from points where the curve $\hat{z} = g(z)$ lies *below* the diagonal line $\hat{z} = z$. Here, the sequence of points that track the audience size will move downward, again converging to the first crossing point it reaches; again, this will be a stable equilibrium. Notice that, around the unstable equilibrium point in the figure, the trajectories of points move *away* from it on either side – consistent with our view of unstable equilibria, there is no way to reach this point unless you start right at it.

Thus, this simple dynamics for updating the audience size – although it is based on myopic behavior by the population – illustrates how stable and unstable equilibria govern the outcomes. Stable equilibria attract the population from both sides, whereas unstable equilibria act like "branch points," with the audience size flowing away from them on either side.

17.5 Industries with Network Goods

The discussion and models thus far provide some useful intuitions about how an industry with network effects might be expected to evolve over time. Let's discuss

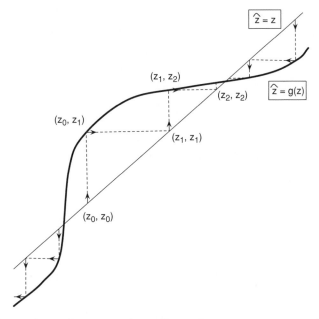

Figure 17.9. Successive updates cause the audience size to converge to a stable equilibrium point (and to move away from the vicinities of unstable ones).

what we can learn at a qualitative level from these models. We'll continue to use "audience size" for the fraction of the population that purchases a product.

Let's start with Figure 17.3 and suppose that a new product is introduced with a high initial cost of production; in particular, suppose the horizontal line at height p^* is above the top of the parabola. In this case the only equilibrium is at audience size $z = 0$. If over time the cost of production falls, then eventually a horizontal line drawn at p^* will intersect the parabola in two points, much like we see in Figure 17.3, and there will be three possible equilibria. But when p^* is large, near the top of the curve in Figure 17.3, it is likely that none of the good will be sold: to have any sales occur consumers would have to expect an audience size of at least z', which will be large when p^* is large (near the fraction of the population where the parabola reaches its peak). Given that none were sold previously – when the cost was above the top of the curve – this seems an unlikely prediction. But as the cost of production continues to fall, the critical point decreases (as z' gets closer to 0), and an audience size of at least z' starts to seem more and more likely. Once consumers expect the good to be viable, with an audience size of at least z', the stable equilibrium is in fact z''. So as costs decline we would expect to initially see no sales, and then once purchases begin we would expect to see sales grow rapidly to the stable point.

Marketing a Product with Network Effects. How can a firm that wants to sell a product with a network effect use these insights to market its product? Suppose you are running a firm that is producing a new product subject to network effects; perhaps it's a new piece of software, communication technology, or social media. The marketing of this product will not succeed unless you can get past the tipping point (at z'). Starting small and hoping to grow slowly is unlikely to succeed, since unless your product is widely used it has little value to any potential purchasers.

Thus, you somehow need to convince a large initial group to adopt your product before others will be willing to buy it. How would you do this? One possibility is to set an initial low, introductory price for the good, perhaps even offering it for free. This price below the cost of producing the good will result in early losses, but if the product catches on – if it gets over the tipping point – then your firm can raise the price and perhaps make enough profit to overcome the initial losses.

Another alternative is to attempt to identify fashion leaders – those whose purchase or use of the good will attract others to use it – and convince them to adopt the good. This strategy also involves network effects, but they are ones that cannot be studied at the population level. Instead we would need to identify a network of connections between potential purchasers and ask who influences whom in this network. We will explore this idea in Chapter 19.

Social Optimality with Network Effects. We saw in Section 17.1 that, for a market with no network effects, the equilibrium is socially optimal. That is, it maximizes the total difference between the reservation prices of the consumers who purchase the good and the total cost of producing the good, over all possible allocations to people.

For goods with network effects, however, the equilibria are typically not optimal. At a high level, the reason is that each consumer's choice affects each other consumer's payoff, and the consequences of this can be analyzed as follows. Suppose we are at an equilibrium in which the audience size is z^*. The consumer named z^* – the purchaser with the least interest in the product – has a reservation price of $r(z^*)f(z^*) = p^*$. Now, consider the set of consumers with names above z^* and below $z^* + c$ for some small constant $c > 0$. None of these consumers want to buy, since $r(z)f(z^*) < p$ for z in this range. But if they all did purchase the good, then all the current purchasers would benefit: the value of the product to each purchaser $x < z^*$ would increase from $r(x)f(z^*)$ to $r(x)f(z^* + c)$. The potential consumers between z^* and $z^* + c$ don't take this effect into account in their respective decisions about purchasing the good.

It is easy to set up situations where this overall benefit to existing purchasers outweighs the overall loss that consumers between z^* and $z^* + c$ would experience from buying the good. In such a case the equilibrium is not socially optimal, since society would be better off if these additional people bought the good. This example illustrates the more general principle that, for goods with network effects, markets typically provide less of the good than is socially optimal.

Network Effects and Competition. Finally, let's ask what might happen if multiple firms develop competing new products, each of which has its own network effects. For example, we could consider two competing social-networking sites that offer similar services, or two technologies that do essentially the same thing, but where the value of each of these technologies depends on how many people use it. There are a number of classic examples of this from technology industries over the past several decades [27]. These include the rise of Microsoft to dominate the market for personal-computer operating systems, and the triumph of VHS over Betamax as the standard videotape format in the 1980s.

In such cases of product competition with network effects, it is likely that one product will dominate the market, as opposed to a scenario in which both products (or even more than two) flourish. The product that first gets over its own tipping point attracts many consumers and this may make the competing product less attractive. Being the first to reach this tipping point is very important – more important than being the "best" in an abstract sense. That is, suppose that if product A has audience size z, then consumer x values it at $r_A(x)f(z)$, whereas if product B has audience size z, then consumer x values it at a larger amount, $r_B(x)f(z) > r_A(x)f(z)$. Let's also suppose that each product can be produced at the same price. Then it seems reasonable to say that product B is the better product. But if product A is on the market first and gets over its tipping point, then product B may not be able to survive.[4]

These considerations help provide some intuition for how markets with strong network effects tend to behave. Writing in the *Harvard Business Review* in 1996, Brian Arthur summarized the "hallmarks" of these markets in a way that reflects the discussion in the previous paragraph: "market instability (the market tilts to favor a product that gets ahead), multiple potential outcomes ([e.g.,] under different events in history different operating systems could have won), unpredictability, the ability to lock in a market, the possible predominance of an inferior product, and fat profits for the winner" [27]. It is not the case that a given market with network effects will necessarily display all these characteristics, but they are phenomena to watch for in this type of setting.

Of course, in our discussion of the dominance of product A over product B, we have assumed that nothing else changes to shift the balance after A achieves dominance. If the firm that makes product B improves its product sufficiently and markets it well, and if the firm that makes product A doesn't respond effectively, then B may still overtake A and become the dominant product.

17.6 Mixing Individual Effects with Population-Level Effects

Thus far we have focused on models of network effects in which the product is useless to consumers when it has an audience size of 0; this is captured by our assumption that $f(0) = 0$. But of course one can also study more general kinds of network effects, in which a product has some value to a person even when he or she is the first purchaser, and its value then increases as more people buy it. We can think of this as a model that mixes individual effects (a person's value for the product on its own) with population-level effects (the increased value a person derives when the product has a large audience size). In such a model, we would have $f(0) > 0$ and have $f(z)$ increasing in z.

We won't attempt to cover all the ways of fleshing out such a model; instead we develop one general class of examples to illustrate how qualitatively new phenomena can arise when we mix individual and population-level effects. In particular, we focus on a phenomenon identified in this type of model by Mark Granovetter [192] and which corresponds to an intuitively natural issue in the marketing of new products with network effects.

---

[4] Exercises 3. and 4. at the end of this chapter offer simple models of this situation.

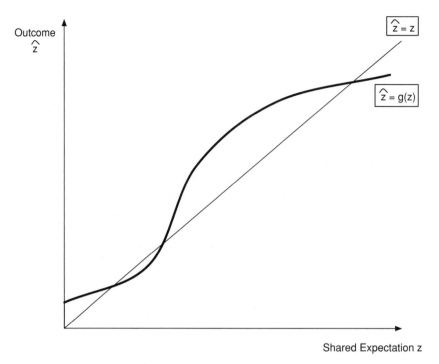

Figure 17.10. When $f(0) > 0$, so that people have value for the product even when they are the only user, the curve $\hat{z} = g(z)$ no longer passes through the point $(0, 0)$, and so an audience size of 0 is no longer an equilibrium.

A Concrete Model. For our example, let's consider a function $f(\cdot)$ of the form $f(z) = 1 + az^2$ for a constant parameter a. We'll continue to use the simple example $r(x) = 1 - x$; so, when the audience size is z, the value of the product to consumer x is

$$r(x)f(z) = (1 - x)(1 + az^2).$$

Now let's apply the analysis from Section 17.4 to this function to get the dynamic behavior of the market. We will assume that the price p^* is strictly between 0 and 1. When everyone expects an audience size of z, the fraction of people who actually use the product is $\hat{z} = g(z)$, where $g(\cdot)$ is defined as in Section 17.4:

$$g(z) = r^{-1}\left(\frac{p^*}{f(z)}\right) \text{ when the condition for a solution } \frac{p^*}{f(z)} \le r(0) \text{ holds;}$$
and $g(z) = 0$ otherwise.

As before, we have $r^{-1}(x) = 1 - x$. Since in our case $r(0) = 1$, $f(z) \ge 1$, and $p^* < 1$, the condition for a solution $\dfrac{p^*}{f(z)} \le r(0)$ always holds. Plugging this into the formula for $g(z)$, we get

$$g(z) = 1 - \frac{p^*}{1 + az^2}.$$

When we plot this function $\hat{z} = g(z)$ together with the 45° line $\hat{z} = z$, we get something that looks like Figure 17.10.

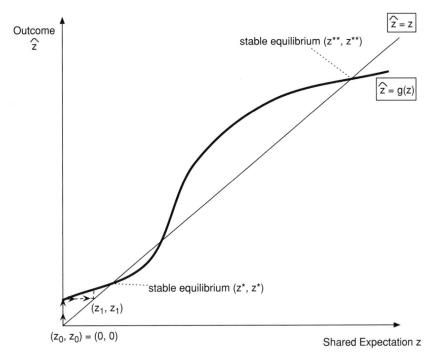

Figure 17.11. The audience grows dynamically from an initial size of zero to a relatively small stable equilibrium size of z^*.

Growing an Audience from Zero. In our earlier model with $f(0) = 0$, an audience size of zero was a stable equilibrium: if everyone expected that no one would use the product, then no one would. But when $f(0) > 0$, so that the product has value to people even when they are the only user, an audience size of zero is no longer an equilibrium (when $p^* < 1$): even if everyone expects no one to use the product, some people will still purchase it.

As a result, it becomes natural to ask what happens when such a product starts at an audience size of zero, and we then follow the dynamics that were defined in Section 17.4. Figure 17.11 shows what happens when we do this: the sequence of audience sizes increases from $z_0 = 0$ up to the first point (z^*, z^*) at which the curve $\hat{z} = g(z)$ crosses the line $\hat{z} = z$. This is the stable equilibrium that is reached when we run the dynamics of the market starting from an audience size of zero.

Notice how the underlying story that we're modeling with this process has no direct analogue in the earlier model when $f(0) = 0$. There, because the product was useless if it had an audience size of zero, a firm marketing the product needed alternate ways to get over its tipping point at the low, unstable equilibrium in order to have any customers at all. But when $f(0) > 0$, the audience can grow from zero up to some larger stable equilibrium z^* through the simple dynamics in Figure 17.11. In other words, we're able to talk here about an audience that grows gradually and organically, starting from no users at all, rather than one that needs to be pushed by other means over an initial tipping point.

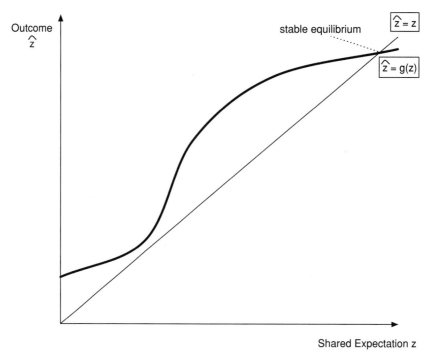

Figure 17.12. If the price is reduced slightly, the curve $\hat{z} = g(z)$ shifts upward so that it no longer crosses the line $\hat{z} = z$ in the vicinity of the point (z^*, z^*).

Bottlenecks and Large Changes. The firm marketing the product in our example, however, may well want more than what it gets in Figure 17.11. Although the audience grows to some size z^* on its own, there is a much higher stable equilibrium, shown in the figure at (z^{**}, z^{**}), that would be much more desirable if only it could be reached. But, starting from zero, the audience doesn't reach this high equilibrium z^{**}, because it is blocked by a "bottleneck" that stops it at z^*.

Here is where we get to the surprising phenomenon at the heart of this example: small changes in the properties of the market can cause enormous changes in the size of the equilibrium audience that is reached, starting from zero [192]. Suppose that the firm is able to lower the price p^* slightly, to some new value $q^* < p^*$. Then we get a new function $h(z)$ mapping shared expectations to outcomes,

$$h(z) = 1 - \frac{q^*}{1 + az^2},$$

which in turn defines a new dynamic process. As q^* is made smaller, the curve $\hat{z} = h(z)$ shifts upward until it no longer crosses the line $\hat{z} = z$ at all in the vicinity of the point (z^*, z^*); this is shown in Figure 17.12. However, $h(\cdot)$ still has a high stable equilibrium close to the high equilibrium (z^{**}, z^{**}) for the function $g(\cdot)$.

As soon as $h(\cdot)$ lifts enough that it no longer crosses $\hat{z} = z$ near (z^*, z^*), the equilibrium audience size starting from zero changes abruptly and dramatically: it suddenly

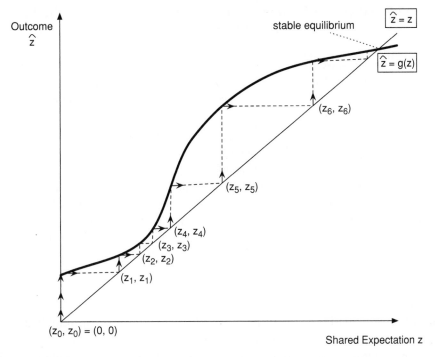

Figure 17.13. The small reduction in price that shifted the curve $\hat{z} = g(z)$ has a huge effect on the equilibrium audience size that is reached when starting from zero.

jumps from a value near z^* to a much higher value near z^{**}. There is a natural reason for this behavior: as shown in Figure 17.13, the bottleneck at (z^*, z^*) has opened into a narrow passageway, and so now the dynamics starting from the point $(0, 0)$ can carry the audience all the way up to the stable equilibrium near (z^{**}, z^{**}).[5]

This phenomenon shows how, in models with network effects, small changes in market conditions can have strong, discontinuous effects on the outcome. The contrast between Figures 17.11 and 17.13 relates to an important issue in the marketing of products with network effects. In Figure 17.11, the product reaches a small group of the most enthusiastic consumers (the ones with the highest values for the product), but it fails to make the leap from this group to the much broader set of people – mainstream, less enthusiastic consumers – who could collectively push the audience size up to the higher equilibrium at z^{**}. However, once the price is lowered very slightly, making the product slightly more attractive to everyone, a passage is opened that enables the success of the product with its most enthusiastic consumers to carry over to this larger mainstream set, driving the equilibrium audience size up to a much larger value.

---

[5] It is not difficult to find specific numbers that cause this effect to happen; for example, you can try $f(z) = 1 + 4z^2$ and $p^* = 0.93$. In this case, the equilibrium audience size starting from zero is around 0.1. If we then lower the price slightly to $q^* = 0.92$, the equilibrium audience size starting from zero jumps to around 0.7.

17.7 Advanced Material: Negative Externalities and the El Farol Bar Problem

In different contexts, we have now analyzed situations with both negative externalities (traffic congestion and the Braess Paradox) and positive externalities (goods with network effects). The settings for these analyses each contained a number of details designed to capture their respective contexts: in our discussion of negative externalities we had the complexity of an underlying network through which the traffic flowed; with positive externalities, we had a heterogeneous population with diverse reservation prices, all reacting to a common market price.

But even after eliminating all these details and reducing the problems to simpler forms, the phenomena that surround negative and positive externalities remain quite different at a more fundamental level. In this section we consider some of these contrasts using stylized, simple examples that enable us to highlight the differences more clearly. In the process, we will also consider the question of how individuals coordinate on equilibrium behavior in each setting.

Simple Scenarios with Negative and Positive Externalities. As our simplified setting for negative externalities, we use the widely studied *El Farol Bar problem* created by Brian Arthur [26]. The problem is named after a bar in Sante Fe that used to have live music every Thursday evening. In the formulation of the problem, the bar has seating for only 60 people, and so showing up for the music is enjoyable only when at most 60 people do so. With more than 60 people in attendance, it becomes unpleasantly crowded, such that it would be preferable to have stayed home. Now, unfortunately, there are 100 people each week who are interested in going to the bar, and they all share the view that going is only worthwhile when at most 60 people show up. How does each person reason in a given week about whether to go or to stay home – knowing that everyone else is reasoning about this decision as well?

The El Farol Bar problem describes a situation with a very simple negative externality: the payoffs to participating in the underlying activity (going to the bar) decrease as the number of participants increases. And despite the appealingly simple statement of the problem, it creates a situation in which the reasoning problem faced by the participants is very complex. To illustrate where some of these complexities come from, it's useful to compare it to a simple analogous situation that contains a positive externality.

In this parallel scenario, let's imagine a division of a large company consisting of 100 people, in which the management is encouraging the employees to use a particular corporate social networking site as part of their workflow. The management would like each employee to create an account and maintain a presence on the site to facilitate increased interaction across the division. The employees each believe that this would be worthwhile provided that enough people in the division participate in the site; otherwise, the effort required would not be worth it. Thus, each employee wants to use the social networking site if at least 60 other employees do so as well. (So counting the employee herself, this means the total number of employees using the site should be strictly greater than 60 in order for it to be worth the effort.) This is closely analogous to the scenarios we've considered in earlier sections of this chapter, concerning goods with network effects, although here, instead of each individual having a distinct reservation price, there is simply a common interest in participating provided the audience size is large enough. (Also, the size of the population is finite rather than infinite.) In a different way, the analogy to the El Farol Bar problem should also be clear: in the scenario of the social networking site we have a positive externality in which a participation level above 60 is good, while in El Farol, we have a negative externality in which a participation level above 60 is bad.

These two examples have been designed in such a way that one exhibits only negative externalities and the other exhibits only positive externalities. It's important to keep in mind, of course, that many real situations in fact display both kinds of externalities – some level of participation by others is good, but too much is bad. For example, the El Farol Bar might be most enjoyable if a reasonable crowd shows up, provided it does not exceed 60. Similarly, an online social media site with limited infrastructure might be most enjoyable if it has a reasonably large audience, but not so large that connecting to the Web site becomes very slow due to the congestion. To keep the discussion here as clean as possible, we are keeping the two kinds of externalities separate, but understanding how they work in combination is an important topic of ongoing research [229]. We also consider a simple way of combining the two effects in Exercise 2 at the end of this chapter.

Basic Comparisons Between the Two Scenarios. The contrasts between the two scenarios – El Farol and corporate social networking – translate into significant differences in how we should expect people to behave. Let's first think about these differences informally; later we'll carry out the analysis in more detail.

Reasoning about the social networking scenario using what we've seen earlier in this chapter, we find that there are two very natural equilibria the group of 100 people could exhibit. If everyone participates, then everyone has an interest in participating; similarly, if no one participates, then no one has an interest in participating. (There are also other more complex equilibria, as we'll see later, but these two all-or-nothing equilibria are by far the two most natural.)

On the other hand, neither of these outcomes is an equilibrium in the El Farol Bar problem. If everyone were to attend, then everyone would have an incentive to stay home; if no one were to attend, then everyone would have an incentive to attend. Instead, the equilibria have a more complex structure in which individuals need to break the underlying symmetry in such a way that some people attend and some stay home.

There is a second, essentially equivalent way to describe this contrast, using the idea of shared expectations from earlier in the chapter. In the social networking scenario, if the individuals have a shared expectation that everyone will participate, then this expectation is self-fulfilling: everyone will in fact participate. On the other hand, if they have a shared expectation that no one will participate, this expectation too will be self-fulfilling. As we've seen, understanding such self-fulfilling expectations is a key part of reasoning about situations with positive externalities.

The negative externalities in the El Farol Bar problem, in contrast, pose problems for shared expectations. In particular, individuals cannot have a fixed, shared expectation of the audience size at El Farol that will be self-fulfilling. If everyone expects an audience size of at most 60, then everyone will show up, thereby negating this prediction. Similarly, if everyone expects an audience size above 60, then everyone will stay home, negating this prediction too.[6]

These are fundamental contrasts: with positive externalities, there exist self-fulfilling expectations and a natural set of outcomes to coordinate on; with negative externalities, any shared expectation of a fixed audience size will be self-negating, and the individuals must instead sort themselves out in much more complicated ways. Given this complexity, the El Farol Bar problem has become a testing ground for a variety of models of individual behavior. We now describe some of these models and styles of analysis in more detail.

Nash Equilibria in the El Farol Bar Problem. First, let's consider how to model the El Farol Bar problem as a game that will be played once by the set of 100 people. (We could imagine that, instead of the bar having music every Thursday, it is simply hosting a single concert, and everyone needs to decide in advance whether to attend.) Each person has two possible strategies, Go (to the bar) or Stay (home), and his payoffs are as follows.

- If he chooses Stay, then he receives a payoff of 0 in all outcomes.
- If he chooses Go, then he receives a payoff of $x > 0$ when at most 60 people choose Go, and a payoff of $-y < 0$ when more than 60 people choose Go.

There are many different pure-strategy Nash equilibria for this game. There is no equilibrium in which all players use the same pure strategy, but any outcome in which exactly 60 people choose Go and 40 people choose Stay is a pure-strategy Nash equilibrium. Of course, it is far from clear how the group would settle on this set of heterogeneous strategies, since at the outset of the game, they are all identical. We will return to the question of how heterogeneous strategies might arise later in this section.

There is, however, an equilibrium in which all players behave symmetrically, and this is through the use of mixed strategies, in which each player chooses Go with the same probability p. In this case too, there are some subtleties. It would be natural to guess that the shared probability p in this mixed-strategy equilibrium would be 0.6, but this is not necessarily the case. Instead, p depends on the payoffs x and $-y$: following the reasoning we saw in Chapter 6, we need to choose p so that each player is indifferent between choosing Go and choosing Stay. This ensures that no one has an incentive to deviate from randomizing between the two alternatives.

Since the payoff for Stay is always 0, we need to choose p so that the expected payoff from Go is also 0. Therefore, we need to choose p so that the equation

$$x \cdot \Pr\left[\textit{at most 60 go}\right] - y \cdot \Pr\left[\textit{more than 60 go}\right] = 0 \qquad (17.3)$$

holds. Using the fact that

$$\Pr\left[\textit{more than 60 go}\right] = 1 - \Pr\left[\textit{at most 60 go}\right],$$

---

[6] As Brian Arthur notes, this latter possibility is a reflection of the same phenomenon that the baseball player Yogi Berra invoked when he quipped about a popular restaurant, "Nobody goes there anymore; it's too crowded" [26, 105].

we can rearrange Equation (17.3) to get

$$\Pr\left[at\ most\ 60\ go\right] = \frac{y}{x + y}. \tag{17.4}$$

So in order to have a mixed-strategy equilibrium, we must choose p so that Equation (17.4) holds. When $x = y$, choosing $p = 0.6$ will work [212]. But suppose that x and y are different; for example, perhaps the music at El Farol is pleasant, but the nights on which it is crowded are truly unbearable, so that y is significantly larger than x. In this case, p must be chosen so that the probability at most 60 people go is very high, and so p will be significantly less than 0.6. Since the expected number of people attending is $100p$, this means that, in expectation, significantly fewer than 60 people will be showing up. So with $y > x$, the bar will be significantly underutilized in the mixed-strategy equilibrium due to the shared fear of overcrowding.

The existence of this mixed-strategy equilibrium is a useful counterpoint to our earlier informal discussion about the difficulty of forming a shared expectation in the El Farol Bar problem. It's true that any shared expectation consisting of a fixed number representing the audience size – the kind of shared expectation we used earlier in this chapter – will be negated by what actually happens. But if we allow more complicated kinds of expectations, then in fact there is a shared expectation that will be self-fulfilling – the expectation that everyone plans to randomize their decision to attend the bar, choosing to go with the probability p that makes Equation (17.4) come true.

Analogies with Equilibria in Related Games. To get some intuition about the equilibria we've found, it's useful to compare them to the equilibria of some related games.

First, suppose we model the corporate social networking scenario from earlier in this section as a similar one-shot game: the two possible strategies are Join or Don't Join (the site); the payoff to Don't Join is always 0, the payoff to Join is y when more than 60 people join, and the payoff to Join is $-x$ when at most 60 join. In this case, corresponding to what we saw in our informal discussion earlier, there are just two pure-strategy equilibria: one in which everyone chooses Join, and one in which everyone chooses Don't Join. Interestingly, the same mixed-strategy equilibrium that applied to the El Farol Bar problem also holds here: if everyone chooses Join with a probability p for which

$$-x \cdot \Pr\left[at\ most\ 60\ join\right] + y \cdot \Pr\left[more\ than\ 60\ join\right] = 0, \tag{17.5}$$

then everyone is indifferent between joining and not joining, and so this is an equilibrium. Since Equations (17.3) and (17.5) are equivalent (they are simply negations of each other), we get the same value of p that we did in the El Farol Bar problem.

Since games with 100 players are inherently complex, it's also instructive to ask what the two-player versions of these games look like. Specifically, in the two-player version of the El Farol Bar problem, each player wants to attend the bar as long as the other player doesn't; in the two-player social networking game, each player wants to use the site as long as the other one does. Scaled down to this size, each of these situations corresponds to one of the fundamental games introduced in Chapter 6: the two-player El Farol Bar problem is a Hawk–Dove game, in which the two players try

Player 2

		Stay	Go
Player 1	Stay	$0, 0$	$0, x$
	Go	$x, 0$	$-y, -y$

Figure 17.14. Two-player El Farol problem.

to make their actions different, while the two-player social networking scenario is a coordination game, in which the two players try to make their actions the same.

Each of these games has pure-strategy equilibria, as well as a mixed-strategy equilibrium in which the players randomize over their two available strategies. For example, in the two-player version of the El Farol Bar problem, the payoff matrix is shown in Figure 17.14.

The two pure-strategy equilibria consist of one player choosing Go while the other chooses Stay. For the mixed-strategy equilibrium, each player chooses Go with a probability p that causes the expected payoff from Go to be equal to zero:

$$x(1 - p) - yp = 0,$$

and hence $p = x/(x + y)$. By analogy with the multiplayer version, p is not equal to $\frac{1}{2}$ unless $x = y$. Also, just as there will be random fluctuations in the actual attendance at the bar around the mean of $100p$ in the multiplayer game, there is significant variation in how many people choose Go in the two-player version as well. Specifically, with probability p^2 both players choose Go, and with probability $(1 - p)^2$ both choose Stay.

Repeated El Farol Problems. Although the existence of a mixed-strategy equilibrium in which all 100 people follow the same strategy is an important observation about the El Farol Bar problem, it can't be the whole story. It's not clear why, or whether, a group of people would actually arrive at this mixed-strategy equilibrium, or at any other particular equilibrium or pattern of behavior from among the many that are possible. Once the group is playing an equilibrium, no one has an incentive to deviate – that's what it means for the behaviors to be in equilibrium. But how do they coordinate on equilibrium behavior in the first place?

To formulate models that address these questions, it is useful to think about a setting in which the El Farol game is played repeatedly. That is, suppose that each Thursday night the same 100 people must each decide whether to go to the bar or to stay home, and each receives a payoff of x (from going as part of a group of at most 60), $-y$ (from going as part of a group of more than 60), or 0 (from staying home). Each person also knows the history of what has happened on each prior Thursday, so they can use this information in making their decision for the current Thursday. By reasoning about decisions over time in this repeated El Farol game, we might hope to see how a pattern of behavior gradually emerges from rules that take past experience into account.

There are a number of different formalisms that can be used to study the repeated El Farol game. One approach is to view the full sequence of Thursdays as a dynamic game of the type studied in Section 6.10, in which players choose sequences of strategies – in this case, one for each Thursday – and correspondingly receive payoffs over time. We could consider Nash equilibria in this dynamic game and see whether the play of the game eventually settles down to repeated play of some equilibrium of the one-shot El Farol game. Essentially, we would be asking if equilibrium play by sophisticated players in the dynamic game converges to something that looks simple. Although learning can go on during the play of an equilibrium in a dynamic game [175], this approach can't fully answer our underlying question of how the individuals come to play a Nash equilibrium at all – since the learning here would be taking place within a Nash equilibrium of the larger dynamic game.

An alternate approach is to ask what might happen if the players are potentially more naive. A useful way to think about how players – sophisticated or naive – behave in a repeated game is to decompose their choice of strategy into a *forecasting rule* and a choice of action given the forecasting rule. A forecasting rule is any function that maps the past history of play to a prediction about the actions that all other players will take in the future. Forecasting rules can in principle be very complex. An individual could take all past behavior into account in generating a forecast and he may also forecast that how others will behave in the future depends on how he behaves now. Alternatively, a very naive player may forecast that each other player will simply use a fixed action forever. From an individual's forecasting rule, we can then make a prediction about his behavior: we assume that each individual behaves optimally given his forecasting rule. That is, he chooses an action that maximizes his expected payoff given whatever he forecasts about the behavior of others.

For the repeated El Farol game, most attention has focused on forecasting rules that work with audience sizes: a given forecasting rule is a function which maps the sequence of past audience sizes to a prediction about the number of other people who will go to the bar on the upcoming Thursday. (Thus, each forecasting rule produces a number between 0 and 99 when given a history of past audience sizes.) This is a bit less expressive than a forecasting rule that predicts, for each other person individually, whether they will go to the bar or stay home, but it captures the main quantity of interest, which is the total number of people who show up. For an individual using any such forecasting rule, his choice of action is easy to describe: he goes to the bar if his forecasting rule produces a number that is at most 59, and he stays home if it produces a number that is 60 or more.

In keeping with our informal discussion earlier in the section about self-fulfilling and self-negating expectations, we observe first of all that if everyone uses the same forecasting rule for the audience size then everyone will make very bad predictions. In any given situation, this common forecasting rule will predict either 59 or fewer others in attendance, or at least 60 others in attendance. In the first case, everyone will show up, and in the second case, everyone will stay home; in both cases, the forecasting rule is wrong. So to make any progress, we need the players to use a diversity of different forecasting rules.

A long line of research has considered how the group behaves when they use different classes of forecasting rules; the goal is to understand whether the system converges to a state in which, on any given Thursday, roughly 60% of the agents produce a forecast that causes them to go the bar, and roughly 40% produce a forecast that causes them to stay home (e.g., [26, 104, 167]). This investigation has been carried out both mathematically and by computer simulation, with some of the analysis becoming quite complex. In general, researchers have found that under a variety of conditions, the system converges to a state where the average attendance varies around 60 – in other words, providing near-optimal utilization of the bar over time.

While we won't go into the details of this analysis, it is not hard to get some intuition for why an average attendance of 60 arises very naturally when agents select from a diversity of forecasting rules. To do this, we can analyze perhaps the simplest model of individual forecasting, in which each person chooses a fixed prediction k for the number of others who will show up, and uses this prediction every week. That is, he will ignore the past history and always predict that k other people will be in attendance. Now, if each person picks their fixed value of k uniformly at random from the 100 natural numbers between 0 and 99, what is the expected audience size at the bar each week? The audience will consist of all people whose forecasting rule is based on a value of k between 0 and 59, and the expected number of such people is 60. Thus, with this very naive forecasting, we in fact get an expected attendance of 60 each Thursday, as desired.

Of course, this analysis is based on people who make extremely naive forecasts, but it shows how diversity in the set of forecasting rules can naturally lead to the right level of attendance. One can also ask what happens when individuals select random forecasts from a more complex space of possibilities, in which the prediction is based on the past several audience sizes. Under fairly general assumptions, an average attendance of 60 continues to hold, although establishing this is significantly more complicated [104].

17.8 Exercises

1. Consider a product that has network effects in the sense of our model from Chapter 17. Consumers are named using real numbers between 0 and 1; the reservation price for consumer x when a fraction z of the popuation uses the product is given by the formula $r(x) f(z)$, where $r(x) = 1 - x$ and $f(z) = z$.

   (a) Let's suppose that this good is sold at cost $\frac{1}{4}$ to any consumer who wants to buy a unit. What are the possible equilibrium numbers of purchasers of the good?

   (b) Suppose that the cost falls to $\frac{2}{9}$ and that the good is sold at this cost to any consumer who wants to buy a unit. What are the possible equilibrium numbers of purchasers of the good?

   (c) Briefly explain why the answers to parts (a) and (b) are qualitatively different.

   (d) Which of the equilibria you found in parts (a) and (b) are stable? Explain your answer.

2. In Chapter 17, we focused on goods with positive network effects – ones for which additional users made the good more attractive for everyone. But we know from our earlier discussion of Braess's paradox that network effects can sometimes be

negative: more users can sometimes make an alternative less rather than more attractive. Some goods actually have both effects; that is, the good may become more attractive as more people use it as long there aren't too many users, and then once there are too many users it becomes less attractive as more people use it. Think of a club in which being a member is more desirable if there is a reasonable number of other members, but once the number of members gets too large the club begins to seem crowded and less attractive. Here we explore how our model of network effects can incorporate such a combination of effects.

In keeping with the notation in Chapter 17, let's assume that consumers are named using real numbers between 0 and 1. Individual x has the reservation price $r(x) = 1 - x$ before we consider the network effect. The network effect is given by $f(z) = z$ for $z \leq \frac{1}{4}$ and by $f(z) = (\frac{1}{2}) - z$ for $z \geq \frac{1}{4}$. So the network benefit to being a user is maximized when the fraction of the population using the product is $z = \frac{1}{4}$; once the fraction is beyond $\frac{1}{4}$ the benefit declines, and it becomes negative if more than $\frac{1}{2}$ of the population is using it. Suppose that the price of this good is p, where $0 < p < \frac{1}{16}$.

(a) How many equilibria are there? Why? [You do not need to solve for the number(s) of users; a graph and explanation are fine.]

(b) Which equilibria are stable? Why?

(c) Consider an equilibrium in which someone is using the good. Is social welfare maximized at this number of users, or would it go up if there were more users, or would it go up if there were fewer users? Explain. (Again no calculations are necessary; a careful explanation is sufficient.)

3. You have developed a new product which performs the same service as an established product and your product is much better than the established product. Specifically, if the number of users of the two products were the same, then each potential purchaser's reservation price for your product would be twice their reservation price for the existing product. The difficulty that you face is that these are products with network effects and no one wants to use more than one of the two products. Currently, 80% of the people in the population are using the established product. Your cost of production and your competitor's costs of production are exactly the same, and let's suppose that they are equal to the price at which your competitor's product is sold.

If all of the current users of the established product switched to your product, the maximum price that you could charge (and still have all of them buy your product) would be twice the current price. So clearly you could make a nice profit if you could attract these potential purchasers. How would you attempt to convince users to switch to your product? You do not need to construct a formal model of the situation described in this question. It is sufficient to describe the strategies that you would try, and to explain why you think they might succeed in terms of network effects.

4. In the model of network effects that we covered in Chapter 17, there was only one product. Now let's ask what may happen if there are two competing products which both have network effects. Assume the following for each product:

(a) If no one is expected to use the product, then no one places a positive value on the product.

(b) If one-half of the consumers are expected to use the product, then exactly one-half of the consumers would buy the product.

(c) If all of the consumers are expected to use the product, then all consumers would buy the product.

Using an analysis of network effects, describe the possible equilibrium configurations of numbers of consumers using each product and briefly discuss which of these equilibria you would expect to be stable and which you would expect to be unstable. You do not need to build a formal model to answer this question. Just describe in words what may happen in this market.

CHAPTER 18

Power Laws and Rich-Get-Richer Phenomena

18.1 Popularity as a Network Phenomenon

For the past two chapters, we have been studying situations in which a person's behavior or decisions depend on the choices made by other people – either because the person's rewards are dependent on what other people do or because the choices of other people convey information that is useful in the decision-making process. We've seen that these types of coupled decisions, where behavior is correlated across a population, can lead to outcomes very different from what we find in cases where individuals make independent decisions.

Here we apply this network approach to analyze the general notion of *popularity*. Popularity is a phenomenon characterized by extreme imbalances: while almost everyone goes through life known only to people in their immediate social circles, a few people achieve wider visibility, and a very, very few attain global name recognition. Analogous things could be said of books, movies, or almost anything that commands an audience. How can we quantify these imbalances? Why do they arise? Are they somehow intrinsic to the whole idea of popularity?

We will see that some basic models of network behavior can provide significant insight into these questions. To begin the discussion, we focus on the Web as a concrete domain in which it is possible to measure popularity very accurately. While it may be difficult to estimate the number of people worldwide who have heard of famous individuals such as Barack Obama or Bill Gates, it is easy to take a snapshot of the full Web and simply count the number of links to high-profile Web sites such as Google, Amazon, or Wikipedia. We will refer to the full set of links pointing to a given Web page as the *in-links* to the page. Thus, we will start by using the number of in-links to a Web page as a measure of the page's popularity, keeping in mind, however, that this is just one example of a much broader phenomenon.

Early in the Web's history, people had already begun to ask a very basic version of the page popularity question, phrased as follows:

As a function of k, what fraction of pages on the Web have k in-links?

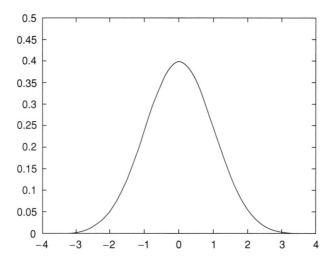

Figure 18.1. The density of values in the normal distribution.

Larger values of k indicate greater popularity, so this is precisely the question of how popularity is distributed over the set of Web pages.

A Simple Hypothesis: The Normal Distribution. Before trying to resolve this question, it's useful to ask what we should expect the answer to be. A natural guess is the *normal*, or *Gaussian*, distribution – the so-called bell curve used widely throughout probability and statistics. While we won't need many details about the normal distribution here, it's worth recalling that it's characterized by two quantities: a mean value and a standard deviation around this mean. Figure 18.1 shows a plot of the density of values in the normal distribution, scaled so that the mean is 0 and the standard deviation is 1. The basic fact about normal distributions is that the probability of observing a value that exceeds the mean by more than c times the standard deviation decreases exponentially in c.

The normal distribution is a natural guess in our case, since it is ubiquitous across the natural sciences. A result from the early 1900s, the Central Limit Theorem, provides a fundamental explanation for its appearance in so many settings: roughly speaking (and suppressing the full details), the Central Limit Theorem says that if we take any sequence of small independent random quantities, then in the limit their sum (or average) will be distributed according to the normal distribution. In other words, any quantity that can be viewed as the sum of many small independent random effects will be well approximated by the normal distribution. Thus, for example, if one performs repeated measurements of a fixed physical quantity, and if the variations in the measurements across trials are the cumulative result of many independent sources of error in each trial, then the distribution of measured values should be approximately normal.

How would we apply this in the case of Web pages? If we model the link structure of the Web, for example, by assuming that each page decides independently at random whether to link to any other given page, then the number of in-links to a given page is the sum of many independent random quantities (i.e., the presence or absence of a link from each other page); hence, we'd expect it to be normally distributed. In particular, this would suggest a hypothesis for the answer to our original question: if we believe this model, then the number of pages with k in-links should decrease exponentially in k, as k grows large.

18.2 Power Laws

When people measured the distribution of links on the Web, however, they found something very different from the predictions of the Central Limit Theorem. In studies over many different Web snapshots, taken at different points in the Web's history, the recurring finding is that the fraction of Web pages that have k in-links is approximately proportional to $1/k^2$ [80]. (More precisely, the exponent on k is generally a number slightly larger than 2.)

Why is this so different from the normal distribution? The crucial point is that $1/k^2$ decreases much more slowly as k increases, so pages with very large numbers of in-links are much more common than we'd expect with a normal distribution. For example, $1/k^2$ is only one in a million for $k = 1000$, whereas an exponentially decaying function like 2^{-k} is unimaginably tiny for $k = 1000$. A function that decreases as k to some fixed power, such as $1/k^2$ in the present case, is called a *power law*; when used to measure the fraction of items having value k, it says, qualitatively, that it's possible to see very large values of k.

This provides a quantitative form for one of the points we made initially: popularity seems to exhibit extreme imbalances, in which very large values are likely to arise. And it accords with our intuition about the Web, where there are certainly a reasonably large number of extremely popular pages. One sees similar power laws arising in measures of popularity in many other domains as well: for example, the fraction of telephone numbers that receive k calls per day is roughly proportional to $1/k^2$; the fraction of books that are bought by k people is roughly proportional to $1/k^3$; the fraction of scientific papers that receive k citations in total is roughly proportional to $1/k^3$; and there are many related examples [10, 320].

Indeed, just as the normal distribution is widespread in a family of settings in the natural sciences, power laws seem to dominate in cases where the quantity being measured can be viewed as a type of popularity. Hence, if you are handed data of this sort – say, for example, that someone gives you a table showing the number of monthly downloads for each song at a large online music site that they're hosting – one of the first things that's worth doing is to test whether it's approximately a power law $1/k^c$ for some c, and if so, to estimate the exponent c.

There's a simple method that provides at least a quick test for whether a data set exhibits a power-law distribution. Let $f(k)$ be the fraction of items that have value k, and suppose you want to know whether the equation $f(k) = a/k^c$ approximately holds, for some exponent c and constant of proportionality, a. Then, if we write this as $f(k) = ak^{-c}$ and take the logarithms of both sides of this equation, we get

$$\log f(k) = \log a - c \log k.$$

This says that if we have a power-law relationship, and we plot $\log f(k)$ as a function of $\log k$, then we should see a straight line: $-c$ will be the slope, and $\log a$ will be the

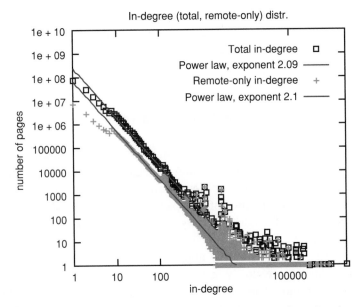

Figure 18.2. A power-law distribution (such as this one for the number of Web page in-links, from Broder et al. [80]) shows up as a straight line on a log-log plot. (Courtesy of Elsevier Limited.)

y-intercept. Such a "log-log" plot thus provides a quick way to see if one's data set exhibits an approximate power-law: it is easy to see if one has an approximately straight line, and one can read off the exponent from the slope. For example, Figure 18.2 does this for the fraction of Web pages with k in-links [80].

But if we are going to accept that power laws are so widespread, we also need a simple explanation for what is causing them: just as the Central Limit Theorem gave us a very basic reason to expect the normal distribution, we'd like something comparable for power laws. For example, it's striking how closely the plot in Figure 18.2 follows a straight line for much of the distribution, especially considering how many utterly uncontrollable factors come into play in the formation of the Web's link structure. What underlying process is keeping the line so straight?

18.3 Rich-Get-Richer Models

Ideas from the analysis of information cascades and network effects provide the basis for a very natural mechanism to generate power laws. Just as normal distributions arise from many independent random decisions averaging out, we will find that power laws arise from the feedback introduced by correlated decisions across a population.

It is actually an open and interesting research question to provide a fully satisfactory model of power laws starting from simple models of individual decision making (as we did for information cascades). Instead, we will build our model not from the internals of each person's decision-making process but from the observable consequences of decision-making in the presence of cascades: we will assume simply that people have a tendency to copy the decisions of people who act before them.

Based on this idea, here is a simple model for the creation of links among Web pages [42, 265, 300, 340, 371].

1. Pages are created in order, and named $1, 2, 3, \ldots, N$.
2. When page j is created, it produces a link to an earlier Web page by choosing between actions (a) and (b) below according to the following probabilistic rule (controlled by a single number p between 0 and 1):

   (a) With probability p, page j chooses a page i uniformly at random from among all earlier pages, and creates a link to this page i.

   (b) With probability $1 - p$, page j instead chooses a page i uniformly at random from among all earlier pages and creates a link *to the page that i points to*.

   (c) This describes the creation of a single link from page j; one can repeat this process to create multiple, independently generated links from page j. (However, to keep things simple, we will suppose that each page creates just one outbound link.)

Part 2(b) of this process is the key: after finding a random earlier page i in the population, the author of page j does not link to i, but instead copies the decision made by the author of page i – linking to the same page that i did.

The main result about this model is that if we run it for many pages, the fraction of pages with k in-links will be distributed approximately according to a power law $1/k^c$, where the value of the exponent c depends on the choice of p [68]. This dependence goes in an intuitively natural direction: as p gets smaller, so that copying becomes more frequent, the exponent c gets smaller as well, making one more likely to see extremely popular pages.

Proving this result would require more intricate analysis than we'll be able to do here, but it is useful to work through some of the informal ideas behind this analysis. First of all, the copying mechanism in 2(b) is really an implementation of the following "rich-get-richer" dynamics: when you copy the decision of a random earlier page, the probability that you end up linking to some page ℓ is directly proportional to the total number of pages that currently link to ℓ. Thus, an equivalent way to write our copying process would have been to phrase 2(b) as

2. ...

   (b) With probability $1 - p$, page j chooses a page ℓ with probability proportional to ℓ's current number of in-links, and creates a link to ℓ.

Why do we call this a "rich-get-richer" rule? Because the probability that page ℓ experiences an increase in popularity is directly proportional to ℓ's current popularity. This phenomenon is also known as *preferential attachment* [42], in the sense that links are formed "preferentially" to pages that already have high popularity. And the copying model provides an operational story for why popularity should exhibit such rich-get-richer dynamics: essentially, the more well known someone is, the more likely you are to hear their name come up in conversation, and hence the more likely you are to end up knowing about them as well. The same holds for Web pages – the specific focus of our model here.

The remaining intuition behind the analysis runs as follows. With the rich-get-richer dynamics in place, our model predicts that popularity should grow according to the same rule that governs the growth of bacterial colonies and compound interest: a page's popularity grows at a rate proportional to its current value, and hence exponentially with time. A page that gets a small lead over others will therefore tend to extend this lead; whereas the crux of the Central Limit Theorem is that small independent random values tend to cancel each other out, the rich-get-richer nature of copying actually amplifies the effects of large values, making them even larger. In Section 18.7 at the end of this chapter, we show how to turn this reasoning into a calculation that produces the correct exponent on the power-law distribution.

As with any simple model, the goal is not to capture all the reasons why people create links on the Web, or in any other network, but to show that a simple and very natural principle behind link creation leads directly to power laws – and hence one should not find them as surprising as they might first appear.

Indeed, rich-get-richer models can suggest a basis for power laws in a wide array of settings, including some that have nothing at all to do with human decision-making. For example, the populations of cities have been observed to follow a power-law distribution: the fraction of cities with population k is roughly $1/k^c$ for some constant c [371]. If we assume that cities are formed at different times – and that, once formed, a city grows in proportion to its current size simply as a result of people having children – then we have almost precisely the same rich-get-richer model; hence, we should not be surprised to see the power law that is in fact present in reality. To take a very different example, researchers in biology have argued (though the data is still too sparse to be sure) that the number of copies of a gene in a genome approximately follows a power-law distribution [99]. If we believe that gene copies arise in large part through mutational events in which a random segment of DNA is accidentally duplicated, then a gene that already has many copies is proportionally more likely to be lying in a random stretch of DNA that gets copied – so "rich" genes (those with many copies) get "richer," and again we should not be surprised to see a power law.

A priori, finding similar laws governing Web page popularity, city populations, and gene copies is quite mysterious, but if one views all these as outcomes of processes exhibiting rich-get-richer effects, then the picture starts to become clearer. Again, one must stress that these are still simple models designed just to approximate what's going on, and moreover, there are other classes of simple models designed to capture power-law behavior that we have not discussed here. For example, a parallel thread of research has argued how power laws can arise from systems that are being *optimized* in the presence of constraints [96, 136, 151, 284, 300]. But what all these simple models suggest is that, when one sees a power law in data, the possible reasons *why* it's there can often be more important than the simple fact *that* it's there.

18.4 The Unpredictability of Rich-Get-Richer Effects

Given the nature of the feedback effects that produce power laws, it's natural to suspect that, for a Web page, a book, a song, or any other object of popular attention, the initial phase of its rise to popularity is a relatively fragile thing. Once any one of these items is well established, the rich-get-richer dynamics of popularity are likely to push it even higher, but getting this rich-get-richer process ignited in the first place seems like a precarious process, full of potential accidents and near misses.

This sensitivity to unpredictable initial fluctuations is something that we saw in the previous two chapters as well: information cascades can depend on the outcome of a small number of initial decisions in the population, and a worse technology can win because it reaches a certain critical audience size before its competitors do. The dynamics of popularity suggest that random effects early in the process should play a role here as well. For example, if we could roll time back 15 years and then run history forward again, would the Harry Potter books again sell hundreds of millions of copies, or would they languish in obscurity while some other works of children's fiction achieved major success? One's intuition suggests the latter. More generally, if history were to be replayed multiple times, it seems likely that there would be a power-law distribution of popularity each of these times, but it's far from clear that the most popular items would always be the same.

Thought experiments of this type are useful in considering the consequences of our models, but, needless to say, it's difficult to actually implement them as real experiments. Recently, however, Salgankik, Dodds, and Watts performed an experiment that begins to provide some empirical support for this intuition [359]. They created a music download site, populated with 48 obscure songs of varying quality written by actual performing groups. Visitors to the site were presented with a list of the songs and given the opportunity to listen to them. Each visitor was also shown a table listing the current "download count" for each song – the number of times it had been downloaded from the site thus far. At the end of a session, the visitor was given the opportunity to download copies of the songs that he or she liked.

Now, unbeknownst to the visitors, upon arrival they were actually being assigned at random to one of eight "parallel" copies of the site. The parallel copies started out identically, with the same songs and with each song having a download count of zero. However, each parallel copy then evolved differently as users arrived. In a controlled, small-scale setting, then, this experiment provided a way to observe what happens to the popularities of 48 songs when you get to run history forward eight different times. And in fact, it was found that the "market share" of the different songs varied considerably across the different parallel copies, although the best songs never ended up at the bottom and the worst songs never ended up at the top.

Salganik et al. also used this approach to show that, overall, feedback produced greater inequality in outcomes. Specifically, they assigned some users to a ninth version of the site in which no feedback about download counts was provided at all. In this version of the site, there was no direct opportunity for users to contribute to rich-get-richer dynamics, and indeed there was significantly less variation in the market share of different songs.

There are clear implications for popularity in less controlled environments, parallel to some of the conclusions we've drawn from our models – specifically, that the future success of a book, movie, celebrity, or Web site is strongly influenced by these types of feedback effects, and hence may to some extent be inherently unpredictable.

Closer Relationships Between Power Laws and Information Cascades? Considerations of this sort suggest an important question for further research: understanding the relationship between power laws and information cascades at a deeper level. When we looked at information cascades, we saw how a population in which people were aware of earlier decisions made between two alternatives (e.g., accepting an idea or rejecting it) could end up in a cascade, even if each person is making an optimal decision given what they've observed. Our copying model for power laws draws on the intuition behind this model, but it differs in several respects. First, a model for popularity should include choices among many possible options (e.g., all possible Web pages) rather than just two options. Second, the copying model involves a set of people who engage in very limited observation of the population: when you create a new Web page, the model assumes you consult the decision of just one other randomly selected person. And third, the copying model is based on the idea that later people imitate the decisions of earlier people, but it doesn't derive this imitation from a more fundamental model of rational decision making.

The first two of these differences simply reflect the specifics of the problem being modeled here – the way in which popularity evolves over time. But it would be very interesting to overcome the third of these differences – constructing a copying-style model to produce power laws on top of a base model of individual decision making. Such an approach could shed further insight into the mechanisms behind rich-get-richer dynamics and provide a picture of popularity as arising from competing information cascades whose intensities vary according to the power laws that we observe in real systems.

18.5 The Long Tail

The distribution of popularity can have important business consequences, particularly in the media industry. In particular, let's imagine a media company with a large inventory – a giant retailer of books or music, for example – and consider the following question: are most sales being generated by a small set of items that are enormously popular, or by a much larger population of items that are each individually less popular? In the former case, the company is basing its success on selling "hits" – a small number of blockbusters that create huge revenues. In the latter case, the company is basing its success on a multitude of "niche products," each of which appeals to a small segment of the audience.

In a widely-read 2004 article entitled "The Long Tail," Chris Anderson argued that Internet-based distribution and other factors were driving the media and entertainment industries toward a world in which the latter alternative would be dominant, with a "long tail" of obscure products driving the bulk of audience interest [13]. As he wrote, "You can find everything out there on the Long Tail. There's the back catalog, older albums still fondly remembered by longtime fans or rediscovered by new ones. There are live tracks, B-sides, remixes, even (gasp) covers. There are niches by the thousands, genre within genre within genre: Imagine an entire Tower Records devoted to '80s hair bands or ambient dub."

Although sales data indicates that the trends are in fact somewhat complex [146], this tension between hits and niche products makes for a compelling organizing framework. It also accords with the fundamental models of companies like Amazon or Netflix, where the ability to carry huge inventories – without the restrictions imposed by

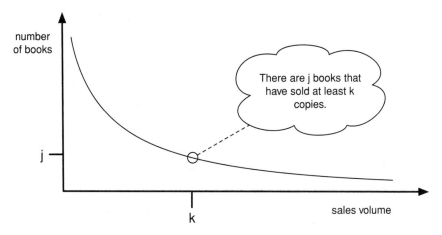

Figure 18.3. The distribution of popularity: how many items have sold at least k copies?

physical stores – makes it feasible to sell an astronomical diversity of products even when very few of them generate much volume on their own. And ultimately, quantifying the importance of the Long Tail comes down to an analysis of power laws.

Visualizing the Long Tail. The first thing to notice, when we compare this discussion of the Long Tail to our earlier analysis of power laws, is that in some sense we're now viewing things out the opposite end of the telescope. Initially, we started from a baseline in which we expected to see Gaussian distributions and tight concentration around the average, and then we observed that the number of highly popular items was much higher than this baseline would suggest. Now, on the other hand, we're starting from a very different default view of the world – a sort of stereotype of the media business in which only blockbusters matter – and we're observing that the total sales volume of *unpopular* items, taken together, is really very significant. In terms of the plot in Figure 18.2, this new view focuses on the upper-left part of the plot, whereas before we were primarily focused on the lower right.

Once you recognize that this contrast is going on, it's not hard to reconcile the two views [4]. First, let's modify our original definition of the popularity curve slightly, in a way that doesn't fundamentally change what we're measuring. Rather than asking

As a function of k, what fraction of items have popularity exactly k?

let's instead ask

As a function of k, what number of items have popularity at least k?

Notice that we've changed two things: "fraction" to "number" (a completely inconsequential change), and "exactly k" to "at least k". This second change modifies the function we're considering, but while we won't go through the derivation here, it's possible to show that if the original function was a power law, then this new one is too. We show a schematic plot of this new function in Figure 18.3; if we're talking about the popularity of some item like books, then a point (k, j) on this curve means, by definition, "there are j books that have sold at least k copies."

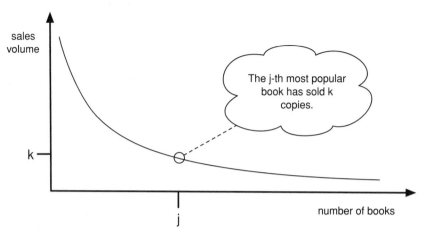

Figure 18.4. The distribution of popularity: how many copies of the *j*th most popular item have been sold?

So far, this is still the conceptual view from the previous section: as we follow the *x*-axis of the curve to the right, we're essentially asking, "As you look at larger and larger sales volumes, how few books do you find?" To capture the discussions of the Long Tail more directly, we want to ask the following question as we follow the *x*-axis to the right: "As you look at less and less popular items, what sales volumes do you see?"

If we think about it, this simply involves switching the two axes. That is, suppose that we plot exactly the same curve, but we interchange the roles of the *x*- and *y*-axes, as shown in Figure 18.4. Interpreting this new curve literally from its definition, a point (j, k) on the curve says, "The *j*th most popular book has sold *k* copies." This is exactly what we want: we order the books by "sales rank," and then we look at the popularity of books as we move out to larger and larger sales ranks – into the niche products.[1] And the characteristic shape of this curve, tailing off slowly downward to the right, is the visual basis for the term "Long Tail."

One can now easily discuss trends in sales volume, and their consequences, in terms of the curve in Figure 18.4. Essentially, the area under the curve from some point *j* outward is the total volume of sales generated by all items of sales-rank *j* and higher, and so a concrete version of the hits-versus-niche question, for a particular set of products, is whether there is significantly more area under the left part of this curve (hits) or the right (niche products). And the debate over trends toward niche products becomes a question of whether this curve is changing shape over time, adding more area under the right at the expense of the left.

It is worth noting that curves of the type in Figure 18.4 – with the axes ordered so that the variable on the *x*-axis is rank rather than popularity – have a long history. They are often called *Zipf plots* after the linguist George Kingsley Zipf, who produced

---

[1] Our notion of "sales rank" simply reflects the sorted, decreasing order of all items by sales volume. When the term *sales rank* is used by online retailers such as Amazon, it tends to be a more complex measure that incorporates other factors as well.

such curves for a number of human activities [423]. Most famously, he identified the empirical principle known as *Zipf's Law* which states that the frequency of the jth most common word in English (or most other widespread human languages) is proportional to $1/j$. Thus, perhaps not surprisingly, the debate within the media industry about curves like this echoes earlier fascination in other areas.

18.6 The Effect of Search Tools and Recommendation Systems

We conclude by briefly discussing a further question that has been growing in importance as people consider popularity and its distribution: are Internet search tools making the rich-get-richer dynamics of popularity more extreme or less extreme? What is interesting is that there are two compelling but juxtaposed sides to this question, and its ultimate resolution will likely involve decisions about how individuals and corporations design and deploy future generations of search tools.

On one side of this question, we've seen that a model in which people copy links from uniformly random Web pages already gives an advantage to popular pages. But once people are using search engines such as Google to find pages, then even the choice of what to copy from becomes highly skewed: as we've seen, Google uses popularity measures to rank Web pages, and the highly-ranked pages are in turn the main ones that users see in order to formulate their own decisions about linking. A similar argument can be made for other media in which a few very popular items have the potential to crowd out all others. In simple models, this kind of feedback can accentuate rich-get-richer dynamics, producing even more inequality in popularity [103].

There are other forces at work, however. To begin with, users type a very wide range of queries into Google, and so there isn't a single list of "top pages on Google"; rather, by getting results for relatively obscure queries, users are being led to pages that they are likely never to have discovered through browsing alone. Search tools used in this style – targeted more closely to users' specific interests – can in fact provide ways around universally popular pages, enabling people to find unpopular items more easily and potentially counteracting the rich-get-richer dynamics. Here too, simple mathematical models have demonstrated how such effects can work [165].

This latter view also forms an important part of Anderson's Long-Tail argument: in order to make money from a giant inventory of niche products, a company crucially needs for its customers to be aware of these products and to have some reasonable way to explore them [13]. Viewed in this light, the types of *recommendation systems* that companies like Amazon and Netflix have popularized can be seen as integral to their business strategies: they are essentially search tools designed to expose people to items that may not be generally popular, but which match user interests as inferred from their history of past purchases.

Ultimately, the design of search tools is an example of a kind of higher-order feedback effect: by causing people to process their available options in one way or another, we can reduce rich-get-richer effects, or amplify them, or potentially steer them in different directions altogether. These are among the subtle consequences that take place when we inject sophisticated information systems into what is an already complex social system.

18.7 Advanced Material: Analysis of Rich-Get-Richer Processes

In Section 18.3, we described a simple model of a growing directed network based on copying – or equivalently, based on rich-get-richer dynamics. We claimed there that the fraction of nodes with k in-links is distributed approximately according to a power law $1/k^c$, where c depends on the behavior of nodes in the model. Here we provide a heuristic argument that analyzes the behavior of the model to indicate why the power law arises, and in fact goes further to show how the power-law exponent c is related to more basic features of the model. The analysis is based on the simple differential equation governing exponential growth that one sees in introductory calculus.

First, let's reprise the description of the model from Section 18.3, as follows.

1. Pages are created in order, and named $1, 2, 3, \ldots, N$.
2. When page j is created, it produces a link to an earlier Web page by choosing between actions (a) and (b) below according to the following probabilistic rule (which is controlled by a single number p between 0 and 1):
    (a) With probability p, page j chooses a page i uniformly at random from among all earlier pages and creates a link to this page i.
    (b) With probability $1 - p$, page j instead chooses a page ℓ with probability proportional to ℓ's current number of in-links and creates a link to ℓ.
    (c) This describes the creation of a single link from page j; one can repeat this process to create multiple, independently generated links from page j. (However, to keep things simple, we will suppose that each page creates just one outbound link.)

Note that here we are using the rich-get-richer version of step 2(b) rather than the original copying version. Recall that the two formulations are equivalent, but for our purposes, it is easier to analyze the phrasing of the model as we have it here.

At one level, we now have a purely probabilistic question: we have specified a randomized process that runs for N steps (as the N pages are created one at a time), and we can simply determine the expected number of pages with k in-links at the end of the process (or analyze the distribution of this quantity). While several groups of researchers have performed this analysis [68], it is a bit more intricate than what we can feasibly cover here. Instead, we describe how an approximation to the model allows for a much simpler calculation that gives the correct value for the exponent c in the power law. This approximate analysis was the first one to be carried out [42], and it thus provided heuristic evidence for the power-law effect that was then verified by more rigorous analysis of the full probabilistic model.

A Deterministic Approximation of the Rich-Get-Richer Process. Before describing the approximation to the model, let's discuss some simple properties of the original probabilistic model itself. First, the number of in-links to a node j at a time step $t \geq j$ is a random variable $X_j(t)$. Let's observe two facts about $X_j(t)$.

   (a) *The initial condition.* Since node j starts with no in-links when it is first created at time j, we know that $X_j(j) = 0$.

(b) *The expected change to X_j over time.* Node j gains an in-link in step $t + 1$ if and only if the link from the newly created node $t + 1$ points to it. What is the probability that this happens? With probability p, node $t + 1$ links to an earlier node chosen uniformly at random, and with probability $1 - p$ it instead links to an earlier node with probability proportional to the node's current number of in-links. In the former case, node $t + 1$ links to node j with probability $1/t$. For the latter case, we observe that at the moment node $t + 1$ is created, the total number of links in the network is t (one out of each prior node), and of these, $X_j(t)$ point to node j. Thus, in the latter case, node $t + 1$ links to node j with probability $X_j(t)/t$. Therefore, the overall probability that node $t + 1$ links to node j is

$$\frac{p}{t} + \frac{(1 - p)X_j(t)}{t}.$$

The basic plan in building an approximation to the model is to analyze a different, closely analogous, but simpler rich-get-richer process in which it is correspondingly easier to discover the power law. Again, this does not directly imply that the original model behaves the same way, but the similarities between the two models offer evidence that can then be verified by further analysis of the original model.

The central idea in formulating the simpler model is to make it *deterministic* – a model in which there are no probabilities, but in which everything instead evolves in a fixed way over time, like an idealized physical system that behaves according to some "equations of motion" starting from a set of initial conditions. To do this, we have time run continuously from 0 to N (rather than in the discrete steps $1, 2, 3, \ldots$), and we approximate $X_j(t)$, the number of in-links of node j, by a continuous function of time, $x_j(t)$. We characterize the function x_j by two properties that seek to approximate the initial conditions and expected change over time that we described earlier for $X_j(t)$. The two properties of the function x_j are the following:

(a) *The initial condition.* Recall that $X_j(j) = 0$. We define $x_j(j) = 0$ as well.
(b) *The growth equation.* Recall that, when node $t + 1$ arrives, the number of in-links to node j increases with probability

$$\frac{p}{t} + \frac{(1 - p)X_j(t)}{t}.$$

In the determinstic approximation provided by the function x_j, we model this rate of growth by the differential equation

$$\frac{dx_j}{dt} = \frac{p}{t} + \frac{(1 - p)x_j}{t}. \tag{18.1}$$

Using differential equations, we have thus specified the behavior of x_j, our deterministic approximation to the number of in-links to node j over time. Essentially, rather than dealing with random variables $X_j(t)$ that move in small probabilistic "jumps" at discrete points in time, we get to work with a quantity x_j that grows completely smoothly over time, at a rate tuned to match the expected changes in the corresponding random variables.

We now explore the consequences of the differential equation defining x_j; this leads quickly to the kind of power-law distribution we want.

Solving the Deterministic Approximation. We begin by solving the differential equation (18.1) governing x_j. For notational simplicity, let's write $q = 1 - p$, so that the differential equation becomes

$$\frac{dx_j}{dt} = \frac{p + qx_j}{t}.$$

Dividing both sides by $p + qx_j$, we get

$$\frac{1}{p + qx_j} \frac{dx_j}{dt} = \frac{1}{t}.$$

Integrating both sides

$$\int \frac{1}{p + qx_j} \frac{dx_j}{dt} dt = \int \frac{1}{t} dt,$$

we get

$$\ln(p + qx_j) = q \ln t + c$$

for a constant c. Exponentiating, and writing $A = e^c$, we get

$$p + qx_j = At^q$$

and hence

$$x_j(t) = \frac{1}{q} \left(At^q - p \right). \tag{18.2}$$

Now we can determine the value of the constant A by using the initial condition $x_j(j) = 0$. This condition gives us the equation

$$0 = x_j(j) = \frac{1}{q} \left(Aj^q - p \right)$$

and hence $A = p/j^q$. Plugging this value for A into Equation (18.2), we get

$$x_j(t) = \frac{1}{q} \left(\frac{p}{j^q} \cdot t^q - p \right) = \frac{p}{q} \left[\left(\frac{t}{j} \right)^q - 1 \right]. \tag{18.3}$$

Identifying a Power Law in the Deterministic Approximation. Equation (18.3) is a significant intermediate step in the analysis, because it gives us a closed-form expression for how each x_j grows over time. Now we want to use this to ask the following question: For a given value of k, and a time t, what fraction of all nodes have at least k in-links at time t? Since x_j approximates the number of in-links of node j, the analogue to this question that we consider in our simplified model is the following: For a given value of k, and a time t, what fraction of all functions x_j satisfy $x_j(t) \geq k$?

Using Equation (18.3), this corresponds to the inequality

$$x_j(t) = \frac{p}{q} \left[\left(\frac{t}{j} \right)^q - 1 \right] \geq k,$$

or, rewriting in terms of j,

$$j \leq t \left[\frac{q}{p} \cdot k + 1 \right]^{-1/q}.$$

Out of all the functions $x_1, x_2, \ldots, x_t$ at time t, the fraction of values j that satisfy this is simply

$$\frac{1}{t} \cdot t \left[\frac{q}{p} \cdot k + 1 \right]^{-1/q} = \left[\frac{q}{p} \cdot k + 1 \right]^{-1/q}. \qquad (18.4)$$

We can already see the power law taking shape here: since p and q are constants, the expression inside brackets on the right-hand side is proportional to k, and so the fraction of x_j that is at least k is proportional to $k^{-1/q}$.

For the final step, note that this has so far been about the fraction of nodes $F(k)$ with *at least* k in-links. But from this we can directly approximate the fraction of nodes $f(k)$ with *exactly* k in-links simply by taking the derivative – in other words, approximating $f(k)$ by $-dF/dk$. Differentiating the expression in Equation (18.4), we get

$$\frac{1}{q} \frac{q}{p} \left[\frac{q}{p} \cdot k + 1 \right]^{-1-1/q}.$$

In other words, the deterministic model predicts that the fraction of nodes with k in-links is proportional to $k^{-(1+1/q)}$ – a power law with exponent

$$1 + \frac{1}{q} = 1 + \frac{1}{1-p}.$$

Subsequent analysis of the original probabilistic model showed that, with high probability over the random formation of links, the fraction of nodes with k in-links is indeed proportional to $k^{-[1+1/(1-p)]}$ [68]. The heuristic argument supplied by the deterministic approximation to the model thus provides a simple way to see where this power-law exponent $1 + 1/(1-p)$ comes from.

The behavior of this exponent also makes sense intuitively as we vary p. When p is close to 1, link formation is mainly based on uniform random choices, and so the role of rich-get-richer dynamics is muted. Correspondingly, the power-law exponent tends to infinity, showing that nodes with very large numbers of in-links become increasingly rare. However, when p is close to 0, the growth of the network is strongly governed by rich-get-richer behavior, and the power-law exponent decreases toward 2, allowing for many nodes with very large numbers of in-links. The fact that 2 is a natural limit for the exponent as rich-get-richer dynamics become stronger also provides a nice way to think about the fact that many power-law exponents in real networks (such as for the number of in-links to a Web page) tend to be slightly above 2.

A final appealing feature of this deterministic analysis is that it is very malleable – it can be easily modified to cover extensions of the model – and this has been the subject of considerable further research [10].

18.8 Exercises

1. Consider an online news site, such as cnn.com or nytimes.com, which consists of a front page with links to many different articles. The people who operate such sites generally track the popularity of the various articles that get posted, asking questions like the ones that we've seen in this chapter: "As a function of k, what fraction of all

articles have been viewed by k people?" Let's call this the *popularity distribution* of the articles.

Now suppose that the operators of such a news site are considering changing the front page, so that next to each link is a counter showing how many people have clicked on the link. (For example, next to each link it will say something like, "30,480 people have viewed this story," with the number getting updated over time.)

First, what effect do you think this change will have on the behavior of people using the site? Second, do you expect that adding this feature will cause the popularity distribution of the articles to follow a power-law distribution more closely or less closely, compared to the version of the site before these counters were added? Give an explanation for your answer.

2. When we covered power laws in Chapter 18, we discussed a number of cases in which power laws arise, generally reflecting some notion of "popularity" or a close analog. Consider, for example, the fraction of news articles each day that are read by k people: if $f(k)$ represents this fraction as a function of k, then $f(k)$ approximately follows a power-law distribution of the form $f(k) \approx k^{-c}$ for some exponent c.

Let's think about this example in more detail, and in particular consider the following questions. What mechanisms for providing news to the public will tend to accentuate this power-law effect, causing the most widely read articles to be even more widely read? What mechanisms will tend to diminish the power-law effect, more evenly balancing readership across more and less widely read articles? Give an explanation for your answer.

This is an open-ended question in the sense that the range of possible correct answers is quite broad; also, it is fine for your answer to be informally stated, provided the explanation is clear.

3. Suppose that some researchers studying educational institutions decide to collect data to address the following two questions.

(a) As a function of k, what fraction of Cornell classes have k students enrolled?
(b) As a function of k, what fraction of third-grade elementary school classrooms in New York State have k pupils?

Which one of these would you expect to more closely follow a power-law distribution as a function of k? Give a brief explanation for your answer, using some of the ideas about power-law distributions developed in Chapter 18.

PART SIX

Network Dynamics: Structural Models

CHAPTER 19

Cascading Behavior in Networks

19.1 Diffusion in Networks

A basic issue in the preceding several chapters has been the way in which an individual's choices depend on what other people do. This has informed our use of information cascades, network effects, and rich-get-richer dynamics to model the processes by which new ideas and innovations are adopted by a population. When we perform this type of analysis, the underlying social network can be considered at two conceptually very different levels of resolution: one in which we view the network as a relatively amorphous population of individuals and look at effects in aggregate, and another in which we move closer to the fine structure of the network as a graph and look at how individuals are influenced by their particular network neighbors. Our focus in these past few chapters has been mainly on the first of these levels of resolution – capturing choices in which each individual is at least implicitly aware of the previous choices made by everyone else, and everyone takes these into account. In the next few chapters, we bring the analysis closer to the detailed network level.

What do we gain by considering this second level of resolution, oriented around network structure? To begin with, we can address a number of phenomena that can't be modeled well at the level of homogeneous populations. Many of our interactions with the rest of the world happen at a local, rather than a global, level: we often don't care as much about the full population's decisions as about the decisions made by friends and colleagues. For example, in a work setting we may choose technology to be compatible with the people we directly collaborate with, rather than the universally most popular technology. Similarly, we may adopt political views that are aligned with those of our friends, even if they are nationally in the minority.

In this way, considering individual choices with explicit network structure merges the models of the past several chapters with a distinct line of thinking begun in Chapter 4, when we examined how people link to others who are like them and in turn can become more similar to their neighbors over time. The framework in Chapter 4 dealt explicitly with network connections, but it did not explore the individual decision making that leads people to become similar to their neighbors: a tendency toward favoring similarity was invoked there as a basic assumption rather than being derived from more fundamental principles. In contrast, the past several chapters have developed principles that show how, at an aggregate population level, becoming similar to one's neighbors can arise from the behavior of individuals who are seeking to maximize their utility in given situations. We saw in fact that there are two distinct kinds of reasons why imitating the behavior of others can be beneficial: *informational effects*, based on the fact that the choices made by others can provide indirect information about what they know, and *direct-benefit effects*, in which there are direct payoffs from copying the decisions of others (for example, payoffs that arise from using compatible technologies instead of incompatible ones).

We now connect these two approaches by exploring some of the principles that can be used to model individual decision making in a social network, leading people to align their behaviors with those of their network neighbors.

The Diffusion of Innovations. We will consider specifically how new behaviors, practices, opinions, conventions, and technologies spread from person to person through a social network, as people influence their friends to adopt new ideas. Our understanding of how this process works is built on a rich area of empirical work in sociology known as the *diffusion of innovations* [115, 351, 382]. A number of now-classic studies done in the middle of the twentieth century established a basic research strategy for studying the spread of a new technology or idea through a group of people, and analyzing the factors that facilitated or impeded its progress.

Some of these early studies focused on cases in which the person-to-person influence was due primarily to informational effects: as people observed the decisions of their network neighbors, they obtained indirect information that led them to try the innovation as well. Two of the most influential early pieces of research to capture such informational effects were Ryan and Gross's study of the adoption of hybrid seed corn among farmers in Iowa [358] and Coleman, Katz, and Menzel's study of the adoption of tetracycline by physicians in the United States [115]. In Ryan and Gross's study, they interviewed farmers to determine how and when they decided to begin using hybrid seed corn; they found that while most of the farmers in their study first learned about hybrid seed corn from salesmen, most were first convinced to try using it based on the experience of neighbors in their community. Coleman, Katz, and Menzel went further when they studied the adoption of a new drug by doctors, in that they mapped out the social connections among the doctors making decisions about adoption. While these two studies clearly concerned very different communities and very different innovations, they – like other important studies of that period – shared a number of basic ingredients. In both cases, the novelty and initial lack of understanding of the innovation made it risky to adopt, but it was ultimately highly beneficial; in both cases, the early adopters had certain general characteristics, including higher socioeconomic status and a tendency to travel more widely; and in both cases, decisions about adoption were made in the context of a social structure where people could observe what their neighbors, friends, and colleagues were doing.

Other important studies in the diffusion of innovations focused on settings in which decisions about adoption were driven primarily by direct-benefit effects rather than informational ones. A long line of diffusion research on communication technologies has explored such direct-benefit effects; the spread of technologies such as the telephone, the fax machine, and e-mail has depended on the incentives people have to communicate with friends who have already adopted the technology [162, 285].

As studies of this type began proliferating, researchers started to identify some of the common principles that applied across many different domains. In his influential book on the diffusion of innovations, Everett Rogers gathered together and articulated a number of these principles [351], including a set of recurring reasons why an innovation can fail to spread through a population, even when it is has significant *relative advantage* compared to existing practices. In particular, the success of an innovation also depends on its *complexity* for people to understand and implement; its *observability*, so that people can become aware that others are using it; its *trialability*, so that people can mitigate its risks by adopting it gradually and incrementally; and, perhaps most crucially, its overall *compatibility* with the social system that it is entering. Related to these issues, the principle of homophily that we encountered in earlier chapters can sometimes act as a barrier to diffusion: since people tend to interact with others who are like themselves, while new innovations tend to arrive from "outside" the system, it can be difficult for these innovations to make their way into a tightly-knit social community.

With these considerations in mind, we now begin the process of formulating a model for the spread of an innovation through a social network.

19.2 Modeling Diffusion through a Network

We build our model for the diffusion of a new behavior in terms of a more basic, underlying model of individual decision making: as individuals make decisions based on the choices of their neighbors, a particular pattern of behavior can begin to spread across the links of the network. To formulate such an individual-level model, it is possible to start from either informational effects [2, 38, 186] or direct-benefit effects [62, 147, 308, 420]. In this chapter, we will focus on the latter, beginning with a natural model of direct-benefit effects in networks due to Stephen Morris [308].

Network models based on direct-benefit effects involve the following underlying consideration: you have certain social network neighbors – friends, acquaintances, or colleagues – and the benefits to you of adopting a new behavior increase as more and more of these neighbors adopt it. In such a case, simple self-interest will dictate that you should adopt the new behavior once a sufficient proportion of your neighbors have done so. For example, you may find it easier to collaborate with co-workers if you are using compatible technologies; similarly, you may find it easier to engage in social interaction – all else being equal – with people whose beliefs and opinions are similar to yours.

A Networked Coordination Game. These ideas can be captured very naturally by using a coordination game – a concept we first encountered in Section 6.5. In an underlying social network, we will study a situation in which each node has a choice between two possible behaviors, labeled A and B. If nodes v and w are linked by an edge, then there is an incentive for them to have their behaviors match. We represent

$$w$$

	A	B
A	a, a	$0, 0$
B	$0, 0$	b, b

v

Figure 19.1. A-B coordination game.

this using a game in which v and w are the players and A and B are the possible strategies. The payoffs are defined as follows:

- if v and w both adopt behavior A, they each get a payoff of $a > 0$;
- if they both adopt B, they each get a payoff of $b > 0$; and
- if they adopt opposite behaviors, they each get a payoff of 0.

We can write this in terms of a payoff matrix, as in Figure 19.1. Of course, it is easy to imagine many more general models for coordination, but for now we are trying to keep things as simple as possible.

This describes what happens on a single edge of the network, but the point is that each node v is playing a copy of this game with each of its neighbors, and its payoff is the sum of its payoffs in the games played on each edge. Hence, v's choice of strategy will be based on the choices made by all of its neighbors, taken together.

The basic question faced by v is the following: suppose that some of its neighbors adopt A, and some adopt B; what should v do in order to maximize its payoff? This clearly depends on the relative number of neighbors doing each, and on the relation between the payoff values a and b. With a little bit of algebra, we can make up a decision rule for v quite easily, as follows. Suppose that a p fraction of v's neighbors have behavior A, and a $(1 - p)$ fraction have behavior B; that is, if v has d neighbors, then pd adopt A and $(1 - p)d$ adopt B, as shown in Figure 19.2. So if v chooses A, it

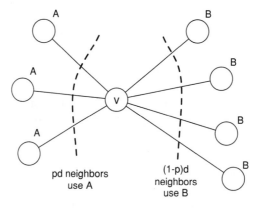

Figure 19.2. Node v must choose between behavior A and behavior B, based on what its neighbors are doing.

gets a payoff of pda, and if it chooses B, it gets a payoff of $(1 - p)db$. Thus, A is the better choice if

$$pda \geq (1 - p)db,$$

or, rearranging terms, if

$$p \geq \frac{b}{a + b}.$$

We'll use q to denote this expression on the right-hand side. This inequality describes a very simple threshold rule: it says that if a fraction of at least $q = b/(a + b)$ of your neighbors follow behavior A, then you should, too. And it makes sense intuitively: when q is small, then A is the much more enticing behavior, and it only takes a small fraction of your neighbors engaging in A for you to do so as well. However, if q is large, then the opposite holds: B is the attractive behavior, and you need a lot of your friends to engage in A before you switch to A. There is a tie-breaking question when exactly a q fraction of a node's neighbors follow A; in this case, we will adopt the convention that the node chooses A rather than B.

Notice that this is in fact a very simple – and in particular, myopic – model of individual decision making. Each node is optimally updating its decision based on the immediate consideration of what its neighbors are currently doing, but it is an interesting research question to think about richer models in which nodes try to incorporate more long-range considerations into their decisions about switching from B to A.

Cascading Behavior. In any network, there are two obvious equilibria to this network-wide coordination game: one in which everyone adopts A, and another in which everyone adopts B. Guided by diffusion questions, we want to understand how easy it is, in a given situation, to "tip" the network from one of these equilibria to the other. We also want to understand what other "intermediate" equilibria look like – states of coexistence where A is adopted in some parts of the network and B is adopted in others.

Specifically, we consider the following type of situation. Suppose that everyone in the network is initially using B as a default behavior. Then a small set of "initial adopters" all decide to use A. We will assume that the initial adopters have switched to A for some reason outside the definition of the coordination game – they have somehow switched due to a belief in A's superiority, rather than by following payoffs – but we'll assume that all other nodes continue to evaluate their payoffs using the coordination game. Given the fact that the initial adopters are now using A, some of their neighbors may decide to switch to A as well, and then some of their neighbors may switch, and so forth, in a potentially cascading fashion. When does this result in every node in the entire network eventually switching over to A? And when this isn't the result, what causes the spread of A to stop? Clearly the answer depends on the network structure, the choice of initial adopters, and the value of the threshold q that nodes use for deciding whether to switch to A.

The preceding discussion describes the full model. An initial set of nodes adopts A while everyone else adopts B. Time then runs forward in unit steps; in each step, each

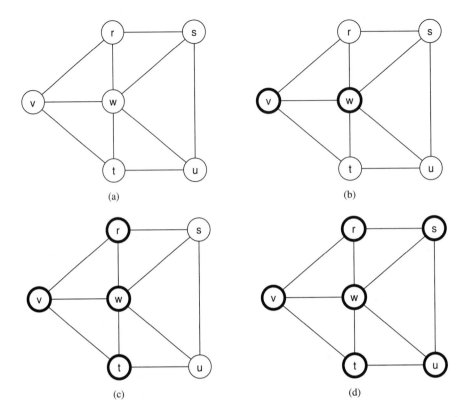

Figure 19.3. Starting with v and w as the initial adopters, and payoffs $a = 3$ and $b = 2$, the new behavior A spreads to all nodes in two steps. Nodes adopting A in a given step are drawn with dark borders; nodes adopting B are drawn with light borders. (a) The underlying network; (b) two nodes are the initial adopters; (c) after one step, two more nodes have adopted; and (d) after a second step, everyone has adopted.

node uses the threshold rule to decide whether to switch from B to A.[1] The process stops either when every node has switched to A or when we reach a step where no node wants to switch, at which point things have stabilized on coexistence between A and B.

Let's consider an example of this process using the social network in Figure 19.3(a).

- Suppose that the coordination game is set up so that $a = 3$ and $b = 2$; that is, the payoff to nodes interacting using behavior A is $\frac{3}{2}$ times what it is with behavior B. Using the threshold formula, we see that nodes will switch from B to A if at least a fraction $q = \frac{2}{(3+2)} = \frac{2}{5}$ of their neighbors are using A.

---

[1] Although we won't go through the details here, it is not hard to show that no node that switches to A at some point during this process will ever switch back to B at a later point – hence, what we're studying is indeed a strictly progressive sequence of switches from A to B. Informally, this fact is based on the observation that, for any node that switches to A at some point in time, the number of neighbors of this node that follow A only continues to increase as time moves forward beyond this point – so if the threshold rule said to switch to A at some point in time, it will only say this more strongly at future times. This is the informal version of the argument, but it is not hard to turn this into a proof.

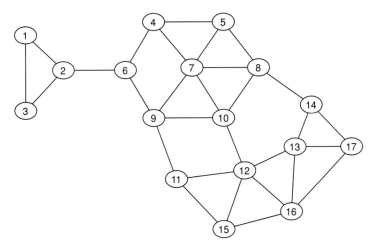

Figure 19.4. A larger example of a graph on which a new behavior may spread.

- Now, suppose that nodes v and w form the set of initial adopters of behavior A, while everyone else uses B. [See Figure 19.3(b), where dark circles denote nodes adopting A and lighter circles denote nodes adopting B.] Then after one step, in which each of the other nodes evaluates its behavior using the threshold rule, nodes r and t will switch to A: for each of them, $\frac{2}{3} > \frac{2}{5}$ of their neighbors are now using A. Nodes s and u do not switch, on the other hand, because for each of them, only $\frac{1}{3} < \frac{2}{5}$ of their neighbors are using A.
- In the next step, however, nodes s and u each have $\frac{2}{3} > \frac{2}{5}$ of their neighbors using A, and so they switch. The process now comes to an end, with everyone in the network using A.

Notice how the process really is a chain reaction: nodes v and w aren't able to get s and u to switch by themselves, but once they've converted r and t, this provides enough leverage.

It's also instructive to consider an example in which the adoption of A continues for a while but then stops. Consider the social network in Figure 19.4, and again let's suppose that in the A-B coordination game we have $a = 3$ and $b = 2$, leading to a threshold of $q = \frac{2}{5}$. If we start from nodes 7 and 8 as initial adopters [Figure 19.5(a)], then in the next three steps we will first see (respectively) nodes 5 and 10 switch to A, then nodes 4 and 9, and then node 6. At this point, no further nodes will be willing to switch, leading to the outcome in Figure 19.5(b).

We call this chain reaction of switches to A a *cascade* of adoptions of A, and we'd like to distinguish between two fundamental possibilities: (i) that the cascade runs for a while but stops while there are still nodes using B, or (ii) that there is a *complete cascade*, in which every node in the network switches to A. We introduce the following terminology for referring to the second possibility.

> Consider a set of initial adopters who start with a new behavior A, while every other node starts with behavior B. Nodes then repeatedly evaluate the decision to switch from B to A using a threshold of q. If the resulting cascade

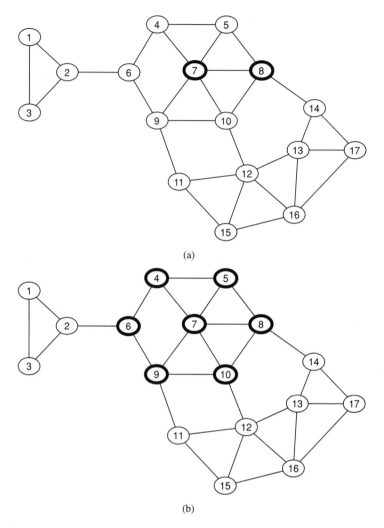

(a)

(b)

Figure 19.5. Starting with nodes 7 and 8 as the initial adopters, the new behavior A spreads to some but not all of the remaining nodes. (a) The two nodes labeled 7 and 8 are the initial adopters and (b) the process ends after three steps.

of adoptions of A eventually causes every node to switch from B to A, then we say that the set of initial adopters *causes a complete cascade at threshold q*.

Cascading Behavior and "Viral Marketing." There are a few general observations to note about the larger example in Figure 19.5. First, it nicely illustrates a point from the opening section that tightly-knit communities in the network can work to hinder the spread of an innovation. Summarizing the process informally, A was able to spread to a set of nodes where there was sufficiently dense internal connectivity, but it was never able to leap across the "shores" in the network that separate nodes 8–10 from nodes 11–14 or that separate node 6 from node 2. As a result, we get coexistence between A and B, with boundaries in the network where the two meet. One can see reflections of this in many instances of diffusion – for example, in different dominant political views between adjacent communities. Or, in a more technological setting, consider the ways in which different social networking sites are dominated by different age groups and lifestyles – people have an incentive to be on the sites their friends are using, even when large parts of the rest of the world are using something else. Similarly, certain industries heavily use Apple Macintosh computers despite the general prevalence of Windows: if most of the people you directly interact with use Apple software, it's in your interest to do so as well, despite the increased difficulty of interoperating with the rest of the world.

This discussion also suggests some of the strategies that might be useful if A and B in Figure 19.5 were competing technologies and the firm producing A wanted to push its adoption past the point at which it has become stuck in Figure 19.5(b). Perhaps the most direct way, when possible, would be for the maker of A to raise the quality of its product slightly. For example, if we change the payoff a in the underlying coordination game from $a = 3$ to $a = 4$, then resulting threshold for adopting A drops from $q = \frac{2}{5}$ down to $q = \frac{1}{3}$. With this threshold, we could check that all nodes would eventually switch to A starting from the situation in Figure 19.5(b). In other words, at this lower threshold, A would be able to break into the other parts of the network that are currently resisting it. This captures an interesting sense in which making an existing innovation slightly more attractive can greatly increase its reach. It also shows that our discussion about the coexistence between A and B along a natural boundary in the network depended not just on the network structure but also on the relative payoffs of coordinating on A versus B.

When it's not possible to raise the quality of A – in other words, when the marketer of A can't change the threshold – a different strategy for increasing the spread of A would be to convince a small number of key people in the part of the network using B to switch to A, choosing these people carefully so as to get the cascade going again. For example, in Figure 19.5(b), we can check that if the marketer of A were to focus its efforts on convincing node 12 or 13 to switch to A, then the cascading adoption of A would start up again, eventually causing all of nodes 11–17 to switch. On the other hand, if the marketer of A spent effort getting node 11 or 14 to switch to A, then it would have no further consequences on the rest of the network; all other nodes using B would still be below their threshold of $q = \frac{2}{5}$ for switching to A. This indicates that the question of how to choose the key nodes to switch to a new product can be subtle, and based intrinsically on their position in the underlying network. Such issues are important in discussions of "viral marketing" [230] and have been analyzed in models of the type we are considering here [71, 132, 240, 309, 348].

Finally, it is useful to reflect on some of the contrasts between population-level network effects in technology adoption, as we formulated them in Chapter 17, and network-level cascading adoption as illustrated here. In a population-level model, when everyone is evaluating their adoption decisions based on the fraction of the entire population that is using a particular technology, it can be very hard for a new technology to get started, even when it is an improvement over the status quo. In a network, however, where you only care about what your immediate neighbors are doing, it's possible for a small set of initial adopters to essentially start a long fuse running that eventually spreads the innovation globally. This idea that a new idea is initially propagated at a local level along social network links is something one sees in many settings where an innovation gains eventual widespread acceptance.

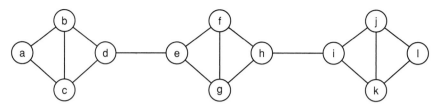

Figure 19.6. A collection of four-node clusters, each of density $\frac{2}{3}$.

19.3 Cascades and Clusters

We continue exploring some of the consequences of our simple model of cascading behavior from the previous section: now that we've seen how cascades form, we look more deeply at what makes them stop. Our specific goal will be to formalize something that is intuitively apparent in Figure 19.5 – that the spread of a new behavior can stall when it tries to break into a tightly-knit community within the network. This in fact will provide a way of formalizing a qualitative principle discussed earlier – that homophily can often serve as a barrier to diffusion by making it hard for innovations to arrive from outside densely connected communities.

As a first step, let's think about how to make the idea of a "densely connected community" precise, so that we can talk about it in the context of our model. A key property of such communities is that when you belong to one, many of your friends also tend to belong. We can take this as the basis of a concrete definition, as follows.

> We say that a *cluster of density* p is a set of nodes such that each node in the set has at least a fraction p of its network neighbors in the set.

For example, the set of nodes a, b, c, d forms a cluster of density $\frac{2}{3}$ in the network in Figure 19.6. The sets e, f, g, h and i, j, k, l each form clusters of density $\frac{2}{3}$ as well.

As with any formal definition, it's important to notice the ways in which it captures our motivation as well as some of the ways in which it may not. Each node in a cluster does have a prescribed fraction of its friends residing in the cluster as well, implying some level of internal "cohesion." On the other hand, our definition does not imply that any two particular nodes in the same cluster necessarily have much in common. For example, in any network, the set of *all* nodes is always a cluster of density 1 – after all, by definition, all your network neighbors reside in the network. Also, if you have two clusters of density p, then the union of these two clusters (i.e., the set of nodes that lie in at least one of them) is also a cluster of density p. These observations are consistent with the notion that clusters in networks can exist simultaneously at many different scales.

The Relationship Between Clusters and Cascades. The example in Figure 19.7 hints at how the cluster structure of a network may tell us something about the success or failure of a cascade. In this example, we see two communities, each of density $\frac{2}{3}$, in the network from Figure 19.4. These correspond precisely to the parts of the network that the cascading behavior A was unable to break into, starting from nodes 7 and 8 as initial adopters. Could this be a general principle?

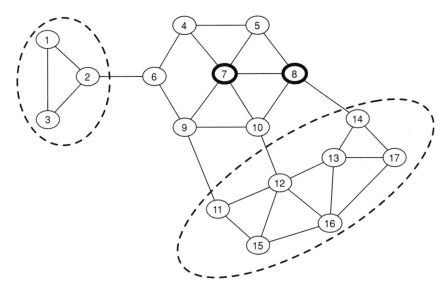

Figure 19.7. Two clusters of density $\frac{2}{3}$ in the network from Figure 19.4.

In fact it is, at least within the context of the model we've developed. We now formulate a result saying, essentially, that a cascade comes to a stop when it runs into a dense cluster, and, furthermore, that this is the only thing that causes cascades to stop [308]. In other words, clusters are the natural obstacles to cascades. Here is the precise statement, phrased in terms of the set of initial adopters and the *remaining network* – the portion of the network consisting of all nodes other than these initial adopters.

> *Claim:* Consider a set of initial adopters of behavior A, with a threshold of q for nodes in the remaining network to adopt behavior A.
>
> (i) If the remaining network contains a cluster of density greater than $1 - q$, then the set of initial adopters will not cause a complete cascade.
> (ii) Moreover, whenever a set of initial adopters does not cause a complete cascade with threshold q, the remaining network must contain a cluster of density greater than $1 - q$.

It is appealing how this result gives a precise characterization for the success or failure of a cascade, in our simple model, using a natural feature of the network structure. Furthermore, it does so by concretely formalizing a sense in which tightly-knit communities block the spread of cascades.

We now prove this result by separately establishing parts (i) and (ii). In going through the proofs of the two parts, it's useful to think about them both in general, and also in light of the example in Figure 19.7, where clusters of density greater than $1 - \frac{2}{5} = \frac{3}{5}$ block the spread of A at threshold $\frac{2}{5}$.

We begin with part (i).

Part (i): Clusters Are Obstacles to Cascades. Consider an arbitrary network in which behavior A is spreading with threshold q, starting from a set of initial adopters. Suppose

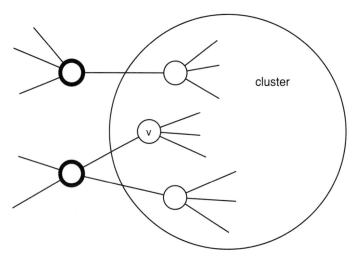

Figure 19.8. The spread of a new behavior, when nodes have threshold q, stops when it reaches a cluster of density greater than $(1 - q)$.

that the remaining network contains a cluster of density greater than $1 - q$. We now argue that no node inside the cluster will ever adopt A.

Indeed, assume the opposite – that some node inside the cluster does eventually adopt A – and consider the earliest time step t at which some node inside the cluster does so. Let v be the name of a node in the cluster that adopts A at time t. The situation is depicted schematically in Figure 19.8 – essentially, we want to argue that, at the time v adopted, it could not possibly have had enough neighbors using A to trigger its threshold rule. This contradiction will show that v in fact could not have adopted.

Here is how we do this. At the time that v adopted A, its decision was based on the set of nodes who had adopted A by the end of the previous time step, $t - 1$. Since no node in the cluster adopted before v did (that's how we chose v), the only neighbors of v that were using A at the time it decided to switch were *outside* the cluster. But since the cluster has density greater than $1 - q$, more than a $1 - q$ fraction of v's neighbors are inside the cluster, and hence less than a q fraction of v's neighbors are outside the cluster. Since these are the only neighbors who could have been using A, and since the threshold rule requires at least a q fraction of neighbors using v, this is a contradiction. Hence, our original assumption, that some node in the cluster adopted A at some point in time, must be false.

Having established that no node in the cluster ever adopts A, we are done, since this shows that the set of initial adopters does not cause a complete cascade.

Part (ii): Clusters Are the Only Obstacles to Cascades. We now establish part (ii) of our claim, which says in effect that not only are clusters a natural kind of obstacle to cascades – they are in fact the *only* kind of obstacle. From a methodological point of view (although all the details are different), this is reminiscent of a question we asked with matching markets: having found that constricted sets are natural obstacles to perfect matchings, we went on to find that they are in fact the only obstacle.

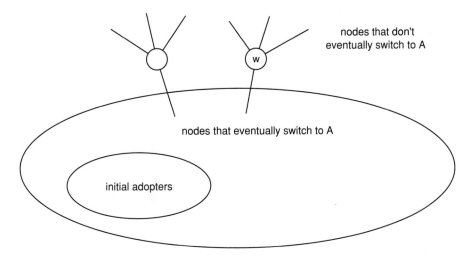

Figure 19.9. If the spread of A stops before filling out the whole network, the set of nodes that remain with B form a cluster of density greater than $1 - q$.

To prove part (ii) we show that whenever a set of initial adopters fails to cause a complete cascade with threshold q, there is a cluster in the remaining network of density greater than $(1 - q)$. In fact, this is not difficult: consider running the process by which A spreads, starting from the initial adopters, until it stops. It stops because there are still nodes using B, but none of the nodes in this set want to switch, as illustrated in Figure 19.9.

Let S denote the set of nodes using B at the end of the process. We want to claim that S is a cluster of density greater than $1 - q$, which will finish the proof of part (ii). To see why this is true, consider any node w in this set S. Since node w doesn't want to switch to A, it must be that the fraction of its neighbors using A is less than q; hence, the fraction of its neighbors using B is greater than $1 - q$. But the only nodes using B in the whole network belong to the set S, so the fraction of w's neighbors belonging to S is greater than $1 - q$. Since this holds for all nodes in S, it follows that S is a cluster of density greater than $1 - q$.

This wraps up our analysis of cascades and clusters; the punch line is that in this model, a set of initial adopters can cause a complete cascade at threshold q if and only if the remaining network contains no cluster of density greater than $1 - q$. So in this sense, cascades and clusters truly are natural opposites: clusters block the spread of cascades, and whenever a cascade comes to a stop, there's a cluster that can be used to explain why.

19.4 Diffusion, Thresholds, and the Role of Weak Ties

One of the fundamental things we learn from studying diffusion is that there is a crucial difference between learning about a new idea and actually deciding to adopt it. This contrast was already important in the early days of diffusion research. For example, Figure 19.10 comes from the original Ryan–Gross study of hybrid seed corn [358]; it

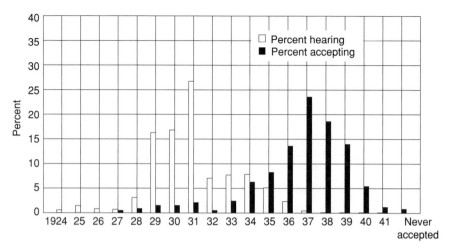

Figure 19.10. The years of first awareness and first adoption for hybrid seed corn in the Ryan–Gross study. (Image from [358]. Scarecrow Press, Inc.)

shows a clear wave of awareness of this innovation that significantly precedes the wave of adoptions.

Our models also illustrate this contrast. If we imagine that people first hear about an innovation when any of their neighbors first adopts, then we see, for example, in Figure 19.5 that nodes 4 and 9 are aware of A as a new behavior right away, but it takes further time for them to actually adopt it. In an even stronger direction, nodes 2 and 11–14 eventually become aware of A but never adopt it.

Centola and Macy [101] and Siegel [369] make the interesting observation that threshold models for diffusion thus highlight an interesting subtlety in the strength-of-weak-ties theory that we discussed in Chapter 3. Recall that the strength of weak ties is rooted in the idea that *weak* social connections, to people we see infrequently, often form local bridges in a social network. They therefore provide access to sources of information – things like new job opportunities – that reside in parts of the network we otherwise wouldn't have access to. To take a canonical picture from Chapter 3, shown here in Figure 19.11, the u-w and v-w edges span tightly-knit communities that wouldn't otherwise be able to communicate, and thus we expect v, for example, to receive information from his edge to w that he wouldn't get from his other edges.

But things look very different if we consider the spread of a new behavior that requires not just awareness but an actual threshold for adoption. Suppose, for example, w and x in Figure 19.11 are the initial adopters of a new behavior that is spreading with a threshold of $\frac{1}{2}$. Then we can check that everyone else in their tightly-knit six-node community will adopt this behavior, but u and v will not. (Nor, therefore, will anyone else lying beyond them in the network.)

This illustrates a natural double-edged aspect to bridges and local bridges in a social network: they are powerful ways to convey awareness of new things, but they are weak at transmitting behaviors that are in some way risky or costly to adopt – behaviors where you need to see a higher threshold of neighbors doing it before you do it as well. In this sense, nodes u and v in Figure 19.11 have strong informational advantages over

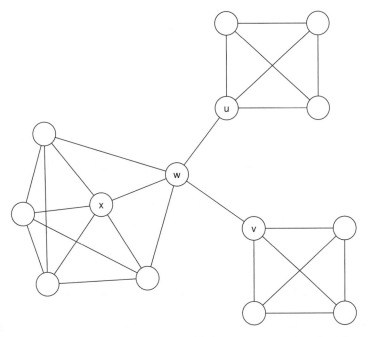

Figure 19.11. The *u-w* and *v-w* edges are more likely to act as conduits for information than for high-threshold innovations.

other members of their respective tightly-knit communities – they can learn from node *w* about a new behavior currently spreading in *w*'s community – but for behaviors with higher thresholds they will still want to align themselves with others in their own community. If we think about it, this is actually remarkably consistent with the picture from Chapter 3, in which local bridges and positions near structural holes can provide access to information that you're not otherwise learning about from your own cluster in the network. For behaviors that spread with high thresholds, a local bridge may well connect you to someone whose network neighborhood has caused them to settle on a different behavior than you have.

The trade-offs inherent in this picture have been used to motivate some of the reasons why many social movements tend to build support locally and relatively slowly. Although a world-spanning system of weak ties in the global friendship network is able to spread awareness of a joke or an online video with remarkable speed, political mobilization moves more sluggishly, needing to gain momentum within neighborhoods and small communities. Thresholds provide a possible reason: social movements tend to be inherently risky undertakings, and hence individuals tend to have higher thresholds for participating; under such conditions, local bridges that connect very different parts of the network are less useful. Such considerations provide a perspective on other well-known observations about social movements in the diffusion literature, such as Hedstrom's findings that such movements often spread geographically [215] and McAdam's conclusion that strong ties, rather than weak ties, played the more significant role in recruitment to student activism during Freedom Summer in the 1960s [290, 291].

$$w$$

		A	B
	A	a_v, a_w	$0, 0$
v	B	$0, 0$	b_v, b_w

Figure 19.12. A-B coordination game.

19.5 Extensions of the Basic Cascade Model

Our discussion thus far has shown how a very simple model of cascades in networks can capture a number of qualitative observations about how new behaviors and innovations diffuse. We now consider how the model can be extended and enriched, keeping its basic points the same while hinting at additional subtleties.

Heterogeneous Thresholds. Thus far we have kept the underlying model of individual behavior as simple as possible – everyone has the same payoffs and the same intensity of interaction with their network neighbors. But we can easily make these assumptions more general while still preserving the structure of the model and the close connection between cascades and clusters.

As the main generalization we consider, suppose that each person in the social network values behaviors A and B differently. Thus, for each node v, we define a payoff a_v – labeled so that it is specific to v – that it receives when it coordinates with someone on behavior A, and we define a payoff b_v that it receives when it coordinates with someone on behavior B. When two nodes v and w interact across an edge in the network, they are thus playing the coordination game in Figure 19.12.

Almost all of the previous analysis carries over with only small modifications; we now briefly survey how these changes go. When we first defined the basic coordination game, with all nodes agreeing on how to value A and B, we next asked how a given node v should choose its behavior based on what its neighbors are doing. A similar question applies here, leading to a similar calculation. If v has d neighbors, of whom a p fraction have behavior A and a $(1 - p)$ fraction have behavior B, then the payoff from choosing A is pda_v while the payoff from choosing B is $(1 - p)db_v$. Thus, A is the better choice if

$$p \geq \frac{b_v}{a_v + b_v}.$$

Using q_v to denote the right-hand side of this inequality, we again have a very simple decision rule – now, each node v has its own *personal* threshold q_v, and it chooses A if at least a fraction q_v of its neighbors have done so. Moreover, the variation in this set of heterogeneous node thresholds has an intuitive meaning in terms of the variation in payoffs: if a node values A more highly relative to B, its threshold q_v is correspondingly lower.

The process now runs as before, starting from a set of initial adopters, with each node evaluating its decision according to its own threshold rule in each time step and

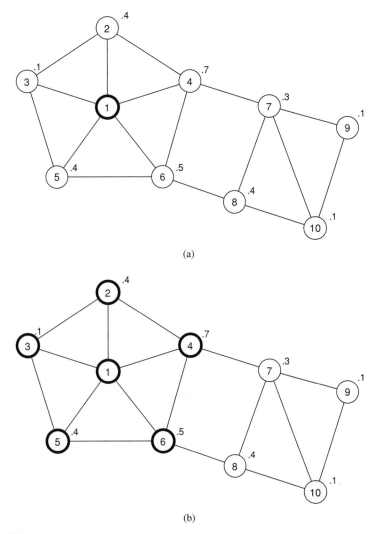

(a)

(b)

Figure 19.13. Starting with node 1 as the unique initial adopter, the new behavior A spreads to some but not all of the remaining nodes. (a) One node is the initial adopter, and (b) the process ends after four steps.

switching to A if its threshold is reached. Figure 19.13 shows an example of this process (where each node's threshold is drawn to the upper right of the node itself).

A number of interesting general observations are suggested by what happens in Figure 19.13. First, the diversity in node thresholds clearly plays an important role that interacts in complex ways with the structure of the network. For example, despite node 1's "central" position, it would not have succeeded in converting anyone at all to A were it not for the extremely low threshold on node 3. This relates closely to a point made in work by Watts and Dodds [409], who argue that for understanding the spread of behaviors in social networks, we need to take into account not just the power of influential nodes but also the extent to which these influential nodes have access to easily *influenceable* people.

It is also instructive to look at how the spread of A comes to a stop in Figure 19.13 and to ask whether the notion of clusters as obstacles to cascades can be extended to hold even in the case when thresholds are heterogeneous. In fact, this is possible, by formulating the notion of a cluster in this setting as follows. Given a set of node thresholds, let's say that a *blocking cluster* in the network is a set of nodes for which each node v has more than a $1 - q_v$ fraction of its friends also in the set. (Notice how the notion of cluster density – like the notion of thresholds – becomes heterogeneous as well: each node has a different requirement for the fraction of friends it needs to have in the cluster.) By a fairly direct adaptation of the analysis from Section 19.3, one can show that a set of initial adopters will cause a complete cascade – with a given set of node thresholds – if and only if the remaining network does not contain a blocking cluster.

19.6 Knowledge, Thresholds, and Collective Action

We now switch our discussion to a related topic that integrates network effects at both the population level and the local network level. We consider situations for which coordination across a large segment of the population is important, and the underlying social network serves to transmit information about people's willingness to participate.

Collective Action and Pluralistic Ignorance. A useful motivating example is the problem of organizing a protest, uprising, or revolt under a repressive regime [109, 110, 192]. Imagine that you are living in such a society, and you are aware of a public demonstration against the government that is planned for tomorrow. If an enormous number of people show up, then the government will be seriously weakened, and everyone in society – including the demonstrators – will benefit. But if only a few hundred show up, then the demonstrators will simply all be arrested (or worse), and it would have been better had everyone stayed home. In such circumstances, what should you do?

This is an example of a *collective action* problem, where an activity produces benefits only if enough people participate. In this way, it is reminiscent of our analysis in Chapter 17 of population-level network effects: as with joining a large-scale demonstration, you only want to buy a fax machine if enough other people do. The starker setting of the present example highlights a few points, however. In the case of a fax machine, you can watch the experience of early adopters; you can read reviews and advertisements; you can canvass a wide array of friends and colleagues to see what they plan to do. Due to the much stronger negative payoffs associated with opposing a repressive government, many of these options are closed to you – you can talk about the idea with a small number of close friends whom you trust, but beyond this your decision about whether to show up for the demonstration is made difficult by a lack of knowledge of other people's willingness to participate, or of their criteria for deciding whether to participate.

These considerations illustrate some of the reasons why repressive governments work so hard to limit communication among their citizens. It is possible, for example, that a large fraction of the population is strong enough in its opposition to be willing to take extreme measures, but that most of these people believe they're in a small minority,

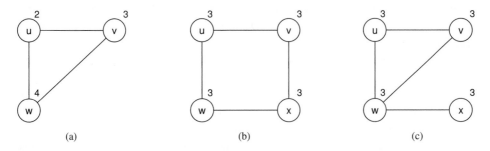

Figure 19.14. Each node in the network has a threshold for participation but only knows the threshold of itself and its neighbors. For three different networks, an uprising will not occur in (a) or (b), but can occur in (c).

and hence view opposition as too risky. In this way, a government could survive long after there is enough strong opposition in principle to get rid of it.

This phenomenon is known as *pluralistic ignorance* [330], in which people have wildly erroneous estimates about the prevalence of certain opinions in the population at large. It is a principle that applies widely, not just in settings where a central authority is actively working to restrict information. For example, a survey conducted in the United States in 1970 (and replicated several times in the surrounding years with similar results) showed that while only a minority of white Americans at that point personally favored racial segregation, significantly more than 50% believed that it was favored by a majority of white Americans in their region of the country [331].

A Model for the Effect of Knowledge on Collective Action. Let's consider how the structure of the underlying social network can affect the way people make decisions about collective action, following a model and a set of illustrative examples proposed by Michael Chwe [109, 110]. Suppose that each person in a social network knows about a potential upcoming protest against the government, and she has a personal *threshold* which encodes her willingness to participate. A threshold of k means, "I will show up for the protest if I am sure that at least k people in total (including myself) will show up."

The links in the social network encode strong ties, where the two endpoints of each link trust each other. Thus, we assume that each person in the network knows the thresholds of all her neighbors in the network, but – due to the risky nature of communication about dissent in this society – does not know the thresholds of anyone else. Now, given a network with a set of thresholds, how should we reason about what is likely to happen?

Let's consider the examples in Figure 19.14, which show some of the subtleties that arise here. Scaling down our notion of "uprising" to a size commensurate with these 3- to 4-person examples, suppose that each node represents one of the senior vice presidents at a company, each of whom must decide whether to actively confront the unpopular CEO at the next day's board meeting. It would be disastrous to do so without reasonable support from the others, so each is willing to confront the CEO provided that at least a certain number of them do so in total. We'll also assume that each node knows what the social network looks like.

First, Figure 19.14(a) indicates some of the reasoning that nodes must do about the decisions being made by other nodes. Here, node w would only join the protest if at least four people do; because there are only three people in total, this means he will never join. Node v knows that w's threshold is 4, so v knows that w won't participate. Because v requires three people in order to be willing to join, v won't participate either. Finally, u only requires two people in order to participate, but she knows the thresholds of both other nodes and hence can determine that neither will participate. So she doesn't either. Hence, the protest doesn't happen.

Figure 19.14(b) introduces even more subtle considerations, in which nodes must reason about what other nodes *know* in order to reason about what they will do. In particular, consider the situation from u's perspective (since it's symmetric for all nodes). She knows that v and w each have a threshold of 3, and so each of u, v, and w would feel safe taking part in a protest that contained all three of them. But she also knows that v and w don't know each other's thresholds, and so they can't engage in the same reasoning that she can.

Is it safe for u to join the protest? The answer is no, for the following reason. Since u doesn't know x's threshold, there's the possibility that it's something very high, like 5. In this case, node v, seeing neighbors with thresholds of 3 and 5, would not join the protest. Neither would w. So in this case, if u joined the protest, she'd be the only one – a disaster for her. Hence, u can't take this chance, and so she doesn't join the protest.

Since the situation is symmetric for all four nodes in Figure 19.14(b), we can conclude that no node will join the protest, and so no protest happens. There is something striking about this: each node in the network knows the fact that there are three nodes with thresholds of 3 – enough for a protest to form – but each holds back because they cannot be sure that any other nodes know this fact.

Things would turn out very differently if the link from v to x were shifted to instead connect v and w, resulting in the network of Figure 19.14(c). Now, each of u, v, and w not only knows the fact that there are three nodes with thresholds of 3, but this fact is *common knowledge* [29, 154, 276]: among the set of nodes consisting of u, v, and w, each node knows this fact, each node knows that each node knows it, each node knows that each node knows that each node knows it, and so on indefinitely. We touched on common knowledge briefly in the context of game theory in Chapter 6; as we see here, it also plays an important role in interactions designed to achieve coordination.

So the differences between the examples in Figures 19.14(b) and 19.14(c) are subtle and come down to the different networks' consequences for the knowledge that nodes have about what others know. This contrast also highlights another way of thinking about the power of strong ties and tightly-knit communities for encouraging participation in high-risk activities, a topic that we discussed in Section 19.4. Weak ties have informational advantages since your strong ties are to people who know things that heavily overlap with what you know. But for collective action, such overlaps in knowledge can be precisely what is needed.

This model for common knowledge and coordination has been developed in further research [110]; understanding the precise interaction of knowledge with collective action remains an interesting direction of study.

Common Knowledge and Social Institutions. Building on these models, Chwe and others have argued that a broad range of social institutions in fact serve the role of helping people achieve common knowledge [111]. A widely publicized speech, or an article in a high-circulation newspaper, has the effect not just of transmitting a message, but of making the listeners or readers realize that many others have gotten the message as well.

This is a useful context for thinking about freedom of the press and freedom of assembly, and their relationship to open societies. But institutions relatively far from the political sphere can also have strong roles as generators of common knowledge. For example, Chwe argues that Super Bowl commercials are often used to advertise products where there are strong network effects – things like cell-phone plans and other goods where it's in your interest to be one of a large population of adopters [111]. For example, the Apple Macintosh was introduced during the 1984 Super Bowl in a commercial directed by Ridley Scott. (Years later, it was declared the "Greatest Television Commercial of All Time" by both *TV Guide* and *Advertising Age* magazine.) As Chwe writes of the event, "The Macintosh was completely incompatible with existing personal computers: Macintosh users could easily exchange data only with other Macintosh users, and if few people bought the Macintosh, there would be little available software. Thus, a potential buyer would be more likely to buy if others bought them also; the group of potential Macintosh buyers faced a coordination problem. By airing the commercial during the Super Bowl, Apple did not simply inform each viewer about the Macintosh; Apple also told each viewer that many other viewers were informed about the Macintosh" [111].

Recently, David Patel used principles of common knowledge to argue that differences between the organization of Sunni and Shiite religious institutions can help explain much about the power dynamics that followed the 2003 U.S. invasion of Iraq [339]. In particular, strong organizational structures enabled Friday sermons at Shiite mosques to be centrally coordinated, while the Sunni religious establishment lacked comparable structures: "Shiite Ayatollahs, controlling hierarchical networks of clerical deputies, can reliably and consistently disseminate similar messages in different mosques, generating common knowledge and coordination across dispersed Shiite congregations on national-level issues like federalism and voting strategies. Through mosque networks, Shiites reliably know what Shiites in far distant areas know" [339]. Patel thus argues that these mechanisms for facilitating shared knowledge enabled Shiites to achieve coordination on goals at a national scale, in a way that other groups in post-invasion Iraq lacked the institutional power to do.

Through all of this, we're seeing that social networks don't simply allow for interaction and the flow of information, but that these processes in turn allow individuals to base decisions on what others know, and on how they expect others to behave as a result. The potential of this framework for studying social processes and social institutions is still being actively explored.

19.7 Advanced Material: The Cascade Capacity

If we go back to the basic model of this chapter, in which nodes choose between behaviors A and B based on thresholds derived from a networked coordination game, an interesting perspective is to understand how different network structures are more or less hospitable to cascades. A first version of this perspective is the analysis in

Figure 19.15. An infinite path with a set of early adopters of behavior A (shaded).

Section 19.3, where we showed that clusters in the network structure form the natural obstacles to cascades. Here we take a different approach; given a network, we ask: what is the largest threshold at which any "small" set of initial adopters can cause a complete cascade? This maximum threshold is thus an inherent property of the network, indicating the outer limit on its ability to support cascades; we will refer to it as the *cascade capacity* of the network.

To make this idea work at a technical level, we clearly need to be careful about what we mean by a "small" set. For example, clearly if we take the set of initial adopters to be the full set of nodes, or (in most cases) something that is almost the full set of nodes, then we can get cascades even at thresholds approaching or equal to 1.

It turns out that the cleanest way to formalize the question is in fact to consider infinite networks in which each node has a finite number of neighbors. We can then define the cascade capacity as the largest threshold at which a *finite* set of nodes can cause a complete cascade. In this way, "small" will mean finite, in the context of a network where the full node set is infinite.

A. Cascades on Infinite Networks

With this goal in mind, we now describe the model in general. The social network will be modeled as a connected graph on an infinite set of nodes; although the node set is infinite, each individual node is only connected to a finite number of other nodes.

The model of node behavior is the same one that we defined earlier in the chapter. The fact that the node set is infinite doesn't pose any problems, since each node only has a finite set of neighbors, and it only makes decisions based on the behavior of these neighbors. To be concrete, initially, a finite set S of nodes has behavior A (this is the small set of early adopters), and all other nodes adopt B. Time then runs forward in steps $t = 1, 2, 3, \ldots$. In each step t, each node other than those in S uses the decision rule with threshold q to decide whether to adopt behavior A or B. (As before, we assume that the nodes in S are committed to A and they never reevaluate this decision.) Finally, we say that the set S *causes a complete cascade* if, starting from S as the early adopters of A, every node in the network eventually switches permanently to A. (Given the fact that the node set is infinite, we must be careful to be clear on what this means: for every node v, there is some time t after which v is always using behavior A.)

The Cascade Capacity. The key definition is now the following. We say that the *cascade capacity* of the network is the largest value of the threshold q for which some finite set of early adopters can cause a complete cascade. To illustrate this definition, let's consider two simple examples. First, in Figure 19.15, we have a network consisting of a path that extends infinitely in both directions. Suppose that the two shaded nodes are early adopters of A, and that all other nodes start out adopting B. What will happen?

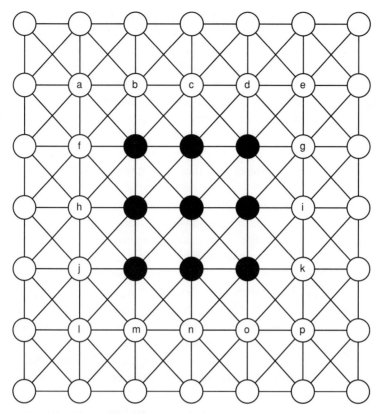

Figure 19.16. An infinite grid with a set of early adopters of behavior A (shaded).

It's not hard to check that if $q \leq \frac{1}{2}$, then nodes u and v will switch to A, after which nodes w and x will switch, and the switches will simply propagate all the way down the path: for each node, there will come some time at which it chooses to switch permanently to A. So the cascade capacity of the infinite path is at least $\frac{1}{2}$, since we have just seen a finite set of initial adopters that causes a complete cascade at threshold $\frac{1}{2}$. In fact, $\frac{1}{2}$ is the exact value of the cascade capacity of the infinite path: with $q > \frac{1}{2}$, *no* finite set of initial adopters can get any node to their right to switch to A, and so A clearly cannot spread to all nodes.

Figure 19.16 shows a second simple example: a network consisting of an infinite grid in which each node is connected to its eight nearest neighbors. Suppose that the nine shaded nodes are early adopters of A and that all other nodes start out adopting B. You can check that if the threshold q is at most $\frac{3}{8}$, then behavior A gradually pushes its way out to the neighbors of the shaded nodes: first to the nodes labeled c, h, i, and n; then to the nodes b, d, f, g, j, k, m, and o; and then to other nodes from there, until every node in the grid is eventually converted to A. (With a smaller threshold – when $q \leq \frac{2}{8}$, for example – behavior A spreads even faster.) We can check that in fact $\frac{3}{8}$ is the cascade capacity of the infinite grid: given any finite set of initial adopters, they are contained in some rectangle of the grid, and if $q > \frac{3}{8}$, no node outside this rectangle will ever choose to adopt A.

Note that the cascade capacity is an intrinsic property of the network itself. A network with a large cascade capacity is one in which cascades happen more "easily"; in other words, they happen even for behaviors A that don't offer much payoff advantage over the default behavior B. As we discussed in Section 19.2, the fact that a small set of initial adopters can eventually cause the whole population to switch illustrates how a better technology (A, when $q < \frac{1}{2}$) can displace an existing, inferior one (B). Viewed in this sense, the example of the grid in Figure 19.16 can be viewed as a kind of failure of social optimality. The fact that the cascade capacity of the grid is $\frac{3}{8}$ means that, when q is strictly between $\frac{3}{8}$ and $\frac{1}{2}$, A is the better technology, but the structure of the network makes B so heavily entrenched that no finite set of initial adopters of A can cause A to win.

We now consider the following fundamental question: how large can a network's cascade capacity be? The infinite path shows that there are networks in which the cascade capacity can be as large as $\frac{1}{2}$: a new behavior A can displace an existing behavior B even when the two confer essentially equivalent benefits (with A having only the "tie-breaking" advantage such that when a node has an equal number of neighbors using A and B, it chooses A). Does there exist any network with a higher cascade capacity? This would be a bit surprising, since such a network would have the property that an inferior technology can displace a superior one, even when the inferior technology starts at only a small set of initial adopters.

In fact, we will show that no network has a cascade capacity larger than $\frac{1}{2}$. In other words, regardless of the structure of the underlying network, if a new behavior requires 51% of someone's friends to adopt it before they do, then it can't spread very far through the population. Despite the fact that this is perhaps an intuitively natural fact, proving it is a bit subtle; it requires a way to bound the extent of a behavior that is spreading at a threshold beyond $\frac{1}{2}$.

B. How Large Can the Cascade Capacity Be?

We now formulate and prove this basic fact about the cascade capacity.

Claim: There is no network in which the cascade capacity exceeds $\frac{1}{2}$.

Although we motivated this claim as a natural one just above, it is less clear why it is true. After all, it's certainly imaginable a priori that there could be some cleverly constructed network, set up in just the right way, so that even though each node needs 51% of its neighbors to adopt before it does, the cascade rolls on steadily, eventually causing everyone to switch. What we really need to show is the following: if $q > \frac{1}{2}$, then regardless of what the underlying network looks like, a new behavior starting at a finite set of nodes will not spread to every other node.

Analyzing the Interface. We're going to approach this question by tracking the "interface" where adopters of A are linked to adopters of B. At a very high level, we're going to show that, as the process runs, this interface becomes narrower and narrower, eventually shrinking to the point where the process must stop, having failed to reach all nodes.

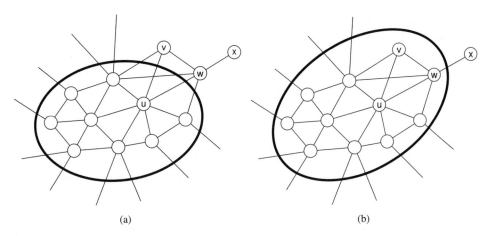

Figure 19.17. Let the nodes inside the dark oval be the adopters of *A*. Part (a) shows the situation before one step of the process, during which nodes *v* and *w* adopt A. After they adopt, as shown in (b), the size of the interface has strictly decreased. In general, the size of the interface strictly decreases with each step of the process when $q > \frac{1}{2}$.

More precisely, suppose the behavior A spreads from a finite initial set S with threshold $q > \frac{1}{2}$. As time moves forward in steps $t = 1, 2, 3, \ldots$, potentially larger and larger sets become adopters of A. At any given point in time, each edge in the network can be described as an A-A edge (connecting two adopters of A), a B-B edge (connecting two adopters of B), or an A-B edge (connecting an adopter of A to an adopter of B). We define the *interface* to be the set of A-B edges. Figure 19.17 shows a useful way to picture the interface: if the set of adopters of A consists of the nodes inside the dark oval, then the edges in the interface are the ones that cross the oval.

What we're going to show is that, in each step, the size of the interface i.e., the number of edges it contains – must strictly decrease. This will be enough to show what we need, for the following reason. The size of the interface clearly starts at some number I_0: since there is some finite set of initial adopters S, and since each of these has a finite set of neighbors, the set of A-B edges is finite and has some size I_0. The size of the interface is always a nonnegative whole number, so if it strictly decreases in each step, the spread of A can run for at most I_0 steps before terminating. Since each step only results in a finite number of nodes converting to A, the process terminates with only a finite set of nodes having adopted A. (So in fact we'll get something stronger than we needed: not only does A not spread everywhere, it only reaches a finite set starting from S.)

The Size of the Interface Decreases in Each Step. So the crux of this is to consider one step of the process and show that the size of the interface strictly decreases. What happens in one step of the process? Figure 19.17 illustrates a way to think about this question. Certain nodes that are currently adopters of B discover, for the first time, that at least a q fraction of their neighbors are now adopters of A, and so they too switch to A.

This causes the interface to change in the following way. When a node w switches from B to A, its edges to nodes that remain with B change from being B-B edges to being A-B edges – so this causes them to join the interface. (An example is the edge linking w and x in Figure 19.17.) On the other hand, the edges from w to nodes that were already with A change from being A-B edges to being A-A edges; in other words, they leave the interface. (See, for example, the edge linking u and w.) Each edge that joins or leaves the interface in this step can be accounted for in this way by exactly one node that switches from B to A.

So to analyze the change in the size of the interface, we can separately consider the contribution from those edges accounted for by each individual node that switches. Thus, consider a node w that switches; suppose that, before the switch, it had a edges to nodes that were already adopters of A, and b edges to nodes that will remain adopters of B at the end of the step. So node w accounts for b edges joining the interface and a edges leaving it. But since $q > \frac{1}{2}$, and node w decided to switch to A in this step, it must be that w had more edges to adopters of A than to adopters of B; therefore $a > b$, and hence w accounts for more edges leaving the interface than edges joining the interface. But this is true for each node that switches in this step, and so the overall size of the interface goes down.

This is what we needed to show. Chaining back through the earlier arguments, since the interface starts at some fixed size I_0, the process can only go for at most I_0 steps before running out of steam and stopping, not having reached all nodes.

Some Final Thoughts. We've shown that when $q > \frac{1}{2}$, no finite set of nodes can cause a complete cascade, in any network. In terms of an underlying story about users choosing between technologies A and B, the situation in which $q > \frac{1}{2}$ corresponds intuitively to the case in which the new technology A is in fact worse: the payoff from an A-A interaction is lower than that of a B-B interaction, and so you only switch to A in cases where more than half your friends already have. So at least in the simple model we've been studying here, a worse technology will not displace a better technology that's already in widespread use. (However, recall the connection with our earlier discussion of network effects: in networks where the cascade capacity is strictly less than $\frac{1}{2}$, it is possible for a better technology to be unable to displace a worse one that is already in widespread use.)

It is also interesting to reflect a bit on the way in which we argued that A can't spread to all nodes when $q > \frac{1}{2}$; there's a methodological parallel here to our discussion of matching markets (though again the details are completely different). There too we had a process – the bipartite auction procedure that updated prices – and we wanted to show that it must come to a halt. Lacking any obvious measure of progress on the process, we invented a nonobvious one – a kind of "potential energy" that steadily drained out of the process as it ran, eventually forcing it to terminate. In retrospect, we used a very similar strategy here, with the size of the interface serving as the potential energy function that steadily decreases until the process has to stop.

C. Compatibility and Its Role in Cascades

We've gotten a lot of mileage in this chapter from taking a game that is fundamentally very simple – a coordination game with two possible strategies – and analyzing how it is played across the edges of a potentially complex network. There are many directions in which the game can be extended and generalized, and most of these lead quickly to current research and open questions. To illustrate how even small extensions to the underlying game can introduce new sources of subtlety, we discuss here an extension that takes into account the notion that a single individual can sometimes choose a combination of two available behaviors [225].

To illustrate what we mean, let's go back to the extended example we considered in Figure 19.5, and the discussion at the end of Section 19.2 of how behaviors A and B ended up coexisting in the network. Coexistence is a common outcome, and it is interesting to ask what things look like along the boundaries between A and B. For example, A and B could be different languages coexisting along a national border, or A and B could be social networking sites that appeal respectively to students in college and to students in high school. Our current model says that anyone positioned along the interface between A and B in the network – for example, nodes 8–14 in Figure 19.5 – will receive positive payoffs from neighbors who adopt the same behavior, but payoffs of zero from their interactions with neighbors who adopt different behaviors.

Experience suggests that when people are actually faced with such situations, they often choose an option that corresponds to neither A nor B – rather, they become *bilingual*, adopting both A and B. In some cases, bilinguality is meant literally: for example, someone who lives near speakers of both French and German is reasonably likely to speak (some amount of) both. But technological versions of bilinguality abound as well: people with friends on two incompatible Instant Messenger systems, or two different social networking sites, will likely have accounts on both; people whose work requires dealing with two different computer operating systems will likely have a way to run both. The common feature of all these examples is that an individual chooses to use some form of both available behaviors, trading off the greater ease of interaction with people of multiple types against the cost of having to acquire and maintain both forms of behavior (i.e., the costs of having to learn an additional language, maintain two different versions of a technology, and so forth). What effect does this bilingual option have on the spread of a behavior through a network?

Modeling the Bilingual Option. In fact, it is not hard to set up a model that captures the possibility that a node will choose to be bilingual. On each edge, connecting two nodes v and w, we still imagine a game being played, but now there are three available strategies: A, B, and AB. The strategies A and B are the same as before, whereas the strategy AB represents a decision to adopt both behaviors. The payoffs follow naturally from the intuition discussed earlier: the nodes can interact with each other using any behavior that is available to both of them. If they interact using A, they each get a payoff of a, while if they interact using B, they each get a payoff of b. In other words, two bilingual nodes can interact using the better of the two behaviors; a bilingual node and a monolingual node can only interact using the monolingual node's behavior; and two monolingual nodes can only interact at all if they have the same behavior. Written as a payoff matrix, the game is shown in Figure 19.18, where we use the notation $(a, b)^+$ to denote the larger of a and b.

It's easy to see that AB is a dominant strategy in this game: why not be bilingual when it gives you the best of both worlds? However, to model the trade-off discussed earlier, we need to also incorporate the notion that bilinguality comes with a cost.

w

		A	B	AB
	A	a, a	$0, 0$	a, a
v	B	$0, 0$	b, b	b, b
	AB	a, a	b, b	$(a, b)^+, (a, b)^+$

Figure 19.18. A coordination game with a bilingual option. Here the notation $(a, b)^+$ denotes the larger of a and b.

The meaning of the cost varies with the context, but the cost in general corresponds to the additional effort and resource expenditure needed to maintain two different behaviors. Thus, we assume that each node v will play a copy of this three-strategy bilingual coordination game with each of its neighbors; as in our models earlier in the chapter, v must use the same strategy in each copy of the game it plays. Its payoff will be equal to the sum of its payoffs in its game with each neighbor, minus a single cost of c if v chooses to play the strategy AB. It is this cost that creates incentives not to play AB, balancing the incentives that exist in the payoff matrix to play it.

The remainder of the model works as before. We assume that every node in an infinite network starts with the default behavior B, and then (for nonstrategic reasons) a finite set S of initial adopters begins using A. We now run time forward in steps $t = 1, 2, 3, \ldots$; in each of these steps, each node outside S chooses the strategy that will provide it the highest payoff, given what its neighbors were doing in the previous step. We are interested in how nodes choose strategies as time progresses, and particularly which nodes eventually decide to switch permanently from B to A or AB.

An Example. To get some practice with the model, let's try it on the infinite path shown in Figure 19.19. Let's suppose that nodes r and s are the initial adopters of A, and that the payoffs are defined by the quantities $a = 2$, $b = 3$, and $c = 1$.

Here is how nodes behave as time progresses. In the first time step, the only interesting decisions are the ones faced by nodes u and v, since all other nodes are either initial adopters (who are hard-wired to play A) or nodes that have all neighbors using B. The decisions faced by u and v are symmetric; for each of them, we can check that the strategy AB provides the highest payoff. (It yields a payoff of $2 + 3 - 1 = 4$ from being able to interact with both neighbors, but having to pay a cost of 1 to be bilingual.) In the second time step, nodes w and x have a fresh decision to make, since they now have neighbors using AB, but we can check that B still yields the highest payoff for each of them. From here on, no node will change its behavior in any future time steps. So with these payoffs, the new behavior A does not spread very far: the decision by the initial adopters to use A caused their neighbors to become bilingual, but after that further progress stopped.

Figure 19.19. An infinite path, with nodes r and s as initial adopters of A.

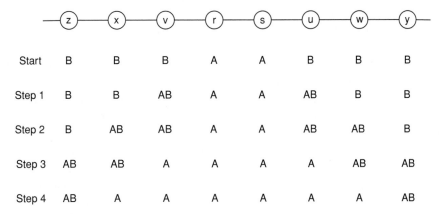

	z	x	v	r	s	u	w	y
Start	B	B	B	A	A	B	B	B
Step 1	B	B	AB	A	A	AB	B	B
Step 2	B	AB	AB	A	A	AB	AB	B
Step 3	AB	AB	A	A	A	A	AB	AB
Step 4	AB	A	A	A	A	A	A	AB

Figure 19.20. With payoffs $a = 5$ and $b = 3$ for interaction using A and B, respectively, and a cost $c = 1$ for being bilingual, the strategy A spreads outward from the initial adopters r and s through a two-phase structure. First, strategy AB spreads, and then behind it, nodes switch permanently from AB to A.

We can further experiment with this example by keeping the network the same but changing the payoffs so that A becomes much more desirable: specifically, let's set $a = 5$, and keep $b = 3$ and $c = 1$. What happens in this case is more complex, as depicted in Figure 19.20. (For the discussion that follows, we will only talk about what happens to the right of the initial adopters, since what's going on to the left is symmetric.)

- In the first step, node u will switch to AB, since it receives a payoff of $5 + 3 - 1 = 7$ from doing so. As a result, in the second step, node w also switches to AB.
- From the third step onward, strategy AB continues to move to the right, one node at a time. However, something additional happens starting in the third step. Because node w switched to AB in the second step, node u faces a new decision: it has one neighbor using A and the other using AB, and so now u's best choice is to switch from AB to A. Essentially, there's no point in being bilingual anymore if all your neighbors now have the higher-payoff behavior available to them (A in this case).
- In the fourth step, node w also switches from AB to A and, more generally, strategy A moves to the right, two steps behind strategy AB. No other changes in strategy happen, so each node switches first to AB (as the wave of bilinguality passes through it), and then permanently switches to A (the higher-payoff monolingual option) two steps later.

Here is one way to view what is happening in this version of the example: as AB spreads through the nodes, B becomes *vestigial* – there is no longer any point for a node to use it. Thus, nodes abandon B completely over time, and so in the long run only A persists.

A Two-Dimensional Version of the Cascade Capacity. In the basic model earlier in this chapter, with the underlying coordination game based just on strategies A and B, we formulated the following question. We are given an infinite graph; for which payoff values a and b is it possible for a finite set of nodes to cause a complete cascade of adoptions of A? Phrased this way, the question appears to depend on two numbers (a and b), but we saw earlier that in fact it depends only on the single number $q = b/(a + b)$.

We can ask the analogous question for our model that includes the strategy AB: given an infinite graph, for which payoff values a, b, and c is it possible for a finite set of nodes to cause a complete cascade of adoptions of A? As with our earlier question, we can eliminate one of the numbers from this question quite easily. The easiest way to do this is to note that the answer to our question remains the same if we were to multiply each of a, b, and c by the same fixed factor. (For example, it does not matter if we multiply each of a, b, and c by 100 and measure the payoffs in cents instead of dollars.) Therefore, we can assume that $b = 1$, fixing this as our basic "unit of currency," and ask how the possibility of a cascade depends on A and C. Choosing b as the number that we fix equal to 1 makes some intuitive sense, since it is the payoff from using the default behavior B; in this way, we're essentially asking: how much better does the new behavior A have to be (the payoff a) and how compatible should it be with B (the payoff c) in order for a cascade to have a possibility of forming?

This question has recently been studied for graphs in general [225], and an interesting qualitative conclusion arises from the model: strategy A does better when it has a higher payoff (this is natural), but in general it has a particularly hard time cascading when the level of compatibility is "intermediate" – when the value of c is neither too high nor too low. Rather than describing the general analysis of this phenomenon, we show how it happens on the infinite path, where the analysis is much simpler and where the main effects are already apparent. We then discuss some possible interpretations of this effect.

When Do Cascades Happen on an Infinite Path? The infinite path is an extremely simple graph, and we saw earlier in this section that in the model with only the strategies A and B, the condition for A to cascade is correspondingly very simple: a cascade of A's can occur precisely when the threshold q is at most $\frac{1}{2}$ – or, equivalently, when $a \geq b$. In other words, a better technology will always spread on the path.

Once we add strategy AB as an option, however, the situation becomes more subtle. Because we are only concerned with whether some finite set of initial adopters can cause a complete cascade of A's, we can assume that this set of initial adopters forms a contiguous interval of nodes on the path. (If not, we can take the left- and rightmost initial adopters and study the situation in which every node in between is also an initial adopter – this set is still finite, and it has just as good a chance of causing a complete cascade.) So changes in nodes' strategies will spread outward symmetrically to the left and right of the initial adopters, and we simply need to account for the possible decisions that nodes make in evaluating their strategies as this happens. Because of the symmetry, we will only think about how strategy changes occur to the right of the initial adopters, since what is going on to the left is the same.

There are two kinds of node-level decisions that are particularly useful for our analysis.

- First, we have to think about nodes like w in Figure 19.21, with a left neighbor using A and a right neighbor using B. (For example, this happens in the first step of

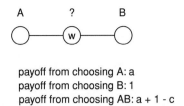

payoff from choosing A: a
payoff from choosing B: 1
payoff from choosing AB: a + 1 - c

Figure 19.21. The payoffs to a node on the infinite path with two neighbors using A and B.

the cascade with the node immediately to the right of the initial adopters.) In this situation, node w receives a payoff of a from choosing A (because it can interact with its left neighbor), a payoff of 1 from choosing B (because it can interact with its right neighbor), and a payoff of $a + 1 - c$ from choosing AB (because it can interact with both neighbors, but pays a cost of c to be bilingual).

Node w will choose the strategy that provides the highest payoff, and that's determined by the relationship between a and c. In other words, we should be asking the following: for which values of a and c will node w choose A, for which will it choose B, and for which will it choose AB? This question can be answered easily if we plot the comparisons among the payoffs in the (a, c)-plane as shown in Figure 19.22(a), with the value of a on the x-axis and the value of c on the y-axis. The break-even point between strategies AB and B, for example, is given by the line defined by setting the two payoffs equal: $a + 1 - c = 1$, or equivalently $a - c = 0$. This is the diagonal line in the figure. Similarly, we draw lines for the break-even point between strategies A and B ($a = 1$) and between strategies A and AB ($a = a + 1 - c$, or equivalently $c = 1$).

These three lines all meet at the point $(1, 1)$, and so we see that they divide the (a, c)-plane into six regions. As shown in Figure 19.22(b), A is the best strategy

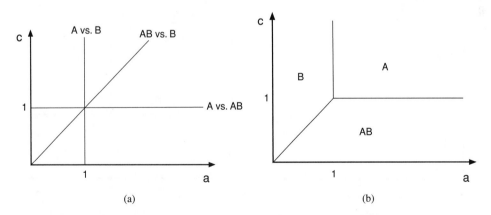

Figure 19.22. Given a node with neighbors using A and B, the values of a and c determine which of the strategies A, B, or AB it will choose. (Here, by rescaling, we can assume $b = 1$.) We can represent the choice of strategy as a function of a and c by dividing up the (a, c)-plane into regions corresponding to different choices. (a) Lines showing break-even points between strategies and (b) regions defining the best choice of strategy.

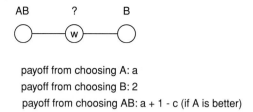

payoff from choosing A: a
payoff from choosing B: 2
payoff from choosing AB: a + 1 - c (if A is better)

Figure 19.23. The payoffs to a node on the infinite path with two neighbors using AB and B.

in two of these regions, B is the best strategy in two of them, and AB is the best strategy in two of them.

- If AB begins to spread, then we'll also have to think about the situation pictured in Figure 19.23: a node whose left-hand neighbor is using AB and whose right-hand neighbor is using B.

   Now, if $a < 1$, then B provides node w with the highest payoff regardless of the value of the cost c (as long as it is positive). So let's consider the more interesting alternative, when $a \geq 1$. This is very similar to the previous case, when w's left-hand neighbor was using A; the one change is that the payoff to w for using B has now gone up to 2, because now w can use B to interact with both neighbors rather than just one.

   As a result, the lines in the (a, c)-plane defining the break-even points between B and the other strategies shift to the right (they are now $a = 2$ and $a + 1 - c = 2$). This in turn shifts the three regions of the (a, c)-plane that define which strategy will be chosen by w, as shown in Figure 19.24.

We are now in a position to determine the values of a and c for which a cascade of A's can occur. We start with a contiguous interval of initial adopters of A, and we consider the node u immediately to the right of the initial adopters. (Again, everything here also applies to the left of the initial adopters by symmetry.)

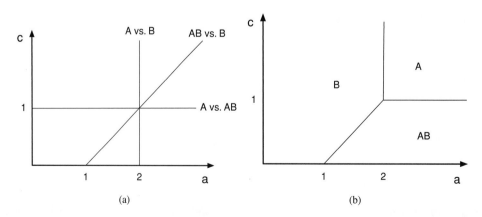

(a)   (b)

Figure 19.24. Given a node with neighbors using AB and B, the values of a and c determine which of the strategies A, B, or AB it will choose, as shown by this division of the (a, c)-plane into regions. (a) Lines showing break-even points between strategies and (b) regions defining the best choice of strategy.

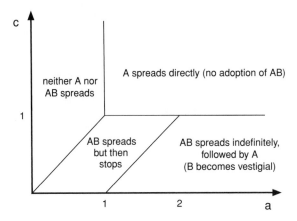

Figure 19.25. There are four possible outcomes for how A spreads or fails to spread on the infinite path, indicated by this division of the (a, c)-plane into four regions.

- If we are in the B region of Figure 19.22(b), then node u will favor B as its strategy, so it will stick with this and the new strategy A will not spread at all.
- If we are in the A region of Figure 19.22(b), then node u will favor A as its strategy, and it will switch to A. So in the next time step we have exactly the same situation shifted one node to the right, and as a result the new strategy A spreads all the way down the path: a cascade occurs.
- Most interestingly, suppose we are in the AB region of Figure 19.22(b). Then, in the next time step, the situation will look different: the crucial decision will now be faced by the next node w to the right of u, who will have its left-hand neighbor (u) now using AB, and its right-hand neighbor still using B.

    To understand what w will do, based on values of a and c, we consult the regions in Figure 19.24(b). But crucially, since we know that AB was the best choice in the first step, we know that the values of a and c lie in the AB region from Figure 19.22(b) – so when we consider Figure 19.24(b), we are concerned not with how its regions carve up the full (a, c)-plane, but only how they carve up the AB region from Figure 19.22(b).

    In fact, they divide the AB region from Figure 19.22(b) by a diagonal line segment from the point $(1, 0)$ to the point $(2, 1)$, as shown in Figure 19.25. To the left of this line segment, B wins and the cascade stops. To the left of this line segment, AB wins – so AB continues spreading to the right, and behind this wave of ABs, nodes will steadily drop B and use only A. This is the scenario that we saw in our example, where B fails to persist because it becomes vestigial in a bilingual world.

Figure 19.25 in fact summarizes the four possible cascade outcomes, based on the values of a and c [i.e., where they lie in the (a, c)-plane]: (i) B is favored by all nodes outside the initial adopter set, (ii) A spreads directly without help from AB, (iii) AB spreads for one step beyond the initial adopter set, but then B is favored by all nodes after that, or (iv) AB spreads indefinitely to the right, with nodes subsequently switching to A.

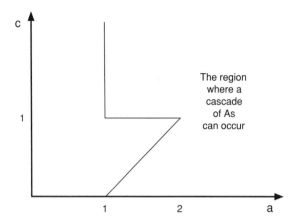

Figure 19.26. The set of values for which a cascade of As can occur defines a region in the (a, c)-plane consisting of a vertical line with a triangular cutout.

So a cascade of As can occur if the pair of values (a, c) lies in one of the two regions described by outcomes (ii) and (iv). This means that the portion of the (a, c)-plane where a cascade can occur looks as depicted in Figure 19.26: it lies to the right of a vertical line with a strange triangular "cutout." The vertical line makes a lot of sense: it corresponds to $a \geq 1$, or, in other words, the requirement that interaction using A produces a higher payoff than interaction using B. But what does the triangular cutout mean? Formally, it says that when the cost of bilinguality is neither too high nor too low, the new strategy A has to be "extra good" – it must produce a payoff a significantly higher than 1 – in order to spread. Moreover, although we won't consider more complex graphs here, the region of the (a, c)-plane where a cascade of As can occur in any graph turns out to have some kind of indentation analogous to the triangular cutout, though the particular boundary of the indentation depends on the structure of the graph [225].

This triangular cutout region has a natural qualitative interpretation that provides potential insight into how compatibility and bilinguality affect the process of diffusion in a network. We discuss this interpretation now.

Interpretations of the Cascade Region. One way to appreciate what's going on in the triangular cutout region is to consider the following question, phrased in terms of technology adoption. Suppose that you're the firm manufacturing the default technology B, and the payoff from interacting via B is equal to 1. Now a new technology A with payoff $a = 1.5$ begins to appear. For which values of the bilinguality cost c should you expect B to survive?

Even without performing any concrete calculations, you could reason as follows. If it's extremely easy to maintain both technologies simultaneously, then adoption of AB will become widespread, and once it is sufficiently widespread, people will begin dropping B altogether, since A is better and it's possible to interact with everyone using A. Essentially, A will have won through "infiltration," working its way into the population via coexistence with B. On the other hand, if it's extremely hard to maintain both technologies simultaneously, then people on the boundary between the two user populations – those who have friends using both technologies – will have to simply choose one or the other. And in this case, you could expect that they may well choose A, because it's in fact better. In this case, A will win through a kind of "direct conquest," simply eliminating B as it goes.

But in between – when it's neither extremely easy nor extremely hard to maintain both technologies – something more favorable to B can happen. Specifically, a bilingual "buffer zone" may form between people who adopt only A and those who adopt only B. On the B side of this buffer zone, no one will have an incentive to change what they're doing, because by using B they can interact with all their neighbors – the bilingual ones and the ones using only B – rather than interacting with only a fraction of their neighbors by switching to the marginally better technology, A. In other words, the inferior technology B has survived because it was neither too compatible nor too incompatible with A – rather, by partially accommodating A, it prevented A from spreading too far.[2]

One can tell this story about nontechnological settings as well. For example, discourse in a succession of geographically adjacent towns may switch from a traditional language B to a more global language A that confers benefits beyond the immediate community – or it may end up with bilingual inhabitants who use both. In a related vein, one could even consider how a more traditional set of cultural practices (B) may persist in the face of more modern ones (A), depending on how easy it is for a person to observe both.

Of course, the model we are discussing is extremely simple, and the full story in any of these scenarios would include many additional factors. For example, in studying competition between technology firms, there has been a long line of work on the role that compatibility and incompatibility can play [143, 235, 415], including case studies of technologies including instant messaging [158] and electronic imaging [283]. But, as with many of our earlier analyses, the streamlined nature of the model helps provide insight into principles that have reflections in more complex settings as well. In this particular case, the model also shows how detailed network structure can play a role in a setting that has otherwise been analyzed primarily at the population level, treating individuals as interacting in aggregate.

Finally, the discussion shows how the basic diffusion model – based on a simple coordination game – is amenable to extensions that capture additional features of real situations where diffusion can take place. Even small extensions such as the one considered here can introduce significant new sources of complexity, and the development of even richer extensions is an open area of research.

---

[2] On the infinite path, the bilingual buffer zones that form are very simple – just one node thick. But in general graphs, the buffer zones can have a more complex structure. In fact, it is possible to prove an analog of the result from Section 19.3, where we showed that clusters are the only obstacle to cascades in the two-strategy model. The more general result is that, with an additional bilingual option AB, a structure consisting of a cluster and a bilingual buffer zone accompanying it is the only obstacle to a cascade of As [225].

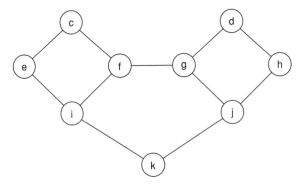

Figure 19.27. Starting from nodes e and f, the new behavior A fails to spread to the entire graph.

19.8 Exercises

1. Consider the network depicted in Figure 19.27; suppose that each node starts with the behavior B, and each node has a threshold of $q = \frac{1}{2}$ for switching to behavior A.

    (a) Now, let e and f form a two-node set S of initial adopters of behavior A. If other nodes follow the threshold rule for choosing behaviors, which nodes will eventually switch to A?
    (b) Find a cluster of density greater than $1 - q = \frac{1}{2}$ in the part of the graph outside S that blocks behavior A from spreading to all nodes, starting from S, at threshold q.

2. Consider the model from Chapter 19 for the spread of a new behavior through a social network. Suppose we have the social network depicted in Figure 19.28; suppose that each node starts with the behavior B, and each node has a threshold of $q = \frac{2}{5}$ for switching to behavior A.

    (a) Now, let c and d form a two-node set S of initial adopters of behavior A. If other nodes follow the threshold rule for choosing behaviors, which nodes will eventually switch to A? Give a brief (one- to two-sentence) explanation for your answer.

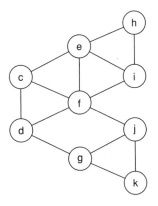

Figure 19.28. Starting from nodes c and d, the new behavior A fails to spread to the entire graph.

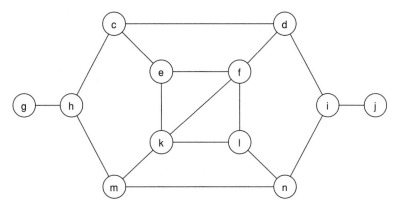

Figure 19.29. A social network in which a new behavior is spreading.

(b) Find a cluster of density greater than $1 - q = \frac{3}{5}$ in the part of the graph outside S that blocks behavior A from spreading to all nodes, starting from S, at threshold q. Give a brief (one- to two-sentence) explanation for your answer.

(c) Suppose you were allowed to add a single edge to the given network, connecting one of nodes c or d to any one node that it is not currently connected to. Could you do this in such a way that now behavior A, starting from S and spreading with a threshold of $\frac{2}{5}$, would reach all nodes? Give a brief explanation for your answer.

3. Consider the model from Chapter 19 for the diffusion of a new behavior through a social network. Recall that for this we have a network, a behavior B that everyone starts with, and a threshold q for switching to a new behavior A; that is, any node will switch to A if at least a fraction q of its neighbors have adopted A.

Consider the network depicted in Figure 19.29; suppose that each node starts with the behavior B, and each node has a threshold of $q = \frac{2}{5}$ for switching to behavior A. Now, let e and f form a two-node set S of initial adopters of behavior A.

(a) If other nodes follow the threshold rule for choosing behaviors, which nodes will eventually switch to A?

(b) Find a cluster of density greater than $1 - q = \frac{3}{5}$ in the part of the graph outside S that blocks behavior A from spreading to all nodes, starting from S, at threshold q.

(c) Suppose you're allowed to add one node to the set S of initial adopters, which currently consists of e and f. Can you do this in such a way that the new three-node set causes a cascade at threshold $q = \frac{2}{5}$?

Provide an explanation for your answer, either by giving the name of a third node that can be added, together with an explanation for what will happen, or by explaining why there is no choice for a third node that will work to cause a cascade.

4. Consider the model from Chapter 19 for the diffusion of a new behavior through a social network.

Suppose that initially everyone is using behavior B in the social network in Figure 19.30, and then a new behavior A is introduced. This behavior has a threshold of $q = \frac{1}{2}$: any node will switch to A if at least $\frac{1}{2}$ of its neighbors are using it.

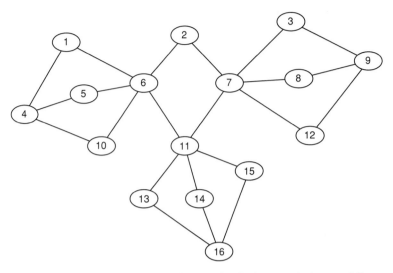

Figure 19.30. A social network through which a new behavior diffuses.

(a) Find a set of three nodes in the network with the property that if they act as the three initial adopters of A then it will spread to all nodes. (In other words, find three nodes that are capable of causing a cascade of adoptions of A.)

(b) Is the set of three nodes you found in part (a) the only set of three initial adopters capable of causing a cascade of A, or can you find a different set of three initial adopters that could also cause a cascade of A?

(c) Find three clusters in the network, each of density greater than $\frac{1}{2}$, with the property that no node belongs to more than one of these clusters.

(d) How does your answer to part (c) help explain why there is no set consisting of only two nodes in the network that would be capable of causing a cascade of adoptions of A (that is, only two nodes that could cause the entire network to adopt A)?

5. Continuing with the diffusion model from Chapter 19, recall that the threshold q was derived from a coordination game that each node plays with each of its neighbors. Specifically, if nodes v and w are each trying to decide whether to choose behaviors A and B, then

- if v and w both adopt behavior A, they each get a payoff of $a > 0$;
- if they both adopt B, they each get a payoff of $b > 0$; and
- if they adopt opposite behaviors, they each get a payoff of 0.

The total payoff for any one node is determined by adding up the payoffs it gets from the coordination game with each neighbor.

Let's now consider a slightly more general version of the model, in which the payoff for choosing opposite behaviors is not 0, but some small positive number x. Specifically, suppose we replace the third point above with the following:

- if they adopt opposite behaviors, they each get a payoff of x, where x is a positive number that is less than both a and B.

Here's the question: in this variant of the model with these more general payoffs, is each node's decision still based on a threshold rule? Specifically, is it possible to write a formula for a threshold q, in terms of the three quantities a, B, and x, so that each node v will adopt behavior A if at least a fraction q of its neighbors are adopting A, and it will adopt B otherwise?

In your answer, either provide a formula for a threshold q in terms of a, B, and x, or explain why, in this more general model, a node's decision can't be expressed as a threshold in this way.

6. A group of twenty students living on the third and fourth floors of a college dorm like to play online games. When a new game appears on campus, each of these students needs to decide whether to join, by registering, creating a player account, and taking a few other steps necessary in order to start playing.

When a student evaluates whether to join a new online game, she bases her decision on how many of her friends in this group are involved in the game as well. (Not all pairs of people in this twenty-person group are friends, and it is more important if your friends are playing than if many people in the group overall are playing.)

To make the story concrete, let's suppose that each game goes through the following "life cycle" within this group of students:

(a) The game has some initial players in the group, who have discovered it and are already involved in it.
(b) Each other student outside this set of initial players is willing to join the game if at least half of her friends in the group are playing it.
(c) Rule (b) is applied repeatedly over time, as in our model from Chapter 19 for the diffusion of a new behavior through a social network.

Suppose that in this group of twenty students, ten live on the third floor of the dorm and ten live on the fourth floor. Suppose that each student in this group has two friends on their own floor, and one friend on the other floor. Now, a new game appears, and five students all living on the fourth floor each begin playing it.

If the other students use the preceding rule to evaluate whether to join the game, will this new game eventually be adopted by all twenty students in the group? There are three possible answers to this question: yes, no, or there is not information in the setup of the question to be able to tell. Say which answer you think is correct, and explain.

7. Some friends of yours have gone to work at a large online game company, and they're hoping to draw on your understanding of networks to help them better understand the user population in one of their games.

Each character in the game chooses a series of *quests* to go on, generally as part of a group of characters who work together on them; there are many options for quests to choose from, but once a character goes on a quest with a group, it can generally last for a couple of weeks.

Your friends working at the game company have also mapped the social network of the game, and they've invented what they find is a useful way of classifying each player's friends: a *reinforced* friend is one with whom the player has at least one other friend in common, and an *unreinforced* friend is one with whom the player has no other friends in common. For example, Figure 19.31 shows the friends of a player A: players B, C, and D would count as reinforced friends, while player E would be an unreinforced friend.

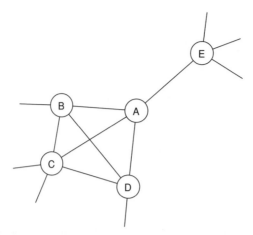

Figure 19.31. A small portion of the social network in an online game.

Now, your friends are particularly interested in what causes players to choose particular quests instead of others, and they are also interested in how players learn about particular methods of cheating along the way – general tricks outside the rules of the game that make it easier to accumulate points, usually regardless of which particular quest they're on. To do some market research on this, they've anonymously surveyed players of the game, asking them two questions:

 (a) How did you first learn about the current quest that you're taking part in?
 (b) How have you learned about ways of cheating in the game?

To their surprise, the answers to these questions were quite different. For question (a), 80% of respondents said that they first found out about the current quest they're on from a reinforced friend, whereas for question (b), 60% of respondents said that they found out about ways of cheating from an unreinforced friend.

Your friends thought you might be able to shed some light on these findings. Why did the answers to these two questions turn out differently? Is the difference specific to this particular game, or could it be predicted from general principles of social networks? In one to two paragraphs, describe how particular ideas from the book can shed light on why the answers to these questions turned out the way they did.

CHAPTER 20

The Small-World Phenomenon

20.1 Six Degrees of Separation

In the previous chapter, we considered how social networks can serve as conduits by which ideas and innovations flow through groups of people. To develop this idea more fully, we now relate it to another basic structural issue – the fact that these groups can be connected by very short paths through the social network. When people try to use these short paths to reach others who are socially distant, they are engaging in a kind of "focused" search that is much more targeted than the broad spreading pattern exhibited by the diffusion of information or a new behavior. Understanding the relationship between targeted search and wide-ranging diffusion is important in thinking more generally about the way things flow through social networks.

As we saw in Chapter 2, the fact that social networks are so rich in short paths is known as the *small-world phenomenon*, or the "six degrees of separation," and it has long been the subject of both anecdotal and scientific fascination. To briefly recapitulate what we discussed in that earlier chapter, the first significant empirical study of the small-world phenomenon was undertaken the social psychologist Stanley Milgram [297, 391], who asked randomly chosen "starter" individuals to each try forwarding a letter to a designated "target" person living in the town of Sharon, Massachusetts, a suburb of Boston. He provided the target's name, address, occupation, and some personal information, but stipulated that the participants could not mail the letter directly to the target; rather, each participant could only advance the letter by forwarding it to a single acquaintance that he or she knew on a first-name basis, with the goal of reaching the target as rapidly as possible. Roughly a third of the letters eventually arrived at the target, in a median of six steps, and this has since served as basic experimental evidence for the existence of short paths in the global friendship network, linking all (or almost all) of us together in society. This style of experiment – constructing paths through social networks to distant target people – has been repeated by a number of other groups in subsequent decades [131, 178, 257].

Milgram's experiment really demonstrated two striking facts about large social networks: first, that short paths are there in abundance; and second, that people, acting without any sort of global "map" of the network, are effective at collectively finding these short paths. It is easy to imagine a social network where the first of these facts is true but the second isn't – a world where the short paths are there, but where a letter forwarded from thousands of miles away might simply wander from one acquaintance to another, lost in a maze of social connections [248]. A large social networking site in which everyone is known only by nine-digit pseudonyms would be like this: if you were told, "Forward this letter to user number 482285204, using only people you know on a first-name basis," the task would clearly be hopeless. The real global friendship network contains enough clues about how people fit together in larger structures – both geographic and social – to allow the process of search to focus in on distant targets. Indeed, when Killworth and Bernard performed follow-up work on the Milgram experiment by studying the strategies that people employ for choosing how to forward a message toward a target, they found a mixture of primarily geographic and occupational features being used, with different features being favored depending on the characteristics of the target in relation to the sender [243].

We begin by developing models for both of these principles – the existence of short paths and also the fact that they can be found. We then look at how some of these models are borne out to a surprising extent on large-scale social-network data. Finally, in Section 20.6, we look at some of the fragility of the small-world phenomenon and the caveats that must be considered in thinking about it – particularly the fact that people are most successful at finding paths when the target is of high status and socially accessible [255]. The picture implied by these difficulties raises interesting additional points about the global structure of social networks, and suggests questions for further research.

20.2 Structure and Randomness

Let's start with models for the existence of short paths. Should we be surprised by the fact that the paths between seemingly arbitrary pairs of people are so short? Figure 20.1(a) illustrates a basic argument suggesting that short paths are at least compatible with intuition. Suppose each of us knows more than 100 other people on a first-name basis (in fact, for most people, the number is significantly larger). Then, taking into account the fact that each of your friends has at least 100 friends other than you, you could in principle be two steps away from more than $100 \times 100 = 10,000$ people. Taking into account the 100 friends of these people brings us to more than $100 \times 100 \times 100 = 1,000,000$ people who in principle could be three steps away. In other words, the numbers are growing by powers of 100 with each step, bringing us to 100 million after four steps, and 10 billion after five steps.

There's nothing mathematically wrong with this reasoning, but it's not clear how much it tells us about real social networks. The difficulty already manifests itself with the second step, where we conclude that there may be more than 10,000 people within two steps of you. As we've seen, social networks abound in triangles – sets of three people who mutually know each other – and in particular, many of your 100 friends will know each other. As a result, when we think about the nodes you can reach by following edges from your friends, many of these edges go from one friend to another,

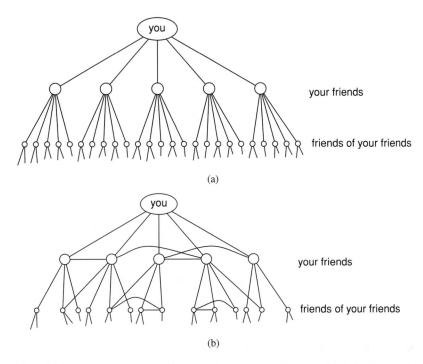

Figure 20.1. Social networks expand to reach many people in only a few steps. (a) Pure exponential growth produces a small world, and (b) triadic closure reduces the growth rate.

not to the rest of world, as illustrated schematically in Figure 20.1(b). The number 10,000 came from assuming that each of your 100 friends was linked to 100 *new* people; without this assumption, the number of friends you could reach in two steps could be much smaller.

So the effect of triadic closure in social networks works to limit the number of people you can reach by following short paths, as shown by the contrast between Figures 20.1(a) and 20.1(b). And indeed, at an implicit level, this is a large part of what makes the small-world phenomenon surprising to many people when they first hear it: the social network appears from the local perspective of any one individual to be highly clustered, not the kind of massively branching structure that would more obviously reach many nodes along very short paths.

The Watts–Strogatz Model. Can we make up a simple model that exhibits both of the features we've been discussing – many closed triads, but also very short paths? In 1998, Duncan Watts and Steve Strogatz argued [411] that such a model follows naturally from a combination of two basic social-network ideas that we saw in Chapters 3 and 4: homophily (the principle that we connect to others who are like ourselves) and weak ties (the links to acquaintances that connect us to parts of the network that would otherwise be far away). Homophily creates many triangles, while the weak ties still produce the kind of widely branching structure that reaches many nodes in a few steps.

Watts and Strogatz made this proposal concrete in a very simple model that generates random networks with the desired properties. Paraphrasing their original formulation

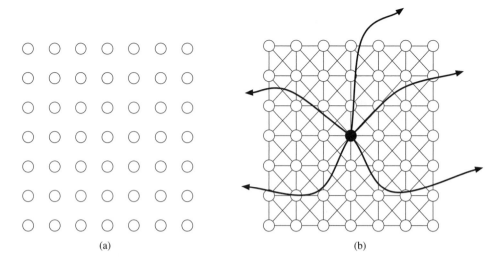

Figure 20.2. The Watts–Strogatz model arises from a highly clustered network (such as the grid), with a small number of random links added in. (a) Nodes arranged in a grid and (b) a network built from local structure and random edges.

slightly (but keeping the main idea intact), let's suppose that everyone lives on a two-dimensional grid. We can imagine the grid as a model of geographic proximity, or potentially some more abstract kind of social proximity, but in any case it represents a notion of similarity that guides the formation of links. Figure 20.2(a) shows the set of nodes arranged on a grid; we say that two nodes are one *grid step* apart if they are directly adjacent to each other in either the horizontal or vertical direction.

We now create a network by giving each node two kinds of links: those explainable purely by homophily and those that constitute weak ties. Homophily is captured by having each node form a link to all other nodes that lie within a radius of up to r grid steps away, for some constant value of r: these are the links you form to people because you are similar to them. Then, for some other constant value k, each node also forms a link to k other nodes selected uniformly at random from the grid. These links correspond to weak ties, connecting nodes that lie very far apart on the grid.

Figure 20.2(b) gives a schematic picture of the resulting network – a hybrid structure consisting of a small amount of randomness (the weak ties) sprinkled onto an underlying structured pattern (the homophilous links). Watts and Strogatz observed first that the network has many triangles: any two neighboring nodes (or nearby nodes) will have many common friends, where their neighborhoods of radius r overlap, and this produces many triangles. But they also find that there are – with high probability – very short paths connecting every pair of nodes in the network. Roughly, the argument is as follows. Suppose we start tracing paths outward from a starting node v, using only the k random weak ties out of each node. Since these edges link to nodes chosen uniformly at random, we are very unlikely to ever see a node twice in the first few steps outward from v. As a result, these first few steps look almost like the picture in Figure 20.1(a), when there was no triadic closure, and so a huge number of nodes are reached in a small number of steps. A mathematically precise version of this argument was carried out by Bollobás and Chung [67], who determined the typical path lengths that it implies.

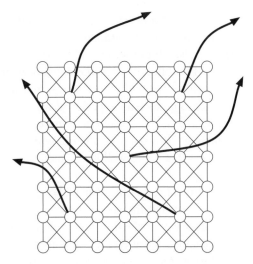

Figure 20.3. The general conclusions of the Watts–Strogatz model still follow even if only a small fraction of the nodes on the grid each have a *single* random link.

Once we understand how this type of hybrid network leads to short paths, we in fact find that a surprisingly small amount of randomness is needed to achieve the same qualitative effect. Suppose, for example, that instead of allowing each node to have k random friends, we only allow one out of every k nodes to have a *single* random friend – keeping the proximity-based edges as before, as illustrated schematically in Figure 20.3. Loosely speaking, we can think of this model with fewer random friends as corresponding to a technologically earlier time, when most people only knew their near neighbors, and a few people knew someone far away. Even this network will have short paths between all pairs of nodes. To see why, suppose that we conceptually group $k \times k$ subsquares of the grid into "towns." Now, consider the small-world phenomenon at the level of towns. Each town contains approximately k people who each have a random friend, and so the town collectively has k links to other towns selected uniformly at random. This is just like the previous model, except that towns are now playing the role of individual nodes, and so we can find short paths between any pair of towns. But now, to find a short path between any two people, we first find a short path between the two towns they inhabit and then use the proximity-based edges to turn this into an actual path in the network of individual people.

This, then, is the crux of the Watts–Strogatz model: introducing a tiny amount of randomness – in the form of long-range weak ties – is enough to make the world "small," with short paths between every pair of nodes.

20.3 Decentralized Search

Let's now consider the second basic aspect of the Milgram small-world experiment – the fact that people were actually able to collectively find short paths to the designated target. This novel kind of "social search" task was a necessary consequence of the way

Milgram formulated the experiment for his participants. To really find the *shortest* path from a starting person to the target, one would have to instruct the starter to forward a letter to *all* of his or her friends, who in turn should have forwarded the letter to all of their friends, and so forth. This "flooding" of the network would have reached the target as rapidly as possible – it is essentially the *breadth-first search* procedure from Chapter 2 – but for obvious reasons, such an experiment was not a feasible option. As a result, Milgram was forced to embark on the much more interesting experiment of constructing paths by "tunneling" through the network, with the letter advancing just one person at a time – a process that could well have failed to reach the target, even if a short path existed.

So the success of the experiment raises fundamental questions about the power of collective search: even if we posit that the social network contains short paths, why should it have been structured so as to make this type of *decentralized search* so effective? Clearly the network contained some type of "gradient" that helped participants guide messages toward the target. As with the Watts–Strogatz model, which sought to provide a simple framework for thinking about short paths in highly clustered networks, this type of search is also something we can try to model: can we construct a random network in which decentralized routing succeeds, and if so, what are the qualitative properties that are crucial for success?

A Model for Decentralized Search. To begin with, it is not difficult to model the kind of decentralized search that took place in the Milgram experiment. Starting with the grid-based model of Watts and Strogatz, we suppose that a starting node s is given a message that it must forward to a target node t, passing it along edges of the network. Initially s only knows the location of t on the grid, but, crucially, it does not know the random edges out of any node other than itself. Each intermediate node along the path has this partial information as well, and it must choose which of its neighbors to send the message to next. These choices amount to a collective procedure for finding a path from s to t – just as the participants in the Milgram experiment collectively constructed paths to the target person. We will evaluate different search procedures according to their *delivery time* – the expected number of steps required to reach the target, over a randomly generated set of long-range contacts, and randomly chosen starting and target nodes.

Unfortunately, given this setup, one can prove that decentralized search in the Watts–Strogatz model will necessarily require a large number of steps to reach a target – much larger than the true length of the shortest path [248]. As a mathematical model, the Watts–Strogatz network is thus effective at capturing the density of triangles and the existence of short paths, but not the ability of people, working together in the network, to actually find the paths. Essentially, the problem is that the weak ties that make the world small are "too random" in this model: since they're completely unrelated to the similarity among nodes that produces the homophily-based links, they're hard for people to use reliably.

One way to think about this is in terms of Figure 20.4, a hand-drawn image from Milgram's original article in *Psychology Today*. To reach a far-off target, one must use long-range weak ties in a fairly structured, methodical way, constantly reducing the distance to the target. As Milgram observed in the discussion accompanying this picture, "The geographic movement of the [letter] from Nebraska to Massachusetts

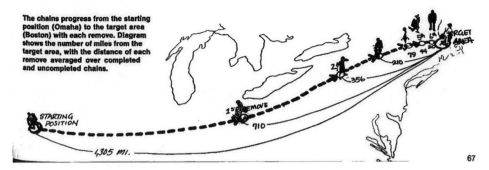

The chains progress from the starting position (Omaha) to the target area (Boston) with each remove. Diagram shows the number of miles from the target area, with the distance of each remove averaged over completed and uncompleted chains.

STARTING POSITION

1,305 mi.

67

Figure 20.4. An image from Milgram's original article in *Psychology Today*, showing a "composite" of the successful paths converging on the target person. Each intermediate step is positioned at the average distance of all chains that completed that number of steps. (Image from [297].)

is striking. There is a progressive closing in on the target area as each new person is added to the chain" [297]. So it is not enough to have a network model in which weak ties span only the very long ranges; it is necessary to span all the intermediate ranges of scale as well. Is there a simple way to adapt the model to take this into account?

20.4 Modeling the Process of Decentralized Search

Although the Watts–Strogatz model does not provide a structure where decentralized search can be performed effectively, a mild generalization of the model in fact exhibits both the properties we want: the networks contain short paths, and these short paths can be found using decentralized search [248].

Generalizing the Network Model. We adapt the model by introducing one extra quantity that controls the "scales" spanned by the long-range weak ties. We have nodes on a grid as before, and each node still has edges to each other node within r grid steps. But now, each of its k random edges is generated in a way that decays with distance, controlled by a *clustering exponent* q as follows. For two nodes v and w, let $d(v, w)$ denote the number of grid steps between them. (This is their distance if one had to walk along adjacent nodes on the grid.) In generating a random edge out of v, we have this edge link to w with probability proportional to $d(v, w)^{-q}$.

So we in fact have a different model for each value of q. The original grid-based model corresponds to $q = 0$, since then the links are chosen uniformly at random; varying q is like turning a knob that controls how uniform the random links are. In particular, when q is very small, the long-range links are "too random" and can't be used effectively for decentralized search (as we saw specifically for the case $q = 0$ earlier); when q is large, the long-range links are "not random enough," since they simply don't provide enough of the long-distance jumps that are needed to create a small world. Pictorially, this variation in q can be seen in the difference between the two networks in Figure 20.5. Is there an optimal operating point for the network where the distribution of long-range links is sufficiently balanced between these extremes to allow for rapid decentralized search?

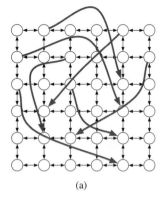

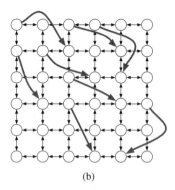

(a)   (b)

Figure 20.5. For (a) a small clustering exponent, the random edges tend to span long distances on the grid; as it increases to (b) a large clustering exponent, the random edges become shorter.

In fact, there is. The main result for this model is that, in the limit of large network size, decentralized search is most efficient when $q = 2$ (so that random links follow an inverse-square distribution). Figure 20.6 shows the performance of a basic decentralized search method across different values of q, for a network of several hundred million nodes. In keeping with the nature of the result – which only holds in the limit as the network size goes to infinity – decentralized search has about the same efficiency on networks of this size across all exponents q between 1.5 and 2.0. (And at this size, it's best for a value of q slightly less than 2.) But the overall trend is already clear, and as the network size increases, the best performance occurs at exponents q closer and closer to 2.

A Rough Calculation Motivating the Inverse-Square Network. It is natural to wonder what's special about the exponent $q = 2$ that makes it best for decentralized

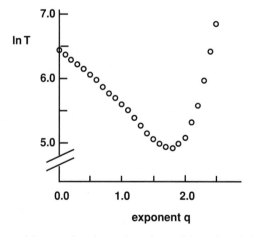

Figure 20.6. Simulation of decentralized search in the grid-based model with clustering exponent q. Each point is the average of 1,000 runs on (a slight variant of) a grid with 400 million nodes. The delivery time is best in the vicinity of exponent $q = 2$, as expected; but even with this number of nodes, the delivery time is comparable over the range between 1.5 and 2 [248].

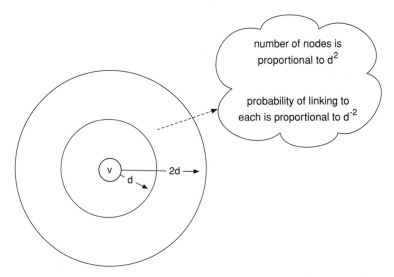

Figure 20.7. The concentric scales of resolution around a particular node.

search. In Section 20.7 at the end of this chapter, we describe a proof that decentralized search is efficient when $q = 2$, and we sketch why search is more efficient with $q = 2$ – in the limit of large network size – than with any other exponent. But even without the full details of the proof, there's a short calculation that suggests why the number 2 is important. We describe this now.

In the real world where the Milgram experiment was conducted, we mentally organize distances into different "scales of resolution": something can be around the world, across the country, across the state, across town, or down the block. A reasonable way to think about these scales of resolution in a network model – from the perspective of a particular node v – is to consider the groups of all nodes at increasingly large ranges of distance from v: nodes at distance 2–4, 4–8, 8–16, and so forth. The connection of this organizational scheme to decentralized search is suggested by Figure 20.4: effective decentralized search "funnels inward" through these different scales of resolution, as we see from the way the letter depicted in this figure reduces its distance to the target by approximately a factor of 2 with each step.

So now let's look at how the inverse-square exponent $q = 2$ interacts with these scales of resolution. We can work concretely with a single scale by taking a node v in the network, and a fixed distance d, and considering the group of nodes lying at distances between d and $2d$ from v, as shown in Figure 20.7.

Now, what is the probability that v forms a link to some node inside this group? Since area in the plane grows like the square of the radius, the total *number* of nodes in this group is proportional to d^2. On the other hand, the probability that v links to any one node in the group varies depending on exactly how far out it is, but each individual probability is proportional to d^{-2}. These two terms – the number of nodes in the group, and the probability of linking to any one of them – approximately cancel out, and we conclude that the probability that a random edge links into *some node* in this ring is approximately independent of the value of d.

This, then, suggests a qualitative way of thinking about the network that arises when $q = 2$: long-range weak ties are being formed in a way that's spread roughly uniformly over all different scales of resolution. This allows the people fowarding the message to consistently find ways of reducing their distance to the target, no matter how near or far they are from it. In this way, it's not unlike how the U.S. Postal Service uses the address on an envelope for delivering a message: a typical postal address exactly specifies scales of resolution, including the country, state, city, street, and finally the street number. But the point is that the postal system is centrally designed and maintained at considerable cost to do precisely this job; the corresponding patterns that guide messages through the inverse-square network arise spontaneously from a completely random pattern of links.

20.5 Empirical Analysis and Generalized Models

The results we've seen thus far have been for stylized models, but they raise a number of qualitative issues that one can try corroborating with data from real social networks. In this section we discuss empirical studies that analyze geographic data to look for evidence of the exponent $q = 2$, as well as more general versions of these models that incorporate nongeographic notions of social distance.

Geographic Data on Friendship. In the past few years, the rich amount of data available on social networking sites has made it much easier to get large-scale data sets that provide insight into how friendship links scale with distance. Liben-Nowell et al. [277] used the blogging site LiveJournal for precisely this purpose, analyzing roughly 500,000 users who provided a U.S. ZIP code for their home address, as well as links to their friends on the system. Note that LiveJournal serves here primarily as a very useful "model system," containing data on the geographic basis of friendship links on a scale that would be enormously difficult to obtain by more traditional survey methods. From a methodological point of view, it is an interesting and fairly unresolved issue to understand how closely the structure of friendships defined in online communities corresponds to the structure of friendships as we understand them in offline settings.

A number of things have to be done in order to align the LiveJournal data with the basic grid model, and perhaps the most subtle involves the fact that the population density of the users is extremely nonuniform (as it is for the United States as a whole). See Figure 20.8 for a visualization of the population density in the LiveJournal data. In particular, the inverse-square distribution is useful for finding targets when nodes are uniformly spaced in two dimensions. But what's a reasonable generalization to the case in which they can be spread very nonuniformly?

Rank-Based Friendship. One approach that works well is to determine link probabilities not by physical distance but by *rank*. Let's suppose that, as node v looks out at all other nodes, it ranks them by proximity: the rank of node w, denoted rank(w), is equal to the number of other nodes that are closer to v than w is. For example, in Figure 20.9(a), node w would have rank 7, since seven others nodes (including v itself) are closer to v than w is. Now, suppose that for some exponent p, node v creates a random

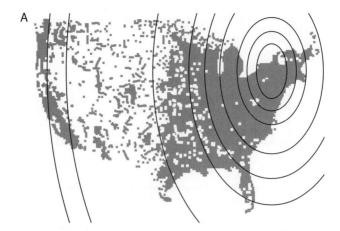

Figure 20.8. The population density of the LiveJournal network studied by Liben-Nowell et al. (Image from [277], National Academy of Sciences.)

link as follows: it chooses a node w as the other end with probability proportional to rank$(w)^{-p}$. We will call this *rank-based friendship* with exponent p.

Which choice of exponent p would generalize the inverse-square distribution for uniformly spaced nodes? As Figure 20.9(b) shows, if a node w in a uniformly spaced grid is at distance d from v, then it lies on the circumference of a disc of radius d, which contains about d^2 closer nodes – so its rank is approximately d^2. Thus, linking to w with probability proportional to d^{-2} is approximately the same as linking with probability rank$(w)^{-1}$, so this suggests that exponent $p = 1$ is the correct generalization of the inverse-square distribution. In fact, Liben-Nowell et al. were able to prove that for essentially any population density, if random links are constructed using rank-based friendship with exponent 1, the resulting network allows for efficient decentralized search with high probability. In addition to generalizing the inverse-square result for

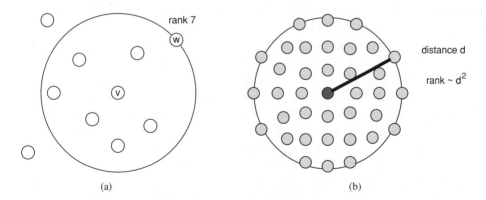

(a)

(b)

Figure 20.9. When the population density is nonuniform, it can be useful to understand how far w is from v in terms of its *rank* rather than its physical distance. In (a), we say that w has rank 7 with respect to v because it is the 7th closest node to v, counting outward in order of distance. In (b), we see for the original version of the model, in which the nodes have a uniform population density, that node w at distance d from v will have a rank that is proportional to d^2, because all the nodes inside the circle of radius d will be closer to v than w is.

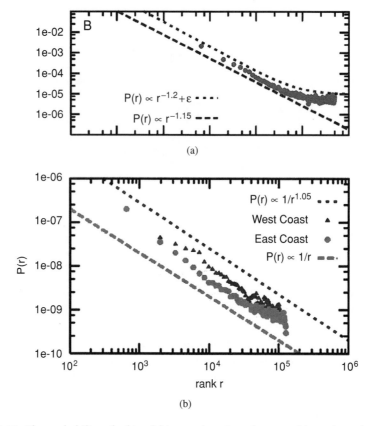

Figure 20.10. The probability of a friendship as a function of geographic rank on the blogging site LiveJournal: rank-based friendship (a) for the full population and (b) for the East and West Coasts separately. (Image from [277]. National Academy of Sciences.)

the grid, this result has a nice qualitative summary: to construct a network that is efficiently searchable, create a link to each node with probability that is inversely proportional to the number of closer nodes.

Now one can go back to LiveJournal and see how well rank-based friendship fits the distribution of actual social network links: we consider pairs of nodes where one assigns the other a rank of r, and we ask what fraction f of these pairs are actually friends, as a function of r. Does this fraction decrease approximately like r^{-1}? Since we're looking for a power-law relationship between the rank r and the fraction of edges, f, we can proceed as in Chapter 18: rather than plotting f as a function of r, we can plot $\log f$ as a function of $\log r$, see if we find an approximately straight line, and then estimate the exponent p as the slope of this line.

Figure 20.10(a) shows this result for the LiveJournal data; we see that much of the body of the curve is approximately a straight line sandwiched between slopes of -1.15 and -1.2, and hence close to the optimal exponent of -1. It is also interesting to work separately with the more structurally homogeneous subsets of the data consisting of West Coast users and East Coast users. When one does so, the exponent becomes very close to the optimal value of -1. Figure 20.10(b) shows this result. The lower dotted line is what you should see if the points followed the distribution r^{-1}, and the upper dotted line is what you should see if the points followed the distribution $r^{-1.05}$. The proximity of the rank-based exponent on real networks to the optimal value of -1 has also been corroborated by subsequent research. In particular, as part of a recent large-scale study of several geographic phenomena in the Facebook social network, Backstrom et al. [33] returned to the question of rank-based friendship and again found an exponent very close to -1; in their case, the bulk of the distribution was closely approximated by rank$^{-0.95}$.

The plots in Figure 20.10, and their follow-ups, are thus the conclusion of a sequence of steps in which we start from an experiment (Milgram's), build mathematical models based on this experiment (combining local and long-range links), make a prediction based on the models (the value of the exponent controlling the long-range links), and then validate this prediction using real data (from LiveJournal and Facebook, after generalizing the model to use rank-based friendship). This is very much how one would hope for such an interplay of experiments, theories, and measurements to play out. But it is also a bit striking to see the close alignment of theory and measurement in this particular case, since the predictions come from a highly simplified model of the underlying social network, yet they are approximately borne out on data arising from real social networks.

Indeed, there remains a mystery at the heart of these findings. While the fact that the distributions are so close does not necessarily imply the existence of any particular organizing mechanism [70], it is still natural to ask why real social networks have arranged themselves in a pattern of friendships across distance that is close to optimal for forwarding messages to far-off targets. Furthermore, whatever the users of LiveJournal and Facebook are doing, they are not explicitly trying to run versions of the Milgram experiment – if there are dynamic forces or selective pressures driving the network toward this shape, they must be more implicit, and it remains a fascinating open problem to determine whether such forces exist and how they might operate. One intriguing approach to this question has been suggested by Oskar Sandberg, who analyzes a model in which a network constantly rewires itself as people perform decentralized searches in it. He argues that over time the network essentially begins to "adapt" to the pattern of searches; eventually the searches become more efficient, and the arrangement of the long-range links begins to approach a structure that can be approximated by rank-based friendship with the optimal exponent [361].

Social Foci and Social Distance. When we first discussed the Watts–Strogatz model in Section 20.2, we noted that the grid of nodes was intended to serve as a stylized notion of similarity among individuals. Clearly it is most easily identified with geographic proximity, but subsequent models have explored other types of similarity and the ways in which they can produce small-world effects in networks [250, 410].

The notion of *social foci* from Chapter 4 provides a flexible and general way to produce models of networks exhibiting both an abundance of short paths and efficient decentralized search. Recall that a social focus is any type of community, occupational pursuit, neighborhood, shared interest, or activity that serves to organize social life around it [161]. Foci are a way of summarizing the many possible reasons that two

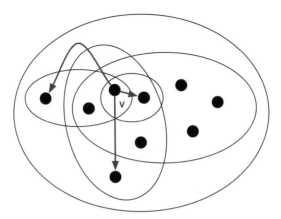

Figure 20.11. When nodes belong to multiple foci, we can define the social distance between two nodes to be the smallest focus that contains both of them. In the figure, the foci are represented by ovals; the node labeled v belongs to five foci of sizes 2, 3, 5, 7, and 9 (with the largest focus containing all the nodes shown).

people can know each other or become friends: because they live on the same block, work at the same company, frequent the same cafe, or attend the same kinds of concerts. Now, two people may have many possible foci in common, but all else being equal, it is likely that the shared foci with only a few members are the strongest generators of new social ties. For example, two people may both work for the same thousand-person company and live in the same million-person city, but it is the fact that they both belong to the same twenty-person literacy tutoring organization that makes it most probable they know each other. Thus, a natural way to define the *social distance* between two people is to declare it to be the size of the *smallest* focus that includes both of them.

In the previous sections, we've used models that build links in a social network from an underlying notion of geographic distance. Let's consider how this might work with this more general notion of social distance. Suppose we have a collection of nodes and a collection of foci to which they belong – each focus is simply a set containing some of the nodes. We let dist(v, w) denote the social distance between nodes v and w as defined in terms of shared foci: dist(v, w) is the size of the smallest focus that contains both v and w. Now, following the style of earlier models, let's construct a link between each pair of nodes v and w with probability proportional to dist(v, w)$^{-p}$. For example, in Figure 20.11, the node labeled v constructs links to three other nodes at social distances 2, 3, and 5. One can now show, subject to some technical assumptions on the structure of the foci, that when links are generated this way with exponent $p = 1$, the resulting network supports efficient decentralized search with high probability [250].

There are aspects of this result that are similar to what we've just seen for rank-based friendship. First, as with rank-based friendship, there is a simple description of the underlying principle: when nodes link to each other with probability inversely proportional to their social distance, the resulting network is efficiently searchable. Second, the exponent $p = 1$ is again the natural generalization of the inverse-square law for the simple grid model. To see why, suppose we take a grid of nodes and define a set of foci as follows: for each location v on the grid, and each possible radius r around

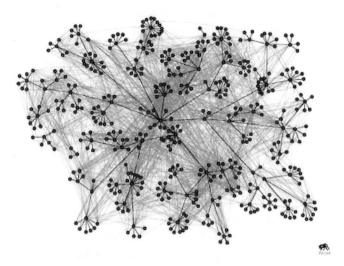

Figure 20.12. The pattern of e-mail communication among 436 employees of Hewlett Packard Research Lab is superimposed on the official organizational hierarchy, showing how network links span different social foci [6]. (Image from http://www-personal. umich.edu/ ladamic/img/hplabsemailhierarchy.jpg, courtesy of Elsevier Science and Technology Journals.)

that location, there is a focus consisting of all nodes who are within distance r of v. (Essentially, these are foci consisting of everyone who lives together in neighborhoods and locales of various sizes.) Then for two nodes who are a distance d apart, their smallest shared focus has a number of nodes proportional to d^2, so this is their social distance. Thus, linking with probability proportional to d^{-2} is essentially the same as linking with probability inversely proportional to their social distance.

Recent studies of who-talks-to-whom data have fit this model to social network structures. In particular, Adamic and Adar analyzed a social network on the employees of Hewlett Packard Research Lab that we discussed briefly in Chapter 1, connecting two people if they exchanged e-mail at least six times over a three-month period [6] (see Figure 20.12). They then defined a focus for each of the groups within the organizational structure (i.e., a group of employees all reporting a common manager). They found that the probability of a link between two employees at social distance d within the organization scaled proportionally to $d^{-3/4}$. In other words, the exponent on the probability for this network is close to, but smaller than, the best exponent for making decentralized search within the network efficient.

These increasingly general models thus provide a way to look at social-network data and speak quantitatively about the ways in which the links span different levels of distance. This is important for understanding not just the small-world properties of these networks, but also more generally for the ways in which homophily and weak ties combine to produce the kinds of structures we find in real networks.

Search as an Instance of Decentralized Problem Solving. While the Milgram experiment was designed to test the hypothesis that people are connected by short paths in the global social network, our discussion here shows that it also served as an empirical study of people's ability to collectively solve a problem – in this case, searching for a path to a far-off individual – using only very local information and by communicating only with their neighbors in the social network. In addition to the kinds of search methods discussed here, based on aiming as closely to the target as possible in each step, researchers have also studied the effectiveness of path-finding strategies in which people send messages to friends who have a particularly large number of edges (on the premise that they will be "better connected" in general) [6, 7], as well as strategies that explicitly trade off the proximity of a person against their number of edges [370].

The notion that social networks can be effective at this type of decentralized problem solving is an intriguing and general premise that applies more broadly than just to the problem of path-finding that Milgram considered. There are many possible problems that people interacting in a network could try to solve, and it is natural to suppose that their effectiveness will depend both on the difficulty of the problem being solved and on the network that connects them. There is a long history of experimental interest in collective problem solving [47], and indeed one way to view the bargaining experiments described in Chapter 12 is as an investigation of the ability of a group of people to collectively find a mutually compatible set of exchanges when their interaction is constrained by a network. Recent experiments have explored this issue for a range of basic problems, across multiple kinds of network structures [236, 237], and there is also a growing line of work on the design of systems that can exploit the power of collective human problem solving by very large on-line populations [402, 403].

20.6 Core–Periphery Structures and Difficulties in Decentralized Search

In the four decades since the Milgram experiment, the research community has come to appreciate both the robustness and the delicacy of the "six degrees" principle. As we noted in Chapter 2, many studies of large-scale social-network data have confirmed the pervasiveness of very short paths in almost every setting. On the other hand, the ability of people to find these paths from within the network is a subtle phenomenon: it is striking that it should happen at all, and the conditions that facilitate it are not fully understood.

As Judith Kleinfeld has noted in her recent critique of the Milgram experiment [255], the success rate at finding targets in re-creations of the experiment has often been much lower than it was in the original work. Much of the difficulty can be explained by lack of participation: many people, asked to forward a letter as part of the experiment, will simply throw it away. This is consistent with lack of participation in any type of survey or activity carried out by mail; assuming this process is more or less random, it has a predictable effect on the results, and one can correct for it [131, 416].

But there are also more fundamental difficulties at work, pointing to questions about large social networks that may help inform a richer understanding of network structure. In particular, Milgram-style search in a network is most successful when the target person is affluent and of socially high status. For example, in the largest small-world experiment to date [131], eighteen different targets were used, drawn from

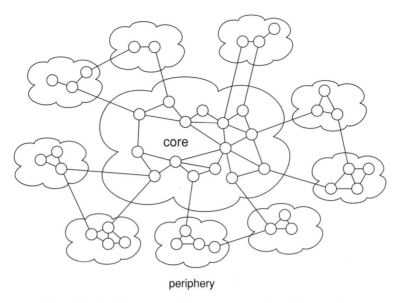

Figure 20.13. The core–periphery structure of social networks.

a wide range of backgrounds. Completion rates to all targets were small, due to lack of participation in the e-mail–based forwarding of messages, but they were highest for targets who were college professors and journalists, and particularly small for low-status targets.

Core–Periphery Structures. This wide variation in the success rates of search to different targets does not simply arise from variations in individual attributes of the respective people; it is based on the fact that social networks are structured to make high-status individuals much easier to find than low-status ones. Homophily suggests that high-status people will mainly know other high-status people, and low-status people will mainly know other low-status people, but this does not imply that the two groups occupy symmetric or interchangeable positions in the social network. Rather, large social networks tend to be organized in what is called a *core–periphery structure* [72], in which the high-status people are linked in a densely connected *core*, while the low-status people are atomized around the *periphery* of the network. Figure 20.13 gives a schematic picture of such a structure. High-status people have the resources to travel widely; to meet each other through shared foci around clubs, interests, and educational and occupational pursuits; and more generally to establish links in the network that span geographic and social boundaries. Low-status people tend to form links that are much more clustered and local. As a result, the shortest paths connecting two low-status people who are geographically or socially far apart will tend to go into the core and then come back out again.

All this has clear implications for people's ability to find paths to targets in the network. In particular, it indicates some of the deep structural reasons why it is harder for Milgram-style decentralized search to find low-status targets than high-status targets. As you move toward a high-status target, the link structure tends to become richer, based on connections with an increasing array of underlying social reasons. In trying to find a low-status target, on the other hand, the link structure becomes structurally more impoverished as you move toward the periphery.

These considerations suggest an opportunity for richer models that take status effects more directly into account. The models we have seen capture the process by which people can find each other when they are all embedded in an underlying social structure and motivated to continue a path toward a specific destination. But as the social structure begins to fray around the periphery, an understanding of how we find our way through it has the potential to shed light not just on the networks themselves, but also on the way that network structure is intertwined with status and the varied positions that different groups occupy in society as a whole.

20.7 Advanced Material: Analysis of Decentralized Search

In Section 20.4, we gave some basic intuition for why an inverse-square distribution of links with distance makes effective decentralized search possible. Even given this way of thinking about it, however, it still requires further work to really see why search succeeds with this distribution. In this section, we describe the complete analysis of the process [249].

To make the calculations a bit simpler, we vary the model in one respect: we place the nodes in one dimension rather than two. In fact, the argument is essentially the same no matter how many dimensions the nodes are in, but one dimension makes things the cleanest (even if not the best match for the actual geographic structure of a real population). It turns out, as we will argue more generally later in this section, that the best exponent for search is equal to the dimension, so in our one-dimensional analysis we will use an exponent of $q = 1$ rather than $q = 2$. At the end, we will discuss the minor ways in which the argument needs to be adapted in two or higher dimensions.

We should also mention, recalling the discussion earlier in the chapter, that there is a second fundamental part of this analysis as well – showing that this choice of q is in fact the best for decentralized search in the limit of increasing network size. At the end, we sketch why this is true, but the full details are beyond what we will cover here.

A. The Optimal Exponent in One Dimension

Here, then, is the model we will be looking at. A set of n nodes are arranged on a one-dimensional ring as shown in Figure 20.14(a), with each node connected by directed edges to the two others immediately adjacent to it. Each node v also has a single directed edge to some other node on the ring; the probability that v links to any particular node w is proportional to $d(v, w)^{-1}$, where $d(v, w)$ is their distance apart on the ring. We will call the nodes to which v has an edge its *contacts*: the two nodes adjacent to it on the ring are its *local contacts*, and the other one is its *long-range contact*. The overall structure is thus a ring that is augmented with random edges, as

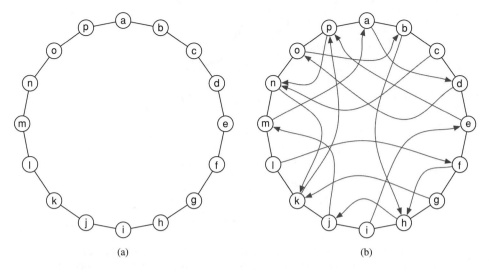

Figure 20.14. The analysis of decentralized search is a bit cleaner in one dimension than in two, although it is conceptually easy to adapt the arguments to two dimensions. As a result, we focus most of the discussion on (a) a set of nodes arranged in a one-dimensional ring (b) augmented with random long-range links.

shown in Figure 20.14(b). Again, this is essentially just a one-dimensional version of the grid with random edges that we saw in Figure 20.5.[1]

Myopic Search. Let's choose a random start node s and a random target node t on this augmented ring network. The goal, as in the Milgram experiment, is to forward a message from the start to the target, with each intermediate node on the way only knowing the locations of its own neighbors, and the location of t, and nothing else about the full network.

The forwarding strategy that we analyze, which works well on the ring when $q = 1$, is a simple technique that we call *myopic search*: when a node v is holding the message, it passes it to the contact that lies as close to t on the ring as possible. Myopic search can clearly be performed even by nodes that know nothing about the network other than the locations of their friends and the location of t, and it is a reasonable approximation to the strategies used by most people in Milgram-style experiments [243].

For example, Figure 20.15 shows the myopic path that would be constructed if we chose a as the start node and i as the target node in the network from Figure 20.14(b).

1. Node a first sends the message to node d, since among a's contacts p, b, and d, node d lies closest to i on the ring.
2. Then node d passes the message to its local contact e, and e likewise passes the message to its local contact f, since the long-range contacts of both d and e lead away from i on the ring, not closer to it.

---

[1] We could also analyze a model in which nodes have more outgoing edges, but this only makes the search problem easier; our result here will show that, even when each node has only two local contacts and a single long-range contact, search can still be very efficient.

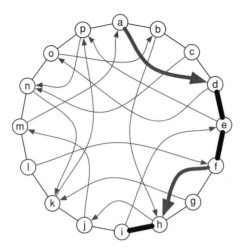

Figure 20.15. In myopic search, the current message holder chooses the contact that lies closest to the target (as measured on the ring), and it forwards the message to this contact.

3. Node f has a long-range contact h that proves useful, so it passes the message to h. Node h actually has the target as a local contact, so it hands it directly to i, completing the path in five steps.

Notice that this myopic path is not the shortest path from a to i. If node a had known that its friend b in fact had h as a contact, it could have handed the message to b, thereby taking the first step in the three-step a-b-h-i path. It is precisely this lack of knowledge about the full network structure that prevents myopic search from finding the true shortest path in general.

Despite this, however, we will see next that in expectation, myopic search finds paths that are surprisingly short.

Analyzing Myopic Search: The Basic Plan. We now have a completely well-defined probabilistic question to analyze, as follows. We generate a random network by adding long-range edges to a ring as before. We then choose a random start node s and random target node t in this network. The number of steps required by myopic search is now a random variable X, and we are interested in showing that $E[X]$, the expected value of X, is relatively small.

Our plan for putting a bound on the expected value of X follows the idea contained in Milgram's picture from Figure 20.4: we track how long it takes for the message to reduce its distance by factors of 2 as it closes in on the target. Specifically, as the message moves from s to t, we say that it's in *phase j* of the search if its distance from the target is between 2^j and 2^{j+1}. See Figure 20.16 for an illustration of this division of the search into phases. Notice that the number of different phases is at most $\log_2 n$, or the number of doublings needed to go from 1 to n. (In what follows, we will drop the base of the logarithm and simply write $\log n$ to denote $\log_2 n$.)

We can write X, the number of steps taken by the full search, as

$$X = X_1 + X_2 + \cdots + X_{\log n};$$

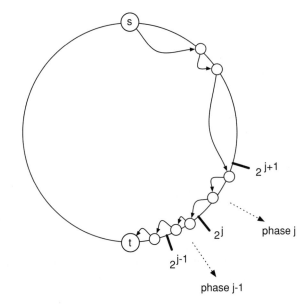

Figure 20.16. We analyze the progress of myopic search in *phases*. Phase j consists of the portion of the search in which the message's distance from the target is between 2^j and 2^{j+1}.

that is, the total time taken by the search is simply the sum of the times taken in each phase. Linearity of expectation says that the expectation of a sum of random variables is equal to the sum of their individual expectations, and so we have

$$E[X] = E[X_1 + X_2 + \cdots + X_{\log n}] = E[X_1] + E[X_2] + \cdots + E[X_{\log n}].$$

We will now show – and this is the crux of the argument – that the expected value of each X_j is at most proportional to $\log n$. In this way, $E[X]$ will be a sum of $\log n$ terms, each at most proportional to $\log n$, and so we will have shown that $E[X]$ is at most proportional to $(\log n)^2$.

This will achieve our overall goal of showing that myopic search is very efficient with the given distribution of links: the full network has n nodes, but myopic search constructs a path that is *exponentially* smaller – proportional to the square of $\log n$.

Intermediate Step: The Normalizing Constant. In implementing this high-level strategy, the first thing we need to work out is in fact something very basic: we've been saying all along that v forms its long-range link to w with probability *proportional to* $d(v, w)^{-1}$, but what is the constant of proportionality? As in any case when we know a set of probabilities up to a missing constant of proportionality $1/Z$, the value of Z here is simply the sum of $d(v, u)^{-1}$ over all nodes $u \neq v$ on the ring. Dividing everything down by this normalizing constant Z, the probability of v linking to w is then equal to $\frac{1}{Z} d(v, w)^{-1}$.

To work out the value of Z, we note that there are two nodes at distance 1 from v, two at distance 2, and more generally two at each distance d up to $n/2$. Assuming

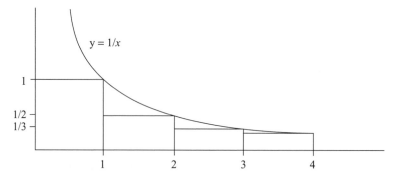

Figure 20.17. Determining the normalizing constant for the probability of links involves evaluating the sum of the first $n/2$ reciprocals. An upper bound on the value of this sum can be determined from the area under the curve $y = 1/x$.

n is even, there is also a single node at distance $n/2$ from v – the node diametrically opposite it on the ring. Therefore, we have

$$Z \leq 2 \left(1 + \frac{1}{2} + \frac{1}{3} + \frac{1}{4} + \cdots + \frac{1}{n/2} \right). \tag{20.1}$$

The quantity inside parentheses on the right is a common expression in probabilistic calculations: the sum of the first k reciprocals for some k, in this case $n/2$. To put an upper bound on its size, we can compare it to the area under the curve $y = 1/x$, as shown in Figure 20.17. As that figure indicates, a sequence of rectangles of unit widths and heights $\frac{1}{2}, \frac{1}{3}, \frac{1}{4}, \ldots, \frac{1}{k}$ fits under the curve $y = 1/x$ as x ranges from 1 to k. Combined with a single rectangle of height and width 1, we see that

$$1 + \frac{1}{2} + \frac{1}{3} + \frac{1}{4} + \cdots + \frac{1}{k} \leq 1 + \int_1^k \frac{1}{x} dx = 1 + \ln k.$$

Plugging in $k = n/2$ to the expression on the right-hand side of inequality (20.1), we get

$$Z \leq 2(1 + \ln(n/2)) = 2 + 2\ln(n/2).$$

For simplicity, we'll use a slightly weaker bound on Z, which follows simply from the observation that $\ln x \leq \log_2 x$:

$$Z \leq 2 + 2\log_2(n/2) = 2 + 2(\log_2 n) - 2(\log_2 2) = 2\log_2 n.$$

Thus, we now have an expression for the actual probability that v links to w (including its constant of proportionality):

$$\frac{1}{Z} d(v, w)^{-1} \geq \frac{1}{2 \log n} d(v, w)^{-1}.$$

Analyzing the Time Spent in One Phase of Myopic Search. Finally, we come to the last and central step of the analysis: showing that the time spent by the search in any one phase is not very large. Let's choose a particular phase j of the search, when the message is at a node v whose distance to the target t is some number d between 2^j and

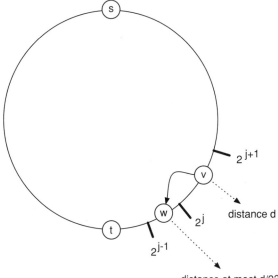

Figure 20.18. At any given point in time, the search is in some phase j, with the message residing at a node v at distance d from the target. The phase will come to an end if v's long-range contact lies at distance less than or equal to $\frac{d}{2}$ from the target t, and so arguing that the probability of this event is large provides a way to show that the phase will not last too long.

2^{j+1}. (See Figure 20.18 for an illustration of all this notation in context.) The phase will come to an end once the distance to the target decreases below 2^j, and we want to show that this happens relatively quickly.

One way for the phase to come to an end immediately would be for v's long-range contact w to be at distance less than or equal to $\frac{d}{2}$ from t. In this case, v would necessarily be the last node to belong to phase j. So let's show that this immediate halving of the distance in fact happens with reasonably large probability.

The argument is pictured in Figure 20.19. Let I be the set of nodes at distance less than or equal to $\frac{d}{2}$ from t; this is where we hope v's long-range contact is located. There are $d + 1$ nodes in I: this includes node t itself, and $\frac{d}{2}$ nodes consecutively on each side of it. Each node w in I has distance at most $\frac{3d}{2}$ from v: the farthest one is on the "far side" of t from v, at distance $d + \frac{d}{2}$. Therefore, each node w in I has probability at least

$$\frac{1}{2 \log n} d(v, w)^{-1} \geq \frac{1}{2 \log n} \times \frac{1}{3d/2} = \frac{1}{3d \log n}$$

of being the long-range contact of v. Since there are more than d nodes in I, the probability that *one of them* is the long-range contact of v is at least

$$d \times \frac{1}{3d \log n} = \frac{1}{3 \log n}.$$

If one of these nodes is the long-range contact of v, then phase j ends immediately in this step. Therefore, for each step that it proceeds, phase j has a probability of at least $1/(3 \log n)$ of coming to an end, independently of what has happened so far. To

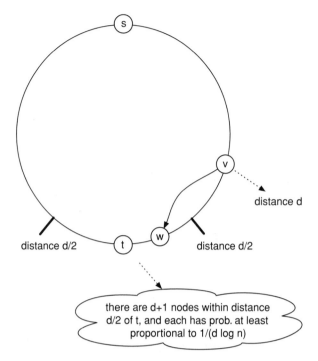

there are d+1 nodes within distance
d/2 of t, and each has prob. at least
proportional to 1/(d log n)

Figure 20.19. With reasonable probability, v's long-range contact lies within half the distance to the target.

run for at least i steps, phase j has to fail to come to an end $i - 1$ times in a row, and so the probability that phase j runs for at least i steps is at most

$$\left(1 - \frac{1}{3 \log n}\right)^{i-1}.$$

Now we conclude by just using the formula for the expected value of a random variable:

$$E[X_j] = 1 \times \Pr[X_j = 1] + 2 \times \Pr[X_j = 2] + 3 \times \Pr[X_j = 3] + \cdots. \quad (20.2)$$

There is a useful alternate way to write this formula. Notice that in the expression

$$\Pr[X_j \geq 1] + \Pr[X_j \geq 2] + \Pr[X_j \geq 3] + \cdots \quad (20.3)$$

the quantity $\Pr[X_j = 1]$ is accounted for once (in the first term only), the quantity $\Pr[X_j = 2]$ is accounted for twice (in the first two terms only), and so forth. Therefore, the expressions in Equations (20.2) and (20.3) are the same thing, and so we have

$$E[X_j] = \Pr[X_j \geq 1] + \Pr[X_j \geq 2] + \Pr[X_j \geq 3] + \cdots. \quad (20.4)$$

Now, we've just argued earlier that

$$\Pr[X_j \geq i] \leq \left(1 - \frac{1}{3 \log n}\right)^{i-1},$$

and so

$$E\left[X_j\right] \leq 1 + \left(1 - \frac{1}{3\log n}\right) + \left(1 - \frac{1}{3\log n}\right)^2 + \left(1 - \frac{1}{3\log n}\right)^3 + \cdots.$$

The right-hand side is a geometric sum with multiplier $1 - \dfrac{1}{3\log n}$, and so it converges to

$$\frac{1}{1 - \left(1 - \frac{1}{3\log n}\right)} = 3\log n.$$

Thus, we have

$$E\left[X_j\right] \leq 3\log n.$$

And now we're done. $E[X]$ is a sum of the $\log n$ terms $E[X_1] + E[X_2] + \cdots + E[X_{\log n}]$, and we've just argued that each of them is at most $3\log n$. Therefore, $E[X] \leq (3\log n)^2$, a quantity proportional to $(\log n)^2$, as we wanted to show.

B. Higher Dimensions and Other Exponents

Using the analysis we've just completed, we now discuss two further issues. First, we sketch how it can be used to analyze networks built by adding long-range contacts to nodes arranged in two dimensions. Then we show how, in the limit of increasing network size, search is more efficient when q is equal to the underlying dimension than when it is equal to any other value.

The Analysis in Two Dimensions. It's not hard to adapt our analysis for the one-dimensional ring directly to the case of the two-dimensional grid. Essentially, we only used the fact that we were in one dimension in two distinct places in the analysis. First, we used it when we determined the normalizing constant Z. Second, and in the end most crucially, we used it to argue that there were at least d nodes within distance $\frac{d}{2}$ of target t. This factor of d canceled the d^{-1} in the link probability, allowing us to conclude that the probability of halving the distance to the target in any given step was at least proportional to $1/(\log n)$, *regardless* of the value of d.

At a qualitative level, this last point is the heart of the analysis: with link probability d^{-1} on the ring, the probability of linking to any one node exactly offsets the number of nodes close to t, and so myopic search makes progress at every possible distance away from the target.

When we go to two dimensions, the number of nodes within distance $\frac{d}{2}$ of the target is proportional to d^2. This suggests that, to get the same nice cancellation property, we should have v link to each node w with probability proportional to $d(v, w)^{-2}$, and this exponent of -2 is what we will use.

With the preceding ideas in mind, and with this change in the exponent to -2, the analysis for two dimensions is almost exactly the same as what we just saw for the one-dimensional ring. First, although we won't go through the calculations here, the normalizing constant Z is still proportional to $\log n$ when the probability of v linking to w is proportional to $d(v, w)^{-2}$. We then consider $\log n$ different phases as before, and

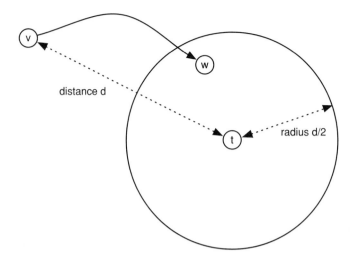

Figure 20.20. The analysis for the one-dimensional ring can be carried over almost directly to the two-dimensional grid. In two dimensions, with the message at a current distance d from target t, we again look at the set of nodes within distance $\frac{d}{2}$ of t and argue that the probability of entering this set in a single step is reasonably large.

as depicted in Figure 20.20, we consider the probability that, at any given moment, the current message holder v has a long-range contact w that halves the distance to the target, ending the phase immediately. Now we use the calculation foreshadowed in the previous paragraph: the number of nodes within distance $\frac{d}{2}$ of the target is proportional to d^2, and the probability that v links to each is proportional to $1/(d^2 \log n)$. Therefore, the probability that the message halves its distance to the target in this step is at least proportional to $d^2/(d^2 \log n) = 1/(\log n)$, and the rest of the analysis then finishes as before.

A similarly direct adaptation of the analysis shows that decentralized search is efficient for networks built by adding long-range contacts to grids in $D > 2$ dimensions, when the exponent q is equal to D.

Why Search Is Less Efficient with Other Exponents. Finally, let's sketch why decentralized search is less efficient when the exponent is anything else. For concreteness, we'll focus on why search doesn't work well when $q = 0$ – the original Watts–Strogatz model when long-range links are chosen uniformly at random. Also, we'll talk again about the one-dimensional ring rather than the two-dimensional grid, since things are a bit cleaner in one dimension, although again the analysis in two dimensions is essentially the same.

The key idea, as with the "good" exponent $q = 1$, is to consider the set of all nodes within some distance of the target t. But whereas in the case of $q = 1$ we wanted to argue that it is easy to enter smaller and smaller sets centered around t, here we want to identify a set of nodes centered at t that is somehow "impenetrable" – a set that is very hard for the search to enter.

In fact, this is not difficult to do. The basic idea is depicted in Figure 20.21; we sketch how the argument works, but without going into all the details. (The details can be

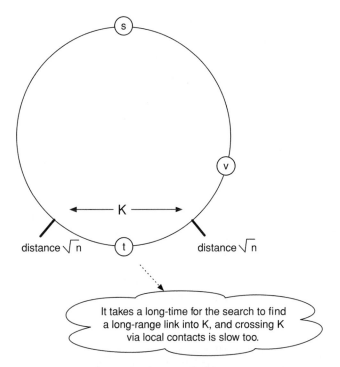

Figure 20.21. To show that decentralized search strategies require large amounts of time with exponent $q = 0$, we argue that it is difficult for the search to cross the set of $\sqrt{n}$ nodes closest to the target. Similar arguments hold for other exponents $q < 1$.

found in [249].) Let K be the set of all nodes within distance less than $\sqrt{n}$ of the target t. Now, with high probability, the starting point of the search lies outside K. Because long-range contacts are created uniformly at random (since $q = 0$), the probability that any one node has a long-range contact inside K is equal to the size of K divided by n: so it is less than $2\sqrt{n}/n = 2/\sqrt{n}$. Therefore, any decentralized search strategy will need at least $\sqrt{n}/2$ steps in expectation to find a node with a long-range contact in K. But as long as it doesn't find a long-range link leading into K, it can't reach the target in less than $\sqrt{n}$ steps, since it would take this long to "walk" step-by-step through K using only the connections among local contacts. Using this argument, one can show that the expected time for any decentralized search strategy to reach t must be at least proportional to $\sqrt{n}$.

There are similar arguments for every other exponent $q \neq 1$. When q is strictly between 0 and 1, a version of the preceding argument works, with a set K centered at t whose width depends on the value of q. And when $q > 1$, decentralized search is inefficient for a different reason: since even the long-range links are relatively short, it takes a long time for decentralized search to find links that span sufficiently long distances. This makes it hard to quickly traverse the distance from the starting node to the target.

Overall, one can show that, for every exponent $q \neq 1$, there is a constant $c > 0$ (depending on q), so that it takes a number of steps at least proportional to n^c in expectation for any decentralized search strategy to reach the target in a network generated with exponent q. So in the limit as n becomes large, decentralized search with exponent $q = 1$ requires time that grows like a polynomial in $\log n$, whereas decentralized search at any other exponent requires a time that grows like a polynomial in n – exponentially worse.[2] The exponent $q = 1$ on the ring – or $q = 2$ in the plane – is optimally balanced between producing networks that are "too random" for search and those that are not random enough.

20.8 Exercises

1. In the basic six-degrees-of-separation question, one asks whether most pairs of people in the world are connected by a path of at most six edges in the social network, where an edge joins any two people who know each other on a first-name basis.

    Now let's consider a variation on this question. Suppose that we consider the full population of the world, and suppose that from each person in the world we create a directed edge only to their ten closest friends (but not to anyone else they know on a first-name basis). In the resulting "closest-friend" version of the social network, is it possible that for each pair of people in the world, there is a path of at most six edges connecting this pair of people? Explain.

2. In the basic six-degrees-of-separation question, one asks whether most pairs of people in the world are connected by a path of at most six edges in the social network, where an edge joins any two people who know each other on a first-name basis.

    Now let's consider a variation on this question. For each person in the world, we ask them to rank the thirty people they know best, in descending order of how well they know them. (Let's suppose for purposes of this question that each person is able to think of thirty people to list.) We then construct two different social networks:

    (a) The "close-friend" network: from each person we create a directed edge only to their ten closest friends on the list.
    (b) The "distant-friend" network: from each person we create a directed edge only to the ten people listed in positions 21 through 30 on their list.

    Let's think about how the small-world phenomenon might differ in these two networks. In particular, let C be the average number of people that a person can reach in six steps in the close-friend network, and let D be the average number of people that a person can reach in six steps in the distant-friend network (taking the average over all people in the world).

    When researchers have done empirical studies to compare these two types of networks (and the exact details often differ from one study to another), they tend to find that one of C or D is consistently larger than the other. Which of the two quantities, C or D, do you expect to be larger? Give a brief explanation for your answer.

3. Suppose you're working with a group of researchers studying social communication networks, with a particular focus on the distances between people in such networks, and the broader implications for the small-world phenomenon.

---

[2] Of course, it can take very large values of n for this distinction to become truly pronounced; recall Figure 20.6, which showed the results of simulations on networks with 400 million nodes.

The research group is currently negotiating an agreement with a large mobile phone carrier to get a snapshot of their "who-calls-whom" graph. Specifically, under a strict confidentiality agreement, the carrier is offering to provide a graph in which there is a node representing each of the carrier's customers, and each edge represents a pair of people who called each other over a fixed one-year period. (The edges will be annotated with the number of calls and the time at which each one happened. No personal identification will be provided with the nodes.)

Recently, the carrier has proposed that, instead of providing all the data, it will only provide edges corresponding to pairs of people who called each other at least once a week on average over the course of the year. (That is, all nodes will be present, but there will only be edges for pairs of people who talked at least 52 times.) The carrier understands that this is not the full network, but they would prefer to release less information and they argue that this is a good approximation to the full network.

Your research group objects, but the carrier is not inclined to change its position unless your group can identify specific research findings that are likely to be misleading if they are drawn from this reduced data set. The leader of your research group asks you to prepare a brief response to the carrier, identifying some concrete ways in which misleading conclusions might be reached from the reduced data set.

What would you say in your response?

CHAPTER 21

Epidemics

The study of epidemic disease has always been a topic that mixes biological issues with social ones. When we talk about epidemic disease, we will be thinking of contagious diseases caused by biological pathogens – things like influenza, measles, and sexually transmitted diseases – which spread from person to person. Epidemics can pass explosively through a population, or they can persist over long time periods at low levels; they can experience sudden flare-ups or even wavelike cyclic patterns of increasing and decreasing prevalence. In extreme cases, a single disease outbreak can have a significant effect on a whole civilization, as with the epidemics started by the arrival of Europeans in the Americas [130], or the outbreak of bubonic plague that killed 20% of the population of Europe over a seven-year period in the 1300s [293].

21.1 Diseases and the Networks That Transmit Them

The patterns by which epidemics spread through groups of people is determined not just by the properties of the pathogen carrying it – including its contagiousness, the length of its infectious period, and its severity – but also by network structures within the population it is affecting. The social network within a population – recording who knows whom – determines a lot about how the disease is likely to spread from one person to another. But more generally, the opportunities for a disease to spread are given by a *contact network*: there is a node for each person, and an edge if two people come into contact with each other in a way that makes it possible for the disease to spread from one to the other.

This suggests that accurately modeling the underlying network is crucial to understanding the spread of an epidemic. This has led to research studying how travel patterns within a city [149, 295] or via the worldwide airline network [119] could affect the spread of a fast-moving disease. Contact networks are also important in understanding how diseases spread through animal populations – with researchers tracing out the interactions within livestock populations during epidemics such as the 2001 foot-and-mouth outbreak in the United Kingdom [211] – as well as plant populations, where the affected individuals occupy fixed locations and diseases tend to have a much clearer spatial footprint [139]. And similar models have been employed for studying the spread of computer viruses, with malicious software spreading between computers across an underlying communication network [241].

The pathogen and the network are closely intertwined: even within the same population, the contact networks for two different diseases can have very different structures, depending on the diseases' respective modes of transmission. For a highly contagious disease, involving airborne transmission based on coughs and sneezes, the contact network will include a huge number of links, including any pair of people who sat together on a bus or an airplane. For a disease requiring close contact, or a sexually transmitted disease, the contact network will be much sparser, with many fewer pairs of people connected by links. Similar distinctions arise in studying computer viruses; a piece of software infecting computers across the Internet, for example, has a much broader contact network than one that spreads by short-range wireless communication between nearby mobile devices [251].

Connections to the Diffusion of Ideas and Behaviors. There are clear connections between epidemic disease and the diffusion of ideas through social networks. Both diseases and ideas can spread from person to person, across similar kinds of networks that connect people, and in this respect, they exhibit very similar structural mechanisms – to the extent that the spread of ideas is often referred to as "social contagion" [85]. Having considered the diffusion of ideas, innovations, and new behaviors in Chapter 19, why then are we revisiting this topic afresh in the context of diseases?

In the context of our discussions here about networks, the biggest difference between biological and social contagion lies in the process by which one person "infects" another. With social contagion, people are making decisions to adopt a new idea or innovation, and our models in Chapter 19 were focused on relating the underlying decision-making processes to the larger effects at the network level. With diseases, on the other hand, not only is there a lack of decision-making in the transmission of the disease from one person to another, but the process is sufficiently complex and unobservable at the person-to-person level that it is most useful to model it as *random*. That is, we will generally assume that when two people are directly linked in the contact network, and one of them has the disease, there is a given probability that he or she will pass it to the other. This use of randomness allows us to abstract away questions about the mechanics of how one person catches a disease from another for which we have no useful simple models.

This approach, then, will be the concrete difference in our discussion of biological as opposed to social contagion – not so much the new context as the new classes of models, based on random processes in networks, that will be employed. In the next three sections, we discuss some of the most basic probabilistic models for epidemics in networks; we then consider how these models provide insight into some basic qualitative issues in the spread of disease, including synchronization, timing, and concurrency in transmission. Finally, we discuss how some of the models developed here are related to similar issues in genetic inheritance, for which a kind of randomized propagation takes place through genealogical networks.

Before moving on, it is worth noting that randomized models can also sometimes be useful in studying social contagion, particularly in cases where the underlying decision processes of the individuals are hard to model and hence are more usefully abstracted as random processes. Often the two approaches – decision-based and probabilistic – produce related results, and they can sometimes be used in conjunction (e.g., [62, 408]). Understanding the relationship between these methodologies at a deeper level is an interesting direction for further research.

21.2 Branching Processes

We begin with perhaps the simplest model of contagion, which we refer to as a *branching process*. It works as follows.

- *First wave.* Suppose that a person carrying a new disease enters a population and transmits it to each person he meets independently with probability p. Furthermore, suppose that he meets k people while he is contagious; let's call these k people the *first wave* of the epidemic. Based on the random transmission of the disease from the initial person, some of the people in the first wave may get infected with the disease, while others may not.
- *Second wave.* Now, each person in the first wave goes out into the population and meets k different people, resulting in a *second wave* of $k \times k = k^2$ people. Each infected person in the first wave passes the disease independently to each of the k second-wave people they meet, again independently with probability p.
- *Subsequent waves.* Further waves are formed in the same way, by having each person in the current wave meet k new people and pass the disease to each independently with probability p.

Thus, the contact network for this epidemic can be drawn as in Figure 21.1(a) (with $k = 3$ and only the first three waves shown). We refer to such a network as a *tree*: it has a single node at the top called the *root*, every node is connected to a set of nodes in the level below it, and every node but the root is also connected to a *single* node in the level above it. The tree that forms the contact network for the branching process is in fact infinite, since we continue defining waves indefinitely.

Now, what is the behavior of an epidemic in this model? We can picture the spread of the epidemic by highlighting the edges of the contact network over which the disease passes successfully from one person to another. (Recall that each of these infections happens independently with probability p.) Thus, Figure 21.1(b) shows an aggressive epidemic that infects two people in the first wave, three in the second wave, five in the third wave, and presumably more in future waves (not shown in the picture). Figure 21.1(c), on the other hand, shows a much milder epidemic (for a less contagious disease, with a smaller value of p): of the two people infected in the first wave, one doesn't infect anyone else, and the other infects only one further person who in turn doesn't pass it on. This disease has completely vanished from the population after the second wave, having infected only four people in total.

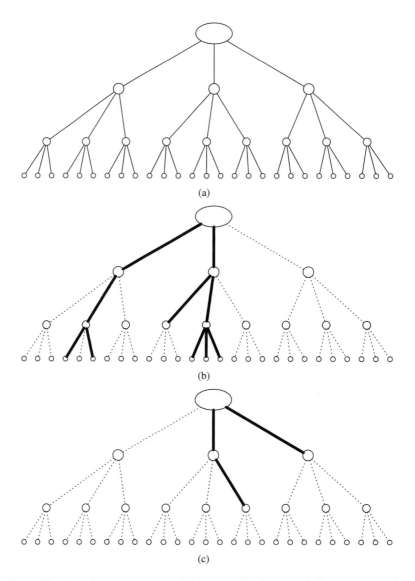

Figure 21.1. The branching process model is a simple framework for reasoning about the spread of an epidemic as one varies both the amount of contact among individuals and the level of contagion. Part (a) shows the contact network for a branching process, for which (b) with high contagion probability, the infection spreads widely, and (c) with low contagion probability, the infection is likely to die out quickly.

The Basic Reproductive Number and a Dichotomy for Branching Processes. Our last observation about Figure 21.1(c) reflects a fundamental property of branching processes. If the disease in a branching process ever reaches a wave where it fails to infect anyone, then it has died out; since people in future waves can only catch the disease from others higher up in the tree, no one in any future wave will be infected either.

So there are really only two possibilities for a disease in the branching process model: it reaches a wave where it infects no one, thus dying out after a finite number of steps, or it continues to infect people in *every* wave, proceeding infinitely through the contact network. And it turns out that there is a simple condition to tell these two possibilities apart, based on a quantity called the *basic reproductive number* of the disease.

The basic reproductive number, denoted R_0, is the expected number of new cases of the disease caused by a single individual. Since everyone in our model meets k new people and infects each with probability p, the basic reproductive number here is given by $R_0 = pk$. The outcome of the disease in a branching process model is determined by whether the basic reproductive number is smaller or larger than 1.

> *Claim:* If $R_0 < 1$, then with probability 1, the disease dies out after a finite number of waves. If $R_0 > 1$, then with probability greater than 0 the disease persists by infecting at least one person in each wave.

We give a proof of this claim in Section 21.8. Even without the details of the proof, however, we can see that the basic condition expressed in the claim – comparing R_0 to 1 – has a natural intuitive basis. When $R_0 < 1$, the disease isn't able to replenish itself: each infected person produces less than one new case in expectation, and so – even if it grows briefly due to the outcome of random fluctuations – the size of the outbreak is constantly trending downward. When $R_0 > 1$, on the other hand, the size of the outbreak is constantly trending upward. Notice, however, that even when $R_0 > 1$, the conclusion is simply that the disease persists with positive probability, not with absolute certainty: whenever $p < 1$, there is always some chance that none of the first few infected people will succeed in infecting anyone else, causing the disease to die out. In other words, even an ultracontagious disease can simply get "unlucky" and vanish from the population before it has a chance to really get going.

The dichotomy expressed by this condition has an interesting "knife-edge" quality to it when R_0 is close to 1. In particular, suppose we have a branching process where R_0 is very slightly below 1, and we increase the contagion probability p by a little bit; the result could push R_0 above 1, suddenly resulting in a positive probability of an enormous outbreak. The same effect can happen in the reverse direction as well, where slightly reducing the contagiousness of a disease to push R_0 below 1 can eliminate the risk of a large epidemic. And because R_0 is the product of p and k, small changes in the number of people k that each person comes into contact with can also have a large effect when R_0 is near 1.

All this suggests that around the critical value, $R_0 = 1$, it can be worth investing large amounts of effort even to produce small shifts in the basic reproductive number. Since R_0 is the product of the two terms p and k, it is in fact easy to interpret two basic kinds of public-health measures in terms of reductions to R_0: quarantining people, which reduces the quantity k, and encouraging behavioral measures such as better sanitary practices to reduce the spread of germs, which reduces the quantity p.

The branching process model is clearly a very simplified model of disease spread; the structure of the contact network, with no triangles at all, is reminiscent of our first pass at a model for the small-world phenomenon in Chapter 20. Thus, in the next few sections, we will look at models that can handle more complex contact networks. For these models, a dichotomy as simple as the one in the preceding claim does not hold. However, the notion of the basic reproductive number is still a useful heuristic guide to the behavior of more complex models; even when epidemiological modelers do not have a precise condition governing when an epidemic will persist and when it will die out, they find the reproductive number R_0 to be a useful approximate indication of the spreading power of the disease.

21.3 The SIR Epidemic Model

We now develop an epidemic model that can be applied to any network structure. To do this, we preserve the basic ingredients of the branching process model at the level of individual nodes, but we make the contact structure much more general. An individual node in the branching process model goes through three potential stages during the course of the epidemic:

- *Susceptible.* Before the node has caught the disease, it is susceptible to infection from its neighbors.
- *Infectious.* Once the node has caught the disease, it is infectious and has some probability of infecting each of its susceptible neighbors.
- *Removed.* After a particular node has experienced the full infectious period, this node is removed from consideration, since it no longer poses a threat of future infection.

Using this three-stage "life cycle" for the disease at each node, we now define a model for epidemics on networks. We are given a directed graph representing the contact network; an edge pointing from v to w in the graph means that if v becomes infected at some point, the disease has the potential to spread directly to w. To represent a symmetric contact between people, where either has the potential to directly infect the other, we can put in directed edges pointing each way: both from v to w and also from w to v. Since contacts between people are often symmetric, it is fine to use networks where most edges appear in each direction, but it is sometimes convenient to be able to express asymmetric contacts as well.

Now, each node has the potential to go through the susceptible–infectious–removed cycle, where we abbreviate these three states as S, I, and R. The progress of the epidemic is controlled by the contact network structure and by two additional quantities: p (the probability of contagion) and t_I (the length of the infection).

- Initially, some nodes are in the I state and all others are in the S state.
- Each node v that enters the I state remains infectious for a fixed number of steps t_I.
- During each of these t_I steps, node v has a probability p of passing the disease to each of its susceptible neighbors.
- After t_I steps, node v is no longer infectious or susceptible to further bouts of the disease; we describe it as *removed* (R), since it is now an inert node in the contact network that can no longer catch or transmit the disease.

This describes the full model; we refer to it as the *SIR model*, after the three disease states experienced by the nodes. Figure 21.2 shows an example of the SIR model unfolding in a particular contact network through successive steps; in each step, shaded nodes

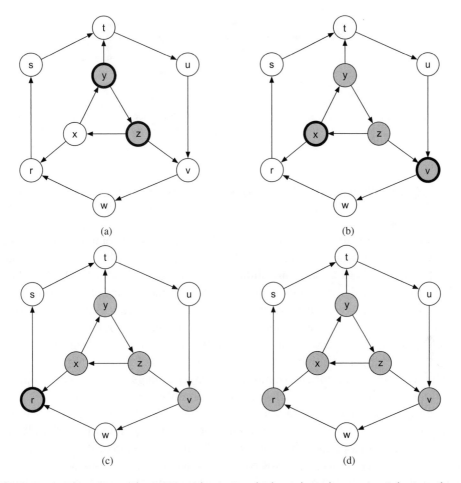

Figure 21.2. The course of an SIR epidemic in which each node remains infectious for a number of steps equal to $t_I = 1$. Starting with nodes y and z initially infected, the epidemic spreads to some but not all of the remaining nodes. In each step, shaded nodes with dark borders are in the infectious (I) state and shaded nodes with thin borders are in the removed (R) state.

with dark borders are in the I state and shaded nodes with thin borders are in the R state.

The SIR model is clearly most appropriate for a disease that each individual only catches once in their lifetime; after being infected, a node is removed either because it has acquired lifetime immunity or because the disease has killed it. In the next section, we will consider a related model for diseases that can be caught multiple times by the same person. Notice also that the branching process model from Section 21.2 is a special case of the SIR model: it simply corresponds to the SIR model where $t_I = 1$ and the contact network is an infinite tree, with each node connected to a fixed number of neighbors in the level below.

Extensions to the SIR Model. Although the contact network in the general SIR model can be arbitrarily complex, the disease dynamics are still being modeled in a simple

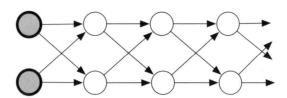

Figure 21.3. In this network, the epidemic is forced to pass through a narrow "channel" of nodes. In such a structure, even a highly contagious disease will tend to die out relatively quickly.

way. Contagion probabilities are set to a uniform value p, and contagiousness has a kind of "on/off" property: a node is equally contagious for each of the t_I steps while it has the disease.

However, it is not difficult to extend the model to handle more complex assumptions. First, we can easily capture the idea that contagion is more likely between certain pairs of nodes by assigning a separate probability $p_{v,w}$ to each pair of nodes v and w for which v links to w in the directed contact network. Here, higher values of $p_{v,w}$ correspond to closer contact and more likely contagion, while lower values indicate less intensive contact. We can also choose to model the infectious period as random in length by assuming that an infected node has a probability q of recovering in each step while it is infected, and leaving the other details of the model as they are.

More elaborate extensions to the model involve separating the I state into a sequence of several states (e.g., early, middle, and late periods of the infection) and allowing the contagion probabilities to vary across these states [238]. This could be used, for example, to model a disease with a highly contagious incubation period, followed by a less contagious period while symptoms are being expressed. Researchers have also considered variations on the SIR model in which the disease-causing pathogen is mutating (and thus changing its disease characteristics) over the course of the outbreak [183].

The Role of the Basic Reproductive Number. We now discuss some observations about the SIR model, focusing on the most basic version of the model in an arbitrary network. First, let's recall the claim, made at the end of Section 21.2, that in networks that do not have a tree structure, the simple dichotomy in epidemic behavior determined by the basic reproductive number R_0 does not necessarily hold. In fact, it is not difficult to construct an example showing how this dichotomy breaks down. To do this, let's start with the network depicted in Figure 21.3, and suppose that these layers of two nodes at a time continue indefinitely to the right. Let's consider an SIR epidemic in which $t_I = 1$, the infection probability p is $\frac{2}{3}$, and the two nodes at the far left are the ones that are initially infected.

When we don't have a tree network, we need to decide how to define an analog of the basic reproductive number. In a network as highly structured as the one in Figure 21.3, we can work directly from the definition of R_0 as the expected number of new cases of the disease caused by a single individual. (For less structured networks, one can consider R_0 to be the expected number of new cases caused by a randomly chosen individual from the population.) In Figure 21.3, each infected node has edges to two nodes in the next layer; since it infects each with probability $\frac{2}{3}$, the expected number of new cases caused by this node is $\frac{4}{3}$.

So in our example, $R_0 > 1$. Despite this fact, however, it is easy to see that the disease will die out almost surely after reaching only a finite number of steps. In each layer, there are four edges leading to the next layer, and each will independently fail to transmit the disease with probability $\frac{1}{3}$. Therefore, with probability $\left(\frac{1}{3}\right)^4 = \frac{1}{81}$, all four edges will fail to transmit the disease; at this point, these four edges become a "roadblock" guaranteeing the disease can never reach the portion of the network beyond them. Thus, as the disease moves along in a layer-by-layer fashion, there is a probability of at least $\frac{1}{81}$ that each layer will be its last. Therefore, with probability 1, it must come to an end after a finite number of layers.

This is a very simple example, but it already indicates how different network structures can be more or less conducive to the spread of a disease – even taking contagiousness and other disease properties as given. Whereas the contact network of the simple branching process from Section 21.2 was a tree that expanded rapidly in all directions, the network in Figure 21.3 forces the disease to pass through a narrow "channel" in which a small breakdown in contagion can wipe it out. Understanding how specific types of network structure interact with disease dynamics remains a challenging research question – and one that affects predictions about the course of real epidemics.

SIR Epidemics and Percolation. Thus far we have been thinking about SIR epidemics as dynamic processes, in which the state of the network evolves step by step over time. This captures the temporal dynamics of the disease itself as it spreads through a population. Interestingly, however, there is an equivalent and completely static view of these epidemics that is often very useful from a modeling point of view [44, 173].

We now describe how to arrive at this static view of the process, focusing on the basic SIR model in which $t_I = 1$. Consider a point in an SIR epidemic when a node v has just become infectious, and it has a susceptible neighbor w. Node v has one chance to infect w (since $t_I = 1$), and it succeeds with probability p. We can view the outcome of this random event as being determined by flipping a coin that has a probability p of coming up "heads" and observing the outcome. From the point of view of the process, it clearly does not matter whether the coin was flipped at the moment that node v first became infectious or whether it was flipped at the very beginning of the whole process and is only being revealed now. Continuing this reasoning, we can in fact assume that for *each* edge in the contact network – from a node v to a node w – a coin with "heads" probability p is flipped at the very beginning of the process (independently of the coins for all other pairs of neighbors), and the result is stored so that it can be later checked *in the event* that node v becomes infectious while node w is susceptible.

With all the coins flipped in advance, the SIR process can be viewed as follows. The edges in the contact network for which the coin flip is successful are declared to be *open*; the remaining edges are declared to be *blocked*. The situation is now as pictured in Figure 21.4, which shows a sample result of coin flips consistent with the pattern of

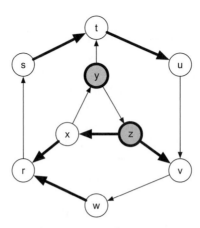

Figure 21.4. An equivalent way to view an SIR epidemic is in terms of *percolation*, where we decide in advance which edges transmit infection (should the opportunity arise) and which do not.

infections in the example from Figure 21.2. And we can now see how to make use of the open and blocked edges to represent the course of the epidemic:

> A node v will become infected during the epidemic if and only if there is a path to v from one of the initially infected nodes that consists entirely of open edges.

Thus, while Figure 21.4 looks superficially different from the sequence of stages in Figure 21.2, it is in fact a beautifully compact way to summarize the course of the epidemic: the nodes that are eventually infected are precisely those that can be reached from the initially infected nodes along a sequence of open edges in the network.

This static view of the model is often referred to as *percolation*, due to the following physical analogy. If we think of the contact network as a system of pipes, and the pathogen as a fluid moving through these pipes, then the edges in the contact network for which contagion succeeds are the "open" pipes and the edges for which it fails are the "blocked" pipes. We now want to know which nodes the fluid will reach, given that it can only pass through open pipes. In fact, this is not simply an illustrative metaphor; percolation is a topic that has been extensively studied by physicists and mathematicians as a model for the flow of fluids through certain types of porous media [69, 173]. It is both an interesting topic in its own right and useful for its role as an equivalent view of the progress of an epidemic.

21.4 The SIS Epidemic Model

In the previous sections we have considered models for epidemics in which each individual contracts the disease at most once. However, a simple variation on these models allows us to reason about epidemics in which nodes can be reinfected multiple times.

To represent such epidemics, we have nodes that simply alternate between two possible states: susceptible (S) and infectious (I). There is no *removed* state here;

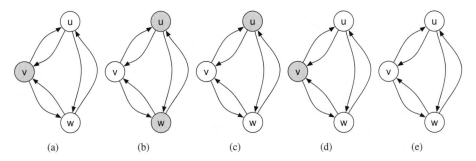

    (a)   (b)   (c)   (d)   (e)

Figure 21.5. In an SIS epidemic, nodes can be infected, recover, and then be infected again. In each step, the nodes in the infectious state are shaded.

rather, after a node is done with the infectious state, it cycles back to the susceptible state and is ready to catch the disease again. Because of this alternation between the S and I states, we refer to the model as the *SIS model*.

Aside from the lack of an R state, the mechanics of the model follow the SIR process very closely:

- Initially, some nodes are in the I state and all others are in the S state.
- Each node v that enters the I state remains infectious for a fixed number of steps t_I.
- During each of these t_I steps, node v has a probability p of passing the disease to each of its susceptible neighbors.
- After t_I steps, node v is no longer infectious, and it returns to the S state.

Figure 21.5 shows an example of the SIS model unfolding on a three-node contact network with $t_I = 1$. Notice how node v starts out infected, recovers, and later becomes infected again – we can imagine this as the contact network within a three-person apartment, or a three-person family, where people pass a disease on to others they're living with and then get it back from them later.

As with the SIR model, the SIS model can be extended to handle more general kinds of assumptions: different contagion probabilities between different pairs of people; probabilistic recovery from the disease, in which each infected node transitions back to the susceptible state with probability q at each step; and multiple stages of infection, with varying disease properties across them.

Life Cycles of SIR and SIS Epidemics. The examples in this section and the preceding one suggest that the overall "trajectories" of SIR and SIS epidemics on (finite-size) graphs are qualitatively quite different. An SIR epidemic on a finite graph is burning through a bounded supply of nodes – since nodes can never be reinfected – and therefore it must come to an end after a relatively small number of steps. An SIS epidemic, on the other hand, can run for an extremely long time as it cycles through the nodes potentially multiple times. But as Figure 21.5(e) illustrates, if there ever comes a point in an SIS epidemic when all nodes are simultaneously free of the disease, then the epidemic has died forever: there are no longer any infected individuals to pass the disease to others. And on a finite graph, there will eventually (with probability 1) come a point in time when all contagion attempts simultaneously fail for t_I steps in a row, and at this point it will be over. Thus, a key question with an SIS epidemic on a given contact network is to understand how long the outbreak will last and how many individuals will be affected at different points in time.

For contact networks where the structure is mathematically tractable, researchers have in fact proved "knife-edge" results for the SIS model similar to our dichotomy for branching processes. These results, for particular classes of contact networks, show that at a particular critical value of the contagion probability p, an SIS epidemic on the network will undergo a rapid shift from one that dies out quickly to one that persists for a very long time [52, 278]. This type of analysis tends to be mathematically quite complex, and this critical value of the contagion probability p depends in subtle ways on the structure of the network.

A Connection Between SIR and SIS Epidemics. Despite the differences between the SIR and SIS models, in fact it is possible to represent some of the basic variants of the SIS model as special cases of the SIR model. This surprising relationship is further evidence of the flexibility of the basic epidemic models, in which formalisms defined in different ways turn out to have very close connections to each other.

We describe the relationship for the SIS model with $t_I = 1$, when each node is infectious for a single step before recovering. The key insight is that if we think about a node v as in fact being a "different individual" at each time step, then we can represent things so that nodes are never reinfected. Specifically, given an instance of the SIS model with $t_I = 1$, we create a separate copy of each node for each time step $t = 0, 1, 2, 3$ and onward. We will call this the *time-expanded contact network*. Now, for each edge in the original contact network, linking a node v to a node w, we create edges in the time-expanded contact network from the copy of v at time t to the copy of w at time $t + 1$; this simply encodes the idea that node w can potentially catch the disease at time $t + 1$ if node v is infected at time t. Figure 21.6(a) shows this construction applied to the contact network from Figure 21.5.

The point is that the same SIS disease dynamics that previously circulated around in the original contact network can now flow forward in time through the time-expanded contact network, with copies of nodes that are in the I state at time t producing new infections in copies of nodes at time $t + 1$. But on this time-expanded graph we have an SIR process, since any copy of a node can be treated as removed (R) once its one time step of infection is over; with this view of the process, we have the same distribution of outcomes as the original SIS process. Figure 21.6(b) shows the course of the SIR epidemic that corresponds to the SIS epidemic in Figure 21.5.

21.5 Synchronization

The models we've developed give us a framework for thinking about various broader issues in the spread of disease. We already encountered one of these issues in the dichotomy for branching processes, which provided a formal basis for the sensitivity of outbreaks to small variations in contagiousness and for the crucial role of the basic reproductive number. We now look at a related issue in the global dynamics of a

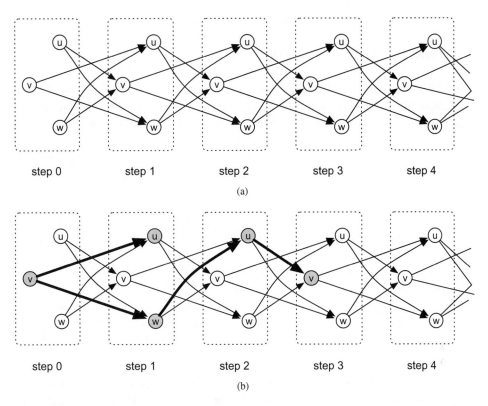

Figure 21.6. An SIS epidemic can be represented in the SIR model by (a) creating a separate copy of the contact network for each time step (using a time-expanded contact network). A node at time t can infect its contact neighbors at time $t + 1$. (b) The SIS epidemic can then be modeled as an SIR epidemic on this time-expanded network.

disease – the tendency for epidemics of certain diseases to synchronize across a population, sometimes producing strong oscillations in the number of affected individuals over time. Such effects are well known for diseases such as measles [196, 213] and syphilis [195].

When looking at public-health data, it is natural to look at periodic oscillations in the number of cases of a disease and to try positing external causes for the effect. For example, cycles in the prevalence of syphilis across the United States over the past 50 years have traditionally been attributed to large-scale societal changes, including changes in sexual mores and other forces [195]. While such factors clearly play a role, recent research has shown that oscillations and synchronization over time can in fact result largely from the contagion dynamics of the disease itself, and that similar patterns can be created in direct simulations of the disease using the types of models we have been considering here [195, 267].

We now describe how such effects can be produced using simple epidemic models. The crucial ingredients appear to be a combination of temporary immunity and long-range links in the contact network. Roughly, long-range links produce coordination in the timing of flare-ups across dispersed parts of the network; when these subside, the temporary immunity produces a network-wide deficit in the number and connectivity of susceptible individuals, yielding a large "trough" in the size of the outbreak that directly follows the "peak" from the earlier flare-ups. We now describe how to make this intuitive picture concrete using simple models.

The SIRS Epidemic Model. The first step in producing a model with oscillations is to allow the disease to confer temporary but not permanent immunity on infected individuals – a feature of many real diseases. To do this, we combine elements of the SIR and SIS models in a simple way: after an infected node recovers, it passes briefly through the R state on its way back to the S state. We call the resulting model the *SIRS model* [267], since nodes pass through the sequence S-I-R-S as the epidemic proceeds. In detail, the model works as follows.

- Initially, some nodes are in the I state and all others are in the S state.
- Each node v that enters the I state remains infectious for a fixed number of steps t_I.
- During each of these t_I steps, node v has a probability p of passing the disease to each of its susceptible neighbors.
- *(The new feature of the model.)* After t_I steps, node v is no longer infectious. It then enters the R state for a fixed number of steps t_R. During this time, it cannot be infected with the disease, nor does it transmit the disease to other nodes. After t_R steps in the R state, node v returns to the S state.

For an SIRS epidemic, the course of the disease through a population is clearly affected not just by the quantities p and t_I, but also by the length t_R of the temporary immunity that is conferred.

Small-World Contact Networks. Temporary immunity can produce oscillations in very localized parts of the network, with patches of immunity following large numbers of infections in a concentrated area. But to produce large fluctuations that can be seen at the level of the full network, the flare-ups of the disease have to be coordinated so that they happen at roughly the same time in many different places. A natural mechanism to produce this kind of coordination is to have a network that is rich in long-range connections, linking otherwise far-apart sections of the network.

This kind of structure is familiar from our discussion of small-world properties in Chapter 20. There, we considered network models where many of the links were "local" and clustered – connecting nodes with very similar social and geographic characteristics, according to the principle of homophily – while some were long-range links, corresponding to weak ties that link very different parts of the network. In Chapter 20 we focused on the effect this kind of structure has on the distances between nodes. But there is a closely related consequence: long-range links make it possible for things that happen in one part of the network to quickly affect what is happening elsewhere.

Watts and Strogatz observed the relevance of small-world properties to synchronization in their original paper on the topic [411], and Kuperman and Abramson showed how it could naturally lead to synchronization and oscillation in epidemics [267]. For their analysis they constructed random networks with small-world properties, in a manner very similar to the grid-plus-random-edges construction discussed in Chapter 20.

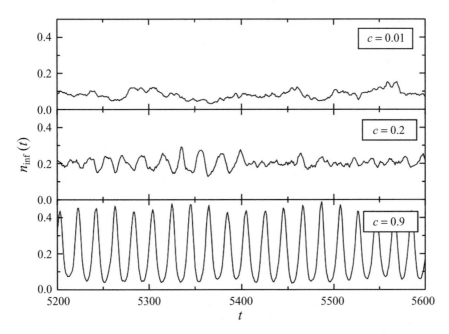

Figure 21.7. These plots depict the number of infected people over time (the quantity $n_{inf}(t)$ on the y-axis) by SIRS epidemics in networks with different proportions of long-range links. With c representing the fraction of long-range links, we see an absence of oscillations for small c ($c = 0.01$), wide oscillations for large c ($c = 0.9$), and a transitional region ($c = 0.2$) where oscillations intermittently appear and then disappear. (Results and image from [267], courtesy of the American Physical Society.)

Instead of the version from that chapter, however, they more closely followed the original construction of Watts and Strogatz, in which a ring network is rewired to produce random shortcuts [411]. Specifically, they started with a graph in which the nodes are arranged in a ring, and each node is connected to its neighbors for some number of steps in each direction. These are all homophilous links, in that they connect nodes that are very close together on the ring. Then, independently with some probability c, they turned each edge into a weak tie by rewiring one end of it to a node chosen uniformly at random. Thus, the probability c controls the fraction of links in the network that serve as long-range weak ties.

When the SIRS model is run on this kind of network, one finds very different behavior depending on the value of c, as indicated in Figure 21.7. When c is very small, disease transmission through the network occurs mainly via the short-range local edges, and so flare-ups of the disease in one part of the network never become coordinated with flare-ups in other parts. As c increases, these flare-ups start to synchronize, and since each burst produces a large number of nodes with temporary immunity, there is a subsequent trough as the disease has difficulty making its way through the sparser set of available targets. For very large values of c (such as $c = 0.9$ in Figure 21.7), there are clear waves in the number of affected individuals; for intermediate values of c (such as $c = 0.2$), one observes interesting effects in which the system achieves network-wide synchronization for a period, and then seems to fall back "out of sync" for reasons that are hard to quantify.

These results show how fairly complex epidemic dynamics can arise from simple models of contagion and contact structure. There are, however, a number of interesting open questions; the results discussed here have been primarily found through simulation, and analyzing the onset of synchronization mathematically in this model remains largely unexplored.

Sychronization in Epidemic Data. It is possible to study these effects empirically – and evaluate proposed models – using extensive records of disease prevalence that reach back many years. Grassly, Fraser, and Garnett [195] performed an instructive comparison of syphilis and gonorrhea that illustrates a number of synchronization principles. The prevalence of syphilis exhibits prominent oscillations on an 8- to 11-year cycle, whereas gonorrhea exhibits very little in the way of periodic behavior. Yet the two diseases affect similar populations and are presumably subject to very similar societal forces.

These differences are consistent, however, with the fact that syphilis confers limited temporary immunity after infection, while gonorrhea does not. Moreover, the timing of the syphilis cycles fits well with the timing of the immune properties associated with it. And from the cyclic patterns, one finds that the extent of synchronization between different regions of the United States increases over time, suggesting that the contact network over which it spread became increasingly connected with cross-country links over the second half of the twentieth century [195].

There are many further directions in which research on epidemic synchronization is proceeding, including attempts to model more complex temporal phenomena. For example, data sets for some diseases such as measles show that epidemics in different cities can synchronize so as to be *out of phase*, with the flare-ups in one city consistently coinciding with troughs in the other [196]. More than simply long-range contacts are required to explain such properties [213]. There is also the question of how immunization, prevention programs, and other medical interventions can take advantage of these timing properties – another way in which insights from even simple models can help to inform decision making in this area.

21.6 Transient Contacts and the Dangers of Concurrency

Thus far, our epidemic models have taken the underlying contact network to be a relatively static object, in which all the links in the contact network are present throughout the course of the epidemic. This is a reasonable simplifying assumption for diseases that are relatively contagious and spread quickly, at a rate faster than the typical creation or dissolution of a contact.

But as we move down the spectrum toward diseases that spread through a population over longer time scales, it is useful to revisit these assumptions. For a disease like HIV/AIDS, the epidemic progresses over many years, and its course is heavily dependent on the properties of the sexual contact network. Most people have zero, one, or very few contacts at any single point in time (a few people have many, which is important as well), and the identities of these contacts can shift significantly while the disease progresses, as new sexual partnerships are formed and others break up.

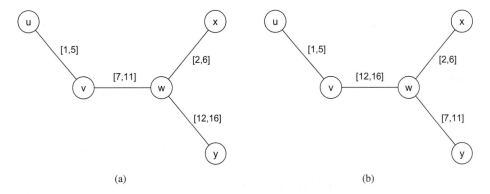

Figure 21.8. (a) In a contact network, we can annotate the edges with time windows during which they existed. (b) The same network as in (a), except that the timing of the *w–v* and *w–y* partnerships have been reversed. Different timings for the edges in a contact network can affect the potential for a disease to spread among individuals. For example, in (a) the disease can potentially pass all the way from node *u* to node *y*, while in (b) it cannot.

So for modeling the contact network in such diseases, it is important to take into account the fact that contacts are *transient* – they do not necessarily last through the whole course of the epidemic, but only for particular windows of time. Thus, we will consider contact networks in which each edge is annotated with the *period of time* during which it existed – the time range over which it was possible for one endpoint of the edge to have passed the disease directly to the other.

Figure 21.8(a) shows an example of this kind of annotation, with the numbers inside square brackets indicating the time ranges when each edge exists. Thus the *u–v* and *w–x* partnerships happen first, and they overlap in time; after this, node *w* has a partnership with node *v* and then later with node *y*. Note also that for this section – in keeping with the motivation from HIV/AIDS and simiar diseases – we assume the edges to be undirected rather than directed, to indicate that infection can pass in either direction between a pair of people in a partnership. (As in previous sections, we could also accomplish this by having directed edges pointing in both directions between each pair of connected people, but since everything here will be symmetric, it is more convenient to use undirected edges.)

The Consequences of Transient Contacts. A little experimentation with the example in Figure 21.8(a) indicates how the timing of different edges can affect the spread of a disease. For example, if node *u* has the disease at time 1, it is possible for it to spread all the way to node *y*, through nodes *v* and *w* as intermediaries. (Of course, if contagion is probabilistic as before, it will not necessarily succeed in spreading, but it has the potential to do so.) On the other hand, node *u* cannot spread the disease to node *x*: node *u* could pass the disease to node *v*, which could pass it to node *w*, but by the time it reaches node *w*, the partnership of *w* and *x* is long over.

Moreover, changing the timing of partnerships can change the possible transmission pathways, even as the set of underlying contacts remains the same. For instance, the example in Figure 21.8(b) differs from the one in Figure 21.8(a) only in that the temporal order of the *w–v* and *w–y* partnerships has been reversed. But notice that

(a) (b)

Figure 21.9. A disease tends to be able to spread more widely with concurrent partnerships than with serial partnerships: node *v*'s two partnerships are shown happening either (a) serially or (b) concurrently.

while node *u* was able to pass the disease all the way to node *y* in Figure 21.8(a), it cannot do so in Figure 21.8(b): in the latter case, the *w–y* partnership is over by the time the disease could possibly get from node *u* to node *w*.

Such considerations are crucial for health workers and epidemiologists to map out the contact networks associated with a disease such as HIV/AIDS. For example, we can see from the difference between Figures 21.8(a) and 21.8(b) that in order for node *y* to know whether he or she is at risk from a disease carried by node *u*, it is not enough to map out the full set of sexual partnerships; it is crucial to know information about the order of events as well. Or if we go back to the striking Figure 2.7 from Chapter 2, mapping out the relationships within a high school, we can appreciate that the image itself is not enough to fully chart the potential spread of diseases through this population – we would also need to know the timing of these relationships.

Networks in which the edges only exist for specific periods of time have been the subject of modeling efforts in many areas, including sociology [182, 305, 258], epidemiology [307, 406], mathematics [106], and computer science [53, 239]. It is an issue that is relevant not just to the spread of disease but also to a wide range of settings that are modeled by networks. For example, the diffusion of information, ideas, and behaviors through social networks clearly also depends on how the timing of different communications between people either enables or blocks the flow of information to different parts of the population.

Concurrency. Differences in the timing of contacts do not just affect who has the potential to spread a disease to whom; the pattern of timing can influence the severity of the overall epidemic itself. A timing pattern of particular interest – and concern – to HIV researchers is *concurrency* [307, 406].

A person is involved in *concurrent* partnerships if he or she has two or more active partnerships that overlap in time. For example, in each of Figures 21.9(a) and 21.9(b), node *v* has partnerships with each of nodes *u* and *w*. But in the first of these figures, the partnerships happen serially – first one, then the other – whereas in the second, they happen concurrently, overlapping in time. The concurrent pattern causes the disease to circulate more vigorously through this three-person network. Nodes *u* and *w* may not be aware of each other's existence, but the concurrent partnerships make it possible for either node *u* or node *w* to spread the disease to the other; the serial partnerships only allow spreading from node *u* to node *w*, but not the other way. In larger examples one can find more extreme effects; for example, Figure 21.10(b) differs from Figure 21.10(a) only in that the time windows of the partnerships have been "pushed together" so that they all overlap. But the effect is considerable: where the pattern in Figure 21.10(a) allowed different parts of the network to be "walled off" from each other by the timing

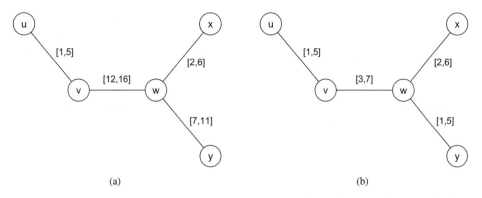

Figure 21.10. In larger networks, the effects of concurrency on disease spreading can become particularly pronounced. (a) No node is involved in any concurrent partnerships; (b) all partnerships overlap in time.

effects, the concurrent partnerships make it possible for any node with the disease to potentially spread it to any other.

In simulations with various notions of concurrency, Morris and Kretzschmar found that small changes in the amount of concurrency – keeping other variables like the average number and duration of partnerships fixed – could produce large changes in the size of the epidemic [307]. Qualitatively, this aligns well with the intuition from earlier sections – changing the average number of new cases of a disease caused by an infected individual even slightly can sometimes have significant consequences. For some of the simplest models, such as the branching process, it is possible to make this intuition precise; for more complex models, such as the present one involving concurrency in arbitrary networks, it remains the topic of ongoing research.

Concurrency is just one particular kind of pattern to be found in the timing of relationships in a contact network. Further research in this area could possibly uncover more subtle patterns as well; the interaction of timing and network structure has the potential to provide further insights into the way diseases spread through the changing contacts within a population.

21.7 Genealogy, Genetic Inheritance, and Mitochondrial Eve

Our discussion of epidemics has provided us with a way of thinking about processes that spread randomly over time through a network. As mentioned earlier, this framework is useful for modeling many kinds of things that spread, not just diseases. The spread of information can be modeled this way, as an alternative to the approaches based on explicit decision rules discussed in Chapter 19. In such settings, adapting the ideas from this chapter can be relatively straightforward but still very informative.

In this section, instead, we apply the perspective of random spreading to a situation where the connection is at first a bit more subtle; it takes a little work to precisely identify the network and the process that is spreading through it. The setting is that of genetic inheritance. What we will find is that if we view the inheritance of traits as a random process that takes place on a network linking organisms in successive generations – in other words, with edges connecting parents to their offspring – then we can obtain insight into some fundamental hereditary processes. We start with a story that illustrates some of the basic genetic issues we'll consider.

Mitochondrial Eve. In 1987, Rebecca Cann, Mark Stoneking, and Allan Wilson published a paper in the journal *Nature* [94] in which they provided evidence for a rather striking proposition. Consider following your maternal ancestry backward in time through human history, producing a trail that goes from you to your mother, to her mother (i.e., your maternal grandmother), to *her* mother, and so on indefinitely. Each of us in principle can produce such a maternal ancestry trail, which we'll call a maternal *lineage*. Now, the claim of Cann, Stoneking, and Wilson was that all these lineages in fact meet at a single woman who lived between 100,000 and 200,000 years ago, probably in Africa. She is at the root of all our maternal ancestries.

Let's first ask how they reached this conclusion, and then consider what it signifies. One way to infer facts about maternal ancestries is to study the DNA found not in our cells' nuclei but in the much smaller, separate genome that each of us has in our cells' mitochondria. Unlike nuclear DNA, which contains parts of both our parents' genomes, this mitochondrial DNA is (to a first approximation) passed to children entirely from their mothers. So roughly speaking, aside from random mutations, you have your mother's DNA, she has her mother's DNA, and so on through your maternal ancestry. With this in mind, Cann, Stoneking, and Wilson analyzed the mitochondrial DNA of people drawn from a wide sample of geographic and ethnic backgrounds; using standard techniques to estimate the rate at which genetic sequences will diverge through random mutations over many generations, they concluded that all the mitochondrial DNA in this population likely had a common origin roughly 100,000 to 200,000 years ago. By "common origin" here, we mean a single mitochondrial genome belonging to a single human being; because she is the source of the mitochondrial DNA of everyone on Earth, researchers standardly refer to this woman as *Mitochondrial Eve*.

This finding caught the public imagination when it was first announced; it received a fair amount of media attention at the time, and its implications have been nicely explored in general books about human history [333]. The analysis involved in the original finding has since been refined by a number of other research groups; caveats have been introduced due to the fact that the inheritance of mitochondrial DNA may be more complicated than originally thought, but the basic conclusion has been mainly accepted at a general level.

As to what this finding signifies: on first hearing, it takes a bit of thought to sort out what it implies and what it doesn't. It is indeed striking to be able to posit the existence of a single person from the not-so-distant evolutionary past who is an ancestor of everyone. Mitochondrial Eve (in contrast to her namesake Eve from the Bible) was not asserted to be the only living woman in her time; there were presumably many other women living at the same time as her. But from the point of view of present-day mitochondrial DNA, all these women are genetically irrelevant: somewhere along the line from then to now, each of their lines of mitchondrial DNA died out.

On the other hand, one also needs to be careful before attributing too much to the relatively recent existence of Mitochondrial Eve. In particular, although her contemporaries were genetically irrelevant to our mitochondrial DNA, they are not irrelevant to

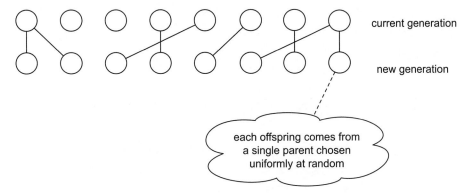

Figure 21.11. In the basic Wright–Fisher model of single-parent ancestry, time moves step by step in generations; there are a fixed number of individuals in each generation, and each offspring in a new generation comes from a single parent in the current generation.

the remainder of our genomes; each of us has genetic contributions from a large number of ancestors. (Though even here there is more going on than meets the eye, as we'll discuss shortly.) Moreover, the overlapping patterns of our respective ancestries are complex and still not well understood; what we learn from Mitochondrial Eve is that all our ancestries are pinned together along their maternal lines, a couple of hundred thousand years into the past.

Ultimately, the identification of Mitochondrial Eve was in a sense a showcase of ideas that had been emerging in the genetics community over the previous decade [245, 325]. These ideas were based on models that could predict the existence of common ancestors and make estimates about their recency. And they showed at a mathematical level, independent of the difficulty of establishing evidence from genetic data, that the existence of someone like Mitochondrial Eve was not only natural, but in fact – as we will see next – essentially inevitable. At their core, these models were built from a probabilistic formalism involving networks; indeed, even in a qualitative sense, one can appreciate something epidemic-like about the way in which copies of different people's mitochondrial DNA can spread through subsequent generations, inhabiting future offspring, until one eventually crowds out all the others. We now describe the basic versions of these models and how they connect to questions about ancestry.

A Model of Single-Parent Ancestry. We use a fundamental model of ancestry known in population genetics as the *Wright–Fisher model* [325]. To remain tractable, the model involves a number of simplifying assumptions. Consider a population that is constrained by resources to maintain a fixed size N in each generation. Time moves step by step from one generation to the next; each new generation is formed by having the current set of N individuals produce N offspring in total. Each offspring in this new generation is produced from a single parent, and this parent is selected independently and uniformly at random from among those in the current generation. Figure 21.11 depicts this process; as shown in the figure, we can draw the relationship of one generation to the next as a graph, with a node for each individual, and an edge connecting each offspring to their parent chosen uniformly at random from the previous generation. Notice that, because of this rule for selecting parents, certain

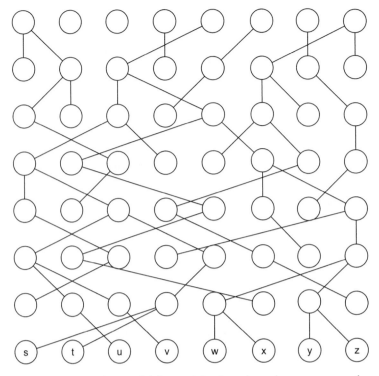

Figure 21.12. We can run the model forward in time through a sequence of generations, ending in a set of present-day individuals. Each present-day individual can then follow its single-parent lineage by following edges leading upward through the network.

individuals in the upper generation can have multiple children (such as the first and last in Figure 21.11), while others may have none.

The structure of this model reflects a few underlying assumptions. First, we're assuming a *neutral model* in which no individual has a selective advantage in reproduction; everyone has the same chance of producing offspring. Furthermore, we're modeling a situation in which each individual is produced from a *single* parent, as opposed to two parents in a sexually reproducing population. This is consistent with several possible interpretations.

- First, and most directly, it can be used to model species that engage in asexual reproduction, with each organism arising from a single parent.
- Second, it can be used to model single-parent inheritance even in sexually reproducing populations, including the inheritance of mitochondrial DNA among women as in our preceding discussion. In this interpretation, each node represents a human woman, with women linked to their mothers in the previous generation. Moreover, as we will discuss later, there is in fact a much more general way to use this model to think about inheritance in sexually reproducing populations.
- Third, it can be used to model purely "social" forms of inheritance, such as master–apprentice relationships. For example, if you receive a Ph.D. in an academic field, you generally have a single primary advisor. If you model students as being

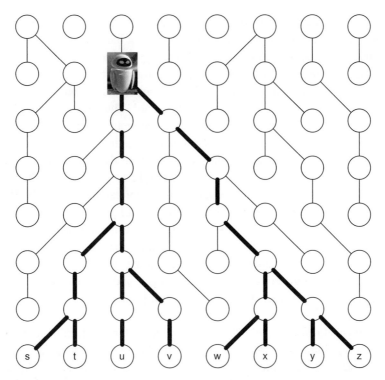

Figure 21.13. A redrawing of the single-parent network from Figure 21.12. As we move back in time, lineages of different present-day individuals coalesce until they have all converged at the most recent common ancestor.

"descended" from advisors, than we can trace ancestries through sequences of advisors back into the past – just as we traced maternal lineages.

Now, if we run this model forward in time through multiple generations, we get a network such as the one pictured in Figure 21.12. Each individual is connected to one parent in the previous generation; time runs from top to bottom, with N present-day individuals in the lowest layer (named s through z in the figure). Notice that from any one of these individuals at the bottom we can trace its single-parent lineage backward in time by following edges upward, always taking the single edge leading up out of each node we encounter.

If we imagine the individuals in the bottom row of Figure 21.12 to be present-day women, then Mitochondrial Eve would be the lowest node in the figure where all the maternal lineages first fully converge. It's a bit tricky, visually, to find this node in Figure 21.12, but we can re-draw the same ancestries with the paths unscrambled in Figure 21.13, and then the location of Eve becomes easy to see: she's the third node in the second row from the top (with the lineages leading back to her consisting of the darkened edges).

These examples indicate how the existence of common ancestors – and even the number of generations needed to reach them – can be predicted from the Wright–Fisher model. To do this, we employ a useful trick for reasoning about the model: we think of the ancestries as being built *backward* in time, rather than forward. In other words, an equivalent view of the model is to take a set of present-day individuals and construct earlier generations one at a time by having each current individual choose its parent in the previous generation independently and uniformly at random.

We can see how this works by moving upward through the levels of Figure 21.13. Whenever two individuals happen to choose the same parent, then their lineages *coalesce* into a common lineage from that point onward. Thus, we start with N distinct lineages in the present, but as we build generations going backward in time, the number of distinct lineages decreases whenever individuals of distinct lineages choose the same parent. This coalescence happens rapidly at first, when there are many lineages and the probability of a collision between lineages is high; as time goes on, the number of distinct lineages of present-day individuals shrinks more and more slowly. But whenever there is more than one distinct lineage, there is a finite expected time until two of them collide, and so the process must eventually reach a single lineage. The node at which this first happens is called the *most recent common ancestor* – the analog of Mitochondrial Eve in this model. The model is simple enough that one can estimate the expected time until the collisions among lineages, and hence the expected number of generations to the most recent common ancestor [245, 325].

Genetic Interpretations. While the maternal inheritance of mitochondrial DNA makes for a very simple single-parent process, the Wright–Fisher model is relevant to sexually reproducing populations for a much more fundamental reason. Although the chromosomes of your parents recombined to produce your genome, making your chromosomes a patchwork of theirs, any *single* point in your genome – a single nucleotide on one of your chromosomes – was inherited from just one of either your mother or your father. They, in turn, inherited it from just one of their mother or father, and so on. As a result, if we want to trace the ancestry of a single point in your genome, we are following a single-parent lineage, even though offspring are produced by sexual reproduction. The most recent common ancestor for this particular point, looking across a population of N individuals, thus follows from the same analysis we've just seen, as it did for mitochrondrial DNA.

Because of recombination, the lineages for one point in the genome may differ from the lineages for even a nearby point; hence, the most recent common ancestors may differ as well. One can develop probabilistic models for how these lineages relate to each other, but the analysis becomes much more complex [418].

There are many other issues that arise when extending these simplified models to more complex genetic applications. For example, geographic barriers in a population can isolate individuals from each other, and this can have an effect on the patterns of interaction among lineages [354]. More generally, spatial constraints on the interactions among individuals can affect these patterns, providing another setting in which network properties can potentially inform broader conclusions about genetic outcomes.

21.8 Advanced Material: Analysis of Branching and Coalescent Processes

In this section, we analyze two of the basic processes discussed in this chapter: the *branching process* for the spread of an epidemic with simplified contact network structure, and the *coalescent process* for the merging of lineages back to a common ancestor. Both of these analyses are based on probabilistic reasoning involving branching tree structures: the first as the epidemic spreads forward through individuals, and the second as the lineages travel backward in time.

A. Analysis of Branching Processes

Recall the branching process model that we considered in Section 21.2: each infected individual meets k others and infects each with probability p. Thus, the expected number of new cases of the disease caused by each infected individual is $R_0 = pk$, the *basic reproductive number*. We want to show that the persistence of the disease depends critically on whether R_0 is smaller or larger than 1, a notion that we will formulate as follows.

Recall that the population in this model is organized into a *tree* [as shown in Figure 21.1(a)] in which every node is connected to k nodes just below it. Let q_n denote the probability that the epidemic survives for at least n waves – in other words, that some individual in the nth level of the tree becomes infected. Let q^* be the limit of q_n as n goes to infinity; we can think of this as the probability that the disease persists indefinitely. We will prove the following claim.

Claim: (a) If $R_0 < 1$ then $q^* = 0$. (b) If $R_0 > 1$ then $q^* > 0$.

This establishes the "knife-edge" quality of R_0 that we discussed in Section 21.2.

The Expected Number of Infected Individuals. We start by considering an approach to this problem that gets us partway to a proof of the claim: considering the expected number of infected individuals at each level of the tree.

First, let's consider the total number of individuals at each level. The number of individuals at any given level exceeds the number at the previous level by a factor of k, and therefore the number who are at level n is k^n. (This is also true at level $n = 0$; the top level consists of just the root, and $k^0 = 1$.)

Now, let X_n be a random variable equal to the number of infected individuals at level n. One way to think about the expected value $E[X_n]$ is to write X_n as a sum of simpler random variables as follows. For each individual j at level n, let Y_{nj} be a random variable equal to 1 if j is infected, and equal to 0 otherwise. Then

$$X_n = Y_{n1} + Y_{n2} + \cdots + Y_{nm},$$

where $m = k^n$, since the right-hand side simply counts, one by one, the number of infected individuals at level n. Linearity of expectation says that the expectation of the sum of a set of random variables is equal to the sum of their expectations, and so

$$E[X_n] = E[Y_{n1} + Y_{n2} + \cdots + Y_{nm}] = E[Y_{n1}] + E[Y_{n2}] + \cdots + E[Y_{nm}]. \quad (21.1)$$

The reason to write things this way is that each expectation on the right-hand side is extremely easy to work out: $E[Y_{nj}] = 1 \times \Pr[Y_{nj} = 1] + 0 \times \Pr[Y_{nj} = 0] = \Pr[Y_n = 1]$, and so the expectation of each Y_{nj} is just the probability that individual j gets infected.

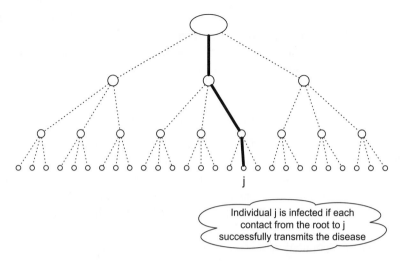

Figure 21.14. To determine the probability that a particular node is infected, we multiply the (independent) probabilities of infection on each edge leading from the root to the node.

Individual j at depth n gets infected precisely when all of the n contacts leading from the root to j successfully transmit the disease, as shown in Figure 21.14. Since each contact transmits the disease independently with probability p, individual j is infected with probability p^n. Therefore, $E\left[Y_{nj}\right] = p^n$. We have already concluded that there are k^n individuals at level n of the tree, and hence k^n terms on the right-hand side of Equation (21.1). Therefore, as summed up in Figure 21.15, we conclude that

$$E\left[X_n\right] = p^n k^n = (pk)^n = R_0^n. \tag{21.2}$$

From Expected Values to Probabilities of Persistence. Equation (21.2) suggests the importance of the basic reproductive number R_0 in reasoning about the spread of an

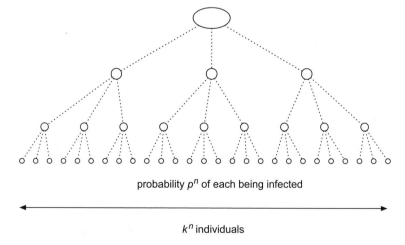

Figure 21.15. The expected number of individuals infected at level n is the product of the number of individuals at that level (k^n) and the probability that each is infected (p^n).

epidemic in the branching process model. Now let's consider what this tells us about q^*, the probability that the epidemic persists indefinitely.

First, the fact that $E[X_n] = R_0^n$ immediately establishes part (a) the claim we are trying to prove, that when $R_0 < 1$ we have $q^* = 0$. To see why, we go back to the definition of $E[X_n]$ and apply a fact that we also found useful in Section 20.7. To recap the discussion there, the definition for the expected value is

$$E[X_n] = 1 \times \Pr[X_n = 1] + 2 \times \Pr[X_n = 2] + 3 \times \Pr[X_n = 3] + \cdots \quad (21.3)$$

and an alternate but equivalent way to write the right-hand side is

$$\Pr[X_n \geq 1] + \Pr[X_n \geq 2] + \Pr[X_n \geq 3] + \cdots, \quad (21.4)$$

since we observe that each term $\Pr[X_n = i]$ contributes exactly i copies of itself to the sum in (21.4). Therefore, we have

$$E[X_n] = \Pr[X_n \geq 1] + \Pr[X_n \geq 2] + \Pr[X_n \geq 3] + \cdots. \quad (21.5)$$

From Equation (21.5) we observe that $E[X_n]$ must be at least as large as the first term on the right-hand side, and so $E[X_n] \geq \Pr[X_n \geq 1]$. Notice also that $\Pr[X_n \geq 1]$ is precisely the definition of q_n, and so $E[X_n] \geq q_n$. But $E[X_n] = R_0^n$, which is converging to 0 as n grows; hence, q_n must also be converging to 0. This shows that $q^* = 0$ when $R_0 < 1$.

Now, when $R_0 > 1$, the expected values $E[X_n] = R_0^n$ go to infinity as n grows. *However*, this fact by itself is not enough to show that $q^* > 0$. It is entirely possible to have a sequence of random variables for which $E[X_n]$ goes to infinity but $\Pr[X_n > 0]$ converges to 0 as n grows. (As a simple example, suppose that X_n were a random variable taking the value 4^n with probability 2^{-n}, and taking the value 0 otherwise. Then $E[X_n] = (4/2)^n = 2^n$, which goes to infinity, while $\Pr[X_n > 0] = 2^{-n}$, which goes to 0.)

This effect doesn't happen in our case, but these considerations do say that to establish $q^* > 0$ when $R_0 > 1$ we need to use something more specific about the process than simply the expected number of infected individuals. We do this now by developing a formula for q_n that in the end allows us to determine the value of q^* exactly.

A Formula for q_n. The quantity q_n depends on three more fundamental quantities: the number of contacts per individual k; the contagion probability p; and the level of the tree, n. In fact, it's difficult to write a direct formula for q_n in terms of these quantities, but it's not hard to express q_n in terms of q_{n-1}, which is what we'll do first.

Consider the root node, and let's first ask what it would take for the following event to hold:

(∗) The disease spreads through the root node's first contact j and then continues to persist down to n levels *in the part of the tree reachable through j*.

This event is illustrated in Figure 21.16. First, for the event (∗) to hold, it would require that j catches the disease directly from the root, which happens with probability p. At this point, j becomes completely analogous to the root node of its own branching process, consisting of all nodes reachable from it downward in the tree. So for event (∗) to hold, after j is infected, it is then necessary that the disease persists for $n - 1$

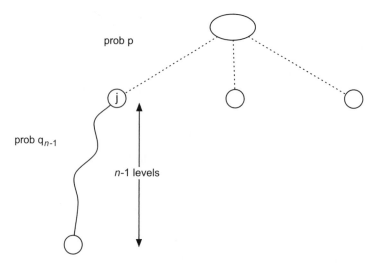

Figure 21.16. For an infection to occur at level n, the root must infect one of its immediate descendants, and then this descendant must, recursively, produce an infection at level $n - 1$.

levels in the version of the branching process in which we view node j as the root. This happens with probability q_{n-1}, by the definition of q_{n-1}. Therefore, the probability of the event (∗) is pq_{n-1}. Or, taking the complementary view, event (∗) fails to hold with probability

$$1 - pq_{n-1}.$$

Now, there is a copy of event (∗) for each of the direct contacts of the root node, and each fails to hold with probability $1 - pq_{n-1}$. Since they're independent, the probability that they *all* fail to hold is

$$(1 - pq_{n-1})^k.$$

At this point, we're almost done. The disease fails to persist down to level n of the tree, starting at the root, if it fails to reach level n through any of the root's direct contacts. In other words, the disease fails to persist to level n precisely when all the copies of event (∗), for each direct contact of the root, fail to hold. Again, we just determined that this probability is $(1 - pq_{n-1})^k$. But this probability is also $1 - q_n$, since by the definition of q_n, the quantity $1 - q_n$ is exactly the probability that the disease fails to persist to n levels. Therefore,

$$1 - q_n = (1 - pq_{n-1})^k$$

and solving for q_n we get

$$q_n = 1 - (1 - pq_{n-1})^k. \tag{21.6}$$

Since we are assuming that the root is infected, and we can treat the root as level 0 of the tree, we have $q_0 = 1$; this simply says that the root is infected with probability 1. Starting from $q_0 = 1$, we can then build up the values $q_1, q_2, q_3, \ldots$ in order, determining each from the previous value in the list using Equation (21.6). Simply being able to determine the values of each q_n this way, however, doesn't immediately tell us

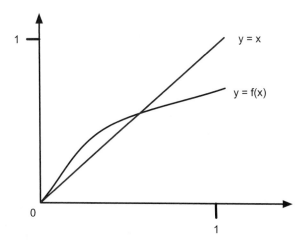

Figure 21.17. To determine the limiting probability of an infection at depth n, as n goes to infinity, we need to repeatedly apply the function $f(x) = 1 - (1 - px)^k$, which is the basis for the recurrence $q_n = f(q_{n-1})$.

where they're headed as n goes to infinity. For that we need a technique that looks at the limiting value of this sequence.

Following the Values q_n to a Limit. If we define the function $f(x) = 1 - (1 - px)^k$, then we can write Equation (21.6) as follows: $q_n = f(q_{n-1})$. This suggests a very clean, purely algebraic way of formulating our question about q^*. We have a function $f(x) = 1 - (1 - px)^k$, and we simply want to study the sequence of values $1, f(1), f(f(1)), f(f(f(1))), \ldots$, obtained by applying f repeatedly.

To get started thinking about this, let's plot the function f on a pair of x–y-axes, as in Figure 21.17. The following are some basic facts about f that help in producing this plot.

- First, $f(0) = 0$ and $f(1) = 1 - (1 - p)^k < 1$. This means that the plot of f passes through the origin but lies below the line $y = x$ once $x = 1$, as shown in Figure 21.17.
- Second, the derivative of f is $f'(x) = pk(1 - px)^k$. Notice that, as x ranges between 0 and 1, the quantity $f'(x)$ is positive but monotonically decreasing. This means that f has the increasing but concave shape depicted in Figure 21.17.
- Finally, the slope of f at $x = 0$ is equal to $f'(0) = pk = R_0$. So in the case when $R_0 > 1$, which is what we're focusing on now, the function f starts out above the line $y = x$ for small positive values of x.

When $R_0 > 1$, we can take these points together (that $y = f(x)$ starts out above $y = x$ for small positive values of x but ends up below it by the time we get to $x = 1$) and conclude that $y = f(x)$ must cross $y = x$ somewhere in the interval between 0 and 1, at a point $x^* > 0$.

Now, using this plot, let's take a geometric view of the sequence of values

$$1, f(1), f(f(1)), f(f(f(1))), \ldots$$

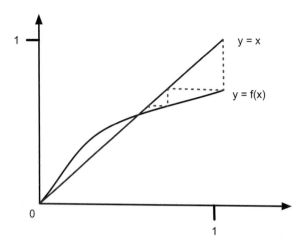

Figure 21.18. When we repeatedly apply the function $f(x)$, starting at $x = 1$, we can follow its trajectory by tracing out the sequence of steps between the curves $y = f(x)$ and $y = x$.

that we're analyzing. In particular, let's track this sequence on the line $y = x$. If we're currently at a particular point (x, x) on the line $y = x$, and we want to get to the point $(f(x), f(x))$, we can proceed as follows. We first move vertically to the curve $y = f(x)$, which puts us at the point $(x, f(x))$. We then move horizontally back to the line $y = x$, which puts us at the point $(f(x), f(x))$, as desired. This two-step vertical–horizontal motion is depicted as the first two parts of the dashed line in Figure 21.18. Continuing this process, we pass through all the points in the sequence x, $f(x)$, $f(f(x))$, ... along the line $y = x$.

If we start this from $x = 1$, as indicated in Figure 21.18, the process converges to the point (x^*, x^*) where the line $y = x$ meets the curve $y = f(x)$. Now we can go back to the interpretation of all this in terms of the branching process. The sequence of values 1, $f(1)$, $f(f(1))$, ... is precisely the sequence $q_0, q_1, q_2, \ldots$, as we argued earlier, and so we have concluded that it converges to $x^* > 0$: the unique point at which $f(x) = x$ in the interval strictly between 0 and 1.

This concludes the argument that when $R_0 > 1$, the probability that the epidemic persists for n levels converges to a positive value as n goes to infinity.

It is also worth noticing that this style of analysis shows that $q^* = 0$ when $R_0 < 1$. Indeed, when $R_0 < 1$, the curve $y = f(x)$ looks much like it does in Figure 21.17, *except* that its derivative at 0 is $R_0 < 1$, and so it lies below the line $y = x$ for the whole interval between 0 and 1. This means that when we follow the sequence of values 1, $f(1)$, $f(f(1))$, ... as the dashed lines do in Figure 21.18, it descends all the way to $x = 0$ without stopping at any intermediate point (see Figure 21.19). This shows that the resulting limit, which is q^*, is equal to 0 in this case.

B. Analysis of Coalescent Processes

We now analyze a different process from earlier in the chapter – the merging of ancestral lineages discussed in Section 21.7. In particular, we will derive an estimate of

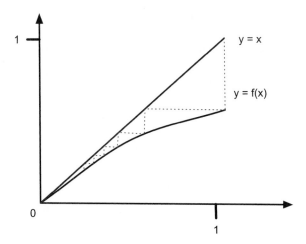

Figure 21.19. When $y = f(x)$ only intersects $y = x$ at 0, the repeated application of $f(x)$ starting at $x = 1$ converges to 0.

the expected number of generations one has to go back in order to find the most recent common ancestor for a set of individuals in the model from that section [245, 325]. Like the analysis of branching processes, this approach will require probabilistic calculations on trees. In this case, however, it is tricky to get an exact answer, and we will make use of two approximations as we estimate the required number of generations. (In fact, these approximations still allow for a very accurate estimate.)

In addition to the approximations, which we'll specify in context later, we start by varying the statement of the problem slightly, following the original work on the topic. Specifically, we will focus on a small sample of k individuals in a large population of size N; rather than analyzing the time until all lineages in the full population merge into a common ancestor, we will consider the time until the lineages of these k individuals merge into a common ancestor. This is reasonable from the point of view of applications, since generally one is only ever studying a fixed-size sample of a large population; also, the calculations involved provide insight into the question for the full population as well.

To recall the model from Section 21.7, adapted to the plan of looking at fixed-size samples of k individuals, we can pose the question as follows. There are N individuals in each generation. For each of the k individuals in the initial sample, we choose a parent for each uniformly at random from the previous generation. We continue working backward in time this way, extending each of the k lineages through earlier generations. Whenever we get to a generation where two individuals happen to choose the same parent, their lineages merge (since their ancestors will now be the same), and so the process continues with fewer distinct lineages to track. Finally, we stop when we first reach a point where the number of lineages has been reduced to one, a moment that we call *coalescence*. We want to estimate the expected time until coalescence occurs. Figure 21.20 illustrates this on an example with $k = 6$ initial present-day individuals (in the bottom row) and a population size of $N = 27$ (the number of nodes in each row).

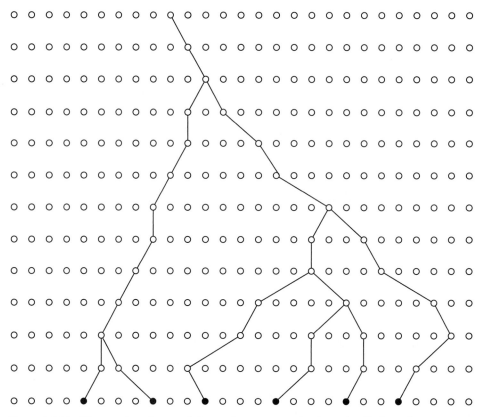

Figure 21.20. We can view the search for coalescence as a backward walk through a sequence of earlier generations, following lineages as they collide with each other.

The Probability That Lineages Collide in One Step. The key to this analysis is to consider a single step, in which we have a set of j distinct lineages that we're tracking; we want to estimate the probability that at least two of them will choose a common parent in the previous generation. (We will call this a *collision* between two lineages.)

The easiest case to think about is $j = 2$. Suppose we view the random choice as being made sequentially by the two lineages under consideration. The first lineage chooses a parent uniformly at random, and then there is only a collision if the second lineage picks the same parent uniformly at random from the N available choices. The probability that this occurs is therefore exactly $1/N$.

Things get more complicated when j is larger than 2. First, let's compute the probability that no two lineages collide by imagining that the lineages choose their parents one at a time. For no two lineages to collide, it must be the case that, after the first lineage chooses a parent, the second chooses a parent distinct from this one, the third chooses a parent distinct from these two, and so forth, up to the jth lineage, who must choose a parent distinct from the first $j - 1$. The probability that this happens is

$$\left(1 - \frac{1}{N}\right)\left(1 - \frac{2}{N}\right)\left(1 - \frac{3}{N}\right) \cdots \left(1 - \frac{j-1}{N}\right).$$

Expanding out this product, we see that it is equal to

$$1 - \left(\frac{1 + 2 + 3 + \cdots + j - 1}{N}\right) + \text{(terms with } N^2 \text{ or higher in the denominator)}.$$

In particular, it is at most

$$1 - \left(\frac{1 + 2 + 3 + \cdots + j - 1}{N}\right) + \frac{g(j)}{N^2}$$

for a function $g(\cdot)$ that depends only on j. So far this calculation has been exact, but here we come to the first of two approximations, following [245]: rather than deal with the complexity of this last term, we observe that when the population size N is much larger than j, expressions of the form $g(j)/N^2$ are negligible compared to $(1 + 2 + \cdots + j - 1)/N$. We therefore ignore them, and we approximate the probability that no two lineages collide by

$$1 - \left(\frac{1 + 2 + 3 + \cdots + j - 1}{N}\right) = 1 - \frac{j(j-1)}{2N}. \tag{21.7}$$

Now, when two lineages do in fact collide, there are a number of possibilities: it could be that there is simply a two-way collision between two of the lineages while all the others remain distinct, or it could be that more than two lineages collide in a single generation. We now describe how the latter scenario can come to pass, and then argue that it is very unlikely.

- First, it could be that three lineages all choose the same parent in a single generation. For any particular set of three lineages, the probability this happens is exactly $1/N^2$: if we imagine the choice being made sequentially, the first lineage can pick any parent, and then the second and third must independently pick this same parent from the N available choices. Now, since there are fewer than j^3 sets of three lineages, the probability that any three-way collision happens in a given generation is less than j^3/N^2. When N is much larger than j, this quantity is negligible compared to expressions in Equation (21.7) that only have N in the denominator.

- Alternately, it could be that two different pairs of lineages each have a separate, two-way collision in the same generation: suppose that lineage A collides with lineage B, and lineage C collides with lineage D. The collision of A and B has probability $1/N$, and the collision of C and D is an independent event, also with probability $1/N$. Therefore, for this particular choice of four lineages, both collisions happen with probability $1/N^2$. Since there are fewer than j^4 ways of choosing A, B, C, and D, the probability that there are simultaneous two-way collisions involving any choice of four lineages is less than j^4/N^2. Again, since N is much larger than j, this quantity is negligible compared to expressions that only have N in the denominator.

These arguments lead to our second approximation: we will assume there is never a generation prior to the most recent common ancestor in which we have more than a single two-way collision among lineages.

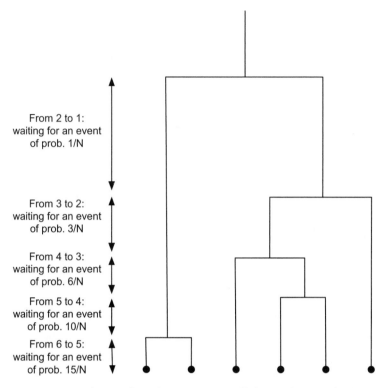

From 2 to 1:
waiting for an event
of prob. 1/N

From 3 to 2:
waiting for an event
of prob. 3/N

From 4 to 3:
waiting for an event
of prob. 6/N

From 5 to 4:
waiting for an event
of prob. 10/N

From 6 to 5:
waiting for an event
of prob. 15/N

Figure 21.21. Assuming that no three lineages ever collide simultaneously, the time to coalescence can be computed as the time for a sequence of distinct collision events to occur.

This means that when we have a generation in which the j current lineages fail to remain completely distinct, it happens because exactly two of them choose a common parent, reducing the number of lineages from j to $j - 1$.

The Expected Time Until Coalescence. Our two approximations have led to a very clean view of the process as it works backward in time. In this approximate view, we start with k distinct lineages and wait until two of them collide. This happens with probability $\frac{k(k-1)}{2N}$ in each generation. Once a collision happens, we have $k - 1$ distinct lineages, and we wait for two of them to collide with probability $\frac{(k-1)(k-2)}{2N}$ per generation. Things continue this way until we are down to two distinct lineages, at which point we wait for them to collide with probability $\frac{2}{2N} = \frac{1}{N}$ per generation. The overall process is shown, for our example with $k = 6$, in Figure 21.21.

Guided by this view of the process, we can analyze it as follows. Let W be a random variable equal to the number of generations back until coalescence. We can write

$$W = W_k + W_{k-1} + W_{k-2} + \cdots + W_2,$$

where W_j is a random variable equal to the number of generations during which there are exactly j distinct lineages. By linearity of expectation, we have

$$E[W] = E[W_k] + E[W_{k-1}] + \cdots + E[W_2].$$

So it remains to figure out the terms on the right-hand side.

Each random variable of the form W_j can be viewed in the following way: when we have j distinct lineages, we move backward through successive generations, waiting until a particular event (a collision) first happens. We now make use of our approximations: W_j is very close to a simpler random variable in which we have j lineages, we count the number of steps until this number of lineages is reduced to $j - 1$, and in each generation this reduction of lineages occurs with probability exactly equal to $p = \frac{j(j-1)}{2N}$. We let X_j denote this closely related, simpler random variable; we write

$$X = X_k + X_{k-1} + X_{k-2} + \cdots + X_2,$$

and we will be interested in determining the expectation

$$E[X] = E[X_k] + E[X_{k-1}] + \cdots + E[X_2]$$

rather than the expectation $E[W]$.

How should we think about the expectation of one of these simpler random variables X_j? It is precisely as though we have a coin that comes up "heads" with a fixed probability $p = \frac{j(j-1)}{2N}$ per flip, and we want to know the expected number of flips until we see the first heads. To compute this expectation, we recall Equation (21.5) from earlier in this section, applied to the current random variable X_j:

$$E[X_j] = \Pr[X_j \geq 1] + \Pr[X_j \geq 2] + \Pr[X_j \geq 3] + \cdots$$

The probability that X_j is at least some value i is just the probability that the coin comes up "tails" on its first i flips, which is $(1 - p)^i$. Therefore,

$$E[X_j] = 1 + (1 - p) + (1 - p)^2 + (1 - p)^3 + \cdots = \frac{1}{1 - (1 - p)} = \frac{1}{p}.$$

This is a very intuitive relationship: the expected time to see the first heads on a coin with a heads probability of p is simply $\frac{1}{p}$.

The random variable X_j describes precisely this process with $p = \frac{j(j-1)}{2N}$. Therefore,

$$E[X_j] = \frac{2N}{j(j - 1)},$$

and so

$$E[X] = \frac{2N}{2 \times 1} + \frac{2N}{3 \times 2} + \frac{2N}{4 \times 3} + \cdots + \frac{2N}{j(j - 1)} + \cdots + \frac{2N}{k(k - 1)} \qquad (21.8)$$

$$= 2N\left[\frac{1}{2 \times 1} + \frac{1}{3 \times 2} + \frac{1}{4 \times 3} + \cdots + \frac{1}{j(j - 1)} + \cdots + \frac{1}{k(k - 1)}\right]. \qquad (21.9)$$

This last sum can be evaluated by noticing that

$$\frac{1}{j(j - 1)} = \frac{1}{j - 1} - \frac{1}{j}$$

and applying this identity to each term in Equation (21.9) we get

$$E[X] = 2N\left[\left(\frac{1}{1} - \frac{1}{2}\right) + \left(\frac{1}{2} - \frac{1}{3}\right) + \cdots + \left(\frac{1}{j-1} - \frac{1}{j}\right)\right.$$
$$\left. + \left(\frac{1}{j} - \frac{1}{j+1}\right) + \cdots + \left(\frac{1}{k-1} - \frac{1}{k}\right)\right].$$

In this new way of writing the sum, almost all the terms inside the parentheses cancel each other out, and the only two that survive are 1 and $-\frac{1}{k}$. Hence, we conclude that

$$E[X] = 2N\left(1 - \frac{1}{k}\right).$$

This gives us the result we were looking for – the approximate number of generations until coalescence – and so we can conclude with just a few final observations. First, once k becomes moderately large, the expected time to coalescence depends only very weakly on k; it is roughly $2N$ as k grows. Second, the breakdown of X into $X_k + X_{k-1} + \cdots + X_2$ lets us appreciate where most of the time is being spent in the merging to a common ancestor. As we begin moving backward in time, collisions happen relatively quickly at first; but as we continue moving backward, we find that essentially half the expected time is being spent once the lineages have merged down to just two, and these two are searching for a final collision point at the most recent common ancestor. Third, the approximations provide us with a very simple way to build trees according to this process: we simply follow the recipe in Figure 21.21, drawing parallel lines backward in time until the outcome of a coin flip tells us to pick two of the lines uniformly at random and merge them into one.

Finally, we should note that, although we have introduced some approximations into the original formulation of the problem, subsequent work has shown that the final estimates are very close to the exact results one gets through much more intricate analysis [91, 174].

21.9 Exercises

1. Suppose you are studying the spread of a rare disease among the set of people pictured in Figure 21.22. The contacts among these people are as depicted in the network in the figure, with a time interval on each edge showing when the period of contact occurred. We assume that the period of observation runs from time 0 to time 20.

   (a) Suppose that node s is the only individual who had the disease at time 0. Which nodes could potentially have acquired the disease by the end of the observation period, at time 20?

   (b) Suppose that you find, in fact, that all nodes have the disease at time 20. You're fairly certain that the disease couldn't have been introduced into this group from other sources, and so you suspect instead that a value you're using as the start or end of one of the time intervals is incorrect. Can you find a single number, designating the start or end of one of the time intervals, that you could change so that in the resulting network it's possible for the disease to have flowed from node s to every other node?

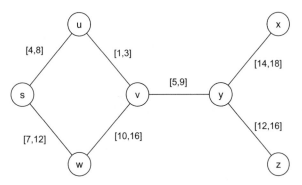

Figure 21.22. Contacts among a set of people, with time intervals showing when the contacts occurred.

2. Imagine that you know a contact graph of a set of people, but you don't know exactly the times during which contacts happened. Suppose you have a hypothesis that a particular disease passed between certain pairs of people, but not between certain other pairs. (Let's call the first set of pairs *positive*, and the second set of pairs *negative*.) It's natural to ask whether it's possible to find a set of time intervals for the edges that support this hypothesis in a strong sense: they make it possible for the disease to flow between the positive pairs, but not between the negative pairs.

   Let's try this genre of question out on the simple contact graph among five people shown in Figure 21.23.

   (a) Can you find time intervals for the edges that make it possible for the disease to flow *from* every node *to* every other node, with the one exception that it is not possible for it to flow from node a to node e? If you think it is possible, describe such a set of time intervals; if you think it is not possible, explain why no such set of time intervals exists.

   (b) Can you find time intervals for the edges that make it possible for the disease to flow from node a to node d and from node b to node e, but not from node a to node c? Again, if you think it is possible, describe such a set of time intervals; if you think it is not possible, explain why no such set of time intervals exists.

3. Imagine that you're advising a group of agricultural officials who are investigating measures to control the outbreak of an epidemic in its early stages within a livestock population. On short notice, they are able to try controlling the extent to which the animals come in contact with each other, and they are also able to introduce higher levels of sanitization to reduce the probability that one animal passes the disease to another.

   Both of these measures cost money, and the estimates of the costs are as follows. If the officials spend x dollars controlling the extent to which animals come into

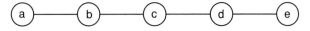

Figure 21.23. A contact graph on five people.

contact with each other, then they expect each animal to come into contact with

$$40 - \frac{x}{200,000}$$

others. If the officials spend y dollars introducing sanitization measures to reduce the probability of transmission, then they expect the probability an infected animal passes the disease to another animal contact to be

$$0.04 - \frac{y}{100,000,000}.$$

The officials have $2 million budgeted for this activity. Their current plan is to spend $1 million on each of the two kinds of measures. Using what you know about epidemics, would you advise them that this is a good use of the available money? If so, why? If not, can you suggest a better way to allocate the money?

PART SEVEN

Institutions and Aggregate Behavior

CHAPTER 22

Markets and Information

In this final part of the book, we build on the principles developed thus far to consider the design of institutions and how different institutions can produce different forms of aggregate behavior. By an *institution*, we mean something very general – any set of rules, conventions, or mechanisms that synthesizes individual behavior across a population into an overall outcome. In the next three chapters, we will focus on three fundamental classes of institutions: markets, voting, and property rights.

We begin by discussing markets, and specifically their role in aggregating and conveying information across a population. Each individual participant in the market arrives with certain beliefs and expectations – about the value of assets or products, and about the likelihood of events that may affect these values. The markets we study will be structured so as to combine this set of beliefs into an overall outcome – generally in the form of market prices – that represents a kind of synthesis of the underlying information.

This is part of a broad issue we have seen several times so far: the fact that individuals' expectations affect their behavior. For example, we saw this in Chapter 8 with Braess's Paradox, where the optimal route depends on which routes others are expected to choose; in Chapter 16 on information cascades, where people draw inferences about the unknown desirability of alternatives (restaurants or fashions) from the behavior of others; and in Chapter 17 on network effects, where the unknown value of a product (a fax machine or a social networking site) depends on how many others are also expected to use the product. In each of these cases, individuals have to decide what to do without knowing exactly what will happen. Will the route be crowded or not? Is the restaurant good or bad? Will others also join the social networking site? In all of these situations, individuals' expectations about payoffs matter for how they will choose.

Along with the similarities among these settings, there is also an important difference that will be fundamental to our discussion here: whether the unknown desirability of the different alternatives is *exogenous* or *endogenous*. Exogenous desirability means that a given alternative is inherently a good idea or a bad idea, regardless of how the individuals make their decisions. Thus, for example, in our model of information cascades, people decided whether to accept or reject an option that was in fact fundamentally either good or bad, and the desirability of the option wasn't affected by whether people accepted it or not. Endogenous desirability is different, and somewhat more subtle: it means that the desirability of an alternative depends on the actual decisions people make about it. In our model of network traffic and Braess's Paradox, no particular route is a priori crowded or not; a route becomes crowded if many people choose it. Similarly, we can't tell whether a product with network effects – like a fax machine – is worth purchasing or not until we know whether many people in fact purchase it.

We consider both types of cases in this chapter. First we will look at what happens in asset markets where the desirability of the assets is exogenous, but unknown. We begin this analysis by focusing on betting markets as a simple, stylized domain with exogenous but uncertain outcomes. We describe how individuals behave and how prices are set in betting markets, and then we discuss how the ideas we develop about betting markets provide insight into more complex settings like stock markets. After this, we will consider what happens in markets in which the desirability of the items is endogenous. The issue we focus on in this case is the role of asymmetric information.

The next two chapters in this part of the book will discuss voting and the role of property rights. Markets and voting mechanisms are alternative institutions that aggregate individual behavior into outcomes for the group. One important difference between them is that voting mechanisms are typically used to produce a single group decision, while in markets each individual may choose a different outcome. The final chapter discusses the role of property rights in influencing what outcomes are possible.

22.1 Markets with Exogenous Events

In this section we begin by examining how markets aggregate opinions about events in settings where the underlying events are exogenous – the probabilities of the events are not affected by the outcomes in the market. *Prediction markets* are one basic example of this setting. These are markets for (generally very simple) assets which have been created to aggregate individuals' predictions about a future event into a single group, or market, opinion. In a prediction market, individuals bet on the outcome of some event by trading claims to monetary amounts that are conditional on the outcome of the event.

One of the most well-known uses of prediction markets has been for the forecasting of election results. For example, the Iowa Electronic Markets[1] ran a market (one of many with this structure) in which individuals could buy or sell a contract that would pay $1 in the event that a Democrat won the 2008 U.S. Presidential election, and would pay nothing if this event did not occur. An individual who bought this contract was betting that a Democrat would win the election. The corresponding contract that paid $1 if a Republican won was also available. In Figure 1.13 from Chapter 1, we saw a plot of the prices for these two contracts over time, and we saw how the movement of the prices followed the – exogenous – course of events affecting the perceived likelihood of the election outcome.

In a prediction market, or any other market, there are two sides to any trade: what someone buys, someone else sells. So a trade in a prediction market means that two

---

[1] www.biz.uiowa.edu/iem/

people disagree about which side of the bet they want to take. But note that at the price where the trade actually occurs, both the buyer and the seller find the trade desirable. In a sense that we will make precise later, the price *separates their beliefs*: their beliefs are on opposite sides of the price, and we can view the price as an average of their beliefs. This is the motivation for the usual interpretation that the price in a prediction market is an average prediction about the probability of the event occurring. So, if the price of the Democrat-wins contract is 60 cents, the usual interpretation is that "the market" believes that the probability of a Democrat winning the election is 0.6. Of course, the market itself does not have beliefs – it's simply an institution, a place where trade is conducted under a particular set of rules. So when we say that the market believes something about a future event, this phrase really means that the market price represents an average belief.

Betting markets for sporting events such as horse races are also markets that aggregate diverse opinions into a price. As is the case with prediction markets, the outcome of the sporting event is independent of the betting behavior of the participants. Of course, some bettors may have more accurate beliefs than other bettors. But, assuming that there is no cheating, what happens in the betting market does not affect the outcome of the sporting event.

Markets for stocks are similar to prediction markets or betting at horse races, and we will use the understanding we develop for these betting markets to help us understand how the stock market works. In both betting markets and the stock market, individuals make decisions under uncertainty about the value of a contract, bet, or stock, and the market aggregates their diverse opinions about the value of the asset. But there is also an important difference between the stock market and gambling. The price set in a gambling market, and who holds what bets, are both interesting, but they do not affect the allocation of real capital. On the other hand, the stock market allocates the available shares of stock in a company. The market price for these shares determines the cost of equity capital for the company; it is the expected rate of return that investors demand in order to hold the existing shares of stock or to buy new shares of stock. The financial capital that the company receives for its shares of stock affects its real investment decisions and thus the future value of the stock. So there is an indirect link between the aggregate opinion in the market about the company, its stock price, and the actual value of the company. But this link is really quite indirect, and for a first pass at understanding stock market prices it is reasonable to ignore it. (In fact, much of the academic literature on asset pricing also ignores this effect.)

As we will see, we can interpret the price of the asset being traded, whether it's a stock, a contract that pays out if a Democrat wins, or a betting ticket at a racetrack, as a market prediction about some event. In the next section, we examine how these markets work and we build an understanding of the circumstances under which they do a good or bad job of producing a useful aggregate prediction.

22.2 Horse Races, Betting, and Beliefs

It is easiest to understand what goes on in these markets if we begin with the simple example of betting on a two-horse race [64]. Suppose that two horses, whom we call A and B, will run a race that one of them will win (we ignore the possibility of a tie).

How should a bettor who has w dollars available to bet allocate his wealth between bets on the two horses?

We make the assumption that the bettor plans to bet all of this money w on the two horses in some fashion. We let r be a number between 0 and 1 representing the fraction of his wealth that he bets on horse A; the remaining $1 - r$ fraction of his wealth will be bet on horse B. The bettor could bet all of his money on horse A ($r = 1$), all of it on horse B ($r = 0$), or he could split it up and bet some on each horse (by choosing r strictly between 0 and 1). The only thing the bettor cannot do is save some of the money and not bet it. We will see later that in our model there is a betting strategy that returns his wealth for sure, so this lack of a direct way to not bet is not really a constraint.

It seems reasonable to expect a bettor's choice of bet will depend on what the bettor believes about the likelihood of each horse winning the race. Let's suppose that the bettor believes that horse A will win with probability a, and that horse B will win with probability $b = 1 - a$. It seems sensible to suppose that the fraction of wealth r bet on horse A won't decrease if the probability of A winning increases, and r should be equal to 1 if $a = 1$ because then betting on horse A is a sure thing. But if neither horse is a sure thing, what should the bet look like? The answer to this question depends on more than the probability of A or B winning the race; in particular, it may depend on two other factors.

First, the bettor's choice of bet may depend on the odds. If the odds on horse A are, for example, three-to-one, then a one-dollar bet on horse A will pay three dollars if horse A wins and nothing if horse A loses. More generally, if the odds on horse A are o_A, and the odds on horse B are o_B, then a bet of x dollars on horse A will pay $o_A x$ dollars if A wins, and a bet of y dollars on horse B will pay $o_B y$ dollars if horse B wins. A bettor may find high odds attractive and bet a lot on a horse with high odds in the hope of winning a large sum of money. But if he does this then he will have little left to bet on a horse with low odds, and if that horse wins the race he will be left with very little money. How a bettor evaluates the different levels of risk in these options is the topic we turn to next.

Modeling Risk and Evaluating the Utility of Wealth. A bettor's reaction to risk is the second factor that influences his choice of bets. It seems reasonable to suppose that a bettor who is very risk-averse will bet so as to have some money left no matter which horse wins, by betting some money on each horse. Someone who does not care as much about risk may place a bet more skewed toward one of the horses, and a person who does not care about risk at all might even bet everything on one horse. This issue of characterizing risk will become even more important when we move from the simple example of betting on horse races to investing in financial markets. Individuals invest significant amounts of their wealth in a wide variety of assets, all of which are subject to some risk, and it is very natural to assume that most people will not want to choose investment strategies where there is a plausible scenario in which their savings are reduced to zero. We can formulate the same issues in our current example, considering the bets on horses A or B as the alternatives that contain risk, while keeping in mind that the whole example is a simply formulated metaphor for markets with exogenous events in general.

How do we model the bettor's attitude toward risk? We saw a simple version of this question in Chapter 6 in which we asked how a player in a game evaluates the payoff of a strategy with random payoffs. Our answer was that the player evaluates each strategy according to the expected value of its payoff, and we will use the same idea here. We assume that the bettor evaluates a bet according to the expected value of the payoff on the bet. But here we need to be a bit careful. What is really the payoff on the bet? Is it the amount of money won or lost, or is it how the bettor feels about the amount of money?

Presumably the bettor prefers outcomes in which he obtains larger amounts of money, but how does his actual evaluation of the outcome depend on the amount of wealth he acquires? To make this precise, we need to define a numerical way of specifying the bettor's evaluation of the outcome as a function of his wealth, and then use this numerical measure as the bettor's payoff. We will do this with a *utility function* $U(\cdot)$: when a bettor has a wealth w, his evaluation of the outcomes – his payoff – is equal to the quantity $U(w)$.

The simplest example of a utility function is the linear function $U(w) = w$, in which a bettor's utility for wealth is exactly its value. We could also consider more general linear utility functions, of the form $U(w) = aw + b$ for some positive number a. With such functions, the bettor's utility increase from gaining a dollar is precisely equal to his utility decrease from losing a dollar. At first glance, it might seem strange to use any other utility function, but in fact linear utility functions predict behavior that doesn't align well with either empirical evidence or common sense.

An easy way to see this is to ask whether a bettor would accept a fair gamble. We consider a particular instance of a fair gamble to illustrate the issue; other examples show similar effects. Suppose that a bettor's current total wealth is w, and he is offered a gamble in which he gains w dollars with probability $\frac{1}{2}$, and loses w dollars with probability $\frac{1}{2}$. In other words, with probability $\frac{1}{2}$, his wealth after the bet will be $2w$, and with probability $\frac{1}{2}$, his wealth after the bet will be 0. We call this "fair" in the sense that the expected value of the better's wealth after the bet is $\frac{1}{2} \times (2w) + \frac{1}{2} \times 0 = w$. Now, a bettor with the linear utility function $U(w) = w$ would be indifferent between accepting and rejecting this gamble, since his expected utility from accepting the gamble would be

$$\frac{1}{2}U(2w) + \frac{1}{2}U(0) = \frac{1}{2} \times (2w) + \frac{1}{2} \times 0 = w,$$

which is the same as his expected utility from passing up the opportunity to gamble. The same would hold for any linear utility function. But if we imagine our scenario serving as a model for the behavior of an individual investing his wealth in a financial market, then our calculation corresponds to the following premise: an investor whose total net worth is \$1 million would be indifferent between accepting and rejecting an investment strategy in which he gains or loses a million dollars with equal probability. This isn't a good model for investor behavior; we'd much prefer a model in which the investor views the downside of such a strategy – having his net worth reduced to zero – as far outweighing the upside of potentially doubling his net worth. In other words, we want to model the idea that the investor, at least to some extent, views this strategy as highly risky despite its expected net change of zero to his wealth.

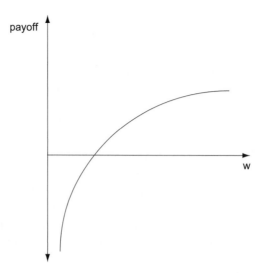

Figure 22.1. When we assume that an individual's utility is logarithmic in his wealth, this means that utility grows at a decreasing rate as wealth increases.

We can capture this kind of behavior by assuming that the bettor's utility grows at a decreasing rate as a function of his wealth w. Examples of utility functions that have this property are $U(w) = w^{1/2}$ and $U(w) = \ln(w)$, the natural logarithm of wealth. In these cases utility still increases as a function of wealth; it is simply that the rate of increase slows down as wealth increases: the appeal of gaining each extra dollar goes down as you become wealthier. With a bit of analysis, we can check that a bettor with this type of utility would reject a fair gamble. For example, if $U(w) = w^{1/2}$, then he would evaluate the expected utility from accepting the bet discussed earlier as

$$\frac{1}{2}U(2w) + \frac{1}{2}U(0) = \frac{1}{2} \times (2w)^{1/2} + \frac{1}{2} \times 0 = 2^{-1/2} \times w^{1/2}.$$

This is less than his current utility of $w^{1/2}$, which he could maintain simply by refusing to bet. Thus, with this kind of utility function, which grows at a decreasing rate in the wealth w, the bettor would reject the gamble.

We will use these types of utility functions in our analysis here. It's important to remember, however, that regardless of how we model utility as a function of wealth, we assume that the bettor evaluates bets according to the expected value of the utility; the difference is simply in the shape of the bettor's utility function.

Logarithmic Utility. To build a simple model of how a bettor might behave, we'll suppose in particular that the bettor's utility function is the natural logarithm of wealth, $\ln(w)$, where $w > 0$ is the bettor's wealth. This utility function is plotted in Figure 22.1; as noted above, it grows with the wealth, but the rate of growth slows down with increasing wealth. This logarithmic form for utility has a simple intuitive property: the bettor receives the same utility benefit from doubling his wealth, regardless of how much he currently has. In other words, the value of each additional dollar declines as wealth increases, but the value of doubling one's wealth is always the same. To see why this is true, we use the following basic fact about logarithms:

$$\ln(x) - \ln(y) = \ln(x/y) \tag{22.1}$$

for any x and y. Given this fact, the increase in utility from doubling your money, when your current wealth is w, is equal to

$$\ln(2w) - \ln(w) = \ln(2w/w) = \ln(2),$$

where the first equality follows by plugging $x = 2w$ and $y = w$ into Equation (22.1). A similar argument would hold for any multiplicative increase or decrease in the bettor's wealth: the change in utility doesn't depend on the current wealth.

The logarithmic utility function will make our analysis particularly clean, although the general ideas of the analysis apply equally well to any utility function that grows at a decreasing rate in wealth.

The Optimal Strategy: Betting Your Beliefs. Let's now figure out the optimal strategy for our bettor, given the logarithmic utility of wealth, the odds being offered, and the bettor's beliefs about the respective probabilities that horses A and B will win.

Recall that the odds on horse A are o_A and the odds on horse B are o_B. Suppose that the bettor bets a fraction r of his wealth on horse A. Then since the amount bet on A is rw, the bettor's wealth will be rwo_A if horse A wins. The amount bet on B is $(1 - r)w$, so the bettor's wealth will be $(1 - r)wo_B$ if horse B wins. The bettor believes there is a probability a that horse A will win, and a probability $b = 1 - a$ that horse B will win. So with the given betting strategy r and with these probabilities, the bettor ends up with a utility of $\ln(rwo_A)$ with probability a (in the event horse A wins), and a utility of $\ln((1 - r)wo_B)$ with probability $1 - a$ (in the event horse B wins). Adding these up, the expected utility after the bet is

$$a \ln(rwo_A) + (1 - a) \ln((1 - r)wo_B). \tag{22.2}$$

The bettor wants to choose r to maximize the value of this expression.

As a step toward maximizing this value, we can use another basic fact about logarithms, closely related to Equation (22.1):

$$\ln(x) + \ln(y) = \ln(xy) \tag{22.3}$$

for any x and y. As a result, we can unpack the products of variables inside the logarithms in Formula (22.2), arriving at an equivalent way to write the expected utility that the bettor wants to maximize:

$$a \ln(r) + (1 - a) \ln(1 - r) + a \ln(wo_A) + (1 - a) \ln(wo_B). \tag{22.4}$$

Something interesting is already happening here. The third and fourth terms of this expression do not contain the value r, and this value r is the only thing the bettor has control over. So the bettor's maximization problem is really just to maximize the first two terms: he needs to choose r to maximize

$$a \ln(r) + (1 - a) \ln(1 - r). \tag{22.5}$$

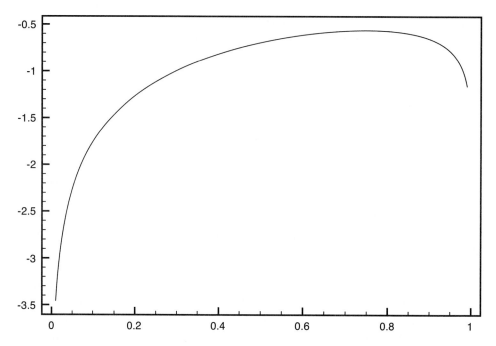

Figure 22.2. A plot of $a \ln(r) + b \ln(1 - r)$ as a function of r, when $a = 0.75$. The maximum is achieved when $r = a$.

This leads to a counterintuitive conclusion, but one that follows directly from our assumption of a logarithmic utility function: Formula (22.5) does not contain the odds o_A and o_B, and so when the bettor determines the optimal choice of r by maximizing this formula, it will not depend on the value of the odds. This makes sense once we think further about what logarithmic utility really means. We can interpret the odds of o_A on horse A as follows: In the event that horse A wins, you will first be paid rw dollars, and then your wealth will be further increased by a factor of o_A. But we just argued that, with logarithmic utilities, the benefit from a multiplicative increase in your wealth is a fixed amount independent of how much you have. So while this final multiplicative boost of o_A is a nice bonus, the value you assign to it is independent of how much money you have at the time; hence, it does not affect your choice of r.

So let's go back to the bettor's problem of maximizing Formula (22.5). Its typical shape as a function of r is shown in Figure 22.2: it drops steeply near $r = 0$ and $r = 1$, and it assumes a unique maximum in between. With some very simple calculus, one can show that it is maximized at $r = a$. In what follows, we'll use this result in a "black-box" fashion, without worrying how it is obtained, but the argument is very short. The derivative of the expression in formula (22.5) with respect to r is

$$\frac{a}{r} - \frac{1 - a}{1 - r}. \tag{22.6}$$

If we set this to zero, we get an equation that is solved simply by setting $r = a$, and this is the maximum point.

This result has a nice interpretation: *the bettor bets his beliefs.* The fraction of wealth bet on horse A is the bettor's belief about the probability that horse A wins. Note also that the optimal bet has the sensible property that the amount bet on A increases with the probability of A winning, and it approaches the bettor's full wealth as this probability approaches 1.

We now use this basic result to study what happens in markets with many participants. Throughout this analysis we will continue to assume that all bettors have logarithmic utility. If we were to use a different utility function, the overall results to follow would still have the same qualitative behavior, but the analysis would become much more elaborate and some of the specific facts we use would no longer hold. In particular, with a different utility function, the bettors' decisions would no longer necessarily be independent of the odds, and this would lead to more complex reasoning about bettor behavior.

22.3 Aggregate Beliefs and the "Wisdom of Crowds"

When there is only one bettor, we can learn about the bettor's beliefs by observing his optimal strategy, but with only one bettor the racetrack cannot be said to be aggregating multiple opinions. To understand how aggregation works, we now consider systems with multiple bettors.

Let's suppose that there are N bettors named $1, 2, 3, \ldots, N$, and that each bettor n believes there is a probability of a_n that horse A will win, and thus a probability of $b_n = 1 - a_n$ that B will win. We allow the bettors to disagree about the probability of winning, but we don't require that they actually do disagree.[2] As we will see, if they agree, then although they wouldn't be willing to take opposite sides of a bet with respect to each other, we can determine the market odds and the aggregate opinion – it is simply the commonly held opinion.

There is no reason to assume that the bettors all have the same wealth, and once they begin betting there will be winners and losers, so eventually their wealths will have to differ. So we might as well allow for different wealths at the beginning. Suppose that bettor n has wealth w_n and thus the total wealth is the sum of all w_n, which we write

$$w = w_1 + w_2 + \cdots + w_N.$$

We will assume that all of the bettors evaluate wealth using the same utility function, and we will continue to use the natural logarithm of wealth, $\ln(w)$, for this utility.

In Section 22.2, we saw that the optimal betting strategy for bettor n with belief a_n is $r_n = a_n$: that is, bettor n will bet $a_n w_n$ on horse A. Correspondingly, bettor n will bet $(1 - a_n)w_n$ on horse B. So the amount that all the bettors together bet on horse A is the sum

$$a_1 w_1 + a_2 w_2 + \cdots + a_N w_N,$$

[2] We take bettors' disagreement about the probabilities as exogenously given. It is also interesting to ask what happens if any disagreements are generated by differing information. But this case is much more complex, because here bettors also need to make inferences about the information of others from whatever market statistics they can observe [345].

and the total amount bet on horse B is the sum

$$b_1 w_1 + b_2 w_2 + \cdots + b_N w_N.$$

Since each bettor bets all of his wealth, the total amount bet is the aggregate wealth w.

The Odds Determined by the Racetrack. Now we would like to determine the odds that the racetrack should offer on horses A and B if it wants to break even – that is, if it wants to pay out to the bettors exactly the total amount bet, no matter which horse wins. We assume that the racetrack collects the bets from the bettors, and so it has w in total bets. It then uses this money to pay off the winning bets. We will assume that no matter which horse wins the race, the racetrack pays out everything that it collects; that is, it has no cost and makes no profit.

If horse A wins, the amount that is owed to bettor n is $a_n w_n o_A$. The total amount owed to the bettors is the sum of their winnings, which is equal to

$$a_1 w_1 o_A + \cdots + a_N w_N o_A.$$

In order to have the amount that is paid out to bettors in the event that horse A wins equal the amount of money w that the track collected, the odds on horse A must solve

$$a_1 w_1 o_A + \cdots + a_N w_N o_A = w. \tag{22.7}$$

That is, the equilibrium odds on horse A are determined so that the track just breaks even if A wins. Solving for the inverse of the equilibrium odds on horse A (which produces a somewhat nicer expression than the formula for the actual odds), we get

$$\frac{a_1 w_1}{w} + \cdots + \frac{a_N w_N}{w} = o_A^{-1}. \tag{22.8}$$

If we write $f_n = w_n / w$ for the share of the total wealth held by bettor n, then this can be written as

$$a_1 f_1 + \cdots + a_N f_N = o_A^{-1}. \tag{22.9}$$

An analogous calculation shows that the equilibrium inverse odds on horse B are

$$b_1 f_1 + \cdots + b_N f_N = o_B^{-1}. \tag{22.10}$$

These inverse odds have a nice interpretation. If the odds on horse A are 4 (i.e., four-to-one, with a one-dollar bet paying four dollars), then in order to have a one-dollar payout in the event that horse A wins, the bettor would need to bet one-fourth of a dollar on horse A. This amount is the inverse of the odds for A: that is, a bet of o_A^{-1} dollars on horse A will result in a payment of \$1 in the event that horse A wins the race. Thus, the inverse odds on A are the price of a dollar to be paid in the event that A wins, and similarly the inverse odds on B are the price of a dollar to be paid in the event that B wins.

State Prices. Let's denote these "prices of a dollar" by $\rho_A = o_A^{-1}$ for the event that horse A wins and $\rho_B = o_B^{-1}$ for the event that horse B wins. These prices are usually called *state prices*, since they are the price of a dollar in the event that a certain future state of the world is reached [24].

There is one more feature of equilibrium odds that is important. Let's ask how much a bettor would have to pay now to get one dollar for sure after the race. To do this the bettor needs to bet enough on horse A to receive one dollar if A wins, and enough on horse B to receive one dollar if horse B wins. These amounts are, as we saw before, o_A^{-1} and o_B^{-1}. So the amount needed to guarantee receiving one dollar in either case – regardless of the outcome – is $o_A^{-1} + o_B^{-1}$. Let's use the equilibrium values of odds to figure out how much money this takes:

$$\begin{aligned}
o_A^{-1} + o_B^{-1} &= (a_1 f_1 + \cdots + a_N f_N) + (b_1 f_1 + \cdots + b_N f_N) \\
&= (a_1 + b_1) f_1 + \cdots + (a_N + b_N) f_N \\
&= (1 \times f_1) + \cdots + (1 \times f_N) \\
&= 1.
\end{aligned}$$

This calculation shows there is a betting strategy that will turn one dollar before the race into one dollar for sure after the race. This is the sense in which our assumption that the bettors actually bet all of their wealth is not a constraint. Any portion of their wealth that they don't want to risk they can bet according to the inverse odds. This calculation also gives us the very useful property that inverse odds, or state prices, sum to 1.

Now having done all of these calculations we are in a position to interpret the state prices. First, note that if every bettor believes that the probability that horse A will win is a, then $\rho_A = a$. That is, if the bettors agree about the probabilities then the market accurately reflects these beliefs, with the state price equal to the common belief. Second, because the wealth shares sum to one, the state prices are *weighted averages* of the bettors' beliefs. The weight on bettor n's beliefs is bettor n's share, f_n, of the aggregate wealth. In particular, if a bettor has no wealth then the state price is not influenced by his beliefs as he cannot bet. Alternatively, if a bettor controls all of the wealth then the state price is his probability. More generally, how much influence a bettor's beliefs have on the state price depends on how much of the aggregate wealth is controlled by that bettor.

So it really does make sense to think of the state prices as the market's averaging of individual beliefs – or, in the more typical phrasing, they can be interpreted as the *market's beliefs*. For our horse-race market (with the logarithmic utility function), this market probability is the weighted average of the investors' beliefs, with each investor's weight determined by his share of the wealth.[3]

The Relationship to the "Wisdom of Crowds."

What does this analysis say about the intuition popularized by recent books such as James Surowiecki's *The Wisdom of Crowds* [383]? The basic argument there, drawing on a long history of intuition about markets, is that the aggregate behavior of many people, each with limited information, can produce very accurate beliefs.

---

[3] The logarithmic utility function is important for the exact form of this relationship. With other utility functions, state prices also depend on individuals' attitudes toward risk.

Our results on state prices illustrate some of the technical basis for this intuition. In particular, we found that the crowd at the racetrack determines the odds, or the state prices, and these odds are an average of the opinions in the crowd. If the opinions in the crowd about the probability of horse A winning are independently drawn from a distribution whose mean is equal to the true probability of horse A winning, and if wealth shares are equal, then the state prices actually do converge to the true probabilities as the size of the crowd grows. This occurs because the state prices are actually the average belief in the crowd, and this average converges to the truth with the size of the crowd.[4]

But these claims have two important qualifications embedded in them, both of which are important for understanding the limitations of the wisdom of crowds. First, it is important that the opinions are independent. We explored the subtleties of noninde- pendent opinions in Chapter 16, noting the difficulties they pose in reasoning about the behavior of crowds, and the fact that they can lead to poor aggregate predictions even when many people participate. Second, it is important that all beliefs are equally weighted. If some bettors have more wealth than others, then state prices place more weight on their beliefs than on the beliefs of those who have little wealth. Whether this reduces or improves the accuracy of state prices depends on whether the beliefs of these wealthy bettors are more or less accurate than those of the poorer bettors. One might expect that over time those bettors with more accurate beliefs would become rich as they tend to make better bets than do those with less accurate beliefs. If this oc- curs, then more accurate beliefs will have more weight placed on them and the market price will become a better and better predictor. We investigate this idea more fully in Section 22.10.

It is also interesting to think about what happens over time to state prices as the bettors watch horse races and learn about the likelihood of each horse winning. Suppose, for example, that horses A and B run a race against each other every week, and that the outcomes of the races are independent. If the true probability of horse A winning is a, then the fraction of times that A wins the race will converge to a. A bettor who watches the races, and who initially forecasts a winning probability for A that is not a, should modify his beliefs in light of his experience. In our examination of Bayesian learning in Chapter 16, we argued that over time an observer who watches independent events and employs Bayes' rule learns the true probability. (This result is reviewed and expanded on in Section 22.10.) So over time, each bettor's belief about the probability of A winning will converge to a, and similarly each bettor's belief about the probability of B winning will converge to b. The state prices are weighted averages of these beliefs, so they too converge to a and b.

22.4 Prediction Markets and Stock Markets

Thus far we have been telling a story about horse races, but there is a direct analogy to any market in which participants purchase assets whose future value depends on the

---

[4] In this discussion we treat bettors' beliefs as fixed and exogenously given. If instead, bettors' beliefs differ because they have differing information, then bettors should learn from prices. In the case in which beliefs are independent samples from a distribution with mean equal to the true probability, the market price reveals the average belief, and all bettors should use it to update their individual beliefs via the market price.

outcome of uncertain events. Two specific examples are prediction markets and – by far the most consequential application of these ideas – stock markets. In both cases, we will see that state prices play a key role in how we reason about what takes place in the market.

Prediction Markets. In a prediction market, individuals trade claims to a one-dollar return conditional on the occurrence of some event. For example, as we discussed at the beginning of the chapter, participants may trade claims to a one-dollar return in the event that a Democrat wins the next U.S. Presidential election. The institutional structure of prediction markets differs from the structure of a betting market at a racetrack. In a prediction market, individuals trade with each other through the market, whereas at a racetrack, individuals place bets directly with the track. Nonetheless, prices play the same role in both markets. The inverse odds on a horse are the cost of a one-dollar return in the event that the horse wins the race. Similarly, the price of a contract in a prediction market is the price of a one-dollar return in the event specified in the contract (such as a particular outcome of an election). In both cases the prices reflect an averaging of the beliefs of the participants in the market.

Here, we will ignore the various institutional structures of prediction markets and instead see how much we can discover about them by applying our analysis of horse races via state prices. Consider, for example, the prediction market for the 2008 U.S. Presidential election with two possible outcomes: a Democrat wins or a Republican wins. (The same analysis can handle prediction markets with many plausible outcomes, such as the earlier prediction market for the identity of the Democratic and Republican nominees for President in 2008.)

Let f_n be the share of the total wealth bet in the prediction market that is bet by trader n. Let a_n and b_n be trader n's probabilities of a Democrat and a Republican winning, respectively. Then, just as was the case for horse races, the market price ρ^D for the contract on a Democratic winner will be the wealth-share weighted average of the investors' probabilities of a Democrat winning the election. That is,

$$\rho^D = a_1 f_1 + \cdots + a_N f_N. \tag{22.11}$$

Similarly, the price of the contract on a Republican winner will be the wealth-share weighted average of the investors' probabilities of a Republican winning the election. In this discussion we are looking at a snapshot of the prediction market at one point in time, which we can think of as a point just before the event occurs. We can also examine the dynamic behavior of the market over periods of time during which beliefs and wealth shares are both likely to change; such dynamic questions are the focus of Section 22.10 at the end of this chapter.

Are the prices of these contracts good predictors of the outcome of the election? They are weighted averages of the beliefs of the investors in the markets, but as we saw with horse races this doesn't necessarily make them either good or bad predictors. It depends on the dispersion of beliefs in the population of investors and on how wealth shares are distributed across those investors. One way to address this question empirically is to look at the predictions made by real prediction markets and ask how well they have done at predicting the outcome of actual events. An interesting paper by Berg, Nelson, and Rietz [51] shows that for the period 1988–2004, the Iowa Electronic

Markets did a significantly better job of predicting the outcome of U.S. Presidential elections than was done by an average of the major national polls.

Stock Markets. Stock markets also provide individuals with the opportunity to bet on future states of the world, but these are more complicated bets because stocks don't just offer a one-dollar return in the event that a particular state occurs. Instead a share of stock in a company offers a monetary amount that will vary depending on which of possibly many states occurs. These states may be things like "the company's current investment in research and development succeeds," "a strong new competitor enters the market," "the demand for the goods produced by the company grows more rapidly than expected," or "the workers go on strike." Each of these states would have an impact on the future value of the stock in the company, and so it's reasonable to think of the stock as providing a different amount conditional on each state. The difference between a bet on a two-horse race and a share of stock, then, is that there are many states, as there would be in a many-horse race, and the amount of money that the owner of a share of stock has a claim to is not given by explicit odds but instead is determined by the value of the stock in each of these states.[5]

If we knew the price of a dollar in each of these states (the state prices), and the value of the stock in each state, we would know how much investors should be willing to pay for the stock conditional on each state: it would be the value of the stock in that state times the price of a dollar in that state. The price of the stock today would be the sum of these terms across all the states. As long as the collection of stocks traded are rich enough, it is possible to determine the state prices from the prices of stocks, and conversely to determine stock prices from state prices. We now give a sense for how this works by means of a simple example.

State Prices in the Stock Market. The general framework for determining state prices from stock prices and vice versa, and for specifying when a set of stocks is "rich enough" to be able to perform this determination, is complex. Here is a streamlined example that conveys the central idea.

Suppose there are two companies, named 1 and 2, whose stock is being traded. There are also two possible states, which we'll call s_1 and s_2. To be concrete, we can imagine that state s_1 is "company 1 does well," and state s_2 is "company 2 does well." Suppose that stock in company 1 is worth one dollar in state s_1 and worth nothing in state s_2; and stock in company 2 is worth one dollar in state s_2 and nothing in state s_1. Then the stocks are equivalent to the contracts traded in a prediction market and, just as we saw for a prediction market, their prices are the market probabilities of the states.

Now let's suppose, more realistically, that each stock is worth something in each state. Suppose that stock in company 1 is worth two dollars in state s_1 and one dollar in state s_2, and stock in company 2 is worth one dollar in state s_1 and two dollars in state s_2. If we know the state prices we can determine the price of each stock. Let's call these prices v_1 for stock in company 1 and v_2 for stock in company 2, and let's write

---

[5] Here, just as in the case of horse races, we are taking the value of the stock in each event as being given exogenously. This is an important simplification, since in reality the value of the stock in each event is endogenous and is determined in the market equilibrium that arises in that state.

ρ_1 and ρ_2 to denote the state prices for states s_1 and s_2. The price of a share of stock in company 1 is the value now of the future worth of the company, which is $2\rho_1 + 1\rho_2$. Intuitively, this is because we can think of a share of stock in company 1 as simply a "package deal" that offers two dollars in state 1 and one dollar in state 2; the price of this package is just the price of its constituent ingredients, which if sold separately would require the purchase of two one-dollar contracts for state 1, at a price of $2\rho_1$, plus the purchase of a single one-dollar contract for state 2, at a price of ρ_2. (Of course, these contracts based on the states themselves are not sold separately; the point is that they only come implicitly "bundled" into the price of the stock.) Similarly, the price of a share of company 2 is $1\rho_1 + 2\rho_2$.

Conversely, if we know the price of each stock we can determine the state prices by solving the system of equations

$$v_1 = 2\rho_1 + 1\rho_2$$
$$v_2 = 1\rho_1 + 2\rho_2$$

for the state prices ρ_1 and ρ_2. The solutions are

$$\rho_1 = \frac{2v_1 - v_2}{3}$$

$$\rho_2 = \frac{2v_2 - v_1}{3}.$$

With these examples in mind we can now get some idea of what is meant by "a rich enough set of stocks." Essentially, we need a set of stocks such that when we write down their prices as functions of the underlying state prices, we get a system of equations like the preceding one that can be solved by a unique set of state prices. If we can do this, then stock prices determine state prices and investors will be able to use trades in stocks to move money across states in any way that they want. Indeed, in this case, we can essentially imagine that there is a big prediction market with a contract for each state, find the equilibrium state prices, and then determine stock prices from these state prices.

The conclusion of our analysis here is that stock markets, prediction markets, and betting markets are all essentially the same. They each give individuals the opportunity to place bets, and they all produce prices which can be interpreted as aggregate predictions about the likelihood of future states. This point of view also provides us with some intuition about what causes prices to change: they change if the distribution of wealth changes (and individuals' beliefs differ) or if individuals' beliefs about the probability of states change. If individuals suddenly believe, for whatever reason, that states with high payoffs are less likely, then prices will fall. Conversely, if individuals become more optimistic, then prices will rise. Of course, this leaves us with the question of why individuals' beliefs change. One possibility is that they are learning about the likelihood of states using Bayes' rule.[6] If their observations cause them to predict a less optimistic probability, then prices will fall. If they are in an environment in which information cascades can occur, then as we saw in Chapter 16, even small events may be able to cause large changes in predictions.

---

[6] This topic is explored in more detail in Section 22.10 at the end of this chapter.

22.5 Markets with Endogenous Events

As we noted at the beginning of this chapter, sometimes the events that individuals have beliefs about are endogenous – that is, whether they come true depends on the aggregate behavior of the individuals themselves. To take an example from our discussion of network effects, if no one expects anyone else to join a particular social networking site, then no one expects a positive payoff from joining the site; consequently, no one joins and the payoff to joining is indeed low. Alternately, if many people expect a large membership at the social networking site, then they expect a large payoff; as a result, many people join and the payoff is indeed high.

Here's a different example, from a setting in which there is a market with buyers and sellers. Suppose that people expect used cars offered for sale to be of uniformly low quality. Then no one will be willing to pay a high price for a used car. As a result, no one with a good used car will offer it for sale (since it would get a price below what it's worth), and so in fact the market will contain only low-quality used cars for sale. On the other hand, if people expect used cars to have some reasonable average quality, then they may be willing to pay a price high enough to induce sellers with both good and bad used cars to put them on the market.

An important common theme in these two stories is the notion of *self-fulfilling expectations* – and in particular, the presence of multiple different self-fulfilling ex-pectations equilibria. This concept was central to our discussion of network effects in Chapter 17, and we see it again in the example of the used-car market. With one set of expectations, the world turns out in a certain way that makes the expectations come true, but with a different set of expectations, the world would have turned out in a different way that would have made *those* expectations come true.

Asymmetric Information. There is, however, an important difference between these two stories. In the case of the social networking site, it seems reasonable to suppose that most people have similar information about the payoffs to joining the site. This information may be more or less accurate, but there is no a priori reason to suppose that some large fraction of the population is intrinsically better informed than some other large fraction. In the case of the used-car market, however, each seller of a used car knows something about his or her own car – its quality – that potential buyers do not know. This is an inherent feature of how the market works: there is *asymmetric information*.

In Chapter 17 we studied self-fulfilling expectations equilibria in settings without asymmetric information. In the rest of this chapter, we add asymmetric information to the picture; this turns out to be a basic ingredient in the way that beliefs about endogenous events can manifest themselves in markets. There is a fundamental reason for this: in many settings where buyers and sellers interact, one side of the market has better information about the goods or services being traded than the other side does. In the market for used cars, sellers know more than buyers do about the sellers' cars. On electronic markets for goods, such as eBay, sellers often know more than buyers do about the goods they are offering for sale. In the market for health insurance, on the other hand, buyers of insurance often know more than sellers do about the value of the good (health insurance) being purchased, since a buyer may well know more about his or her inherent health risks than the company offering the insurance does. In the stock market, either side of a transaction could have information about the future value of the stock that is not known to the other side of the transaction (a feature that we ignored in our earlier discussion of the stock market). In all of these cases, uninformed traders need to form expectations about the value of the good being traded, and these expectations should take into account the behavior of better-informed traders.

22.6 The Market for Lemons

At the beginning of the chapter, we started with a simple scenario involving horse racing and then showed how the resulting principles extended to much larger and more complex systems such as the stock market. For considering the role of asymmetric information, we'll follow a similar strategy, first developing the case of the used-car market as a simple, stylized example, and then showing how the same principles apply to a range of more complex and fundamental markets.

In focusing first on used cars, we're following the rhetorical lead of the economist George Akerlof, who published a foundational paper on asymmetric information [9] for which he shared the 2001 Nobel Prize in Economics. His leading example in the paper was the market for used cars – or, as he called it, the "market for lemons." (A used car that is particularly bad is called a lemon.) The idea behind this phrase is old, probably as old as trading itself, but Akerlof was the first to clearly articulate the underlying principle and its implications for how markets work – or, in some cases, how they fail to work. Once we develop the basic ideas for the example of the used car market, we will then discuss how to apply these ideas to other markets.

Let's suppose that there are two types of used cars: *good cars* and *bad cars*. Each seller knows the quality of his or her own car. Buyers do not know the quality of any seller's car, but they are aware of the fact that sellers know the quality of their own cars. Market participants – the buyers and sellers – value used cars differently. To keep the analysis simple we will pick the following specific values for used cars.

- Sellers value good cars at 10 and bad cars at 4. (We can imagine these as multiples of a thousand dollars, for example.) These values can be interpreted as sellers' reservation prices for their cars. That is, a seller with a good car would be willing to sell it for a price of at least 10, but at any lower price would prefer to hold onto it. Similarly, a seller with a bad car would be willing to sell it for a price of at least 4, but at any lower price would prefer to hold onto it.
- Buyers value good cars at 12 and bad cars at 6. These values can be interpreted as buyers' reservation prices for cars. Thus, a buyer would be willing to buy a car that is known to be a good car if and only if the price is no more than 12, and a bad car if and only if the price is no more than 6.

Note that we have assumed that, for any type of car, all buyers place the same value on it and this value is more than the common value that all sellers place on it. This simplification is not necessary for our analysis, but it will make our example of market failure more striking.

Let's suppose that a fraction g of used cars are good cars, and hence a fraction $1 - g$ are bad cars. We'll also assume that everyone knows g. Finally, let's suppose that there are more buyers than used cars (or more buyers than sellers, since each seller has one used car).

The Market with Symmetric Information. As an initial baseline, let's consider the simple case in which the type of each car is known to everyone. In this case, since there are more buyers than sellers, every car could be sold to some buyer.

How would the market work under this assumption? We would expect to observe different prices for good cars and bad cars. The price of good cars will clearly be between 10 and 12 because only at prices in this range can all good cars be sold. Similarly, the price of bad cars will be between 4 and 6. Since there are more buyers than sellers, some buyers will not be able to purchase a car, and so we would expect prices of each type of car to be bid up to the upper limit of the range of prices. That is, the price of good cars will be 12 and the price of bad cars will be 6.

The Market with Asymmetric Information. But what happens if buyers cannot tell in advance of a purchase what type of car they are buying? Since cars are indistinguishable to buyers, there can only be one price for a used car – all cars that trade will have to trade at that price. Furthermore, because a buyer can't tell the quality of the car she is buying, the quality of the car she gets is random, based on the mixture of qualities on the market. Given this random aspect to the outcome, we need to consider how buyers evaluate risk, just as we did when considering bettors and horse races. To keep the analysis simple in the current case of the used-car market, we will assume that buyers do not care about risk; they simply evaluate the expected value of the used cars they are considering. We could also introduce utility functions that capture the notion that buyers are concerned with risk, as we did in the earlier parts of this chapter, but in the present case it would complicate the model without significantly changing our qualitative conclusions.

Let's consider what the market looks like in the case that buyers can't distinguish among different types of cars. First, the fraction of good cars in the population of used cars for sale is some number h. This fraction h might be the same as g – the fraction of good cars in the overall used-car population – but it might not, since not all sellers of good used cars will necessarily put their cars up for sale. Given this fraction h, the value that any buyer places on a used car is

$$12h + 6(1 - h) = 6 + 6h. \tag{22.12}$$

Thus, in order for buyers to know how much they should be willing to pay for a used car, they need to have a prediction for the value of h.

This puts us into the domain of self-fulfilling expectations equilibria, similarly to what we saw in discussing network effects in Chapter 17 (but here with the added issue of information asymmetry). We need to look for a shared expectation h by the buyers that is self-fulfilling, in that if each buyer expects a fraction h of the cars on the market to be good, then indeed an h fraction of the cars on the market will be good.

Characterizing the Self-Fulfilling Expectations Equilibria. One candidate for an equilibrium of this form is $h = g$. This would be a correct prediction by the buyers if all sellers indeed choose to offer their car for sale. If this occurs, then we can plug $h = g$ into Equation (22.12) and see that buyers would be willing to pay $6 + 6g$ for a car. Let's call this price p^*. For the prediction $h = g$ to be correct, it must be the case that at a price of p^* both sellers who own good cars and sellers who own bad cars offer them for sale. A seller with a good car would offer it for sale at p^* provided that

$$p^* = 6 + 6g \geq 10,$$

or, equivalently, if $g \geq \frac{2}{3}$. It is easy to see that if a seller with a good car would sell it at p^* then a seller with a bad car would also be happy to make a sale. So, if $g \geq \frac{2}{3}$, there is a self-fulfilling expectations equilibrium in which all cars are offered for sale.

Now let's consider what happens if $g < \frac{2}{3}$. Could there be a self-fulfilling expectations equilibrium in which $h = g$; that is, in which all cars are offered for sale? We can analyze this as follows. When $g < \frac{2}{3}$, the price that buyers would be willing to pay if they believe that all cars will be offered for sale, using Equation (22.12), is

$$p^* = 6 + 6g < 10.$$

However, owners of good cars would not be willing to sell for a price below 10, and so when $g < \frac{2}{3}$ they will keep them off the market – meaning that h, the fraction of good cars on the market, would not be equal to g. So in this case, there cannot be a self-fulfilling expectations equilibrium in which $h = g$.

However, for any value of g, there is always a self-fulfilling expectations equilibrium in which $h = 0$; that is, in which only bad cars are sold. To see why, note that if buyers expect only bad cars to be on the market, then they are willing to pay 6 for a car. At this price, sellers of bad cars would be willing to sell, but sellers of good cars would not, and so the market would consist only of bad cars. Thus, this is a self-fulfilling expectations equilibrium with $h = 0$.

So to summarize, the value $g = \frac{2}{3}$ is a critical point in this example. If $g \geq \frac{2}{3}$, there are two possible self-fulfilling expectations equilibria: one in which all cars are sold, and one in which only bad cars are sold. If $g < \frac{2}{3}$, on the other hand, then the only equilibrium is the one in which only bad cars are sold. In this latter case, the abundance of bad cars, combined with buyers' inability to distinguish good cars from bad cars, has driven the good cars out of the market.

Complete Market Failure. Our example with good and bad cars illustrates the basic idea of how equilibria with asymmetric information work, but it doesn't fully capture the possible extent of market failure, or how bad the effect can get. To explore this, let's consider an example in which there are now three types of used cars: good cars, bad cars, and *lemons*. Good cars and bad cars still play the same basic role as in our previous example, whereas lemons are completely worthless to both buyers and sellers: a market in which only lemons are offered for sale is in fact not a functioning market at all, since it consists only of opportunities to trade items of value 0.

For this example with three types of used cars, let's suppose the following:

- One-third of the cars are good, one-third are bad, and one-third are lemons.
- Sellers value good cars at 10, bad cars at 4, and lemons at 0.
- Buyers value good cars at 12, bad cars at 6, and lemons at 0.
- There are more buyers than there are used cars.

So if there were complete information, we would expect all good and bad cars to be sold at prices of 12 and 6, respectively, since there are more buyers than sellers, and the buyers value each type of car at least as much as the sellers do. Whether the lemons are sold is a question of buyer and seller indifference, since they are worth 0 to everyone.

But with asymmetric information, we need to consider the possible self-fulfilling expectations equilibria. There are three candidates for an equilibrium: (a) all cars are offered for sale, (b) only bad cars and lemons are offered for sale, or (c) only lemons are offered for sale. Again, note that option (c) represents the complete failure of the market, since all items on the market would have value 0. Let's consider each of these in turn and see which are actually possible.

(a) First, suppose buyers expect all cars to be on the market. Then the expected value of a car to a buyer would be

$$\frac{12 + 6 + 0}{3} = 6.$$

This is less than the value that sellers of good cars places on their cars, and so they would not put them on the market, meaning that this expectation would not be borne out by what happens. Hence, this is not an equilibrium.

(b) Alternately, suppose buyers expect bad cars and lemons to be on the market. Then the expected value of a car to a buyer would be

$$\frac{6 + 0}{2} = 3.$$

But this is less than the value that sellers of bad cars place on bad cars, and so they would not put them on the market, meaning again that this expectation would not be borne out by what happens. So this too is not an equilibrium.

(c) Finally, as in our previous example with two types of cars, it is clearly an equilibrium if buyers expect only lemons to be sold. In this case, their expected value for a car is 0, and if this is what they are willing to pay, then the market will consist completely of lemons.

Notice how the market has been subverted by a kind of chain reaction: good cars can't survive on the market because of the frequency of bad cars and lemons, and even without the good cars, the bad cars can't survive on the market because of the frequency of lemons. It is not hard to produce this effect with even larger numbers of types of cars: things can chain together so that, in Akerlof's words, "it is ... possible to have the bad driving out the not-so-bad driving out the medium driving out the not-so-good driving out the good in such a sequence of events that no market exists at all" [9].

Summary: Ingredients of the Market for Lemons. In the next section, we'll take the lessons from our used-car examples and apply them to markets that are much larger and more fundamental. To do this, it's useful to review the key features of the current examples that led to market failure:

   (i) The items that can be offered for sale have varying qualities.

  (ii) For any given level of quality, the buyers value the items of that quality at least as much as the sellers do – so with complete information, the market would succeed in allocating items from sellers to buyers, potentially with different prices for different levels of quality.

 (iii) There is asymmetric information about the quality of the items – only one side in a transaction can reliably determine the quality of what is being sold. (In the used-car example, the seller in a potential buyer–seller transaction could tell the quality of what he was selling. In the next section, we'll also talk about other basic markets in which it is the buyer who has this power relative to the seller.)

 (iv) Because of feature (iii), the items all must be sold for the same uniform price, and sellers will only put their items up for sale if they value them at or below this uniform price.

The market does not necessarily fail when these ingredients are present. It depends on whether there is an equilibrium where the buyers expect a mixture of qualities – and hence a price they are willing to pay – that induces the sellers to put their items up for sale. Market failure becomes more likely when the fraction of low-quality items is higher, and also when the difference between buyer and seller values is smaller.

In our discussion we have implicitly compared the market outcome with an outcome that can be achieved only with full information about each seller's car. But only the seller knows the value of his car, so any allocation procedure – not just a market – has to deal with this problem. Any procedure has to at least implicitly reward sellers for revealing their information, and this reward drives a wedge between the compensation needed to convince sellers to participate and the amount that buyers are willing to pay. Determining exactly which assignments are possible is complicated, but the optimal allocation that would be possible with full information cannot always be achieved.

22.7 Asymmetric Information in Other Markets

The ideas behind the market for lemons turn out to be fundamental to some of society's most important markets. Once you start thinking about interactions in which one party to the transaction knows something that the other party cares about, you realize that the phenomenon we're discussing is far from exceptional; in fact, it occurs all the time.

The Labor Market. One example where these ideas apply very naturally is to the labor market, in which people seeking jobs play the role of the sellers, and companies seeking employees play the role of the buyers. That is, we think of the process of employment as a market where people offer their skills for sale to employers, who pay them wages in return. Let's consider the basic assumptions of the market for lemons – numbered (i)–(iv) at the end of the previous section – in the context of the labor market.

(i) There are different qualities of workers; some are very productive while others are less productive, and this affects the value they will produce for the company that hires them.

(ii) It is natural to consider a setting where there are different kinds of jobs at different levels of wages, and where companies would be willing to hire any given prospective employee if they could accurately determine which jobs and wage levels were appropriate for them.

(iii) There is asymmetric information: a person generally has a better sense for how productive they are than a prospective employer does.

(iv) If we take a strong but plausible version of assumption (iii), where employers can't reliably determine the quality of the people they are hiring, then employers can't hire only productive workers and wages can't directly depend on the quality of the person being hired. Rather, a uniform wage will be offered, and only applicants who believe this wage acceptably values their skills will take the job.

In this analysis we are assuming that, although workers have differing productivities, each individual's productivity is a fixed, given amount and not affected by anything that the worker chooses to do. It is plausible that workers can affect their productivity by varying the amount of effort that they put into their job, but we will ignore this issue for the sake of the present formulation. Thus, the key issue is point (iv), which – as in the case of the used-car market – can be viewed as a problem of *adverse selection*. The firm cannot select for a population consisting only of high-productivity workers; instead, if it hires any workers at all, the only thing it can be sure of is getting those with low productivity.

It's useful to work through the consequences of information asymmetry in the labor market through a simple example whose structure closely parallels our used-car example. Suppose a firm hires workers from a large pool of potential employees. Suppose further that workers come in two types, productive and unproductive, and that half the workers in the population are of each type. Each productive worker hired by the firm will generate $80,000 of revenue per year for the firm, while each unproductive worker will generate $40,000 of revenue per year for the firm.

Each worker knows his own type. Also, each worker could choose not to work for the firm and instead generate an alternative income by being self-employed. Workers who are more productive will get more value from being self-employed: suppose that each productive worker could produce an income of $55,000 per year through self-employment, while each unproductive worker could produce an income of $25,000 per year through self-employment. So if the firm could accurately determine the type of each job applicant, the situation would be straightforward: the firm could offer a salary between $55,000 and $80,000 to each productive applicant, and a salary between $25,000 and $40,000 to each unproductive applicant, all job offers would be accepted, and both workers and the firm would benefit from each job that is taken at the firm.

Unfortunately for the firm, it cannot reliably determine the type of each worker. So the firm has to offer a uniform wage of w and simply hire workers who are willing to work at wage w. The firm is willing to offer a given wage w if and only if the average revenue it receives from the workers it hires at this wage is at least w.

Equilibria in the Labor Market. In our example, what wages can be offered, and which workers will be willing to work for the firm? The reasoning is very similar to the case of used cars. We start by looking for a self-fulfilling expectations equilibrium. If the firm expects all workers to be on the job market, then – because there are equal numbers of the two types of workers – its expected revenue per employee will be

$$\frac{80,000 + 40,000}{2} = 60,000,$$

and hence it can offer a uniform wage of \$60,000 per year. At this wage, both types of workers will be willing to accept the firm's offers, and so the expectation will be confirmed by what happens – we have an equilibrium in which all workers are hired.

By analogy with the used-car example, there is also another – less socially desirable – equilibrium. If the firm expects only unproductive workers to be on the job market, then it expects to make only \$40,000 per year per employee, and so this is the maximum wage it will offer. At this wage, only unproductive workers will be willing to accept jobs, and so again the firm's expectations are confirmed. So there are two possible equilibria here – a high one and a low one, with different mixtures of workers in the applicant pool in the two equilibria. Essentially, the firm's a priori level of confidence in the quality of its job applicants is self-fulfilling.

Things change if we shift the relative fractions of productive and unproductive workers in the population. Suppose that only $\frac{1}{4}$ of the workers are productive and $\frac{3}{4}$ are unproductive. There is still an equilibrium in which only unproductive workers are hired. But is there also one in which all workers are hired? If the firm were to expect all workers to be on the market, then its expected revenue per employee would be

$$\frac{1}{4} \times 80,000 + \frac{3}{4} \times 40,000 = 50,000,$$

and so this is the highest wage it could offer. But at this wage, the productive workers wouldn't be willing to accept the firm's offers, and so in fact not all workers would be on the market. In other words, there is no equilibrium in which the productive workers apply for jobs at the firm – just as with good used cars, they have been driven out of the market by the high frequency of unproductive workers.

The Market for Insurance. There are many markets that we can analyze in a similar fashion. For example, asymmetric information plays an important role in the market for health insurance. Health insurance companies generally know much less about the health of those they insure than the insured know about their own health. Health insurance companies are very good at predicting the average cost of insuring a pool of people, but it is difficult for them to predict the cost of insuring any particular individual. They group people into risk categories based on their medical history, but within any group each individual knows more about his or her own history, and about how he or she will behave in the future, than the insurance company knows.

So we have all the ingredients of the market for lemons: individuals in a given risk category can be more or less costly to insure, but the insurance company cannot reliably make these fine-grained distinctions. We should also notice an interesting twist in the case of health insurance: it is the *buyers* of health insurance, rather than the sellers, who have the additional information. But the consequence is the same. For any risk category, the insurance company has to essentially charge a uniform price for the insurance that is sufficient to cover the average cost of providing health care for the group. This means that the healthiest individuals in the group are being charged a price that is greater than the expected cost of providing care for them, and so they may be unwilling to buy insurance. Then, because these relatively healthy people do not participate, the average quality of the remaining pool goes down; the insurance company would need to set a higher price for this less healthy pool. Now the healthiest people in this remaining pool may be unwilling to pay this higher price; they too may choose to not buy insurance, and the average quality in the pool goes down further. As in the case of the used-car market, the market for health insurance can unravel to the point that no one buys insurance. Of course, whether this actually happens depends on the actual numbers: how much it costs to provide the insurance, and how much people value the insurance compared to their alternatives. But just as in our earlier examples, we see how socially undesirable outcomes can occur in the market when there are imbalances in information.

The information asymmetry we have focused on in the market for health insurance leads, just as in cases of used cars or employment, to a type of adverse selection. Insurance companies cannot select for a population consisting only of healthy individuals; rather, if anyone buys insurance at all, the only thing one can be sure of is that it will be bought by those who are less healthy. There is another type of information asymmetry that occurs in the market for health insurance that we have so far ignored in our discussion. As in the previous examples, we have treated the health status of each individual, and thus his or her cost to insure, as fixed and given. But individuals can take actions which affect their health. If these actions are not observable to the insurance company then we have a new source of information asymmetry, since each individual knows more about his future behavior than the insurance company does. Once an individual purchases health insurance, his incentive to undertake costly actions to maintain his health is reduced, since he no longer bears the full cost of poor health. This introduces an effect known as *moral hazard*: when you're shielded from the full cost of your potential bad behavior, you have less incentive to avoid engaging in it.

Information Asymmetry in Trading and the Stock Market. It is useful to reflect further on these examples in light of one of the basic lessons of this chapter: that in any trade, each trader should ask why whoever is on the other side of the trade wants to make the trade. As we noted at the beginning of this chapter, if one trader is buying then the other trader is selling, and vice versa. So the actions of the two traders are exactly the opposite of each other. Understanding the motivation behind the other trader's action may be crucial to understanding whether the trade is actually a good idea. For example, in the used-car market, a buyer should ask why any seller wants to sell. The same question can be asked by sellers when they are at a potential information disadvantage: for example, companies selling health insurance cannot be sure exactly why any one individual is seeking to buy their insurance.

All these issues play an important role in another market we discussed earlier in the chapter – the market for financial assets such as stocks or bonds. Here too, for every buyer there is a seller, and each should be curious about the other's motivation. A seller of a stock could be selling because of a desire to adjust their portfolio or a need for cash. A seller of a stock could be selling because their opinion differs from the opinion reflected in the market price (the market belief), even though they do not have private information. Alternatively, a seller could be selling because they have some private information that suggests that the price of the stock will fall in the future. Similarly, a buyer could want to buy because they have extra cash to invest, because they simply happen to have a different belief about the market, or because they are taking advantage of information that suggests the price of the stock will rise in the future.

When one side in such stock trades has better information, the other party would value the stock differently if they too had the information. Determining what the other party to the transaction knows is often impossible, but understanding that sometimes the other party knows something is not impossible. Once each party to the transaction takes this into account, it is possible that no trade occurs, just as we saw with the example of used cars [299].

22.8 Signaling Quality

Given how powerfully information asymmetry can affect the operation of a market, it is natural to consider methods for alleviating it. One fundamental approach, useful in a number of settings, is to create a kind of certification mechanism: a way for a seller to provide a signal about the quality of the good that he or she is offering for sale.

To return to the case of used cars, for example, we can identify a variety of such possible signals. One that dealers sometimes offer is a guarantee that a given car is a "certified used car." Dealers certify that these cars have been checked for a number of possible defects and that any problems have been repaired. Another signaling mechanism is to offer a warranty promising that if the car needs to be repaired during some period after the sale, then the seller will pay for, or provide for free, the needed repair. Both of these quality assurances are directly valuable to buyers, but their value is more than you might imagine. It is less expensive for sellers who have good cars to provide these guarantees or warranties than it is for sellers who have bad cars. Either fewer repairs are needed before the car is sold or fewer repairs are expected to be needed after the car is sold. If it is too expensive for sellers of bad cars to provide these signals, then only good cars will have the signals – or at least, applying a milder form of this reasoning, the population of cars with these signals will contain a higher proportion of good cars compared to the population as a whole. Thus, buyers can make inferences about the quality of the car from the existence of the signal. These inferences raise the expected value of the car to the buyer even more than the direct value of the completed or promised future repairs.

Thus, the overall system of warranties may be crucial for breaking down information asymmetries that could otherwise cause the market to fail.

Signaling in the Labor Market. This idea of signaling applies to many settings other than just the used-car market. Perhaps its most important application is to the labor market, in which education can serve as a signal; Michael Spence developed this idea and shared the 2001 Nobel Prize in Economics (with George Akerlof and Joseph Stiglitz) for his work on this topic [379].

Spence's idea is easy to understand in the context of our earlier labor market example, where firms cannot initially distinguish productive workers from unproductive ones. Suppose that it is easier for productive workers to obtain education than it is for unproductive workers. (Perhaps productive workers also perform better in school, and they can obtain a degree with less effort.) In this case, education provides a credible signal of productivity, and employers would be willing to pay higher wages to workers with more education than to workers with less education.

Notice that this signaling mechanism works even if education has no direct effect on a worker's productivity. Of course, education is also intrinsically valuable, but when we take information asymmetry into account, we see that education has a kind of twofold power in the market. It trains workers for future employment, but beyond this, it also reduces information asymmetry about worker quality in a way that can potentially be necessary for the labor market to function effectively at all.

22.9 Quality Uncertainty Online: Reputation Systems and Other Mechanisms

Once we adopt the perspective that the availability of information is crucial in many markets, we can begin to appreciate that many of the standard mechanisms used in Web sites for online commerce are in fact motivated by considerations of asymmetric information and signaling. In this section we discuss two of these mechanisms: reputation systems, and the role of ad-quality measures in sponsored-search advertising.

Reputation Systems. One of the clearest examples of these ideas at work in an online setting is the development of *reputation systems* for sites like eBay [171]. Since eBay is designed to facilitate trade between arbitrary people who have never met and may never meet again, a buyer faces a risk that he is dealing with a bad seller (like a seller of a lemon) who will provide an item of lower quality than advertised, or possibly fail to provide a promised item at all. Thus, we have a situation that corresponds closely to the market for lemons: if buyers believe that the chance of receiving bad products (or of being cheated outright) is too high, then the price they will be willing to pay for an arbitrary item on eBay will be so low that no seller of reasonable items will want to participate. In this case, eBay's market could fail completely.

Reputation systems are a kind of feature provided by Web sites like eBay to offer a certification mechanism for alleviating this problem. After each purchase, the buyer can provide an evaluation of the seller, reporting whether the transaction and the item they received met the expectations that were conveyed. The evaluations received by a seller are synthesized by an algorithm at the heart of the system to provide an overall *reputation score* for the seller. A seller's reputation score evolves over time: favorable evaluations cause the score to go up while unfavorable ones cause it to go down. Thus, a good reputation score serves as a signal; in principle, it is costly to obtain, since it requires engaging in a sequence of transactions that cause the respective buyers to be satisfied. If it's cheaper for good sellers to acquire a good reputation than it is for bad sellers to acquire the same reputation, then reputation can serve as a signal of seller quality, just as a seller certifying his used car or a worker paying for education serves as a signal. In this way, if a site like eBay can convince buyers to have confidence in the reliability of the reputation system, then the resulting scores can reduce some of the strong information asymmetries inherent in the site.

There are many challenges in creating a reputation system that functions effectively, and a number of these challenges arise from the online nature of the application itself [171]. In particular, participants on a site like eBay can generally create multiple identities by registering for multiple user accounts on the system, and this leads to several approaches for subverting the goals of the reputation system. First, a seller interested in misbehaving can build up the reputation of a particular identity so that buyers will trust it, then behave badly until its reputation gets seriously damaged, discard the identity in favor of a freshly created one, and start the process again. In other words, the reputational consequences of bad behavior can be mitigated online if there is an easy way to "start over" by simply registering a new identity on the site. This ability to start over adds a severe moral-hazard feature to the online transaction problem, just like the ability of an individual to affect his health status adds a moral-hazard component to health insurance. This makes the problem of creating a reliable reputation system more difficult than it would be if there were only an adverse-selection problem. In addition, the design of a reputation system is further complicated by the potential for other kinds of misleading seller behavior. In particular, a seller can operate several identities simultaneously and have the different identities engage in transactions with one another purely for the purpose of having them lavish positive feedback on each other. The seller can thereby obtain identities with high reputation scores despite no genuine history of good behavior.

In spirit, these types of strategies are reminiscent of what we saw in our discussion of link analysis for Web search – they are extreme versions of the general principle that when people's behavior is being evaluated by an algorithm, we should expect that many people will react and adapt to the criteria of the algorithm in ways that benefit them. Designing reputation systems that are robust in the presence of these kinds of difficulties is an ongoing research question.

Ad Quality in Keyword-Based Advertising. The ideas behind the market for lemons also show up clearly in the systems that search engines use for keyword-based advertising, and in fact this makes for an interesting case study in how these ideas have influenced a large online market. Specifically, we talked in Chapter 15 about the problem of ad quality – how the ranking of an ad on a page should not be based purely on the bid offered by the advertiser, but also on an estimate of the true clickthrough rates that this ad will have in a given position, compared to other ads. Otherwise, an unappealing ad based on a high bid could end up clogging the top slot on the page, generating very little revenue for the search engine because almost no one clicks on it.

But when you look at how the search industry actually runs the market for advertising, you quickly appreciate that the notion of "ad quality" is not just a proxy for the estimated rate of clicks the ad will get – it is a more subtle concept that is based on a broader estimate of overall user satisfaction with the ad. A common scenario here is as follows. There can be an advertiser that bids very highly for an ad on a certain query, *and* this ad has enticing text that causes it to get clicked on at a rapid rate by users from the search results page. A high bid per click multiplied by a high rate of clicks generates significant revenue for the search engine. However, the actual page the ad links to (the *landing page* that users reach when they click on the ad) is of low quality – not fraudulent, just not actually very relevant to the query with which the ad is associated. Consider, for example, an advertiser that places a high bid on an ad for the query "Caribbean vacations" and includes ad text on the Google results page saying "Dream vacations here" – but when you click on the ad, you get to a page that's trying to rent vacation properties in some completely different part of the world. It would be natural for most users to be disappointed when they click on this ad.

In such scenarios, the current strategy of search engines is to significantly lower the placement of such an ad on the page, or to not display it, *even though* this apparently causes them to lose the high rate of price-per-click revenue that the ad would generate in a high position. Their reason for this is the following: If users learn from experience that clicking on ads often takes them to low-quality landing pages, then they won't click on ads as much in general, and this overall effect on user behavior will have a huge negative effect on revenue in the long run. Essentially, the short-term gain in revenue from high-clickthrough low-quality ads is being traded off against the long-term losses due to user perceptions of quality.

The problem of asymmetric information is a fundamental issue behind this trade-off, and in fact the market for search advertising exhibits the basic ingredients of the market for lemons. Although clicking on a single search ad is a much less significant action than purchasing a car or hiring a new employee – as in our earlier examples of the used-car market and the labor market – it is still an activity that a user (the buyer) will undertake only if she believes that what she will find at the other end of the resulting link (the item being offered by the seller) is worth her effort. And just as a buyer can't tell the true quality of a used car until she purchases it, a user can't tell how well the ad text reflects the true quality of the landing page until she clicks on the ad. In this respect, advertisers have more information about the quality of their landing pages than the users of search engines do, and users implicitly form a mental estimate of how much they expect the ad text to reflect the quality of the landing page.

Notice, therefore, that while the analogy to the market for lemons is quite natural, it is also a bit subtle. In particular, it is not about the relationship between the advertisers and the search engine (though one can look for information asymmetry there too), but between the users and the advertisers, with user effort in clicking on ads as the quantity being valued. In aggregate, of course, all these user decisions to click are crucial, since they add up to a large portion of the search industry's revenue.

Now, we have seen in our earlier analyses that there can be multiple self-fulfilling expectations equilibria in these types of markets: some where buyers predict high average quality and there are in fact high-quality items for sale, and some where buyers predict low average quality and only low-quality items are on the market. Such equilibria are based on the assumption that consumers make correct predictions, which makes sense in the case of search advertising if users have time to learn the distribution of ad quality. Since the search engines have control over the ads they display, they are trying to maintain a mixture of ads of reasonable quality, thereby selecting an equilibrium for the overall market in which users expect high-quality ads, and advertisers with high-quality content are correspondingly willing to advertise via search engines.

22.10 Advanced Material: Wealth Dynamics in Markets

When we considered markets for assets such as stocks, shares in a prediction market, or bets in a horse race, we observed that market prices serve to aggregate the beliefs of the market participants. Essentially, the market produces a weighted average of the participants' beliefs, with the weights determined by the participants' relative shares of wealth. Now, if we were to watch the market as it runs over time, certain participants would do better than others, their wealth shares would increase, and as a result their overall effect on the aggregate market price would increase. If we expect that people with more accurate beliefs will do better in the market, then this reweighting as wealth shifts toward them should in fact produce more accurate market prices.

This intuition about market evolution over time was developed in the writings of a number of economists in the mid-twentieth century [11, 157, 172]. The basic argument is that markets impose a kind of "natural selection" that favors traders whose decisions are closest to optimal. Early writers used this idea to argue that one tends to find rational investors in markets (because the others will have been driven out of the market) and that stock markets tend to be efficient (because prices are determined by the traders who have survived over the long run).

It has only been relatively recently, however, that this general idea has been explored more precisely, and its scope and limitations have begun to be understood. In this section, we describe a basic mathematical analysis that formalizes the intuition at the heart of these ideas [64]. The analysis will work by developing a close analogy between wealth dynamics in a market and the use of Bayes' rule by an individual who learns over time. Recall from Chapter 16 that Bayes' rule provides a systematic way to make use of new observations in decision-making. We will see that as wealth moves between participants in a market, their contributions to the aggregate market price change over time exactly like the probabilities assigned to different hypotheses would change according to Bayes' rule.

So in a precise sense, although the market is simply an institution that facilitates trade, it can also be viewed as acting like an artificially intelligent Bayesian agent that aggregates information. Moreover, if there is a set of traders who have correct beliefs, then over time their fraction of the wealth converges to 1, and the market price converges to reflect their (correct) beliefs. This provides a concrete expression of the general idea that markets for assets tend to work well at synthesizing the information held by groups of people.

A. Bayesian Learning in a Market

We begin the analysis by considering how a Bayesian learner – that is, someone applying Bayes' rule – would update his beliefs over time in a market. Once we've done this, we'll draw an analogy to how the wealth of participants changes over time.

We discussed Bayes's rule in Chapter 16, but here we'll cast it in the notation of this chapter and also extend some of the conclusions. Since horse races have served as a useful example to suggest the phenomena at work in more complex settings like the stock market, we'll continue to use horse races in the discussion here. Thus, suppose that two horses, A and B, will run a race every week; suppose that the outcomes of these races are independent; and suppose that A wins each one with probability a (and hence B wins with probability $b = 1 - a$).

Now, our Bayesian learner does not know the values of a and b; rather, he wants to learn them over time by watching the outcomes of races. He begins with a set of N possible hypotheses for the probabilities, which we will denote by

$$(a_1, b_1), (a_2, b_2), \ldots, (a_N, b_N).$$

For now, let's assume in fact that one of these hypotheses is correct (although the learner does not know which it is); we relabel them if necessary so that $(a_1, b_1) = (a, b)$.

The learner begins with a *prior probability* for each hypothesis; let f_n be the prior probability of hypothesis (a_n, b_n). We assume that each prior probability f_n is greater than zero, indicating that the learner considers it to be a possible description of the true probability. Because these prior probabilities form an initial weighted average over the hypotheses, the learner's initial predicted probability of A winning is

$$a_1 f_1 + a_2 f_2 + \cdots + a_N f_N.$$

Now, suppose that T races are run, and we observe a sequence S of outcomes of these races, in which horse A wins a total of k times and horse B wins a total of ℓ times. Then using Bayes' rule as in Chapter 16, we can compute the posterior probability of the hypothesis (a_n, b_n), conditional on the sequence S, as follows:

$$\Pr\left[(a_n, b_n) \mid S\right] = \frac{f_n \Pr\left[S \mid (a_n, b_n)\right]}{\Pr\left[S\right]}$$

$$= \frac{f_n \Pr\left[S \mid (a_n, b_n)\right]}{f_1 \Pr\left[S \mid (a_1, b_1)\right] + f_2 \Pr\left[S \mid (a_2, b_2)\right] + \cdots + f_N \Pr\left[S \mid (a_N, b_N)\right]}.$$

Now, the probability of S given a hypothesis (a_n, b_n) is simply the probability it assigns to the sequence of wins in S: since horse A wins a total of k times and horse B wins a total of ℓ times, this probability is just $a_n^k b_n^\ell$. Therefore, we have

$$\Pr\left[(a_n, b_n) \mid S\right] = \frac{f_n a_n^k b_n^\ell}{f_1 a_1^k b_1^\ell + f_2 a_2^k b_2^\ell + \cdots + f_N a_N^k b_N^\ell}. \tag{22.13}$$

Moreover, after this sequence S of observed outcomes, the learner's predicted probability for horse A is

$$a_1 \Pr\left[(a_1, b_1) \mid S\right] + a_2 \Pr\left[(a_2, b_2) \mid S\right] + \cdots + a_N \Pr\left[(a_N, b_N) \mid S\right]. \tag{22.14}$$

This is the sense in which the learner is Bayesian: as he observes outcomes, he updates his predicted probability according to Bayes' rule.

Convergence to the Correct Hypothesis. Now, let's consider how the posterior probabilities of the different hypotheses fare as horse races are run over a long period of time. The easiest way to do this is to consider the ratios of these probabilities. After a sequence S of observed outcomes, with k wins by A and ℓ wins by B, the ratio of the posterior probability of hypothesis (a_m, b_m) to the posterior probability of hypothesis (a_n, b_n) can be computed simply by taking the ratios of the respective expressions given by Equation (22.13) and noticing that the two expressions have the same denominator:

$$\frac{\Pr[(a_m, b_m) \mid S]}{\Pr[(a_n, b_n) \mid S]} = \frac{f_m a_m^k b_m^\ell}{f_n a_n^k b_n^\ell}. \tag{22.15}$$

We will be particularly interested in ratios that compare the correct hypothesis (a_1, b_1) to an alternate hypothesis (a_n, b_n):

$$\frac{\Pr[(a_1, b_1) \mid S]}{\Pr[(a_n, b_n) \mid S]} = \frac{f_1 a_1^k b_1^\ell}{f_n a_n^k b_n^\ell}. \tag{22.16}$$

We call this ratio $R_n[S]$. Taking logarithms yields something known as the *log odds ratio* of the two hypotheses, given the sequence of observed outcomes S:

$$\ln(R_n[S]) = \ln\left(\frac{f_1}{f_n}\right) + k\ln\left(\frac{a_1}{a_n}\right) + \ell\ln\left(\frac{b_1}{b_n}\right).$$

Now, let's divide both sides by the total number of observations T, obtaining

$$\frac{1}{T}\ln(R_n[S]) = \frac{1}{T}\ln\left(\frac{f_1}{f_n}\right) + \frac{k}{T}\ln\left(\frac{a_1}{a_n}\right) + \frac{\ell}{T}\ln\left(\frac{b_1}{b_n}\right). \tag{22.17}$$

We're interested in what happens as T goes to infinity, and in this case the right-hand side of this equation can be simplified as follows. The first term is just a fixed constant $\ln(f_1/f_n)$ divided by T, so it converges to 0 as T grows. To analyze the second and third terms, we observe, using the Law of Large Numbers, that k/T converges almost surely to the true probability of horse A winning, which is a, and ℓ/T converges almost surely to the true probability of horse B winning, which is b. So the entire right-hand side of Equation (22.17) converges almost surely to

$$a\ln\left(\frac{a_1}{a_n}\right) + b\ln\left(\frac{b_1}{b_n}\right) = a\ln(a_1) + b\ln(b_1) - [a\ln(a_n) + b\ln(b_n)]. \tag{22.18}$$

We want to know whether this limit is positive, negative, or zero, since that will let us reason about what's happening to the left-hand side of Equation (22.17). Here is how we can think about this limit. The first two terms have the form $a\ln(x) + (1-a)\ln(1-x)$, with $x = a_1$, and the third and fourth terms have this form as well, with $x = a_n$. But we know from Section 22.2, and specifically the discussion around Equation (22.5), that the expression $a\ln(x) + (1-a)\ln(1-x)$ is maximized when $x = a$, and it is strictly smaller than this maximum for all other values of x. Since $a_1 = a$, the sum of the first two terms therefore achieves this maximum, and since $a_n \neq a$, the third and fourth terms that are being subtracted off don't achieve the maximum. Therefore, the expression in Equation (22.18) is strictly positive (since the first two terms outweigh the latter two), and so returning to Equation (22.17), we conclude that

$$\frac{1}{T}\ln(R_n[S]) > 0$$

almost surely as T goes to infinity.

It follows that, as T goes to infinity, $\ln(R_n[S])$, and hence $R_n[S]$ itself, must be diverging to positive infinity. Moreover, this takes place for every $n > 1$ – that is, for every incorrect hypothesis. How can this happen? Each $R_n[S]$ is the ratio of two probabilities, so in order for one of the probabilities (on (a_1, b_1)) to become larger than all the others by an arbitrary factor, it must be that the probability on hypothesis (a_1, b_1) is converging to 1 while the probability on each of the others is converging to 0.

The conclusion from this analysis is that the Bayesian learner will, in the limit, assign a posterior probability of 1 to the correct hypothesis. Moreover, this means that his predicted probability for horse A, as computed by Equation (22.14), is converging to $a_1 = a$.

Convergence Without a Correct Hypothesis. If we think about it, the preceding analysis in fact shows something stronger than we've claimed. For the learner to converge to a posterior probability of 1 on the hypothesis (a_1, b_1), it is not necessary that (a_1, b_1) actually be correct. We simply need that the expression in Equation(22.18) is positive for all competing hypotheses $n > 1$.

The interpretation of this stronger claim is usually expressed in terms of a notion of "distance" between hypotheses, as follows. For a given hypothesis (a_n, b_n), we define the *relative entropy* $D_{(a,b)}(a_n, b_n)$ between (a_n, b_n) and the true hypothesis (a, b) to be

$$D_{(a,b)}(a_n, b_n) = a \ln(a) + b \ln(b) - [a \ln(a_n) + b \ln(b_n)]. \tag{22.19}$$

By our earlier observation about the maximization of $a \ln(x) + (1 - a) \ln(1 - x)$, we see that the contribution of the first two terms must always outweigh the negative effect of the third and fourth terms, and so $D_{(a,b)}(a_n, b_n)$ is always a nonnegative number, and it is zero when $(a_n, b_n) = (a, b)$. We can therefore interpret the relative entropy as a nonlinear measure of how far a given hypothesis is from the truth: smaller relative entropies indicate better agreement with the true hypothesis.

Going back to Equations (22.17) and (22.18), we see that, even when (a_1, b_1) is not the correct hypothesis, the quantity $\ln(R_n[S])/T$ is converging almost surely to

$$D_{(a,b)}(a_n, b_n) - D_{(a,b)}(a_1, b_1).$$

Therefore, suppose that $a_1 \neq a$, but that the hypothesis (a_1, b_1) is closer than any other (a_n, b_n) to the true hypothesis in relative entropy: that is,

$$D_{(a,b)}(a_1, b_1) < D_{(a,b)}(a_n, b_n)$$

for all $n > 1$. Then just as before, we have

$$\frac{1}{T} \ln(R_n[S]) > 0$$

almost surely as T goes to infinity. And from this we draw the same conclusion as before: that the posterior probability the learner places on (a_1, b_1) converges to 1.

In other words, when no hypothesis is correct but some hypothesis is uniquely closest to the truth in relative entropy, a Bayesian learner will assign a posterior probability of 1 to this hypothesis in the limit.

B. Wealth Dynamics

We have now seen how a Bayesian learner aggregates information about events taking place in a market: the learner maintains a weighted average of the probabilities assigned by different hypotheses, updating the weights using Bayes' rule. Earlier in the chapter, we saw that the odds computed by the market are also a weighted average – in that case an average of bettors' beliefs weighted by their wealth shares. As time runs forward, the weights in this weighted average are updated simply because the bettors are gaining and losing money. We now show that this updating works exactly the way Bayes' rule does, which is why the aggregate behavior of the market itself can be viewed as that of a Bayesian learner.

Evolution of Wealth Shares. Let's use the framework of betting markets from Sections 22.2 and 22.3 (again as a stand-in for more complex settings like stock markets). There are N bettors; each bettor n has a fixed belief that horse A will win with probability a_n (and hence that horse B will win with probability $b_n = 1 - a_n$). Bettor n has an initial wealth of w_n; if the total wealth of all bettors is w, then this corresponds to a share $f_n = w_n/w$ of the total wealth.

Now, horses A and B race each other in each of time steps $t = 1, 2, 3, \ldots$. At the start of each time step t, before the tth race, the market determines odds $o_A^{\langle t \rangle}$ and $o_B^{\langle t \rangle}$ on horses A and B; note that the odds may be different in each step, and as we saw in Section 22.3 they may depend on who the bettors are and how much they are betting. Also at the start of each step t, each bettor n has a current wealth $w_n^{\langle t \rangle}$; he bets this wealth optimally given his beliefs (a_n, b_n). As we saw in Section 22.2, this corresponds to putting a bet of $a_n w_n^{\langle t \rangle}$ on horse A and a bet of $b_n w_n^{\langle t \rangle}$ on horse B. Consequently, bettor n's new wealth $w_n^{\langle t+1 \rangle}$ after this race is equal to $a_n w_n^{\langle t \rangle} o_A^{\langle t \rangle}$ if A wins, and it is equal to $b_n w_n^{\langle t \rangle} o_B^{\langle t \rangle}$ if B wins.

Let's consider two bettors m and n, with initial wealth shares f_m and f_n, and suppose that by step t, due to the results of their bets on the first $t - 1$ races, their wealth shares are $f_m^{\langle t \rangle}$ and $f_n^{\langle t \rangle}$, respectively. Let's consider the two possible outcomes of race t.

- If horse A wins race t, the wealth of bettor m is multiplied by $a_m o_A^{\langle t \rangle}$ and the wealth of bettor n is multiplied by $a_n o_A^{\langle t \rangle}$. Therefore, in this case, the ratio of the wealth shares of m and n changes from $f_m^{\langle t \rangle}/f_m^{\langle t \rangle}$ to $a_m f_m^{\langle t \rangle}/a_n f_m^{\langle t \rangle}$. (Notice that the odds cancel out of this ratio, since they apply equally to both bettors.) In other words, the ratio is multiplied by a_m/a_n.
- If horse B wins race t, the wealth of bettor m is multiplied by $b_m o_B^{\langle t \rangle}$ and the wealth of bettor n is multiplied by $b_n o_B^{\langle t \rangle}$. Therefore, in this case, the ratio of the wealth shares of m and n changes from $f_m^{\langle t \rangle}/f_m^{\langle t \rangle}$ to $b_m f_m^{\langle t \rangle}/b_n f_m^{\langle t \rangle}$. In other words, the ratio is multiplied by b_m/b_n.

So we see that whenever horse A wins a race, the ratio of wealth shares of bettors m and n changes by a factor of a_m/a_n, while whenever horse B wins a race, the ratio of their wealth shares changes by a factor of b_m/b_n.

Suppose we apply these changes, starting from wealth shares f_m and f_n, over a sequence of races S in which A wins k times and B wins ℓ times. Then we end up with a ratio of wealth shares that's equal to

$$\frac{f_m a_m^k b_m^\ell}{f_n a_n^k b_n^\ell}. \tag{22.20}$$

The point is that this is exactly the same as Equation (22.15), describing the ratio of posterior probabilities that a Bayesian learner puts on the hypotheses (a_m, b_m) and (a_n, b_n), starting from prior probabilities of f_m and f_n. So the analogy is perfect: the wealth shares of the bettors evolve exactly like the posterior probabilities on hypotheses under Bayes' rule. That is, the market treats each bettor as a hypothesis about the two horses, and in response to the outcome of the race it adjusts that bettor's wealth share in exactly the same way that a Bayesian learner would adjust the probability on the hypothesis.

We can draw two main conclusions from this result.

- First, the inverse odds maintained by the market are computed from the wealth-share weighted average of the bettors' beliefs, using Equation (22.9) from Section 22.3. This equation is parallel to the Bayesian learner's Equation (22.14) by which he determines the predicted probability for horse A. Hence, the market's inverse odds follow the results of Bayesian learning as well.

- Because the ratios of wealth shares evolve just as the posterior probabilities of hypotheses, we can conclude that if there is a unique bettor whose beliefs are closest in relative entropy to the correct probabilities (a, b), then in the limit the wealth share of this bettor will converge to 1. So the market is selecting for bettors with more accurate beliefs, where "accuracy" here refers to the bettor's distance from the truth in relative entropy. Combined with our previous observation about the inverse odds, we see that in the limit, the assets (i.e., the possible bets) are priced according to the most accurate information held by any of the market participants.

It is also important to note that in the special case when one of the bettors has correct beliefs, this bettor will acquire a wealth share of 1 in the limit, and the market will come to reflect the bettor's (correct) beliefs.

Extensions and Interpretations. We have kept the model very simple so as to make the calculations clear. But it is possible to extend the model to incorporate a number of further considerations.

First, we are assuming that the bettors have fixed beliefs and do not learn from observing the outcomes of races. This makes it easy to isolate the effect of wealth dynamics in the market, distinguishing it from the learning dynamics of individual participants. But while it is a bit messy, it is not particularly difficult to combine this analysis of wealth dynamics with Bayesian learning by the bettors. Second, our analysis assumes that each bettor reinvests his entire wealth in the market in each time step. However, this too can be extended to a model in which bettors must decide both how much to reinvest in the market, as well as how to allocate this investment across the different options [64].

Our overall conclusion – that the market selects for the trader with the most accurate beliefs, and asymptotically prices assets according to these beliefs – applies equally well in other settings such as prediction markets. Notice that the argument here about the performance of the market is not based on the benefits of averaging, as in our previous discussion of the "wisdom of crowds." Rather, in the analysis here, the crowd is exactly as smart as its smartest participant in the limit, since in the limit it is only this participant whose beliefs affect the market's predictions. As noted earlier, this idea draws on a long history of economic arguments for market efficiency based on natural selection [11, 157, 172], in which smarter traders come to hold an increasingly large fraction of the wealth in the market and thereby exert an increasingly large influence on the market. The model here puts this intuition on more precise footing [64], and subsequent research has expanded on it in important ways [65, 362].

While these expanded models are too complex to describe in detail here, they relate in interesting ways to some of the issues from earlier in the chapter. First, and rather surprisingly, the more complex models show that the assumption of logarithmic utility, on which the model here is based, is in fact not important for the general conclusion about market selection. A more general and abstract analysis shows that we only need the assumption that traders are risk averse – that is, their utility gain from increased wealth decreases as their wealth grows. The recent line of research also shows that these results apply to more complex markets, provided that there is a rich enough set of assets being traded. Intuitively, if there aren't enough traded assets, there may not be enough ways for traders with better beliefs to take advantage of traders with worse beliefs, and thus the traders with worse beliefs may not be driven out of the market. The richness condition that is needed for stock markets is exactly the condition discussed in Section 22.4. The conclusion of this analysis is that if there is a rich enough set of assets traded in the stock market, then in the long run the market prices assets as correctly as possible given the collection of traders' beliefs that are made available to the market.

22.11 Exercises

1. Consider a betting market with two horses A and B and two bettors 1 and 2, as in Section 22.3. Let's suppose that each bettor has wealth w. Bettor 1 believes there is a probability of $\frac{1}{2}$ that horse A will win, and a probability of $\frac{1}{2}$ that horse B will win. Bettor 2 believes there is a probability of $\frac{1}{4}$ that horse A will win, and a probability of $\frac{3}{4}$ that horse B will win. Both bettors have logarithmic utility for wealth, and they each choose bets to maximize the expected utility of wealth given their beliefs.

   (a) How much money should bettors 1 and 2 each bet on horses A and B, respectively?
   (b) Find the equilibrium inverse odds on horse A and on horse B.
   (c) How much money will bettor 1 have after the race if horse A wins? How about if horse B wins?

2. Consider a betting market with two horses, A and B, and two bettors, 1 and 2, as in Section 22.3. Let's suppose that each bettor has wealth w. Bettor 1's beliefs are (a_1, b_1), where the first number in the pair is bettor 1's probability of horse A winning

the race. Both bettors have logarithmic utility for wealth. Bettor 1 chooses his bets to maximize his expected utility of wealth using his beliefs, as in the chapter. Bettor 2, however, behaves differently; he believes that the inverse odds are the correct probabilities and he maximizes his expected utility using these inverse odds.

(a) Bettor 1's optimal bet on horse A is some function of his wealth and his beliefs. Let's call this function $f_1(w, a_1)$. Determine this function.

(b) Suppose that bettor 2 knows the equilibrium inverse odds on horse A, which we call ρ_A. Bettor 2's optimal bet on horse A is some function of his wealth and the equilibrium inverse odds on horse A. Let's call this function $f_2(w, \rho_A)$. Determine this function.

(c) If we take Equation (22.8) from Section 22.3 and apply it to the betting rules in question, then we see that the equilibrium inverse odds on horse A must solve the equation

$$\frac{f_1(w, a_1)}{2w} + \frac{f_2(w, \rho_A)}{2w} = \rho_A.$$

Using this observation, find the equilibrium inverse odds on horse A.

(d) Now let's generalize this idea to many bettors. Suppose that most bettors are like bettor 2; they trust that the inverse odds are in some sense correct and they use them in deciding how to bet. Only a few bettors are like bettor 1; they have beliefs and they bet according to their beliefs. Would you expect the "wisdom of crowds" idea to be more or less likely to be true in this market than in a market in which each bettor has beliefs and bets according to their own beliefs? Does your answer depend on which bettors bet using inverse odds as their beliefs and which ones use their own beliefs? (Think about which bettors are more likely to have correct beliefs.)

3. Consider the model of the market for lemons. Suppose that there are three types of used cars: good ones, medium ones, and lemons, and that sellers know which type of car they have. Buyers do not know which type of car a seller has. The fraction of used cars of each type is $\frac{1}{3}$ and buyers know this. Let's suppose that a seller who has a good car values it at $8,000, a seller with a medium car values it at $5,000, and a seller with a lemon values the lemon at $1,000. A seller is willing to sell his car for any price greater than or equal to his value for the car; the seller is not willing to sell the car at a price below the value of the car. Buyers' values for good cars, medium cars, and lemons are, $9,000, $8,000, and $4,000, respectively. As in Chapter 22 we assume that buyers are risk neutral; that is, they are willing to pay their expected value of a car.

(a) Is there an equilibrium in the used-car market in which all types of cars are sold? Explain briefly.

(b) Is there an equilibrium in the used-car market in which only medium-quality cars and lemons are sold? Explain briefly.

(c) Is there an equilibrium in the used-car market in which only lemons are sold? Explain briefly.

4. Consider the model of the market for lemons from Chapter 22. Suppose that there are two types of used cars – good ones and lemons – and that sellers know which type of car they have. Buyers do not know which type of car a seller has. The fraction of used cars of each type is $\frac{1}{2}$ and buyers know this. Let's suppose that a seller who has a good car values it at $10,000 and a seller with a lemon values the lemon

at $5,000. A seller is willing to sell his car for any price greater than or equal to his value for the car; the seller is not willing to sell the car at a price below the value of the car. Buyers' values for good cars and lemons are $14,000 and $8,000, respectively. As in Chapter 22 we assume that buyers are risk neutral; that is, they are willing to pay their expected value of a car.

(a) Is there an equilibrium in the used-car market in which all types of cars are sold? Briefly explain.
(b) Is there an equilibrium in the used-car market in which only lemons are sold? Briefly explain.

5. Consider the model of the market for lemons. Suppose that there are three types of used cars: good ones, medium ones, and lemons, and that sellers know which type of car they have. Buyers do not know which type of car a seller has. The fraction of used cars of each type is $\frac{1}{3}$ and buyers know this. Let's suppose that a seller who has a good car values it at $4,000, a seller with a medium car values it at $3,000, and a seller with a lemon values it at $0. A seller is willing to sell his car for any price greater than or equal to his value for the car; the seller is not willing to sell the car at a price below the value of the car. Buyers values for good cars, medium cars, and lemons are $10,000, $4,000, and $1,000, respectively. As in Chapter 22 we assume that buyers are willing to pay their expected value of a car. We also assume that there are at least as many buyers as used cars.

(a) Is there an equilibrium in the used-car market in which all types of used cars are sold? If so, find some equilibrium price for used cars such that all used cars are sold, together with a brief explanation of why all cars are sold. If not, explain why not.
(b) Now suppose that someone develops a way for sellers of good used cars to certify that their cars are good cars. All sellers of good used cars do this and they are no longer part of the general market for uncertified used cars, which now consists only of medium-quality used cars and lemons in equal numbers. Is there an equilibrium in the market for these remaining, uncertified used cars in which both medium-quality used cars and lemons are sold? If so, find some equilibrium price for used cars such that medium-quality used cars and lemons are sold, together with a brief explanation. If not, explain why not.

6. Consider the model of the market for lemons. Suppose that there are two types of used cars, good ones and lemons, and that sellers know which type of car they have. Buyers do not know which type of car a seller has. The fraction of used cars that are good cars is g and buyers know this fraction. Let's suppose that a seller who has a good car values it at $10,000 and that a seller with a lemon values the lemon at $4,000. A seller is willing to sell his car for any price greater than or equal to his value for the car; the seller is not willing to sell the car at a price below the value of the car. Buyers' values for good cars and lemons are $12,000 and $5,000, respectively. As in Chapter 22 we assume that buyers are risk neutral; that is, they are willing to pay their expected value of a car.

(a) Suppose that you observe that used cars sell for a price of $10,000. What can you say about the fraction of used cars that are lemons?
(b) Suppose instead that the fraction of used cars that are lemons is $g = 0.5$. What is the maximum selling price for used cars?

7. In this question we are going to examine how a tax on the purchase of used cars may affect the price and quantity of used cars traded. Suppose that there are two types of used cars: good ones and bad ones. Sellers of used cars know the type of car that they own. Buyers do not know which type of car any particular seller has. Buyers do know that there are good and bad used cars, and they know that, of the 100 people who own used cars and are interested in selling their car, 50 have good cars and 50 have bad cars. Let's suppose that there are 200 possible buyers of used cars. (As in Chapter 22 we want to assume that there are more buyers than sellers to make the analysis straightforward.) A seller who has a good used car values it at $8,000 and a seller who has a bad used car values it at $3,000. A seller is willing to sell his car for any price greater than or equal to his value for the car; no seller is willing to sell his car for a price less than his value for the car. Buyers' values for good and bad used cars are $10,000 and $6,000, respectively. As in Chapter 22 we assume that buyers each want at most one used car and they are willing to pay their expected value for a used car.

   (a) Find all of the equilibria in the market for used cars. For each equilibrium provide the price of used cars and the number of used cars traded.
   (b) Now suppose that the government places a tax of $100 on the purchase of used cars. That is, anyone who buys a used car must pay a tax of $100 on the purchase of the car. This effectively lowers the values that buyers place on any type of used car by $100. Find all of the equilibria in the market for used cars.
   (c) Now let's change the setup of the problem a bit so that there are three types of used cars: good ones, bad ones, and lemons. There are 50 sellers with good cars, 50 with bad cars, and 50 with lemons. Buyers' and sellers' values for good and bad used cars are the same as before. Everyone (both buyers and sellers) values a lemon at $0. There are still 200 buyers.

      (i) There is no tax on the purchase of used cars. Find all of the equilibria in the market for used cars.
      (ii) Now the government imposes a tax of $100 on the purchase of used cars. Find all of the equilibria in the market for used cars.

8. A group of researchers have been investigating the quality and seaworthiness of five-year-old boats in the United States. They classify the boats into five possible categories: excellent, good, medium, poor, and dangerous. They have concluded that there are no excellent five-year-old boats, and that most of these boats are of medium and/or lower quality. To conduct their study, these researchers pretended to be potential buyers of five-year-old boats. They examined a very large number of five-year-old boats offered for sale both by private sellers (individuals) and by boat dealers. Based on the results of their study this group of researchers has concluded that there should be an investigation by the U.S. Coast Guard into the quality of these older boats. What concerns do you have about the methodology the researchers used in their study? Can you suggest an alternative approach that they may have used in order to draw a more careful conclusion about the actual quality distribution of five-year-old boats?

CHAPTER 23

Voting

In the previous chapter, we saw a first example of an institution that can synthesize information held by many people, through the ways in which markets serve to aggregate the individual beliefs of investors. We now turn to a second fundamental institution: voting.

23.1 Voting for Group Decision Making

Like markets, voting systems also serve to aggregate information across a group, and as a result, it's hard to draw a perfectly clear dividing line between these two kinds of institutions. But there are definite distinctions between the respective settings in which they are typically applied. A first important distinction is that voting is generally used in situations where a group of people is expressly trying to reach a single decision that in a sense will speak for the group. When a population votes on a set of candidates or ballot initiatives, a legislative body votes on whether to pass a bill, a jury votes on a verdict in a trial, a prize committee votes on the recipient of an award, or a group of critics votes on the top movies of the past century, the resulting decision is a single outcome that stands for the group and has some kind of binding effect going forward. In contrast, markets synthesize the opinions of a group more indirectly, as investors' beliefs are conveyed implicitly through their transactions in the market – choosing how much to invest or to bet, choosing whether to buy or not to buy, and so forth. The overt goal of the market is to enable these transactions, rather than any broader synthesis or group decision that may in fact arise from the transactions in aggregate.

There are other important distinctions as well. A simple but important one is that the choices in a market are often numerical in nature (how much money to transact in various ways), and the synthesis that takes place generally involves arithmetic performed on these quantities – weighted averages and other measures. Many of the key applications of voting, on the other hand, take place in situations in which there is no natural way to "average" the preferences of individuals – because the preferences are over different people, different policy decisions, or different options under a largely

645

subjective criterion. Indeed, as we will see in this chapter, much of the richness of the theory of voting comes from precisely this attempt to combine preferences in the absence of simple metaphors like averaging.

The notion of voting encompasses a broad class of methods for reaching a group decision. For example, the methods to reach a jury verdict, an outcome in a U.S. Presidential election, or a winner of college football's Heisman Trophy are all distinct, and these distinctions have effects on both the process and the result. Moreover, voting can be used in settings where a single "winner" must be chosen, as well as in situations where the goal is to produce a ranked list. Examples of the latter include the ranking of college sports teams by aggregating multiple polls, or published rankings of the greatest movies, songs, or albums of all time by combining the opinions of many critics.

Voting is often used in situations where the voters disagree because of genuine divergence in their subjective evaluations. For example, film critics who disagree on whether to rank *Citizen Kane* or *The Godfather* as the greatest movie of all time are generally not disagreeing because they lack relevant information about the two movies – we can expect that they are closely familiar with both – but because of differing aesthetic evaluations of them. In other cases, however, voting is used to achieve group decisions where the difficulty is a lack of information – where the members of the group would likely be unanimous if they had all the information relevant to the decision. For example, jury verdicts in criminal trials often hinge on genuine uncertainty as to whether the defendant committed the crime; in such cases one expects that jurors all have approximately the same goal in mind (determining the correct verdict), and the differences are in their access to and processing of the available information. We will consider both of these settings in this chapter.

Ideas from the theory of voting have been adopted in a number of recent online applications [140]. Different Web search engines produce different rankings of results; a line of work on *meta-search* has developed tools for combining these rankings into a single aggregate ranking. Recommendation systems for books, music, and other items – such as Amazon's product recommendation system – have employed related ideas for aggregating preferences. In this case, a recommendation system determines a set of users whose past history indicates tastes similar to yours and then uses voting methods to combine the preferences of these other users to produce a ranked list of recommendations (or a single best recommendation) for you. Note that in this case, the goal is not a single aggregate ranking for the whole population, but instead an aggregate ranking for each user, based on the preferences of similar users.

Across all of these different contexts in which voting arises, one sees a recurring set of questions. How should we produce a single ranking from the conflicting opinions provided by multiple voters? Is some version of majority voting a good mechanism? Is there a better one? And ultimately, what does it even mean for a voting system to be good? These are some of the questions we address in this chapter.

23.2 Individual Preferences

The goal of a voting system, for our purposes, can be described as follows. A group of people is evaluating a finite set of possible *alternatives*; these alternatives could correspond to political candidates, possible verdicts in a trial, amounts of money to spend on national defense, nominees for an award, or any other set of options in a decision. The people involved wish to produce a single *group ranking* that orders the alternatives from best to worst and that in some sense reflects the collective opinion of the group. Of course, the challenge will be to define what it means to "reflect" the multiple opinions held by members of the group.

To begin with, let's consider how to model the opinions of any one member of the group. We suppose that each individual is able to determine a preference between any two alternatives when presented with these two as a pair. If individual i prefers alternative X to alternative Y, then we write $X \succ_i Y$. (Sometimes, for ease of discussion, we say that X "defeats" Y according to i's preferences.) Thus, for example, if a set of film critics are each given a large list of movies and asked to express preferences, we could write *Citizen Kane* $\succ_i$ *The Godfather* to express the fact that critic i prefers the former movie to the latter. We will sometimes refer to an individual's preferences over all pairs of alternatives, represented by $\succ_i$, as this individual's *preference relation* over the alternatives.

Completeness and Transitivity. We require that individual preferences satisfy two properties. The first is that each person's preferences are *complete*: for each pair of distinct alternatives X and Y, either she prefers X to Y or she prefers Y to X, but not both. It is possible to extend the theory here to consider the possibility that an individual has ties in her preferences (i.e., for some pairs of alternatives, she likes them equally) and also the possibility that for some pairs of alternatives, an individual has no preference (perhaps because individual i has no knowledge of one of X or Y). Both of these extensions introduce interesting complications, but for this chapter we focus on the case in which each individual has a preference between each pair of alternatives.

The second requirement is that each individual's preferences be *transitive*: if an individual i prefers X to Y and Y to Z, then i should also prefer X to Z. This seems like a very sensible restriction to impose on preferences, because otherwise we could have situations in which an individual had no apparent favorite alternative. In other words, suppose we were evaluating preferences over flavors of ice cream, and we had an individual i for whom chocolate $\succ_i$ vanilla, and vanilla $\succ_i$ strawberry – and, in a violation of transitivity, also strawberry $\succ_i$ chocolate. A simple informal argument for why such preferences seem pathological is the following: if individual i were to walk up to the counter at an ice cream shop and see all three flavors on display, which would she choose? This would in some sense have to be her favorite, despite the fact that each of the three flavors is defeated by some other flavor in her preferences. There has been a long line of work exploring the philosophical and psychological basis for transitive preferences, as well as identifying natural situations in which nontransitive preferences can in fact arise [12, 41, 163]. For our purposes, we will assume that each individual's preferences are transitive.

Individual Rankings. Thus far we have been expressing an individual's opinions about a set of alternatives in terms of his or her preferences over pairs. An alternate model for opinions would be to imagine that each individual produces a completely ranked list of all the alternatives, ranking them from best to worst.

Notice that from such a ranked list we could define a preference relation $\succ_i$ very simply: we'd say that $X \succ_i Y$ if alternative X comes before alternative Y in i's ranked list. In this case, we say that the *preference relation arises from the ranked list*. It's not hard to see that if a preference relation arises from a ranked list of the alternatives, then it must be complete and transitive: completeness holds because, for each pair of alternatives, one precedes the other in the list, and transitivity holds because if X precedes Y and Y precedes Z in the list, then X must also precede Z.

What is somewhat less obvious is that this fact holds in the opposite direction as well:

> If a preference relation is complete and transitive, then it arises from some ranked list of the alternatives.

The way to see why this is true is to consider the following method for constructing a ranked list from a complete and transitive preference relation. First, we identify the alternative X that defeats the most other alternatives in pairwise comparisons – that is, the X such that $X \succ_i Y$ for the most other choices of Y. We claim that this X in fact defeats all the other alternatives: $X \succ_i Y$ for all other Y.

We'll see why this is true in a moment; but first, let's see why this fact lets us construct the ranked list we want. To begin with, having established that X defeats all other alternatives, we can safely put it at the front of the ranked list. We now remove X from the set of alternatives and repeat exactly the same process on the remaining alternatives. The preferences defined by $\succ_i$ are still complete and transitive on the remaining alternatives, so we can apply our claim again on this smaller set: for the alternative Y that defeats the most others in this set, it in fact defeats every remaining alternative. Hence, Y defeats every alternative in the original set except for X, so we can put Y second in the list, remove it too from the set of alternatives, and continue in this way until we exhaust the finite set of alternatives. The way we've constructed the list, each alternative is preferred to all the alternatives that come after it, and so $\succ_i$ arises from this ranked list.

All of this depends on showing that, for any complete and transitive preferences over a set of alternatives (including the original preferences, and the ones we get as we remove alternatives), the alternative X that defeats the most others in fact defeats all of them. Here is an argument showing why this is true (and illustrated in Figure 23.1). We suppose, for the sake of contradiction, that it were not true; then there would be some alternative W that defeats X. But then, for every Y that is defeated by X, we'd have $W \succ_i X$ and $X \succ_i Y$, and so by transitivity $W \succ_i Y$. The conclusion is that W would defeat everything X defeats, and also defeat X; so W would defeat more alternatives than X does. This is a contradiction, because we chose X as the alternative that defeats the most others. Therefore, our assumption that some W defeats X cannot be correct, and so X in fact defeats all other alternatives. This argument justifies our construction of the ranked list.

In view of all this, when we have a complete and transitive preference relation, we can equally well view it as a ranked list. Both of these views will be useful in the discussion to follow.

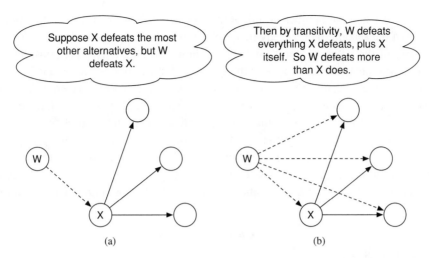

Figure 23.1. With complete and transitive preferences, the alternative X that defeats the most others in fact defeats all of them. If not, (a) some other alternative W would defeat X, but then by transitivity (b) W would defeat more alternatives than X does.

23.3 Voting Systems: Majority Rule

In the previous section we developed a way to talk about the individual preference relations that we're seeking to combine. We can now describe a *voting system* (also called an *aggregation procedure*) as follows: it is any method that takes a collection of complete and transitive individual preference relations – or equivalently, a collection of individual rankings – and produces a *group ranking*.

This definition is very general, and at this level of generality it may be hard to see what makes for a "reasonable" voting system. So we begin, in this section and the next, by discussing two of the most common classes of voting systems. By considering these, we'll start to identify some of the principles – and pathologies – at work in voting more generally.

Majority Rule and the Condorcet Paradox. When there are only two alternatives, the most widely used voting system – and arguably the most natural – is *majority rule*. Under majority rule, we take the alternative that is preferred by a majority of the voters and rank it first, placing the other alternative second. For this discussion we will assume that the number of voters is odd, so that we won't have to worry about the possibility of majority rule producing ties.

Since majority rule is so natural in the case of two alternatives, it is natural to try designing a voting system based on majority rule when there are more than two alternatives. This, however, turns out to be remarkably tricky. Probably the most direct approach is to first create *group preferences*, by applying majority rule to each pair of alternatives, and then trying to turn these group preferences into a group ranking. That is, we create a group preference relation $\succ$ out of all the individual preferences $\succ_i$ as follows. For each pair of alternatives X and Y, we count the number of individuals for whom $X \succ_i Y$ and the number of individuals for whom $Y \succ_i X$. If the first number is larger than the second, then we say that the group preference $\succ$ satisfies $X \succ Y$, since a majority of the voters prefer X to Y when these two alternatives are considered in isolation. Similarly, we say $Y \succ X$ is the group preference if $Y \succ_i X$ for a majority of the individuals i. Because the number of voters is odd, we can't have equal numbers favoring X and favoring Y. So for every distinct pair of alternatives we have exactly one of $X \succ Y$ or $Y \succ X$. That is, the group preference relation is complete.

There's no problem getting this far; the surprising difficulty is that the group preferences might not be transitive, even when each individual's preferences are transitive. To see how this can happen, suppose that we have three individuals named 1, 2, and 3, and three alternatives named X, Y, and Z. Suppose further that individual 1's ranking is

$$X \succ_1 Y \succ_1 Z, \tag{23.1}$$

individual 2's ranking is

$$Y \succ_2 Z \succ_2 X, \tag{23.2}$$

and individual 3's ranking is

$$Z \succ_3 X \succ_3 Y. \tag{23.3}$$

Then using majority rule to define group preferences, we'd have $X \succ Y$ (since X is preferred to Y by both 1 and 3), $Y \succ Z$ (since Y is preferred to Z by both 1 and 2), and $Z \succ X$ (since Z is preferred to X by both 2 and 3). This violates transitivity, which would require $X \succ Z$ once we have $X \succ Y$ and $Y \succ Z$.

The possibility of nontransitive group preferences arising from transitive individual preferences is called the *Condorcet Paradox*, after the Marquis de Condorcet, a French political philosopher who discussed it in the 1700s. And there's something genuinely counterintuitive about it. If we recall our earlier discussion of nontransitive preferences as being somehow "incoherent," the Condorcet Paradox describes a simple scenario in which a set of people, each with perfectly plausible preferences, manages to behave incoherently when forced to express their collective preferences through majority rule. For example, let's return to our example of an individual who prefers chocolate to vanilla to strawberry to chocolate. Even if we were to assume that no one individually behaves this way, the Condorcet Paradox shows how this can arise very naturally as the group preferences of a set of ice cream–eating friends, when they plan to share a pint of ice cream and decide on which flavor to buy using majority rule.

The Condorcet Paradox has in fact also been used to show how a single person can naturally be led to form nontransitive individual preferences [41, 163]. Consider, for example, a student deciding which college to attend. She prefers to go to a college that is highly ranked, that has a small average class size, and that offers her a significant amount in scholarship money. Suppose she has been admitted to the following three colleges, with characteristics as described in Figure 23.2.

In comparing colleges, the student was planning to decide between pairs of colleges by favoring the one that did better on a majority of these three criteria. Unfortunately, this leads to the preferences $X \succ_i Y$ (since X is better than Y on ranking and scholarship money), $Y \succ_i Z$ (since Y is better than Z on ranking and average class size), and $Z \succ_i X$

College	National Ranking	Average Class Size	Scholarship Money Offered
X	4	40	$3,000
Y	8	18	$1,000
Z	12	24	$8,000

Figure 23.2. When a single individual is making decisions based on multiple criteria, the Condorcet Paradox can lead to nontransitive preferences. Here, if a college applicants wants a school with a high ranking, small average class size, and a large scholarship offer, it is possible for each option to be defeated by one of the others on a majority of the criteria.

(since Z is better than X on average class size and scholarship money). It's not hard to see the analogy: each criterion is like a voter, and the student's "individual preference relation" is really the group preference relation synthesized from these three criteria. But it does show some of the complications that arise even when one individual engages in decision making in the presence of multiple criteria.

Voting Systems Based on Majority Rule. The Condorcet Paradox portends trouble for the design of voting systems in general, but given that we need some way to produce an actual group ranking (including an actual top-ranked alternative), it's still worth exploring what can be done using majority rule. We'll focus on methods for selecting a top-ranked alternative, which we'll think of as the "group favorite"; to produce a full ranked list, one could first select a group favorite, remove it from the available alternatives, and then apply the procedure repeatedly to what's left.

One natural approach for finding a group favorite is as follows. We arrange all the alternatives in some order, and then eliminate them one by one in this order using majority rule. Thus, we compare the first two alternatives by majority vote, compare the winner of this vote to the third alternative, compare the winner of that to the fourth alternative, and so on. The winner of the final comparison is deemed to be the group favorite. We can represent this in a pictorial way as in Figure 23.3(a), showing the sequence of eliminations in a four-alternative example, with alternatives A and B compared first, then the winner compared to C, and then that winner compared to D. We can think of this as an agenda for a meeting in which pairs of alternatives are proposed to the group, majority votes are taken, and a group favorite emerges from this process.

This is an example of a more general strategy for using majority rule over pairs of alternatives to find a group favorite: we can arrange them in any kind of "elimination tournament," in which alternatives are paired off against each other in some fashion, with the winner advancing to a subsequent round while the loser is eliminated. The alternative that eventually emerges as the overall winner of this tournament is declared to be the group favorite. The system we were just discussing, shown in Figure 23.3(a), is one such way to structure an elimination tournament; Figure 23.3(b) depicts another.

Pathologies in Voting Systems Based on Majority Rule. These systems do produce a group favorite (and, by repeatedly invoking the system on the remaining alternatives, also produce a group ranking). The Condorcet Paradox, however, can be used to uncover

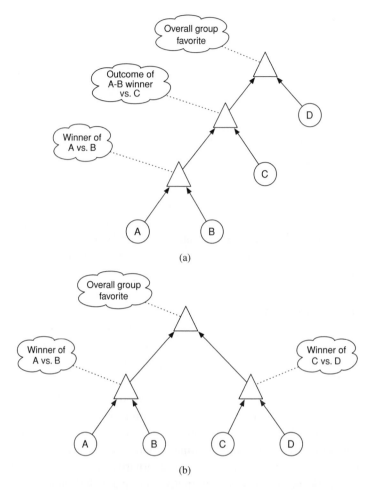

Figure 23.3. One can use majority rule for pairs to build voting systems on three or more alternatives. The alternatives are considered according to a particular "agenda" (in the form of an elimination tournament), and they are eliminated by pairwise majority vote according to this agenda. This produces an eventual winner that serves as the overall group favorite. As shown in (a) and (b), there can be many different orders in which to pair off the alternatives against each other.

an important pathology that such systems exhibit: their outcomes are susceptible to a kind of *strategic agenda setting*. Let's go back to our original example of the Condorcet Paradox, where three voters had the individual rankings over alternatives X, Y, and Z given by lists (23.1)–(23.3). They decide to choose a group favorite using a version of the system shown in Figure 23.3(a), scaled down to three alternatives: they will first perform a majority vote between two of the alternatives, and then perform a majority vote between the winner of this first vote and the remaining alternative.

The question then becomes how to set the agenda for this process. That is, which two of alternatives X, Y, and Z will be voted on first, and which one will be held until the final vote? Because of the structure of the individual preferences, the choice of agenda in this case has a decisive effect on the outcome. If, as in Figure 23.4(a), alternatives

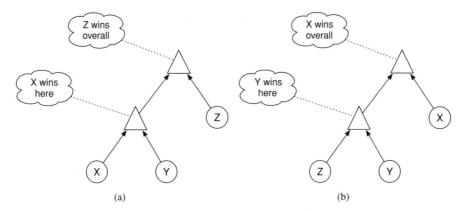

Figure 23.4. With individual rankings as in the Condorcet Paradox, the winner of the elimination tournament depends entirely on how the agenda is set: (a) an agenda in which Z wins and (b) an agenda in which X wins.

X and Y are paired off first, then X will win this first vote but then be defeated by Z as the group favorite. On the other hand, if alternatives Y and Z are paired off first [as in Figure 23.4(b)], then Y will win this first vote but then be defeated by X as the group favorite. (We could do a similar thing to have Y be the group favorite.)

So with individual preferences as in the Condorcet Paradox, the overall winner is determined entirely by how the votes between pairs are sequenced. To put it a different way, if the voter who likes Z best gets to set the agenda, then she can sequence the votes so Z wins, but if the voter who likes X or Y best gets to set the agenda, then he can sequence the votes so his respective favorite wins. The group favorite is thus determined by the individual who controls the agenda. Nor can this be remedied by using a system in which voters can reintroduce alternatives once they've been eliminated: with preferences as in the Condorcet Paradox, there's always an alternative that can be reintroduced to defeat the current candidate for the group favorite, and so a process in which alternatives can be reintroduced for consideration would never come to an end.

Earlier in this section – using an example of a student choosing colleges based on multiple criteria, in Figure 23.2 – we observed that the Condorcet Paradox can also capture pathologies in the decisions made by a single individual, rather than a group. The problem of agenda setting has an analog in the context of such individual decisions as well. Suppose, for example, that the student in our earlier college-choice example makes the natural decision to eliminate choices one at a time as acceptance offers come in. Then if the acceptances arrive in the order X, Y, Z, she will eliminate Y in favor of X when Y arrives (X has a higher ranking and a higher scholarship offer) and then eliminate X in favor of Z when the acceptance from Z arrives (since Z has a smaller average class size and a higher scholarship offer). Each of these makes sense as a pairwise decision, and it leads to Z as her overall decision – but it has the property that Y, which she eliminated first, is in fact a choice she preferred to Z. This is precisely the problem of having a final decision that depends on the agenda by which alternatives are considered.

23.4 Voting Systems: Positional Voting

A different class of voting systems tries to produce a group ranking directly from the individual rankings, rather than building up the group ranking from pairwise comparisons of alternatives. In this type of system, each alternative receives a certain *weight* based on its positions in all the individual rankings, and the alternatives are then ordered according to their total weight. A simple example of such a system is the *Borda Count*, named for Jean-Charles de Borda, who proposed it in 1770. The Borda Count is often used to choose the winners of sports awards, such as the Heisman trophy in college football; a variant of it is used to select the Most Valuable Player in professional baseball; and it is used by the Associated Press and United Press International to rank sports teams.

In the Borda Count, if there are k alternatives in total, then individual i's ranking confers a weight of $k - 1$ on her first-ranked alternative, a weight of $k - 2$ on her second-ranked alternative, and so on down to a weight of 1 on her second-to-last alternative, and a weight of 0 on her last alternative. In other words, each alternative receives a weight from individual i equal to the number of other alternatives ranked lower by i. The total weight of each alternative is simply the sum of the weights it receives from each of the individuals. The alternatives are then ordered according to their total weights. (We will suppose that if two alternatives receive the same total weight, then some tie-breaking system arranged in advance is used to decide which of these two alternatives to place in front of the other.)

For example, suppose there are four alternatives, named A, B, C, and D, and there are two voters with the individual rankings

$$A \succ_1 B \succ_1 C \succ_1 D$$

and

$$B \succ_2 C \succ_2 A \succ_2 D.$$

Then the weight assigned by the Borda Count to alternative A is $3 + 1 = 4$, the weight assigned to B is 5, the weight assigned to C is 3, and the weight assigned to D is 0. Therefore, sorting the weights in descending order, the group ranking is

$$B \succ A \succ C \succ D.$$

It is easy to create variants of the Borda Count that retain its basic flavor: we can assign any number of "points" to each position in each list and then rank the alternatives by the total number of points they receive based on their positions in all lists. The Borda Count assigns $k - 1$ points for first, $k - 2$ points for second, and so forth, but one could imagine versions that assign points differently: for example, to make only the top three positions in each individual ranking matter, one could assign 3 points for first, 2 for second, 1 for third, and 0 points for all other positions, with the group ranking still determined by the total number of points the alternatives receive. We refer to any system of this type as a *positional voting system*, since the alternatives receive numerical weights based on their positions on the individual rankings.

A key appealing feature of the Borda Count is that – ignoring ties – it always produces a complete, transitive ranking for a set of alternatives. This is simply by its definition, since it creates a single numerical criterion along which to sort the alternatives (including, as noted previously, a rule for tie-breaking). But the Borda Count also has some fundamental pathologies, as we now discuss.

Pathologies in Positional Voting Systems. Most of the problems with the Borda Count, and with positional voting systems more generally, arise from the fact that competition for top spots in the group ranking can depend critically on the rankings of alternatives that are further down in the list.

Here's a hypothetical scenario illustrating how this can happen. Suppose that a magazine writes a column in which it asks five film critics to discuss their choice for the greatest movie of all time; the two movies discussed in the column are *Citizen Kane* and *The Godfather*, and the column ends with a majority-vote decision on the winner. Critics 1, 2, and 3 favor *Citizen Kane*, while critics 4 and 5 favor *The Godfather*.

At the last minute, however, the editors decide the column needs a more "modern" feel, so they introduce *Pulp Fiction* as a third option that needs to be discussed and evaluated. Since there are now three options, the magazine decides to have each critic produce a ranking, and then use the Borda Count for the overall decision that will serve as the punch line of the column. The first three critics (who all prefer older movies) each report the ranking

$$Citizen\ Kane \succ_i The\ Godfather \succ_i Pulp\ Fiction.$$

Critics 4 and 5 (who only like movies made in the past 40 years) each report the ranking

$$The\ Godfather \succ_i Pulp\ Fiction \succ_i Citizen\ Kane.$$

Applying the Borda Count, we see that *Citizen Kane* receives a weight of 2 from each of the first three critics, and a weight of 0 from the last two, for a total of 6. *The Godfather* receives a weight of 1 from each of the first three critics, and a weight of 2 from the last two, for a total of 7. *Pulp Fiction* receives a weight of 0 from each of the first three critics, and a weight of 1 from the last two, for a total of 2. As a result, the Borda Count produces *The Godfather* as the overall group favorite.

Notice what's happened here. The outcome of the head-to-head comparison between *Citizen Kane* and *The Godfather* remains the same as before – *Citizen Kane* is favored by a vote of three to two. But because a third alternative was introduced, the identity of the group favorite has changed. Moreover, this is not because the group was particularly fond of this new, third alternative – the third alternative loses in a head-to-head vote against *each* of the two existing alternatives. To put the difficulty in another way: *Citizen Kane* fails to rank first in the Borda Count even though it defeats each of the other two alternatives in a head-to-head comparison under majority rule. So what we find is that the outcome in the Borda Count can depend on the presence of alternatives that intuitively seem "irrelevant" – weak alternatives that essentially act as "spoilers" in shifting the outcome from one higher-ranked alternative to another.

The possibility of such a result suggests further difficulties with the Borda Count – specifically, the problem of *strategic misreporting of preferences*. To see how this happens, let's consider a slightly different scenario. Suppose in our previous story that critics 4 and 5 actually had the true ranking

$$\text{The Godfather} \succ_i \text{Citizen Kane} \succ_i \text{Pulp Fiction}.$$

In other words, in this version of the story, all five critics agree that *Pulp Fiction* should be ranked last among these three movies. If we were to run the Borda Count on this set of five individual rankings, the group ranking would place *Citizen Kane* first (it would receive a total weight of $3 \times 2 + 2 \times 1 = 8$ to *The Godfather*'s $3 \times 1 + 2 \times 2 = 7$). However, suppose that critics 4 and 5 understand the pathologies that are possible with the Borda Count, and they decide in advance to misreport their rankings as

$$\text{The Godfather} \succ_i \text{Pulp Fiction} \succ_i \text{Citizen Kane}.$$

Then we have the individual rankings from the previous scenario, and *The Godfather* ends up being ranked first.

The underlying point is that voters in the Borda Count can sometimes benefit by lying about their true preferences, particularly so as to downgrade the overall group ranking of an alternative that many other voters will put at the top of their individual rankings.

Examples from U.S. Presidential Elections. Versions of these pathologies are familiar from U.S. Presidential elections as well. The full Presidential election process in the United States has a complex specification, but if we think about how states choose their electors in the general election – how they choose which candidate will receive the state's electoral votes – it is generally done using *plurality voting*: the candidate who is top ranked by the most voters wins. (The U.S. Constitution doesn't require this, and some states have considered other methods and used others in the past, but this is the typical system.)

If we think about it, plurality voting is in fact a positional voting system, since an equivalent way to run it is as follows. We ask each voter to report an individual ranking of all the candidates. Each individual ranking then confers a weight of 1 to the candidate at the top of the ranking and a weight of 0 to all the other candidates. The candidate with the greatest total weight from these rankings is declared the winner. Note that this is just a different way of saying that the candidate who is top ranked by the most voters wins, but it makes it clear that this system fits the structure of a positional method.

Plurality voting exhibits difficulties analogous to what we observed for the Borda Count. With only two candidates, plurality voting is the same as majority rule, but with more than two candidates, one sees recurring "third-party" effects: an alternative that is the favorite of very few people can potentially shift the outcome from one of the two leading contenders to the other. In turn, this causes some voters to make their choices strategically, misreporting their top-ranked choice so as to favor a candidate with a better chance of winning. Such issues have been present in recent U.S. Presidential elections, and their effects in important earlier elections, such as the election of Abraham Lincoln in 1860, have also been studied [384].

23.5 Arrow's Impossibility Theorem

We have now looked at a number of different voting systems, and we've seen that when there are more than two alternatives under consideration, they all exhibit pathological behavior. If we were to consider further voting systems used in practice, we'd find they too suffered from inherent problems in the way they produce a group ranking. At some point, however, it makes sense to step back from specific voting systems and ask a more general question: is there *any* voting system that produces a group ranking for three or more alternatives and avoids all of the pathologies we've seen thus far?

Making this question concrete requires that we precisely specify all the relevant definitions. We've already discussed the precise definition of a voting system: for a fixed number of voters k, it is any function that takes a set of k individual rankings and produces a group ranking. The other thing we need to do is to specify what it means for a voting system to be free of pathologies. We will do this by specifying two properties that we would like a reasonable voting system to satisfy:

- First, if there is any pair of alternatives X and Y for which $X \succ_i Y$ in the rankings of every individual i, then the group ranking should also have $X \succ Y$. This is a very natural condition, known as the *Pareto Principle*, or *Unanimity*; it simply requires that if everyone prefers X to Y, then the group ranking should reflect this preference. One can think of Unanimity, as ensuring that the group ranking be responsive to the individual rankings in at least a minimal way.
- Second, we require that, for each pair of alternatives, the ordering of X and Y in the group ranking should depend only on how each individual ranks X and Y relative to each other. In other words, suppose we have a set of individual rankings that produces a group ranking in which $X \succ Y$. If we then take some third alternative Z and shift its position in some of the individual rankings, while leaving the relative ordering of X and Y unchanged, then the voting system should still produce $X \succ Y$ for this new set of individual rankings.

  This condition is called Independence of Irrelevant Alternatives (IIA), because it requires that the group ranking of X and Y should depend only on voter preferences between X and Y, not on how they evaluate other alternatives. IIA is more subtle than Unanimity, but the failure of IIA is in fact responsible for most of the pathological behavior we saw in our earlier discussions of specific voting systems. It was clearly at work in the strategic misreporting of preferences for the Borda Count since there the shift in ranking of a third alternative Z was sufficient to change the outcome between two other alternatives X and Y. It also plays a role in the problem of strategic agenda setting for elimination systems based on majority rule: the key idea there was to choose an agenda that eliminated one alternative X early, before it could be paired against an alternative Y that it would in fact defeat.

Voting Systems That Satisfy Unanimity and IIA. Since Unanimity and IIA are both reasonable properties, it's natural to ask what voting systems satisfy them. When there are only two alternatives, majority rule clearly satisfies both: it favors X to Y when all voters do, and – since there are only two alternatives – the group ranking of X and Y clearly does not depend on any other alternatives.

When there are three or more alternatives, it's trickier to find a voting system that satisfies these two properties: neither the positional systems nor the systems based on majority rule that we've considered will work. There is, however, a voting system that satisfies the two properties: dictatorship. That is, we pick one of the individuals i, and we simply declare the group ranking to be equal to the ranking provided by individual i. Notice that there are really k different possible voting systems based on dictatorship – one in which each of the k possible voters is chosen as the dictator.

We can easily check that each of these k dictatorship systems satisfies Unanimity and IIA. First, if everyone prefers X to Y, then the dictator does, and hence the group ranking does. Second, the group ranking of X and Y depends only on how the dictator ranks X and Y and does not depend on how any other alternative Z is ranked.

Arrow's Theorem. In the 1950s, Kenneth Arrow proved the following remarkable result [22, 23], which clarifies why it's so hard to find voting systems that are free of pathological behavior.

> *Arrow's Theorem:* If there are at least three alternatives, then any voting system that satisfies both Unanimity and IIA must correspond to dictatorship by one individual.

In other words, dictatorship is the only voting system that satisfies both Unanimity and IIA.

Because dictatorship is also generally viewed as an undesirable property, Arrow's Theorem is often phrased as an impossibility result. That is, suppose we say a voting system satisfies *Non-dictatorship* if there is no individual i for which the group ranking always coincides with i's ranking. Then we can phrase Arrow's Theorem as follows.

> *Arrow's Theorem (equivalent version):* If there are at least three alternatives, then there is no voting system that satisfies Unanimity, IIA, and Non-dictatorship.

Ultimately, what Arrow's Theorem shows us is not that voting is necessarily "impossible" but that it is subject to unavoidable trade-offs: any system we choose will exhibit certain forms of undesirable behavior. It therefore helps to focus discussions of voting on how to manage these trade-offs and to evaluate different voting systems in light of them.

23.6 Single-Peaked Preferences and the Median Voter Theorem

Condorcet's Paradox and Arrow's Theorem are facts of nature; we cannot make them go away. However, a common approach when faced with an impossibility result is to consider reasonable special cases of the problem where the underlying difficulties do not arise. There has been a long line of research in voting that follows this direction.

The starting point for this line of research is the observation that there's something a bit unusual about the individual rankings used in the setup of the Condorcet Paradox.

Recall that with three alternatives X, Y, and Z, and three voters 1, 2, and 3, we had

$$X \succ_1 Y \succ_1 Z,$$

$$Y \succ_2 Z \succ_2 X,$$

$$Z \succ_3 X \succ_3 Y.$$

Suppose that X, Y, and Z correspond to amounts of money to spend on education or national defense, with X corresponding to a small amount, Y to a medium amount, and Z to a large amount. Then the preferences of voter 1 make sense: she is happiest with the smallest amount, and second-happiest with a medium amount. The preferences of voter 2 also make sense: he is happiest with a medium amount, but if not medium, then he prefers a large amount. The preferences of voter 3, on the other hand, are harder to justify in a simple way: he prefers a large amount, but his second choice is a small amount, with medium coming last. In other words, the first two voters have preferences that can be explained by proximity to a fixed number: each of them has an "ideal" amount that they'd like, and they evaluate the alternatives by how close they come to this ideal. The third voter's preferences can't be explained this way: there's no "ideal" quantity such that both large and small are close to it, but medium isn't. This is not to say that a person couldn't hold these preferences (e.g., "if we're not willing to invest enough in education to do it right, we shouldn't spend anything at all"), but they're more unusual.

Similar reasoning would apply if X, Y, and Z were political candidates arranged in order on a political spectrum, with X the liberal candidate, Y the moderate candidate, and Z the conservative candidate. In this case, voter 1 prefers more liberal candidates; voter 2 prefers moderates and leans conservative when forced to choose between extremes, but voter 3 favors the conservative candidate, followed next by the liberal candidate, with the moderate candidate last. Again, the preferences of voters 1 and 2 can be explained by assuming that each evaluates candidates by their proximity to a personal "ideal" point on the political spectrum, but voter 3's preferences are less natural in that they can't be explained this way.

We now describe a way to formalize the "unusualness" in voter 3's ranking, and we then show that for rankings that do not contain this structure, the Condorcet Paradox cannot arise.

Single-Peaked Preferences. For alternatives corresponding to numerical quantities or linear orderings like a political spectrum, it is reasonable to assume that individual preferences tend to look like the preferences of voters 1 and 2 in our example: each has a particular favorite point in the range of alternatives, and they evaluate alternatives by their proximity to this point. In fact, for our discussion here, it is enough to assume something weaker: simply that each voter's preferences "fall away" consistently on both sides of their favorite alternative.

To make this precise, let's assume that the k alternatives are named $X_1, X_2, \ldots, X_k$, and that voters all perceive them as being arranged in this order. (Again, we'll think of the examples of numerical quantities or candidates on a political spectrum.) We

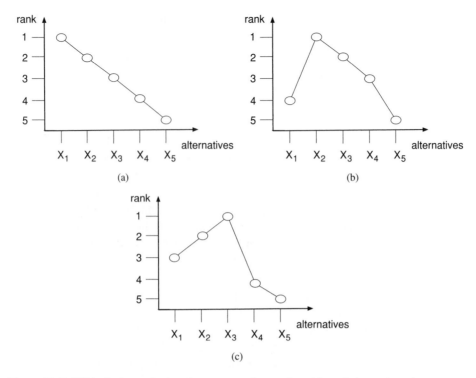

Figure 23.5. With single-peaked preferences, each voter's ranking of alternatives decreases on both sides of a "peak" corresponding to her favorite choice: (a) voter 1's ranking, (b) voter 2's ranking, and (c) voter 3's ranking.

say that a voter has *single-peaked preferences* if there is no alternative X_s for which both neighboring alternatives X_{s-1} and X_{s+1} are ranked above X_s. In other words, a voter never prefers two options that lie on opposite sides of a middle option. (Since we are assuming voters have complete and transitive preferences, we will also refer to single-peaked preferences as single-peaked rankings.)

Such preferences are called single-peaked because the condition we impose is equivalent to the following: each voter i has a top-ranked option X_t, and her preferences fall off on both sides of X_t:

$$X_t \succ_i X_{t+1} \succ_i X_{t+2} \succ_i \cdots$$

and

$$X_t \succ_i X_{t-1} \succ_i X_{t-2} \succ_i \cdots .$$

Pictorially, this can be represented as in Figure 23.5. The example shown there has three voters, with preferences

$$X_1 \succ_1 X_2 \succ_1 X_3 \succ_1 X_4 \succ_1 X_5,$$

$$X_2 \succ_2 X_3 \succ_2 X_4 \succ_2 X_1 \succ_2 X_5,$$

$$X_3 \succ_3 X_2 \succ_3 X_1 \succ_3 X_4 \succ_3 X_5,$$

and each of the three plots shows one of these sets of individual preferences. In the plots, there is an oval for each alternative, and its height corresponds to its position in the list. As drawn, the single peak in an individual's ranking emerges visually as a peak in the plot.

Majority Rule with Single-Peaked Preferences. Single-peaked preferences are natural as a model for many kinds of rankings, but their significance in the theory of voting lies in the following observation, made by Duncan Black in 1948 [61].

Recall our first, most basic attempt at synthesizing a group ranking from a set of individual rankings, back in Section 23.3: we would compare each pair of alternatives X and Y to each other, using majority rule to produce a group preference of the form $X \succ Y$ or $Y \succ X$ (depending on which alternative is preferred by more voters). As before, we'll suppose that the number of voters is odd, so that we don't have to worry about the possibility of ties. Our hope was that the resulting group preference relation $\succ$ would be complete and transitive, so that we could produce a group ranking from it. Unfortunately, the Condorcet Paradox showed that this hope was in vain: transitive individual preferences can give rise to group preferences that are non-transitive.

But here's the point of the framework we've developed in this section: with single-peaked preferences, our original plan works perfectly. This is the content of the following result.

> *Claim:* If all individual rankings are single-peaked, then majority rule applied to all pairs of alternatives produces a group preference relation $\succ$ that is complete and transitive.

It is not initially clear why this striking fact should be true, but in fact it follows for an intuitively natural reason, as we now describe.

The Median Individual Favorite. As in other attempts to construct group rankings, we start by figuring out how to identify a group favorite – an alternative that can be placed at the top of the ranking – and then proceed to fill in further slots of the ranking. Finding a group favorite is the crux of the problem, since it requires us to identify an alternative that defeats every other alternative in a pairwise majority vote.

Let's consider the top-ranked alternative for each voter and sort this set of individual favorites from left to right, along our linear order. Notice that if several voters have the same alternative as their respective individual favorite, then this alternative will appear multiple times in the sorted list: it is fine for the list to have repetitions. Now consider the individual favorite that forms the *median* of this list – the individual favorite that lies exactly at the halfway point in the sorted order. For example, in the preferences from Figure 23.5, the sorted list of individual favorites would be X_1, X_2, X_3, and so the median is X_2. With more voters, if the individual favorites were (for example) $X_1, X_1, X_2, X_2, X_3, X_4, X_5$, then the median would also be X_2, since we are considering the median of the list with all the repetitions included.

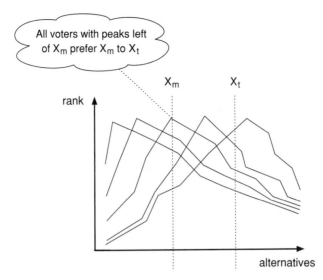

Figure 23.6. The proof that the median individual favorite X_m defeats every other alternative X_t in a pairwise majority vote: if X_t is to the right of X_m, then X_m is preferred by all voters whose peak is on X_m or to its left. (The symmetric argument applies when X_t is to the left of X_m.)

The median individual favorite is a natural idea to consider as a potential group favorite, since it naturally "compromises" between more extreme individual favorites on either side. And in fact it works very well for this purpose:

> *The Median Voter Theorem:* With single-peaked rankings, the median individual favorite defeats every other alternative in a pairwise majority vote.

To see why this is true, let X_m be the median individual favorite, and let X_t be any other alternative. Let's suppose that X_t lies to the right of X_m; that is, $t > m$. (The case in which it lies to the left has a completely symmetric argument.) Let's also order the voters in the sorted order of their individual favorites.

The argument is now depicted schematically in Figure 23.6. The number of voters k is odd, and we know that, because it is the median, X_m is in position $(k + 1)/2$ of the sorted list of individual favorites. This means that, for everyone in the first $(k + 1)/2$ positions, X_m is either their favorite, or their favorite lies to the left of X_m. For each voter in this latter group, X_m and X_t are both on the right-hand "down-slope" of this voter's preferences, but X_m is closer to the peak than X_t is, so X_m is preferred to X_t. It follows that everyone in the first $(k + 1)/2$ positions prefers X_m to X_t. But this is a strict majority of the voters, and so X_m defeats X_t in a pairwise majority vote.

To put it succinctly: the median individual favorite X_m can always count on gathering a majority of support against any other alternative X_t, because for more than half the voters, X_m lies between X_t and each of their respective favorites.

From this fact about the median individual favorite, it is easy to see why majority rule among all pairs produces a complete and transitive group ranking: we simply build up the group ranking by identifying group favorites one at a time. That is, we start by finding the median individual favorite and placing it at the top of the group ranking.

This is safe to do because the Median Voter Theorem guarantees that it defeats all other alternatives that will come later in the list. Now we remove this alternative from each individual ranking. Notice that when we do this, the rankings all remain single peaked: essentially, we have simply "decapitated" the peak from each ranking, and the second item in each voter's ranking becomes their new peak. We now have a version of the same problem we faced before, with single-peaked rankings on a set of alternatives that is one smaller. So we find the median individual favorite on the remaining alternatives, place it second in the group ranking, and continue in this way until we exhaust the finite set of alternatives.

For example, applying this approach to the three voters in Figure 23.5, we would identify X_2 as the median individual favorite, and we'd place it first in the group ranking. Once we remove this alternative, we have three single-peaked rankings on the alternatives X_1, X_3, X_4, and X_5. The individual favorites in this reduced set are X_1, X_3, and X_3, so X_3 is the new median individual favorite, and we place it second in the group ranking. Proceeding in this way, we end up with the group ranking

$$X_2 \succ X_3 \succ X_1 \succ X_4 \succ X_5.$$

Since voter 2 was the original "median voter" in the sense of having the original median individual favorite, the start of the group ranking necessarily agrees with the start of voter 2's individual ranking: they both place X_2 first. However, the full group ranking does not coincide with voter 2's full individual ranking: for example, voters 1 and 3 both prefer X_1 to X_4, even through voter 2 doesn't, and the group ranking reflects this fact.

23.7 Voting as a Form of Information Aggregation

Thus far, we have focused primarily on situations in which voting is used to aggregate fundamentally and genuinely different opinions within a group of people. But there are contexts in which voting is used by a group of people who have a shared goal – where it is reasonable to suppose that there is a true best ranking of the alternatives, and the purpose of the voting system is to discover it. This is unlikely to be appropriate for the ranking of political candidates or works of art, but it can be a good model of jury deliberations in cases where the decision hinges on genuine uncertainty about the facts. It can also be a good model for decisions made by a board of advisers to a company, evaluating business plans that each yield an uncertain future payoff.

In settings like these, where we imagine that there is a true best ranking, it's reasonable to suppose that the individual rankings differ only because they are based on different information, or based on different evaluations of the available information. If everyone in such a case had the same information and evaluated it in the same way, they would have the same ranking.

We will see that these considerations can lead to some potentially complex effects in the way individuals reason about their votes. As a starting baseline, we begin with a simple model in which individuals vote simultaneously, and based purely on their own individual rankings. We then discuss what happens in situations where one or both of these assumptions do not hold – when voting is done sequentially, or when knowledge of other rankings would cause an individual to change her own ranking.

Simultaneous, Sincere Voting: The Condorcet Jury Theorem. We begin with a simple setting in which there are two alternatives X and Y; one of these two is genuinely the best choice, and each voter will cast a vote for what she believes to be this best choice.

To model the idea that voters possess different but uncertain information, we use a general framework that worked well in Chapter 16 on information cascades. We suppose first that there is a *prior probability* of X being the best choice, and that this is known to all voters. For simplicity, we'll take this prior probability to be $\frac{1}{2}$ in our analysis here; this means that initially, X and Y are equally likely to be the best choice. Then, each voter receives an independent, private *signal* about which of X or Y is better. For some value $q > \frac{1}{2}$, signals favoring the best choice occur with probability q; writing this in terms of conditional probability as in Chapter 16, we have

$$\Pr\left[X\text{-}signal \text{ is observed} \mid X \text{ is best}\right] = q$$

and

$$\Pr\left[Y\text{-}signal \text{ is observed} \mid Y \text{ is best}\right] = q.$$

(We can imagine each voter's signal as behaving like the flip of a biased coin: for each voter, it lands on the side indicating the better alternative with probability q.)

Unlike the case in Chapter 16, all the votes in our current analysis are being made simultaneously: no voter is able to see the decisions made by any other voter before reaching her own decision. Also, we assume that everyone is voting *sincerely*: each voter will choose the alternative she believes to be better, based on the information she has available (in the form of her private signal). To model sincere voting by an individual, we can use conditional probabilities just as in Chapter 16. When a voter observes a signal favoring X, she first evaluates the conditional probability

$$\Pr\left[X \text{ is best} \mid X\text{-}signal \text{ is observed}\right].$$

She then decides to vote in favor of X if this probability is greater than $\frac{1}{2}$, and in favor of Y if this probability is less than $\frac{1}{2}$. The analogous reasoning applies if she observes a signal favoring Y; we focus just on the case of an X-signal, since the analysis is symmetric in the two cases.

We can evaluate the conditional probability underlying the voter's decision using Bayes' rule, by strict analogy with the calculations we did in Section 16.3. We have

$$\Pr\left[X \text{ is best} \mid X\text{-}signal \text{ is observed}\right]$$
$$= \frac{\Pr\left[X \text{ is best}\right] \times \Pr\left[X\text{-}signal \text{ is observed} \mid X \text{ is best}\right]}{\Pr\left[X\text{-}signal \text{ is observed}\right]}.$$

By our assumption about the prior probability, we know that $\Pr\left[X \text{ is best}\right] = \frac{1}{2}$. By the definition of the signals, we know that $\Pr\left[X\text{-}signal \text{ is observed} \mid X \text{ is best}\right] = q$.

Finally, there are two ways for an X-signal to be observed: if X is best, or if Y is best. Therefore,

$$\Pr[\textit{X-signal is observed}] = \Pr[\textit{X is best}] \times \Pr[\textit{X-signal is observed} \mid \textit{X is best}]$$
$$+ \Pr[\textit{Y is best}] \times \Pr[\textit{X-signal is observed} \mid \textit{Y is best}]$$
$$= \frac{1}{2}q + \frac{1}{2}(1-q) = \frac{1}{2}.$$

Putting all this together, we get

$$\Pr[\textit{X is best} \mid \textit{X-signal is observed}] = \frac{(1/2)q}{1/2} = q.$$

The conclusion – which is completely natural – is that the voter will favor the alternative that is reinforced by the signal she receives. In fact, the calculation using Bayes' rule gives us more than just this conclusion; it also shows how much probability she should assign to this favored alternative based on the signal.

The Marquis de Condorcet wrote about this type of scenario in 1785. In his version, he took as a given the assumption that each voter chooses the best alternative with some probability $q > \frac{1}{2}$, rather than deriving it from the assumption of a private signal – but the model based on either of these starting assumptions is effectively the same. Condorcet's interest was in showing that majority rule is effective when there are many voters who favor the better of two choices at a rate slightly greater than half. His probabilistic formulation of individuals' decisions was a novel step – probability was still a relatively new idea in his time – and his main observation, now known as the *Condorcet Jury Theorem*, is the following. Suppose that X is the best alternative (the case for Y being symmetric). Then as the number of voters increases, the fraction of voters choosing X will converge almost surely to the probability of receiving an X-signal, which is $q > \frac{1}{2}$. In particular, this means that the probability of the majority reaching a correct decision converges to 1 as the number of voters grows. In this sense, Condorcet's Jury Theorem is perhaps one of the oldest explicit formulations of the "wisdom of crowds" idea: aggregating the estimates of many people can lead to a decision of higher quality than that of any individual expert.

23.8 Insincere Voting for Information Aggregation

One of the assumptions behind the Condorcet Jury Theorem in the previous section is that all individuals are voting sincerely: each is choosing the alternative he or she believes to be best, given the information available. On the surface, this seems like a mild assumption. If the voters could share all their signals, they would reach a unanimous evaluation of the best alternative, but because they aren't able to communicate with each other and have access only to their own private signals, why should a voter do anything anything other than follow her best guess based on her own signal?

In fact, however, there are very natural situations in which an individual should actually choose to vote insincerely – favoring the alternative she believes to be worse – *even though her goal is to maximize the probability that the group as a whole selects the best alternative.* This is clearly a counterintuitive claim, and its underlying basis has only been elucidated relatively recently [30, 159, 160]. To explain how this phenomenon can arise, we begin with a hypothetical experiment, modeled on a scenario described by Austen-Smith and Banks [30].

An Experiment That Encourages Insincere Voting. Here's how the experiment works. An experimenter announces that an urn with 10 marbles will be placed at the front of a room; there is a 50% chance the urn will contain ten white marbles, and a 50% chance that it will contain nine green marbles and one white marble. (We describe the first kind of urn as "pure" and the second kind as "mixed.")

The experimenter asks a group of three people to collectively guess which kind of urn it is. Their group decision will be made according to the following protocol. First, each of the three people is allowed to draw one marble from the urn, look at it (without showing it to the other two), and then replace it in the urn. Then, the three people are asked to cast simultaneous votes, without communicating, each guessing which type of urn they think it is. If a majority of the votes are for the correct type of urn, then all three people win a monetary prize; if a majority of the votes are for the wrong type of urn, then all three people get nothing. (Note that each person gets nothing if the majority is wrong, even if they personally voted for the correct alternative.)

One can see that the experiment is designed to create a set of independent private signals for the voters: the color of the marble drawn by each voter is her private signal, and she cannot communicate this signal to any of the other voters. Rather, the group decision must be reached by majority vote, with each voter having access to these different and potentially conflicting probabilistic signals.

We now ask how an individual should reason about the conditional probabilities of the different urn types based on the marble she draws; after this, we'll consider how she should actually vote.

Conditional Probabilities and Decisions About Voting. First, suppose that you (as one of the three people in the experiment) draw a white marble. While we won't go through the precise calculations, it's not hard to work out, using Bayes' rule just as we did in the previous section, that the urn in this case is significantly more likely to be pure than mixed. (Intuitively, if you see a white marble, it's much more likely to have been from the all-white pure urn than to be the single white marble in the mixed urn.) On the other hand, if you draw a green marble, then in fact you know for certain that the urn is mixed – since green marbles are only found in mixed urns.

Therefore, if you were to vote sincerely, you would vote "pure" on drawing a white marble and "mixed" if you draw a green marble. But suppose you knew that the other two people in the group were going to vote sincerely, and you wanted to choose your vote to maximize the chance that the majority among the three of you produced the right answer. Then a useful question to ask yourself is, "In what situations does my vote actually affect the outcome?" If you think about it, your vote only affects the outcome when the other two (sincere) votes are split – when there is one vote for pure and one vote for mixed. In this case, however, one of your two partners in the experiments actually drew a green marble, and so the urn must be mixed. Here's the conclusion from this reasoning: whenever your vote actually matters to the outcome, the urn is mixed!

So if you know your two partners will be voting sincerely, you can best help the group by always voting "mixed," so as to give a single draw of a green marble the chance to sway the majority outcome. In other words, you're manipulating the group choice by voting strategically. You're not doing this to take advantage of the other voters; indeed, you're doing it to make it more likely the group will make the best choice. But nonetheless, it is not optimal for you to vote sincerely in this case, if your two partners are voting sincerely.

Interpretations of the Voting Experiment. Once we appreciate what's going on here, it becomes natural to think of voting with a shared objective in terms of game theory. The voters correspond to players, their possible strategies are the possible ways of choosing votes based on private information, and they receive payoffs based on the votes selected by everyone. The experiment we've just considered constructs a scenario in which sincere voting is not an equilibrium. Notice that while our analysis has therefore ruled out the most natural candidate for an equilibrium, it hasn't actually determined what an equilibrium looks like for this game. In fact, there are multiple equilibria, some of which are a bit complicated to compute, and we won't try to work them out here.

There are a few further points worth reflecting on from this discussion. First, the experiment presents the phenomenon of insincere voting in a very clean and stylized form, which has the advantage of clearly exposing what's going on. But versions of this scenario arise in real-world situations as well, when a highly symmetric decision process like majority rule clashes with a pair of alternatives that has an asymmetric structure – like the pure and mixed urns here. Suppose, for example, that a corporate advisory board has to decide between a risky and a safe course of action for the company, and they decide to use majority rule. Suppose further that board members have their own private evidence in favor of one option or the other, and in fact if anyone were to have genuine evidence in favor of the risky option, then it would clearly be the better choice. If you're a board member in this case, and you know that the other board members will be voting sincerely, then your vote will only matter in the case when half of the rest of the board has evidence in favor of the risky option – in which case, the risky option is the better idea. So the group would be better served if you voted insincerely in favor of the risky option, to improve its chances of being chosen when it should be. Of course, viewing the process of voting as a game, you should appreciate that the situation is in fact more complicated: rather than assuming that the other board members will vote sincerely, you may want to assume that they are also going through this reasoning. Determining how to behave, given this, is a complex problem.

Finally, it's worth highlighting a key methodological point in this analysis – the underlying principle in which you evaluate the consequences of your actions only in the cases where they actually affect the outcome. This was the clarifying insight that exposed why insincere voting was the correct decision. Researchers have observed that the use of this principle for voting forms a parallel with reasoning in other game-theoretic contexts as well, including the "winner's curse" for auctions that we saw in Chapter 9 [159]. There, when many people bid on an item that has a common value (such as oil-drilling rights for a tract of land), the value of your bid only matters if you win, in which case your estimate of the true value of the item is more likely to be an overestimate than an underestimate. Hence, you should take this into account when bidding, and bid lower than your estimate of the true value. This type of insincerity in bidding is analogous to the insincerity in voting that we've been discussing here; in both cases, they arise because you're evaluating your decision contingent on its actually affecting the outcome, which provides additional implicit information that needs to be taken into account.

23.9 Jury Decisions and the Unanimity Rule

Jury decisions in criminal trials were an important initial example to motivate this discussion: they form a natural class of instances where a group of voters (the jurors) agree in principle that there is a "best" decision for the group – the defendant should be convicted if guilty and acquitted if innocent – and they want to aggregate their individual opinions to try arriving at this best decision. Given what we've just seen, it is natural to ask: can insincere voting arise in this case, and if so, what are its consequences? As Feddersen and Pesendorfer have argued, insincere voting in fact can arise naturally as a strategy for jurors who want their vote to contribute to the best overall group decision [160]. We describe the basic structure of their analysis here.

Verdicts, Unanimity, and Private Signals. If we compare jury decisions in criminal trials with the setup for the Condorcet Jury Theorem from Section 23.7, we notice two basic differences, both of which arise from institutional features of the criminal-justice system designed to help avoid convicting innocent defendants.

The first difference is that it generally requires a unanimous vote in order to convict a defendant. So if we have k jurors, and the two options *acquittal* and *conviction*, each juror votes for one of these options, and conviction is chosen by the group only if each juror votes for it. The second difference is in the criterion that jurors are asked to use for evaluating the two alternatives. In the model from Section 23.7, if each voter could observe all the available information, she would choose alternative X if

$$\Pr\left[X \text{ is best} \mid \text{all available information}\right] > \frac{1}{2}.$$

In a criminal trial, however, the instructions to a jury are not, "the defendant should be convicted if he is more likely to be guilty than innocent," but instead "the defendant should be convicted if he is guilty beyond a reasonable doubt." This means that jurors should not be asking whether

$$\Pr\left[\text{defendant is guilty} \mid \text{all available information}\right] > \frac{1}{2},$$

but whether

$$\Pr\left[\text{defendant is guilty} \mid \text{all available information}\right] > z,$$

for some larger number z.

We now consider how to model the information available to each juror. Following the framework used for the Condorcet Jury Theorem in Section 23.7, we assume that each juror receives an independent private signal suggesting guilt (a G-signal) or innocence (an I-signal). The defendant, in reality, is of course either guilty or innocent, and we assume that signals favoring the truth are more abundant than signals favoring the wrong answer: for some number $q > \frac{1}{2}$, we have

$$\Pr\left[G\text{-signal} \mid \text{defendant is guilty}\right] = q$$

and

$$\Pr\left[I\text{-signal} \mid \text{defendant is innocent}\right] = q.$$

A juror who observes a G-signal is interested in the conditional probability of guilt given the signal, namely $\Pr\left[\text{defendant is guilty} \mid G\text{-signal}\right]$. Let's assume a prior probability of $\frac{1}{2}$ that the defendant is guilty – that is, in the absence of any signals. Then the argument using Bayes' rule from Section 23.7 (with conviction and acquittal playing the roles of the two alternatives X and Y from that section) applies directly here, showing that

$$\Pr\left[\text{defendant is guilty} \mid G\text{-signal}\right] = q,$$

and similarly that

$$\Pr\left[\text{defendant is innocent} \mid I\text{-signal}\right] = q.$$

The conclusions of the analysis to follow would remain essentially the same, with slightly different calculations, if we were to assume any prior probability between 0 and 1.

Before proceeding with the analysis, it's fair to ask whether the modeling assumption that jurors receive independent, private signals about guilt or innocence is reasonable; after all, they sit through the trial together, and they all see the same evidence being presented. Clearly, the assumption of private signals is a simplified approximation, but it is also clear that jurors in real trials can and do form widely divergent views of the facts in a case. This is natural: despite seeing the same evidence, jurors form different interpretations and inferences based on their own personal intuitions and decision-making styles – things that cannot necessarily be transmitted as facts from one person to another [160]. So in this case we can think of the private signals as representing private *interpretations* of the information presented, rather than some personal source of additional information. A rational juror is thus guided by her own signal, but she would also be influenced by knowledge of the signals of others – by knowledge that others had interpreted things the same or differently.

Modeling a Juror's Decision. As noted above, the unanimity rule is designed to make it hard for an innocent defendant to be convicted, since such a result would require every single juror to "erroneously" favor conviction. On the surface, this informal principle makes sense; but as we saw in Section 23.8, reasoning about such principles can become subtle when we assume that individuals are choosing their votes with the overall group decision in mind.

In particular, things become complicated for the following reason. Suppose that you're one of the k jurors, and you received an I-signal. At first, it seems clear that you should vote to acquit: after all, your I-signal on its own gives you a conditional probability of $q > \frac{1}{2}$ that the defendant is innocent. But then you remember two things. First, the criterion for conviction by the group is

$$\Pr\,[\textit{defendant is guilty} \mid \textit{available information}] > z,$$

which means that in principle the unobserved signals of everyone else – if only you knew what they were – could be enough to push the conditional probability of guilt above z, despite your I-signal. Second, you ask yourself the key question from Section 23.8: "In what situations does my vote actually affect the outcome?" Given the unanimity rule, your vote only affects the outcome when every juror but you is voting to convict. If you believe that everyone else's vote will reflect the signal they received, then you can work out exactly what the full set of signals is in the event that your vote affects the outcome: it consists of $k - 1$ G-signals and your one I-signal.

What is the probability the defendant is guilty in this case? We can use Bayes' rule to say that

$$\Pr\,[\textit{defendant is guilty} \mid \textit{you have the only I-signal}]$$
$$= \frac{\Pr\,[\textit{defendant is guilty}] \times \Pr\,[\textit{you have the only I-signal} \mid \textit{defendant is guilty}]}{\Pr\,[\textit{you have the only I-signal}]}.$$

Our assumption is that $\Pr\,[\textit{defendant is guilty}] = \frac{1}{2}$, and since the G-signals are independent, we have $\Pr\,[\textit{you have the only I-signal} \mid \textit{defendant is guilty}] = q^{k-1}(1 - q)$. (For this latter calculation, there is a probability of q^{k-1} that each of the $k - 1$ other jurors gets a G-signal, times a probability of $1 - q$ that you get an I-signal.) Finally, as usual in Bayes' rule calculations, we determine the two different ways in which all jurors but you receive G-signals: if the defendant is guilty, or if he is innocent:

$$\Pr\,[\textit{you have the only I-signal}]$$
$$= \Pr\,[\textit{defendant is guilty}] \times \Pr\,[\textit{you have the only I-signal} \mid \textit{defendant is guilty}]$$
$$+ \Pr\,[\textit{defendant is innocent}]$$
$$\times \Pr\,[\textit{you have the only I-signal} \mid \textit{defendant is innocent}]$$
$$= \frac{1}{2}q^{k-1}(1 - q) + \frac{1}{2}(1 - q)^{k-1}q.$$

(The second term in the preceding expression arises from an analogous calculation to what we used for the first term: if the defendant is innocent, there is a probability of $(1 - q)^{k-1}$ that each of the $k - 1$ jurors other than you gets a G-signal, times a probability of q that you get an I-signal.) Putting these quantities together, we have

$$\Pr\,[\textit{defendant is guilty} \mid \textit{you have the only I-signal}] = \frac{\frac{1}{2}q^{k-1}(1 - q)}{\frac{1}{2}q^{k-1}(1 - q) + \frac{1}{2}(1 - q)^{k-1}q}$$
$$= \frac{q^{k-2}}{q^{k-2} + (1 - q)^{k-2}},$$

where the second quality follows just by canceling $q(1 - q)/2$ from both the numerator and denominator.

Now, since $q > \frac{1}{2}$, the term $(1-q)^{k-2}$ represents an arbitrarily small portion of the total denominator as the jury size k goes to infinity – and so in particular

$$\Pr[\textit{defendant is guilty} \mid \textit{you have the only I-signal}]$$

converges to 1 as k goes to infinity. Hence, if the jury size k is large enough, it follows that $\Pr[\textit{defendant is guilty} \mid \textit{you have the only I-signal}] > z$.

We conclude from this calculation that if you believe everyone else is voting their signals, and if there are enough other jurors, then in the only case where your vote to acquit affects the outcome, the defendant is in fact guilty beyond a reasonable doubt. So if you were to vote with the actual instructions to the jury in mind, you should ignore your signal and vote to convict. Of course, you should do this with even more confidence in the event that you receive a G-signal, and so we can summarize the conclusion even more starkly: if you believe everyone else is voting their signals, and the jury size is large enough, you should always ignore your signal and vote to convict.

Intuitively, what's going on is that you only affect the outcome of a unanimous vote when everyone else holds the opposite opinion; on the assumption that everyone else is as well informed as you are, and voting their true opinion, the conclusion is that they're probably (collectively) right, and you're wrong. As with our earlier example in Section 23.8, this serves as an interesting reminder that, when you design a procedure or protocol for a group of people to follow, you should expect that they'll adapt their behavior in light of the rules you define. Here, the voting system based on unanimity was designed to help prevent erroneous convictions, but in fact it creates an incentive for people to disregard signals that the defendant is innocent.

Equilibria for Voting Under Unanimity and Other Systems. As in Section 23.8, we've shown that (for large enough juries) voting your signal is not an equilibrium – if everyone else is doing it, then you should always vote to convict. In their analysis of this problem, Feddersen and Pesendorfer went further and worked out what the equilibria for jury voting in this model actually look like.

First, there's an equilibrium that's easy to find but a bit pathological: if everyone decides to ignore their signals and vote to acquit, this is an equilibrium. To see why, notice that no juror can affect the outcome by changing her behavior; hence, there is no incentive for any juror to change what she is doing.

More interestingly, there is a unique equilibrium with the properties that (i) all jurors use the same strategy and (ii) each juror's behavior actually depends on the signal she receives. This is a mixed-strategy equilibrium, in which each juror always votes to convict on a G-signal, and votes to convict with some probability between 0 and 1 on an I-signal. The idea is that each juror with an I-signal may randomly choose to disregard it, effectively correcting for the possibility that she is wrong. One can show that when jurors follow this equilibrium, the probability that their group decision convicts an innocent defendant is a positive number that does not converge to zero as the size of the jury goes to infinity. This forms a sharp contrast to the Condorcet Jury Theorem, for which the probability of a correct decision converges to 1 as the number of voters grows. The problem here is that the unanimity rule encourages voters to "overcorrect" so strongly for the chance that they might be wrong, it leads to a noticeable probability that the group as a whole reaches the wrong decision.

Moreover, the unanimity rule is particularly bad in this regard. Specifically, with further analysis, we can study voting systems in which convicting a defendant requires only that an f fraction of the jurors vote for conviction, for different values of f with $0 < f < 1$. For a given choice of f, we'll call such a system the f-*majority rule*. There is still an equilibrium here in which jurors employ randomization, sometimes disregarding their signals to correct for the possibility that they are wrong. But with the f-majority rule, a juror's vote affects the outcome when the remaining jurors are divided between convicting and acquitting in a ratio of f to $(1 - f)$ – a much less extreme split than under the unanimity rule, where a juror's vote affects the outcome only in the event that she is singular in her opposition to convicting. As a result, the randomized correction used by jurors is correspondingly less extreme, and one can show that, as the jury size goes to infinity, the probability of the group decision being wrong goes to 0 [160].

This result offers a further reason to question the appropriateness of the unanimity rule – the result suggests that a decision rule for juries requiring conviction by a wide majority, rather than a unanimous vote, might actually induce behavior in which there is a lower probability of erroneous convictions. It is again an indication of the subtle issues that arise when one evaluates the trade-offs between different social institutions in light of the behaviors they induce in the people who take part in them.

23.10 Sequential Voting and the Relation to Information Cascades

Let's return to the original formulation of the Condorcet Jury Theorem, with individuals who vote simultaneously and sincerely over two alternatives X and Y. In the previous two sections, we've examined what happens when we remove the assumption of sincerity. It's also interesting to instead remove the assumption of simultaneity and see what happens. We'll keep sincerity in this discussion, since this simplifies the analysis by only changing one aspect of the model at a time. Each voter will cast a vote for the alternative she believes to be the best choice.

When we assume that voters act sincerely but sequentially, we have a model that closely aligns with the formulation of information cascades from Chapter 16. In our model for information cascades, we assumed that voters make choices sequentially: they are able to observe the choices (but not the private signals) of earlier voters, and they can choose to disregard their own signals if it increases the chance that they personally choose the better alternative. Note that in this model of cascades, voters are still behaving sincerely in the sense that they are trying to choose the alternative that is more likely to be correct, based on everything they are able to observe.

Aside from this distinction between simultaneous and sequential voting, the setup for the Condorcet Jury Theorem from Section 23.7 is otherwise quite similar to the model for information cascades from Chapter 16. In both models, there is a given prior probability for X to be correct, and there are private signals favoring the correct alternative with probability greater than $\frac{1}{2}$. Therefore, we can invoke our analysis from

Section 16.5 to argue that if voters act sequentially, two initial votes in favor of X will cause a cascade in which all subsequent votes are for X as well – regardless of whether X is the correct decision. More generally, once the number of votes for one alternative first exceeds the number of votes for the other alternative by at least two, a cascade will form in which all subsequent voters will strategically choose to disregard their own signals.

The fact that cascades begin when one alternative leads the other by exactly two votes depends on the specific structure of our simplified model from Chapter 16. The broader principle, however, is quite general. In sequential voting of the type we're describing, a cascade will eventually develop. And cascades can be wrong: even if Y is the best alternative, a cascade for X can develop. Moreover, increasing the number of voters does essentially nothing to stop this cascade. So the principle behind the Condorcet Jury Theorem does not apply in this setting: there is no reason to expect that a large crowd of sequential voters will get the answer right.

23.11 Advanced Material: A Proof of Arrow's Impossibility Theorem

In this section we give a proof of Arrow's Theorem [22, 23], which was stated in Section 23.5. The proof we present is not Arrow's original one; instead, we follow a shorter proof found more recently by John Geanakoplos [179].

Let's begin by stating the theorem in a language that will help in discussing the ideas in the proof. We start with a finite set of alternatives. We have a set of k individuals, whom we can assume to be numbered $1, 2, 3, \ldots, k$; each individual has a ranking of the possible alternatives. We'll call the collection of all k rankings a *profile*. In this terminology, a *voting system* is simply a function that takes a profile and produces a *group ranking*: a single ranking of the alternatives.[1] The voting system satisfies Unanimity if it puts $X \succ Y$ in the group ranking whenever $X \succ_i Y$ according to the ranking of each individual i. The voting system satisfies Independence of Irrelevant Alternatives (IIA) if the ordering of alternatives X and Y in the group ranking depends only on the ordering of X and Y in each individual ranking, and not on their position relative to any other alternatives.

Here's a slightly different but equivalent way to describe IIA, which will be useful in our discussion. Consider a profile of rankings, and any two alternatives X and Y. We say that an individual's ranking *restricted to X and Y* consists of a copy of his or her ranking in which we erase all the alternatives other than X and Y. A profile *restricted to X and Y* is the profile consisting of all individual rankings restricted to X and Y. Then, as illustrated in Figure 23.7, if a voting system satisfies IIA, it must produce the same ordering of X and Y for any two profiles that are the same when restricted to X and Y. (In other words, the profile restricted to X and Y is the only information the voting system can look at in ordering X and Y in the group ranking.)

---

[1] As in earlier sections of this chapter, we consider the case in which individual rankings have no ties, and the voting system is required to produce a group ranking that has no ties either.

Profile 1:

Individual	Ranking	Ranking restricted to X and Y
1	W ≻ X ≻ Y ≻ Z	X ≻ Y
2	W ≻ Z ≻ Y ≻ X	Y ≻ X
3	X ≻ W ≻ Z ≻ Y	X ≻ Y

Profile 2:

Individual	Ranking	Ranking restricted to X and Y
1	X ≻ Y ≻ W ≻ Z	X ≻ Y
2	Z ≻ Y ≻ X ≻ W	Y ≻ X
3	W ≻ X ≻ Y ≻ Z	X ≻ Y

Figure 23.7. These two profiles involve quite different rankings, but, for each individual, her ranking restricted to X and Y in the first profile is the same as her ranking restricted to X and Y in the second profile. If the voting system satisfies IIA, then it must produce the same ordering of X and Y in the group ranking for both profiles.

Recall from Section 23.5 that a voting system can satisfy both Unanimity and IIA via *dictatorship*: it selects some individual j in advance, and for any profile of individual rankings, it simply declares the group ranking to be j's ranking. There are k different dictatorship procedures, depending on which of the k individuals is chosen in advance to be the dictator. Arrow's Theorem is that the k dictatorship procedures are the only voting systems that satisfy Unanimity and IIA. This is the statement we prove here.

The challenge in proving Arrow's Theorem is that the Unanimity and IIA conditions are both quite simple, and hence they give us relatively little to work with. Despite this challenge, we need to take an arbitrary voting system satisfying these two properties and show that it in fact coincides with dictatorship by a single individual.

Our proof will consists of three main steps. First we show the following interesting fact; its utility in the proof is not immediately apparent, but it plays a crucial role. Let's call X a *polarizing alternative* if it is ranked either first or last by every individual. Profiles P and P' in Figure 23.8 are examples of profiles in which X is a polarizing alternative. We'll show that if a voting system satisfies Unanimity and IIA, then it must place any polarizing alternative in either first or last place in the group ranking. In other words, such a voting system can't find a way to "average" and place a polarizing alternative somewhere in the middle of the group ranking. Note that many profiles don't contain a polarizing alternative; this fact only applies to those that do. In the second step of the proof, we then use this fact to identify a natural candidate for the role of dictator, and in the third step, we prove that this individual is in fact a dictator.

First Step: Polarizing Alternatives. For the remainder of the proof, let F be a voting system satisfying Unanimity and IIA. We will use P to denote a profile of individual rankings, and use $F(P)$ to denote the group ranking that F produces as a function of

Profile P:

Individual	Ranking
1	$X \succ \cdots \succ Y \succ \cdots \succ Z \succ \cdots$
2	$X \succ \cdots \succ Z \succ \cdots \succ Y \succ \cdots$
3	$\cdots \succ Y \succ \cdots \succ Z \succ \cdots \succ X$

Profile P':

Individual	Ranking
1	$X \succ \cdots \succ Z \succ Y \succ \cdots$
2	$X \succ \cdots \succ Z \succ \cdots \succ Y \succ \cdots$
3	$\cdots \succ Z \succ Y \succ \cdots \succ X$

Figure 23.8. A polarizing alternative is one that appears at the beginning or end of every individual ranking. A voting system that satisfies IIA must put such an alternative at the beginning or end of the group ranking as well. The figure shows the key step in the proof of this fact, based on rearranging individual rankings while keeping the polarizing alternative in its original position.

this profile. We will work toward identifying an individual j with the property that F simply consists of dictatorship by j.

First, let P be a profile in which X is a polarizing alternative, and suppose by way of contradiction that F does not place X in either first or last place in the group ranking $F(P)$. This means that there are other alternatives Y and Z so that $Y \succ X \succ Z$ in the group ranking $F(P)$.

Now, for any individual ranking that puts Y ahead of Z, let's change it by sliding Z to the position just ahead of Y. This produces a new profile P', as sketched in Figure 23.8. Since X is a polarizing alternative, the relative order of X and Z does not change in any individual ranking when we do this, nor does the relative order of X and Y. Therefore, by IIA, we still have $Y \succ X \succ Z$ in the group ranking $F(P')$. But in P', alternative Z is ahead of alternative Y in every individual ranking, and so by Unanimity we have $Z \succ Y$ in the group ranking $F(P')$. Putting these together, the group ranking $F(P')$ has $Y \succ X \succ Z \succ Y$, which contradicts the fact that the voting system F always produces a transitive group ranking.

This contradiction shows that our original assumption of alternatives Y and Z with $Y \succ X \succ Z$ in $F(P)$ cannot be correct, and so X must appear in either the first or last position in the group ranking $F(P)$.

Second Step: Identifying a Potential Dictator. In the next step, we create a sequence of profiles with the property that each differs from the next by very little, and we watch how the group ranking (according to F) changes as we move through this sequence. As we track these changes, a natural candidate for the dictator will emerge.

Here is how the sequence of profiles is constructed. We pick one of the alternatives, X, and we start with any profile P_0 that has X at the end of each individual ranking.

Profile P_0:

Individual	Ranking
1	$\cdots \succ Y \succ \cdots \succ Z \succ \cdots \succ X$
2	$\cdots \succ Z \succ \cdots \succ Y \succ \cdots \succ X$
3	$\cdots \succ Y \succ \cdots \succ Z \succ \cdots \succ X$

Profile P_1:

Individual	Ranking
1	$X \succ \cdots \succ Y \succ \cdots \succ Z \succ \cdots$
2	$\cdots \succ Z \succ \cdots \succ Y \succ \cdots \succ X$
3	$\cdots \succ Y \succ \cdots \succ Z \succ \cdots \succ X$

Profile P_2:

Individual	Ranking
1	$X \succ \cdots \succ Y \succ \cdots \succ Z \succ \cdots$
2	$X \succ \cdots \succ Z \succ \cdots \succ Y \succ \cdots$
3	$\cdots \succ Y \succ \cdots \succ Z \succ \cdots \succ X$

Profile P_3:

Individual	Ranking
1	$X \succ \cdots \succ Y \succ \cdots \succ Z \succ \cdots$
2	$X \succ \cdots \succ Z \succ \cdots \succ Y \succ \cdots$
3	$X \succ \cdots \succ Y \succ \cdots \succ Z \succ \cdots$

Figure 23.9. To find a potential dictator, one can study how a voting system behaves when we start with an alternative at the end of each individual ranking, and then gradually (one person at a time) move it to the front of people's rankings.

Now, one individual ranking at a time, we move X from last place to first place while leaving all other parts of the rankings the same, as shown in Figure 23.9. This produces a sequence of rankings $P_0, P_1, P_2, \ldots, P_k$, where P_i

   (i)   has X at the front of the individual rankings of $1, 2, \ldots, i$;
   (ii)   has X at the end of the individual rankings of $i + 1, i + 2, \ldots, k$; and
   (iii)   has the same order as P_0 on all other alternatives.

So in other words, P_{i-1} and P_i differ only in that individual i ranks X last in P_{i-1}, and he ranks it first in P_i.

Now, by Unanimity, X must be last in the group ranking $F(P_0)$, and it must be first in the group ranking $F(P_k)$. So somewhere along this sequence there is a first profile in which X is not in last place in the group ranking; suppose this first profile is P_j. Since X is a polarizing alternative in P_j, and it is not in last place in $F(P_j)$, it must be in first place.

So individual j has a huge amount of power over the outcome for alternative X, at least in this sequence of rankings: by switching her own ranking of X from last to first, she causes X to move from last to first in the group ranking. In the final step of the proof, we will show that j is in fact a dictator.

Third Step: Establishing That j Is a Dictator. The key argument in showing that j is a dictator is to show that for any profile Q, and any alternatives Y and Z that are different from X, the ordering of Y and Z in the group ranking $F(Q)$ is the same as the ordering of Y and Z in j's individual ranking in Q. After that, we'll show that the same also holds for pairs of alternatives in which one of the alternatives is X. In this way, we'll have established that the ordering of each pair is determined entirely by j's ordering and, hence, j is a dictator.

So let Q be any profile, and let Y and Z be alternatives not equal to X such that j ranks Y ahead of Z. We show that $F(Q)$ puts Y ahead of Z as well.

We create an additional profile Q' that is a variant of Q; this new profile will help us understand how j controls the ordering of Y and Z. First, we take Q, move X to the front of the individual rankings of $1, 2, \ldots, j$, and move X to the end of the individual rankings of $j + 1, j + 2, \ldots, k$. Then, we move Y to the front of j's individual ranking (just ahead of X). We call the resulting profile Q'.

Now, we make the following observations.

- We know that X comes first in the group ranking $F(P_j)$. Since Q' and P_j are the same when restricted to X and Z, it follows from IIA that $X \succ Z$ in $F(Q')$.
- We know that X comes last in the group ranking $F(P_{j-1})$. Since Q' and P_{j-1} are the same when restricted to X and Y, it follows from IIA that $Y \succ X$ in $F(Q')$.
- By transitivity, we conclude that $Y \succ Z$ in $F(Q')$.
- Q and Q' are the same when restricted to Y and Z, since we produced Q' from Q without ever swapping the order of Y and Z in any individual ranking. By IIA, it follows that $Y \succ Z$ in $F(Q)$.
- Since Q was any profile, and Y and Z were any alternatives (other than X) subject only to the condition that j ranks Y ahead of Z, it follows that the ordering of Y and Z in the group ranking is always the same as j's.

Thus, we've shown that j is a dictator over all pairs that do not involve X. We're almost done; we just have to show that j is also a dictator over all pairs involving X as well.

To show this, first observe that we can run the argument thus far with respect to any other alternative W different from X, and thereby establish that there is also an individual ℓ who is a dictator over all pairs not involving W. Suppose that ℓ is not equal to j. Now, for X and some third alternative Y different from X and W, we know that the profiles P_{j-1} and P_j differ only in j's individual ranking, yet the ordering of X and Y is different between the group rankings $F(P_{j-1})$ and $F(P_j)$. In one of these two group rankings, the ordering of X and Y must therefore differ from the ordering of X and Y in ℓ's individual ranking, contradicting the fact that ℓ is a dictator for the pair X and Y. Hence, our assumption that ℓ is different from j must be false and, thus, j is in fact a dictator over all pairs.

23.12 Exercises

1. In this chapter, we discussed how voting systems based on majority rule are suscep-tible to strategic agenda setting. Let's explore how one may do this with some basic examples.

    (a) Suppose there are four alternatives, named A, B, C, and D. There are three voters who have the following individual rankings:

    $$B \succ_1 C \succ_1 D \succ_1 A,$$

    $$C \succ_2 D \succ_2 A \succ_2 B,$$

    $$D \succ_3 A \succ_3 B \succ_3 C.$$

    You're in charge of designing an agenda for considering the alternatives in pairs and eliminating them using majority vote, via an elimination tourna-ment in the style of the examples shown in Figure 23.3.
        You would like alternative A to win. Can you design an agenda (i.e., an elimination tournament) in which A wins? If so, describe how you would structure it; if not, explain why it is not possible.

    (b) Now, consider the same question but for a slightly different set of individual rankings in which the last two positions in voter 3's ranking have been swapped. That is, we have

    $$B \succ_1 C \succ_1 D \succ_1 A,$$

    $$C \succ_2 D \succ_2 A \succ_2 B,$$

    $$D \succ_3 A \succ_3 C \succ_3 B.$$

    We now ask the same question: Can you design an agenda in which A wins? If so, describe how you would structure it; if not, explain why it is not possible.

2. The Borda Count is susceptible to strategic misreporting of preferences. Here are some examples to practice how this works.

    (a) Suppose you are one of three people voting on a set of four alternatives named A, B, C, and D. The Borda Count will be used as the voting system. The other two voters have the rankings

    $$D \succ_1 C \succ_1 A \succ_1 B,$$

    $$D \succ_2 B \succ_2 A \succ_2 C.$$

    You are voter 3 and would like alternative A to appear first in the group ranking, as determined by the Borda Count. Can you construct an individ-ual ranking for yourself so that this will be the result? If so, explain how you would choose your individual ranking; if not, explain why it is not possible.

(b) Let's consider the same question, but with different rankings for the other two voters, as follows:

$$D \succ_1 A \succ_1 C \succ_1 B,$$

$$B \succ_2 D \succ_2 A \succ_2 C.$$

Again, as voter 3, you would like alternative A to appear first in the group ranking determined by the Borda Count. Can you construct an individual ranking for yourself so that this will be the result? If so, explain how you would choose your individual ranking; if not, explain why it is not possible.

3. In Section 23.6, we considered a setting in which alternatives are arranged on a line. Each voter has an "ideal" point on the line, and she ranks alternatives by the distance of these alternatives to her ideal point. An interesting property of this setting is that the Condorcet Paradox cannot arise; more strongly, majority voting over pairs of alternatives always produces group preferences that are complete and transitive.

Suppose we try to generalize this by allowing alternatives and voters to be positioned in two dimensions rather than one. That is, suppose that each alternative corresponds to a point in two-dimensional space. (For example, perhaps the alternatives are different versions of a piece of legislation, and they differ in two distinct characteristics, corresponding to the two dimensions.) As before, each voter has an "ideal" point in the two-dimensional plane where the alternatives reside, and she evaluates the alternatives by their respective distances (in the plane) to this ideal point.

Unfortunately, the desirable properties that applied to one-dimensional preferences no longer hold here. Show how to construct a set of three alternatives in two dimensions, and a set of three voters, each with an ideal point, so that the resulting set of individual preferences produces the preferences that we saw in the Condorcet Paradox.

CHAPTER 24

Property Rights

The final broad class of social institutions we consider is concerned with the allocation of resources in a society via *property rights*. Property rights give the holder of the right the ability to use a resource, the ability to exclude others from using it, and usually the right to sell or transfer the resource to another person. Property can take many forms, ranging from physical property such as a plot of land or a can of Diet Coke, to intellectual property such as a song or a manufacturing process. In this chapter we examine how the existence and form of property rights, or the lack of property rights, can affect social outcomes for each of these types of property. The central message of this chapter is that the property rights a society chooses to establish will affect the allocations that occur, and some property rights are more likely than others to result in socially optimal allocations.

24.1 Externalities and the Coase Theorem

In Chapter 17 we argued that the allocation of goods that arises in a market equilibrium (for an economy without network effects) is socially optimal. In a market equilibrium, the goods that are produced are assigned to the consumers who value them the most, and any unit of a good that is produced costs society less to produce than it is worth to the consumer who receives the good. This results in maximum total social surplus. The intuition for this fact comes from the observation that, at a market equilibrium allocation, each person who consumes a unit of a good pays the cost to society of producing a unit of the good, and anyone who is not consuming the good is unwilling to pay the cost of producing a unit of the good. In this discussion, and in Chapter 17, we have assumed (implicitly) that: the cost of producing the good correctly reflects the true cost to society of producing the good; an individual's willingness to pay for a unit of the good correctly reflects the value to society of allowing that individual to consume the good; a producer of a good owns it (has the property right to it) and can sell it at the market price; and, in order to consume the good, an individual must buy the good at the market price.

These are important qualifications to the social optimality of market equilibria. To see why getting the values right is so important, let's tell the story of production and trade in slightly different terms. When an individual consumes a can of Diet Coke, the individual creates a personal benefit (otherwise she would not voluntarily consume it), and she creates a harm to the rest of society because there is now one less can of Diet Coke that could be consumed by another member of the society. However, if the price that the consumer pays for the can of Diet Coke is equal to the cost to society of producing another can of Diet Coke, then the consumer who buys and consumes the can of Diet Coke compensates the rest of society correctly for the harm she imposes. Well-defined property rights play an important role beneath the surface of this story. One important role that they play is that every good that is produced or consumed is covered by a clear property right. If property rights to the can of Diet Coke are clear, and if no one else is affected by the actions of the Diet Coke producer and the Diet Coke consumer, then property rights cover this transaction completely. If instead the actions of either the producer or the consumer of our can of Diet Coke affect others in a way that is not covered by some property right, then the resulting equilibrium need not be socially optimal. When the welfare of some individuals or firms is affected by the actions of other individuals or firms without a property right that requires mutually agreeable compensation, then we say that an *externality* occurs. Externalities can be negative, as we saw in Chapter 8 when we discussed traffic congestion, or positive, as we focused on in Chapter 17 when we discussed goods with network effects. In this chapter we will discuss externalities at a more general level.

Externalities and Nonoptimal Allocations. Let's explore several examples to see how externalities may arise and why they can create nonoptimal allocations. First, suppose someone decides to smoke a cigar in a restaurant in which there is one other diner. The smoker purchased the cigar at a price which presumably covered the cost of producing the cigar, so at least between the smoker and the producer there is no externality created by the sale of the cigar. But in the act of consuming the cigar in the restaurant the smoker imposes a harm on the other diner without compensating this person for the harm. Whether the resulting allocation is socially optimal or not depends on the amounts of harm and benefit created.

Suppose that the amount of harm suffered by the other diner is $10; that is, if the other diner received a compensation of $10 for the harm created by the smoke, then this person would be just as well off as he would be if the other diner didn't smoke the cigar in the restaurant. On the other hand, suppose the benefit that the smoker receives from smoking the cigar, above the price he paid for it, is only $5. Then smoking the cigar reduces total social surplus by $5: the difference between the harm of $10 created by the smoke and the benefit of $5 received from creating the smoke. In this case, social optimality requires a smoke-free environment in the restaurant. One mechanism that would achieve this goal is a law that prohibits smoking in restaurants.

An alternative mechanism that would achieve the same goal would be to establish a property right to smoke-free air in restaurants and to make this property right tradeable. In this case, the other diner can choose whether or not to allow the smoker to smoke his cigar by agreeing to abandon the property right in exchange for suitable compensation – that is, by selling the property right. Since we're assuming the smoker only values the ability to smoke at $5, there would be no smoking in the restaurant in this case, because the smoker would not be willing to pay enough to compensate the other diner for the ($10) harm caused by the smoke. Of course, if the benefit the smoker received from smoking were $15, rather than $5, then there would be a trade. The smoker would pay the other diner an amount between $10 and $15 for the clean air right, the smoker would smoke his cigar, both parties would be happy with this outcome, and we would have a socially optimal allocation.[1]

In the smoking example, establishing a property right to smoke-free air results in a socially optimal allocation no matter what the individual's values are for smoking and smoke-free air. Alternatively, a property right that allows the smoker to smoke would also work, because after negotiation between the smoker and the other diner, smoking occurs exactly when it is socially optimal for it to occur. The possible lack of social optimality arises when there is no clear property right or no property right at all. In this case, the individuals may simply disagree about whether smoking is allowed or not and negotiation to a socially optimal allocation seems unlikely to occur.

Finally, a law that prohibits smoking in restaurants will result in a socially optimal allocation if the values are such that the optimal allocation requires no smoking, but it will fail to provide an optimal allocation in the case in which smoking is optimal. In practice, smoking in restaurants is banned in parts of the United States, and it is useful to relate this to the issue of optimal allocations. There are several possible motivations for a smoking ban, phrased in terms of the preceding discussion. Maybe the underlying values are such that the optimal allocation always or almost always requires smoke-free air; maybe policy makers believe that individuals consistently undervalue smoke-free air and so would make mistakes if they were allowed to trade; or maybe the costs of enforcing and trading a property right to smoke-free air in restaurants would be so expensive that it is better to just outlaw smoking in restaurants.

Let's explore the last of these motivations – the cost of establishing the property right – in a bit more detail. In our example there was only one other diner. What if instead there were many other diners and employees in the restaurant? Then, no matter who owns the property right (the smoker or the others in the restaurant), a complex negotiation would be required, and if diners come and go, the negotiation would have to be conducted repeatedly. This could easily be so costly as to simply be infeasible, and instead establishing a law banning smoking could be the next best alternative. It is quite likely to be the best we can do if social optimality would typically result in a smoke-free environment anyhow.

Our example of smoking in a restaurant is a simplified story capturing some of the issues that arise in a broad and important domain where property rights play a role: the problem of environmental impact from activities like industrial production. Similar issues can arise here when property rights are not clearly defined and enforced. For example, consider a power-generating plant that pollutes the air and water. The power plant pays for many of the goods that it uses in the process of generating power; goods such as labor, capital equipment, and fuel are purchased on the market at prices that compensate the sellers of these goods for the harm they suffer in giving them up. But

---

[1] In this discussion, and in the rest of this chapter, we will assume that individuals' values are independent of their wealth.

the power plant also implicitly uses up clean air and clean water in the process of production. If the power plant had to pay a price that reflected the harm it causes to others – both to individuals and to other firms – by converting clean air and water into dirty air and water, then the allocation of power, air, and water would be socially optimal. Just as in the case of smoking in a restaurant, establishing a property right to either clean air and water or a property right giving the power plant the right to pollute the air and water would in principle work to produce a socially optimal allocation of both power and the degree of pollution of air and water. It is worth pointing out that social optimality is unlikely to mean there would be no pollution. Instead, it simply requires that the amount of pollution, like the amount of all other goods, is determined so that there is no reallocation that improves welfare. But also, just as in the case of the restaurant, the transaction costs involved in negotiation between the power plant and all those affected by its activities may be prohibitive.

Mechanisms for Determining Socially Optimal Allocations. One difficulty with using property rights and mutually agreeable compensation to determine the socially optimal allocation in our power plant example is the following: how do we discover the true amount of harm created by the pollution? If we simply ask people how much harm they suffer from pollution, and attempt to use this information to decide whether or not to allow the pollution, then each person who is harmed has an incentive to overstate the amount of harm. Similarly, the firm creating the pollution has an incentive to overstate the cost of reducing its pollution. However, there is a procedure that can be used to address this incentive problem and we have already analyzed a special case of it.

In Chapter 15, we demonstrated that the Vickrey–Clark–Groves (VCG) mechanism results in an efficient matching of sellers to buyers in a matching market (in the specific context of advertising slots and advertisers), even when the buyers' valuations for items are not known. This occurs because VCG pricing makes truth-telling a dominant strategy for buyers. A similar mechanism can be used to induce truth-telling for polluters and for those who suffer the harm created by pollution. The pollution setting is a bit more complex because the valuations of both the buyers (polluters) and the sellers (affected individuals) are unknown. Here we might imagine the government running the mechanism, collecting revenue from the polluter and providing compensation to individuals harmed by the pollution. The goal of this mechanism is to determine the socially optimal amount of pollution; it is not to use the money collected from the polluter to fully compensate those who are harmed by the pollution. In fact, individuals may be better or worse off once the mechanism is run and the payments occur. In addition, the amount of revenue collected may not equal the amount of compensation, so the government may run either a surplus or a deficit.[2]

Actually running the VCG mechanism to determine the optimal amount of pollution would be difficult and costly. The first problem is to determine who is potentially harmed by the pollution and thus who should be included in the mechanism. Next, the mechanism would have to be rerun every time the group of affected individuals changes

---

[2] For an accessible discussion of the issues involved in designing an optimal mechanism, see the Nobel Prize Committee's Scientific Background statement in support of the 2007 Nobel Prize in Economics [329], which was awarded for work in mechanism design.

and every time the polluter wants to change the amount of pollution. This would have to be done for every polluter. The cost of running these mechanisms over and over would be large. Instead, some governments use a more market-based approach in which firms can buy the right to pollute at market prices. These are called cap-and-trade systems. The United States uses a cap-and-trade system for sulfur dioxide emissions [394]. In a cap-and-trade system, the government provides a number of pollution emissions permits, allows the firms to trade these permits, and requires that any firm emitting pollution must own a number of permits equal to the pollution it emits. If the initial number of permits is set correctly, then this too achieves a socially optimal allocation of pollution.

The central idea behind the use of property rights or tradeable pollution permits as a device to solve problems created by externalities is *Coase's Theorem* [113], which roughly says that if tradeable property rights are established and enforced, then negotiation between the parties affected by the externality will lead to a socially optimal outcome no matter who initially owns the property rights. For example, in our earlier scenario of the smoker in the restaurant, all that was necessary for social optimality was to establish and enforce the right to smoke or the right to have smoke-free air. Then trade between the parties would result in a socially optimal allocation. Of course, who owns the right will affect how well off each of the parties is in the resulting equilibrium and they will certainly disagree about who should initially own the right. But, no matter who it is given to, smoking will occur if and only if it is socially optimal. The same idea applies to pollution emission permits. If property rights are clearly established with someone as the initial owner then trade will lead to optimality. Again the initial allocation of permits will make some better off and some worse off, and it is sure to be politically contentious [81].

The one qualification that is necessary in Coase's argument (that initial ownership is irrelevant) is that it ignores transaction costs and simply assumes that negotiation beginning from any assignment of property rights will lead to an efficient outcome. As we noted in the smoking example, this is not plausible when many individuals are involved in the negotiation. Similarly, in the case of pollution, establishing marketable pollution rights is more likely to minimize transaction costs and lead to socially optimal outcomes.

24.2 The Tragedy of the Commons

In a 1968 article in *Science*, entitled "The Tragedy of the Commons" [205], Garrett Hardin offered a compelling story about the inevitable "tragedy" of commonly shared resources. In his story there is a village commons on which any herdsman can freely graze his cattle.[3] Hardin noted that inevitably the commons will be overused to the detriment of all the villagers. He then argued that establishing property rights would solve the problem. These property rights could be privately held, the commons could be sold to some individual, or they could be publicly held. However, if the village

---

[3] The term *commons* comes from the common use of a village green in Europe. Many old villages still have them, although generally not for use by cattle anymore.

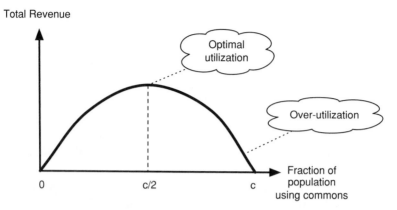

Figure 24.1. In "The Tragedy of the Commons," a freely shared resource can easily be overused unless some form of property right is established.

continues to own the commons it must carefully limit the use of the commons if we are to have a socially optimal allocation.

A Model for the Commons. Let's construct a simple example to see how Hardin's story plays out. Suppose that there is a village with N people, for some large number N, and each villager owns one cow. If an x fraction of this population of N cows grazes on the commons, then the revenue generated per cow is equal to $f(x)$ for some function $f(\cdot)$. Hardin noted that the fewer cows there are on the commons, the more grass there is per cow, and so the greater revenue per cow. That is, the function $f(\cdot)$ is decreasing. Let's suppose, for example, that $f(x) = c - x$ for some number $c < 1$. This means that the revenue per cow remains positive until x reaches c, at which point it becomes zero; increasing the fraction of cattle using the commons beyond $x = c$ will cause a negative revenue per cow due to the crowding of the commons.

So the total revenue generated, if the commons is used by an x fraction of all cattle, is equal to $f(x)(xN)$, which in our example is $(cx - x^2)N$. Figure 24.1 shows the curve $y = (cx - x^2)N$. If the goal of using the commons is to generate revenue from the cattle that graze there, then the socially optimal fraction of cattle on the commons is the value x^* that maximizes the function $f(x)(xN)$; in our case, as we see from the figure, this maximum is achieved midway between the two points where the curve crosses the x-axis, at $x^* = c/2$. Thus, the maximum revenue is

$$f(x^*)(x^*N) = \left(c - \frac{c}{2}\right)\left(\frac{c}{2}\right)N = \frac{c^2N}{4}.$$

We analyzed a similar function in Chapter 17 to describe the maximum price that users would pay for a good with network effects when an x fraction of the population is using it. In that setting there is also an externality, since each individual's willingness to pay for the good is affected by the total number of users. There are key differences, however, between the setting of network effects and the issues involving the commons. With network effects, each additional user had a positive effect on the people already using the product, due to the positive externality. Here, on the other hand, increasing the population on the commons has a negative effect on each individual already there, due to the crowding. Revenue is maximized when the increased crowding due to extra cattle is traded off against the greater revenue from having more cattle using the commons – and this maximum occurs at a fraction $x = c/2$ of the population in the case of our simple example.

This is what happens if we are able to choose a quantity of cattle on the commons that maximizes the total revenue. But what happens if the commons is freely available to all the villagers? In this case, villagers will add cattle to the commons as long as the revenue from doing so is positive. This will eventually lead to the revenue per cow being driven to zero (as long as there are enough cows available, which in our example is true). To see why this must happen, note that if there is presently a fraction x of cattle on the commons and $f(x) > 0$, then there are villagers whose cows are not currently using the commons, and it would be in the interest of any one of these villagers to add his cow to the commons in order to reap even a small bit of positive revenue. This can stop only when the fraction of cattle on the commons reaches the number $\bar{x}$ for which $f(\bar{x}) = 0$, which in our example is $\bar{x} = c$. At that point, there will be twice as many cows on the commons as is socially optimal and the total revenue from the collective use of the commons is $f(\bar{x})(\bar{x}N) = 0$. This is Hardin's tragedy. The village owns a resource which is clearly valuable, but because its use is not restricted, everyone who uses it receives zero reward from using it.

Avoiding the Tragedy. A further "tragic" aspect to this loss of social optimality is that the village could easily solve the problem. There are two obvious ways to do it and several variations on each approach.

One approach is for the village to continue to own the commons jointly but somehow limit the quantity of cattle to the socially optimal number. This could be done either by charging a price for grazing on the commons or by simply setting the fraction of cattle that are allowed on the commons at the optimal value x^*, which in our example is equal to $c/2$. If the village charges a price, the optimal price to charge is $c/2$ per cow. To see why this is optimal, note that a villager will add his cow to the commons if and only if the revenue from grazing a cow on the commons is greater than the price. Thus, in an equilibrium, the revenue from grazing a cow on the commons must be equal to the price. So the equilibrium will be the value of x that solves $f(x) = c/2$, which is $x = c/2$. Alternatively, the village could sell grazing rights for x^*N cows. Again, the maximum price per cow the village could charge for such grazing rights is $c/2$ per cow, as we have just found. Either variation on this method results in the socially optimal use of the commons and a revenue to the village of $c^2N/4$.

Instead of owning it jointly, the village could sell the commons to a large owner of livestock who has many cows. This livestock owner who buys the commons would put x^*N cows on the commons too, since this is the number of cows that maximizes his revenue. The maximum price that the village could sell the commons for is the revenue that the buyer would receive from optimal use of the commons, which is again $c^2N/4$. So in either approach – joint ownership by the village with an appropriate price charged per cow for grazing, or outright sale to an individual – the village receives a revenue of $c^2N/4$, and the commons is used by the optimal fraction of cattle.

In Hardin's village commons example, all that is needed to avoid the tragedy is to establish a property right. It can either be a property right held by some form of government which optimally limits use of the resource or it can be a privately held property right. Just as with Coase's argument, it does not matter (for social optimality) who owns the property; all that matters is that someone owns it. Hardin uses this story to argue why too much pollution is produced, why national parks are overused (if there are no admission charges or limits on the number of users), why there is overfishing, and, more controversially, to argue that overpopulation and thus overuse of the world's resources is inevitable. In each of these examples there is an externality as the actions of any one firm or individual affect others, and if there are no property rights, there is no compensation, and thus no reason to use the resource optimally.

24.3 Intellectual Property

The property that we discussed in our exploration of Coase's Theorem or Hardin's tragedy existed independently of investment by individuals or firms. The air in the restaurant, and the air or water that might be polluted by the power plant, were there regardless of what property rights society creates. Similarly, once the village green is established, it exists independently of any actions by the villagers. But there is a difference between the green and the air or water; and, as we will see, there is yet another difference between either of these examples and intellectual property.

To this point in our analysis we have focused on the efficient use of resources without regard to where theses resources came from. For air and water this seems reasonable. These natural resources are not created by any human effort, and no effort is needed to make them useful. The village green is also a natural resource, but human effort can reasonably make it more or less valuable. Cutting the grass regularly, removing weeds, and applying chemical or natural fertilizer can all make the green more productive. What property rights are established will matter for whether these activities are carried out. If no one owns the green, then no one can fully benefit from undertaking these costly but productivity-enhancing investments, and it seems likely that they will not occur. Solving the property rights problem by assigning the property rights to someone solves the problem of inefficient use of the resource and it also solves the problem of a lack of incentives for productivity-enhancing investment. If an individual owns the green, then that individual reaps the reward of investment in the green, and this provides the individual with the proper incentive to make exactly those investments that are worthwhile. The individual will undertake any investment in the green that generates more revenue than the investment costs. Similarly, if the village owns the green jointly, but sells rights to use it, the village also has the proper incentives to maintain the green. So assigning property rights to the village green is even more important for social optimality than our earlier discussion indicated.

Rivalrous and Nonrivalrous Goods. Perhaps surprisingly given our focus to this point on the desirability of assigning and enforcing property rights, there are commodities for which assigning property rights can lead to less efficient use than would occur if there were no ownership at all. Consider, for example, the result of a creative process. This could be a book, a song, a new computer program, a new variety of crop, a new drug to treat cancer, or a new manufacturing process to produce batteries. The use by one individual or firm of the outcome of the creative process (not the physical object, if one exists, but the idea that is captured in the physical object) does not affect the ability of anyone else to use it.[4] The same process for making a battery or making a drug, for example, can be used by an unlimited number of people. Everyone can listen to a song downloaded from the Internet, or read a book online, without affecting the ability of anyone else to listen to the song or to read the book. In contrast, the can of Diet Coke that one person drinks cannot be consumed by anyone else. The grass on the village green that one villager's cow consumes cannot be consumed by another cow. Goods such that their use or consumption by one user precludes use or consumption by any other potential user are called *rivalrous goods*; goods that can be used or consumed over and over are called *nonrivalrous goods*.

For nonrivalrous goods, establishing property rights can interfere with efficient use of the goods. The owner of the good can charge for use of the good, and any nonzero price may result in some potential users not purchasing the good, and thus not using it (or at least not using it legally). This results in an inefficiency, since there is no cost to society in allowing everyone to use the good, and so prohibiting anyone from using it is wasteful. This contrasts with the socially optimal use of the village green in which it was necessary to limit the use of the good (the green) to achieve social optimality. In that case, the good was rivalrous. But for nonrivalrous goods, Hardin's ideas do not apply.

This is, of course, not the end of the story about property rights for nonrivalrous goods. We also have to ask where the good came from and whether it would exist without property rights. If the creator of a nonrivalrous good does not own it, then the creator's ability to profit from his creation is limited. Even so, the creator may receive some benefit from his creation. Humans discovered many useful ideas (using fire to cook meat, for example) long before there was any legal protection for the creators of the results of these ideas. These early inventors received a direct benefit from their own use of their inventions. Plato wrote and Mozart created music with little or no protection for their works. They too received benefits both directly and from users of their work. So some creative activity will exist, and creators will receive some benefits from creation without property rights that protect intellectual property. But it is not obvious that the socially optimal amount of creative activity will occur without these property rights, nor is it obvious what form those rights should take in order to generate the optimal amount of creative activity.

The relevant question is the trade-off between providing incentives for creative activity and allowing efficient use of the creation once it exists. No one will have the creation unless the creator releases it, so the creator at least can benefit from the first use of a valuable good. If there are no protections, then eventually the good will become publicly available and the creator's ability to charge for it will vanish. Thus, without property rights, the financial reward for creative activity may be small, and in the modern economy, with the advent of fast and inexpensive copying and communication, that ability may be very small indeed. Instituting property rights to creative activity

---

[4] Use by many people may of course affect how profitable it is to use the result of the creative process, but it does not affect the feasibility of use by others.

increases the creator's incentives, but it does so at the cost of inefficient use of the creation once it exists.

Copyrights. Rather than attempt to determine how this balancing should occur in the abstract, we will look at several examples. First, let's consider the case of books, songs, plays, television shows, and movies. In the United States, all of these creations are covered by the *copyright law* (currently the Copyright Act of 1976), which gives the creator of the work the exclusive right to copy the work, to distribute it, to modify it, or – in the case of songs, plays, television shows, and movies – to perform the work. This right lasts for 70 years beyond the lifetime of the creator of the work. The owner of the copyright has the right to transfer this right to others.

It is important to be careful about what use of copyrighted works is allowed and what uses are illegal without permission of the holder of the copyright. First, the copyright holder's exclusive right to copy the work does not actually prohibit all copying. The doctrine of *fair use* has evolved over time to permit limited copying for noncommercial use of parts of a copyrighted work. For example, it is permissible to quote a copyrighted work in a review of the work, in a scholarly article, or in a classroom. The doctrine of fair use is outlined in Section 107 of Title 17 of the Copyright Act of 1976 (the entire law can be found at http://www.copyright.gov/title17/). This law does not define exactly what is or is not fair use; instead, whether a use of a copyrighted work is fair or not is to be determined on a case-by-case basis, with the intent of the copier a critical factor in making the determination. Second, copyright law does not prohibit the owner of a copy of a work from reselling that copy. (This is distinct from making another copy and selling the new copy, which is prohibited.) So although it is illegal to copy a book or CD and transfer that copy to someone else, selling a legally obtained copy of the book or CD is permitted.

Copyright law grants a monopoly (single seller) to the holder of the copyright. Generally monopolies are harmful as the monopolist artificially restricts the use of the good by setting a price above the socially optimal price. For copyrighted works, the socially optimal price would clearly be zero if this price had no effect on the creation of the work. The extent to which the protection afforded by a copyright is necessary to provide sufficient incentives to produce goods that are currently copyrighted is unclear. Some authors, such as Boldrin and Levine [66], for example, argue that copyrights should not exist at all because they believe that copyrights are not necessary for innovation and they prevent efficient use of works once they are created. The more common view is that copyrights are a necessary evil: they do prevent efficient use, but without them the amount of resources devoted to creative activities would be inefficiently small.

Patents. Next, let's consider inventions such as a new drug, a new manufacturing process, or a new piece of computer hardware. The inventor can apply to the U.S. Patent and Trademark Office for a patent on the invention, and, if the patent is granted, the inventor has the right to exclude others from using the invention for a fixed period of time, usually 20 years. The Web site of the U.S. Patent and Trademark Office (http://www.uspto.gov/main/patents.htm) provides a description of the law.

The economic role of patents is much like that of copyrights. They increase the reward to inventive activity at the expense of inefficient use of the patented invention once it is created. However, patents are different from copyrights in several ways. First, granting of copyrights for original work is automatic; the creator only needs to indicate that the work is copyrighted. Patents are obtained by filing an application with the U.S. Patent and Trademark Office, which reviews the application for originality of the work. Second, enforcement of copyrights and patents is generally left to the holder of the copyright or patent. The primary exception to this is copyright infringement of songs and movies over the Internet, and the creation of devices or procedures that can be used to circumvent digital rights management (technologies designed to prevent copying). These activities have been partially criminalized by the Digital Millennium Copyright Act of 1998. Third, the investment in research and development (R&D) needed to create many patentable commodities is very large relative to the investment needed to create most works of art. The pharmaceutical industry, for example, spends large sums on R&D and it seems likely that this would not occur without the ability to patent discoveries. So the case for restrictive and strongly enforced patent law is more compelling than that for copyright law. As with many other aspects of property rights, the trade-offs here are complex, and they remain the subject of active consideration.

24.4 Exercises

1. Consider an airport that is trying to sell exclusive rights to operate a wireless access network in its terminals. Depending on what proportion of all travelers use the network, it can become congested and result in a low-quality experience for everyone. Specifically, suppose for simplicity that there are N travelers at any given time during normal hours in the airport, and if a fraction x of them attempt to use the network concurrently, then the payoff to each of them will be $\frac{1}{2} - x$. (We can view this payoff as the amount they'd be willing to pay for the service.)

   (a) When the airport sells the rights to operate the network to a third-party access provider, this provider will make back what it pays for the rights by charging travelers in the airport a fee to connect to the networks. How much should the airport expect to be able to sell the rights for, how much will the third-party access provider in turn charge to travelers, and what will be the resulting sum of payoffs to all travelers? Explain.

   (b) Suppose instead that the airport were to let people use the service for free. What would be the sum of payoffs to all travelers in this case? Explain.

2. Consider the setup from Exercise 1, but now let's change the scenario a bit to suppose that there are two populations among the travelers through the airport, with members of one population valuing the wireless access service more than members of the other.

   In particular, suppose that travelers of type 1 receive a payoff of $\frac{1}{2} - x$ when a fraction x of all travelers use the service. (Here, the fraction x is based on the total usage by travelers of both types, because travelers of both types contribute to the shared congestion.) Travelers of type 2 receive twice this payoff, $1 - 2x$, when a fraction x of all travelers use the service. Notice that both payoffs become 0 when x

reaches $\frac{1}{2}$, because at that point the high congestion makes the service useless for everyone.

As in Exercise 1, the airport is going to sell the right to operate the network to an access provider, who will then charge a single price to all travelers (regardless of which type they are).

(a) Suppose that the airport and the access provider know that half of all travelers are of type 1 and half are of type 2. How much can the airport expect to sell the rights for, and how much will the access provider charge?

(b) Now let's consider a variation: suppose instead that only 5% of all travelers are of type 2, and the rest are of type 1. Again, both the airport and the access provider know this. Now how much can the airport expect to sell the rights for, and how much will the access provider charge?

Bibliography

[1] James Abello, Adam L. Buchsbaum, and Jeffery Westbrook. A functional approach to external graph algorithms. In *Proc. 6th European Symposium on Algorithms*, pages 332–343, 1998.

[2] Daron Acemoglu, Munther A. Dahleh, Ilan Lobel, and Asuman Ozdaglar. Bayesian learning in social networks. Technical Report 2780, MIT Laboratory for Information and Decision Systems (LIDS), May 2008.

[3] Theodore B. Achacoso and William S. Yamamoto. *AY's Neuroanatomy of C. elegans for Computation*. CRC Press, 1991.

[4] Lada Adamic. Zipf, power-laws, and Pareto: A ranking tutorial, 2000. Online at http://www.hpl.hp.com/research/idl/papers/ranking/ranking.html.

[5] Lada Adamic and Natalie Glance. The political blogosphere and the 2004 U.S. election: Divided they blog. In *Proceedings of the 3rd International Workshop on Link Discovery*, pages 36–43, 2005.

[6] Lada A. Adamic and Eytan Adar. How to search a social network. *Social Networks*, 27(3):187–203, 2005.

[7] Lada A. Adamic, Rajan M. Lukose, Amit R. Puniyani, and Bernardo A. Huberman. Search in power-law networks. *Physical Review E*, 64:046135, 2001.

[8] Ravindra K. Ahuja, Thomas L. Magnanti, and James B. Orlin. *Network Flows: Theory, Algorithms, and Applications*. Prentice Hall, 1993.

[9] George Akerlof. The market for 'lemons': Quality uncertainty and the market mechanism. *Quarterly Journal of Economics*, 84:488–500, 1970.

[10] Réka Albert and Albert-László Barabási. Statistical mechanics of complex networks. *Reviews of Modern Physics*, 74:47–97, 2002.

[11] Armen A. Alchian. Uncertainty, evolution, and economic theory. *Journal of Political Economy*, 58:211–221, 1950.

[12] Paul Anand. *Foundations of Rational Choice Under Risk*. Oxford University Press, 1993.

[13] Chris Anderson. The long tail. *Wired*, October 2004.

[14] Lisa R. Anderson and Charles A. Holt. Classroom games: Information cascades. *Journal of Economic Perspectives*, 10(4):187–193, Fall 1996.

[15] Lisa R. Anderson and Charles A. Holt. Information cascades in the laboratory. *American Economic Review*, 87(5):847–862, December 1997.

[16] McKenzie Andre, Kashef Ijaz, Jon D. Tillinghast, Valdis E. Krebs, Lois A. Diem, Beverly Metchock, Theresa Crisp, and Peter D. McElroy. Transmission network analysis to complement

routine tuberculosis contact investigations. *American Journal of Public Health*, 97(3):470–477, 2007.

[17] Helmut K. Anheier, Jürgen Gerhards, and Frank P. Romo. Forms of capital and social structure in cultural fields: Examining Bourdieu's social topography. *American Journal of Sociology*, 100(4):859–903, January 1995.

[18] Elliot Anshelevich, Anirban Dasgupta, Jon M. Kleinberg, Éva Tardos, Tom Wexler, and Tim Roughgarden. The price of stability for network design with fair cost allocation. In *Proc. 45th IEEE Symposium on Foundations of Computer Science*, pages 295–304, 2004.

[19] Elliot Anshelevich, Anirban Dasgupta, Éva Tardos, and Tom Wexler. Near-optimal network design with selfish agents. In *Proc. 35th ACM Symposium on Theory of Computing*, pages 511–520, 2003.

[20] Tibor Antal, Paul Krapivsky, and Sidney Redner. Social balance on networks: The dynamics of friendship and enmity. *Physica D*, 224(130), 2006.

[21] Sinan Aral, Lev Muchnik, and Arun Sundararajan. Distinguishing influence-based contagion from homophily-driven diffusion in dynamic networks. *Proc. Natl. Acad. Sci. USA*, 106(51):21544–21549, December 2009.

[22] Kenneth J. Arrow. A difficulty in the concept of social welfare. *Journal of Political Economy*, 58(4):328–346, August 1950.

[23] Kenneth J. Arrow. *Social Choice and Individual Values*. John Wiley & Sons, second edition, 1963.

[24] Kenneth J. Arrow. The role of securities in the optimal allocation of risk-bearing. *Review of Economic Studies*, 31(2):91–96, April 1964.

[25] Brian Arthur. Positive feedbacks in the economy. *Scientific American*, pages 92–99, February 1990.

[26] W. Brian Arthur. Inductive reasoning and bounded rationality. *American Economic Review*, 84:406–411, 1994.

[27] W. Brian Arthur. Increasing returns and the two worlds of business. *Harvard Business Review*, 74(4):100–109, July–August 1996.

[28] Robert Aumann and Adam Brandenberger. Epistemic conditions for Nash equilibrium. *Econometrica*, 63(5):1161–1180, 1995.

[29] Robert J. Aumann. Agreeing to disagree. *Annals of Statistics*, 4:1236–1239, 1976.

[30] David Austen-Smith and Jeffrey S. Banks. Information aggregation, rationality, and the Condorcet Jury Theorem. *American Political Science Review*, 90(1):34–45, March 1996.

[31] Yossi Azar, Benjamin Birnbaum, L. Elisa Celis, Nikhil R. Devanur, and Yuval Peres. Convergence of local dynamics to balanced outcomes in exchange networks. In *Proc. 50th IEEE Symposium on Foundations of Computer Science*, 2009.

[32] Lars Backstrom, Dan Huttenlocher, Jon Kleinberg, and Xiangyang Lan. Group formation in large social networks: Membership, growth, and evolution. In *Proc. 12th ACM SIGKDD International Conference on Knowledge Discovery and Data Mining*, 2006.

[33] Lars Backstrom, Eric Sun, and Cameron Marlow. Find me if you can: Improving geographical prediction with social and spatial proximity. In *Proc. 19th International World Wide Web Conference*, 2010.

[34] David A. Bader, Shiva Kintali, Kamesh Madduri, and Milena Mihail. Approximating betweenness centrality. In *Proc. 5th Workshop on Algorithms and Models for the Web Graph*, pages 124–137, 2007.

[35] David A. Bader and Kamesh Madduri. SNAP: Small-world network analysis and partitioning: An open-source parallel graph framework for the exploration of large-scale networks. In *Proc. 22nd IEEE International Symposium on Parallel and Distributed Processing*, pages 1–12, 2008.

[36] Ricardo Baeza-Yates and Berthier Ribeiro-Neto. *Modern Information Retrieval*. Addison Wesley, 1999.

[37] Linda Baker. Removing roads and traffic lights speeds urban travel. *Scientific American*, pages 20–21, February 2009.

[38] Venkatesh Bala and Sanjeev Goyal. Learning from neighbours. *Review of Economic Studies*, 65(3):595–621, 1998.

[39] Venkatesh Bala and Sanjeev Goyal. A non-cooperative model of network formation. *Econometrica*, 68:1181–1229, September 2000.

[40] Abhijit Banerjee. A simple model of herd behavior. *Quarterly Journal of Economics*, 107:797–817, 1992.

[41] Maya Bar-Hillel and Avishai Margalit. How vicious are cycles of intransitive choice? *Theory and Decision*, 24:119–145, 1988.

[42] Albert-László Barabási and Réka Albert. Emergence of scaling in random networks. *Science*, 286:509–512, 1999.

[43] Albert-László Barabási and Zoltan Oltvai. Network biology: Understanding the cell's functional organization. *Nature Reviews Genetics*, 5:101–113, 2004.

[44] A. D. Barbour and D. Mollison. Epidemics and random graphs. In *Stochastic Processes in Epidemic Theory*, volume 86 of *Lecture Notes in Biomathematics*, pages 86–89. Springer, 1990.

[45] John A. Barnes. *Social Networks*. Number 26 in Modules in Anthropology. Addison Wesley, 1972.

[46] Chris Barrett and E. Mutambatsere. Agricultural markets in developing countries. In Lawrence E. Blume and Steven N. Durlauf, editors, *The New Palgrave Dictionary of Economics*. Oxford University Press, second edition, 2008.

[47] Alex Bavelas. Communication patterns in task-oriented groups. *Journal of the Acoustical Society of America*, 22(6):725–730, November 1950.

[48] Peter Bearman and James Moody. Suicide and friendships among American adolescents. *American Journal of Public Health*, 94(1):89–95, 2004.

[49] Peter Bearman, James Moody, and Katherine Stovel. Chains of affection: The structure of adolescent romantic and sexual networks. *American Journal of Sociology*, 110(1):44–99, 2004.

[50] Morton L. Bech and Enghin Atalay. The topology of the federal funds market. Technical Report 354, Federal Reserve Bank of New York, November 2008.

[51] Joyce E. Berg, Forrest D. Nelson, and Thomas A. Rietz. Prediction market accuracy in the long run. *International Journal of Forecasting*, 24(2):285–300, April–June 2008.

[52] Noam Berger, Christian Borgs, Jennifer T. Chayes, and Amin Saberi. On the spread of viruses on the Internet. In *Proc. 16th ACM-SIAM Symposium on Discrete Algorithms*, pages 301–310, 2005.

[53] Kenneth Berman. Vulnerability of scheduled networks and a generalization of Menger's theorem. *Networks*, 28:125–134, 1996.

[54] Tim Berners-Lee, Robert Cailliau, Ari Luotonen, Henrik Frystyk Nielsen, and Arthur Secret. The World-Wide Web. *Communications of the ACM*, 37(8):76–82, 1994.

[55] Tim Berners-Lee and Mark Fischetti. *Weaving the Web*. Harper Collins, 1999.

[56] Krishna Bharat, Bay-Wei Chang, Monika Rauch Henzinger, and Matthias Ruhl. Who links to whom: Mining linkage between Web sites. In *Proc. IEEE International Conference on Data Mining*, pages 51–58, 2001.

[57] Krishna Bharat and Monika Rauch Henzinger. Improved algorithms for topic distillation in a hyperlinked environment. In *Proc. 21st ACM SIGIR Conference on Research and Development in Information Retrieval*, pages 104–111, 1998.

[58] Krishna Bharat and George A. Mihaila. When experts agree: Using non-affiliated experts to rank popular topics. In *Proc. 10th International World Wide Web Conference*, pages 597–602, 2001.

[59] Sushil Bikhchandani, David Hirshleifer, and Ivo Welch. A theory of fads, fashion, custom and cultural change as information cascades. *Journal of Political Economy*, 100:992–1026, 1992.

[60] Ken Binmore, Ariel Rubinstein, and Asher Wolinsky. The Nash bargaining solution in economic modeling. *RAND Journal of Economics*, 17:176–188, 1986.

[61] Duncan Black. On the rationale of group decision-making. *Journal of Political Economy*, 56:23–34, 1948.

[62] Lawrence Blume. The statistical mechanics of strategic interaction. *Games and Economic Behavior*, 5:387–424, 1993.

[63] Lawrence Blume, David Easley, Jon M. Kleinberg, and Éva Tardos. Trading networks with price-setting agents. In *Proc. 8th ACM Conference on Electronic Commerce*, pages 143–151, 2007.

[64] Lawrence Blume and David Easley. Evolution and market behavior. *Journal of Economic Theory*, 58:9–40, 1992.

[65] Lawrence Blume and David Easley. If you're so smart, why aren't you rich? Belief selection in complete and incomplete markets. *Econometrica*, 74:929–966, 2006.

[66] Michele Boldrin and David K. Levine. *Against Intellectual Monopoly*. Cambridge University Press, 2008.

[67] Bela Bollobás and Fan R. K. Chung. The diameter of a cycle plus a random matching. *SIAM Journal on Discrete Mathematics*, 1(3):328–333, August 1988.

[68] Bela Bollobás and Oliver Riordan. Mathematical results on scale-free random graphs. In Stefan Bornholdt and Hans Georg Schuster, editors, *Handbook of Graphs and Networks*, pages 1–34. John Wiley & Sons, 2005.

[69] Bela Bollobás and Oliver Riordan. *Percolation*. Cambridge University Press, 2006.

[70] Abraham Bookstein. Informetric distributions, Part II: Resilience to ambiguity. *Journal of the American Society for Information Science*, 41(5):376–386, 1990.

[71] Stephen P. Borgatti. Identifying sets of key players in a network. *Computational and Mathematical Organization Theory*, 12(4):21–34, 2006.

[72] Stephen P. Borgatti and Martin G. Everett. Models of core/periphery structures. *Social Networks*, 21(4):375–395, October 2000.

[73] Stephen P. Borgatti and Martin G. Everett. A graph-theoretic perspective on centrality. *Social Networks*, 28(4):466–484, 2006.

[74] Stephen P. Borgatti, Candace Jones, and Martin G. Everett. Network measures of social capital. *Connections*, 21(2):27–36, 1998.

[75] Pierre Bourdieu. The forms of capital. In J. E. Richardson, editor, *Handbook of Theory of Research for the Sociology of Education*, pages 241–258. Greenwood Press, 1986.

[76] Dietrich Braess. Über ein paradoxon aus der verkehrsplanung. *Unternehmensforschung*, 12:258–268, 1968.

[77] Ulrich Brandes. A faster algorithm for betweenness centrality. *Journal of Mathematical Sociology*, 25:163–177, 2001.

[78] Ronald L. Breiger. The duality of persons and groups. *Social Forces*, 53:181–190, 1974.

[79] Sergey Brin and Lawrence Page. The anatomy of a large-scale hypertextual Web search engine. In *Proc. 7th International World Wide Web Conference*, pages 107–117, 1998.

[80] Andrei Broder, Ravi Kumar, Farzin Maghoul, Prabhakar Raghavan, Sridhar Rajagopalan, Raymie Stata, Andrew Tomkins, and Janet Wiener. Graph structure in the Web. In *Proc. 9th International World Wide Web Conference*, pages 309–320, 2000.

[81] John M. Broder. From a theory to a consensus on emissions. *New York Times*, 16 May 2009.

[82] Chris Brown. Run/pass balance and a little game theory, 10 July 2006. http://smartfootball .blogspot.com/2006/07/runpass-balance-and-little-game-theory.html.

[83] Luciana S. Buriol, Carlos Castillo, Debora Donato, Stefano Leonardi, and Stefano Millozzi. Temporal analysis of the wikigraph. In *Proc. IEEE/WIC/ACM International Conference on Web Intelligence*, pages 45–51, 2006.

[84] Brian Burke. Game theory and run/pass balance, 13 June 2008. http://www.advancednflstats .com/2008/06/game-theory-and-runpass-balance.html.

[85] Ronald S. Burt. Social contagion and innovation: Cohesion versus structural equivalence. *American Journal of Sociology*, 92(6):1287–1335, May 1987.

[86] Ronald S. Burt. *Structural Holes: The Social Structure of Competition*. Harvard University Press, 1992.

[87] Ronald S. Burt. The network structure of social capital. *Research in Organizational Studies*, 22:345–423, 2000.

[88] Ronald S. Burt. Structural holes and good ideas. *American Journal of Sociology*, 110(2):349–99, September 2004.

[89] Vannevar Bush. As we may think. *Atlantic Monthly*, 176(1):101–108, July 1945.

[90] Vincent Buskens and Arnout van de Rijt. Dynamics of networks if everyone strives for structural holes. *American Journal of Sociology*, 114(2):371–407, 2009.

[91] Samuel R. Buss and Peter Clote. Solving the Fisher–Wright and coalescence problems with a discrete Markov chain analysis. *Advances in Applied Probability*, 36:1175–1197, 2004.

[92] Robert B. Cairns and Beverly D. Cairns. *Lifelines and Risks: Pathways of Youth in our Time*. Cambridge University Press, 1995.

[93] Colin Camerer. *Behavioral Game Theory: Experiments in Strategic Interaction*. Princeton University Press, 2003.

[94] Rebecca L. Cann, Mark Stoneking, and Allan C. Wilson. Mitochondrial DNA and human evolution. *Nature*, 325:31–36, January 1987.

[95] E. C. Capen, R. V. Clapp, and W. M. Campbell. Competitive bidding in high-risk situations. *Journal of Petroleum Technology*, 23:641–653, June 1971.

[96] Jean M. Carlson and John Doyle. Highly optimized tolerance: A mechanism for power laws in designed systems. *Physical Review E*, 60(2):1412–1427, 1999.

[97] Dorwin Cartwright and Frank Harary. Structure balance: A generalization of Heider's theory. *Psychological Review*, 63(5):277–293, September 1956.

[98] James Cassing and Richard W. Douglas. Implications of the auction mechanism in baseball's free agent draft. *Southern Economic Journal*, 47:110–121, July 1980.

[99] Stanislaw Cebrat, Jan P. Radomski, and Dietrich Stauffer. Genetic paralog analysis and simulations. In *International Conference on Computational Science*, pages 709–717, 2004.

[100] Bogachan Celen and Shachar Kariv. Distinguishing informational cascades from herd behavior in the laboratory. *American Economic Review*, 94(3):484–498, June 2004.

[101] Damon Centola and Michael Macy. Complex contagions and the weakness of long ties. *American Journal of Sociology*, 113:702–734, 2007.

[102] Soumen Chakrabarti, Byron Dom, Prabhakar Raghavan, Sridhar Rajagopalan, David Gibson, and Jon M. Kleinberg. Automatic resource compilation by analyzing hyperlink structure and associated text. In *Proc. 7th International World Wide Web Conference*, pages 65–74, 1998.

[103] Soumen Chakrabarti, Alan M. Frieze, and Juan Vera. The influence of search engines on preferential attachment. In *Proc. 16th ACM-SIAM Symposium on Discrete Algorithms*, pages 293–300, 2005.

[104] Damien Challet, M. Marsili, and Gabriele Ottino. Shedding light on El Farol. *Physica A*, 332:469–482, 2004.

[105] Murray Chass. View of sport: It's over now that it's over. *New York Times*, 1 October 1989.

[106] Eddie Cheng, Jerrold W. Grossman, and Marc J. Lipman. Time-stamped graphs and their associated influence digraphs. *Discrete Applied Mathematics*, 128:317–335, 2003.

[107] P.A. Chiappori, S. Levitt, and T. Groseclose. Testing mixed-strategy equilibria when players are heterogeneous: The case of penalty kicks in soccer. *American Economic Review*, 92:1138–1151, 2002.

[108] Nicholas A. Christakis and James H. Fowler. The spread of obesity in a large social network over 32 years. *New England Journal of Medicine*, 357(4):3700–379, July 2007.

[109] Michael Suk-Young Chwe. Structure and strategy in collective action. *American Journal of Sociology*, 105(1):128–156, July 1999.

[110] Michael Suk-Young Chwe. Communication and coordination in social networks. *Review of Economic Studies*, 67:1–16, 2000.

[111] Michael Suk-Young Chwe. *Rational Ritual: Culture, Coordination, and Common Knowledge.* Princeton University Press, 2001.

[112] Edward H. Clarke. Multipart pricing of public goods. *Public Choice*, 11:17–33, Fall 1971.

[113] Ronald Coase. The problem of social cost. *Journal of Law and Economics*, 1:1–44, 1960.

[114] Jere M. Cohen. Sources of peer group homogeneity. *Sociology in Education*, 50:227–241, October 1977.

[115] James S. Coleman, Herbert Menzel, and Elihu Katz. *Medical Innovations: A Diffusion Study.* Bobbs Merrill, 1966.

[116] James S. Coleman. *The Adolescent Society.* Free Press, 1961.

[117] James S. Coleman. Social capital in the creation of human capital. *American Journal of Sociology*, 94(S1):S95–S120, 1988.

[118] James S. Coleman. *Foundations of Social Theory.* Harvard University Press, 1990.

[119] Vittoria Colizza, Alain Barrat, Marc Barthélemy, and Alessandro Vespignani. The role of the airline transportation network in the prediction and predictability of global epidemics. *Proc. Natl. Acad. Sci. USA*, 103(7):2015–2020, 2006.

[120] Karen S. Cook and Toshio Yamagishi. Power in exchange networks: A power-dependence formulation. *Social Networks*, 14:245–265, 1992.

[121] Jacomo Corbo and David C. Parkes. The price of selfish behavior in bilateral network formation. In *Proc. 24th ACM Symposium on Principles of Distributed Computing*, pages 99–107, 2005.

[122] David Crandall, Dan Cosley, Dan Huttenlocher, Jon Kleinberg, Xiangyang Lan, and Siddharth Suri. Feedback effects between similarity and social influence in online communities. In *Proc. 14th ACM SIGKDD International Conference on Knowledge Discovery and Data Mining*, 2008.

[123] Vincent P. Crawford. Lying for strategic advantage: Rational and boundedly rational misrepresentation of intentions. *American Economic Review*, 93(1):133–149, 2003.

[124] Partha Dasgupta, Peter Hammond, and Eric Maskin. The implementation of social choice rules: Some general results on incentive compatibility. *Review of Economic Studies*, 46:216, 1979.

[125] Ian Davis. Talis, Web 2.0, and all that, 4 July 2005. Internet Alchemy blog, http://internetalchemy.org/2005/07/talis-web-20-and-all-that.

[126] James A. Davis. Structural balance, mechanical solidarity, and interpersonal relations. *American Journal of Sociology*, 68:444–462, 1963.

[127] James A. Davis. Clustering and structural balance in graphs. *Human Relations*, 20(2):181–187, 1967.

[128] Gabrielle Demange. Strategyproofness in the assignment market game, 1982. Laboratoire d'Econometrie de l'Ecole Polytechnique.

[129] Gabrielle Demange, David Gale, and Marilda Sotomayor. Multi-item auctions. *Journal of Political Economy*, 94(4):863–872, 1986.

[130] Jared Diamond. *Guns, Germs, and Steel: The Fates of Human Societies*. W. W. Norton & Company, 1999.

[131] Peter Dodds, Roby Muhamad, and Duncan Watts. An experimental study of search in global social networks. *Science*, 301:827–829, 2003.

[132] Pedro Domingos and Matt Richardson. Mining the network value of customers. In *Proc. 7th ACM SIGKDD International Conference on Knowledge Discovery and Data Mining*, pages 57–66, 2001.

[133] Debora Donato, Luigi Laura, Stefano Leonardi, and Stefano Millozzi. The Web as a graph: How far we are. *ACM Transactions on Internet Technology*, 7(1), 2007.

[134] Shawn M. Douglas, Gaetano T. Montelione, and Mark Gerstein. PubNet: A flexible system for visualizing literature derived networks. *Genome Biology*, 6(9), 2005.

[135] Zvi Drezner (editor). *Facility location: a survey of applications and methods*. Springer, 1995.

[136] Raissa M. D'Souza, Christian Borgs, Jennifer T. Chayes, Noam Berger, and Robert D. Kleinberg. Emergence of tempered preferential attachment from optimization. *Proc. Natl. Acad. Sci. USA*, 104(15):6112–6117, April 2007.

[137] Jennifer A. Dunne. The network structure of food webs. In Mercedes Pascual and Jennifer A. Dunne, editors, *Ecological Networks: Linking Structure to Dynamics in Food Webs*, pages 27–86. Oxford University Press, 2006.

[138] Steven Durlauf and Marcel Fafchamps. Social capital. In Phillippe Agion and Steven Durlauf, editors, *Handbook of Economic Growth*. Elsevier, 2004.

[139] Richard Durrett. Stochastic spatial models. *SIAM Review*, 41(4):677–718, 1999.

[140] Cynthia Dwork, Ravi Kumar, Moni Naor, and D. Sivakumar. Rank aggregation methods for the Web. In *Proc. 10th International World Wide Web Conference*, pages 613–622, 2001.

[141] Nathan Eagle and Alex Pentland. Reality mining: Sensing complex social systems. *Personal and Ubiquitous Computing*, 10(4), May 2006.

[142] Nathan Eagle, Alex Pentland, and David Lazer. Mobile phone data for inferring social network structure. In John J. Salerno, Huan Liu and Michael J. Young, editors, *Social Computing, Behavioral Modeling, and Prediction*, pages 79–88. Springer, 2008.

[143] Nicholas Economides. Desirability of compatibility in the absence of network externalities. *American Economic Review*, 79(5):1165–1181, December 1989.

[144] Ben Edelman, Michael Ostrovsky, and Michael Schwarz. Internet advertising and the generalized second price auction: Selling billions of dollars worth of keywords. *American Economic Review*, 97(1):242–259, March 2007.

[145] Leo Egghe and Ronald Rousseau. *Introduction to Informetrics: Quantitative Methods in Library, Documentation and Information Science*. Elsevier, 1990.

[146] Anita Elberse. Should you invest in the long tail? *Harvard Business Review*, 86(7/8):88–96, Jul-Aug 2008.

[147] Glenn Ellison. Learning, local interaction, and coordination. *Econometrica*, 61:1047–1071, 1993.

[148] Richard M. Emerson. Power-dependence relations. *American Sociological Review*, 27:31–40, 1962.

[149] Stephen Eubank, Hasan Guclu, V. S. Anil Kumar, Madhav V. Marathe, Aravind Srinivasan, Zoltan Toroczkai, and Nan Wang. Modelling disease outbreaks in realistic urban social networks. *Nature*, 429:180–184, 2004.

[150] Eyal Even-Dar, Michael Kearns, and Siddharth Suri. A network formation game for bipartite exchange economies. In *Proc. 18th ACM-SIAM Symposium on Discrete Algorithms*, pages 697–706, 2007.

[151] Alex Fabrikant, Elias Koutsoupias, and Christos H. Papadimitriou. Heuristically optimized trade-offs: A new paradigm for power laws in the Internet. In *Proc. 29th Intl. Colloq. on Automata, Languages and Programming*, pages 110–122, 2002.

[152] Alex Fabrikant, Ankur Luthra, Elitza N. Maneva, Christos H. Papadimitriou, and Scott Shenker. On a network creation game. In *Proc. 22nd ACM Symposium on Principles of Distributed Computing*, pages 347–351, 2003.

[153] Marcel Fafchamps and Eleni Gabre-Madhin. Agricultural markets in Benin and Malawi. *African Journal of Agricultural and Resource Economics*, 1(1):67–94, 2006.

[154] Ronald Fagin, Joseph Y. Halpern, Yoram Moses, and Moshe Y. Vardi. *Reasoning About Knowledge*. MIT Press, 1995.

[155] Michalis Faloutsos, Petros Faloutsos, and Christos Faloutsos. On power-law relationships of the Internet topology. In *Proc. ACM SIGCOMM Conference on Applications, Technologies, Architectures, and Protocols for Computer Communication*, pages 251–262, 1999.

[156] Daniel S. Falster and Mark Westoby. Plant height and evolutionary games. *Trends in Ecology and Evolution*, 18(7):337–343, July 2003.

[157] Eugene F. Fama. The behavior of stock market prices. *Journal of Business*, 38:34–105, 1965.

[158] Gerald R. Faulhaber. Network effects and merger analysis: Instant messaging and the AOL Time Warner case. *Telecommunication Policy*, 26:311–333, June/July 2002.

[159] Timothy J. Feddersen and Wolfgang Pesendorfer. The swing voter's curse. *American Economic Review*, 86(3):408–424, June 1996.

[160] Timothy J. Feddersen and Wolfgang Pesendorfer. Convicting the innocent: The inferiority of unanimous jury verdicts under strategic voting. *American Political Science Review*, 92(1):23–35, March 1998.

[161] Scott L. Feld. The focused organization of social ties. *American Journal of Sociology*, 86(5):1015–1035, 1981.

[162] Claude S. Fischer. *America Calling: A Social History of the Telephone to 1940*. University of California Press, 1992.

[163] Peter C. Fishburn. Nontransitive preferences in decision theory. *Journal of Risk and Uncertainty*, 4:113–134, 1991.

[164] Lester R. Ford and D. Ray Fulkerson. *Flows in Networks*. Princeton University Press, 1962.

[165] S. Fortunato, A. Flammini, F. Menczer, and A. Vespignani. Topical interests and the mitigation of search engine bias. *Proc. Natl. Acad. Sci. USA*, 103(34):12684–12689, 2006.

[166] James H. Fowler and Sangick Jeon. The authority of Supreme Court precedent. *Social Networks*, 30:16–30, 2008.

[167] Reiner Franke. Reinforcement learning in the El Farol model. *Journal of Economic Behavior and Organization*, 51:367–388, 2003.

[168] Linton C. Freeman. A set of measure of centrality based on betweenness. *Sociometry*, 40(1):35–41, 1977.

[169] Linton C. Freeman. Centrality in social networks: Conceptual clarification. *Social Networks*, 1:215–239, 1979.

[170] Noah Friedkin. *A Structural Theory of Social Influence*. Cambridge University Press, 1998.

[171] Eric Friedman, Paul Resnick, and Rahul Sami. Manipulation-resistant reputation systems. In Noam Nisan, Tim Roughgarden, Éva Tardos, and Vijay Vazirani, editors, *Algorithmic Game Theory*, pages 677–698. Cambridge University Press, 2007.

[172] Milton Friedman. *Essays in Positive Economics*. University of Chicago Press, 1953.

[173] H. L. Frisch and J. M. Hammersley. Percolation processes and related topics. *SIAM Journal on Applied Mathematics*, 11(4):894–918, 1963.

[174] Yun-Xin Fu. Exact coalescent for the Wright–Fisher model. *Theoretical Population Biology*, 69:385–394, 2006.

[175] Drew Fudenberg and David Levine. *The Theory of Learning in Games*. The MIT Press, 1998.

[176] Douglas Gale and Shachar Kariv. Financial networks. *American Economic Review: Papers and Proceedings*, 97(2):99–103, May 2007.

[177] Eugene Garfield. Citation analysis as a tool in journal evaluation. *Science*, 178:471–479, 1972.

[178] Eugene Garfield. It's a small world after all. *Current Contents*, 43:5–10, 1979.

[179] John Geanakoplos. Three brief proofs of Arrow's impossibility theorem. *Economic Theory*, 26(1):211–215, 2005.

[180] Nancy Geller. On the citation influence methodology of Pinski and Narin. *Information Processing and Management*, 14:93–95, 1978.

[181] Mordechai Gersani, Joel S. Brown, Erin E. O'Brien, Godfrey M. Maina, and Zvika Abramski. Tragedy of the commons as a result of root competition. *Journal of Ecology*, 89:660–669, 2001.

[182] David Gibson. Concurrency and commitment: Network scheduling and its consequences for diffusion. *Journal of Mathematical Sociology*, 29(4):295–323, 2005.

[183] Michelle Girvan, Duncan Callaway, Mark E. J. Newman, and Steven H. Strogatz. Simple model of epidemics with pathogen mutation. *Physical Review E*, 65:031915, 2002.

[184] Michelle Girvan and Mark E. J. Newman. Community structure in social and biological networks. *Proc. Natl. Acad. Sci. USA*, 99(12):7821–7826, June 2002.

[185] Scott A. Golder, Dennis Wilkinson, and Bernardo A. Huberman. Rhythms of social interaction: Messaging within a massive online network. In *Proc. 3rd International Conference on Communities and Technologies*, 2007.

[186] Benjamin Golub and Matthew O. Jackson. Naive learning in social networks: Convergence, influence and the wisdom of crowds. *American Economic Journal: Microeconomics*, 2(1):112–49, 2010.

[187] Joshua Goodman, Gordon Cormack, and David Heckerman. Spam and the ongoing battle for the inbox. *Communications of the ACM*, 50(2):24–33, February 2007.

[188] Sanjeev Goyal and Fernando Vega-Redondo. Structural holes in social networks. *Journal of Economic Theory*, 137(1):460–492, 2007.

[189] Ronald L. Graham. On properties of a well-known graph, or, What is your Ramsey number? *Annals of the New York Academy of Sciences*, 328(1):166–172, June 1979.

[190] Mark Granovetter. The strength of weak ties. *American Journal of Sociology*, 78:1360–1380, 1973.

[191] Mark Granovetter. *Getting a Job: A Study of Contacts and Careers*. University of Chicago Press, 1974.

[192] Mark Granovetter. Threshold models of collective behavior. *American Journal of Sociology*, 83:1420–1443, 1978.

[193] Mark Granovetter. Economic action and social structure: The problem of embeddedness. *American Journal of Sociology*, 91(3):481–510, November 1985.

[194] Mark Granovetter. Problems of explanation in economic sociology. In Nitin Nohria and Robert G. Eccles, editors, *Networks and Organization*, pages 29–56. Harvard Business School Press, 1992.

[195] Nicholas C. Grassly, Christophe Fraser, and Geoffrey P. Garnett. Host immunity and synchronized epidemics of syphilis across the United States. *Nature*, 433:417–421, January 2005.

[196] B. T. Grenfell, O. N. Bjornstad, and J. Kappey. Travelling waves and spatial hierarchies in measles epidemics. *Nature*, 414:716–723, December 2001.

[197] David Griffeath. Ultimate Bacon: The giant component of a complex network. http://psoup.math.wisc.edu/archive/recipe59.html.

[198] Jerrold W. Grossman and Patrick D. F. Ion. On a portion of the well-known collaboration graph. *Congressus Numerantium*, 108:129–131, 1995.

[199] Theodore Groves. Incentives in teams. *Econometrica*, 41:617–631, July 1973.

[200] John Guare. *Six Degrees of Separation: A Play*. Vintage Books, 1990.

[201] R. V. Guha, Ravi Kumar, Prabhakar Raghavan, and Andrew Tomkins. Propagation of trust and distrust. In *Proc. 13th International World Wide Web Conference*, 2004.

[202] Sunetra Gupta, Roy M. Anderson, and Robert M. May. Networks of sexual contacts: Implications for the pattern of spread of HIV. *AIDS*, 3:807–817, 1989.

[203] Werner Güth, Rolf Schmittberger, and Bernd Schwarze. An experimental analysis of ultimatum bargaining. *Journal of Economic Behavior and Organization*, 3:367–388, 1982.

[204] Frank Harary. On the notion of balance of a signed graph. *Michigan Mathematical Journal*, 2(2):143–146, 1953.

[205] Garrett Hardin. The tragedy of the commons. *Science*, 162(3859):1243–1248, 1968.

[206] Larry Harris. *Trading and Exchanges: Market Microstructure for Practitioners*. Oxford University Press, 2002.

[207] Milton Harris and Robert M. Townsend. Resource allocation under asymmetric information. *Econometrica*, 49:33–64, 1981.

[208] John C. Harsanyi. Game with incomplete information played by "Bayesian" players, I–III. Part I: The basic model. *Management Science*, 14(3):159–182, November 1967.

[209] Joel Hasbrouck. *Empirical Market Microstructure: The Institutions, Economics, and Econometrics of Securities Trading*. Oxford University Press, 2007.

[210] Kjetil K. Haugen. The performance-enhancing drug game. *Journal of Sports Economics*, 5(1):67–86, 2004.

[211] D. T. Haydon, M. Chase-Topping, D. J. Shaw, L. Matthews, J. K. Friar, J. Wilesmith, and M. E. J. Woolhouse. The construction and analysis of epidemic trees with reference to the 2001 UK foot-and-mouth outbreak. *Proc. Royal Soc. London B*, 270:121–127, 2003.

[212] Kais Hazma. The smallest uniform upper bound on the distance between the mean and the median of the binomial and Poisson distributions. *Statistics and Probability Letters*, 23:21–25, 1995.

[213] Daihai He and Lewi Stone. Spatio-temporal synchronization of recurrent epidemics. *Proc. Royal Soc. London B*, 270:1519–1526, 2003.

[214] F. Heart, A. McKenzie, J. McQuillian, and D. Walden. *ARPANET Completion Report*. Bolt, Beranek and Newman, 1978.

[215] Peter Hedstrom. Contagious collectivities: On the spatial diffusion of Swedish trade unions. *American Journal of Sociology*, 99:1157–1179, 1994.

[216] Fritz Heider. Attitudes and cognitive organization. *Journal of Psychology*, 21:107–112, 1946.

[217] Fritz Heider. *The Psychology of Interpersonal Relations*. John Wiley & Sons, 1958.

[218] Robert Heinsohn and Craig Packer. Complex cooperative strategies in group-territorial African lions. *Science*, 269:1260–1262, September 1995.

[219] Miguel Helft. Google and Apple eliminate another tie. *New York Times*, 12 October 2009.

[220] James Hendler, Nigel Shadbolt, Wendy Hall, Tim Berners-Lee, and Daniel Weitzner. Web science: An interdisciplinary approach to understanding the Web. *Communications of the ACM*, 51(7):60–69, 2008.

[221] Douglas Hofstadter. *Gödel, Escher, Bach: An Eternal Golden Braid*. Basic Books, 1979.

[222] Bernardo A. Huberman, Daniel M. Romero, and Fang Wu. Social networks that matter: Twitter under the microscope. *First Monday*, 14(1), January 2009.

[223] Steffen Huck and Jorg Oechssler. Informational cascades in the laboratory: Do they occur for the right reasons? *Journal of Economic Psychology*, 21(6):661–671, 2000.

[224] Robert Huckfeldt and John Sprague. Networks in context: The social flow of political information. *American Political Science Review*, 81(4):1197–1216, December 1987.

[225] Nicole Immorlica, Jon Kleinberg, Mohammad Mahdian, and Tom Wexler. The role of compatibility in the diffusion of technologies through social networks. In *Proc. 8th ACM Conference on Electronic Commerce*, 2007.

[226] Y. Iwasa, D. Cohen, and J. A. Leon. Tree height and crown shape, as results of competitive games. *Journal of Theoretical Biology*, 112:279–298, 1985.

[227] Matthew O. Jackson and Asher Wolinsky. A strategic model of social and economic networks. *Journal of Economic Theory*, 71(1):44–74, 1996.

[228] Thorsten Joachims. Optimizing search engines using clickthrough data. In *Proc. 8th ACM SIGKDD International Conference on Knowledge Discovery and Data Mining*, pages 133–142, 2002.

[229] Ramesh Johari and Sunil Kumar. Congestible Services and Network Effects. In *Proc. 11th ACM Conference on Electronic Commerce*, 2010.

[230] Steve Jurvetson. What exactly is viral marketing? *Red Herring*, 78:110–112, 2000.

[231] Daniel Kahneman and Amos Tversky. On the psychology of prediction. *Psychological Review*, 80(4):237–251, 1973.

[232] Sham M. Kakade, Michael J. Kearns, Luis E. Ortiz, Robin Pemantle, and Siddharth Suri. Economic properties of social networks. In *Proc. 17th Advances in Neural Information Processing Systems*, 2004.

[233] Denise B. Kandel. Homophily, selection, and socialization in adolescent friendships. *American Journal of Sociology*, 84(2):427–436, September 1978.

[234] Yakar Kannai. The core and balancedness. In Robert J. Aumman and Sergiu Hart, editors, *Handbook of Game Theory*, volume 1, pages 355–395. Elsevier, 1992.

[235] Michael L. Katz and Carl Shapiro. Network externalities, competition, and compatibility. *American Economic Review*, 75(3):424–440, June 1985.

[236] Michael Kearns, Stephen Judd, Jinsong Tan, and Jennifer Wortman. Behavioral experiments on biased voting in networks. *Proc. Natl. Acad. Sci. USA*, 106(5):1347–1352, February 2009.

[237] Michael Kearns, Siddharth Suri, and Nick Montfort. An experimental study of the coloring problem on human subject networks. *Science*, 313(5788):824–827, 2006.

[238] Matt J. Keeling and Ken T. D. Eames. Network and epidemic models. *J. Royal Soc. Interface*, 2:295–307, 2005.

[239] David Kempe, Jon Kleinberg, and Amit Kumar. Connectivity and inference problems for temporal networks. In *Proc. 32nd ACM Symposium on Theory of Computing*, pages 504–513, 2000.

[240] David Kempe, Jon Kleinberg, and Éva Tardos. Maximizing the spread of influence in a social network. In *Proc. 9th ACM SIGKDD International Conference on Knowledge Discovery and Data Mining*, pages 137–146, 2003.

[241] Jeffrey Kephart, Gregory Sorkin, David Chess, and Steve White. Fighting computer viruses. *Scientific American*, pages 88–93, November 1997.

[242] Walter Kern and Daniël Palusma. Matching games: The least core and the nucleolus. *Mathematics of Operations Research*, 28(2):294–308, 2003.

[243] Peter D. Killworth and H. Russell Bernard. Reverse small world experiment. *Social Networks*, 1:159–192, 1978.

[244] Peter D. Killworth, Eugene C. Johnsen, H. Russell Bernard, Gene Ann Shelley, and Christopher McCarty. Estimating the size of personal networks. *Social Networks*, 12(4):289–312, December 1990.

[245] John F. C. Kingman. The coalescent. *Stochastic Processes and their Applications*, 13:235–248, 1982.

[246] Aniket Kittur and Robert E. Kraut. Harnessing the wisdom of crowds in Wikipedia: Quality through coordination. In *Proc. CSCW'08: ACM Conference on Computer-Supported Cooperative Work*, 2008.

[247] Jon Kleinberg. Authoritative sources in a hyperlinked environment. *Journal of the ACM*, 46(5):604–632, 1999. A preliminary version appears in the Proceedings of the 9th ACM-SIAM Symposium on Discrete Algorithms, Jan. 1998.

[248] Jon Kleinberg. Navigation in a small world. *Nature*, 406:845, 2000.

[249] Jon Kleinberg. The small-world phenomenon: an algorithmic perspective. In *Proc. 32nd ACM Symposium on Theory of Computing*, pages 163–170, 2000.

[250] Jon Kleinberg. Small-world phenomena and the dynamics of information. In *Proc. 14th Advances in Neural Information Processing Systems*, pages 431–438, 2001.

[251] Jon Kleinberg. The wireless epidemic. *Nature (News & Views)*, 449:287–288, 2007.

[252] Jon Kleinberg, Siddharth Suri, Éva Tardos, and Tom Wexler. Strategic network formation with structural holes. In *Proc. 9th ACM Conference on Electronic Commerce*, 2008.

[253] Jon Kleinberg and Éva Tardos. *Algorithm Design*. Addison Wesley, 2006.

[254] Jon Kleinberg and Éva Tardos. Balanced outcomes in social exchange networks. In *Proc. 40th ACM Symposium on Theory of Computing*, 2008.

[255] Judith Kleinfeld. Could it be a big world after all? The 'six degrees of separation' myth. *Society*, 39(2):61–66, January 2002.

[256] Paul Klemperer. *Auctions: Theory and Practice*. Princeton University Press, 2004. On-line at www.paulklemperer.org.

[257] Charles Korte and Stanley Milgram. Acquaintance networks between racial groups: Application of the small world method. *Journal of Personality and Social Psychology*, 15, 1978.

[258] Gueorgi Kossinets, Jon Kleinberg, and Duncan Watts. The structure of information pathways in a social communication network. In *Proc. 14th ACM SIGKDD International Conference on Knowledge Discovery and Data Mining*, 2008.

[259] Gueorgi Kossinets and Duncan Watts. Empirical analysis of an evolving social network. *Science*, 311:88–90, 2006.

[260] Dexter Kozen. *The Design and Analysis of Algorithms*. Springer, 1990.

[261] Rachel Kranton and Deborah Minehart. A theory of buyer-seller networks. *American Economic Review*, 91(3):485–508, June 2001.

[262] Lothar Krempel and Thomas Plümper. Exploring the dynamics of international trade by combining the comparative advantages of multivariate statistics and network visualizations. *Journal of Social Structure*, 4(1), 2003.

[263] David Kreps. *A Course in Microeconomic Theory*. Princeton University Press, 1990.

[264] Ravi Kumar, Jasmine Novak, Prabhakar Raghavan, and Andrew Tomkins. Structure and evolution of blogspace. *Communications of the ACM*, 47(12):35–39, 2004.

[265] Ravi Kumar, Prabhakar Raghavan, Sridhar Rajagopalan, D. Sivakumar, Andrew Tomkins, and Eli Upfal. Random graph models for the Web graph. In *Proc. 41st IEEE Symposium on Foundations of Computer Science*, pages 57–65, 2000.

[266] Jérôme Kunegis, Andreas Lommatzsch, and Christian Bauckhage. The Slashdot Zoo: Mining a social network with negative edges. In *Proc. 18th International World Wide Web Conference*, pages 741–750, 2009.

[267] Marcelo Kuperman and Guillermo Abramson. Small world effect in an epidemiological model. *Physical Review Letters*, 86(13):2909–2912, March 2001.

[268] Amy N. Langville and Carl D. Meyer. *Google's PageRank and Beyond: The Science of Search Engine Rankings*. Princeton University Press, 2006.

[269] Paul Lazarsfeld and Robert K. Merton. Friendship as a social process: A substantive and methodological analysis. In Morroe Berger, Theodore Abel, and Charles H. Page, editors, *Freedom and Control in Modern Society*, pages 18–66. Van Nostrand, 1954.

[270] Herman B. Leonard. Elicitation of honest preferences for the assignment of individuals to positions. *Journal of Political Economy*, 91(3):461–479, 1983.

[271] Jure Leskovec, Lada Adamic, and Bernardo Huberman. The dynamics of viral marketing. *ACM Transactions on the Web*, 1(1), May 2007.

[272] Jure Leskovec, Lars Backstrom, Ravi Kumar, and Andrew Tomkins. Microscopic evolution of social networks. In *Proc. 14th ACM SIGKDD International Conference on Knowledge Discovery and Data Mining*, pages 462–470, 2008.

[273] Jure Leskovec and Eric Horvitz. Worldwide buzz: Planetary-scale views on an instant-messaging network. In *Proc. 17th International World Wide Web Conference*, 2008.

[274] Jure Leskovec, Dan Huttenlocher, and Jon Kleinberg. Signed networks in social media. In *Proc. 28th ACM SIGCHI Conference on Human Factors in Computing Systems*, 2010.

[275] Jure Leskovec, Kevin J. Lang, Anirban Dasgupta, and Michael W. Mahoney. Statistical properties of community structure in large social and information networks. In *Proc. 17th International World Wide Web Conference*, pages 695–704, 2008.

[276] David Lewis. *Convention: A Philosophical Study*. Oxford University Press, 1969.

[277] David Liben-Nowell, Jasmine Novak, Ravi Kumar, Prabhakar Raghavan, and Andrew Tomkins. Geographic routing in social networks. *Proc. Natl. Acad. Sci. USA*, 102(33):11623–11628, August 2005.

[278] Thomas Liggett. *Stochastic Interacting Systems: Contact, Voter and Exclusion Processes*. Springer, 1999.

[279] Nan Lin. *Social Capital: A Theory of Social Structure and Action*. Cambridge University Press, 2002.

[280] László Lovász and Michael Plummer. *Matching Theory*. North-Holland, 1986.

[281] Jeffrey W. Lucas, C. Wesley Younts, Michael J. Lovaglia, and Barry Markovsky. Lines of power in exchange networks. *Social Forces*, 80(11):185–214, 2001.

[282] Sean Luke. Schelling segregation applet. http://www.cs.gmu.edu/eclab/projects/mason/projects/schelling/.

[283] Jeffrey K. MacKie-Mason and John Metzler. Links between markets and aftermarkets: Kodak (1997). In John E. Kwoka and Lawrence J. White, editors, *The Antitrust Revolution*, pages 558–583. Oxford University Press, fifth edition, 2004.

[284] Benoit B. Mandelbrot. An informational theory of the statistical structure of languages. In W. Jackson, editor, *Communication Theory*, pages 486–502. Butterworth, 1953.

[285] M. Lynne Markus. Toward a "critical mass" theory of interactive media: Universal access, interdependence and diffusion. *Communication Research*, 14(5):491–511, 1987.

[286] Cameron Marlow, Lee Byron, Tom Lento, and Itamar Rosenn. Maintained relationships on Facebook 2009. Online at http://overstated.net/2009/03/09/maintained-relationships-on-facebook.

[287] Seth A. Marvel, Steven H. Strogatz, and Jon M. Kleinberg. The energy landscape of social balance. *Physical Review Letters*, 103(19):198701, 2009.

[288] Andreu Mas-Collel, Michael Whinston, and Jerry Green. *Microeconomic Theory*. Oxford University Press, 1995.

[289] Michael Maschler. The bargaining set, kernel, and nucleolus. In Robert J. Aumann and Sergiu Hart, editors, *Handbook of Game Theory*, volume 1, pages 592–667. Elsevier, 1992.

[290] Doug McAdam. Recruitment to high-risk activism: The case of Freedom Summer. *American Journal of Sociology*, 92:64–90, 1986.

[291] Doug McAdam. *Freedom Summer*. Oxford University Press, 1988.

[292] Preston McAfee and John McMillan. Auctions and bidding. *Journal of Economic Literature*, 25:708–747, 1987.

[293] Colin McEvedy. The bubonic plague. *Scientific American*, 258(2):118–123, February 1988.

[294] Miller McPherson, Lynn Smith-Lovin, and James M. Cook. Birds of a feather: Homophily in social networks. *Annual Review of Sociology*, 27:415–444, 2001.

[295] Lauren Ancel Meyers, Babak Pourbohloul, Mark E. J. Newman, Danuta M. Skowronski, and Robert C. Brunham. Network theory and SARS: Predicting outbreak diversity. *Journal of Theoretical Biology*, 232:71–81, 2005.

[296] Donna Miles. Bush outlines strategy for victory in terror war. *American Forces Press Service*, 6 October 2005.

[297] Stanley Milgram. The small-world problem. *Psychology Today*, 2:60–67, 1967.

[298] Stanley Milgram, Leonard Bickman, and Lawrence Berkowitz. Note on the drawing power of crowds of different size. *Journal of Personality and Social Psychology*, 13(2):79–82, October 1969.

[299] Paul Milgrom and Nancy Stokey. Information, trade and common knowledge. *Journal of Economic Theory*, 26:17–27, 1982.

[300] Michael Mitzenmacher. A brief history of generative models for power law and lognormal distributions. *Internet Mathematics*, 1(2):226–251, 2004.

[301] Mark S. Mizruchi. What do interlocks do? An analysis, critique, and assessment of research on interlocking directorates. *Annual Review of Sociology*, 22:271–298, 1996.

[302] Markus M. Möbius and Tanya S. Rosenblat. The process of ghetto formation: Evidence from Chicago, 2001. Working paper.

[303] Dov Monderer and Lloyd S. Shapley. Potential games. *Games and Economic Behavior*, 14:124–143, 1996.

[304] James Moody. Race, school integration, and friendship segregation in america. *American Journal of Sociology*, 107(3):679–716, November 2001.

[305] James Moody. The importance of relationship timing for diffusion. *Social Forces*, 81:25–56, 2002.

[306] Michael Moore. An international application of Heider's balance theory. *European Journal of Social Psychology*, 8:401–405, 1978.

[307] Martina Morris and Mirjam Kretzschmar. Concurrent partnerships and the spread of HIV. *AIDS*, 11(4):641–648, 1997.

[308] Stephen Morris. Contagion. *Review of Economic Studies*, 67:57–78, 2000.

[309] Elchanan Mossel and Sebastien Roch. On the submodularity of influence in social networks. In *Proc. 39th ACM Symposium on Theory of Computing*, 2007.

[310] Roger Myerson. Incentive compatibility and the bargaining problem. *Econometrica*, 47:61–73, 1979.

[311] Roger Myerson. Optimal auction design. *Mathematics of Operations Research*, 6:58–73, 1981.

[312] John Nash. The bargaining problem. *Econometrica*, 18:155–162, 1950.

[313] John Nash. Equilibrium points in n-person games. *Proc. Natl. Acad. Sci. USA*, 36:48–49, 1950.

[314] John Nash. Non-cooperative games. *Annals of Mathematics*, 54:286–295, 1951.

[315] National Research Council Committee on Technical and Privacy Dimensions of Information for Terrorism Prevention and Other National Goals. *Protecting Individual Privacy in the Struggle Against Terrorists: A Framework for Program Assessment*. National Academies Press, 2008.

[316] Ted Nelson. *Literary Machines*. Mindful Press, 1981.

[317] Mark E. J. Newman. Scientific collaboration networks: II. Shortest paths, weighted networks, and centrality. *Physical Review E*, 64:016132, 2001.

[318] Mark E. J. Newman. The structure of scientific collaboration networks. *Proc. Natl. Acad. Sci. USA*, 98(2):404–409, January 2001.

[319] Mark E. J. Newman. Mixing patterns in networks. *Physical Review E*, 67:026126, 2003.

[320] Mark E. J. Newman. The structure and function of complex networks. *SIAM Review*, 45:167–256, 2003.

[321] Mark E. J. Newman. Fast algorithm for detecting community structure in networks. *Physical Review E*, 69:066133, 2004.

[322] Mark E. J. Newman and Michelle Girvan. Finding and evaluating community structure in networks. *Physical Review E*, 69(2):026113, 2004.

[323] Mark E. J. Newman, Duncan J. Watts, and Steven H. Strogatz. Random graph models of social networks. *Proc. Natl. Acad. Sci. USA*, 99(Suppl.1):2566–2572, February 2002.

[324] Jakob Nielsen. The art of navigating through hypertext. *Communications of the ACM*, 33(3):296–310, 1990.

[325] Magnus Nordborg. Coalescent theory. In David J. Balding, Martin Bishop, and Chris Canning, editors, *Handbook of Statistical Genetics*, pages 179–212. John Wiley & Sons, 2001.

[326] Martin A. Nowak and Karl Sigmund. Phage-lift for game theory. *Nature*, 398:367–368, April 1999.

[327] Martin A. Nowak and Karl Sigmund. Evolutionary dynamics of biological games. *Science*, 303:793–799, February 2004.

[328] Barack Obama. Inaugural address, 20 January 2009.

[329] Prize Committee of the Royal Swedish Academy of Sciences. Mechanism design theory, 15 October 2007. Online at http://nobelprize.org/nobel_prizes/economics/laureates/2007/sci.html.

[330] Hubert J. O'Gorman. The discovery of pluralistic ignorance: An ironic lesson. *Journal of the History of the Behavioral Sciences*, 22:333–347, 1986.

[331] Hubert J. O'Gorman and Stephen L. Garry. Pluralistic ignorance – A replication and extension. *Public Opinion Quarterly*, 40:449–458, 1976.

[332] Maureen O'Hara. *Market Microstructure Theory*. Wiley, 1998.

[333] Steve Olson. *Mapping Human History: Genes, Race, and our Common Origins*. Houghton Mifflin, 2002.

[334] J.-P. Onnela, J. Saramaki, J. Hyvonen, G. Szabo, D. Lazer, K. Kaski, J. Kertesz, and A.-L. Barabasi. Structure and tie strengths in mobile communication networks. *Proc. Natl. Acad. Sci. USA*, 104:7332–7336, 2007.

[335] Tim O'Reilly. What is Web 2.0: Design patterns and business models for the next generation of software. *Communication and Strategy*, 1:17, 2007.

[336] Martin Osboren and Ariel Rubinstein. *A Course in Game Theory*. The MIT Press, 1994.

[337] I. Palacios-Huerta. Professionals play minimax. *Review of Economic Studies*, 70:395–415, 2003.

[338] Christopher R. Palmer, Phillip B. Gibbons, and Christos Faloutsos. ANF: A fast and scalable tool for data mining in massive graphs. In *Proc. 8th ACM SIGKDD International Conference on Knowledge Discovery and Data Mining*, pages 81–90, 2002.

[339] David S. Patel. Ayatollahs on the Pareto frontier: The institutional basis of religious authority in Iraq, 2006. Working paper.

[340] David M. Pennock, Gary W. Flake, Steve Lawrence, Eric J. Glover, and C. Lee Giles. Winners don't take all: Characterizing the competition for links on the Web. *Proc. Natl. Acad. Sci. USA*, 99(8):5207–5211, April 2002.

[341] Gabriel Pinski and Francis Narin. Citation influence for journal aggregates of scientific publications: Theory, with application to the literature of physics. *Information Processing and Management*, 12:297–312, 1976.

[342] Alejandro Portes. Social capital: Its origins and applications in modern sociology. *Annual Review of Sociology*, 24:1–24, 1998.

[343] William Poundstone. *Prisoner's Dilemma*. Doubleday, 1992.

[344] Robert D. Putnam. *Bowling Alone: The Collapse and Revival of American Community*. Simon & Schuster, 2000.

[345] Roy Radner. Rational expectations equilibrium: Generic existence and the information revealed by prices. *Econometrica*, 47:655–678, 1979.

[346] Anatol Rapoport and Albert M. Chammah. *Prisoner's Dilemma*. University of Michigan Press, 1965.

[347] Anatole Rapoport. Spread of information through a population with socio-structural bias I: Assumption of transitivity. *Bulletin of Mathematical Biophysics*, 15(4):523–533, December 1953.

[348] Matt Richardson and Pedro Domingos. Mining knowledge-sharing sites for viral marketing. In *Proc. 8th ACM SIGKDD International Conference on Knowledge Discovery and Data Mining*, pages 61–70, 2002.

[349] Sharon C. Rochford. Symmetrically pairwise-bargained allocations in an assignment market. *Journal of Economic Theory*, 34:262–281, 1984.

[350] John E. Roemer. *Political Competition: Theory and Applications*. Harvard University Press, 2001.

[351] Everett Rogers. *Diffusion of Innovations*. Free Press, fourth edition, 1995.

[352] Tim Roughgarden. *Selfish Routing and the Price of Anarchy*. MIT Press, 2005.

[353] Tim Roughgarden and Éva Tardos. How bad is selfish routing? *Journal of the ACM*, 49(2):236–259, 2002.

[354] Francois Rousset. Inferences from spatial population genetics. In David J. Balding, Martin Bishop, and Chris Canning, editors, *Handbook of Statistical Genetics*, pages 239–270. John Wiley & Sons, 2001.

[355] Matthew C. Rousu. A football play-calling experiment to illustrate the mixed strategy Nash equilibrium. *Journal of the Academy of Business Education*, pages 79–89, Summer 2008.

[356] Ariel Rubinstein. Perfect equilibrium in a bargaining model. *Econometrica*, 50:97–109, 1982.

[357] Paat Rusmevichientong and David P. Williamson. An adaptive algorithm for selecting profitable keywords for search-based advertising services. In *Proc. 7th ACM Conference on Electronic Commerce*, pages 260–269, 2006.

[358] Bryce Ryan and Neal C. Gross. The diffusion of hybrid seed corn in two Iowa communities. *Rural Sociology*, 8:15–24, 1943.

[359] Matthew Salganik, Peter Dodds, and Duncan Watts. Experimental study of inequality and unpredictability in an artificial cultural market. *Science*, 311:854–856, 2006.

[360] Gerard Salton and M.J. McGill. *Introduction to Modern Information Retrieval*. McGraw-Hill, 1983.

[361] Oskar Sandberg. Neighbor selection and hitting probability in small-world graphs. *Annals of Applied Probability*, 18(5):1771–1793, 2008.

[362] Alvaro Sandroni. Do markets favor agents able to make accurate predictions? *Econometrica*, 68:1303–1342, 2000.

[363] Leonard Savage. *The Foundations of Statistics*. Wiley, 1954.

[364] Thomas Schelling. *The Strategy of Conflict*. Harvard University Press, 1960.

[365] Thomas Schelling. Dynamic models of segregation. *Journal of Mathematical Sociology*, 1:143–186, 1972.

[366] Thomas Schelling. *Micromotives and Macrobehavior*. Norton, 1978.

[367] Bruce Schneier. Drugs: Sports' prisoner's dilemma. *Wired*, 10 August 2006.

[368] Carl Shapiro and Hal Varian. *Information Rules: A Strategic Guide to the Network Economy*. Harvard Business School Press, 1998.

[369] David A. Siegel. Social networks and collective action. *American Journal of Political Science*, 53(1):122–138, 2009.

[370] Özgür Simşek and David Jensen. Navigating networks by using homophily and degree. *Proc. Natl. Acad. Sci. USA*, 105(35):12758–12762, September 2008.

[371] Herbert Simon. On a class of skew distribution functions. *Biometrika*, 42:425–440, 1955.

[372] Simon Singh. Erdos-Bacon numbers. *Daily Telegraph*, April 2002.

[373] John Skvoretz and David Willer. Exclusion and power: A test of four theories of power in exchange networks. *American Sociological Review*, 58:801–818, 1993.

[374] Brian Skyrms. *The Stag Hunt and Evolution of Social Structure*. Cambridge University Press, 2003.

[375] John Maynard Smith. *On Evolution*. Edinburgh University Pres, 1972.

[376] John Maynard Smith and G. R. Price. The logic of animal conflict. *Nature*, 246:15–18, 1973.

[377] Thomas A. Smith. The web of law. *San Diego Law Review*, 44(309), 2007.

[378] Tamás Solymosi and Tirukkannamangai E. S. Raghavan. An algorithm for finding the nucleolus of assignment games. *International Journal of Game Theory*, 23:119–143, 1994.

[379] Michael Spence. Job market signaling. *Quarterly Journal of Economics*, 87:355–374, 1973.

[380] Olaf Sporns, Dante R. Chialvo, Marcus Kaiser, and Claus Hilgetag. Organization, development and function of complex brain networks. *Trends in Cognitive Science*, 8:418–425, 2004.

[381] Mark Steyvers and Joshua B. Tenebaum. The large-scale structure of semantic networks: Statistical analyses and a model of semantic growth. *Cognitive Science*, 29(1):41–78, 2005.

[382] David Strang and Sarah Soule. Diffusion in organizations and social movements: From hybrid corn to poison pills. *Annual Review of Sociology*, 24:265–290, 1998.

[383] James Surowiecki. *The Wisdom of Crowds: Why the Many Are Smarter Than the Few and How Collective Wisdom Shapes Business, Economies, Societies and Nations*. Little, Brown, 2004.

[384] Alexander Tabarrok and Lee Spector. Would the Borda Count have avoid the Civil War? *Journal of Theoretical Politics*, 11(2):261–288, 1999.

[385] Éva Tardos and Tom Wexler. Network formation games and the potential function method. In Noam Nisan, Tim Roughgarden, Éva Tardos, and Vijay Vazirani, editors, *Algorithmic Game Theory*, pages 487–516. Cambridge University Press, 2007.

[386] Richard H. Thaler. Anomalies: The ultimatum game. *Journal of Economic Perspectives*, 2(4):195–206, 1988.

[387] Richard H. Thaler. Anomalies: The winner's curse. *Journal of Economic Perspectives*, 2(1):191–202, 1988.

[388] Michael F. Thorpe and Philip M. Duxbury. *Rigidity Theory and Applications*. Springer, 1999.

[389] Shane Thye, Michael Lovaglia, and Barry Markovsky. Responses to social exchange and social exclusion in networks. *Social Forces*, 75:1031–1049, 1997.

[390] Shane Thye, David Willer, and Barry Markovsky. From status to power: New models at the intersection of two theories. *Social Forces*, 84:1471–1495, 2006.

[391] Jeffrey Travers and Stanley Milgram. An experimental study of the small world problem. *Sociometry*, 32(4):425–443, 1969.

[392] Paul E. Turner and Lin Chao. Prisoner's Dilemma in an RNA virus. *Nature*, 398:441–443, April 1999.

[393] Paul E. Turner and Lin Chao. Escape from Prisoner's Dilemma in RNA phage ϕ6. *American Naturalist*, 161(3):497–505, March 2003.

[394] U.S. Environmental Protection Agency. Clean air markets. http://www.epa.gov/airmarkt/.

[395] Brian Uzzi. The sources and consequences of embeddedness for economic performance of organizations: The network effect. *American Sociological Review*, 61(4):674–698, August 1996.

[396] Thomas Valente. *Evaluating Health Promotion Programs*. Oxford University Press, 2002.

[397] Marcel van Assen. Essays on actor models in exchange networks and social dilemmas, 2001. Ph.D. Thesis, Rijksuniversiteit Groningen.

[398] Hal Varian. *Intermediate Microeconomics: A Modern Approach*. Norton, 2003.

[399] Hal Varian. Position auctions. *International Journal of Industrial Organization*, 25:1163–1178, 2007.

[400] William Vickrey. Counterspeculation, auctions, and competitive sealed tenders. *Journal of Finance*, 16:8–37, 1961.

[401] Dejan Vinković and Alan Kirman. A physical analogue of the Schelling model. *Proc. Natl. Acad. Sci. USA*, 103(51):19261–19265, 2006.

[402] Luis von Ahn and Laura Dabbish. Designing games with a purpose. *Communications of the ACM*, 51(8):58–67, 2008.

[403] Luis von Ahn, Ben Maurer, Colin McMillen, David Abraham, and Manuel Blum. reCAPTCHA: Human-based character recognition via Web security measures. *Science*, 321(5895):1465–1468, September 2008.

[404] Jakob Voss. Measuring Wikipedia. In *International Conference of the International Society for Scientometrics and Informetrics*, 2005.

[405] Mark Walker and John Wooders. Minimax play at Wimbledon. *American Economic Review*, 91:1521–1538, 2001.

[406] Charlotte H. Watts and Robert M. May. The influence of concurrent partnerships on the dynamics of HIV/AIDS. *Mathematical Biosciences*, 108:89–104, 1992.

[407] Duncan J. Watts. *Small Worlds: The Dynamics of Networks Between Order and Randomness*. Princeton University Press, 1999.

[408] Duncan J. Watts. A simple model of global cascades on random networks. *Proc. Natl. Acad. Sci. USA*, 99(9):5766–5771, April 2002.

[409] Duncan J. Watts and Peter S. Dodds. Networks, influence, and public opinion formation. *Journal of Consumer Research*, 34(4):441–458, 2007.

[410] Duncan J. Watts, Peter S. Dodds, and Mark E. J. Newman. Identity and search in social networks. *Science*, 296(5571):1302–1305, May 2002.

[411] Duncan J. Watts and Steven H. Strogatz. Collective dynamics of "small-world" networks. *Nature*, 393:440–442, 1998.

[412] Ivo Welch. Sequential sales, learning and cascades. *Journal of Finance*, 47:695–732, 1992.

[413] Barry Wellman. An electronic group is virtually a social network. In Sara Kiesler, editor, *Culture of the Internet*, pages 179–205. Lawrence Erlbaum, 1997.

[414] Barry Wellman, Janet Salaff, Dimitrina Dimitrova, Laura Garton, Milena Gulia, and Caroline Haythornthwaite. Computer networks as social networks: Collaborative work, telework, and virtual community. *Annual Review of Sociology*, 22:213–238, 1996.

[415] Michael D. Whinston. Tying, foreclosure, and exclusion. *American Economic Review*, 80(4):837–859, September 1990.

[416] Harrison C. White. Search parameters for the small world problem. *Social Forces*, 49(2):259–264, December 1970.

[417] David Willer (editor). *Network Exchange Theory*. Praeger, 1999.

[418] Carsten Wiuf and Jotun Hein. On the number of ancestors to a DNA sequence. *Genetics*, 147:1459–1468, 1997.

[419] B. Wotal, H. Green, D. Williams, and N. Contractor. WoW!: The dynamics of knowledge networks in massively multiplayer online role playing games (MMORPG). In *Sunbelt XXVI: International Sunbelt Social Network Conference*, 2006.

[420] H. Peyton Young. *Individual Strategy and Social Structure: An Evolutionary Theory of Institutions*. Princeton University Press, 1998.

[421] Wayne Zachary. An information flow model for conflict and fission in small groups. *Journal of Anthropological Research*, 33(4):452–473, 1977.

[422] Alice X. Zheng, Andrew Y. Ng, and Michael I. Jordan. Stable algorithms for link analysis. In *Proc. 24th ACM SIGIR Conference on Research and Development in Information Retrieval*, pages 258–266, 2001.

[423] George Kingsley Zipf. *Human Behaviour and the Principle of Least Effort: An Introduction to Human Ecology*. Addison Wesley, 1949.

Index